THE SPIRIT OF LAWS

BY CHARLES DE MONTESQUIEU

TRANSLATED BY THOMAS NUGENT

A Digireads.com Book
Digireads.com Publishing

The Spirit of the Laws
By Charles de Montesquieu
Translated by Thomas Nugent
ISBN: 1-4209-3830-4

Please visit *www.digireads.com*

THE TRANSLATOR TO THE READER

BY THOMAS NUGENT

1752

The following work may with the strictest justice be said to have done honor to human nature as well as to the great abilities of the author. The wisest and most learned man, and those most distinguished by birth and the elevation of their stations, have, in every country in Europe, considered it as a most excellent performance. And may we be permitted to add, that a sovereign prince [1] as justly celebrated for his probity and good sense, as for his political and military skill, has declared that from M. de Montesquieu he has learnt the art of government. But had the illustrious author received no such distinguished honor, the numerous editions of this work in French, and their sudden spreading through all Europe, are a sufficient testimony of the high esteem with which it has been received by the public.

[1] The present King of Sardinia.

But notwithstanding the deserved applause which has been so liberally bestowed on the author, there have been some who have not only endeavored to blast his laurels, but have treated him with all that scurrility which bigotry and superstition are apt, on every occasion, to throw out against truth, reason and good sense. These M. de Montesquieu has himself answered, in a separate treatise entitled, *A Defense of the Spirit of Laws*, from whence we have thought proper to extract, for the sake of such as have not seen that treatise, the principal of those objections, and the substance of what has been given in reply: Only first observing, that this defense is divided into three parts, in the first of which he answers the general reproaches that have been thrown out against him; in the second he replies to particular reproaches; and in the third, he gives some reflections on the manner in which his work has been criticized.

The author first complains of his being charged both with espousing the doctrines of Spinoza, and with being a Deist, two opinions directly contradictory to each other. To the former of these he answers, by placing in one view the several passages in the Spirit of Laws directly leveled against the doctrines of Spinoza; and then he replies to the objections that have been made to those passages, upon which this injurious charge is founded.

The critic asserts that our author stumbles at his first setting out, and is offended at his saying, that Laws in their most extensive signification, are the necessary relations derived from the nature of things. To this he replies, that the critic had heard it said that Spinoza had maintained that the world was governed by a blind and necessary principle; and from hence on seeing the word necessary, he concludes that this must be Spinozism; though' what is most surprising, this article is directly leveled at the dangerous principles maintained by Spinoza: That he had Hobbes' system in his eye, a system, which, as it makes all the virtues and vices depend on the establishment of human laws, and as it would prove that men were born in a state of war, and that the first law of nature is a war of all against all, overturns, like Spinoza, all religion, and all morality. Hence he laid down this position, that there were laws of justice and equity before the establishment of positive laws: hence also he has proved that all beings had laws; that even before their creation they had possible laws; and that God himself had laws, that is, the laws which he himself had made. He has shown [2] that nothing can be more false than the assertion that men were born in a state of war; and he has made it appear that wars did not commence till after the establishment of society. His principles are here extremely clear; from whence it follows, that as he has attacked Hobbes' errors, he has consequently those of Spinoza; and he has been so little understood, that they have taken for the opinions of Spinoza, those very objections which were made against Spinozism.

[2] Book i. Chap. 1.

Again, the author has said that the creation which appears to be an arbitrary act, supposes laws as invariable as the fatality of the Atheists. From these words the critic concludes that the author admits the fatality of the Atheists.

To this he answers, that he had just before destroyed this fatality, by representing it as the greatest absurdity to suppose that a blind fatality was capable of producing intelligent beings. Besides, in the passage here censured, he can only be made to say what he really does say: he does not speak of causes, nor does he compare causes; but he speaks of effects and compares effects. The whole article, what goes before and what follows, make it evident, that there is nothing here intended but the laws of motion, which, according to the author, had been established by God: these laws are invariable; this he has asserted, and all natural philosophy has asserted the same thing; they are invariable because God has been pleased to make them so, and because he has pleased to preserve the world. When the author therefore says that the creation which appears to be an arbitrary act, supposes laws as invariable as the fatality of the Atheists, he cannot be understood to say that the creation was a necessary act like the fatality of the Atheists.

Having vindicated himself from the charge of Spinozism, he proceeds to the other accusation, and from a multitude of passages collected together proves that he has not only acknowledged the truth of revealed religion; but that he is in love with Christianity, and endeavors to make it appear amiable in the eyes of others. He then enquires into what his adversaries have said to prove the contrary, observing that the proofs ought to bear some proportion to the accusation; that this accusation is not of a frivolous nature, and that the proofs therefore ought not to be frivolous.

The first objection is, that he has praised the Stoics, who admitted a blind fatality, and that this is the foundation of natural religion. To this he replies, "I will for a moment suppose that this false manner of reasoning has some weight: has the author praised the philosophy and metaphysics of the Stoics? He has praised their morals, and has said that the people reaped great benefit from them: he has said this, and he has said no more: I am mistaken, he has said more, he has at the beginning of his book attacked this fatality, he does not then praise it, when he praises the Stoics."

The second objection is, that he has praised Bayle, in calling him a great man. To this he answers, "It is true that the author has called Bayle a great man, but he has censured his opinions: if he has censured them, he has not espoused them: and since he has censured his opinions, he does not call him a great man because of his opinions. Everybody knows that Bayle had a great genius which he abused; but this genius which he abused, he had: the author has attacked his sophisms, and pities him on account of his errors. I don't love the men who subvert the laws of their country; but I should find great difficulty in believing that Caesar and Cromwell had little minds: I am not in love with conquerors, but it would be very difficult to persuade me to believe that Alexander and Genghis-Khan were men of only a common genius. Besides, I have remarked, that the declamations of angry men make but little impression on any except those who are angry: the greatest part of the readers are men of moderation, and seldom take up a book but when they are in cool blood; for rational and sensible men love reason. Had the author loaded Bayle with a thousand injurious reproaches, it would not have followed from thence, that Bayle had reasoned well or ill; all that his readers would have been able to conclude from it would have been, that the author knew how to be abusive."

The third objection is, that he has not in his first chapter spoken of original sin. To which he replies: "I ask every sensible man if this chapter is a treatise of divinity? if the author had spoken of original sin, they might have imputed it to him as a crime that he had not spoken of redemption."

The next objection takes notice, that "The author has said that in England self-murder is the effect of a distemper, and that it cannot be punished without punishing the effects of madness; the consequence the critic draws from thence is, that a follower of natural religion can never forget that England is the cradle of his sect, and that he rubs a sponge over all the crimes he found there." He replies, "The author does not know that England is the cradle of natural religion; but he knows that England was not his cradle. He is not of the same religious sentiments as an Englishman, any more than an Englishman who speaks of the physical effects he found in France, is not of the same religion as the French. He is not a follower of natural religion; but he wishes that his critic was a follower of natural logic."

These are the principle objections leveled against our author, on this head, from which our readers will sufficiently see on what trifling, what puerile arguments this charge of Deism is founded. He concludes however this article, with a defense of the religion of nature, and such a defense as every rational Christian must undoubtedly approve.

"Before I conclude this first part, I am tempted to make one objection against him who has made so many; but he has so stunned my ears with the words follower of natural religion, that I scarcely dare pronounce them. I shall endeavor however to take courage. Do not the critic's two pieces stand in greater need of an explication, than that which I defend? Does he do well, while speaking of natural religion and revelation, to fall perpetually upon one side of the subject, and to lose all traces of the other? Does he do well never to distinguish those who acknowledge only the religion of nature, from those who acknowledge both natural and revealed religion? Does he do well to turn frantic whenever the author considers man in the state of natural religion, and whenever he explains anything on the principles of natural religion? Does he do well to confound natural religion with Atheism? Have I not heard that we have all natural religion? Have I not heard that Christianity is the perfection of natural religion? Have I not heard that natural religion is employed to prove the truth of revelation against the Deists? and that the same natural religion is employed to prove the existence of a God against the Atheists? He has said that the Stoics were the followers of natural religion; and I say, that they were Atheists, since they believed that a blind fatality governed the universe; and it is by the religion of nature that we ought to attack that of the Stoics. He says that the scheme of natural religion is connected with that of Spinoza; and I say, that they are contradictory to each other, and it is by natural religion that we ought to destroy Spinoza's scheme. I say, that to confound natural religion with Atheism, is to confound the proof with the thing to be proved, and the objections against error with error itself, and that this is to take away the most powerful arms we have against this error."

The author now proceeds to the second part of his defense, in which he has the following remarks. "What has the critic done to give an ample scope to his declamations, and to open the widest door to invectives? he has considered the author, as if he had intended to follow the example of M. Abbadye, and had been writing a treatise on the Christian religion: he has attacked him, as if his two books on religion were two treatises on divinity; he has caviled against him, as if while he had been talking of any religion whatsoever which was not Christian, he should have examined it according to the principles, and doctrines of Christianity; he has judged him as if in his two books relating to religion he ought to have preached to Mahometans and Idolators the doctrines of Christianity. Whenever he has spoken of religion in general, whenever he has made use of the word religion, the critic says, 'that is the Christian religion'; whenever he has compared the religious rites of different nations and has said that they are more conformable to the political government of these countries, than some other rites, the critic again says, 'you approve them then and abandon the Christian faith': when he has spoken of a people who have never embraced Christianity, or who have lived before Christ, again says the critic, 'you don't then acknowledge the morals of Christianity'; when he has canvassed any custom whatsoever, which he has found in a political writer, the critic asks him, 'Is this a doctrine of Christianity?' He might as well add, 'You say you are a civilian, and I will make you a divine in spite of yourself: you have given us elsewhere some very excellent things on the Christian religion, but this was only to conceal your real sentiments, for I know your heart, and penetrate into your thoughts. It is true I do not understand your book, nor it is material that I should discover the good or bad design with which it has been written; but I know the bottom of all your thoughts: I don't know a word of what you have said, but I understand perfectly well, what you have not said.'"

But to proceed. The author has maintained that polygamy is necessarily and in its own nature bad; he has wrote a chapter expressly against it, and afterwards has examined in a philosophical manner, in what countries, in what climates, or in what circumstances it is least pernicious; he has compared climates with climates, and countries with countries, and has found, that there are countries where its effects are less pernicious than in others; because, according to the accounts that have been given of them, the number of men and women not being everywhere equal, it is evident, that if there are places where there are more women than men, polygamy, bad as it is in itself, is there less pernicious than in others. But as the title of this chapter [3] contains these words, "That the law of polygamy is an affair of calculation," they have seized this title as an excellent subject for declamation. Having repeated the chapter itself, against which no objection is made, he proceeds to justify the title and adds: "Polygamy is an affair of calculation when we would know, if it is more or less pernicious in certain climates, in certain countries, in certain circumstances than in others; it is not an affair of calculation when we would decide whether it be good or bad in itself. It is not an affair of calculation when we reason on its nature; it may be an affair of calculation when we combine its effects; in short, it is never an affair of calculation when we inquire into the end of marriage, and it is even less so, when we inquire into marriage as a law established and confirmed by Jesus Christ."

[3] Book xvi. Chap. 4.

Again, the author having said that [4] polygamy is more conformable to nature in some countries than in others, the critic has seized the words more conformable to nature, to make his say, that he approves polygamy. To which he answers, "If I say, that I should like better to have a fever than the scurvy, does this signify that I should like to have a fever? or only that the scurvy is more disagreeable to me than a fever?"

[4] Book xvi. Chap. 4.

Having finished his reply to what had been objected to on the subject of polygamy, he vindicates that excellent part of his work which treats of the climates; when speaking of the influence these have upon religion, he says, "I am very sensible that religion is in its own nature independent of all physical causes whatsoever, that the religion which is good in one country is good in another, and that it cannot be pernicious in one country without being so in all; but yet, I say, that as it is practiced by men, and has a relation to those who do not practice it, any religion whatsoever will find a greater facility in being practiced, either in the whole or in part, in certain circumstances than in others, and that whoever says the contrary must renounce all pretensions to sense and understanding."

But the critic has been greatly offended by our author's saying, [5] that when a state is at liberty to receive or to reject a new religion, it ought to be rejected; when it is received, it ought to be tolerated. From hence he objects, that the author has advised idolatrous princes, not to admit the Christian religion into their dominions. To this he answers first by referring to a passage in which he says, [6] that the best civil and political laws are, next to Christianity, the greatest blessings that men can give or receive; and adds, "If then Christianity is the first and greatest blessing, and the political and civil laws the second, there are no political or civil laws in any state that can or ought to hinder the entrance of the Christian religion."

[5] Book xxv. Ch. 10.
[6] Ibid. Ch. 1.

His second answer is, "That the religion of heaven is not established by the same methods as the religions of the earth; read the history of the church, and you will see the wonders performed by the Christian religion: was she to enter a country, she knew how to open its gates; every instrument was able to effect it; at one time God makes use of a few fisherman, at another he sets an emperor on the throne, and makes him bow down his head under the yolk of the gospel. Does Christianity hide herself in subterranean caverns? Stay a moment, and you see an advocate speaking from the imperial throne on her behalf. She traverses, whenever she pleases, seas, rivers, and mountains; no obstacles here below can stop her progress: implant aversion in the mind, she will conquer this aversion: establish customs, form habits, publish edicts, enact laws, she will triumph over the climate, over the laws which result from it, and over the legislators who have made them. God acting according to decrees which are unknown to us, extends or contracts the limits of his religion."

8

CONTENTS

10

12

14

16

18

20

22

24

PREFACE

If amidst the infinite number of subjects contained in this book there is anything which, contrary to my expectation, may possibly offend, I can at least assure the public that it was not inserted with an ill intention: for I am not naturally of a captious temper. Plato thanked the gods that he was born in the same age with Socrates: and for my part I give thanks to the Supreme that I was born a subject of that government under which I live; and that it is His pleasure I should obey those whom He has made me love.

I beg one favor of my readers, which I fear will not be granted me; this is, that they will not judge by a few hours' reading of the labor of twenty years; that they will approve or condemn the book entire, and not a few particular phrases. If they would search into the design of the author, they can do it in no other way so completely as by searching into the design of the work.

I have first of all considered mankind; and the result of my thoughts has been, that amidst such an infinite diversity of laws and manners, they were not solely conducted by the caprice of fancy.

I have laid down the first principles, and have found that the particular cases follow naturally from them; that the histories of all nations are only consequences of them; and that every particular law is connected with another law, or depends on some other of a more general extent.

When I have been obliged to look back into antiquity, I have endeavored to assume the spirit of the ancients, lest I should consider those things as alike which are really different; and lest I should miss the difference of those which appear to be alike.

I have not drawn my principles from my prejudices, but from the nature of things.

Here a great many truths will not appear till we have seen the chain which connects them with others. The more we enter into particulars, the more we shall perceive the certainty of the principles on which they are founded. I have not even given all these particulars, for who could mention them all without a most insupportable fatigue?

The reader will not here meet with any of those bold flights which seem to characterize the works of the present age. When things are examined with never so small a degree of extent, the sallies of imagination must vanish; these generally arise from the mind's collecting all its powers to view only one side of the subject, while it leaves the other unobserved.

I write not to censure anything established in any country whatsoever. Every nation will here find the reasons on which its maxims are founded; and this will be the natural inference, that to propose alterations belongs only to those who are so happy as to be born with a genius capable of penetrating the entire constitution of a state.

It is not a matter of indifference that the minds of the people be enlightened. The prejudices of magistrates have arisen from national prejudice. In a time of ignorance they have committed even the greatest evils without the least scruple; but in an enlightened age they even tremble while conferring the greatest blessings. They perceive the ancient abuses; they see how they must be reformed; but they are sensible also of the abuses of a reformation. They let the evil continue, if they fear a worse; they are content with a lesser good, if they doubt a greater. They examine into the parts, to judge of them in connection; and they examine all the causes, to discover their different effects.

Could I but succeed so as to afford new reasons to every man to love his prince, his country, his laws; new reasons to render him more sensible in every nation and government of the blessings he enjoys, I should think myself the most happy of mortals.

Could I but succeed so as to persuade those who command, to increase their knowledge in what they ought to prescribe; and those who obey, to find a new pleasure resulting from obedience—I should think myself the most happy of mortals.

The most happy of mortals should I think myself could I contribute to make mankind recover from their prejudices. By prejudices I here mean, not that which renders men ignorant of some particular things, but whatever renders them ignorant of themselves.

It is in endeavoring to instruct mankind that we are best able to practice that general virtue which comprehends the love of all. Man, that flexible being, conforming in society to the thoughts and impressions of others, is equally capable of knowing his own nature, whenever it is laid open to his view; and of losing the very sense of it, when this idea is banished from his mind.

Often have I begun, and as often have I laid aside, this undertaking. I have a thousand times given the leaves I had written to the winds: [7] I, every day, felt my paternal hands fall. [8] I have followed my object without any fixed plan: I have known neither rules nor exceptions; I have found the truth, only to lose it again. But when I once discovered my first principles, everything I sought for appeared; and in the course of twenty years, I have seen my work begun, growing up, advancing to maturity, and finished.

[7] *Ludibria ventis.*
[8] *Bis patriæ cecidere manus——.*

If this work meets with success, I shall owe it chiefly to the grandeur and majesty of the subject. However, I do not think that I have been totally deficient in point of genius. When I have seen what so many great men both in France, England, and Germany have said before me, I have been lost in admiration; but I have not lost my courage: I have said with Correggio, "And I also am a painter." [9]

[9] *Ed io anche son pittore.*

ADVERTISEMENT

1. For the better understanding of the first four books of this work, it is to be observed that what I distinguish by the name of virtue, in a republic, is the love of one's country, that is, the love of equality. It is not a moral, nor a Christian, but a political virtue; and it is the spring which sets the republican government in motion, as honor is the spring which gives motion to monarchy. Hence it is that I have distinguished the love of one's country, and of equality, by the appellation of political virtue. My ideas are new, and therefore I have been obliged to find new words, or to give new acceptations to old terms, in order to convey my meaning. They, who are unacquainted with this particular, have made me say most strange absurdities, such as would be shocking in any part of the world, because in all countries and governments morality is requisite.

2. The reader is also to notice that there is a vast difference between saying that a certain quality, modification of the mind, or virtue, is not the spring by which government is actuated, and affirming that it is not to be found in that government. Were

I to say such a wheel or such a pinion is not the spring which sets the watch going, can you infer thence that they are not to be found in the watch? So far is it from being true that the moral and Christian virtues are excluded from monarchy, that even political virtue is not excluded. In a word, honor is found in a republic, though its spring be political virtue; and political virtue is found in a monarchical government, though it be actuated by honor.

To conclude, the honest man of whom we treat in the third book, chapter 5, is not the Christian, but the political honest man, who is possessed of the political virtue there mentioned. He is the man who loves the laws of his country, and who is actuated by the love of those laws. I have set these matters in a clearer light in the present edition, by giving a more precise meaning to my expression: and in most places where I have made use of the word virtue I have taken care to add the term *political*.

BOOK I.

OF LAWS IN GENERAL

1. *Of the Relation of Laws to different Beings.*

Laws, in their most general signification, are the necessary relations arising from the nature of things. In this sense all beings have their laws: the Deity [10] His laws, the material world its laws, the intelligences superior to man their laws, the beasts their laws, man his laws.

[10] "Law," says Plutarch, "is the king of mortal and immortal beings." See his treatise, *A Discourse to an Unlearned Prince.*

They who assert that *a blind fatality produced the various effects we behold in this world* talk very absurdly; for can anything be more unreasonable than to pretend that a blind fatality could be productive of intelligent beings?

There is, then, a prime reason; and laws are the relations subsisting between it and different beings, and the relations of these to one another.

God is related to the universe, as Creator and Preserver; the laws by which He created all things are those by which He preserves them. He acts according to these rules, because He knows them; He knows them, because He made them; and He made them, because they are in relation to His wisdom and power.

Since we observe that the world, though formed by the motion of matter, and void of understanding, subsists through so long a succession of ages, its motions must certainly be directed by invariable laws; and could we imagine another world, it must also have constant rules, or it would inevitably perish.

Thus the creation, which seems an arbitrary act, supposes laws as invariable as those of the fatality of the Atheists. It would be absurd to say that the Creator might govern the world without those rules, since without them it could not subsist.

These rules are a fixed and invariable relation. In bodies moved, the motion is received, increased, diminished, or lost, according to the relations of the quantity of matter and velocity; each diversity is *uniformity*, each change is *constancy*.

Particular intelligent beings may have laws of their own making, but they have some likewise which they never made. Before there were intelligent beings, they were possible;

they had therefore possible relations, and consequently possible laws. Before laws were made, there were relations of possible justice. To say that there is nothing just or unjust but what is commanded or forbidden by positive laws, is the same as saying that before the describing of a circle all the radii were not equal.

We must therefore acknowledge relations of justice antecedent to the positive law by which they are established: as, for instance, if human societies existed, it would be right to conform to their laws; if there were intelligent beings that had received a benefit of another being, they ought to show their gratitude; if one intelligent being had created another intelligent being, the latter ought to continue in its original state of dependence; if one intelligent being injures another, it deserves a retaliation; and so on.

But the intelligent world is far from being so well governed as the physical. For though the former has also its laws, which of their own nature are invariable, it does not conform to them so exactly as the physical world. This is because, on the one hand, particular intelligent beings are of a finite nature, and consequently liable to error; and on the other, their nature requires them to be free agents. Hence they do not steadily conform to their primitive laws; and even those of their own instituting they frequently infringe.

Whether brutes be governed by the general laws of motion, or by a particular movement, we cannot determine. Be that as it may, they have not a more intimate relation to God than the rest of the material world; and sensation is of no other use to them than in the relation they have either to other particular beings or to themselves.

By the allurement of pleasure they preserve the individual, and by the same allurement they preserve their species. They have natural laws, because they are united by sensation; positive laws they have none, because they are not connected by knowledge. And yet they do not invariably conform to their natural laws; these are better observed by vegetables, that have neither understanding nor sense.

Brutes are deprived of the high advantages which we have; but they have some which we have not. They have not our hopes, but they are without our fears; they are subject like us to death, but without knowing it; even most of them are more attentive than we to self-preservation, and do not make so bad a use of their passions.

Man, as a physical being, is like other bodies governed by invariable laws. As an intelligent being, he incessantly transgresses the laws established by God, and changes those of his own instituting. He is left to his private direction, though a limited being, and subject, like all finite intelligences, to ignorance and error: even his imperfect knowledge he loses; and as a sensible creature, he is hurried away by a thousand impetuous passions. Such a being might every instant forget his Creator; God has therefore reminded him of his duty by the laws of religion. Such a being is liable every moment to forget himself; philosophy has provided against this by the laws of morality. Formed to live in society, he might forget his fellow-creatures; legislators have therefore by political and civil laws confined him to his duty.

2. Of the Laws of Nature.

Antecedent to the above-mentioned laws are those of nature, so called, because they derive their force entirely from our frame and existence. In order to have a perfect knowledge of these laws, we must consider man before the establishment of society: the laws received in such a state would be those of nature.

The law which, impressing on our minds the idea of a Creator, inclines us towards Him, is the first in importance, though not in order, of natural laws. Man in a state of nature would have the faculty of knowing, before he had acquired any knowledge. Plain it is that his first ideas would not be of a speculative nature; he would think of the preservation of his being, before he would investigate its origin. Such a man would feel nothing in himself at first but impotency and weakness; his fears and apprehensions would be excessive; as appears from instances (were there any necessity of proving it) of savages found in forests, [11] trembling at the motion of a leaf, and flying from every shadow.

[11] Witness the savage found in the forests of Hanover, who was carried over to England during the reign of George I.

In this state every man, instead of being sensible of his equality, would fancy himself inferior. There would therefore be no danger of their attacking one another; peace would be the first law of nature.

The natural impulse or desire which Hobbes attributes to mankind of subduing one another is far from being well founded. The idea of empire and dominion is so complex, and depends on so many other notions, that it could never be the first which occurred to the human understanding.

Hobbes [12] inquires, *For what reason go men armed, and have locks and keys to fasten their doors, if they be not naturally in a state of war?* But is it not obvious that he attributes to mankind before the establishment of society what can happen but in consequence of this establishment, which furnishes them with motives for hostile attacks and self-defense?

[12] In præfat. lib. *de Cive.*

Next to a sense of his weakness man would soon find that of his wants. Hence another law of nature would prompt him to seek for nourishment.

Fear, I have observed, would induce men to shun one another; but the marks of this fear being reciprocal, would soon engage them to associate. Besides, this association would quickly follow from. the very pleasure one animal feels at the approach of another of the same species. Again, the attraction arising from the difference of sexes would enhance this pleasure, and the natural inclination they have for each other would form a third law.

Beside the sense or instinct which man possesses in common with brutes, he has the advantage of acquired knowledge; and thence arises a second tie, which brutes have not. Mankind have therefore a new motive of uniting; and a fourth law of nature results from the desire of living in society.

3. *Of Positive Laws.*

As soon as man enters into a state of society he loses the sense of his weakness; equality ceases, and then commences the state of war. [13]

[13] Interpreter and admirer of the social instinct as he was, Montesquieu has not hesitated to avow that war takes simultaneous rise with society. But the true philosophy of this unhappy truth, which Hobbes took advantage of in order to vaunt the serenity of despotism, and Rousseau to celebrate the independence of savage life, gives birth to the

wholesome necessity of laws which are an armistice between states, and a treaty of perpetual peace for the citizens (*Eloge de Montequieu*).

Each particular society begins to feel its strength, whence arises a state of war between different nations. The individuals likewise of each society become sensible of their force; hence the principal advantages of this society they endeavor to convert to their own emolument, which constitutes a state of war between individuals.

These two different kinds of states give rise to human laws. Considered as inhabitants of so great a planet, which necessarily contains a variety of nations, they have laws relating to their mutual intercourse, which is what we call the *law of nations*. As members of a society that must be properly supported, they have laws relating to the governors and the governed, and this we distinguish by the name of *politic law*. They have also another sort of law, as they stand in relation to each other; by which is understood the *civil law*.

The law of nations is naturally founded on this principle, that different nations ought in time of peace to do one another all the good they can, and in time of war as little injury as possible, without prejudicing their real interests.

The object of war is victory; that of victory is conquest; and that of conquest preservation. From this and the preceding principle all those rules are derived which constitute the *law of nations*.

All countries have a law of nations, not excepting the Iroquois themselves, though they devour their prisoners: for they send and receive ambassadors, and understand the rights of war and peace. The mischief is that their law of nations is not founded on true principles.

Besides the law of nations relating to all societies, there is a polity or civil constitution for each particularly considered. No society can subsist without a form of government. *The united strength of individuals*, as Gravina [14] well observes, *constitutes what we call the body politic*.

[14] Italian poet and jurist, 1664-1718.

The general strength may be in the hands of a single person, or of many. Some think that nature having established paternal authority, the most natural government was that of a single person. But the example of paternal authority proves nothing. For if the power of a father relates to a single government, that of brothers after the death of a father, and that of cousins-german after the decease of brothers, refer to a government of many. The political power necessarily comprehends the union of several families.

Better is it to say, that the government most conformable to nature is that which best agrees with the humor and disposition of the people in whose favor it is established.

The strength of individuals cannot be united without a conjunction of all their wills. *The conjunction of those wills*, as Gravina again very justly observes, *is what we call the* CIVIL STATE.

Law in general is human reason, inasmuch as it governs all the inhabitants of the earth: the political and civil laws of each nation ought to be only the particular cases in which human reason is applied.

They should be adapted in such a manner to the people for whom they are framed that it should be a great chance if those of one nation suit another.

They should be in relation to the nature and principle of each government; whether they form it, as may be said of politic laws; or whether they support it, as in the case of civil institutions.

They should be in relation to the climate of each country, to the quality of its soil, to its situation and extent, to the principal occupation of the natives, whether husbandmen, huntsmen, or shepherds: they should have relation to the degree of liberty which the constitution will bear; to the religion of the inhabitants, to their inclinations, riches, numbers, commerce, manners, and customs. In fine, they have relations to each other, as also to their origin, to the intent of the legislator, and to the order of things on which they are established; in all of which different lights they ought to be considered.

This is what I have undertaken to perform in the following work. These relations I shall examine, since all these together constitute what I call the *Spirit of Laws*.

I have not separated the political from the civil institutions, as I do not pretend to treat of laws, but of their spirit; and as this spirit consists in the various relations which the laws may bear to different objects, it is not so much my business to follow the natural order of laws as that of these relations and objects.

I shall first examine the relations which laws bear to the nature and principle of each government; and as this principle has a strong influence on laws, I shall make it my study to understand it thoroughly: and if I can but once establish it, the laws will soon appear to flow thence as from their source. I shall proceed afterwards to other and more particular relations.

BOOK II.

OF LAWS DIRECTLY DERIVED FROM THE NATURE OF GOVERNMENT

1. *Of the Nature of the three different Governments.*

There are three species of government: *republican, monarchical,* and *despotic.* In order to discover their nature, it is sufficient to recollect the common notion, which supposes three definitions, or rather three facts: that a *republican government is that in which the body, or only a part of the people, is possessed of the supreme power; monarchy, that in which a single person governs by fixed and established laws; a despotic government, that in which a single person directs everything by his own will and caprice.*

This is what I call the nature of each government; we must now inquire into those laws which directly conform to this nature, and consequently are the fundamental institutions.

2. *Of the Republican Government, and the Laws in relation to Democracy.* [15]

[15] Compare Aristotle, *Politics*, VI. 2., wherein are exposed the fundamental laws of democratic constitutions.—Ed.

When the body of the people is possessed of the supreme power, it is called a *democracy.* When the supreme power is lodged in the hands of a part of the people, it is then an *aristocracy.*

In a democracy the people are in some respects the sovereign, and in others the subject.

There can be no exercise of sovereignty but by their suffrages, which are their own will; now the sovereign's will is the sovereign himself. The laws therefore which establish the right of suffrage are fundamental to this government. And indeed it is as important to regulate in a republic, in what manner, by whom, to whom, and concerning what, suffrages are to be given, as it is in a monarchy to know who is the prince, and after what manner he ought to govern.

Libanius [16] says that at *Athens a stranger who intermeddled in the assemblies of the people was punished with death*. This is because such a man usurped the rights of sovereignty. [17]

[16] Declamations, 17, 18.
[17] Libanius himself gives the reason for this law. "It was," he avers, "in order to prevent the secrets of the Republic from being divulged."—Ed.

It is an essential point to fix the number of citizens who are to form the public assemblies; otherwise it would be uncertain whether the whole, or only a part of the people, had given their votes. At Sparta the number was fixed at ten thousand. But Rome, designed by Providence to rise from the weakest beginnings to the highest pitch of grandeur; Rome, doomed to experience all the vicissitudes of fortune; Rome, who had sometimes all her inhabitants without her walls, and sometimes all Italy and a considerable part of the world within them; Rome, I say, never fixed the number [18] and this was one of the principal causes of her ruin.

[18] See the Considerations on the Causes of the Grandeur and Decline of the Romans, ch. 9.

The people, in whom the supreme power resides, ought to have the management of everything within their reach: that which exceeds their abilities must be conducted by their ministers.

But they cannot properly be said to have their ministers, without the power of nominating them: it is, therefore, a fundamental maxim in this government, that the people should choose their ministers—that is, their magistrates.

They have occasion, as well as monarchs, and even more so, to be directed by a council or senate. But to have a proper confidence in these, they should have the choosing of the members; whether the election be made by themselves, as at Athens, or by some magistrate deputed for that purpose, as on certain occasions was customary at Rome. [19]

[19] The Roman senators were *invariably* chosen by magistrates in whom the people had vested the power.—Crévier

The people are extremely well qualified for choosing those whom they are to entrust with part of their authority. They have only to be determined by things to which they cannot be strangers, and by facts that are obvious to sense. They can tell when a person has fought many battles, and been crowned with success; they are, therefore, capable of electing a general. They can tell when a judge is assiduous in his office, gives general satisfaction, and has never been charged with bribery: this is sufficient for choosing a prætor. They are struck with the magnificence or riches of a fellow-citizen; no more is requisite for electing an edile. These are facts of which they can have better information in a public forum than a monarch in his palace. But are they capable of conducting an intricate affair, of seizing and improving the opportunity and critical moment of action? No; this surpasses their abilities.

Should we doubt the people's natural capacity, in respect to the discernment of merit, we need only cast an eye on the series of surprising elections made by the Athenians and Romans; which no one surely will attribute to hazard.

We know that though the people of Rome assumed the right of raising plebeians to public offices, yet they never would exert this power; and though at Athens the magistrates were allowed, by the law of Aristides, to be elected from all the different classes of inhabitants, there never was a case, says Xenophon, [20] when the common people petitioned for employments which could endanger either their security or their glory.

[20] Pp. 691, 693, Edit. Wechel, 1596.

As most citizens have sufficient ability to choose, though unqualified to be chosen, so the people, though capable of calling others to an account for their administration, are incapable of conducting the administration themselves.

The public business must be carried on with a certain motion, neither too quick nor too slow. But the motion of the people is always either too remiss or too violent. Sometimes with a hundred thousand arms they overturn all before them; and sometimes with a hundred thousand feet they creep like insects.

In a popular state the inhabitants are divided into certain classes. It is in the manner of making this division that great legislators have signalized themselves; and it is on this the duration and prosperity of democracy have ever depended.

Servius Tullius followed the spirit of aristocracy in the distribution of his classes. We find in Livy [21] and in Dionysius Halicarnassus, [22] in what manner he lodged the right of suffrage in the hands of the principal citizens. He had divided the people of Rome into 193 centuries, which formed six classes; and ranking the rich, who were in smaller numbers, in the first centuries, and those in middling circumstances, who were more numerous, in the next, he flung the indigent multitude into the last; and as each century had but one vote [23] it was property rather than numbers that decided the election.

[21] Bk. i.
[22] Bk. iv, art. 15 et seq.
[23] See in the Considerations on the Causes of the Grandeur and Decline of the Romans, ch. 9, how this spirit of Servius Tullius was preserved in the republic.

Solon divided the people of Athens into four classes. In this he was directed by the spirit of democracy, his intention not being to fix those who were to choose, but such as were eligible: therefore, leaving to every citizen the right of election, he made [24] the judges eligible from each of those four classes; but the magistrates he ordered to be chosen only out of the first three, consisting of persons of easy fortunes. [25]

[24] Dionysius Halicarnassus, Eulogium of Isocrates, ii, p. 97, ed. Wechel. Pollux, viii. 10, art. 130.
[25] See Aristotle's *Politics*, lib. II. 12.

As the division of those who have a right of suffrage is a fundamental law in republics, so the manner of giving this suffrage is another fundamental.

The suffrage by *lot* is natural to democracy; as that by *choice* is to aristocracy. [26]

[26] *Ibid*, lib. IV. 9.

The suffrage by *lot* is a method of electing that offends no one, but animates each citizen with the pleasing hope of serving his country. [27]

[27] The mere suffrage might occasion mortification to those who were excluded, and undue pride to the favored ones. It was in order to avoid this contingency that they had recourse to lot, and thus chance precluded this danger, for it does not deal in humiliation or inflation.—*Servan*

Yet as this method is in itself defective, it has been the endeavor of the most eminent legislators to regulate and amend it.

Solon made a law at Athens that military employments should be conferred by choice; but that senators and judges should be elected by *lot*.

The same legislator ordained that civil magistracies, attended with great expense, should be given by choice; and the others by lot.

In order, however, to amend the suffrage by lot, he made a rule that none but those who presented themselves should be elected; that the person elected should be examined by judges [28] and that everyone should have a right to accuse him if he were unworthy of the office: [29] this participated at the same time of the suffrage by lot, and of that by choice. When the time of their magistracy had expired, they were obliged to submit to another judgment in regard to their conduct. Persons utterly unqualified must have been extremely backward in giving in their names to be drawn by lot.

[28] See the oration of Demosthenes, *De Falsâ legat.*, and the oration against Timarchus.
[29] They used even to draw two tickets for each place, one which gave the place, and the other which named the person who was to succeed, in case the first was rejected. (These two tickets sufficed when the people were called upon to deliberate in a question of law; but in the election of magistrates, each citizen received as many tickets as there were candidates.—*Crévier*)

The law which determines the manner of giving suffrage is likewise fundamental in a democracy. It is a question of some importance whether the suffrages ought to be public or secret. Cicero observes [30] that the laws [31] which rendered them secret towards the close of the republic were the cause of its decline. But as this is differently practiced in different republics, I shall offer here my thoughts concerning this subject.

[30] *De Leg.*, Lib. I, III.

[31] They were called *Leges Tabulares*; two tablets were presented to each citizen, the first marked with an *A*, for *Antique*, or *I forbid it*; and the other with an *U* and an *R*, for *Uti Rogas*, or *Be it as you desire*.

The people's suffrages ought doubtless to be public; [32] and this should be considered as a fundamental law of democracy. The lower class ought to be directed by those of higher rank, and restrained within bounds by the gravity of eminent personages. Hence, by rendering the suffrages secret in the Roman republic, all was lost; it was no longer possible to direct a populace that sought its own destruction. But when the body of the nobles are to vote in an aristocracy, [33] or in a democracy the senate, [34] as the business is then only to prevent intrigues, the suffrages cannot be too secret.

[32] At Athens the people used to lift up their hands.
[33] As at Venice.
[34] The thirty tyrants at Athens ordered the suffrages of the *Areopagites* to be public, in order to manage them as they pleased.—Lysias, *Orat. contra Agorat.* Chap. 8.

Intriguing in a senate is dangerous; it is dangerous also in a body of nobles; but not so among the people, whose nature is to act through passion. In countries where they have no share in the government, we often see them as much inflamed on account of an actor as ever they could be for the welfare of the state. The misfortune of a republic is when intrigues are at an end; which happens when the people are gained by bribery and corruption: in this case they grow indifferent to public affairs, and avarice becomes their predominant passion. Unconcerned about the government and everything belonging to it, they quietly wait for their hire.

It is likewise a fundamental law in democracies, that the people should have the sole power to enact laws. And yet there are a thousand occasions on which it is necessary the senate should have the power of decreeing; nay, it is frequently proper to make some trial of a law before it is established. The constitutions of Rome and Athens were excellent. The decrees of the senate [35] had the force of laws for the space of a year, but did not become perpetual till they were ratified by the consent of the people.

[35] See Dionysius Halicarnassus, lib. iv, ix.

3. *Of the Laws in relation to the Nature of Aristocracy.*

In an aristocracy the supreme power is lodged in the hands of a certain number of persons. These are invested both with the legislative and executive authority; and the rest of the people are, in respect to them, the same as the subjects of a monarchy in regard to the sovereign.

They do not vote here by lot, for this would be productive of inconveniences only. And indeed, in a government where the most mortifying distinctions are already established, though they were to be chosen by lot, still they would not cease to be odious; it is the nobleman they envy, and not the magistrate.

When the nobility are numerous, there must be a senate to regulate the affairs which the body of the nobles are incapable of deciding, and to prepare others for their decision. In this case it may be said that the aristocracy is in some measure in the senate, the democracy in the body of the nobles, and the people are a cipher.

It would be a very happy thing in an aristocracy if the people, in some measure, could be raised from their state of annihilation. Thus at Genoa, the bank of St. George being administered by the people [36] gives them a certain influence in the government, whence their whole prosperity is derived.

[36] See Mr. Addison, *Travels to Italy*, p. 16.

The senators ought by no means to have the right of naming their own members; for this would be the only way to perpetuate abuses. At Rome, which in its early years was a kind of aristocracy, the senate did not fill up the vacant places in their own body; the new members were nominated by the censors. [37]

[37] They were named at first by the consuls.

In a republic, the sudden rise of a private citizen to exorbitant power produces monarchy, or something more than monarchy. In the latter the laws have provided for, or in some measure adapted themselves to, the constitution; and the principle of government checks the monarch: but in a republic, where a private citizen has obtained an exorbitant power, [38] the abuse of this power is much greater, because the laws foresaw it not, and consequently made no provision against it.

[38] This is what ruined the republic of Rome. See Considerations on the Causes of the Grandeur and Decline of the Romans.

There is an exception to this rule, when the constitution is such as to have immediate need of a magistrate invested with extraordinary power. Such was Rome with her dictators, such is Venice with her state inquisitors; these are formidable magistrates, who restore, as it were by violence, the state to its liberty. But how comes it that these magistracies are so very different in these two republics? It is because Rome supported the remains of her aristocracy against the people; whereas Venice employs her state inquisitors to maintain her aristocracy against the nobles. The consequence was that at Rome the dictatorship could be only of short duration, as the people acted through passion and not with design. It was necessary that a magistracy of this kind should be exercised with luster and pomp, the business being to intimidate, and not to punish, the multitude. It was also proper that the dictator should be created only for some particular affair, and for this only should have an unlimited authority, as he was always created upon some sudden emergency. On the contrary, at Venice they have occasion for a permanent magistracy; for here it is that schemes may be set on foot, continued, suspended, and resumed; that the ambition of a single person becomes that of a family, and the ambition of one family that of many. They have occasion for a secret magistracy, the crimes they punish being hatched in secrecy and silence. This magistracy must have a general inquisition, for their business is not to remedy known disorders, but to prevent the unknown. In a word, the latter is designed to punish suspected crimes; whereas the former used rather menaces than punishment even for crimes that were openly avowed.

In all magistracies, the greatness of the power must be compensated by the brevity of the duration. This most legislators have fixed to a year; a longer space would be dangerous, and a shorter would be contrary to the nature of government. For who is it that in the management even of his domestic affairs would be thus confined? At Ragusa [39] the chief magistrate of the republic is changed every month, the other officers every week, and the governor of the castle every day. But this can take place only in a small republic environed [40] by formidable powers, who might easily corrupt such petty and insignificant magistrates.

[39] Tournefort, *Voyages*.
[40] At Lucca the magistrates are chosen only for two months.

The best aristocracy is that in which those who have no share in the legislature are so few and inconsiderable that the governing party have no interest in oppressing them. Thus when [41] Antipater made a law at Athens that whosoever was not worth two thousand drachmæ should have no power to vote, he formed by this method the best aristocracy possible; because this was so small a sum as to exclude very few, and not one of any rank or consideration in the city.

[41] Diodorus, lib. XVIII, p. 601, ed. Rhodoman.

Aristocratic families ought therefore, as much as possible, to level themselves in appearance with the people. The more an aristocracy borders on democracy, the nearer it approaches perfection: and, in proportion as it draws towards monarchy, the more is it imperfect.

But the most imperfect of all is that in which the part of the people that obeys is in a state of civil servitude to those who command, as the aristocracy of Poland, where the peasants are slaves to the nobility.

4. Of the Relation of Laws to the Nature of Monarchical Government.

The intermediate, subordinate, and dependent powers constitute the nature of monarchical government; I mean of that in which a single person governs by fundamental laws. I said the *intermediate, subordinate,* and *dependent powers*. And indeed, in monarchies the prince is the source of all power, political and civil. These fundamental laws necessarily suppose the intermediate channels through which the power flows: for if there be only the momentary and capricious will of a single person to govern the state, nothing can be fixed, and of course there is no fundamental law.

The most natural, intermediate, and subordinate power is that of the nobility. This in some measure seems to be essential to a monarchy, whose fundamental maxim is: *no monarch, no nobility; no nobility, no monarch*; but there may be a despotic prince. [42]

[42] This maxim brings to mind the unfortunate Charles I., who said, "No bishop, no monarch;" while Henry IV. of France declared to the *Seize*, "No nobility, no monarch!"—Voltaire

There are men who have endeavored in some countries in Europe to suppress the jurisdiction of the nobility, not perceiving that they were driving at the very thing that was done by the parliament of England. Abolish the privileges of the lords, the clergy and cities in a monarchy, and you will soon have a popular state, or else a despotic government.

The courts of a considerable kingdom in Europe have, for many ages, been striking at the patrimonial jurisdiction of the lords and clergy. We do not pretend to censure these sage magistrates; but we leave it to the public to judge how far this may alter the constitution.

Far am I from being prejudiced in favor of the privileges of the clergy; however, I should be glad if their jurisdiction were once fixed. The question is not whether their jurisdiction was justly established; but whether it be really established; whether it constitutes a part of the laws of the country, and is in every respect in relation to those laws: whether between two powers acknowledged independent, the conditions ought not to be reciprocal; and whether it be not equally the duty of a good subject to defend the prerogative of the prince, and to maintain the limits which from time immemorial have been prescribed to his authority.

Though the ecclesiastic power be so dangerous in a republic, yet it is extremely proper in a monarchy, especially of the absolute kind. What would become of Spain and Portugal, since the subversion of their laws, were it not for this only barrier against the incursions of arbitrary power? A barrier ever useful when there is no other: for since a despotic government is productive of the most dreadful calamities to human nature, the very evil that restrains it is beneficial to the subject.

In the same manner as the ocean, threatening to overflow the whole earth, is stopped by weeds and pebbles that lie scattered along the shore, [43] so monarchs, whose power seems unbounded, are restrained by the smallest obstacles, and suffer their natural pride to be subdued by supplication and prayer.

[43] Voltaire is inclined to doubt the justice of this comparison.—Ed.

The English, to favor their liberty, have abolished all the intermediate powers of which their monarchy was composed. [44] They have a great deal of reason to be jealous of this liberty; were they ever to be so unhappy as to lose it, they would be one of the most servile nations upon earth.

[44] On the contrary, the English have rendered the power of their spiritual and temporal lords more legal, and have augmented that of the Commons.—*Voltaire*

Mr. Law, through ignorance both of a republican and monarchical constitution, was one of the greatest promoters of absolute power ever known in Europe. Besides the violent and extraordinary changes owing to his direction, he would fain suppress all the intermediate ranks, and abolish the political communities. He was dissolving [45] the monarchy by his chimerical reimbursements, and seemed as if he even wanted to redeem the constitution.

[45] Ferdinand, king of Aragon, made himself grand master of the orders, and that alone changed the constitution.

It is not enough to have intermediate powers in a monarchy; there must be also a depositary of the laws. This depositary can only be the judges of the supreme courts of justice, who promulgate the new laws, and revive the obsolete. The natural ignorance of the nobility, their indolence and contempt of civil government, require that there should be a body invested with the power of reviving and executing the laws, which would be otherwise buried in oblivion. The prince's council are not a proper depositary. They are naturally the depositary of the momentary will of the prince, and not of the fundamental laws. Besides, the prince's council is continually changing; it is neither permanent nor numerous; neither has it a sufficient share of the confidence of the people; consequently it is capable of setting them right in difficult conjunctures, or of reducing them to proper obedience.

Despotic governments, where there are no fundamental laws, have no such kind of depositary. Hence it is that religion has generally so much influence in those countries, because it forms a kind of permanent depositary; and if this cannot be said of religion, it may of the customs that are respected instead of laws.

5. *Of the Laws in relation to the Nature of a despotic Government.*

From the nature of despotic power it follows that the single person, invested with this power, commits the execution of it also to a single person. A man whom his senses continually inform that he himself is everything and that his subjects are nothing, is naturally lazy, voluptuous, and ignorant. In consequence of this, he neglects the management of public affairs. But were he to commit the administration to many, there would be continual disputes among them; each would form intrigues to be his first slave; and he would be obliged to take the reins into his own hands. It is, therefore, more natural for him to resign it to a vizir, [46] and to invest him with the same power as himself. The creation of a vizir is a fundamental law of this government.

[46] The Eastern kings are never without vizirs, says Sir John Chardin.

It is related of a pope that he had started an infinite number of difficulties against his election, from a thorough conviction of his incapacity. At length he was prevailed on to accept of the pontificate, and resigned the administration entirely to his nephew. He was soon struck with surprise, and said, *I should never have thought that these things were so easy.* The same may be said of the princes of the East, who, being educated in a prison where eunuchs corrupt their hearts and debase their understandings, and where they are frequently kept ignorant even of their high rank, when drawn forth in order to be placed on the throne, are at first confounded: but as soon as they have chosen a vizir, and abandoned themselves in their seraglio to the most brutal passions; pursuing, in the midst of a prostituted court, every capricious extravagance, they would never have dreamed that they could find matters so easy.

The more extensive the empire, the larger the seraglio; and consequently the more voluptuous the prince. Hence the more nations such a sovereign has to rule, the less he attends to the cares of government; the more important his affairs, the less he makes them the subject of his deliberations.

BOOK III.

OF THE PRINCIPLES OF THE THREE KINDS OF GOVERNMENT

1. *Difference between the Nature and Principle of Government.*

Having examined the laws in relation to the nature of each government, we must investigate those which relate to its principle.

There is this difference between the nature and principle [47] of government, that the former is that by which it is constituted, the latter that by which it is made to act. One is its particular structure, and the other the human passions which set it in motion.

[47] This is a very important distinction, whence I shall draw many consequences; for it is the key of an infinite number of laws.

Now, laws ought no less to relate to the principle than to the nature of each government. We must, therefore, inquire into this principle, which shall be the subject of this third book.

2. *Of the Principle of different Governments.*

I have already observed that it is the nature of a republican government that either the collective body of the people, or particular families, should be possessed of the supreme power; of a monarchy, that the prince should have this power, but in the execution of it should be directed by established laws; of a despotic government, that a single person should rule according to his own will and caprice. This enables me to discover their three principles; which are thence naturally derived. I shall begin with a republican government, and in particular with that of democracy.

3. *Of the Principle of Democracy.*

There is no great share of probity necessary to support a monarchical or despotic government. The force of laws in one, and the prince's arm in the other, are sufficient to direct and maintain the whole. But in a popular state, one spring more is necessary, namely, *virtue.*

What I have here advanced is confirmed by the unanimous testimony of historians, and is extremely agreeable to the nature of things. [48] For it is clear that in a monarchy, where he who commands the execution of the laws generally thinks himself above them, there is less need of virtue than in a popular government, where the person entrusted with the execution of the laws is sensible of his being subject to their direction.

[48] It has always been argued against Montesquieu that he has said that there can only be virtue in republics, and honor in monarchies, or *vice versa*: whereas he has said nothing of the sort, and to allege it even is to suppose him capable of a great absurdity.—*La Harpe*

Clear is it also that a monarch who, through bad advice or indolence, ceases to enforce the execution of the laws, may easily repair the evil; he has only to follow other advice; or to shake off this indolence. But when, in a popular government, there is a suspension of the laws, as this can proceed only from the corruption of the republic, the state is certainly undone.

A very droll spectacle it was in the last century to behold the impotent efforts of the English towards the establishment of democracy. As they who had a share in the direction of public affairs were void of virtue; as their ambition was inflamed by the success of the most daring of their members; [49] as the prevailing parties were successively animated by the spirit of faction, the government was continually changing: the people, amazed at so many revolutions, in vain attempted to erect a commonwealth. At length, when the country had undergone the most violent shocks, they were obliged to have recourse to the very government which they had so wantonly proscribed.

[49] Cromwell.

When Sylla thought of restoring Rome to her liberty, this unhappy city was incapable of receiving that blessing. She had only the feeble remains of virtue, which were continually diminishing. Instead of being roused from her lethargy by Cæsar, Tiberius, Caius Claudius, Nero, and Domitian, she riveted every day her chains; if she struck some blows, her aim was at the tyrant, not at the tyranny.

The politic Greeks, who lived under a popular government, knew no other support than virtue. The modern inhabitants of that country are entirely taken up with manufacture, commerce, finances, opulence, and luxury.

When virtue is banished, ambition invades the minds of those who are disposed to receive it, and avarice possesses the whole community. The objects of their desires are changed; what they were fond of before has become indifferent; they were free while under the restraint of laws, but they would fain now be free to act against law; and as each citizen is like a slave who has run away from his master, that which was a maxim of equity he calls rigor; that which was a rule of action he styles constraint; and to precaution he gives the name of fear. Frugality, and not the thirst of gain, now passes for avarice. Formerly the wealth of individuals constituted the public treasure; but now this has become the patrimony of private persons. The members of the commonwealth riot on the public spoils, and its strength is only the power of a few, and the license of many.

Athens was possessed of the same number of forces when she triumphed so gloriously as when with such infamy she was enslaved. She had twenty thousand citizens [50] when she defended the Greeks against the Persians, when she contended for empire with Sparta, and invaded Sicily. She had twenty thousand when Demetrius Phalereus numbered them [51] as slaves are told by the head in a market-place. When Philip attempted to lord it over Greece, and appeared at the gates of Athens [52] she had even then lost nothing but time. We may see in Demosthenes how difficult it was to awaken her; she dreaded Philip, not as the enemy of her liberty, but of her pleasures. [53] This famous city, which had withstood so many defeats, and having been so often destroyed had as often risen out of her ashes, was overthrown at Chæronea, and at one blow deprived of all hopes of resource. What does it avail her that Philip sends back her prisoners, if he does not return her men? It was ever after as easy to triumph over the forces of Athens as it had been difficult to subdue her virtue.

[50] Plutarch, Life of Pericles; Plato, in *Critia*.

[51] She had at that time twenty-one thousand citizens, ten thousand strangers, and four hundred thousand slaves. See Athenæus, vi.

[52] She had then twenty thousand citizens. See Demosthenes in *Aristog.*

[53] They had passed a law, which rendered it a capital crime for anyone to propose applying the money designed for the theatres to military

How was it possible for Carthage to maintain her ground? When Hannibal, upon his being made prætor, endeavored to hinder the magistrates from plundering the republic, did not they complain of him to the Romans? Wretches, who would fain be citizens without a city, and be beholden for their riches to their very destroyers! Rome soon insisted upon having three hundred of their principal citizens as hostages; she obliged them next to surrender their arms and ships; and then she declared war. [54] From the desperate efforts of this defenseless city, one may judge of what she might have performed in her full vigor, and assisted by virtue.

[54] This lasted three years.

4. *Of the Principle of Aristocracy.*

As virtue is necessary in a popular government, it is requisite also in an aristocracy. True it is that in the latter it is not so absolutely requisite.

The people, who in respect to the nobility are the same as the subjects with regard to a monarch, are restrained by their laws. They have, therefore, less occasion for virtue than the people in a democracy. But how are the nobility to be restrained? They who are to execute the laws against their colleagues will immediately perceive that they are acting against themselves. Virtue is therefore necessary in this body, from the very nature of the constitution.

An aristocratic government has an inherent vigor, unknown to democracy. The nobles form a body, who by their prerogative, and for their own particular interest, restrain the people; it is sufficient that there are laws in being to see them executed.

But easy as it may be for the body of the nobles to restrain the people, it is difficult to restrain themselves. [55] Such is the nature of this constitution, that it seems to subject the very same persons to the power of the laws, and at the same time to exempt them.

[55] Public crimes may be punished, because it is here a common concern; but private crimes will go unpunished, because it is the common interest not to punish them.

Now such a body as this can restrain itself only in two ways; either by a very eminent virtue, which puts the nobility in some measure on a level with the people, and may be the means of forming a great republic; or by an inferior virtue, which puts them at least upon a level with one another, and upon this their preservation depends.

Moderation is therefore the very soul of this government; a moderation, I mean, founded on virtue, not that which proceeds from indolence and pusillanimity.

5. *That Virtue is not the Principle of a Monarchical Government.*

In monarchies, policy effects great things with as little virtue as possible. Thus in the nicest machines, art has reduced the number of movements, springs, and wheels.

The state subsists independently of the love of our country, of the thirst of true glory, of self-denial, of the sacrifice of our dearest interests, and of all those heroic virtues which we admire in the ancients, and to us are known only by tradition.

The laws supply here the place of those virtues; they are by no means wanted, and the state dispenses with them: an action performed here in secret is in some measure of no consequence.

Though all crimes be in their own nature public, yet there is a distinction between crimes really public and those that are private, which are so called because they are more injurious to individuals than to the community.

Now in republics private crimes are more public, that is, they attack the constitution more than they do individuals; and in monarchies, public crimes are more private, that is, they are more prejudicial to private people than to the constitution.

I beg that no one will be offended with what I have been saying; my observations are founded on the unanimous testimony of historians. I am not ignorant that virtuous princes are so very rare; but I venture to affirm that in a monarchy it is extremely difficult for the people to be virtuous. [56]

[56] I speak here of political virtue, which is also moral virtue as it is directed to the public good; very little of private moral virtue, and not at all of that virtue which relates to revealed truths. This will appear better in book V. chap. 2.

Let us compare what the historians of all ages have asserted concerning the courts of monarchs; let us recollect the conversations and sentiments of people of all countries, in respect to the wretched character of courtiers, and we shall find that these are not airy speculations, but truths confirmed by a sad and melancholy experience.

Ambition in idleness; meanness mixed with pride; a desire of riches without industry; aversion to truth; flattery, perfidy, violation of engagements, contempt of civil duties, fear of the prince's virtue, hope from his weakness, but, above all, a perpetual ridicule cast upon virtue, are, I think, the characteristics by which most courtiers in all ages and countries have been constantly distinguished. Now, it is exceedingly difficult for the leading men of the nation to be knaves, and the inferior sort to be honest; for the former to be cheats, and the latter to rest satisfied with being only dupes.

But if there should chance to be some unlucky honest man [57] among the people. Cardinal Richelieu, in his political testament, seems to hint that a prince should take care not to employ him. [58] So true is it that virtue is not the spring of this government! It is not indeed excluded, but it is not the spring of government.

[57] This is to be understood in the sense of the preceding note.
[58] We must not, says he, employ people of mean extraction; they are too rigid and morose.

6. *In what Manner Virtue is supplied in a Monarchical Government.*

But it is high time for me to have done with this subject, lest I should be suspected of writing a satire against monarchical government. Far be it from me; if monarchy wants one spring, it is provided with another. Honor, that is, the prejudice of every person and rank, supplies the place of the political virtue of which I have been speaking, and is everywhere her representative: here it is capable of inspiring the most glorious actions, and, joined with the force of laws, may lead us to the end of government as well as virtue itself.

Hence, in well-regulated monarchies, they are almost all good subjects, and very few good men; for to be a good man [59] a good intention is necessary, [60] and we should love our country, not so much on our own account, as out of regard to the community.

[59] This word *good man* is understood here in a political sense only.
[60] See Footnote 56.

7. *Of the Principle of Monarchy.*

A monarchical government supposes, as we have already observed, pre-eminences and ranks, as likewise a noble descent. Now since it is the nature of honor to aspire to preferments and titles, [61] it is properly placed in this government.

[61] These preferments, distinctions, and honors, in the days of the Roman republic, were worth quite as much as the *débris* which goes to constitute a kingdom today. Prefectures, consulates, axes, fasces, and triumphs were valued at the price of so many colored ribbons.—*Voltaire*

Ambition is pernicious in a republic. But in a monarchy it has some good effects; it gives life to the government, and is attended with this advantage, that it is in no way dangerous, because it may be continually checked.

It is with this kind of government as with the system of the universe, in which there is a power that constantly repels all bodies from the centre, and a power of gravitation that attracts them to it. Honor sets all the parts of the body politic in motion, and by its very action connects them; thus each individual advances the public good, while he only thinks of promoting his own interest.

True it is that, philosophically speaking, it is a false honor which moves all the parts of the government; but even this false honor is as useful to the public as true honor could possibly be to private persons.

Is it not very exacting to oblige men to perform the most difficult actions, such as require an extraordinary exertion of fortitude and resolution, without other recompense than that of glory and applause?

8. *That Honor is not the Principle of Despotic Government.*

Honor is far from being the principle of despotic government: mankind being here all upon a level, no one person can prefer himself to another; and as on the other hand they are all slaves, they can give themselves no sort of preference.

Besides, as honor has its laws and rules, as it knows not how to submit; as it depends in a great measure on a man's own caprice, and not on that of another person; it can be found only in countries in which the constitution is fixed, and where they are governed by settled laws.

How can despotism abide with honor? The one glories in the contempt of life; and the other is founded on the power of taking it away. How can honor, on the other hand, bear with despotism? The former has its fixed rules, and peculiar caprices; but the latter is directed by no rule, and its own caprices are subversive of all others.

Honor, therefore, a thing unknown in arbitrary governments, some of which have not even a proper word to express it, [62] is the prevailing principle in monarchies; here it gives life to the whole body politic, to the laws, and even to the virtues themselves.

[62] See Perry, p. 447.

9. *Of the Principle of Despotic Government.*

As virtue is necessary in a republic, and in a monarchy honor, so fear is necessary in a despotic government: with regard to virtue, there is no occasion for it, and honor would be extremely dangerous. [63]

[63] It has been thought that Montesquieu anticipated innumerable difficulties, if he entered upon his plan, and in his own style began to refute objections. It is evident that his only desire was to construct a series of his ideas, and that his motives should be conceived.

Here the immense power of the prince devolves entirely upon those whom he is pleased to entrust with the administration. Persons capable of setting a value upon themselves would be likely to create disturbances. Fear must therefore depress their spirits, and extinguish even the least sense of ambition.

A moderate government may, whenever it pleases, and without the least danger, relax its springs. It supports itself by the laws, and by its own internal strength. But when a despotic prince ceases for one single moment to uplift his arm, when he cannot instantly demolish those whom he has entrusted with the first employments, [64] all is over: for as fear, the spring of this government, no longer subsists, the people are left without a protector.

[64] As it often happens in a military aristocracy.

It is probably in this sense the Cadis maintained that the Grand Seignior was not obliged to keep his word or oath, when he limited thereby his authority. [65]

[65] Ricaut on the Ottoman Empire. I, ii.

It is necessary that the people should be judged by laws, and the great men by the caprice of the prince, that the lives of the lowest subject should be safe, and the pasha's head ever in danger. We cannot mention these monstrous governments without horror. The Sophi of Persia, dethroned in our days by Mahomet, the son of Miriveis, saw the constitution subverted before this resolution, because he had been too sparing of blood. [66]

[66] See the history of this revolution by Father Ducerceau.

History informs us that the horrid cruelties of Domitian struck such a terror into the governors that the people recovered themselves a little during his reign. [67] Thus a torrent overflows one side of a country, and on the other leaves fields untouched, where the eye is refreshed by the prospect of fine meadows.

[67] His was a military constitution, which is one of the species of despotic government.

10. *Difference of Obedience in Moderate and Despotic Governments.*

In despotic states, the nature of government requires the most passive obedience; and when once the prince's will is made known, it ought infallibly to produce its effect.

Here they have no limitations or restrictions, no mediums, terms, equivalents, or remonstrances; no change to propose: man is a creature that blindly submits to the absolute will of the sovereign.

In a country like this they are no more allowed to represent their apprehensions of a future danger than to impute their miscarriage to the capriciousness of fortune. Man's portion here, like that of beasts, is instinct, compliance, and punishment.

Little does it then avail to plead the sentiments of nature, filial respect, conjugal or parental tenderness, the laws of honor, or want of health; the order is given, and, that is sufficient.

In Persia, when the king has condemned a person, it is no longer lawful to mention his name, or to intercede in his favor. Even if the prince were intoxicated, or non compos, the decree must be executed; [68] otherwise he would contradict himself, and the law admits of no contradiction. This has been the way of thinking in that country in all ages; as the order which Ahasuerus gave, to exterminate the Jews, could not be revoked, they were allowed the liberty of defending themselves. [69]

[68] See Sir John Chardin.
[69] This order was revoked by a new edict. See Esther xvi. 7.—Ed.

One thing, however, may be sometimes opposed to the prince's will, [70] namely, religion. They will abandon, nay they will slay a parent, if the prince so commands; but he cannot oblige them to drink wine. The laws of religion are of a superior nature, because they bind the sovereign as well as the subject. But with respect to the law of nature, it is otherwise; the prince is no longer supposed to be a man.

[70] See Sir John Chardin.

In monarchical and moderate states, the power is limited by its very spring, I mean by honor, which, like a monarch, reigns over the prince and his people. They will not allege to their sovereign the laws of religion; a courtier would be apprehensive of rendering himself ridiculous. But the laws of honor will be appealed to on all occasions.

Hence arise the restrictions necessary to obedience; honor is naturally subject to whims, by which the subject's submission will be ever directed.

Though the manner of obeying be different in these two kinds of government, the power is the same. On which side soever the monarch turns, he inclines the scale, and is obeyed. The whole difference is that in a monarchy the prince receives instruction, at the same time that his ministers have greater abilities, and are more versed in public affairs, than the ministers of a despotic government.

11. *Reflections on the preceding Chapters.*

Such are the principles of the three sorts of government: which does not imply that in a particular republic they actually are, but that they ought to be, virtuous; nor does it prove that in a particular monarchy they are actuated by honor, or in a particular despotic government by fear; but that they ought to be directed by these principles, otherwise the government is imperfect.

BOOK IV.

THAT THE LAWS OF EDUCATION OUGHT TO BE IN RELATION TO THE PRINCIPLES OF GOVERNMENT

1. *Of the Laws of Education.*

The laws of education are the first impressions we receive; and as they prepare us for civil life, every private family ought to be governed by the plan of that great household which comprehends them all.

If the people in general have a principle, their constituent parts, that is, the several families, will have one also. The laws of education will be therefore different in each species of government: in monarchies they will have honor for their object; in republics, virtue; in despotic governments, fear.

2. *Of Education in Monarchies.*

In monarchies the principal branch of education is not taught in colleges or academies. It commences, in some measure, at our setting out in the world; for this is the school of what we call honor, that universal preceptor which ought everywhere to be our guide.

Here it is that we constantly hear three rules or maxims, viz., *that we should have a certain nobleness in our virtues, a kind of frankness in our morals, and a particular politeness in our behavior.*

The virtues we are here taught are less what we owe to others than to ourselves; they are not so much what draws us towards society, as what distinguishes us from our fellow-citizens.

Here the actions of men are judged, not as virtuous, but as shining; not as just, but as great; not as reasonable, but as extraordinary. When honor here meets with anything noble in our actions, it is either a judge that approves them, or sophist by whom they are excused.

It allows of gallantry when united with the idea of sensible affection, or with that of conquest; this is the reason why we never meet with so strict a purity of morals in monarchies as in republican governments.

It allows of cunning and craft, when joined with the notion of greatness of soul or importance of affairs; as, for instance, in politics, with finesses of which it is far from being offended.

It does not forbid adulation, save when separated from the idea of a large fortune, and connected only with the sense of our mean condition.

With regard to morals, I have observed that the education of monarchies ought to admit of a certain frankness and open carriage. Truth, therefore, in conversation is here a necessary point. But is it for the sake of truth? By no means. Truth is requisite only because a person habituated to veracity has an air of boldness and freedom. And indeed a man of this stamp seems to lay a stress only on the things themselves, not on the manner in which they are received.

Hence it is that in proportion as this kind of frankness is commended, that of the common people is despised, which has nothing but truth and simplicity for its object.

In fine, the education of monarchies requires a certain politeness of behavior. Man, a sociable animal, is formed to please in society; and a person that would break through the rules of decency, so as to shock those he conversed with, would lose the public esteem, and become incapable of doing any good.

But politeness, generally speaking, does not derive its origin from so pure a source. It arises from a desire of distinguishing ourselves. It is pride that renders us polite; we are flattered with being taken notice of for behavior that shows we are not of a mean condition, and that we have not been bred with those who in all ages are considered the scum of the people.

Politeness, in monarchies, is naturalized at court. One man excessively great renders everybody else little. Hence that regard which is paid to our fellow-subjects; hence that politeness, equally pleasing to those by whom, as to those towards whom, it is practiced, because it gives people to understand that a person actually belongs, or at least deserves to belong, to the court.

A courtly air consists in quitting a real for a borrowed greatness. The latter pleases the courtier more than the former. It inspires him with a certain disdainful modesty, which shows itself externally, but whose pride insensibly diminishes in proportion to its distance from the source of this greatness.

At court we find a delicacy of taste in everything—a delicacy arising from the constant use of the superfluities of life, from the variety, and especially the satiety, of pleasures, from the multiplicity and even confusion of fancies, which, if they are but agreeable, are sure of being well received.

These are the things which properly fall within the province of education, in order to form what we call a man of honor, a man possessed of all the qualities and virtues requisite in this kind of government.

Here it is that honor interferes with everything, mixing even with people's manner of thinking, and directing their very principles.

To this whimsical honor it is owing that the virtues are only just what it pleases; it adds rules of its own invention to everything prescribed to us; it extends or limits our duties according to its own fancy, whether they proceed from religion, politics, or morality.

There is nothing so strongly inculcated in monarchies, by the laws, by religion and honor, as submission to the prince's will; but this very honor tells us that the prince never ought to command a dishonorable action, because this would render us incapable of serving him.

Crillon refused to assassinate the Duke of Guise, but offered to fight him. After the massacre of St. Bartholomew, Charles IX, having sent orders to the governors in the several provinces for the Huguenots to be murdered, Viscount Dorte, who commanded at Bayonne, wrote thus to the king: [71] *Sire, among the inhabitants of this town, and your majesty's troops, I could not find so much as one executioner; they are honest citizens and brave soldiers. We jointly, therefore, beseech your majesty to command our arms and lives in things that are practicable.* This great and generous soul looked upon a base action as a thing impossible.

[71] See d'Aubigny's History.

There is nothing that honor more strongly recommends to the nobility than to serve their prince in a military capacity. And, indeed, this is their favorite profession, because its dangers, its success, and even its miscarriages are the road to grandeur. Yet this very law of its own making honor chooses to explain: and in case of any affront, it requires or permits us to retire.

It insists also that we should be at liberty either to seek or to reject employments, a liberty which it prefers even to an ample fortune.

Honor therefore has its supreme laws, to which education is obliged to conform. [72] The chief of these are that we are permitted to set a value upon our fortune, but are absolutely forbidden to set any upon our lives.

[72] We mention here what actually is, and not what ought to be; honor is a prejudice, which religion sometimes endeavors to remove, and at other times to regulate.

The second is, that when we are raised to a post or preferment, we should never do or permit anything which may seem to imply that we look upon ourselves as inferior to the rank we hold.

The third is that those things which honor forbids are more rigorously forbidden, when the laws do not concur in the prohibition; and those it commands are more strongly insisted upon, when they happen not to be commanded by law.

3. Of Education in a Despotic Government.

As education in monarchies tends to raise and ennoble the mind, in despotic governments its only aim is to debase it. Here it must necessarily be servile; even in power such an education will be an advantage, because every tyrant is at the same time a slave.

Excessive obedience supposes ignorance in the person that obeys: [73] the same it supposes in him that commands, for he has no occasion to deliberate, to doubt, to reason; he has only to will.

[73] By excessive obedience, Montesquieu intends *blind* obedience.—*De Dupin.*

In despotic states, each house is a separate government. As education, therefore, consists chiefly in social converse, it must be here very much limited; all it does is to strike the heart with fear, and to imprint on the understanding a very simple notion of a few principles of religion. Learning here proves dangerous, emulation fatal; and as to virtue, Aristotle [74] cannot think that there is any one virtue belonging to slaves; [75] if so, education in despotic countries is confined within a very narrow compass.

[74] Politics, i. 13.
[75] How can this be, asks one, when slaves have no will? —Ed.

Here, therefore, education is in some measure needless: to give something, one must take away everything, and begin with making a bad subject in order to make a good slave.

For why should education take pains in forming a good citizen, only to make him share in the public misery? If he loves his country, he will strive to relax the springs of government; if he miscarries he will be undone; if he succeeds, he must expose himself, the prince, and his country to ruin.

4. Difference between the Effects of Ancient and Modern Education.

Most of the ancients lived under governments that had virtue for their principle; and when this was in full vigor they performed actions unusual in our times, and at which our narrow minds are astonished.

Another advantage their education possessed over ours was that it never could be effaced by contrary impressions. Epaminondas, the last year of his life, said, heard, beheld, and performed the very same things as at the age in which he received the first principles of his education.

In our days we receive three different or contrary educations, namely, of our parents, of our masters, and of the world. What we learn in the latter effaces all the ideas of the former. This, in some measure, arises from the contrast we experience between our religious and worldly engagements, [76] a thing unknown to the ancients.

[76] The Christian religion forbids vengeance and prescribes humility; this is perhaps the point of contrast which the author notes. But these precepts have not made of Europe a world of poltroons. It is well known that officers most attached to the laws of this religion are commonly the most exact in fulfilling the duties of their state, and the most intrepid in danger. —D.

5. Of Education in a Republican Government.

It is in a republican government that the whole power of education is required. The fear of despotic governments naturally arises of itself amidst threats and punishments; the honor of monarchies is favored by the passions, and favors them in its turn; but virtue is a self-renunciation, [77] which is ever arduous and painful.

[77] This virtue, which Montesquieu defines as "love of country," is not self-renunciation; far from urging man to abnegation of his interests, it permits him to see the state flourishing and tranquil. In this public prosperity the citizen often finds his

own peace of mind and independence, the peaceable possession and enjoyment of his property, the hope of increasing it by liberty of commerce, and of being raised to posts of dignity. —D.

This virtue may be defined as the love of the laws and of our country. As such love requires a constant preference of public to private interest, it is the source of all private virtues; for they are nothing more than this very preference itself.

This love is peculiar to democracies. In these alone the government is entrusted to private citizens. Now a government is like everything else: to preserve it we must love it.

Has it ever been known that kings were not fond of monarchy, or that despotic princes hated arbitrary power?

Everything therefore depends on establishing this love in a republic; and to inspire it ought to be the principal business of education: but the surest way of instilling it into children is for parents to set them an example.

People have it generally in their power to communicate their ideas to their children; but they are still better able to transfuse their passions.

If it happens otherwise, it is because the impressions made at home are effaced by those they have received abroad.

It is not the young people that degenerate; they are not spoiled till those of maturer age are already sunk into corruption.

6. *Of some Institutions among the Greeks.*

The ancient Greeks, convinced of the necessity that people who live under a popular government should be trained up to virtue, made very singular institutions in order to inspire it. Upon seeing in the life of Lycurgus the laws that legislator gave to the Lacedæmonians, I imagine I am reading the history of the Sevarambes. [78] The laws of Crete were the model of those of Sparta; and those of Plato reformed them.

[78] See Vairasse d'Allais in his *Voyages Imaginaires*, vol. v. —Ed.

Let us reflect here a little on the extensive genius with which those legislators must have been endowed, to perceive that by striking at received customs, and by confounding all manner of virtues, [79] they should display their wisdom to the universe. Lycurgus, by blending theft with the spirit of justice, the hardest servitude with excess of liberty, the most rigid sentiments with the greatest moderation, gave stability to his city. He seemed to deprive her of all resources, such as arts, commerce, money, and walls; ambition prevailed among the citizens without hopes of improving their fortune; they had natural sentiments without the tie of a son, husband, or father; and chastity was stripped even of modesty and shame. This was the road that led Sparta to grandeur and glory; and so infallible were these institutions, that it signified nothing to gain a victory over that republic without subverting her polity. [80]

[79] The author intends that the Lacedæmonians confounded their virtues and vices. —D.
[80] Philopœmen obliged the Lacedæmonians to change their manner of educating their children, being convinced that if he did not take this measure they would always be noted for their magnanimity.—Plutarch, Philopœmen. See Livy, XXXVIII.

By these laws Crete and Laconia were governed. Sparta was the last that fell a prey to the Macedonians, and Crete to the Romans. [81]

[81] She defended her laws and liberty for the space of three years. See the 98th, 99th, and 100th book of Livy, in Florus's epitome. She made a braver resistance than the greatest kings.

The Samnites had the same institutions, which furnished those very Romans with the subject of four-and-twenty triumphs. [82]

[82] Florus, lib. I. chap. 16.

A character so extraordinary in the institutions of Greece has shown itself lately in the dregs and corruptions of modern times. [83] A very honest legislator has formed a people to whom probity seems as natural as bravery to the Spartans. Mr. Penn is a real Lycurgus: and though the former made peace his principal aim, as the latter did war, yet they resemble one another in the singular way of living to which they reduced their people, in the ascendant they had over free men, in the prejudices they overcame, and in the passions which they subdued.

[83] In *fœce Romuli.*—*Cicero*, Letters to Atticus, II. 1.

Another example we have from Paraguay. This has been the subject of an invidious charge against a society that considers the pleasure of commanding as the only happiness in life: but it will be ever a glorious undertaking to render a government subservient to human happiness. [84]

[84] The Indians of Paraguay do not depend on any particular lord; they pay only a fifth of the taxes, and are allowed the use of firearms to defend themselves.

It is glorious indeed for this society to have been the first in pointing out to those countries the idea of religion joined with that of humanity. By repairing the devastations of the Spaniards, she has begun to heal one of the most dangerous wounds that the human species ever received.

An exquisite sensibility to whatever she distinguishes by the name of honor, joined to her zeal for a religion which is far more humbling in respect to those who receive than to those who preach its doctrines, has set her upon vast undertakings, which she has accomplished with success. She has drawn wild people from their woods, secured them a maintenance, and clothed their nakedness; and had she only by this step improved the industry of mankind, it would have been sufficient to eternize her fame.

They who shall attempt hereafter to introduce like institutions must establish the community of goods as prescribed in Plato's republic; that high respect he required for the gods; that separation from strangers, for the preservation of morals; and an extensive commerce carried on by the community, and not by private citizens: they must give our arts without our luxury, and our wants without our desires.

They must proscribe money, the effects of which are to swell people's fortunes beyond the bounds prescribed by nature; to learn to preserve for no purpose what has been idly hoarded up; to multiply without end our desires; and to supply the sterility of nature, from whom we have received very scanty means of inflaming our passions, and of corrupting each other.

"The Epidamnians, [85] perceiving their morals depraved by conversing with barbarians, chose a magistrate for making all contracts and sales in the name and behalf of the city." Commerce then does not corrupt the constitution, and the constitution does not deprive society of the advantages of commerce. [86]

[85] Plutarch in his Questions Concerning the Greek Affairs. The Epidamnians were the inhabitants of Dyrrachium, now Durazzo.—Ed.
[86] But it does away with competition, and thus ruins commerce.—Anon. Ed. 1764

7. *In what Cases these singular Institutions may be of Service.*

Institutions of this kind may be proper in republics, because they have virtue for their principle; but to excite men to honor in monarchies, or to inspire fear in despotic governments, less trouble is necessary.

Besides, they can take place but in a small state, [87] in which there is a possibility of general education, and of training up the body of the people like a single family.

[87] Such as were formerly the cities of Greece.

The laws of Minos, of Lycurgus, and of Plato suppose a particular attention and care, which the citizens ought to have over one another's conduct. But an attention of this kind cannot be expected in the confusion and multitude of affairs in which a large nation is entangled.

In institutions of this kind, money, as we have above observed, must be banished. But in great societies, the multiplicity, variety, embarrassment, and importance of affairs, as well as the facility of purchasing, and the slowness of exchange, require a common measure. In order to support or extend our power, we must be possessed of the means to which, by the unanimous consent of mankind, this power is annexed.

8. *Explanation of a Paradox of the Ancients in respect to Manners.*

That judicious writer, Polybius, informs us [88] that music was necessary to soften the manners of the Arcadians, who lived in a cold, gloomy country; that the inhabitants of Cynete, who slighted music, were the cruelest of all the Greeks, and that no other town was so immersed in luxury and debauchery. Plato [89] is not afraid to affirm that there is no possibility of making a change in music without altering the frame of government. Aristotle, who seems to have written his Politics only in order to contradict Plato, agrees with him, notwithstanding, in regard to the power and influence of music over the manners of the people. [90] This was also the opinion of Theophrastus, of Plutarch [91] and of all the ancients—an opinion grounded on mature reflection; being one of the principles of their polity. [92] Thus it was they enacted laws, and thus they required that cities should be governed.

[88] Hist. iv. 20 and 21.
[89] *De Repub.* lib. IV.
[90] Lib. VIII. chap. v.

[91] Life of Pelopidas.

[92] Plato, in his fourth book of Laws, says that the præfectures of music and gymnic exercises are the most important employments in the city; and, in his Republic, iii, Damon will tell you, says he, what sounds are capable of corrupting the mind with base sentiments, or of inspiring the contrary virtues.

This I fancy must be explained in the following manner. It is observable that in the cities of Greece, especially those whose .principal object was war, all lucrative arts and professions were considered unworthy of a freeman. *Most arts*, says Xenophon, [93] *corrupt and enervate the bodies of those that exercise them; they oblige them to sit in the shade, or near the fire. They can find no leisure, either for their friends or for the republic.* It was only by the corruption of some democracies that artisans became freemen. This we learn from Aristotle, [94] who maintains that a well-regulated republic will never give them the right and freedom of the city. [95]

[93] Book 5th of Memorable Sayings.
[94] *Politics*, book III. Chap. 4.
[95] Diophantes, says Aristotle, *Politics*, ii. 7, made a law formerly at Athens, that artisans should be slaves to the republic.

Agriculture was likewise a servile profession, and generally practiced by the inhabitants of conquered countries, such as the *Helotes* among the Lacedæmonians, the *Periecians* among the Cretans, the *Penestes* among the Thessalians, and other conquered [96] people in other republics.

[96] Plato, likewise, and Aristotle require slaves to till the land, Laws, viii. *Politics*, vii. 10. True it is that agriculture was not everywhere exercised by slaves: on the contrary, Aristotle observes the best republics were those in which the citizens themselves tilled the land: but this was brought about by the corruption of the ancient governments, which had become democratic: for in earlier times the cities of Greece were subject to an aristocratic government.

In fine, every kind of low commerce [97] was infamous among the Greeks; as it obliged a citizen to serve and wait on a slave, on a lodger, or a stranger. This was a notion that clashed with the spirit of Greek liberty; hence Plato [98] in his Laws orders a citizen to be punished if he attempts to concern himself with trade.

[97] Cauponatio.
[98] Book XI.

Thus in the Greek republics the magistrates were extremely embarrassed. They would not have the citizens apply themselves to trade, to agriculture, or to the arts, and yet they would not have them idle. [99] They found, therefore, employment for them in gymnic and military exercises; and none else were allowed by their institution. [10] Hence the Greeks must be considered as a society of wrestlers and boxers. Now, these exercises having a natural tendency to render people hardy and fierce, there was a necessity for tempering them with others that might soften their manners. [101] For this purpose, music, which influences the mind by means of the corporeal organs, was extremely proper. It is a kind of medium between manly exercises, which harden the body, and speculative sciences, which are apt to render us unsociable and sour. It cannot be said that music inspired virtue, for this would be inconceivable: but it prevented the effects of a savage institution, and enabled the soul to have such a share in the education as it could never have had without the assistance of harmony.

[99] Aristotle, *Politics*. lib. X

[100] "Ars corporum exercendorum gymnastica, variis certaminibus terendorum pœdotribica."—Aristotle, *Politics*. lib. VIII. chap. iii.

[101] Aristotle observes that the children of the Lacedæmonians, who began these exercises at a very tender age, contracted thence too great a ferocity and rudeness of behavior.—*Politics*. lib. VIII. chap. 4.

Let us suppose among ourselves a society of men so passionately fond of hunting as to make it their sole employment; they would doubtless contract thereby a kind of rusticity and fierceness. But if they happen to imbibe a taste for music, we should quickly perceive a sensible difference in their customs and manners. In short, the exercises used by the Greeks could raise but one kind of passions, viz., fierceness, indignation, and cruelty. But music excites all these; and is likewise able to inspire the soul with a sense of pity, lenity, tenderness, and love. Our moral writers, who declaim so vehemently against the stage, sufficiently demonstrate the power of music over the mind.

If the society above mentioned were to have no other music than that of drums, and the sound of the trumpet, would it not be more difficult to accomplish this end than by the more melting tones of softer harmony? The ancients were therefore in the right when, under particular circumstances, they preferred one mode to another in regard to manners.

But some will ask, why should music be pitched upon as preferable to any other entertainment? It is because of all sensible pleasures there is none that less corrupts the soul. We blush to read in Plutarch [102] that the Thebans, in order to soften the manners of their youth, authorized by law a passion which ought to be proscribed by all nations.

[102] Life of Pelopidas.

BOOK V.

THAT THE LAWS GIVEN BY THE LEGISLATOR OUGHT TO BE IN RELATION TO THE PRINCIPLE OF GOVERNMENT

1. *Idea of this Book.*

That the laws of education should relate to the principle of each government has been shown in the preceding book. Now the same may be said of those which the legislator gives to the whole society. The relation of laws to this principle strengthens the several springs of government; and this principle derives thence, in its turn, a new degree of vigor. And thus it is in mechanics, that action is always followed by reaction.

Our design is, to examine this relation in each government, beginning with the republican state, the principle of which is virtue.

2. *What is meant by Virtue in a political State.*

Virtue in a republic is a most simple thing: it is a love of the republic; it is a sensation, and not a consequence of acquired knowledge: a sensation that may be felt by the meanest as well as by the highest person in the state. When the common people adopt good maxims, they adhere to them more steadily than those whom we call gentlemen. It is very rarely that corruption commences with the former: nay, they frequently derive from their imperfect light a stronger attachment to the established laws and customs.

The love of our country is conducive to a purity of morals, and the latter is again conducive to the former. The less we are able to satisfy our private passions, the more we abandon ourselves to those of a general nature. How comes it that monks are so fond of their order? It is owing to the very cause that renders the order insupportable. Their rule debars them from all those things by which the ordinary passions are fed; there remains therefore only this passion for the very rule that torments them. The more austere it is, that is, the more it curbs their inclinations, the more force it gives to the only passion left them.

3. *What is meant by a Love of the Republic in a Democracy.*

A love of the republic in a democracy is a love of the democracy; as the latter is that of equality.

A love of the democracy is likewise that of frugality. Since every individual ought here to enjoy the same happiness and the same advantages, they should consequently taste the same pleasures and form the same hopes, which cannot be expected but from a general frugality.

The love of equality in a democracy limits ambition to the sole desire, to the sole happiness, of doing greater services to our country than the rest of our fellow-citizens. They cannot all render her equal services, but they all ought to serve her with equal alacrity. At our coming into the world, we contract an immense debt to our country, which we can never discharge.

Hence distinctions here arise from the principle of equality, even when it seems to be removed by signal services or superior abilities.

The love of frugality limits the *desire of having* to the study of procuring necessaries to our family, and superfluities to our country. Riches give a power which a citizen cannot use for himself, for then he would be no longer equal. They likewise procure pleasures which he ought not to enjoy, because these would be also repugnant to the equality.

Thus well-regulated democracies, by establishing domestic frugality, made way at the same time for public expenses, as was the case at Rome and Athens, when magnificence and profusion arose from the very fund of frugality. And as religion commands us to have pure and unspotted hands when we make our offerings to the gods, the laws required a frugality of life to enable them to be liberal to our country.

The good sense and happiness of individuals depend greatly upon the mediocrity of their abilities and fortunes. Therefore, as a republic, where the laws have placed many in a middling station, is composed of wise men, it will be wisely governed; as it is composed of happy men, it will be extremely happy.

4. *In what Manner the Love of Equality and Frugality is inspired.*

The love of equality and of a frugal economy is greatly excited by equality and frugality themselves, in societies where both these virtues are established by law.

In monarchies and despotic governments, nobody aims at equality; this does not so much as enter their thoughts; they all aspire to superiority. People of the very lowest condition desire to emerge from their obscurity, only to lord it over their fellow-subjects.

It is the same with respect to frugality. To love it, we must practice and enjoy it. It is not those who are enervated by pleasure that are fond of a frugal life; were this natural and common, Alcibiades would never have been the admiration of the universe. [103] Neither is it those who envy or admire the luxury of the great; people that have present to their view none but rich men, or men miserable like themselves, detest their wretched condition, without loving or knowing the real term or point of misery.

[103] Voltaire takes exception to this adulation of Alcibiades, and holds that Plutarch and Montesquieu do not prevail since his standard of admiration is filled by such men as Cato and Marcus Amelius.—Ed.

A true maxim it is, therefore, that in order to love equality and frugality in a republic, these virtues must have been previously established by law.

5. *In what Manner the Laws establish Equality in a Democracy.*

Some ancient legislators, as Lycurgus and Romulus, made an equal division of lands. A settlement of this kind can never take place except upon the foundation of a new republic; or when the old one is so corrupt, and the minds of the people are so disposed, that the poor think themselves obliged to demand, and the rich obliged to consent to a remedy of this nature.

If the legislator, in making a division of this kind, does not enact laws at the same time to support it, he forms only a temporary constitution; inequality will break in where the laws have not precluded it, and the republic will be utterly undone.

Hence for the preservation of this equality it is absolutely necessary there should be some regulation in respect to women's dowries, donations, successions, testamentary settlements, and all other forms of contracting. For were we once allowed to dispose of our property to whom and how we pleased, the will of each individual would disturb the order of the fundamental law.

Solon, by permitting the Athenians, upon failure of issue [104] to leave their estates to whom they pleased, acted contrary to the ancient laws, by which the estates were ordered to continue in the family of the testator; [105] and even contrary to his own laws, for by abolishing debts he had aimed at equality.

[104] Plutarch, Life of Solon.
[105] Ibid.

The law which prohibited people having two inheritances [106] was extremely well adapted for a democracy. It derived its origin from the equal distribution of lands and portions made to each citizen. The law would not permit a single man to possess more than a single portion.

[106] *Philolaus* of Corinth made a law at Athens that the number of the portions of land and that of inheritances should be always the same.—Aristotle, *Politics*, II. chap. 12. (Philolaus was legislator at Corinth, and not at Athens.—Ed.)

From the same source arose those laws by which the next relative was ordered to marry the heiress. This law was given to the Jews after the like distribution. Plato, [107] who grounds his laws on this division, made the same regulation which had been received as a law by the Athenians.

[107] Republic, book VIII.

At Athens there was a law whose spirit, in my opinion, has not been hitherto rightly understood. It was lawful to marry a sister only by the father's side, but it was not permitted to espouse a sister by the same venter. [108] This custom was originally owing to republics, whose spirit would not permit that two portions of land, and consequently two inheritances, should devolve on the same person. A man who married his sister only by the father's side could inherit but one estate, namely, that of his father; but by espousing his sister by the same venter, it might happen that this sister's father, having no male issue, might leave her his estate, and consequently the brother who married her might be possessed of two.

[108] *Cornelius Nepos in præfat.* This custom began in the earliest times. Thus Abraham says of Sarah, *She is my sister, my father's daughter, but not my mother's.* The same reasons occasioned the establishing the same law among different nations.

Little will it avail to object to what Philo says, [109] that although the Athenians were allowed to marry a sister by the father's side, and not by the mother's, yet the contrary practice prevailed among the Lacedæmonians, who were permitted to espouse a sister by the mother's side, and not by the father's. For I find in Strabo [110] that at Sparta, whenever a woman was married to her brother she had half his portion for her dowry. Plain is it that this second law was made in order to prevent the bad consequences of the former. That the estate belonging to the sister's family might not devolve on the brother's, they gave half the brother's estate to the sister for her dowry.

[109] *De specialibus legibus quæ pertinent ad præceptor Decalogi.*
[110] Lib. X. (Strabo speaks in this connection of the laws of Crete, and not of those of the Lacedæmonians.—Barthélemy.

Seneca [111] speaking of Silanus, who had married his sister, [112] says that the permission was limited at Athens, but general at Alexandria. In a monarchical government there was very little concern about any such thing as a division of estates.

[111] *Athenis dimidium licet, Alexandriæ totum.*—Seneca, *de morte Claudii.*

[112] Montesquieu is here accused of an attempt at satire, since it is Tacitus who says, "Silanus lived in great friendship with his sister, though not criminally, although not without indiscretion."—*Crévier*

Excellent was that law which, in order to maintain this division of lands in a democracy, ordained that a father who had several children should pitch upon one of them to inherit his portion, [] and leave the others to be adopted, to the end that the numbers of citizens might always be kept upon an equality with that of the divisions.

[113] Plato has a law of this kind, lib. XI. *Leg.*

Phaleas of Chalcedon [114] contrived a very extraordinary method of rendering all fortunes equal, in a republic where there was the greatest inequality. This was that the rich should give fortunes with their daughters to the poor, but receive none themselves; and that the poor should receive money for their daughters, instead of giving them fortunes. But I do not remember that a regulation of this kind ever took place in any republic. It lays the citizens under such hard and oppressive conditions as would make them detest the very equality which they designed to establish. It is proper sometimes that the laws should not seem to tend so directly to the end they propose.

[114] Aristotle. lib. II. chap. 7.

Though real equality be the very soul of a democracy, it is so difficult to establish that an extreme exactness in this respect would not be always convenient. Sufficient is it to establish a census [115] which shall reduce or fix the differences to a certain point: it is afterwards the business of particular laws to level, as it were, the inequalities, by the duties laid upon the rich, and by the ease afforded to the poor. It is moderate riches alone that can give or suffer this sort of compensation; for as to men of overgrown estates, everything which does not contribute to advance their power and honor is considered by them as an injury.

[115] Solon made four classes: the first, of those who had an income of 500 minas either in corn or liquid fruits; the second, of those who had 300, and were able to keep a horse; the third, of such as had only 200; the fourth, of all those who lived by their manual labor.—Plutarch, Life of Solon.

All inequality in democracies ought to be derived from the nature of the government, and even from the principle of equality. For example, it may be apprehended that people who are obliged to live by their labor would be too much impoverished by a public employment, or neglect the duties attending it; that artisans would grow insolent, and that too great a number of freemen would overpower the ancient citizens. In this case the equality [116] in a democracy may be suppressed for the good of the state. But this is only an apparent equality; for a man ruined by a public employment would be in a worse condition than his fellow-citizens; and this same man, being obliged to neglect his duty, would reduce the rest to a worse condition than himself, and so on.

[116] Solon excludes from public employments all those of the fourth class.

6. In what Manner the Laws ought to maintain Frugality in a Democracy.

It is not sufficient in a well-regulated democracy that the divisions of land be equal; they ought also to be small, as was customary among the Romans. *God forbid*, said Curius to his soldiers, [117] *that a citizen should look upon that as a small piece of land which is sufficient to maintain him.*

[117] They insisted upon a larger division of the conquered lands.—Plutarch, Lives of the ancient Kings and Commanders.

As equality of fortunes supports frugality, so the latter maintains the former. These things, though in themselves different, are of such a nature as to be unable to subsist separately; they reciprocally act upon each other; if one withdraws itself from a democracy, the other surely follows it.

True is it that when a democracy is founded on commerce, private people may acquire vast riches without a corruption of morals. This is because the spirit of commerce is naturally attended with that of frugality, economy, moderation, labor, prudence, tranquility, order, and rule. So long as this spirit subsists, the riches it produces have no bad effect. The mischief is, when excessive wealth destroys the spirit of commerce, then it is that the inconveniences of inequality begin to be felt.

In order to support this spirit, commerce should be carried on by the principal citizens; this should be their sole aim and study; this the chief object of the laws: and these very laws, by dividing the estates of individuals in proportion to the increase of commerce, should set every poor citizen so far at his ease as to be able to work like the rest, and every wealthy citizen in such a mediocrity as to be obliged to take some pains either in preserving or acquiring a fortune.

It is an excellent law in a trading republic to make an equal division of the paternal estate among the children. The consequence of this is that how great soever a fortune the father has made, his children, being not so rich as he, are induced to avoid luxury, and to work as he has done. I speak here only of trading republics; as to those that have no commerce, the legislator must pursue quite different measures. [118]

[118] In these, the portions or fortunes of women ought to be very much limited.

In Greece there were two sorts of republics: the one military, like Sparta; the other commercial, as Athens. In the former, the citizens were obliged to be idle; in the latter, endeavors were used to inspire them with the love of industry and labor. Solon made idleness a crime, and insisted that each citizen should give an account of his manner of getting a livelihood. And, indeed, in a well-regulated democracy, where people's expenses should extend only to what is necessary, every one ought to have it; for how should their wants be otherwise supplied?

7. Other Methods of favoring the Principle of Democracy.

An equal division of lands cannot be established in all democracies. There are some circumstances in which a regulation of this nature would be impracticable, dangerous, and even subversive of the constitution. We are not always obliged to proceed to extremes. If it appears that this division of lands, which was designed to preserve the people's morals, does not suit the democracy, recourse must be had to other methods.

If a permanent body be established to serve as a rule and pattern of manners; a senate, to which years, virtue, gravity, and eminent services procure admittance; the senators, by being exposed to public view like the statues of the gods, must naturally inspire every family with sentiments of virtue.

Above all, this senate must steadily adhere to the ancient institutions, and mind that the people and the magistrates never swerve from them.

The preservation of the ancient customs is a very considerable point in respect to manners. Since a corrupt people seldom perform any memorable actions, seldom establish societies, build cities, or enact laws; on the contrary, since most institutions are derived from people whose manners are plain and simple, to keep up the ancient customs is the way to preserve the original purity of morals.

Besides, if by some revolution the state has happened to assume a new form, this seldom can be effected without infinite pains and labor, and hardly ever by idle and debauched persons. Even those who had been the instruments of the revolution were desirous it should be relished, which is difficult to compass without good laws. Hence it is that ancient institutions generally tend to reform the people's manners, and those of modern date to corrupt them. In the course of a long administration, the descent to vice is insensible; but there is no reascending to virtue without making the most generous efforts.

It has been questioned whether the members of the senate we are speaking of ought to be for life or only chosen for a time. Doubtless they ought to be for life, as was the custom at Rome, [119] at Sparta, [120] and even at Athens. For we must not confound the senate at Athens, which was a body that changed every three months, with the Areopagus, whose members, as standing patterns, were established for life.

[119] The magistrates there were annual, and the senators for life.
[120] Lycurgus, says Xenophon, de *Repub. Lacedæm.*, ordained that the senators should be chosen from amongst the old men, to the end that they might not be neglected in the decline of life; thus by making them judges of the courage of young people, he rendered the old age of the former more honorable than the strength and vigor of the latter.

Let this be therefore a general maxim; that in a senate designed to be a rule, and the depository, as it were, of manners, the members ought to be chosen for life: in a senate intended for the administration of affairs, the members may be changed.

The spirit, says Aristotle, waxes old as well as the body. This reflection holds good only in regard to a single magistrate, but cannot be applied to a senatorial assembly.

At Athens, besides the Areopagus, there were guardians of the public morals, as well as of the laws. [121] At Sparta, all the old men were censors. At Rome, the censorship was committed to two particular magistrates. As the senate watched over the people, the censors were to have an eye over the people and the senate. Their office was to reform the corruptions of the republic, to stigmatize indolence, to censure neglects, and to correct mistakes; as to flagrant crimes, these were left to the punishment of the laws.

[121] Even the Areopagus itself was subject to their censure.

That Roman law which required the accusations in cases of adultery to be public was admirably well calculated for preserving the purity of morals; it intimidated married women, as well as those who were to watch over their conduct.

Nothing contributes more to the preservation of morals than an extreme subordination of the young to the old. Thus they are both restrained, the former by their respect for those of advanced age, and the latter by their regard for themselves.

Nothing gives a greater force to the law than a perfect subordination between the citizens and the magistrate. *The great difference which Lycurgus established between Sparta and the other cities,* says Xenophon, [122] *consists chiefly in the obedience the citizens show to their laws; they run when the magistrate calls them. But at Athens a rich man would be highly displeased to be thought dependent on the magistrate.*

[122] Republic of the Lacedæmonians.

Paternal authority is likewise of great use towards the preservation of morals. We have already observed that in a republic there is not so coercive a force as in other governments. The laws must therefore endeavor to supply this defect by some means or other; and this is done by paternal authority.

Fathers at Rome had the power of life and death over their children. [123] At Sparta, every father had a right to correct another man's child.

[123] We may see in the Roman History how useful this power was to the republic. I shall give an instance even in the time of its greatest corruption. Aulus Fulvius was set out on his journey in order to join Catiline; his father called him back, and put him to death.—Sallust, d*e Bello Catil.* (The instance is by no means isolated. See Dion. lib. XXXVII. 36.—Ed.

Paternal authority ended at Rome together with the republic. In monarchies, where such a purity of morals is not required, they are controlled by no other authority than that of the magistrates.

The Roman laws, which accustomed young people to dependence, established a long minority. Perhaps we are mistaken in conforming to this custom; there is no necessity for so much constraint in monarchies.

This very subordination in a republic might make it necessary for the father to continue in the possession of his children's fortune during life, as was the custom at Rome. But this is not agreeable to the spirit of monarchy.

8. *In what Manner the Laws should relate to the Principle of Government in an Aristocracy.*

If the people are virtuous in an aristocracy, they enjoy very nearly the same happiness as in a popular government, and the state grows powerful. But as a great share of virtue is very rare where men's fortunes are so unequal, the laws must tend as much as possible to infuse a spirit of moderation, and endeavor to re-establish that equality which was necessarily removed by the constitution.

The spirit of moderation is what we call virtue in an aristocracy; it supplies the place of the spirit of equality in a popular state.

As the pomp and splendor with which kings are surrounded form a part of their power, so modesty and simplicity of manners constitute the strength of an aristocratic nobility. [124] When they affect no distinction, when they mix with the people, dress like them, and with them share all their pleasures, the people are apt to forget their subjection and weakness.

[124] In our days the Venetians, who in many respects may be said to have a very wise government, decided a dispute between a noble Venetian and a gentleman of Terra Firma in respect to precedency in a church, by declaring that out of Venice a noble Venetian had no pre-eminence over any other citizen.

Every government has its nature and principle. An aristocracy must not therefore assume the nature and principle of monarchy; which would be the case were the nobles to be invested with personal privileges distinct from those of their body; privileges ought to be for the senate, and simple respect for the senators.

In aristocratic governments there are two principal sources of disorder: excessive inequality between the governors and the governed; and the same inequality between the different members of the body that governs. From these two inequalities, hatreds and jealousies arise, which the laws ought ever to prevent or repress.

The first inequality is chiefly when the privileges of the nobility are honorable only as they are ignominious to the people. Such was the law at Rome by which the patricians were forbidden to marry plebeians; [125] a law that had no other effect than to render the patricians on the one side more haughty, and on the other more odious. The reader may see what advantages the tribunes derived thence in their harangues.

[125] It was inserted by the decemvirs in the two last tables. See Dionysius Helicarnassus, lib. X.

This inequality occurs likewise when the condition of the citizens differs with regard to taxes, which may happen in four different ways: when the nobles assume the privilege of paying none; when they commit frauds to exempt themselves; [126] when they engross the public money, under pretence of rewards or appointments for their respective employments; in fine, when they render the common people tributary, and divide among their own body the profits arising from the several subsidies. This last case is very rare; an aristocracy so instituted would be the most intolerable of all governments.

[126] As in some aristocracies in our time; nothing is more prejudicial to the government.

While Rome inclined towards aristocracy, she avoided all these inconveniences. The magistrates never received any emoluments from their office. The chief men of the republic were taxed like the rest, nay, more heavily; and sometimes the taxes fell upon them alone. In fine, far from sharing among themselves the revenues of the state, all they could draw from the public treasure, and all the wealth that fortune flung into their laps, they bestowed freely on the people, to be excused from accepting public honors. [127]

[127] See in Strabo, XIV., in what manner the Rhodians behaved in this respect.

It is a fundamental maxim that largesses are pernicious to the people in a democracy, but salutary in an aristocratic government. The former make them forget they are citizens, the latter bring them to a sense of it.

If the revenues of the state are not distributed among the people, they must be convinced at least of their being well administered: to feast their eyes with the public treasure is with them the same thing almost as enjoying it. The golden chain displayed at Venice, the riches exhibited at Rome in public triumphs, the treasures preserved in the temple of Saturn, were in reality the wealth of the people.

It is a very essential point in an aristocracy that the nobles themselves should not levy the taxes. The first order of the state in Rome never concerned themselves with it; the levying of the taxes was committed to the second, and even this in process of time was attended with great inconveniences. In an aristocracy of this kind, where the nobles levied the taxes, the private people would be all at the discretion of persons in public employments; and there would be no such thing as a superior tribunal to check their power. The members appointed to remove the abuses would rather enjoy them. The nobles would be like the princes of despotic governments, who confiscate whatever estates they please.

Soon would the profits hence arising be considered as a patrimony, which avarice would enlarge at pleasure. The farms would be lowered, and the public revenues reduced to nothing. This is the reason that some governments, without having ever received any remarkable shock, have dwindled away to such a degree as not only their neighbors, but even their own subjects, have been surprised at it.

The laws should likewise forbid the nobles all kinds of commerce: merchants of such unbounded credit would monopolize all to themselves. Commerce is a profession of people who are upon an equality; hence among despotic states the most miserable are those in which the prince applies himself to trade.

The laws of Venice debar [128] the nobles from commerce, by which they might even innocently acquire exorbitant wealth.

[128] *Amelot de la Houssaye,* Of the Government of Venice, part III. The *Claudian* law forbade the senators to have any ship at sea that held above forty bushels.—Livy, lib. XXI. chap. 63.

The laws ought to employ the most effectual means for making the nobles do justice to the people. If they have not established a tribune, they ought to be a tribune themselves.

Every sort of asylum in opposition to the execution of the laws destroys aristocracy, and is soon succeeded by tyranny.

They ought always to mortify the lust of dominion. There should be either a temporary or perpetual magistrate to keep the nobles in awe, as the Ephori at Sparta and the State Inquisitors at Venice—magistrates subject to no formalities. This sort of government stands in need of the strongest springs: thus a mouth of stone [129] is open to every informer at Venice—a mouth to which one would be apt to give the appellation of tyranny.

[129] The informers throw their scrolls into it.

These arbitrary magistrates in an aristocracy bear some analogy to the censorship in democracies, [130] which of its own nature is equally independent. And, indeed, the censors ought to be subject to no inquiry in relation to their conduct during their office; they should meet with a thorough confidence, and never be discouraged. In this respect the practice of the Romans deserved admiration; magistrates of all denominations were accountable for their administration, [131] except the censors. [132]

[130] Their vote is secret; whereas at Rome it was public.—Ed.

[131] See Livy, XLIX. A censor could not be troubled even by a censor; each made his remark without taking the opinion of his colleague; and when it otherwise happened, the censorship was in a manner abolished.

[132] At Athens the *Logistæ*, who made all the magistrates accountable for their conduct, gave no account themselves.

There are two very pernicious things in an aristocracy—excess either of poverty, or of wealth in the nobility. To prevent their poverty, it is necessary, above all things, to oblige them to pay their debts in time. To moderate the excess of wealth, prudent and gradual regulations should be made; but no confiscations, no agrarian laws, no expunging of debts; these are productive of infinite mischief.

The laws ought to abolish the right of primogeniture among the nobles, [133] to the end that by a continual division of the inheritances their fortunes may be always upon a level.

[133] It is so practiced at Venice.—*Amelot de la Housaye*, pp. 30, 31.

There should be no substitutions, no powers of redemption, no rights of *Majorasgo*, or adoption. The contrivances for perpetuating the grandeur of families in monarchical governments ought never to be employed in aristocracies. [134]

[134] The main design of some aristocracies seems to be less the support of the state than of their nobility.

When the laws have compassed the equality of families, the next thing is to preserve a proper harmony and union among them. The quarrels of the nobility ought to be quickly decided; otherwise the contests of individuals become those of families. Arbiters may terminate, or even prevent, the rise of disputes.

In fine, the laws must not favor the distinctions raised by vanity among families, under pretence that they are more noble or ancient than others. Pretences of this nature ought to be ranked among the weaknesses of private persons.

We have only to cast an eye upon Sparta; there we may see how the Ephori contrived to check the foibles of the kings, [135] as well as those of the nobility and common people.

[135] These were not kings of Sparta, but pretenders. The true sovereigns were the Ephori, since royalty itself was subservient to them.—Ed.

9. *In what Manner the Laws are in relation to their Principle in Monarchies.*

As honor is the principle of a monarchical government, the laws ought to be in relation to this principle.

They should endeavor to support the nobility, in respect to whom honor may be, in some measure, deemed both child and parent.

They should render the nobility hereditary, not as a boundary between the power of the prince and the weakness of the people, but as the link which connects them both.

In this government, substitutions which preserve the estates of families undivided are extremely useful, though in others not so proper.

Here the power of redemption is of service, as it restores to noble families the lands that had been alienated by the prodigality of a parent.

The land of the nobility ought to have privileges as well as their persons. The monarch's dignity is inseparable from that of his kingdom; and-the dignity of the nobleman from that of his fief.

All these privileges must be peculiar to the nobility, and incommunicable to the people, unless we intend to act contrary to the principle of government, and to diminish the power of the nobles together with that of the people.

Substitutions are a restraint to commerce, the power of redemption produces an infinite number of processes; every estate in land that is sold throughout the kingdom is in some measure without an owner for the space of a year. Privileges annexed to fiefs give a power very burdensome to those governments which tolerate them. These are the inconveniences of nobility—inconveniences, however, that vanish when confronted with its general utility: but when these privileges are communicated to the people, every principle of government is wantonly violated.

In monarchies a person may leave the bulk of his estate to one of his children—a permission improper in any other government.

The laws ought to favor all kinds of commerce [136] consistent with the constitution, to the end that the subjects may, without ruining themselves, be able to satisfy the continual cravings of the prince and his court.

[136] It is tolerated only in the common people. See Leg. 3, Cod. de *Comm. et Mercatoribus*, which is full of good sense.

They should establish some regulation that the manner of collecting the taxes may not be more burdensome than the taxes themselves.

The weight of duties produces labor, labor weariness, and weariness the spirit of indolence.

10. *Of the Expedition peculiar to the Executive Power in Monarchies.*

Great is the advantage which a monarchical government has over a republic: as the state is conducted by a single person, the executive power is thereby enabled to act with greater expedition. But as this expedition may degenerate into rapidity, the laws should use some contrivance to slacken it. They ought not only to favor the nature of each constitution, but likewise to remedy the abuses that might result from this very nature.

Cardinal Richelieu [137] advises monarchs to permit no such things as societies or communities that raise difficulties upon every trifle. If this man's heart had not been bewitched with the love of despotic power, still these arbitrary notions would have filled his head.

[137] *Testament polit.*

The bodies entrusted with the deposition of the laws are never more obedient than when they proceed slowly, and use that reflection in the prince's affairs which can scarcely be expected from the ignorance of a court, or from the precipitation of its councils. [138]

[138] *Barbaris cunctatio servilis, statim exequi regium videtur.*—Tacitus, *Annal.* lib. V. chap. xxxii.

What would have become of the finest monarchy in the world if the magistrates, by their delays, their complaints, and entreaties, had not checked the rapidity even of their princes' virtues, when these monarchs, consulting only the generous impulse of their minds, would fain have given a boundless reward to services performed with an unlimited courage and fidelity?

11. *Of the Excellence of a Monarchical Government.*

Monarchy has a great advantage over a despotic government. As it naturally requires there should be several orders or ranks of subjects, the state is more permanent, the constitution more steady, and the person of him who governs more secure.

Cicero [139] is of opinion that the establishing of the tribunes preserved the republic. *And indeed,* says he, *the violence of a headless people is more terrible. A chief or head is sensible that the affair depends upon himself, and therefore he thinks; but the people in their impetuosity are ignorant of the danger into which they hurry themselves.* This reflection may be applied to a despotic government, which is a people without tribunes; and to a monarchy, where the people have some sort of tribunes.

[139] Lib. III. *de Leg.* 10.

Accordingly it is observable that in the commotions of a despotic government, the people, hurried away by their passions, are apt to push things as far as they can go. The disorders they commit are all extreme; whereas in monarchies matters are seldom carried to excess. The chiefs are apprehensive on their own account; they are afraid of being abandoned, and the intermediate dependent powers [140] do not choose that the populace should have too much the upper hand. It rarely happens that the states of the kingdom are entirely corrupted: the prince adheres to these; and the seditious, who have neither will nor hopes to subvert the government, have neither power nor will to dethrone the prince.

[140] See the first note of book II. chap. 4.

In these circumstances men of prudence and authority interfere; moderate measures are first proposed, then complied with, and things at length are redressed; the laws resume their vigor, and command submission.

Thus all our histories are full of civil wars without revolutions, while the histories of despotic governments abound with revolutions without civil wars.

The writers of the history of the civil wars of some countries, even those who fomented them, sufficiently demonstrate the little foundation princes have to suspect the authority with which they invest particular bodies of men; since, even under the unhappy circumstance of their errors, they sighed only after the laws and their duty; and restrained, more than they were capable of inflaming, the impetuosity of the revolted. [141]

[141] Memoirs of Cardinal de Retz, and other histories.

Cardinal Richelieu, reflecting perhaps that he had too much reduced the states of the kingdom, has recourse to the virtues of the prince and of his ministers for the support [142] of government: but he requires so many things, that indeed there is none but an angel capable of such attention, such resolution and knowledge; and scarcely can we flatter ourselves that we shall ever see such a prince and ministers while monarchy subsists.

[142] *Testament polit.*

As people who live under a good government are happier than those who without rule or leaders wander about the forests, so monarchs who live under the fundamental laws of their country are far happier than despotic princes who have nothing to regulate, neither their own passions nor those of their subjects.

12. *The same Subject continued.*

Let us not look for magnanimity in despotic governments; [143] the prince cannot impart a greatness which he has not himself; with him there is no such thing as glory.

[143] Voltaire maintains that the conqueror of Candia, the Vizir Ibrahim, and many others of despotic sway contradict this statement.—Ed.

It is in monarchies that we behold the subjects encircling the throne, and cheered by the irradiancy of the sovereign; there it is that each person filling, as it were, a larger space, is capable of exercising those virtues which adorn the soul, not with independence, but with true dignity and greatness.

13. *An Idea of Despotic Power.*

When the savages of Lewisiana are desirous of fruit, they cut the tree to the root, and gather the fruit. [144] This is an emblem of despotic government.

[144] Edifying Letters, coll. ii, p. 315.

14. *In what Manner the Laws are in relation to the Principles of Despotic Government.*

The principle of despotic government is fear; but a timid, ignorant, and faint-spirited people have no occasion for a great number of laws.

Everything ought to depend here on two or three ideas; hence there is no necessity that any new notions should be added. When we want to break a horse, we take care not to let him change his master, his lesson, or his pace. Thus an impression is made on his brain by two or three motions, and no more.

If a prince is shut up in a seraglio, he cannot leave his voluptuous abode without alarming those who keep him confined. They will not bear that his person and power should pass into other hands. He seldom therefore wages war in person, and hardly ventures to entrust the command to his generals.

A prince of this stamp, unaccustomed to resistance in his palace, is enraged to see his will opposed by armed force; hence he is generally governed by wrath or vengeance. Besides, he can have no notion of true glory. War therefore is carried on under such a government in its full natural fury, and less extent is given to the law of nations than in other states.

Such a prince has so many imperfections that they are afraid to expose his natural stupidity to public view. He is concealed in his palace, and the people are ignorant of his situation. It is lucky for him that the inhabitants of those countries need only the name of a prince to govern them.

When Charles XII was at Bender, [145] he met with some opposition from the senate of Sweden; upon which he wrote word home that he would send one of his boots to command them. This boot would have governed like a despotic prince.

[145] The king was not then at Bender, but at Demotica.—D.

If the prince is a prisoner, he is supposed to be dead, and another mounts the throne. The treaties made by the prisoner are void, his successor will not ratify them; and indeed, as he is the law, the state, and the prince: when he is no longer a prince, he is nothing: were he not therefore deemed to be deceased, the state would be subverted.

One thing which chiefly determined the Turks to conclude a separate peace with Peter I was the Muscovites telling the Vizir that in Sweden another prince had been placed upon the throne. [146]

[146] Continuation of Puffendorf, introduction to the History of Europe, in the article on Sweden, chap. 10.

The preservation of the state is only the preservation of the prince, or rather of the palace where he is confined. Whatever does not directly menace this palace or the capital makes no impression on ignorant, proud, and prejudiced minds; and as for the concatenation of events, they are unable to trace, to foresee, or even to conceive it. Politics, with its several springs and laws, must here be very much limited; the political government is as simple as the civil. [147]

[147] According to Sir John Chardin, there is no council of state in Persia. (See Chardin, chap. xi.)

The whole is reduced to reconciling the political and civil administration to the domestic government, the officers of state to those of the seraglio.

Such a state is happiest when it can look upon itself as the only one in the world, when it is environed with deserts, and separated from those people whom they call Barbarians. Since it cannot depend on the militia, it is proper it should destroy a part of itself.

As fear is the principle of despotic government, its end is tranquility; but this tranquility cannot be called a peace: no, it is only the silence of those towns which the enemy is ready to invade.

Since strength does not lie in the state, but in the army that founded it, in order to defend the state the army must be preserved, how formidable soever to the prince. How, then, can we reconcile the security of the government to that of the prince's person?

Observe how industriously the Russian government endeavors to temper its arbitrary power, which it finds more burdensome than the people themselves. They have broken their numerous guards, mitigated criminal punishments, erected tribunals, entered into a knowledge of the laws, and instructed the people. But there are particular causes that will probably once more involve them in the very misery which they now endeavor to avoid.

In those states religion has more influence than anywhere else; it is fear added to fear. In Mahomedan countries, it is partly from their religion that the people derive the surprising veneration they have for their prince.

It is religion that amends in some measure the Turkish constitution. The subjects, who have no attachment of honor to the glory and grandeur of the state, are connected with it by the force and principle of religion.

Of all despotic governments there is none that labors more under its own weight than that wherein the prince declares himself proprietor of all the lands, and heir to all his subjects. Hence the neglect of agriculture arises; and if the prince intermeddles likewise in trade, all manner of industry is ruined.

Under this sort of government, nothing is repaired or improved. [148] Houses are built only for the necessity of habitation; there is no digging of ditches or planting of trees; everything is drawn from, but nothing restored to, the earth; the ground lies untilled, and the whole country becomes a desert.

[148] See Ricaut, State of the Ottoman Empire, p. 196.

Is it to be imagined that the laws which abolish the property of land and the succession of estates will diminish the avarice and cupidity of the great? By no means. They will rather stimulate this cupidity and avarice. The great men will be prompted to use a thousand oppressive methods, imagining they have no other property than the gold and silver which they are able to seize upon by violence, or to conceal.

To prevent, therefore, the utter ruin of the state, the avidity of the prince ought to be moderated by some established custom. Thus, in Turkey, the sovereign is satisfied with the right of three per cent on the value of inheritances. [149] But as he gives the greatest part of the lands to his soldiery, and disposes of them as he pleases; as he seizes on all the inheritances of the officers of the empire at their decease; as he has the property of the possessions of those who die without issue, and the daughters have only the usufruct; it thence follows that the greatest part of the estates of the country are held in a precarious manner.

[149] See concerning the inheritances of the Turks, Ancient and Modern Sparta. See also
 Ricaut on the Ottoman empire.

By the laws of Bantam, [150] the king seizes on the whole inheritance, even wife, children, and habitation. In order to elude the cruelest part of this law, they are obliged to marry their children at eight, nine, or ten years of age, and sometimes younger, to the end that they may not be a wretched part of the father's succession.

[150] Collection of Voyages that contributed to the establishment of the East India
 Company, tom. i. The law of Pegu is less cruel; if there happen to be children, the
 king succeeds only to two-thirds. Ibid., iii, p. 1.

In countries where there are no fundamental laws, the succession to the empire cannot be fixed. The crown is then elective, and the right of electing is in the prince, who names a successor either of his own or of some other family. In vain would it be to establish here the succession of the eldest son; the prince might always choose another. The successor is declared by the prince himself, or by a civil war. Hence a despotic state is, upon another account, more liable than a monarchical government to dissolution.

As every prince of the royal family is held equally capable of being chosen, hence it follows that the prince who ascends the throne immediately strangles his brothers, as in Turkey; or puts out their eyes, as in Persia; [151] or bereaves them of their understanding, as in the Mogul's country; or if these precautions are not used, as in Morocco, the vacancy of the throne is always attended with the horrors of a civil war.

[151] Chardin, chap. i. and iii.

By the constitution of Russia [152] the Czar may choose whom he has a mind for his successor, whether of his own or of a strange family. Such a settlement produces a thousand revolutions, and renders the throne as tottering as the succession is arbitrary. The right of succession being one of those things which are of most importance to the people to know, the best is that which most sensibly strikes them. Such as a certain order of birth. A settlement of this kind puts a stop to intrigues, and stifles ambition; the mind of a weak prince is no longer enslaved, nor is he made to speak his will as he is just expiring.

[152] See the different constitutions, especially that of 1722.

When the succession is established by a fundamental law, only one prince is the successor, and his brothers have neither a real nor apparent right to dispute the crown with him. They can neither pretend to nor take any advantage of the will of a father. There is then no more occasion to confine or kill the king's brother than any other subject.

But in despotic governments, where the prince's brothers are equally his slaves and his rivals, prudence requires that their persons be secured; especially in Mahomedan countries, where religion considers victory or success as a divine decision in their favor; so that they have no such thing as a monarch *de jure*, but only *de facto*.

There is a far greater incentive to ambition in countries where the princes of the blood are sensible that if they do not ascend the throne they must be either imprisoned or put to death, than among us, where they are placed in such a station as may satisfy, if not their ambition, at least their moderate desires.

The princes of despotic governments have ever perverted the use of marriage. They generally take a great many wives, especially in that part of the world where absolute power is in some measure naturalized, namely, Asia. Hence they come to have such a multitude of children that they can hardly have any great affection for them, nor the children for one another.

The reigning family resembles the state; it is too weak itself, and its head too powerful; it seems very numerous and extensive, and yet is suddenly extinct. Artaxerxes [153] put all his children to death for conspiring against him. It is not at all probable that fifty children would conspire against their father, and much less that this conspiracy would be owing to his having refused to resign his concubine to his eldest son. It is more natural to believe that the whole was an intrigue of those oriental seraglios, where fraud, treachery, and deceit reign in silence and darkness; and where an old prince, grown every day more infirm, is the first prisoner of the palace.

[153] See Justin.

After what has been said, one would imagine that human nature should perpetually rise up against despotism. But notwithstanding the love of liberty, so natural to mankind, notwithstanding their innate detestation of force and violence, most nations are subject to this very government. This is easily accounted for. To form a moderate government, it is necessary to combine the several powers; to regulate, temper, and set them in motion; to give, as it were, ballast to one, in order to enable it to counterpoise the other. This is a masterpiece of legislation; rarely produced by hazard, and seldom attained by prudence. On the contrary, a despotic government offers itself, as it were, at first sight; it is uniform throughout; and as passions only are requisite to establish it, this is what every capacity may reach.

15. *The same Subject continued.*

In warm climates, where despotic power generally prevails, the passions disclose themselves earlier, and are sooner extinguished; [154] the understanding is sooner ripened; they are less in danger of squandering their fortunes; there is less facility of distinguishing themselves in the world; less communication between young people, who are confined at home; they marry much earlier, and consequently may be sooner of age than in our European climates. In Turkey they are of age at fifteen. [155]

[154] See the book of laws as relative to the nature of the climate. Book XIV, below.
[155] Laquilletiere, Ancient and Modern Sparta, p. 463.

They have no such thing as a cession of goods; in a government where there is no fixed property, people depend rather on the person than on his estate.

The cession of goods is naturally admitted in moderate governments, [156] but especially in republics, because of the greater confidence usually placed in the probity of the citizens, and the lenity and moderation arising from a form of government which every subject seems to have preferred to all others.

[156] The same may be said of compositions in regard to fair bankrupts.

Had the legislators of the Roman republic established the cession of goods, [157] they never would have been exposed to so many seditions and civil discords; neither would they have experienced the danger of the evils, nor the inconvenience of the remedies.

[157] There was no such establishment made till the Julian law, *De Cessione bonorum*; which preserved them from prison and from an ignominious division of their goods.

Poverty and the precariousness of property in a despotic state render usury natural, each person raising the value of his money in proportion to the danger he sees in lending it. Misery therefore pours from all parts into those unhappy countries; they are bereft of everything, even of the resource of borrowing.

Hence it is that a merchant under this government is unable to carry on an extensive commerce; he lives from hand to mouth; and were he to encumber himself with a large quantity of merchandise, he would lose more by the exorbitant interest he must give for money than he could possibly get by the goods. Hence they have no laws here relating to commerce; they are all reduced to what is called the bare police.

A government cannot be unjust without having hands to exercise its injustice. Now, it is impossible but that these hands will be grasping for themselves. The embezzling of the public money is therefore natural in despotic states.

As this is a common crime under such a government, confiscations are very useful. By these the people are eased; the money drawn by this method being a considerable tribute which could hardly be raised on the exhausted subject: neither is there in those countries any one family which the prince would be glad to preserve.

In moderate governments it is quite a different thing. Confiscations would render property uncertain, would strip innocent children, would destroy a whole family, instead of punishing a single criminal. In republics they would be attended with the mischief of subverting equality, which is the very soul of this government, by depriving a citizen of his necessary subsistence.

There is a Roman law [158] against confiscations, except in the case of *crimen majestatis*, or high treason of the most heinous nature. It would be a prudent thing to follow the spirit of this law, and to limit confiscations to particular crimes. [159] In countries where a local custom has rendered real estates alienable, Bodin very justly observes that confiscations should extend only to such as are purchased or acquired. [160]

[158] Authentica bona damnatorum.—Cod. *de bon. damn.*
[159] They seem to have been too fond of confiscations in the republic of Athens.
[160] Book V. chap. iii.

16. *Of the Communication of Power.*

In a despotic government the power is communicated entire to the person entrusted with it. The vizir himself is the despotic prince; and each particular officer is the vizir. In monarchies the power is less immediately applied, being tempered by the monarch as he gives it. [161] He makes such a distribution of his authority as never to communicate a part of it without reserving a greater share to himself.

[161] "Ut esse Phœbi dulcius lumen solet
  Jamjam cadentis ————— Seneca, *Trias*, V. i.

Hence in monarchies the governors of towns are not so dependent on the governor of the province as not to be still more so on the prince; and the private officers or military bodies are not so far subject to their general as not to owe still a greater subjection to their sovereign.

In most monarchies it has been wisely regulated that those who have an extensive command should not belong to any military corps; so that as they have no authority but through the prince's pleasure, and as they may be employed or not, they are in some measure in the service, and in some measure out of it.

This is incompatible with a despotic government. For if those who are not actually employed were still invested with privileges and titles, the consequence must be that there would be men in the state who might be said to be great of themselves; a thing directly opposite to the nature of this government.

Were the governor of a town independent of the pasha, expedients would be daily necessary to make them agree; which is highly absurd in a despotic state. Besides, if a particular governor should refuse to obey, how could the other answer for his province with his head?

In this kind of government, authority must ever be wavering; nor is that of the lowest magistrate more steady than that of the despotic prince. Under moderate governments, the law is prudent in all its parts, and perfectly well known, so that even the pettiest magistrates are capable of following it. But in a despotic state, where the prince's will is the law, though the prince were wise, yet how could the magistrate follow a will he does not know? He must certainly follow his own.

Again, as the law is only the prince's will, and as the prince can only will what he knows, the consequence is that there are an infinite number of people who must will for him, and make their wills keep pace with his. In fine, as the law is the momentary will of the prince, it is necessary that those who will for him should follow his sudden manner of willing.

17. *Of Presents.*

It is a received custom in despotic countries never to address any superior whomsoever, not excepting their kings, without making them a present. [162] The Mogul [163] never receives the petitions of his subjects if they come with empty hands. These princes spoil even their own favors.

[162] Chardin, chap. xi.
[163] Collection of Voyages that Contributed to the Establishment of the East India Company, tom. i, p. 80.

But thus it must ever be in a government where no man is a citizen; where they have all a notion that a superior is under no obligation to an inferior; where men imagine themselves bound by no other tie than the chastisements inflicted by one party upon another; where, in fine, there is very little to do, and where the people have seldom an occasion of presenting themselves before the great, of offering their petitions, and much less their complaints.

In a republic, presents are odious, because virtue stands in no need of them. In monarchies, honor is a much stronger incentive than presents. But in a despotic government, where there is neither honor nor virtue, people cannot be determined to act but through hope of the conveniences of life.

It is in conformity with republican ideas that Plato [164] ordered those who received presents for doing their duty to be punished with death. *They must not take presents,"* says he, *"neither for good nor for evil actions.*

[164] Book XII. of Laws.

A very bad law was that among the Romans [165] which gave the magistrates leave to accept small presents [166] provided they did not exceed one hundred crowns in the whole year. They who receive nothing expect nothing; they who receive a little soon covet more, till at length their desires swell to an exorbitant height. Besides, it is much easier to convict a man who knows himself obliged to accept no present at all, and yet will accept something, than a person who takes more when he ought to take less, and who always finds pretexts, excuses, and plausible reasons in justification of his conduct.

[165] Leg. 5, § ad leg. Jul. repet.
[166] Munuscula.

18. *Of Rewards conferred by the Sovereign.*

In despotic governments, where, as we have already observed, the principal motive of action is the hope of the conveniences of life, the prince who confers rewards has nothing to bestow but money. In monarchies, where honor alone predominates, the prince's rewards would consist only of marks of distinction, if the distinctions established by honor were not attended with luxury, which necessarily brings on its wants: the prince therefore is obliged to confer such honors as lead to wealth. But in a republic where virtue reigns—a motive self-sufficient, and which excludes all others—the recompenses of the state consist only of public attestations of this virtue.

It is a general rule that great rewards in monarchies and republics are a sign of their decline; because they are a proof of their principles being corrupted, and that the idea of honor has no longer the same force in a monarchy, nor the title of citizen the same weight in a republic.

The very worst Roman emperors were those who were most profuse in their largesses; for example, Caligula, Claudius, Nero, Otho, Vitellius, Commodus, Heliogabalus, and Caracalla. The best, as Augustus, Vespasian, Antoninus Pius, Marcus Aurelius, and Pertinax, were economists. Under good emperors the state resumed its principles; all other treasures were supplied by that of honor.

19. *New Consequences of the Principles of the three Governments.*

I cannot conclude this book without making some applications of my three principles.

1st Question.] It is a question whether the laws ought to oblige a subject to accept a public employment. My opinion is that they ought in a republic, but not in a monarchical government. In the former, public employments are attestations of virtue, depositions with which a citizen is entrusted by his country, for whose sake alone he ought to live, to act, and to think, consequently he cannot refuse them. [167] In the latter, public offices are testimonials of honor; now such is the capriciousness of honor that it chooses to accept none of these testimonies but when and in what manner it pleases.

[167] Plato, in his Republic, VIII, ranks these refusals among the marks of the corruption of a republic. In his Laws, VI, he orders them to be punished by a fine; at Venice they are punished with banishment.

The late King of Sardinia [168] inflicted punishments on his subjects who refused the dignities and public offices of the state. In this he unknowingly followed republican ideas: but his method of governing in other respects sufficiently proves that this was not his intention.

[168] Victor Amadeus.

2nd Question.] Secondly, it is questioned whether a subject should be obliged to accept a post in the army inferior to that which he held before. Among the Romans it was usual to see a captain serve the next year under his lieutenant. [169] This is because virtue in republics requires a continual sacrifice of our persons and of our repugnances for the good of the state. But in monarchies, honor, true or false, will never bear with what it calls degrading itself.

[169] Some centurions having appealed to the people for the employments which they had before enjoyed, *It is just, my comrades,* said a centurion, *that you should look upon every post as honorable in which you have an opportunity of defending the republic.*—Livy, dec. 5, XLII.

In despotic governments, where honor, posts, and ranks are equally abused, they indiscriminately make a prince a scullion, and a scullion a prince.

3rd Question.] Thirdly, it may be inquired, whether civil and military employments should be conferred on the same person. In republics I think they should be joined, but in monarchies separated. In the former it would be extremely dangerous to make the profession of arms a particular state, distinct from that of civil functions; and in the latter, no less dangerous would it be to confer these two employments on the same person.

In republics a person takes up arms only with a view to defend his country and its laws; it is because he is a citizen he makes himself for a while a soldier. Were these two distinct states, the person who under arms thinks himself a citizen would soon be made sensible he is only a soldier.

In monarchies, they whose condition engages them in the profession of arms have nothing but glory, or at least honor or fortune, in view. To men, therefore, like these, the prince should never give any civil employments; on the contrary, they ought to be checked by the civil magistrate, that the same persons may not have at the same time the confidence of the people and the power to abuse it. [170]

[170] Ne imperium ad optimos nobilium transferretur, Senatum militia vetuit Gallienus, etiam adire exercitum.—Aurelius Victor, *de virii illustribus.*

We have only to cast an eye on a nation that may be justly called a republic, disguised under the form of monarchy, and we shall see how jealous they are of making a separate order of the profession of arms, and how the military state is constantly allied with that of the citizen, and even sometimes of the magistrate, to the end that these qualities may be a pledge for their country, which should never be forgotten.

The division of civil and military employments, made by the Romans after the extinction of the republic, was not an arbitrary thing. It was a consequence of the change which happened in the constitution of Rome; it was natural to a monarchical government; and what was only commenced under Augustus [171] succeeding emperors [172] were obliged to finish, in order to temper the military government.

[171] Augustus deprived the senators, proconsuls, and governors of the privilege of wearing arms.—Dio, xxxiii.
[172] Constantine. See Zozimus, lib. ii.

Procopius, therefore, the competitor of Valens the emperor, was very much to blame when, conferring the pro-consular dignity [173] upon Hormisdas, a prince of the blood royal of Persia, he restored to this magistracy the military command of which it had been formerly possessed; unless indeed he had very particular reasons for so doing. A person that aspires to the sovereignty concerns himself less about what is serviceable to the state than what is likely to promote his own interest.

[173] Ammianus Marcellinus, xxvi, Et Civilia, *more veterum, et bella recturo.*

4th Question.] Fourthly, it is a question whether public employments should be sold. They ought not, I think, in despotic governments, where the subjects must be instantaneously placed or displaced by the prince.

But in monarchies this custom is not at all improper, by reason it is an inducement to engage in that as a family employment [174] which would not be undertaken through a motive of virtue; it fixes likewise everyone in his duty, and renders the several orders of the kingdom more permanent. Suidas [175] very justly observes that Anastasius had changed the empire into a kind of aristocracy, by selling all public employments.

[174] Voltaire exclaims, "Let us lament that Montesquieu has defamed his work by such paradoxes. But we can forgive him : his uncle purchased the office of President in the country, and left it to him. After all we find the man. No one of us is without his weak point."—Ed.
[175] Fragments taken from the embassies of Constantine Porphyrogenitus.

Plato [176] cannot bear with this prostitution: *This is exactly,* says he, *as if a person were to be made a mariner or pilot of a ship for his money. Is it possible that this rule should be bad in every other employment of life, and hold good only in the administration of a republic?* But Plato speaks of a republic founded on virtue, and we of a monarchy. Now, in monarchies (where, though there were no such thing as a regular sale of public offices, still the indigence and avidity of the courtier would equally prompt him to expose them to sale) chance will furnish better subjects than the prince's choice. In short, the method of attaining to honors through riches inspires and cherishes industry, [177] a thing extremely wanting in this kind of government.

[176] *Republic,* lib. VIII.
[177] We see the laziness of Spain, where all public employments are given away.

5th Question.] The fifth question is in what kind of government censors are necessary. My answer is, that they are necessary in a republic, where the principle of government is virtue. We must not imagine that criminal actions only are destructive of virtue; it is destroyed also by omissions, by neglects, by a certain coolness in the love of our country, by bad examples, and by the seeds of corruption: whatever does not openly violate but elude the laws, does not subvert but weaken them, ought to fall under the inquiry and correction of the censors.

We are surprised at the punishment of the Areopagite for killing a sparrow which, to escape the pursuit of a hawk, had taken shelter in his bosom. Surprised we are also that an Areopagite should put his son to death for putting out the eyes of a little bird. But let us reflect that the question here does not relate to a criminal sentence, but to a judgment concerning manners in a republic founded on manners.

In monarchies there should be no censors; the former are founded on honor, and the nature of honor is to have the whole world for its censor. Every man who fails in this article is subject to the reproaches even of those who are void of honor.

Here the censors would be spoiled by the very people whom they ought to correct: they could not prevail against the corruption of a monarchy; the corruption rather would be too strong against them.

Hence it is obvious that there ought to be no censors in despotic governments. The example of China seems to derogate from this rule; but we shall see, in the course of this work, the particular reasons of that institution.

BOOK VI.

CONSEQUENCES OF THE PRINCIPLES OF DIFFERENT GOVERNMENTS WITH RESPECT TO THE SIMPLICITY OF CIVIL AND CRIMINAL LAWS, THE FORM OF JUDGMENTS, AND THE INFLICTING OF PUNISHMENTS

1. *Of the Simplicity of Civil Laws in different Governments.*

Monarchies do not permit of so great a simplicity of laws as despotic governments. For in monarchies there must be courts of judicature; these must give their decisions; the decisions must be preserved and learned, that we may judge in the same manner to-day as yesterday, and that the lives and property of the citizens may be as certain and fixed as the very constitution of the state.

In monarchies, the administration of justice, which decides not only in whatever belongs to life and property, but likewise to honor, demands very scrupulous inquiries. The delicacy of the judge increases in proportion to the increase of his trust, and of the importance of the interests on which he determines.

We must not, therefore, be surprised to find so many rules, restrictions, and extensions in the laws of those countries—rules that multiply the particular cases, and seem to make of reason itself an art.

The difference of rank, birth, and condition established in monarchical governments is frequently attended with distinctions in the nature of property; and the laws relating to the constitution of this government may augment the number of these distinctions. Hence, among us goods are divided into real estates, purchases, dowries, paraphernalia, paternal and maternal inheritances; movables of different kinds; estates held in fee-simple, or in tail; acquired by descent or conveyance; allodial, or held by soccage; ground rents; or annuities. Each sort of goods is subject to particular rules, which must be complied with in the disposal of them. These things must needs diminish the simplicity of the laws.

In our governments the fiefs have become hereditary. It was necessary that the nobility should have a fixed property, that is, the fief should have a certain consistency, to the end that the proprietor might be always in a capacity of serving the prince. This must have been productive of great varieties; for instance, there are countries where fiefs could not be divided among the brothers; in others, the younger brothers may be allowed a more generous subsistence.

The monarch who knows each of his provinces may establish different laws, or tolerate different customs. But as the despotic prince knows nothing, and can attend to nothing, he must take general measures, and govern by a rigid and inflexible will, which throughout his whole dominions produces the same effect; in short, everything bends under his feet.

In proportion as the decisions of the courts of judicature are multiplied in monarchies, the law is loaded with decrees that sometimes contradict one another; either because succeeding judges are of a different way of thinking, or because the same causes are sometimes well, and at other times ill, defended; or, in fine, by reason of an infinite number of abuses, to which all human regulations are liable. This is a necessary evil, which the legislator redresses from time to time, as contrary even to the spirit of moderate governments. For when people are obliged to have recourse to courts of judicature, this should come from the nature of the constitution, and not from the contradiction or uncertainty of the law.

In governments where there are necessary distinctions of persons, there must likewise be privileges. This also diminishes the simplicity, and creates a thousand exceptions.

One of the privileges least burdensome to society, and especially to him who confers it, is that of pleading in one court in preference to another. Here new difficulties arise, when it becomes a question before which court we shall plead.

Far different is the case of the people under despotic governments. In those countries I can see nothing that the legislator is able to decree, or the magistrate to judge. As the lands belong to the prince, it follows that there are scarcely any civil laws in regard to landed property. From the right the sovereign has to successions, it follows, likewise, that there are none relating to inheritances. The monopolies established by the prince for himself in some countries render all sorts of commercial laws quite useless. The marriages which they usually contract with female slaves are the cause that there are scarcely any civil laws relating to dowries, or to the particular advantage of married women. From the prodigious multitude of slaves, it follows, likewise, that there are very few who have any such thing as a will of their own, and of course are answerable for their conduct before a judge. Most moral actions that are only in consequence of a father's, a husband's, or a master's will, are regulated by them, and not by the magistrates.

I forgot to observe that as what we call honor is a thing hardly known in those countries, the several difficulties relating to this article, though of such importance with us, are with them quite out of the question. Despotic power is self-sufficient; round it there is an absolute vacuum. Hence it is that when travelers favor us with the description of countries where arbitrary sway prevails, they seldom make mention of civil laws. [178]

[178] In Mazulipatam it could never be found out that there was such a thing as a written law. See the Collection of Voyages that Contributed to the Establishment of the East India Company, tom. iv., part I, p. 391. The Indians are regulated in their decisions by certain customs. The Vedan and such books do not contain civil laws, but religious precepts. See *Lettres édifiantes*, 14, collect.

All occasions, therefore, of wrangling and law-suits are here removed. And to this in part is it owing that litigious people in those countries are so roughly handled. As the injustice of their demand is neither screened, palliated, nor protected by an infinite number of laws, of course it is immediately discovered.

2. *Of the Simplicity of Criminal Laws in different Governments.*

We hear it generally said, that justice ought to be administered with us as in Turkey. Is it possible, then, that the most ignorant of all nations should be the most clear-sighted on a point which it most behooves mankind to know?

If we examine the set forms of justice with respect to the trouble the subject undergoes in recovering his property, or in obtaining satisfaction for an injury or affront, we shall find them doubtless too numerous: but if we consider them in the relation they bear to the liberty and security of every individual, we shall often find them too few; and be convinced that the trouble, expense, delays, and even the very dangers of our judiciary proceedings, are the price that each subject pays for his liberty.

In Turkey, where little regard is shown to the honor, life, or estate of the subject, all causes are speedily decided. The method of determining them is a matter of indifference, provided they be determined. The pasha, after a quick hearing, orders which party he pleases to be bastinadoed, and then sends them about their business.

Here it would be dangerous to be of a litigious disposition; this supposes a strong desire of obtaining justice, a settled aversion, an active mind, and a steadiness in pursuing one's point. All this should be avoided in a government where fear ought to be the only prevailing sentiment, and in which popular disturbances are frequently attended with sudden and unforeseen revolutions. Here every man ought to know that the magistrate must not hear his name mentioned, and that his security depends entirely on his being reduced to a kind of annihilation.

But in moderate governments, where the life of the meanest subject is deemed precious, no man is stripped of his honor or property until after a long inquiry; and no man is bereft of life till his very country has attacked him—an attack that is never made without leaving him all possible means of making his defense.

Hence it is that when a person renders himself absolute, [179] he immediately thinks of reducing the number of laws. In a government thus constituted they are more affected with particular inconveniences than with the liberty of the subject, which is very little minded.

[179] Cæsar, Cromwell, and many others.

In republics, it is plain that as many formalities at least are necessary as in monarchies. In both governments they increase in proportion to the value which is set on the honor, fortune, liberty, and life of the subject.

In republican governments, men are all equal; equal they are also in despotic governments: in the former, because they are everything; in the latter, because they are nothing.

3. In what Governments and in what Cases the Judges ought to determine according to the express Letter of the Law.

The nearer a government approaches towards a republic, the more the manner of judging becomes settled and fixed; hence it was a fault in the republic of Sparta for the Ephori to pass such arbitrary judgments without having any laws to direct them. The first consuls at Rome pronounced sentence in the same manner as the Ephori; but the inconvenience of this proceeding was soon felt, and they were obliged to have recourse to express and determinate laws.

In despotic governments there are no laws; the judge himself is his own rule. There are laws in monarchies; and where these are explicit, the judge conforms to them; where they are otherwise, he endeavors to investigate their spirit. In republics, the very nature of the constitution requires the judges to follow the letter of the law; otherwise the law might be explained to the prejudice of every citizen, in cases where their honor, property, or life is concerned.

At Rome the judges had no more to do than to declare that the persons accused were guilty of a particular crime, and then the punishment was found in the laws, as may be seen in divers laws still extant. In England the jury give their verdict whether the fact brought under their cognizance be proved or not; if it be proved, the judge pronounces the punishment inflicted by the law, and for this he needs only to open his eyes.

4. Of the Manner of passing Judgment.

Hence arises the different modes of passing judgment. In monarchies the judges choose the method of arbitration; they deliberate together, they communicate their sentiments for the sake of unanimity; they moderate their opinions, in order to render them conformable to those of others: and the lesser number are obliged to give way to the majority. But this is not agreeable to the nature of a republic. At Rome, and in the cities of Greece, the judges never entered into a consultation; each gave his opinion in one of these three ways: *I absolve, I condemn, It does not appear clear to me:* [180] this was because the people judged, or were supposed to judge. But the people are far from being civilians; all these restrictions and methods of arbitration are above their reach; they must have only one object and one single fact set before them; and then they have only to see whether they ought to condemn, to acquit, or to suspend their judgment.

[180] *Non liquet.*

The Romans introduced set forms of actions, [181] after the example of the Greeks, and established a rule that each cause should be directed by its proper action. This was necessary in their manner of judging; it was necessary to fix the state of the question, that the people might have it always before their eyes. Otherwise, in a long process, this state of the question would continually change, and be no longer distinguished.

[181] *Quas actiones ne populus prout vellet institueret, certas solemnesque esse voluerunt*—Lib. II. § 6., *Digest. de Orig. Jur.*

Hence it followed that the Roman judges granted only the simple demand, without making any addition, deduction, or limitation. But the prætors devised other forms of actions, which were called ex bona fide, in which the method of pronouncing sentence was left to the disposition of the judge. This was more agreeable to the spirit of monarchy. Hence it is a saying among the French lawyers, that in France [182] all actions are ex bona fide.

[182] In France a person, though sued for more than he owes, loses his costs if he has not offered to pay the exact debt.

5. *In what Governments the Sovereign may be Judge.*

Machiavel [183] attributes the loss of the liberty of Florence to the people's not judging in a body in cases of high treason against themselves, as was customary at Rome. For this purpose they had eight judges: *but the few*, says Machiavel, *are corrupted by a few.* I should willingly adopt the maxim of this great man. But as in those cases the political interest prevails in some measure over the civil (for it is always an inconvenience that the people should be judges in their own cause), in order to remedy this evil, the laws must provide as much as possible for the security of individuals.

[183] Discourse on the first decade of Livy, book. i. chap. 7.

With this view the Roman legislators did two things: they gave the persons accused permission to banish themselves [184] before sentence was pronounced; [185] and they ordained that the goods of those who were condemned should be sacred, to prevent their being confiscated to the people. We shall see in Book XI the other limitations that were set to the judicatory power residing in the people.

[184] This is well explained in Cicero's oration *pro Cæcina*, towards the end.
[185] This was the law at Athens, as appears by Demosthenes. Socrates refused to make use of it.

Solon knew how to prevent the abuse which the people might make of their power in criminal judgments. He ordained that the Court of Areopagus should re-examine the affair; that if they believed the party accused was unjustly acquitted [186] they should impeach him again before the people; that if they believed him unjustly condemned [187] they should prevent the execution of the sentence, and make them rejudge the proceeding—an admirable law, that subjected the people to the censure of the magistracy which they most revered, and even to their own!

[186] Demosthenes, *pro Corona*, p. 494, edit. Frankfort, 1604.
[187] See Philostratus, Lives of the Sophists, Book. I., Life of Æschines.

In affairs of this kind it is always proper to throw in some delays, especially when the party accused is under confinement; to the end that the people may grow calm and give their judgment coolly.

In despotic governments, the prince himself may be judge. But in monarchies this cannot be; the constitution by such means would be subverted, and the dependent intermediate powers annihilated; all set forms of judgment would cease; fear would take possession of the people's minds, and paleness spread itself over every countenance: the more confidence, honor, affection, and security in the subject, the more extended is the power of the monarch.

We shall give here a few more reflections on this point. In monarchies, the prince is the party that prosecutes the person accused, and causes him to be punished or acquitted. Now, were he himself to sit upon the trial, he would be both judge and party.

In this government the prince has frequently the benefit of confiscation, so that here again, by determining criminal causes, he would be both judge and party.

Further, by this method he would deprive himself of the most glorious attribute of sovereignty, namely, that of granting pardon, [188] for it would be quite ridiculous of him to make and unmake his decisions; surely he would not choose to contradict himself.

[188] Plato does not think it right that kings, who, as he says, are priests, should preside at trials where people are condemned to death, to exile, or to imprisonment.

Besides, this would be confounding all ideas; it would be impossible to tell whether a man was acquitted, or received his pardon.

Lewis XIII being desirous to sit in judgment upon the trial of the Duke de la Valette, [189] sent for some members of the parliament and of the privy council, to debate the matter; upon their being ordered by the king to give their opinion concerning the warrant for his arrest, the president, De Believre, said "that he found it very strange that a prince should pass sentence upon a subject; that kings had reserved to themselves the power of pardoning, and left that of condemning to their officers; that his majesty wanted to see before him at the bar a person who, by his decision, was to be hurried away into the other world! That the prince's countenance should inspire with hopes, and not confound with fears; that his presence alone removed ecclesiastic censures; and that subjects ought not to go away dissatisfied from the sovereign." When sentence was passed, the same magistrate declared, "This is an unprecedented judgment to see, contrary to the example of past ages—a king of France, in the quality of a judge, condemning a gentleman to death." [190]

[189] See the account of the trial of the Duke de la Valette. It is printed in the Memoirs of Montresor, tom. ii, p. 62.

[190] It was afterwards revoked. See the same account, ii. p. 236. It was ordinarily a right of the peerage that a peer criminally accused should be judged by the king, as Francis II in the trial of the Prince of Condé, and Charles VII in the case of the Duc d'Alençon. To-day, the presence of the king at the trial of a peer, in order to condemn him would seem an act of tyranny.—Voltaire.

Again, sentences passed by the prince would be an inexhaustible source of injustice and abuse; the courtiers by their importunity would always be able to extort his decisions. Some Roman emperors were so mad as to sit as judges themselves; the consequence was that no reigns ever so surprised the world with oppression and injustice.

Claudius, says Tacitus, [191] *having appropriated to himself the determination of lawsuits, and the function of magistrates, gave occasion to all manner of rapine.* But Nero, upon coming to the empire after Claudius, endeavored to conciliate the minds of the people by declaring "that he would take care not to be judge himself in private causes, that the parties might not be exposed within the walls of a palace to the iniquitous influence of a few freedmen." [192]

[191] *Annal.* lib. XI.
[192] *Ibid.*, lib. XIII.

Under the reign of Arcadius, says Zozimus, [193] *a swarm of calumniators spread themselves on every side, and infested the court. Upon a person's decease, it was immediately supposed he had left no children;* [194] *and, in consequence of this, his property was given away by a rescript. For as the prince was surprisingly stupid, and the empress excessively enterprising, she was a slave to the insatiable avarice of her domestics and confidants; insomuch that to an honest man nothing could be more desirable than death.*

[193] Histories, lib. v.
[194] The same disorder happened under Theodosius the younger.

Formerly, says Procopius [195] *there used to be very few people at court; but in Justinian's reign, as the judges had no longer the liberty of administering justice, their tribunals were deserted, while the prince's palace resounded with the litigious clamours of the several parties.* Everybody knows what a prostitution there was of public judgments, and even of the very laws themselves, at that emperor's court.

[195] Secret History.

The laws are the eye of the prince; by them he sees what would otherwise escape his observation. Should he attempt the function of a judge, he would not then labor for himself, but for impostors, whose aim is to deceive him.

6. *That in Monarchies Ministers ought not to sit as Judges.*

It is likewise a very great inconvenience in monarchies for the ministers of the prince to sit as judges. We have still instances of states where there are a great number of judges to decide exchequer causes, and where the ministers nevertheless (a thing most incredible!) would fain determine them. Many are the reflections that here arise; but this single one will suffice for my purpose.

There is in the very nature of things a kind of contrast between a prince's council and his courts of judicature. The king's council ought to be composed of a few persons, and the courts of judicature of a great many. The reason is, in the former, things should be undertaken and conducted with a kind of warmth and passion, which can hardly be expected but from four or five men who make it their sole business. On the contrary, in courts of judicature a certain coolness in requisite, and an indifference, in some measure, to all manner of affairs.

7. Of a single Magistrate.

A magistracy of this kind cannot take place but in a despotic government. We have an instance in the Roman history how far a single magistrate may abuse his power. Might it not be very well expected that Appius on his tribunal should contemn all laws, after having violated that of his own enacting? [196] Livy has given us the iniquitous distinction of the Decemvir. He had suborned a man to reclaim Virginia in his presence as his slave; Virginia's relatives insisted that by virtue of his own law she should be consigned to them, till the definitive judgment was passed. Upon which he declared that his law had been enacted only in favor of the father, and that as Virginius was absent, no application could be made of it to the present case. [197]

[196] See the 2nd law, § 24 ff. de Orig. jur.
[197] "Quod pater puellæ abesset, locum injuriæ esse ratus."—Livius, dec. I, lib. III.

8. Of Accusation in different Governments.

At Rome, [198] it was lawful for one citizen to accuse another. This was agreeable to the spirit of a republic, where each citizen ought to have an unlimited zeal for the public good, and is supposed to hold all the rights of his country in his own hands. Under the emperors, the republican maxims were still pursued; and instantly appeared a pernicious tribe, a swarm of informers. Crafty, wicked men, who could stoop to any indignity to serve the purposes of their ambition, were sure to busy themselves in the search of criminals whose condemnation might be agreeable to the prince; this was the road to honor and preferment, [199] but luckily we are strangers to it in our country.

[198] And in a great many other cities.
[199] See in Tacitus the rewards given to those informers.

We have at present an admirable law, namely, that by which the prince, who is established for the execution of the laws, appoints an officer in each court of judicature to prosecute all sorts of crimes in his name; hence the profession of informers is a thing unknown to us, for if this public avenger were suspected to abuse his office, he would soon be obliged to mention his author.

By Plato's Laws [200] those who neglect to inform or to assist the magistrates are liable to punishment. This would not be so proper in our days. The public prosecutor watches for the safety of the citizens; he proceeds in his office while they enjoy their quiet and ease.

86

9. *Of the Severity of Punishments in different Governments.*

The severity of punishments is fitter for despotic governments, whose principle is terror, than for a monarchy or a republic, whose spring is honor and virtue.

In moderate governments, the love of one's country, shame, and the fear of blame are restraining motives, capable of preventing a multitude of crimes. Here the greatest punishment of a bad action is conviction. The civil laws have therefore a softer way of correcting, and do not require so much force and severity.

In those states a good legislator is less bent upon punishing than preventing crimes; he is more attentive to inspire good morals than to inflict penalties.

It is a constant remark of the Chinese authors [201] that the more the penal laws were increased in their empire, the nearer they drew towards a revolution. This is because punishments were augmented in proportion as the public morals were corrupted.

[201] I shall show hereafter that China is, in this respect, in the same case as a republic or a monarchy.

It would be an easy matter to prove that in all, or almost all, the governments of Europe, penalties have increased or diminished in proportion as those governments favored or discouraged liberty.

In despotic governments, people are so unhappy as to have a greater dread of death than regret for the loss of life; consequently their punishments ought to be more severe. In moderate states they are more afraid of losing their lives than apprehensive of the pain of dying; those punishments, therefore, which deprive them simply of life are sufficient.

Men in excess of happiness or misery are equally inclinable to severity; witness conquerors and monks. It is mediocrity alone, and a mixture of prosperous and adverse fortune, that inspires us with lenity and pity.

What we see practiced by individuals is equally observable in regard to nations. In countries inhabited by savages who lead a very hard life, and in despotic governments, where there is only one person on whom fortune lavishes her favors, while the miserable subjects lie exposed to her insults, people are equally cruel. Lenity reigns in moderate governments.

When in reading history we observe the cruelty of the sultans in administration of justice, we shudder at the very thought of the miseries of human nature.

In moderate governments, a good legislator may make use of everything by way of punishment. Is it not very extraordinary that one of the chief penalties at Sparta was to deprive a person of the power of lending out his wife, or of receiving the wife of another man, and to oblige him to have no company at home but virgins? In short, whatever the law calls a punishment is such effectively.

10. *Of the ancient French Laws.*

In the ancient French laws we find the true spirit of monarchy. In cases relating to pecuniary mulcts, the common people are less severely punished than the nobility. [202] But in criminal [203] cases it is quite the reverse; the nobleman loses his honor and his voice in court, while the peasant, who has no honor to lose, undergoes a corporal punishment.

[202] Suppose, for instance, to prevent the execution of a decree, the common people paid a fine of forty sous, and the nobility of sixty livres.—Somme Rurale, book II. p. 198, edit. Got. of the year 1512.

[203] See the Council of Peter Defontaines, chap. 13, especially the 22nd art.

11. *That when People are virtuous few Punishments are necessary.*

The people of Rome had some share of probity. Such was the force of this probity that the legislator had frequently no further occasion than to point out the right road, and they were sure to follow it; one would imagine that instead of precepts it was sufficient to give them counsels.

The punishments of the regal laws, and those of the Twelve Tables, were almost all abolished in the time of the republic, in consequence either of the Valerian [204] or of the Porcian law. [205] It was never observed that this step did any manner of prejudice to the civil administration.

[204] It was made by Valerius Publicola soon after the expulsion of the kings, and was twice renewed, both times by magistrates of the same family. As Livy observes, lib. X., the question was not to give it a greater force, but to render its injunctions more perfect. "Diligentius sanctum," says Livy, ibid.

[205] "Lex Porcia pro tergo civium lata." It was made in the 454th year of the foundation of Rome.

This Valerian law, which restrained the magistrates from using violent methods against a citizen that had appealed to the people, inflicted no other punishment on the person who infringed it than that of being reputed a dishonest man. [206]

[206] "Nihil ultra quam improbe factum adjecet."—Liv.

12. *Of the Power of Punishments.*

Experience shows that in countries remarkable for the lenity of their laws the spirit of the inhabitants is as much affected by slight penalties as in other countries by severer punishments.

If an inconvenience or abuse arises in the state, a violent government endeavors suddenly to redress it; and instead of putting the old laws in execution, it establishes some cruel punishment, which instantly puts a stop to the evil. But the spring of government hereby loses its elasticity; the imagination grows accustomed to the severe as well as the milder punishment; and as the fear of the latter diminishes, they are soon obliged in every case to have recourse to the former. Robberies on the highway became common in some countries; in order to remedy this evil, they invented the punishment of breaking upon the wheel, the terror of which put a stop for a while to this mischievous practice. But soon after robberies on the highways became as common as ever.

Desertion in our days has grown to a very great height; in consequence of which it was judged proper to punish those delinquents with death; and yet their number did not diminish. The reason is very natural; a soldier, accustomed to venture his life, despises, or affects to despise, the danger of losing it. He is habituated to the fear of shame; it would have been therefore much better to have continued a punishment [207] which branded him with infamy for life; the penalty was pretended to be increased, while it really diminished.

[207] They slit his nose or cut off his ears.

Mankind must not be governed with too much severity; we ought to make a prudent use of the means which nature has given us to conduct them. If we inquire into the cause of all human corruptions, we shall find that they proceed from the impunity of criminals, and not from the moderation of punishments.

Let us follow nature, who has given shame to man for his scourge; and let the heaviest part of the punishment be the infamy attending it.

But if there be some countries where shame is not a consequence of punishment, this must be owing to tyranny, which has inflicted the same penalties on villains and honest men.

And if there are others where men are deterred only by cruel punishments, we may be sure that this must, in a great measure, arise from the violence of the government which has used such penalties for slight transgressions.

It often happens that a legislator, desirous of remedying an abuse, thinks of nothing else; his eyes are open only to this object, and shut to its inconveniences. When the abuse is redressed, you see only the severity of the legislator; yet there remains an evil in the state that has sprung from this severity; the minds of the people are corrupted, and become habituated to despotism.

Lysander [208] having obtained a victory over the Athenians, the prisoners were ordered to be tried, in consequence of an accusation brought against that nation of having thrown all the captives of two galleys down a precipice, and of having resolved in full assembly to cut off the hands of those whom they should chance to make prisoners. The Athenians were therefore all massacred, except Adymantes, who had opposed this decree. Lysander reproached Phylocles, before he was put to death, with having depraved the people's minds, and given lessons of cruelty to all Greece.

[208] Xenophon, *Hist.*, lib. III.

The Argives, says Plutarch, [209] *having put fifteen hundred of their citizens to death, the Athenians ordered sacrifices of expiation,* [210] *that it might please the gods to turn the hearts of the Athenians from so cruel a thought.*

[209] Morals of those who are entrusted with the direction of the state affairs.
[210] Montesquieu appears to have followed Amyot, who was mistaken here. Plutarch says that the Athenians carried the victims of expiation around the assembly. It was done as an act of purification.—*Crévier.*

There are two sorts of corruptions—one when the people do not observe the laws; the other when they are corrupted by the laws: an incurable evil, because it is in the very remedy itself.

13. *Insufficiency of the Laws of Japan.*

Excessive punishments may even corrupt a despotic government; of this we have an instance in Japan.

Here almost all crimes are punished with death, [211] because disobedience to so great an emperor as that of Japan is reckoned an enormous crime. The question is not so much to correct the delinquent as to vindicate the authority of the prince. These notions are derived from servitude, and are owing especially to this, that as the emperor is universal proprietor, almost all crimes are directly against his interests.

[211] See Kempfer.

They punish with death lies spoken before the magistrate; [212] a proceeding contrary to natural defense.

[212] Collection of voyages that contributed to the establishment of the East India Company, tom. iii, p. 428.

Even things which have not the appearance of a crime are severely punished; for instance, a man that ventures his money at play is put to death.

True it is that the character of this people, so amazingly obstinate, capricious, and resolute as to defy all dangers and calamities, seems to absolve their legislators from the imputation of cruelty, notwithstanding the severity of their laws. But are men who have a natural contempt for death, and who rip open their bellies for the least fancy—are such men, I say, mended or deterred, or rather are they not hardened, by the continual prospect of punishments?

The relations of travelers inform us, with respect to the education of the Japanese, that children must be treated there with mildness, because they become hardened to punishment; that their slaves must not be too roughly used, because they immediately stand upon their defense. Would not one imagine that they might easily have judged of the spirit which ought to reign in their political and civil government from that which should prevail in their domestic concerns?

A wise legislator would have endeavored to reclaim people by a just temperature of punishments and rewards; by maxims of philosophy, morality, and religion, adapted to those characters; by a proper application of the rules of honor, and by the enjoyment of ease and tranquility of life. And should he have entertained any apprehension that their minds, being inured to the cruelty of punishments, would no longer be restrained by those of a milder nature, he would have conducted himself [213] in another manner, and gained his point by degrees, in particular cases that admitted of any indulgence, he would have mitigated the punishment, till he should have been able to extend this mitigation to all cases.

[213] Let this be observed as a maxim in practice, with regard to cases where the minds of people have been depraved by too great a severity of punishments.

But these are springs to which despotic power is a stranger; it may abuse itself, and that is all it can do: in Japan it has made its utmost effort, and has surpassed even itself in cruelty.

As the minds of the people grew wild and intractable, they were obliged to have recourse to the most horrid severity.

This is the origin, this the spirit, of the laws of Japan. They had more fury, however, than force. They succeeded the extirpation of Christianity; but such unaccountable efforts are a proof of their insufficiency. They wanted to establish a good policy, and they have shown greater marks of their weakness.

We have only to read the relation of the interview between the Emperor and the Deyro at Meaco. [214] The number of those who were suffocated or murdered in that city by ruffians is incredible; young maids and boys were carried off by force, and found afterwards exposed in public places, at unseasonable hours, quite naked, and sewn in linen bags, to prevent their knowing which way they had passed; robberies were committed in all parts; the bellies of horses were ripped open, to bring their riders to the ground; and coaches were overturned, in order to strip the ladies. The Dutch, who were told they could not pass the night on the scaffolds without exposing themselves to the danger of being assassinated, came down, &c.

[214] Collection of Voyages that Contributed to the Establishment of the East India Company, tom. v, p. 2.

I shall here give one instance more from the same nation. The Emperor having abandoned himself to infamous pleasures, lived unmarried, and was consequently in danger of dying without issue. The Deyro sent him two beautiful damsels; one he married out of respect, but would not meddle with her. His nurse caused the finest women of the empire to be sent for, but all to no purpose. At length, an armourer's daughter having pleased his fancy, [215] he determined to espouse her, and had a son. The ladies belonging to the court, enraged to see a person of such mean extraction preferred to themselves, stifled the child. The crime was concealed from the Emperor; for he would have deluged the land with blood. The excessive severity of the laws hinders, therefore, their execution: when the punishment surpasses all measure, they are frequently obliged to prefer impunity to it.

[215] Ibid. tom. v. p. 2

14. *Of the Spirit of the Roman Senate.*

Under the consulate of Acilius Glabrio and Piso, the Asilian law [216] was made to prevent the intriguing for places. Dio says [217] that the senate engaged the consuls to propose it, by reason that C. Cornelius, the tribune, had resolved to cause more severe punishments to be established against this crime; to which the people seemed greatly inclined. The senate rightly judged that immoderate punishments would strike, indeed, a terror into people's minds, but must have also this effect, that there would be nobody afterwards to accuse or condemn; whereas, by proposing moderate penalties, there would be always judges and accusers.

[216] The guilty were condemned to a fine; they could not be admitted into the rank of senators, nor nominated to any public office.—Dio, XXXVI.

[217] Book XXXVI.

15. *Of the Roman Laws in respect to Punishments.*

I am strongly confirmed in my sentiments upon finding the Romans on my side; and I think that punishments are connected with the nature of governments when I behold this great people changing in this respect their civil laws, in proportion as they altered their form of government.

The *regal* laws, made for fugitives, slaves, and vagabonds, were very severe. The spirit of a republic would have required that the decemvirs should not have inserted those laws in their Twelve Tables; but men who aimed at tyranny were far from conforming to a republican spirit.

Livy says, [218] in relation to the punishment of Metius Suffetius, dictator of Alba, who was condemned by Tullius Hostilius to be fastened to two chariots drawn by horses, and torn asunder, that this was the first and last punishment in which the remembrance of humanity seemed to have been lost. He is mistaken; the Twelve Tables are full of very cruel laws. [219]

[218] Lib I.

[219] We find there the punishment of fire, and generally capital punishments, theft punished with death, &c.

The design of the decemvirs appears more conspicuous in the capital punishment pronounced against libelers and poets. This is not agreeable to the genius of a republic, where the people like to see the great men humbled. But persons who aimed at the subversion of liberty were afraid of writings that might revive its spirit. [220]

[220] Sylla, animated with the same spirit as the decemvirs, followed their example in augmenting the penal laws against satirical writers.

After the expulsion of the decemvirs, almost all the penal laws were abolished. It is true they were not expressly repealed; but as the Porcian law had ordained that no citizen of Rome should be put to death, they were of no further use.

This is exactly the time to which we may refer what Livy says [221] of the Romans, that no people were ever fonder of moderation in punishments.

[221] Book I.

But if to the lenity of penal laws we add the right which the party accused had of withdrawing before judgment was pronounced, we shall find that the Romans followed the spirit which I have observed to be natural to a republic.

Sylla, who confounded tyranny, anarchy, and liberty, made the Cornelian laws. He seemed to have contrived regulations merely with a view to create new crimes. Thus distinguishing an infinite number of actions by the name of murder, he found murderers in all parts; and by a practice too much followed, he laid snares, sowed thorns, and opened precipices, wheresoever the citizens set their feet.

Almost all Sylla's laws contained only the interdiction of fire and water. To this Cæsar added the confiscation of goods [222] because the rich, by preserving their estates in exile, became bolder in the perpetration of crimes.

[222] Pœnas facinorum auxit, cum locupletes eo facilius scelere se obligarent, quod integris patrimoniis exularent.—Suetonius in *Julius Cæsar*.

The emperors, having established a military government, soon found that it was as terrible to the prince as to the subject; they endeavored therefore to temper it, and with this view had recourse to dignities, and to the respect with which those dignities were attended.

The government thus drew nearer a little to monarchy, and punishments were divided into three classes: [223] those which related to the principal persons in the state, [224] which were very mild: those which were inflicted on persons of an inferior rank, [225] and were more severe; and, in fine, such as concerned only persons of the lowest condition, [226] which were the most rigorous.

[223] See the 3rd law, § legis ad leg. Cornel. *de Sicariis*, and a vast number of others in the Digest and in the Codex.
[224] Sublimiores.
[225] Medios.
[226] Infimos. Leg. 3, § legis ad leg. Cornel, *de Sicariis*.

Maximinus, that fierce and stupid prince, increased the rigor of the military government which he ought to have softened. The senate were informed, says Capitolinus, [227] that some had been crucified, others exposed to wild beasts, or sewn up in the skins of beasts lately killed, without any manner of regard to their dignity. It seemed as if he wanted to exercise the military discipline, on the model of which he pretended to regulate the civil administration.

[227] Jul. Cap., Maximini duo.

In 'The Consideration on the Rise and Declension of the Roman Grandeur,' [228] we find in what manner Constantine changed the military despotism into a military and civil government, and drew nearer to monarchy. There we may trace the different revolutions of this state, and see how they fell from rigor to indolence, and from indolence to impunity.

[228] Chapter xvii.

16. *Of the just Proportion between Punishments and Crimes.*

It is an essential point, that there should be a certain proportion in punishments, because it is essential that a great crime should be avoided rather than a smaller, and that which is more pernicious to society rather than that which is less.

"An impostor, [229] who called himself Constantine Ducas, raised a great insurrection at Constantinople. He was taken and condemned to be whipped; but upon informing against several persons of distinction, he was sentenced to be burned as a calumniator." It is very extraordinary that they should thus proportion the punishments between the crime of high treason and that of calumny.

[229] Hist. of Nicephorus, patriarch of Constantinople.

This puts me in mind of a saying of Charles II, King of Great Britain. He saw a man one day standing in the pillory; upon which he asked what crime the man had committed. He was answered, *Please your Majesty, he has written a libel against your ministers. The fool said the King, why did he not write against me? They would have done nothing to him.*

"Seventy persons having conspired against the Emperor Basil, he ordered them to be whipped, and the hair of their heads and beards to be burned. A stag, one day, having taken hold of him by the girdle with his horn, one of his retinue drew his sword, cut the girdle, and saved him; upon which he ordered that person's head to be cut off, for having," said he, "drawn his sword against his sovereign." [230] Who could imagine that the same prince could ever have passed two such different judgments?

[230] In Nicephorus' History.

It is a great abuse amongst us to condemn to the same punishment a person that only robs on the highway and another who robs and murders. Surely, for the public security, some difference should be made in the punishment.

In China, those who add murder to robbery are cut in pieces: [231] but not so the others; to this difference it is owing that though they rob in that country they never murder.

[231] Du Halde, tom. i, p. 6.

In Russia, where the punishment of robbery and murder is the same, they always murder. [232] The dead, say they, tell no tales.

[232] Present State of Russia, by Perry.

Where there is no difference in the penalty, there should be some in the expectation of pardon. In England they never murder on the highway, because robbers have some hopes of transportation, which is not the case in respect to those that commit murder.

Letters of grace are of excellent use in moderate governments. This power which the prince has of pardoning, exercised with prudence, is capable of producing admirable effects. The principle of despotic government, which neither grants nor receives any pardon, deprives it of these advantages.

17. Of the Rack.

The wickedness of mankind makes it necessary for the law to suppose them better than they really are. Hence the deposition of two witnesses is sufficient in the punishment of all crimes. The law believes them, as if they spoke by the mouth of truth. Thus we judge that every child conceived in wedlock is legitimate; the law having a confidence in the mother, as if she were chastity itself. But the use of the rack against criminals cannot be defended on a like plea of necessity.

We have before us the example of a nation blessed with an excellent civil government, [233] where without any inconvenience the practice of racking criminals is rejected. It is not, therefore, in its own nature necessary. [234]

[233] The English.
[234] The citizens of Athens could not be put to the rack (Lysias, *Orat. contra A*gorat.) unless it was for high treason. The torture was used within thirty days after condemnation. (Curius Fortunatus. *Rhetor, scol.*, lib. II.) There was no preparatory torture. In regard to the Romans, the Leg. 3, 4, *ad leg. Jul. majest.*, show that birth, dignity, and the military profession exempted people from the rack, except in cases of high treason. See the prudent restrictions of this practice made by the laws of the Visigoths.

So many men of learning and genius have written against the custom of torturing criminals, that after them I dare not presume to meddle with the subject. I was going to say that it might suit despotic states, where whatever inspires fear is the fittest spring of government. I was going to say that the slaves among the Greeks and Romans—but nature cries out aloud, and asserts her rights.

18. *Of pecuniary and corporal Punishments.*

Our ancestors, the Germans, admitted of none but pecuniary punishments. Those free and warlike people were of opinion that their blood ought not to be spilled but with sword in hand. On the contrary, these punishments are rejected by the Japanese, [235] under pretence that the rich might elude them. But are not the rich afraid of being stripped of their property? And might not pecuniary penalties be proportioned to people's fortunes? And, in fine, might not infamy be added to those punishments?

[235] See Kempfer.

A good legislator takes a just medium; he ordains neither always pecuniary, nor always corporal punishments.

19. *Of the Law of Retaliation.*

The use of the *law of retaliation* [236] is very frequent in despotic countries, where they are fond of simple laws. Moderate governments admit of it sometimes; but with this difference, that the former exercise it in full rigor, whereas among the latter it ever receives some kind of limitation.

[236] It is established in the Koran. See the chapter, Of the Cow.

The law of the Twelve Tables admitted two: first, it never condemned to retaliation, but when the plaintiff could not be satisfied in any other manner. [237] Secondly, after condemnation they might pay damages and interest, [238] and then the corporal was changed into a pecuniary punishment. [239]

[237] "Si membrum rupit, ni cum eo pacit, talio esto." Aulus Gellius, lib. XX chap. i.
[238] Ibid.
[239] See also the law of the Visigoths, book VI, tit. 4, §§ 3 and 5.

20. *Of the Punishment of Fathers for the Crimes of their Children.*

In China, fathers are punished for the crimes of their children. This was likewise the custom of Peru [240]—a custom derived from the notion of despotic power.

[240] See Garcilaso, History of the Civil Wars of the Spaniards.

Little does it signify to say that in China the father is punished for not having exerted that paternal authority which nature has established, and the laws themselves have improved. This still supposes that there is no honor among the Chinese. Amongst us, parents whose children are condemned by the laws of their country, and children [241] whose parents have undergone the like fate, are as severely punished by shame, as they would be in China by the loss of their lives.

[241] "Instead of punishing them," says Plato, "they ought to be commended for not having followed their fathers' example."—Book IX. of Laws.

21. *Of the Clemency of the Prince.*

Clemency is the characteristic of monarchs. In republics, whose principle is virtue, it is not so necessary. In despotic governments, where fear predominates, it is less customary, because the great men are to be restrained by examples of severity. It is more necessary in monarchies, where they are governed by honor, which frequently requires what the very law forbids. Disgrace is here equivalent to chastisement; and even the forms of justice are punishments. This is because particular kinds of penalty are formed by shame, which on every side invades the delinquent.

The great men in monarchies are so heavily punished by disgrace, by the loss (though often imaginary) of their fortune, credit, acquaintances, and pleasures, that rigor in respect to them is needless. It can tend only to divest the subject of the affection he has for the person of his prince, and of the respect he ought to have for public posts and employments.

As the instability of the great is natural to a despotic government, so their security is interwoven with the nature of monarchy.

So many are the advantages which monarchs gain by clemency, so greatly does it raise their fame, and endear them to their subjects, that it is generally happy for them to have an opportunity of displaying it; which in this part of the world is seldom wanting.

Some branch, perhaps, of their authority, but never hardly the whole, will be disputed; and if they sometimes fight for their crown, they do not fight for their life.

But some may ask when it is proper to punish, and when to pardon. This is a point more easily felt that prescribed. When there is danger in the exercise of clemency, it is visible; nothing so easy as to distinguish it from that imbecility which exposes princes to contempt and to the very incapacity of punishing.

The Emperor Maurice [242] made a resolution never to spill the blood of his subjects. Anastasius [243] punished no crimes at all. Isaac Angelus took an oath that no one should be put to death during his reign. Those Greek emperors forgot that it was not for nothing they were entrusted with the sword.

[242] Evagr. Hist.
[243] Fragment of Suidas, in Constantine Porphyrogenitus.

BOOK VII.

CONSEQUENCES OF THE DIFFERENT PRINCIPLES OF THE THREE GOVERNMENTS WITH RESPECT TO SUMPTUARY LAWS, LUXURY, AND THE CONDITION OF WOMEN

1. *Of Luxury.*

Luxury is ever in proportion to the inequality of fortunes. If the riches of a state are equally divided there will be no luxury; for it is founded merely on the conveniences acquired by the labor of others.

In order to have this equal distribution of riches, the law ought to give to each man only what is necessary for nature. If they exceed these bounds, some will spend, and others will acquire, by which means an inequality will be established.

Supposing what is necessary for the support of nature to be equal to a given sum, the luxury of those who have only what is barely necessary will be equal to a cipher: if a person happens to have double that sum, his luxury will be equal to one; he that has double the latter's substance will have a luxury equal to three; if this be still doubled, there will be a luxury equal to seven; so that the property of the subsequent individual being always supposed double to that of the preceding, the luxury will increase double, and a unit be always added, in this progression, 0, 1, 3, 7, 15, 31, 63, 127.

In Plato's republic, [244] luxury might have been exactly calculated. There were four sorts of censuses or rates of estates. The first was exactly the term beyond poverty, the second was double, the third triple, the fourth quadruple to the first. In the first census, luxury was equal to a *cipher*; in the second to one, in the third to two, in the fourth to three: and thus it followed in an arithmetical proportion.

[244] The first census was the hereditary share in land, and Plato would not allow them to have, in other effects, above a triple of the hereditary share. See his Laws, V

Considering the luxury of different nations with respect to one another, it is in each state a compound proportion to the inequality of fortunes among the subjects, and to the inequality of wealth in different states. In Poland, for example, there is an extreme inequality of fortunes, but the poverty of the whole binders them from having so much luxury as in a more opulent government.

Luxury is also in proportion to the populousness of the towns, and especially of the capital; so that it is in a compound proportion to the riches of the state, to the inequality of private fortunes, and to the number of people settled in particular places.

In proportion to the populousness of towns, the inhabitants are filled with notions of vanity, and actuated by an ambition of distinguishing themselves by trifles. [245] If they are very numerous, and most of them strangers to one another, their vanity redoubles, because there are greater hopes of success. As luxury inspires these hopes, each man assumes the marks of a superior condition. But by endeavoring thus at distinction, every one becomes equal, and distinction ceases; as all are desirous of respect, nobody is regarded.

[245] "In large and populous cities," says the author of the Fable of the Bees, i, p. 133, "they wear clothes above their rank, and, consequently, have the pleasure of being esteemed by a vast majority, not as what they are, but what they appear to be. They have the satisfaction of imagining that they appear what they would be: which, to weak minds, is a pleasure almost as substantial as they could reap from the very accomplishment of their wishes."

Hence arises a general inconvenience. Those who excel in a profession set what value they please on their labor; this example is followed by people of inferior abilities, and then there is an end of all proportion between our wants and the means of satisfying them. When I am forced to go to law, I must be able to fee counsel; when I am sick, I must have it in my power to fee a physician.

It is the opinion of several that the assemblage of so great a multitude of people in capital cities is an obstruction to commerce, because the inhabitants are no longer at a proper distance from each other. But I cannot think so; for men have more desires, more wants, more fancies, when they live together.

2. *Of sumptuary Laws in a Democracy.*

We have observed that in a republic, where riches are equally divided, there can be no such thing as luxury; and as we have shown in the 5th Book, [246] that this equal distribution constitutes the excellence of a republican government; hence it follows, that the less luxury there is in a republic, the more it is perfect. There was none among the old Romans, none among the Lacedæmonians; and in republics where this equality is not quite lost, the spirit of commerce, industry, and virtue renders every man able and willing to live on his own property, and consequently prevents the growth of luxury.

[246] Chapters iv. and v.

The laws concerning the new division of lands, insisted upon so eagerly in some republics, were of the most salutary nature. They are dangerous, only as they are sudden. By reducing instantly the wealth of some, and increasing that of others, they form a revolution in each family, and must produce a general one in the state.

In proportion as luxury gains ground in a republic, the minds of the people are turned towards their particular interests. Those who are allowed only what is necessary have nothing but their own reputation and their country's glory in view. But a soul depraved by luxury has many other desires, and soon becomes an enemy to the laws that confine it. The luxury in which the garrison of Rhegium [247] began to live was the cause of their massacring the inhabitants.

[247] The city at the extremity of Italy, nearest Sicily; pillaged by Decius Jubellius with a barbarian legion.—Ed.

No sooner were the Romans corrupted than their desires became boundless and immense. Of this we may judge by the price they set on things. A pitcher of Falernian wine [248] was sold for a hundred Roman denarii; a barrel of salt meat from the kingdom of Pontus cost four hundred; a good cook four talents; and for boys, no price was reckoned too great. When the whole world, impelled by the force of corruption, is immersed in voluptuousness [249] what must then become of virtue?

[248] Fragment of the 36th book of Diodorus, quoted by Constantine Porphyrogenitus, in his Extract of Virtues and Vices.

[249] Cum maximus omnium impetus ad luxuriant esset.—Ibid.

3. *Of sumptuary Laws in an Aristocracy.*

There is this inconvenience in an ill-constituted aristocracy, that the wealth centers in the nobility, and yet they are not allowed to spend; for as luxury is contrary to the spirit of moderation, it must be banished thence. This government comprehends, therefore, only people who are extremely poor and cannot acquire, and people who are vastly rich and cannot spend.

In Venice, they are compelled by the laws to moderation. They are so habituated to parsimony that none but courtesans can make them part with their money. Such is the method made use of for the support of industry; the most contemptible of women may be profuse without danger, whilst those who contribute to their extravagance consume their days in the greatest obscurity.

Admirable in this respect were the institutions of the principal republics of Greece. The rich employed their money in festivals, musical choruses, chariots, horse-races, and chargeable offices. Wealth was, therefore, as burdensome there as poverty.

4. *Of sumptuary Laws in a Monarchy.*

Tacitus says [250] *That the Suiones,* [251] *a German nation, has a particular respect for riches; for which reason they live under the government of one person.* This shows that luxury is extremely proper for monarchies, and that under this government there must be no sumptuary laws.

[250] *De Moribus Germanorum,* 44.

[251] The Suiones were the inhabitants of that part of Europe now known as Sweden.—Ed.

As riches, by the very constitution of monarchies, are unequally divided, there is an absolute necessity for luxury. Were the rich not to be lavish, the poor would starve. It is even necessary here that the expenses of the opulent should be in proportion to the inequality of fortunes, and that luxury, as we have already observed, should increase in this proportion. The augmentation of private wealth is owing to its having deprived one part of the citizens of their necessary support; this must therefore be restored to them.

Hence it is that for the preservation of a monarchical state, luxury ought continually to increase, and to grow more extensive, as it rises from the laborer to the artificer, to the merchant, to the magistrate, to the nobility, to the great officers of state, up to the very prince; otherwise the nation will be undone.

In the reign of Augustus, a proposal was made in the Roman senate, which was composed of grave magistrates, learned civilians, and of men whose heads were filled with the notion of the primitive times, to reform the manners and luxury of women. It is curious to see in Dio, [252] with what art this prince eluded the importunate solicitations of those senators. This was because he was founding a monarchy, and dissolving a republic.

[252] Dio Cassius, lib. LIV.

Under Tiberius, the Ædiles proposed in the senate the re-establishment of the ancient sumptuary laws. [253] This prince, who did not want sense, opposed it. *The state,* said he, *could not possibly subsist in the present situation of things. How could Rome, how could the provinces, live? We were frugal, while we were only masters of one city; now we consume the riches of the whole globe, and employ both the masters and their slaves in our service.* He plainly saw that sumptuary laws would not suit the present form of government.

[253] Tacitus, *Annal.* lib. III.

When a proposal was made under the same emperor to the senate, to prohibit the governors from carrying their wives with them into the provinces, because of the dissoluteness and irregularity which followed those ladies, the proposal was rejected. It was said that the examples of ancient austerity had been changed into a more agreeable method of living. [254] They found there was a necessity for different manners.

[254] *Malta duritiei veterum melius et latius mutata*—Tacitus. *Annal.* lib. III.

Luxury is therefore absolutely necessary in monarchies; as it is also in despotic states. In the former, it is the use of liberty; in the latter, it is the abuse of servitude. A slave appointed by his master to tyrannize over other wretches of the same condition, uncertain of enjoying tomorrow the blessings of to-day, has no other felicity than that of glutting the pride, the passions, and voluptuousness of the present moment.

Hence arises a very natural reflection. Republics end with luxury; monarchies with poverty. [255]

[255] "Opulentia paritura mox egestatem."—Florus, lib. III.

5. *In what Cases sumptuary Laws are useful in a Monarchy.*

Whether it was from a republican spirit, or from some other particular circumstance, sumptuary laws were made in Aragon, in the middle of the thirteenth century. James the First ordained that neither the king nor any of his subjects should have above two sorts of dishes at a meal, and that each dish should be dressed only one way, except it were game of their own killing. [256]

[256] Constitution of James I in the year 1234, art. 6, in *Marca Hispanica*, p. 1429.

In our days, sumptuary laws have been also enacted in Sweden; but with a different view from those of Aragon.

A government may make sumptuary laws with a view to absolute frugality; this is the spirit of sumptuary laws in republics; and the very nature of the thing shows that such was the design of those of Aragon.

Sumptuary laws may likewise be established with a design to promote a relative frugality: when a government, perceiving that foreign merchandise, being at too high a price, will require such an exportation of home manufactures as to deprive them of more advantages by the loss of the latter than they can receive from the possession of the former, they will forbid their being introduced. And this is the spirit of the laws which in our days have been passed in Sweden. [257] Such are the sumptuary laws proper for monarchies.

[257] They have prohibited rich wines and other costly merchandise.

In general, the poorer a state, the more it is ruined by its relative luxury; and consequently the more occasion it has for relative sumptuary laws. The richer a state, the more it thrives by its relative luxury; for which reason it must take particular care not to make any relative sumptuary laws. This we shall better explain in the book on commerce; [258] here we treat only of absolute luxury.

[258] See book XX. Chap. 20.

6. Of the Luxury of China.

Sumptuary laws may, in some governments, be necessary for particular reasons. The people, by the influence of the climate, may grow so numerous, and the means of subsisting may be so uncertain, as to render a universal application to agriculture extremely necessary. As luxury in those countries is dangerous, their sumptuary laws should be very severe. In order, therefore, to be able to judge whether luxury ought to be encouraged or proscribed, we should examine first what relation there is between the number of people and the facility they have of procuring subsistence. In England the soil produces more grain than is necessary for the maintenance of such as cultivate the land, and of those who are employed in the woollen manufactures. This country may be therefore allowed to have some trifling arts, and consequently luxury. In France, likewise, there is corn enough for the support of the husbandman and of the manufacturer. Besides, a foreign trade may bring in so many necessaries in return for toys that there is no danger to be apprehended from luxury.

On the contrary, in China, the women are so prolific, and the human species multiplies so fast, that the lands, though never so much cultivated, are scarcely sufficient to support the inhabitants. Here, therefore, luxury is pernicious, and the spirit of industry and economy is as requisite as in any republic. [259] They are obliged to pursue the necessary arts, and to shun those of luxury and pleasure.

[259] Luxury has been here always prohibited.

This is the spirit of the excellent decrees of the Chinese emperors. *Our ancestors,* says an emperor of the family of the Tangs [260] *held it as a maxim that if there was a man who did not work, or a woman that was idle, somebody must suffer cold or hunger in the empire.* And on this principle he ordered a vast number of the monasteries of Bonzes to be destroyed.

[260] In an ordinance quoted by Father Du Halde, ii, p. 497.

The third emperor of the one-and-twentieth dynasty, [261] to whom some precious stones were brought that had been found in a mine, ordered it to be shut up, not choosing to fatigue his people with working for a thing that could neither feed nor clothe them.

[261] History of China, 21st Dynasty, in Father Du Halde's work, tom. i.

So great is our luxury, says Kiayventi, [262] *that people adorn with embroidery the shoes of boys and girls, whom they are obliged to sell.* Is employing so many people in making clothes for one person the way to prevent a great many from wanting clothes? There are ten men who eat the fruits of the earth to one employed in agriculture; and is this the means of preserving numbers from wanting nourishment?

[262] In a discourse cited by Father Du Halde, tom. iii, p. 418.

7. *Fatal Consequence of Luxury in China.*

In the history of China we find it has had twenty-two successive dynasties, that is, it has experienced twenty-two general, without mentioning a prodigious number of particular, revolutions. The first three dynasties lasted a long time, because they were wisely administered, and the empire had not so great an extent as it afterwards obtained. But we may observe in general that all those dynasties began very well. Virtue, attention, and vigilance are necessary in China; these prevailed in the commencement of the dynasties, and failed in the end. It was natural that emperors trained up in military toil, who had compassed the dethroning of a family immersed in pleasure, should adhere to virtue, which they had found so advantageous, and be afraid of voluptuousness, which they knew had proved so fatal to the family dethroned. But after the three or four first princes, corruption, luxury, indolence, and pleasure possessed their successors; they shut themselves up in a palace; their understanding was impaired; their life was shortened; the family declined; the grandees rose up; the eunuchs gained credit; none but children were set on the throne; the palace was at variance with the empire; a lazy set of people that dwelt there ruined the industrious part of the nation; the emperor was killed or destroyed by a usurper, who founded a family, the third or fourth successor of which went and shut himself up in the very same palace.

8. *Of public Continency.*

So many are the imperfections that attend the loss of virtue in women, and so greatly are their minds depraved when this principal guard is removed, that in a popular state public incontinency may be considered as the last of miseries, and as a certain forerunner of a change in the constitution.

Hence it is that the sage legislators of republican states have ever required of women a particular gravity of manners. They have proscribed not only vice, but the very appearance of it. They have banished even all commerce of gallantry—a commerce that produces idleness, that renders the women corrupters, even before they are corrupted, that gives a value to trifles, and debases things of importance: a commerce, in fine, that makes people act entirely by the maxims of ridicule, in which the women are so perfectly skilled.

9. Of the Condition or State of Women in different Governments.

In monarchies women are subject to very little restraint, because as the distinction of ranks calls them to court, there they assume a spirit of liberty, which is almost the only one tolerated in that place. Each courtier avails himself of their charms and passions, in order to advance his fortune: and as their weakness admits not of pride, but of vanity, luxury constantly attends them.

In despotic governments women do not introduce, but are themselves an object of, luxury. They must be in a state of the most rigorous servitude. Every one follows the spirit of the government, and adopts in his own family the customs he sees elsewhere established. As the laws are very severe and executed on the spot, they are afraid lest the liberty of women should expose them to danger. Their quarrels, indiscretions, repugnancies, jealousies, piques, and that art, in fine, which little souls have of interesting great ones, would be attended there with fatal consequences.

Besides, as princes in those countries make a sport of human nature, they allow themselves a multitude of women; and a thousand considerations oblige them to keep those women in close confinement.

In republics women are free by the laws and restrained by manners; luxury is banished thence, and with it corruption and vice.

In the cities of Greece, where they were not under the restraint of a religion which declares that even amongst men regularity of manners is a part of virtue; where a blind passion triumphed with a boundless insolence, and love appeared only in a shape which we dare not mention, while marriage was considered as nothing more than simple friendship; [263] such was the virtue, simplicity, and chastity of women in those cities, that in this respect hardly any people were ever known to have had a better and wiser polity. [264]

[263] "In respect to true love," says Plutarch, "the women have nothing to say to it." In his Treatise of Love, p. 600. He spoke in the style of his time. See Xenophon in the dialogue intitled Hiero.
[264] At Athens there was a particular magistrate who inspected the conduct of women.

10. Of the domestic Tribunal among the Romans.

The Romans had no particular magistrates, like the Greeks, to inspect the conduct of women. The censors had not an eye over them, as over the rest of the republic.

The institution of the domestic tribunal [265] supplied the magistracy established among the Greeks. [266]

[265] Romulus instituted this tribunal, as appears from Dionysius Halicarnassus, book II, p. 96.

[266] See in Livy, XXXIX, the use that was made of this tribunal at the time of the conspiracy of the Bacchanalians (they gave the name of conspiracy against the republic to assemblies in which the morals of women and young people were debauched.)

The husband summoned the wife's relatives, and tried her in their presence. [267] This tribunal preserved the manners of the republic; and at the same time those very manners maintained this tribunal. For it decided not only in respect to the violation of the laws, but also of manners: now, in order to judge of the violation of the latter, manners are requisite. The penalties inflicted by this tribunal ought to be, and actually were, arbitrary: for all that relates to manners, and to the rules of modesty, can hardly be comprised under one code of laws. It is easy indeed to regulate by laws what we owe to others; but it is very difficult of comprise all we owe to ourselves.

[267] It appears from Dionysius Halicarnassus, lib. II, that Romulus's institution was that in ordinary cases the husband should sit as judge in the presence of the wife's relatives, but that in heinous crimes he should determine in conjunction with five of them. Hence Ulpian, tit. 6, 9, 12, 13, distinguishes in respect to the different judgments of manners between those which he calls important, and those which are less so: *mores graviores, leviores.*

The domestic tribunal inspected the general conduct of women: but there was one crime which, beside the animadversion of this tribunal, was likewise subject to a public accusation. This was adultery; whether that in a republic so great a depravation of manners interested the government; or whether the wife's immorality might render the husband suspected; or whether, in fine, they were afraid lest even honest people might choose that this crime should rather be concealed than punished.

11. *In what Manner the Institutions changed at Rome, together with the Government.*

As manners were supported by the domestic tribunal, they were also supported by the public accusation; and hence it is that these two things fell together with the public manners, and ended with the republic. [268]

[268] *Judicio de moribus (quod antea quidem in antiquis legibus positum erat, non autem frequentabatur) penitus abolito.* Leg. 11. *Cod. de repud.*

The establishing of perpetual questions, that is, the division of jurisdiction among the prætors, and the custom gradually introduced of the prætors determining all causes themselves, [269] weakened the use of the domestic tribunal. This appears by the surprise of historians, who look upon the decisions which Tiberius caused to be given by this tribunal as singular facts, and as a renewal of the ancient course of pleading.

[269] *Judicia extraordinaria.*

The establishment of monarchy and the change of manners put likewise an end to public accusations. It might be apprehended lest a dishonest man, affronted at the slight shown him by a woman, vexed at her refusal, and irritated even by her virtue, should form a design to destroy her. The Julian law ordained that a woman should not be accused of adultery till after her husband had been charged with favoring her irregularities; which limited greatly, and annihilated, as it were, this sort of accusation. [270]

[270] It was entirely abolished by Constantine: "It is a shame," said he, "that settled marriages should be disturbed by the presumption of strangers."

Sextus Quintus seemed to have been desirous of reviving the public accusations. [271] But there needs very little reflection to see that this law would be more improper in such a monarchy as his than in any other.

[271] Sextus Quintus ordained, that if a husband did not come and make his complaint to him of his wife's infidelity, he should be put to death. See Leti.

12. *Of the Guardianship of Women among the Romans.*

The Roman laws subjected women to a perpetual guardianship, except they were under cover and subject to the authority of a husband. [272] This guardianship was given to the nearest of the male relatives; and by a vulgar expression [273] it appears they were very much confined. This was proper for a republic, but not at all necessary in a monarchy. [274]

[272] *Nisi convenissent in manum viri.*
[273] *Ne sis mihi patruus oro.*
[274] The Papian law ordained, under Augustus, that women who had borne three children should be exempt from this tutelage.

That the women among the ancient Germans were likewise under a perpetual tutelage appears from the different codes of the Laws of the Barbarians. [275] This custom was communicated to the monarchies founded by those people; but was not of long duration.

[275] This tutelage was by the Germans called *Mundeburdium.*

13. *Of the Punishments decreed by the Emperors against the Incontinence of Women.*

The Julian law ordained a punishment against adultery. But so far was this law, any more than those afterwards made on the same account, from being a mark of regularity of manners, that on the contrary it was a proof of their depravity.

The whole political system in respect to women received a change in the monarchical state. The question was no longer to oblige them to a regularity of manners, but to punish their crimes. That new laws were made to punish their crimes was owing to their leaving those transgressions unpunished which were not of so criminal a nature.

The frightful dissolution of manners obliged indeed the emperors to enact laws in order to put some stop to lewdness; but it was not their intention to establish a general reformation. Of this the positive facts related by historians are a much stronger proof than all these laws can be of the contrary. We may see in Dio the conduct of Augustus on this occasion, and in what manner he eluded, both in his prætorian and censorian office, the repeated instances that were made him [276] for that purpose.

[276] Upon their bringing before him a young man who had married a woman with whom he had before carried on an illicit commerce, he hesitated a long while, not daring to approve or to punish these things. At length recollecting himself, *Seditions*, says he, *have been the cause of very great evils; let us forget them.* Dio, liv. 16. The senate having desired him to give them some regulations in respect to women's morals, he evaded their petition by telling them that they should chastise their wives in the same manner as he did his; upon which they desired him to tell them how he behaved to his wife. (I think a very indiscreet question.)

It is true that we find in historians very rigid sentences, passed in the reigns of Augustus and Tiberius, against the lewdness of some Roman ladies: but by showing us the spirit of those reigns, at the same time they demonstrate the spirit of those decisions.

The principal design of Augustus and Tiberius was to punish the dissoluteness of their relatives. It was not their immorality they punished, but a particular crime of impiety or high treason [277] of their own invention, which served to promote a respect for majesty, and answered their private revenge. Hence it is that the Roman historians inveigh so bitterly against this tyranny.

[277] Tacitus, Annals, iii. 24.

The penalty of the Julian law was small. [278] The emperors insisted that in passing sentence the judges should increase the penalty of the law. This was the subject of the invectives of historians. They did not examine whether the women were deserving of punishment, but whether they had violated the law, in order to punish them.

[278] This law is given in the Digest, but without mentioning the penalty. It is supposed it was only *relegatio*, because that of incest was only *deportatio*. Leg., *si quis viduam*, ff. de quæst.

One of the most tyrannical proceedings of Tiberius [279] was the abuse he made of the ancient laws. When he wanted to extend the punishment of a Roman lady beyond that inflicted by the Julian law, he revived the domestic tribunal. [280]

[279] "Proprium id Tiberio fuit scelera nuper reperta priscis verbis obtegere."—Tacit.
[280] "Adulterii graviorem pœnam deprecatus, ut exemplo majorum propinquis suis ultra ducentesimum lapidem removeretur, suasit. Adultero Manlio Italiâ atque Africâ interdictum est."—Tacit. *Annal.* lib. II.

These regulations in respect to women concerned only senatorial families, not the common people. Pretences were wanted to accuse the great, which were constantly furnished by the dissolute behavior of the ladies.

In fine, what I have above observed, namely, that regularity of manners is not the principle of monarchy, was never better verified than under those first emperors; and whoever doubts it need only read Tacitus, Suetonius, Juvenal, or Martial.

14. *Sumptuary Laws among the Romans.*

We have spoken of public incontinence because it is the inseparable companion of luxury. If we leave the motions of the heart at liberty, how shall we be able to restrain the weaknesses of the mind?

At Rome, besides the general institutions, the censors prevailed on the magistrates to enact several particular laws for maintaining the frugality of women. This was the design of the Fannian, Licinian, and Oppian laws. We may see in Livy [281] the great ferment the senate was in when the women insisted upon the revocation of the Oppian law. The abrogation of this law is fixed upon by Valerius Maximus as the period whence we may date the luxury of the Romans.

[281] Dec. 4, lib. IV.

15. *Of Dowries and Nuptial Advantages in different Constitutions.*

Dowries ought to be considerable in monarchies, in order to enable husbands to support their rank and the established luxury. In republics, where luxury should never reign, [282] they ought to be moderate; but there should be hardly any at all in despotic governments, where women are in some measure slaves.

[282] Marseilles was the wisest of all the republics in its time; here it was ordained that dowries should not exceed one hundred crowns in money, and five in clothes, as Strabo observes, lib. IV. Strabo further allows a small sum in gold ornaments to serve in the decoration of a bride.

The community of goods introduced by the French laws between man and wife is extremely well adapted to a monarchical government; because the women are thereby interested in domestic affairs, and compelled, as it were, to take care of their family. It is less so in a republic, where women are possessed of more virtue. But it would be quite absurd in despotic governments, where the women themselves generally constitute a part of the master's property.

As women are in a state that furnishes sufficient inducements to marriage, the advantages which the law gives them over the husband's property are of no service to society. But in a republic they would be extremely prejudicial, because riches are productive of luxury. In despotic governments the profits accruing from marriage ought to be mere subsistence, and no more.

16. *An excellent Custom of the Samnites.*

The Samnites had a custom which in so small a republic, and especially in their situation, must have been productive of admirable effects. The young people were all convened in one place, and their conduct was examined. He that was declared the best of the whole assembly had leave given him to take which girl he pleased for his wife; the second best chose after him; and so on. [283] Admirable institution! The only recommendation that young men could have on this occasion was their virtue and the services done their country. He who had the greatest share of these endowments chose which girl he liked out of the whole nation. Love, beauty, chastity, virtue, birth, and even wealth itself, were all, in some measure, the dowry of virtue. A nobler and grander recompense, less chargeable to a petty state, and more capable of influencing both sexes, could scarcely be imagined.

[283] Fragment of Nicolaus Damascenus, taken from Stobæus in the collection of Constantine Porphyrogenitus.

The Samnites were descended from the Lacedæmonians; and Plato, whose institutes are only an improvement of those of Lycurgus, enacted nearly the same law. [284]

[284] He even permits them to have a more frequent interview with one another.

17. *Of Female Administration.*

It is contrary to reason and nature that women should reign in families, as was customary among the Egyptians; but not that they should govern an empire. In the former case the state of their natural weakness does not permit them to have the pre-eminence; in the latter their very weakness generally gives them more lenity and moderation, qualifications fitter for a good administration than roughness and severity.

In the Indies they are very easy under a female government; and it is settled that if the male issue be not of a mother of the same blood, the females born of a mother of the blood-royal must succeed. [285] And then they have a certain number of persons who assist them to bear the weight of the government. According to Mr. Smith, [286] they are very easy in Africa under female administration. If to this we add the example of England and Russia, we shall find that they succeed alike both in moderate and despotic governments.

[285] Edifying Letters, 14th collection.
[286] Voyage to Guinea, part the second, p. 165, of the kingdom of Angola, on the Golden Coast.

BOOK VIII.

OF THE CORRUPTION OF THE PRINCIPLES
OF THE THREE GOVERNMENTS

1. *General Idea of this Book.*

The corruption of this government generally begins with that of the principles.

2. *Of the Corruption of the Principles of Democracy.*

The principle of democracy is corrupted not only when the spirit of equality is extinct, but likewise when they fall into a spirit of extreme equality, and when each citizen would fain be upon a level with those whom he has chosen to command him. Then the people, incapable of bearing the very power they have delegated, want to manage everything themselves, to debate for the senate, to execute for the magistrate, and to decide for the judges.

When this is the case, virtue can no longer subsist in the republic. The people are desirous of exercising the functions of the magistrates, who cease to be revered. The deliberations of the senate are slighted; all respect is then laid aside for the senators, and consequently for old age. If there is no more respect for old age, there will be none presently for parents; deference to husbands will be likewise thrown off, and submission to masters. This license will soon become general, and the trouble of command be as fatiguing as that of obedience. Wives, children, slaves will shake off all subjection. No longer will there be any such thing as manners, order, or virtue.

We find in Xenophon's Banquet a very lively description of a republic in which the people abused their equality. Each guest gives in his turn the reason why he is satisfied. *Content I am,* says Chamides, *because of my poverty. When I was rich, I was obliged to pay my court to informers, knowing I was more liable to be hurt by them than capable of doing them harm. The republic constantly demanded some new tax of me; and I could not decline paying. Since I have grown poor, I have acquired authority; nobody threatens me; I rather threaten others. I can go or stay where I please. The rich already rise from their seats and give me the way. I am a king, I was before a slave: I paid taxes to the republic, now it maintains me: I am no longer afraid of losing: but I hope to acquire.*

The people fall into this misfortune when those in whom they confide, desirous of concealing their own corruption, endeavor to corrupt them. To disguise their own ambition, they speak to them only of the grandeur of the state; to conceal their own avarice, they incessantly flatter theirs.

The corruption will increase among the corruptors, and likewise among those who are already corrupted. The people will divide the public money among themselves, and, having added the administration of affairs to their indolence, will be for blending their poverty with the amusements of luxury. But with their indolence and luxury, nothing but the public treasure will be able to satisfy their demands.

We must not be surprised to see their suffrages given for money. It is impossible to make great largesses to the people without great extortion: and to compass this, the state must be subverted. The greater the advantages they seem to derive from their liberty, the nearer they approach towards the critical moment of losing it. Petty tyrants arise who have all the vices of a single tyrant. The small remains of liberty soon become insupportable; a single tyrant starts up, and the people are stripped of everything, even of the profits of their corruption.

Democracy has, therefore, two excesses to avoid—the spirit of inequality, which leads to aristocracy or monarchy, and the spirit of extreme equality, which leads to despotic power, as the latter is completed by conquest.

True it is that those who corrupted the Greek republics did not always become tyrants. This was because they had a greater passion for eloquence than for the military art. Besides there reigned an implacable hatred in the breasts of the Greeks against those who subverted a republican government; and for this reason anarchy degenerated into annihilation, instead of being changed into tyranny.

But Syracuse being situated in the midst of a great number of petty states, whose government had been changed from oligarchy to tyranny, [287] and being governed by a senate [288] scarcely ever mentioned in history, underwent such miseries as are the consequence of a more than ordinary corruption. This city, ever a prey to licentiousness [289] or oppression, equally laboring under the sudden and alternate succession of liberty and servitude, and notwithstanding her external strength, constantly determined to a revolution by the least foreign power—this city, I say, had in her bosom an immense multitude of people, whose fate it was to have always this cruel alternative, either of choosing a tyrant to govern them, or of acting the tyrant themselves.

[287] See Plutarch in Timoleon and Dio.
[288] It was that of the Six Hundred, of whom mention is made by Diodorus.
[289] Upon the expulsions of the tyrants, they made citizens of strangers and mercenary troops, which gave rise to civil wars.—Aristotle, *Politics*, v. 3. The people having been the cause of the victory over the Athenians, the republic was changed.—*Ibid.*, 4. The passion of two young magistrates, one of whom carried off the other's boy, and in revenge the other debauched his wife, was attended with a change in the form of this republic.—*Ibid.* lib. VII. chap. iv.

3. *Of the Spirit of extreme Equality.*

As distant as heaven is from earth, so is the true spirit of equality from that of extreme equality. The former does not imply that everybody should command, or that no one should be commanded, but that we obey or command our equals. It endeavors not to shake off the authority of a master, but that its masters should be none but its equals.

In the state of nature, indeed, all men are born equal, but they cannot continue in this equality. Society makes them lose it, and they recover it only by the protection of the laws.

Such is the difference between a well-regulated democracy and one that is not so, that in the former men are equal only as citizens, but in the latter they are equal also as magistrates, as senators, as judges, as fathers, as husbands, or as masters.

The natural place of virtue is near to liberty; but it is not nearer to excessive liberty than to servitude.

4. *Particular Cause of the Corruption of the People.*

Great success, especially when chiefly owing to the people, intoxicates them to such a degree that it is impossible to contain them within bounds. Jealous of their magistrates, they soon became jealous likewise of the magistracy; enemies to those who govern, they soon prove enemies also to the constitution. Thus it was that the victory over the Persians in the straits of Salamis corrupted the republic of Athens; [290] and thus the defeat of the Athenians ruined the republic of Syracuse. [291]

[290] Aristotle, *Politics*, lib. V. chap. iv.
[291] Ibid.

Marseilles never experienced those great transitions from lowness to grandeur; this was owing to the prudent conduct of that republic, which always preserved her principles.

5. *Of the Corruption of the Principle of Aristocracy.*

Aristocracy is corrupted if the power of the nobles becomes arbitrary: when this is the case, there can no longer be any virtue either in the governors or the governed.

If the reigning families observe the laws, it is a monarchy with several monarchs, and in its own nature one of the most excellent; for almost all these monarchs are tied down by the laws. But when they do not observe them, it is a despotic state swayed by a great many despotic princes.

In the latter case, the republic consists only in the nobles. The body governing is the republic; and the body governed is the despotic state; which forms two of the most heterogeneous bodies in the world.

The extremity of corruption is when the power of the nobles becomes hereditary; [292] for then they can hardly have any moderation. If they are only a few, their power is greater, but their security less: if they are a larger number, their power is less, and their security greater, insomuch that power goes on increasing, and security diminishing, up to the very despotic prince who is encircled with excess of power and danger.

[292] The aristocracy is changed into an oligarchy.

The great number, therefore, of nobles in an hereditary aristocracy renders the government less violent: but as there is less virtue, they fall into a spirit of supineness and negligence, by which the state loses all its strength and activity. [293]

[293] Venice is one of those republics that has enacted the best laws for correcting the inconveniences of an hereditary aristocracy.

An aristocracy may maintain the full vigor of its constitution if the laws be such as are apt to render the nobles more sensible of the perils and fatigues than of the pleasure of command: and if the government be in such a situation as to have something to dread, while security shelters under its protection, and uncertainty threatens from abroad.

As a certain kind of confidence forms the glory and stability of monarchies, republics, on the contrary, must have something to apprehend. [294] A fear of the

Persians supported the laws of Greece. Carthage and Rome were alarmed, and strengthened by each other. Strange, that the greater security those states enjoyed, the more, like stagnated waters, they were subject to corruption!

[294] Justin attributes the extinction of Athenian virtue to the death of Epaminondas. Having no further emulation, they spent their revenues in feasts, *frequentius cœnam, quam castra visentes.* Then it was that the Macedonians emerged from obscurity, 1. 6.

6. Of the Corruption of the Principle of Monarchy.

As democracies are subverted when the people despoil the senate, the magistrates, the judges of their functions, so monarchies are corrupted when the prince insensibly deprives societies or cities of their privileges. In the former case the multitude usurp the power, in the latter it is usurped by a single person.

The destruction of the dynasties of Tsin and Soui, says a Chinese author, *was owing to this: the princes, instead of confining themselves, like their ancestors, to a general inspection, the only one worthy of a sovereign, wanted to govern everything immediately by themselves.* [295]

[295] Compilation of works made under the Mings, related by Father Du Halde,

The Chinese author gives us in this instance the cause of the corruption of almost all monarchies.

Monarchy is destroyed when a prince thinks he shows a greater exertion of power in changing than in conforming to the order of things; when he deprives some of his subjects of their hereditary employments to bestow them arbitrarily upon others; and when he is fonder of being guided by fancy than judgment.

Again, it is destroyed when the prince, directing everything entirely to himself, calls the state to his capital, the capital to his court, and the court to his own person.

It is destroyed, in fine, when the prince mistakes his authority, his situation and the love of his people, and when he is not fully persuaded that a monarch ought to think himself secure, as a despotic prince ought to think himself in danger.

7. The same Subject continued.

The principle of monarchy is corrupted when the first dignities are marks of the first servitude, when the great men are deprived of public respect, and rendered the low tools of arbitrary power.

It is still more corrupted when honor is set up in contradiction to honors, and when men are capable of being loaded at the very same time with infamy [296] and with dignities.

[296] During the reign of Tiberius statues were erected to, and triumphal ornaments conferred on, informers; which debased these honors to such a degree that those who had really merited them disdained to accept them. Frag. of Dio, LVIII., taken from the Extract of Virtues and Vices, by Constantine Porphyrogenitus. See in Tacitus in what manner Nero, on the discovery and punishment of a pretended conspiracy,

bestowed triumphal ornaments on Petronius Turpilianus, Nerva, and Tigellinus.— *Annal*, XIV. See likewise how the generals refused to serve, because they condemned the military honors: *pervulgatis triumphi insignibus*—Tacit. *Annal*. book XIII.

It is corrupted when the prince changes his justice into severity; when he puts, like the Roman emperors, a Medusa's head on his breast; [297] and when he assumes that menacing and terrible air which Commodus ordered to be given to his statues. [298]

[297] In this state the prince knew extremely well the principle of his government.
[298] Herodian.

Again, it is corrupted when mean and abject souls grow vain of the pomp attending their servitude, and imagine that the motive which induces them to be entirely devoted to their prince exempts them from all duty to their country.

But if it be true (and indeed the experience of all ages has shown it) that in proportion as the power of the monarch becomes boundless and immense, his security diminishes, is the corrupting of this power, and the altering of its very nature, a less crime than that of high treason against the prince?

8. *Danger of the Corruption of the Principle of monarchical Government.*

The danger is not when the state passes from one moderate to another moderate government, as from a republic to a monarchy, or from a monarchy to a republic; but when it is precipitated from a moderate to a despotic government.

Most of the European nations are still governed by the principles of morality. But if from a long abuse of power or the fury of conquest, despotic sway should prevail to a certain degree, neither morals nor climate would be able to withstand its baleful influence: and then human nature would be exposed, for some time at least, even in this beautiful part of the world, to the insults with which she has been abused in the other three.

9. *How ready the Nobility are to defend the Throne.*

The English nobility buried themselves with Charles the First under the ruins of the throne; and before that time, when Philip the Second endeavored to tempt the French with the allurement of liberty, the crown was constantly supported by a nobility who think it an honor to obey a king, but consider it as the lowest disgrace to share the power with the people.

The house of Austria has ever used her endeavors to oppress the Hungarian nobility; little thinking how serviceable that very nobility would be one day to her. She would fain have drained their country of money, of which they had no plenty; but took no notice of the men, with whom it abounded. When princes combined to dismember her dominions, the several parts of that monarchy fell motionless, as it were one upon another. No life was then to be seen but in those very nobles, who, resenting the affronts offered to the sovereign, and forgetting the injuries done to themselves, took up arms to avenge her cause, and considered it the highest glory bravely to die and to forgive.

10. *Of the Corruption of the Principle of despotic Government.*

The principle of despotic government is subject to a continual corruption, because it is even in its nature corrupt. Other governments are destroyed by particular accidents, which do violence to the principles of each constitution; this is ruined by its own intrinsic imperfections, when some accidental causes do not prevent the corrupting of its principles. It maintains itself therefore only when circumstances, drawn from the climate, religion, situation, or genius of the people, oblige it to conform to order, and to admit of some rule. By these things its nature is forced without being changed; its ferocity remains; and it is made tame and tractable only for a time.

11. *Natural Effects of the Goodness and Corruption of the Principles of Government.*

When once the principles of government are corrupted, the very best laws become bad, and turn against the state: but when the principles are sound, even bad laws have the same effect as good; the force of the principle draws everything to it.

The inhabitants of Crete used a very singular method to keep the principal magistrates dependent on the laws, which was that of Insurrection. Part of the citizens rose up in arms, [299] put the magistrates to flight, and obliged them to return to a private life. This was supposed to be done in consequence of the law. One would have imagined that an institution of this nature, which established sedition to hinder the abuse of power, would have subverted any republic whatsoever; and yet it did not subvert that of Crete. The reason is this. [300]

[299] Aristotle, *Politics*, book II. 10.
[300] They always united immediately against foreign enemies, which was called *Syncretism.*—Plutarch *Moralia*, p. 88.

When the ancients would cite a people that had the strongest affection for their country, they were sure to mention the inhabitants of Crete: *Our Country*, said Plato, [301] *a name so dear to the Cretans.* They called it by a name which signifies the love of a mother for her children. [302] Now the love of our country sets everything right.

[301] *Republic*, lib. IX.
[302] Plutarch's Morals, treatise *whether a man advanced in years ought to meddle with public affairs.*

The laws of Poland have likewise their Insurrection: but the inconveniences thence arising plainly show that the people of Crete alone were capable of using such a remedy with success.

The gymnic exercises established among the Greeks had the same dependence on the goodness of the principle of government. *It was the Lacedæmonians and Cretans*, said Plato, [303] *that opened those celebrated academies which gave them so eminent a rank in the world. Modesty at first was alarmed; but it yielded to the public utility.* In Plato's time these institutions were admirable: [304] as they bore a relation to a very important object, which was the military art. But when virtue fled from Greece, the military art was destroyed by these institutions; people appeared then on the arena, not for improvement, but for debauch. [305]

[303] *Republic*, lib. V.
[304] The Gymnic art was divided into two parts, *dancing* and *wrestling*. In Crete they had the armed dances of the Curetes; at Sparta they had those of Castor and Pollux; at Athens the armed dances of Pallas, which were extremely proper for those that were not yet of age for military service. Wrestling is the image of war, said Plato (Laws, Book VII.) He commends antiquity for having established only two dances, the pacific and the Pyrrhic. See how the latter dance was applied to the military art, Plato, *ibid.*
[305] . . . . . Aut libidinosæ. Ladæas Lacedæmonis palæstras.—Mart. lib. IV. ep. 55.

Plutarch informs us [306] that the Romans in his time were of opinion that those games had been the principal cause of the slavery into which the Greeks had fallen. On the contrary, it was the slavery of the Greeks that corrupted those exercises. In Plutarch's time, [307] their fighting naked in the parks, and their wrestling, infected the young people with a spirit of cowardice, inclined them to infamous passions, and made them mere dancers. But under Epaminondas the exercise of wrestling made the Thebans win the famous battle of Leuctra. [308]

[306] Plutarch's Morals, in the treatise entitled *Questions Concerning the Affairs of the Romans*.
[307] Ibid.
[308] Plutarch's Morals, Table Propositions, book II.

There are very few laws which are not good, while the state retains its principles: here I may apply what Epicurus said of riches. *It is not the liquor, but the vessel that is corrupted.*

12. *The same Subject continued.*

In Rome the judges were chosen at first from the order of senators. This privilege the Gracchi transferred to the knights; Drusus gave it to the senators and knights; Sylla to the senators only: Cotta to the senators, knights, and public treasurers; Cæsar excluded the latter; Antony made decuries of senators, knights, and centurions.

When once a republic is corrupted, there is no possibility of remedying any of the growing evils, but by removing the corruption and restoring its lost principles; every other correction is either useless or a new evil. While Rome preserved her principles entire, the judicial power might without any abuse be lodged in the hands of senators; but as soon as this city became corrupt, to whatsoever body that power was transferred, whether to the senate, to the knights, to the treasurers, to two of those bodies, to all three together, or to any other, matters still went wrong. The knights had no more virtue than the senate, the treasurers no more than the knights, and these as little as the centurions.

After the people of Rome had obtained the privilege of sharing the magistracy with the patricians, it was natural to think that their flatterers would immediately become arbiters of the government. But no such thing ever happened.—It was observable that the very people who had rendered the plebeians capable of public offices ever fixed their choice upon the patricians. Because they were virtuous, they were magnanimous; and because they were free, they had a contempt of power. But when their morals were corrupted, the more power they were possessed of, the less prudent was their conduct, till at length, upon becoming their own tyrants and slaves, they lost the strength of liberty to fall into the weakness and impotency of licentiousness.

13. *The Effect of an Oath among virtuous People.*

There is no nation, says Livy, [309] that has been longer uncorrupted than the Romans; no nation where moderation and poverty have been longer respected.

[309] Book I.

Such was the influence of an oath among those people that nothing bound them more strongly to the laws. They often did more for the observance of an oath than they would ever have performed for the thirst of glory or for the love of their country.

When Quintus Cincinnatus, the consul, wanted to raise an army in the city against the Æqui and the Volsci, the tribunes opposed him. *Well*, said he, *let all those who have taken an oath to the consul of the preceding year march under my banner.* [310] In vain did the tribunes cry out that this oath was no longer binding, and that when they took it Quintus was but a private person: the people were more religious than those who pretended to direct them; they would not listen to the distinctions or equivocations of the tribunes.

[310] Livy, book III. 20.

When the same people thought of retiring to the Sacred Mount, they felt some remorse from the oath they had taken to the consuls, that they would follow them into the field. [311] They entered then into a design of killing the consuls; but dropped it when they were given to understand that their oath would still be binding. Now it is easy to judge of the notion they entertained of the violation of an oath from the crime they intended to commit.

[311] Ibid. book III.

After the battle of Cannæ, the people were seized with such a panic that they would fain have retired to Sicily. [312] But Scipio having prevailed upon them to swear they would not stir from Rome, the fear of violating this oath surpassed all other apprehensions. Rome was a ship held by two anchors, religion and morality, in the midst of a furious tempest.

[312] The people here referred to were several young officers, who, in despair, proposed to retire, but were restrained by Scipio.—Crévier.

14. How the smallest Change of the Constitution
is attended with the Ruin of its Principles.

Aristotle mentions the city of Carthage as a well-regulated republic. Polybius tells us [313] that there was this inconvenience at Carthage in the second Punic war, that the senate had lost almost all its authority. We are informed by Livy that when Hannibal returned to Carthage he found that the magistrates and the principal citizens had abused their power, and converted the public revenues to their private emolument. The virtue, therefore, of the magistrates, and the authority of the senate, both fell at the same time; and all was owing to the same cause.

[313] About a hundred years after.

Everyone knows the wonderful effects of the censorship among the Romans. There was a time when it grew burdensome; but still it was supported because there was more luxury than corruption. Claudius [314] weakened its authority, by which means the corruption became greater than the luxury, and the censorship dwindled away of itself. [315] After various interruptions and resumptions, it was entirely laid aside, till it became altogether useless, that is, till the reigns of Augustus and Claudius.

[314] See Book XI, chap. 12.
[315] See Dio, XXXVIII, Cicero in Plutarch, Cicero to Atticus, book IV. letters 10, 15. Asconius on Cicero, *de divinatione*.

15. Sure Methods of preserving the three Principles.

I shall not be able to make myself rightly understood till the reader has perused the four following chapters.

16. Distinctive Properties of a Republic.

It is natural for a republic to have only a small territory; otherwise it cannot long subsist. In an extensive republic there are men of large fortunes, and consequently of less moderation; there are trusts too considerable to be placed in any single subject; he has interests of his own; he soon begins to think that he may be happy and glorious, by oppressing his fellow-citizens; and that he may raise himself to grandeur on the ruins of his country.

In an extensive republic the public good is sacrificed to a thousand private views; it is subordinate to exceptions, and depends on accidents. In a small one, the interest of the public is more obvious, better understood, and more within the reach of every citizen; abuses have less extent, and of course are less protected.

The long duration of the republic of Sparta was owing to her having continued in the same extent of territory after all her wars. The sole aim of Sparta was liberty; and the sole advantage of her liberty, glory.

It was the spirit of the Greek republics to be as contented with their territories as with their laws. Athens was first fired with ambition and gave it to Lacedæmon; but it was an ambition rather of commanding a free people than of governing slaves; rather of directing than of breaking the union. All was lost upon the starting up of monarchy—a government whose spirit is more turned to increase of dominion.

Excepting particular circumstances, [316] it is difficult for any other than a republican government to subsist longer in a single town. A prince of so petty a state would naturally endeavor to oppress his subjects, because his power would be great, while the means of enjoying it or of causing it to be respected would be inconsiderable. The consequence is, he would trample upon his people. On the other hand, such a prince might be easily crushed by a foreign or even a domestic force; the people might any instant unite and rise up against him. Now as soon as the sovereign of a single town is expelled, the quarrel is over; but if he has many towns, it only begins.

[316] As when a petty sovereign supports himself between two great powers by means of their mutual jealousy; but then he has only a precarious existence.

17. *Distinctive Properties of a Monarchy.*

A monarchical state ought to be of moderate extent. Were it small, it would form itself into a republic; were it very large, the nobility, possessed of great estates, far from the eye of the prince, with a private court of their own, and secure, moreover, from sudden executions by the laws and manners of the country—such a nobility, I say, might throw off their allegiance, having nothing to fear from too slow and too distant a punishment.

Thus Charlemagne had scarcely founded his empire when he was obliged to divide it; whether the governors of the provinces refused to obey; or whether, in order to keep them more under subjection, there was a necessity of parceling the empire into several kingdoms.

After the decease of Alexander his empire was divided. How was it possible for those Greek and Macedonian chiefs, who were each of them free and independent, or commanders at least of the victorious bands dispersed throughout that vast extent of conquered land—how was it possible, I say, for them to obey?

Attila's empire was dissolved soon after his death; such a number of kings, who were no longer under restraint, could not resume their fetters.

The sudden establishment of unlimited power is a remedy, which in those cases may prevent a dissolution: but how dreadful the remedy, which after the enlargement of dominion opens a new scene of misery!

The rivers hasten to mingle their waters with the sea; and monarchies lose themselves in despotic power.

18. *Particular Case of the Spanish Monarchy.*

Let not the example of Spain be produced against me, it rather proves what I affirm. To preserve America she did what even despotic power itself does not attempt: she destroyed the inhabitants. To preserve her colony, she was obliged to keep it dependent even for its subsistence.

In the Netherlands, she essayed to render herself arbitrary; and as soon as she abandoned the attempt, her perplexity increased. On the one hand the Walloons would not be governed by Spaniards; and on the other, the Spanish soldiers refused to submit to Walloon officers. [317]

[317] See the History of the United Provinces, by M. Le Clerc.

In Italy she maintained her ground, merely by exhausting herself and by enriching that country. For those who would have been pleased to have got rid of the king of Spain were not in a humor to refuse his gold.

19. *Distinctive Properties of a despotic Government.*

A large empire supposes a despotic authority in the person who governs. It is necessary that the quickness of the prince's resolutions should supply the distance of the places they are sent to; that fear should prevent the remissness of the distant governor or magistrate; that the law should be derived from a single person, and should shift continually, according to the accidents which necessarily multiply in a state in proportion to its extent.

20. *Consequence of the preceding Chapters.*

If it be, therefore, the natural property of small states to be governed as a republic, of middling ones to be subject to a monarch, and of large empires to be swayed by a despotic prince; the consequence is, that in order to preserve the principles of the established government, the state must be supported in the extent it has acquired, and that the spirit of this state will alter in proportion as it contracts or extends its limits.

21. *Of the Empire of China.*

Before I conclude this book, I shall answer an objection that may be made to the foregoing doctrine.

Our missionaries inform us that the government of the vast empire of China is admirable, and that it has a proper mixture of fear, honor, and virtue. Consequently I must have given an idle distinction in establishing the principles of the three governments.

But I cannot conceive what this honor can be among a people who act only through fear of being bastinadoed. [318]

[318] "It is the cudgel that governs China," says Father Du Halde.

Again, our merchants are far from giving us any such accounts of the virtue so much talked of by the missionaries; we need only consult them in relation to the robberies and extortions of the mandarins. [319] I likewise appeal to another unexceptional witness, the great Lord Anson.

[319] Among others, De Lange's relation.

Besides, Father Perennin's letters concerning the emperor's proceedings against some of the princes of the blood [320] who had incurred his displeasure by their conversion, plainly show us a settled plan of tyranny, and barbarities committed by rule, that is, in cold blood.

[320] Of the Family of Sourmama, Edifying Letters, coll. xviii.

We have likewise Monsieur de Mairan's, and the same Father Perennin's, letters on the government of China. I find therefore that after a few proper questions and answers the whole mystery is unfolded.

Might not our missionaries have been deceived by an appearance of order? Might not they have been struck with that constant exercise of a single person's will—an exercise by which they themselves are governed, and which they are so pleased to find in the courts of the Indian princes; because as they go thither only in order to introduce great changes, it is much easier to persuade those princes that there are no bounds to their power, than to convince the people that there are none to their submission. [321]

[321] See in Father Du Halde how the missionaries availed themselves of the authority of Canhi to silence the mandarins, who constantly declared that by the laws of the country no foreign worship could be established in the empire.

In fine, there is frequently some kind of truth even in errors themselves. It may be owing to particular and, perhaps, very extraordinary circumstances that the Chinese government is not so corrupt as one might naturally expect. The climate and some other physical causes may, in that country, have had so strong an influence on their morals as in some measure to produce wonders.

The climate of China is surprisingly favorable to the propagation of the human species. [322] The women are the most prolific in the whole world. The most barbarous tyranny can put no stop to the progress of propagation. The prince cannot say there like Pharaoh, *Let us deal wisely with them, lest they multiply.* He would be rather reduced to Nero's wish, that mankind had all but one head. In spite of tyranny, China by the force of its climate will be ever populous, and triumph over the tyrannical oppressor.

[322] See Lettres Persanes, cxx.

China, like all other countries that live chiefly upon rice, is subject to frequent famines. When the people are ready to starve, they disperse in order to seek for nourishment; in consequence of which, gangs of robbers are formed on every side. Most of them are extirpated in their very infancy; others swell, and are likewise suppressed. And yet in so great a number of such distant provinces, some band or other may happen to meet with success. In that case they maintain their ground, strengthen their party, form themselves into a military body, march up to the capital, and place their leader on the throne.

From the very nature of things, a bad administration is here immediately punished. The want of subsistence in so populous a country produces sudden disorders. The reason why the redress of abuses in other countries is attended with such difficulty is because their effects are not immediately felt; the prince is not informed in so sudden and sensible a manner as in China.

The Emperor of China is not taught like our princes that if he governs ill he will be less happy in the other life, less powerful and less opulent in this. He knows that if his government be not just he will be stripped both of empire and life.

As China grows every day more populous, notwithstanding the exposing of children, [323] the inhabitants are incessantly employed in tilling the lands for their subsistence. This requires a very extraordinary attention in the government. It is their perpetual concern that every man should have it in his power to work, without the apprehension of being deprived of the fruits of his labor. Consequently this is not so much a civil as a domestic government.

[323] See the order of Tsongtou for tilling the land, in the Edifying Letters, 21st collection.

Such has been the origin of those regulations which have been so greatly extolled. They wanted to make the laws reign in conjunction with despotic power; but whatever is joined to the latter loses all its force. In vain did this arbitrary sway, laboring under its own inconveniences, desire to be fettered; it armed itself with its chains, and has become still more terrible.

China is therefore a despotic state, whose principle is fear. Perhaps in the earliest dynasties, when the empire had not so large an extent, the government might have deviated a little from this spirit; but the case is otherwise at present.

BOOK IX.

OF LAWS IN THE RELATION THEY BEAR TO A DEFENSIVE FORCE

1. *In what Manner Republics provide for their Safety.*

If a republic be small, it is destroyed by a foreign force; if it be large, it is ruined by an internal imperfection.

To this twofold inconvenience democracies and aristocracies are equally liable, whether they be good or bad. The evil is in the very thing itself, and no form can redress it.

It is, therefore, very probable that mankind would have been, at length, obliged to live constantly under the government of a single person, had they not contrived a kind of constitution that has all the internal advantages of a republican, together with the external force of a monarchical, government. I mean a confederate republic.

This form of government is a convention by which several petty states agree to become members of a larger one, which they intend to establish. It is a kind of assemblage of societies, that constitute a new one, capable of increasing by means of further associations, till they arrive at such a degree of power as to be able to provide for the security of the whole body.

It was these associations that so long contributed to the prosperity of Greece. By these the Romans attacked the whole globe, and by these alone the whole globe withstood them; for when Rome had arrived at her highest pitch of grandeur, it was the associations beyond the Danube and the Rhine—associations formed by the terror of her arms—that enabled the barbarians to resist her.

Hence it proceeds that Holland, [324] Germany, and the Swiss cantons are considered in Europe as perpetual republics.

[324] It is composed of about fifty different republics, all different from one another.—
M. Janisson, State of the United Provinces. Voltaire notes upon this remark that
Montesquieu has taken each of the independent cities as a republic.—Ed.

The associations of cities were formerly more necessary than in our times. A weak,
defenseless town was exposed to greater danger. By conquest it was deprived not only of
the executive and legislative power, as at present, but moreover of all human property.
[325]

[325] Civil liberty, goods, wives, children, temples, and even burying-places.

A republic of this kind, able to withstand an external force, may support itself
without any internal corruption; the form of this society prevents all manner of
inconveniences.

If a single member should attempt to usurp the supreme power, he could not be
supposed to have an equal authority and credit in all the confederate states. Were he to
have too great an influence over one, this would alarm the rest; were he to subdue a part,
that which would still remain free might oppose him with forces independent of those
which he had usurped, and overpower him before he could be settled in his usurpation.

Should a popular insurrection happen in one of the confederate states, the others are
able to quell it. Should abuses creep into one part, they are reformed by those that remain
sound. The state may be destroyed on one side, and not on the other; the confederacy may
be dissolved, and the confederates preserve their sovereignty.

As this government is composed of petty republics, it enjoys the internal happiness
of each; and with regard to its external situation, by means of the association, it possesses
all the advantages of large monarchies.

2. That a confederate Government ought to be composed of States of the same Nature, especially of the republican Kind.

The Canaanites were destroyed by reason that they were petty monarchies, that had
no union or confederacy for their common defense; and, indeed, a confederacy is not
agreeable to the nature of petty monarchies.

As the confederate republic of Germany consists of free cities, and of petty states
subject to different princes, experience shows us that it is much more imperfect than that
of Holland and Switzerland.

The spirit of monarchy is war and enlargement of dominion: peace and moderation
are the spirit of a republic. These two kinds of government cannot naturally subsist in a
confederate republic.

Thus we observe, in the Roman history, that when the Veientes had chosen a king,
they were immediately abandoned by all the other petty republics of Tuscany. Greece
was undone as soon as the kings of Macedon obtained a seat among the Amphyktyons.

The confederate republic of Germany, composed of princes and free towns, subsists
by means of a chief, who is, in some respects, the magistrate of the union, in others, the
monarch.

3. *Other Requisites in a confederate Republic.*

In the republic of Holland one province cannot conclude an alliance without the consent of the others. This law, which is an excellent one, and even necessary in a confederate republic, is wanting in the Germanic constitution, where it would prevent the misfortunes that may happen to the whole confederacy, through the imprudence, ambition, or avarice of a single member. A republic united by a political confederacy has given itself entirely up, and has nothing more to resign.

It is difficult for the united states to be all of equal power and extent. The Lycian [326] republic was an association of twenty-three towns; the large ones had three votes in the common council, the middling ones two, and the small towns one. The Dutch republic consists of seven provinces of different extent of territory, which have each one voice.

[326] Strabo, lib. XIV.

The cities of Lycia [327] contributed to the expenses of the state, according to the proportion of suffrages. The provinces of the United Netherlands cannot follow this proportion; they must be directed by that of their power.

[327] Ibid.

In Lycia [328] the judges and town magistrates were elected by the common council, and according to the proportion already mentioned. In the republic of Holland they are not chosen by the common council, but each town names its magistrates. Were I to give a model of an excellent confederate republic, I should pitch upon that of Lycia.

[328] Ibid.

4. *In what Manner despotic Governments provide for their Security.*

As republics provide for their security by uniting, despotic governments do it by separating, and by keeping themselves, as it were, single. They sacrifice a part of the country; and by ravaging and desolating the frontiers they render the heart of the empire inaccessible.

It is a received axiom in geometry that the greater the extent of bodies, the more their circumference is relatively small. This practice, therefore, of laying the frontiers waste is more tolerable in large than in middling states.

A despotic government does all the mischief to itself that could be committed by a cruel enemy, whose arms it were unable to resist.

It preserves itself likewise by another kind of separation, which is by putting the most distant provinces into the hands of a great vassal. The Mogul, the king of Persia, and the emperors of China have their feudatories; and the Turks have found their account in putting the Tartars, the Moldavians, the Wallachians, and formerly the Transylvanians, between themselves and their enemies.

5. *In what Manner a Monarchical Government provides for its Security.*

A monarchy never destroys itself like a despotic government. But a kingdom of a moderate extent is liable to sudden invasions: it must therefore have fortresses to defend its frontiers; and troops to garrison those fortresses. The least spot of ground is disputed with military skill and resolution. Despotic states make incursions against one another; it is monarchies only that wage war.

Fortresses are proper for monarchies; despotic governments are afraid of them. They dare not entrust their officers with such a command, as none of them have any affection for the prince or his government.

6. *Of the defensive Force of States in general.*

To preserve a state in its due force, it must have such an extent as to admit of a proportion between the celerity with which it may be invaded, and that with which it may defeat the invasion. As an invader may appear on every side, it is requisite that the state should be able to make on every side its defense; consequently it should be of a moderate extent, proportioned to the degree of velocity that nature has given to man, to enable him to move from one place to another.

France and Spain are exactly of a proper extent. They have so easy a communication for their forces as to be able to convey them immediately to what part they have a mind; the armies unite and pass with rapidity from one frontier to another, without any apprehension of such difficulties as require time to remove.

It is extremely happy for France that the capital stands near to the different frontiers in proportion to their weakness; and the prince has a better view of each part of his country according as it is more exposed.

But when a vast empire, like Persia, is attacked, it is several months before the troops are assembled in a body; and then they are not able to make such forced marches, for that space of time, as they could for fifteen days. Should the army on the frontiers be defeated, it is soon dispersed, because there is no neighboring place of retreat. The victor, meeting with no resistance, advances with all expedition, sits down before the capital, and lays siege to it, when there is scarcely time sufficient to summon the governors of the provinces to its relief. Those who foresee an approaching revolution hasten it by their disobedience. For men whose fidelity is entirely owing to the danger of punishment are easily corrupted as soon as it becomes distant; their aim is their own private interest. The empire is subverted, the capital taken, and the conqueror disputes the several provinces with the governors.

The real power of a prince does not consist so much in the facility he meets with in making conquests as in the difficulty an enemy finds in attacking him, and, if I may so speak, in the immutability of his condition. But the increase of territory obliges a government to lay itself more open to an enemy.

As monarchs therefore ought to be endued with wisdom in order to increase their power, they ought likewise to have an equal share of prudence to confine it within bounds. Upon removing the inconveniences of too small a territory, they should have their eye constantly on the inconveniences which attend its extent.

7. A Reflection.

The enemies of a great prince, whose reign was protracted to an unusual length, have very often accused him, rather, I believe, from their own fears than upon any solid foundation, of having formed and carried on a project of universal monarchy. Had he attained his aim, nothing would have been more fatal to his subjects, to himself, to his family, and to all Europe. Heaven, that knows our true interests, favored him more by preventing the success of his arms than it could have done by crowning him with victories. Instead of raising him to be the only sovereign in Europe, it made him happier by rendering him the most powerful.

The subjects of this prince, who in travelling abroad are never affected but with what they have left at home; who on quitting their own habitations look upon glory as their chief object, and in distant countries as an obstacle to their return; who disgust you even by their good qualities, because they are tainted with so much vanity; who are capable of supporting wounds, perils, and fatigues, but not of foregoing their pleasures; who are supremely fond of gaiety, and comfort themselves for the loss of a battle by a song upon the general: those subjects, I say, would never have the solidity requisite for an enterprise of this kind, which if defeated in one country would be unsuccessful everywhere else; and if once unsuccessful, would be so forever.

8. A particular Case in which the defensive Force of a State is inferior to the offensive.

It was a saying of the Lord of Coucy to King Charles V *that the English are never weaker, nor more easily overcome, than in their own country.* The same was observed of the Romans; the same of the Carthaginians; and the same will happen to every power that sends armies to distant countries, in order to reunite by discipline and military force those who are divided among themselves by political or civil interests. The state finds itself weakened by the disorder that still continues, and more so by the remedy.

The Lord of Coucy's maxim is an exception to the general rule, which disapproves of wars against distant countries. And this exception confirms likewise the rule because it takes place only with regard to those by whom such wars are undertaken.

9. Of the relative Force of States.

All grandeur, force, and power are relative. Care therefore must be taken that in endeavoring to increase the real grandeur, the relative be not diminished.

During the reign of Lewis XIV France was at its highest pitch of relative grandeur. Germany had not yet produced such powerful princes as have since appeared in that country. Italy was in the same case. England and Scotland were not yet formed into one united kingdom. Aragon was not joined to Castile: the distant branches of the Spanish monarchy were weakened by it, and weakened it in their turn; and Muscovy was as little known in Europe as Crim Tartary.

10. *Of the Weakness of neighboring States.*

Whensoever a state lies contiguous to another that happens to be in its decline, the former ought to take particular care not to precipitate the ruin of the latter, because this is the happiest situation imaginable; nothing being so convenient as for one prince to be near another, who receives for him all the rebuffs and insults of fortune. And it seldom happens that by subduing such a state the real power of the conqueror is as much increased as the relative is diminished.

BOOK X.

OF LAWS IN THE RELATION THEY BEAR TO OFFENSIVE FORCE

1. *Of offensive Force.*

Offensive force is regulated by the law of nations, which is the political law of each country considered in its relation to every other.

2. *Of War.*

The life of governments is like that of man. The latter has a right to kill in case of natural defense: the former have a right to wage war for their own preservation.

In the case of natural defense I have a right to kill, because my life is in respect to me what the life of my antagonist is to him: in the same manner a state wages war because its preservation is like that of any other being.

With individuals the right of natural defense does not imply a necessity of attacking. Instead of attacking they need only have recourse to proper tribunals. They cannot therefore exercise this right of defense but in sudden cases, when immediate death would be the consequence of waiting for the assistance of the law. But with states the right of natural defense carries along with it sometimes the necessity of attacking; as for instance, when one nation sees that a continuance of peace will enable another to destroy her, and that to attack that nation instantly is the only way to prevent her own destruction.

Thence it follows that petty states have oftener a right to declare war than great ones, because they are oftener in the case of being afraid of destruction.

The right of war, therefore, is derived from necessity and strict justice. If those who direct the conscience or councils of princes do not abide by this maxim, the consequence is dreadful: when they proceed on arbitrary principles of glory, convenience, and utility, torrents of blood must overspread the earth.

But, above all, let them not plead such an idle pretext as the glory of the prince: his glory is nothing but pride; it is a passion, and not a legitimate right.

It is true the fame of his power might increase the strength of his government; but it might be equally increased by the reputation of his justice.

3. Of the Right of Conquest.

From the right of war comes that of conquest; which is the consequence of that right, and ought therefore to follow its spirit.

The right the conqueror has over a conquered people is directed by four sorts of laws: the law of nature, which makes everything tend to the preservation of the species; the law of natural reason, which teaches us to do to others what we would have done to ourselves; the law that forms political societies, whose duration nature has not limited; and, in fine, the law derived from the nature of the thing itself. Conquest is an acquisition, and carries with it the spirit of preservation and use, not of destruction.

The inhabitants of a conquered country are treated by the conqueror in one of the four following ways: Either he continues to rule them according to their own laws, and assumes to himself only the exercise of the political and civil government; or he gives them new political and civil government; or he destroys and disperses the society; or, in fine, he exterminates the people.

The first way is conformable to the law of nations now followed; the fourth is more agreeable to the law of nations followed by the Romans: in respect to which I leave the reader to judge how far we have improved upon the ancients. We must give due commendations to our modern refinements in reason, religion, philosophy, and manners.

The authors of our public law, guided by ancient histories, without confining themselves to cases of strict necessity, have fallen into very great errors. They have adopted tyrannical and arbitrary principles, by supposing the conquerors to be invested with I know not what right to kill: thence they have drawn consequences as terrible as the very principle, and established maxims which the conquerors themselves, when possessed of the least grain of sense, never presumed to follow. It is a plain case that when the conquest is completed, the conqueror has no longer a right to kill, because he has no longer the plea of natural defense and self-preservation.

What has led them into this mistake is, that they imagined a conqueror had a right to destroy the state; whence they inferred that he had a right to destroy the men that compose it: a wrong consequence from a false principle. For from the destruction of the state it does not at all follow that the people who compose it ought to be also destroyed. The state is the association of men, and not the men themselves; the citizen may perish, and the man remain.

From the right of killing in the case of conquest, politicians have drawn that of reducing to slavery—a consequence as ill-grounded as the principle.

There is no such thing as a right of reducing people to slavery, save when it becomes necessary for the preservation of the conquest. Preservation, and not servitude, is the end of conquest; though servitude may happen sometimes to be a necessary means of preservation.

Even in that case it is contrary to the nature of things that the slavery should be perpetual. The people enslaved ought to be rendered capable of becoming subjects. Slavery in conquests is an accidental thing. When after the expiration of a certain space of time all the parts of the conquering state are connected with the conquered nation, by custom, marriages, laws, associations, and by a certain conformity of disposition, there ought to be an end of the slavery. For the rights of the conqueror are founded entirely on the opposition between the two nations in those very articles, whence prejudices arise, and the want of mutual confidence.

A conqueror, therefore, who reduces the conquered people to slavery, ought always to reserve to himself the means (for means there are without number) of restoring them to their liberty.

These are far from being vague and uncertain notions. Thus our ancestors acted, those ancestors who conquered the Roman empire. The laws they made in the heat and transport of passion and in the insolence of victory were gradually softened; those laws were at first severe, but were afterwards rendered impartial. The Burgundians, Goths, and Lombards would have the Romans continue a conquered people; but the laws of Euric, Gundebald, and Rotharis made the Romans and barbarians fellow-citizens. [329]

[329] See the Code of Barbarian Laws.

Charlemagne, to tame the Saxons, deprived them of their liberty and property. Lewis the Debonnaire made them a free people, [330] and this was one of the most prudent regulations during his whole reign. Time and servitude had softened their manners, and they ever after adhered to him with the greatest fidelity.

[330] See the anonymous author of the Life of Lewis le Debonnaire, in Duchesne's collection, tom. ii, p. 296.

4. Some Advantages of a conquered People.

Instead of inferring such destructive consequences from the right of conquest, much better would it have been for politicians to mention the advantages which this very right may sometimes give to a conquered people—advantages which would be more sensibly and more universally experienced were our law of nations exactly followed, and established in every part of the globe.

Conquered countries are, generally speaking, degenerated from their original institution. Corruption has crept in, the execution of the laws has been neglected, and the government has grown oppressive. Who can question but such a state would be a gainer, and derive some advantages from the very conquest itself, if it did not prove destructive? When a government has arrived at that degree of corruption as to be incapable of reforming itself, it would not lose much by being newly moulded. A conqueror who enters triumphant into a country where the moneyed men have, by a variety of artifices, insensibly arrived at innumerable ways of encroaching on the public, where the miserable people, who see abuses grown into laws, are ready to sink under the weight of impression, yet think they have no right to apply for redress—a conqueror, I say, may make a total change, and then the tyranny of those wretches will be the first thing exposed to his resentment.

We have beheld, for instance, countries oppressed by the farmers of the revenues, and eased afterwards by the conqueror, who had neither the engagements nor wants of the legitimate prince. Even the abuses have been often redressed without any interposition of the conqueror.

Sometimes the frugality of a conquering nation has enabled them to allow the conquered those necessaries of which they had been deprived under a lawful prince.

A conquest may destroy pernicious prejudices, and lay, if I may presume to use the expression, the nation under a better genius.

What good might not the Spaniards have done to the Mexicans? They had a mild religion to impart to them; but they filled their heads with a frantic superstition. They might have set slaves at liberty; they made freemen slaves. They might have undeceived them with regard to the abuse of human sacrifices; instead of that they destroyed them. Never should I have finished, were I to recount all the good they might have done, and all the mischief they committed.

It is a conqueror's business to repair a part of the mischief he has occasioned. The right, therefore, of conquest I define thus: a necessary, lawful, but unhappy power, which leaves the conqueror under a heavy obligation of repairing the injuries done to humanity.

5. *Gelon, King of Syracuse.*

The noblest treaty of peace ever mentioned in history is, in my opinion, that which Gelon made with the Carthaginians. He insisted upon their abolishing the custom of sacrificing their children. [331] Glorious indeed! After having defeated three hundred thousand Carthaginians, he required a condition that was advantageous only to themselves, or rather he stipulated in favor of human nature.

[331] See M. Barbeyrac's collection, art. 112.

The Bactrians exposed their aged fathers to be devoured by large mastiffs—a custom suppressed by Alexander, [332] whereby he obtained a signal triumph over superstition.

[332] Strabo, lib. XI.

6. *Of Conquest made by a Republic.*

It is contrary to the nature of things that in a confederate government one state should make any conquest over another, as in our days we have seen in Switzerland. [333] In mixed confederate republics, where the association is between petty republics and monarchies, of a small extent, this is not so absurd.

[333] With regard to Tockenburg.

Contrary is it also to the nature of things that a democratic republic should conquer towns which cannot enter into the sphere of its democracy. It is necessary that the conquered people should be capable of enjoying the privileges of sovereignty, as was settled in the very beginning among the Romans. The conquest ought to be limited to the number of citizens fixed for the democracy.

If a democratic republic subdues a nation in order to govern them as subjects, it exposes its own liberty; because it entrusts too great a power to those who are appointed to the command of the conquered provinces.

How dangerous would have been the situation of the republic of Carthage had Hannibal made himself master of Rome? What would he not have done in his own country, had he been victorious, he who caused so many revolutions in it after his defeat? [334]

[334] He was at the head of a faction.

Hanno could never have dissuaded the senate from sending succor to Hannibal, had he used no other argument than his own jealousy. The Carthaginian senate, whose wisdom is so highly extolled by Aristotle (and which has been evidently proved by the prosperity of that republic), could never have been determined by other than solid reasons. They must have been stupid not to see that an army at the distance of three hundred leagues would necessarily be exposed to losses which required reparation.

Hanno's party insisted that Hannibal should be delivered up to the Romans. [335] They could not at that time be afraid of the Romans; they were therefore apprehensive of Hannibal.

[335] Hanno wanted to deliver Hannibal up to the Romans, as Cato would fain have delivered up Cæsar to the Gauls.

It was impossible, some will say, for them to imagine that Hannibal had been so successful. But how was it possible for them to doubt it? Could the Carthaginians, a people spread over all the earth, be ignorant of what was transacting in Italy? No: they were sufficiently acquainted with it, and for that reason they did not care to send supplies to Hannibal.

Hanno became more resolute after the battle of Trebia, after the battle of Thrasimenus, after that of Cannæ; it was not his incredulity that increased, but his fear.

7. The same Subject continued.

There is still another inconvenience in conquests made by democracies: their government is ever odious to the conquered states. It is apparently monarchical: but in reality it is much more oppressive than monarchy, as the experience of all ages and countries evinces.

The conquered people are in a melancholy situation; they neither enjoy the advantages of a republic, nor those of a monarchy.

What has been here said of a popular state is applicable to aristocracy.

8. The same Subject continued.

When a republic, therefore, keeps another nation in subjection, it should endeavor to repair the inconveniences arising from the nature of its situation by giving it good laws both for the political and civil government of the people.

We have an instance of an island in the Mediterranean, subject to an Italian republic, whose political and civil laws with regard to the inhabitants of that island were extremely defective. The act of indemnity, [336] by which it ordained that no one should be condemned to bodily punishment in consequence of the private knowledge of the governor, ex informata conscientia, is still recent in everybody's memory. There have been frequent instances of the people's petitioning for privileges; here the sovereign grants only the common right of all nations.

[336] Of the 18th of October, 1738, printed at Genoa by Franchelli: Vietiamo al nostro general governatore in detta Isola di condannare in avvenire solamente ex informata conscientia persona alcuna nazionale in pena afflittiva; potrà bensì arrestare ed

incarcerare le persone che gli saranno sospette, salvo di renderne poi a noi conto sollecitamente.—Art. 6.

9. *Of Conquests made by a Monarchy.*

If a monarchy can long subsist before it is weakened by its increase, it will become formidable; and its strength will remain entire, while pent up by the neighboring monarchies.

It ought not, therefore, to aim at conquests beyond the natural limits of its government. So soon as it has passed these limits, it is prudence to stop.

In this kind of conquest things must be left as they were found—the same courts of judicature, the same laws, the same customs, the same privileges: there ought to be no other alteration than that of the army and of the name of the sovereign.

When a monarchy has extended its limits by the conquest of neighboring provinces, it should treat those provinces with great lenity.

If a monarchy has been long endeavoring at conquest, the provinces of its ancient demesne are generally ill-used. They are obliged to submit both to the new and to the ancient abuses; and to be depopulated by a vast metropolis, that swallows up the whole. Now if, after having made conquests round this demesne, the conquered people were treated like the ancient subjects, the state would be undone; the taxes sent by the conquered provinces to the capital would never return; the inhabitants of the frontiers would be ruined, and consequently the frontiers would be weaker; the people would be disaffected; and the subsistence of the armies designed to act and remain there would become more precarious.

Such is the necessary state of a conquering monarchy: a shocking luxury in the capital; misery in the provinces somewhat distant; and plenty in the most remote. It is the same with such a monarchy as with our planet; fire at the centre, verdure on the surface, and between both a dry, cold, and barren earth.

10. *Of one Monarchy that subdues another.*

Sometimes one monarchy subdues another. The smaller the latter, the better it is overawed by fortresses; and the larger it is, the better will it be preserved by colonies.

11. *Of the Manners of a conquered People.*

It is not sufficient in those conquests to let the conquered nation enjoy their own laws; it is, perhaps, more necessary to leave them also their manners, because people in general have a stronger attachment to these than to their laws.

The French have been driven nine times out of Italy, because, as historians say, [337] of their insolent familiarities with the fair sex. It is too much for a nation to be obliged to bear not only with the pride of conquerors, but with their incontinence and indiscretion; these are, without doubt, most grievous and intolerable, as they are the source of infinite outrages.

[337] See Puffendorff's Universal History.

12. *Of a Law of Cyrus.*

Far am I from thinking that a good law which Cyrus made to oblige the Lydians to practice none but mean or infamous professions. It is true he directed his attention to an object of the greatest importance: he thought of guarding against revolts, and not invasions; but invasions will soon come, when the Persians and Lydians unite and corrupt each other. I would therefore much rather support by laws the simplicity and rudeness of the conquering nation than the effeminacy of the conquered.

Aristodemus, tyrant of Cumæ, [338] used all his endeavors to banish courage, and to enervate the minds of youth. He ordered that boys should let their hair grow in the same manner as girls, that they should deck it with flowers, and wear long robes of different colors down to their heels; that when they went to their masters of music and dancing, they should have women with them to carry their umbrellas, perfumes, and fans, and to present them with combs and looking-glasses whenever they bathed. This education lasted till the age of twenty—an education that could be agreeable to none but to a petty tyrant, who exposes his sovereignty to defend his life.

[338] Dionysius Halicarnassus. lib. VII.

13. *Charles XII.*

This prince, who depended entirely on his own strength, hastened his ruin by forming designs that could never be executed but by a long war—a thing which his kingdom was unable to support.

It was not a declining state he undertook to subvert, but a rising empire. The Russians made use of the war he waged against them as of a military school. Every defeat brought them nearer to victory; and, losing abroad, they learned to defend themselves at home.

Charles, in the deserts of Poland, imagined himself sovereign of the whole world: here he wandered, and with him in some measure wandered Sweden; while his capital enemy acquired new strength against him, locked him up, made settlements along the Baltic, destroyed or subdued Livonia.

Sweden was like a river whose waters are cut off at the fountain head in order to change its course.

It was not the affair of Pultowa that ruined Charles. Had he not been destroyed at that place, he would have been in another. The casualties of fortune are easily repaired; but who can be guarded against events that incessantly arise from the nature of things?

But neither nature nor fortune were ever so much against him as he himself.

He was not directed by the present situation of things, but by a kind of plan of his forming; and even this he followed very ill. He was not an Alexander; but he would have made an excellent soldier under that monarch.

Alexander's project succeeded because it was prudently concerted. [339] The bad success of the Persians in their several invasions of Greece, the conquests of Agesilaus, and the retreat of the ten thousand had shown to demonstration the superiority of the Greeks in their manner of fighting and in their arms; and it was well known that the Persians were too proud to be corrected.

[339] Montesquieu, Voltaire, and Robertson, in his History of America, were the first historians to render justice to this extraordinary general.—*Servan.*

It was no longer possible for them to weaken Greece by divisions: Greece was then united under one head, which could not pitch upon a better method of rendering her insensible to her servitude than by flattering her vanity with the destruction of her hereditary enemy, and with the hopes of the conquest of Asia.

An empire cultivated by the most industrious nation in the world, that followed agriculture from a principle of religion—an empire abounding with every convenience of life, furnished the enemy with all necessary means of subsisting.

It was easy to judge by the pride of those kings, who in vain were mortified by their numerous defeats, that they would precipitate their ruin by their forwardness in venturing battles; and that the flattery of their courtiers would never permit them to doubt of their grandeur.

The project was not only wise, but wisely executed. Alexander, in the rapidity of his conquests, even in the impetuosity of his passion, had, if I may so express myself, a flash of reason by which he was directed, and which those who would fain have made a romance of his history, and whose minds were more corrupt than his, could not conceal from our view. Let us descend more minutely into his history.

14. *Alexander.*

He did not set out upon his expedition till he had secured Macedonia against the neighboring barbarians, and completed the reduction of Greece; he availed himself of this conquest for no other end than for the execution of his grand enterprise; he rendered the jealousy of the Lacedæmonians of no effect; he attacked the maritime provinces; he caused his land forces to keep close to the sea-coast, that they might not be separated from his fleet; he made an admirable use of discipline against numbers; he never wanted provisions; and if it be true that victory gave him everything, he, in his turn, did everything to obtain it.

In the beginning of his enterprise—a time when the least check might have proved his destruction—he trusted very little to fortune; but when his reputation was established by a series of prosperous events, he sometimes had recourse to temerity. When before his departure for Asia he marched against the Triballians and Illyrians, you find he waged war [340] against those people in the very same manner as Cæsar afterwards conducted that against the Gauls. Upon his return to Greece, [341] it was in some measure against his will that he took and destroyed Thebes. When he invested that city, he wanted the inhabitants to come into terms of peace; but they hastened their own ruin. When it was debated whether he should attack the Persian fleet, [342] it is Parmenio who shows his presumption, Alexander his wisdom. His aim was to draw the Persians from the sea-coast, and to lay them under a necessity of abandoning their marine, in which they had a manifest superiority. Tyre being from principle attached to the Persians, who could not subsist without the commerce and navigation of that city, Alexander destroyed it. He subdued Egypt, which Darius had left bare of troops while he was assembling immense armies in another world.

[340] See Arrian, *de expedit. Alexandri,* lib. I.
[341] *Ibid.*

[342] *Ibid.*

To the passage of the Granicus, Alexander owed the conquest of the Greek colonies; to the battle of Issus, the reduction of Tyre and Egypt; to the battle of Arbela, the empire of the world.

After the battle of Issus, he suffered Darius to escape, and employed his time in securing and regulating his conquests: after the battle of Arbela, he pursued him so close [343] as to leave him no place of refuge in his empire. Darius enters his towns, his provinces, to quit them the next moment; and Alexander marches with such rapidity that the empire of the world seems to be rather the prize of an Olympian race than the fruit of a great victory. In this manner he carried on his conquests: let us now see how he preserved them.

[343] *Ibid.* lib. III.

He opposed those who would have had him treat the Greeks as masters [344] and the Persians as slaves. He thought only of uniting the two nations, and of abolishing the distinctions of a conquering and a conquered people. After he had completed his victories, he relinquished all those prejudices that had helped him to obtain them. He assumed the manners of the Persians, that he might not chagrin them too much by obliging them to conform to those of the Greeks. It was this humanity which made him show so great a respect for the wife and mother of Darius; and this that made him so continent. What a conqueror! He is lamented by all the nations he has subdued! What a usurper! At his death the very family he has cast from the throne is all in tears. These were the most glorious passages in his life, and such as history cannot produce an instance of in any other conqueror.

[344] This was Aristotle's advice. Plutarch's Morals, of the fortune and virtue of Alexander.

Nothing consolidates a conquest more than the union formed between the two nations by marriages. Alexander chose his wives from the nation he had subdued; he insisted on his courtiers doing the same; and the rest of the Macedonians followed the example. The Franks and Burgundians permitted those marriages; [345] the Visigoths forbade them in Spain, and afterwards allowed them. [346] By the Lombards they were not only allowed but encouraged. [347] When the Romans wanted to weaken Macedonia, they ordered that there should be no intermarriages between the people of different provinces.

[345] See the Law of the Burgundians, tit. 12, art. 5.
[346] See the Law of the Visigoths, book III, tit. 1, § 1, which abrogates the ancient law that had more regard, it says, to the difference of nations than to that of people's conditions.
[347] See the Law of the Lombards, book II, tit. 7, §§ 1, 2.

Alexander, whose aim was to unite the two nations, thought fit to establish in Persia a great number of Greek colonies. He built, therefore, a multitude of towns; and so strongly were all the parts of this new empire cemented, that after his decease, amidst the disturbances and confusion of the most frightful civil wars, when the Greeks had reduced themselves, as it were, to a state of annihilation, not a single province of Persia revolted.

To prevent Greece and Macedon from being too much exhausted, he sent a colony of Jews [348] to Alexandria; the manners of those people signified nothing to him, provided he could be sure of their fidelity.

[348] The kings of Syria, abandoning the plan laid down by the founder of the empire, resolved to oblige the Jews to conform to the manners of the Greeks—a resolution that gave the most terrible shock to their government.

He not only suffered the conquered nations to retain their own customs and manners, but likewise their civil laws; and frequently the very kings and governors to whom they had been subject: the Macedonians [349] he placed at the head of the troops, and the natives of the country at the head of the government, rather choosing to run the hazard of a particular disloyalty (which sometimes happened) than of a general revolt.

[349] See Arrian, *de expedit.* Alexandri, lib. III, and others.

He paid great respect to the ancient traditions, and to all the public monuments of the glory or vanity of nations. The Persian monarchs having destroyed the temples of the Greeks, Babylonians, and Egyptians, Alexander rebuilt them: [350] few nations submitted to his yoke to whose religion he did not conform; and his conquests seem to have been intended only to make him the particular monarch of each nation, and the first inhabitant of each city. The aim of the Romans in conquest was to destroy, his to preserve; and wherever he directed his victorious arms, his chief view was to achieve something whence that country might derive an increase of prosperity and power. To attain this end, he was enabled first of all by the greatness of his genius; secondly, by his frugality and private economy; [351] thirdly, by his profusion in matters of importance. He was close and reserved in his private expenses, but generous to the highest degree in those of a public nature. In regulating his household, he was the private Macedonian; but in paying the troops, in sharing his conquests with the Greeks, and in his largesses to every soldier in his army, he was Alexander.

[350] *Ibid.*
[351] *Ibid.*

He committed two very bad actions in setting Persepolis on fire and slaying Clitus; but he rendered them famous by his repentance. Hence it is that his crimes are forgotten, while his regard for virtue was recorded: they were considered rather as unlucky accidents than as his own deliberate acts. Posterity, struck with the beauty of his mind, even in the midst of his irregular passion, can view him only with pity, but never with an eye of hatred.

Let us draw a comparison between him and Cæsar. The Roman general, by attempting to imitate the Asiatic monarch, flung his fellow-citizens into a state of despair for a matter of mere ostentation; the Macedonian prince, by the same imitation, did a thing which was quite agreeable to his original scheme of conquest.

15. *New Methods of preserving a Conquest.*

When a monarch has subdued a large country, he may make use of an admirable method, equally proper for moderating despotic power, and for preserving the conquest; it is a method practiced by the conquerors of China.

In order to prevent the vanquished nation from falling into despair, the victors from growing insolent and proud, the government from becoming military, and to contain the two nations within their duty, the Tartar family now on the throne of China has ordained that every military corps in the provinces should be composed half of Chinese and half Tartars, to the end that the jealousy between the two nations may keep them within bounds. The courts of judicature are likewise half Chinese and half Tartars. This is productive of several good effects, 1. The two nations are a check to one another. 2. They both preserve the civil and military power, and one is not destroyed by the other, 3. The conquering nation may spread itself without being weakened and lost. It is likewise enabled to withstand civil and foreign wars. The want of so wise an institution as this has been the ruin of almost all the conquerors that ever existed.

16. *Of Conquests made by a despotic Prince.*

When a conquest happens to be vastly large, it supposes a despotic power; and then the army dispersed in the provinces is not sufficient. There should be always a body of faithful troops near the prince, ready to fall instantly upon any part of the empire that may chance to waver. This military corps ought to awe the rest, and to strike terror into those who through necessity have been entrusted with any authority in the empire. The emperor of China has always a large body of Tartars near his person, ready upon all occasions. In India, in Turkey, in Japan, the prince has always a body-guard independent of the other regular forces. This particular corps keeps the dispersed troops in awe.

17. *The same Subject continued.*

We have observed that the countries subdued by a despotic monarch ought to be held by a vassal. Historians are very lavish of their praises of the generosity of those conquerors who restored the princes to the throne whom they had vanquished. Extremely generous then were the Romans, who made such a number of kings, in order to have instruments of slavery. [352] A proceeding of that kind is absolutely necessary. If the conqueror intends to preserve the country which he has subdued, neither the governors he sends will be able to contain the subjects within duty, nor he himself the governors. He will be obliged to strip his ancient patrimony of troops, in order to secure his new dominions. The miseries of each nation will be common to both; civil broils will spread themselves from one to the other. On the contrary, if the conqueror restores the legitimate prince to the throne, he will of course have an ally; by the junction of whose forces his own power will be augmented. We have a recent instance of this in Shah Nadir, who conquered the Mogul, seized his treasures, and left him in possession of Hindostan.

[352] "Ut haberent instrumenta servitutis et reges."—Tacitus, Life of Agricola, 14.

BOOK XI.

OF THE LAWS WHICH ESTABLISH POLITICAL LIBERTY, WITH REGARD TO THE CONSTITUTION

1. *A general Idea.*

I make a distinction between the laws that establish political liberty, as it relates to the constitution, and those by which it is established, as it relates to the citizen. The former shall be the subject of this book; the latter I shall examine in the next.

2. *Different Significations of the word Liberty.*

There is no word that admits of more various significations, and has made more varied impressions on the human mind, than that of liberty. Some have taken it as a means of deposing a person on whom they had conferred a tyrannical authority; others for the power of choosing a superior whom they are obliged to obey; others for the right of bearing arms, and of being thereby enabled to use violence; others, in fine, for the privilege of being governed by a native of their own country, or by their own laws. [353] A certain nation for a long time thought liberty consisted in the privilege of wearing a long beard. [354] Some have annexed this name to one form of government exclusive of others: those who had a republican taste applied it to this species of polity; those who liked a monarchical state gave it to monarchy. [355] Thus they have all applied the name of *liberty* to the government most suitable to their own customs and inclinations: and as in republics the people have not so constant and so present a view of the causes of their misery, and as the magistrates seem to act only in conformity to the laws, hence liberty is generally said to reside in republics, and to be banished from monarchies. In fine, as in democracies the people seem to act almost as they please, this sort of government has been deemed the most free, and the power of the people has been confounded with their liberty.

[353] "I have copied," says Cicero, "Scævola's edict, which permits the Greeks to terminate their difference among themselves according to their own laws; this makes them consider themselves a free people."
[354] The Russians could not bear that Czar Peter should make them cut it off.
[355] The Cappadocians refused the condition of a republican state, which was offered them by the Romans.

3. *In what Liberty consists.*

It is true that in democracies the people seem to act as they please; but political liberty does not consist in an unlimited freedom. In governments, that is, in societies directed by laws, liberty can consist only in the power of doing what we ought to will, and in not being constrained to do what we ought not to will.

We must have continually present to our minds the difference between independence and liberty. Liberty is a right of doing whatever the laws permit, [356] and if a citizen could do what they forbid he would be no longer possessed of liberty, because all his fellow-citizens would have the same power.

[356] "Omnes legum servi sumus ut liberi esse possimus."—Cicero, *pro Cluentio*, 53.

4. *The same Subject continued.*

Democratic and aristocratic states are not in their own nature free. Political liberty is to be found only in moderate governments; and even in these it is not always found. It is there only when there is no abuse of power. But constant experience shows us that every man invested with power is apt to abuse it, and to carry his authority as far as it will go. Is it not strange, though true, to say that virtue itself has need of limits?

To prevent this abuse, it is necessary from the very nature of things that power should be a check to power. A government may be so constituted, as no man shall be compelled to do things to which the law does not oblige him, nor forced to abstain from things which the law permits.

5. *Of the End or View of different Governments.*

Though all governments have the same general end, which is that of preservation, yet each has another particular object. Increase of dominion was the object of Rome; war, that of Sparta; religion, that of the Jewish laws; commerce, that of Marseilles; public tranquility, that of the laws of China: [357] navigation, that of the laws of Rhodes; natural liberty, that of the policy of the Savages; in general, the pleasures of the prince, that of despotic states; that of monarchies, the prince's and the kingdom's glory; the independence of individuals is the end aimed at by the laws of Poland, thence results the oppression of the whole. [358]

[357] The natural end of a state that has no foreign enemies, or that thinks itself secured against them by barriers.
[358] Inconvenience of the *Liberum veto*.

One nation there is also in the world that has for the direct end of its constitution political liberty. We shall presently examine the principles on which this liberty is founded; if they are sound, liberty will appear in its highest perfection.

To discover political liberty in a constitution, no great labor is requisite. If we are capable of seeing it where it exists, it is soon found, and we need not go far in search of it.

6. *Of the Constitution of England.*

In every government there are three sorts of power: the legislative; the executive in respect to things dependent on the law of nations; and the executive in regard to matters that depend on the civil law.

By virtue of the first, the prince or magistrate enacts temporary or perpetual laws, and amends or abrogates those that have been already enacted. By the second, he makes peace or war, sends or receives embassies, establishes the public security, and provides against invasions. By the third, he punishes criminals, or determines the disputes that arise between individuals. The latter we shall call the judiciary power, and the other simply the executive power of the state.

The political liberty of the subject is a tranquility of mind arising from the opinion each person has of his safety. In order to have this liberty, it is requisite the government be so constituted as one man need not be afraid of another.

When the legislative and executive powers are united in the same person, or in the same body of magistrates, there can be no liberty; because apprehensions may arise, lest the same monarch or senate should enact tyrannical laws, to execute them in a tyrannical manner.

Again, there is no liberty, if the judiciary power be not separated from the legislative and executive. Were it joined with the legislative, the life and liberty of the subject would be exposed to arbitrary control; for the judge would be then the legislator. Were it joined to the executive power, the judge might behave with violence and oppression.

There would be an end of everything, were the same man or the same body, whether of the nobles or of the people, to exercise those three powers, that of enacting laws, that of executing the public resolutions, and of trying the causes of individuals.

Most kingdoms in Europe enjoy a moderate government because the prince who is invested with the two first powers leaves the third to his subjects. In Turkey, where these three powers are united in the Sultan's person, the subjects groan under the most dreadful oppression.

In the republics of Italy, where these three powers are united, there is less liberty than in our monarchies. Hence their government is obliged to have recourse to as violent methods for its support as even that of the Turks; witness the state inquisitors, [359] and the lion's mouth into which every informer may at all hours throw his written accusations.

[359] At Venice.

In what a situation must the poor subject be in those republics! The same body of magistrates are possessed, as executors of the laws, of the whole power they have given themselves in quality of legislators. They may plunder the state by their general determinations; and as they have likewise the judiciary power in their hands, every private citizen may be ruined by their particular decisions.

The whole power is here united in one body; and though there is no external pomp that indicates a despotic sway, yet the people feel the effects of it every moment.

Hence it is that many of the princes of Europe, whose aim has been leveled at arbitrary power, have constantly set out with uniting in their own persons all the branches of magistracy, and all the great offices of state.

I allow indeed that the mere hereditary aristocracy of the Italian republics does not exactly answer to the despotic power of the Eastern princes. The number of magistrates sometimes moderates the power of the magistracy; the whole body of the nobles do not always concur in the same design; and different tribunals are erected, that temper each other. Thus at Venice the legislative power is in the *council*, the executive in the *pregadi*, and the judiciary in the *quarantia*. But the mischief is, that these different tribunals are composed of magistrates all belonging to the same body; which constitutes almost one and the same power.

The judiciary power ought not to be given to a standing senate; it should be exercised by persons taken from the body of the people [360] at certain times of the year, and consistently with a form and manner prescribed by law, in order to erect a tribunal that should last only so long as necessity requires.

[360] As at Athens.

By this method the judicial power, so terrible to mankind, not being annexed to any particular state or profession, becomes, as it were, invisible. People have not then the judges continually present to their view; they fear the office, but not the magistrate.

In accusations of a deep and criminal nature, it is proper the person accused should have the privilege of choosing, in some measure, his judges, in concurrence with the law; or at least he should have a right to except against so great a number that the remaining part may be deemed his own choice.

The other two powers may be given rather to magistrates or permanent bodies, because they are not exercised on any private subject; one being no more than the general will of the state, and the other the execution of that general will.

But though the tribunals ought not to be fixed, the judgments ought; and to such a degree as to be ever conformable to the letter of the law. Were they to be the private opinion of the judge, people would then live in society, without exactly knowing the nature of their obligations.

The judges ought likewise to be of the same rank as the accused, or, in other words, his peers; to the end that he may not imagine he is fallen into the hands of persons inclined to treat him with rigor.

If the legislature leaves the executive power in possession of a right to imprison those subjects who can give security for their good behavior, there is an end of liberty; unless they are taken up, in order to answer without delay to a capital crime, in which case they are really free, being subject only to the power of the law.

But should the legislature think itself in danger by some secret conspiracy against the state, or by a correspondence with a foreign enemy, it might authorize the executive power, for a short and limited time, to imprison suspected persons, who in that case would lose their liberty only for a while, to preserve it forever.

And this is the only reasonable method that can be substituted to the tyrannical magistracy of the Ephori, and to the *state inquisitors* of Venice, who are also despotic.

As in a country of liberty, every man who is supposed a free agent ought to be his own governor; the legislative power should reside in the whole body of the people. But since this is impossible in large states, and in small ones is subject to many inconveniences, it is fit the people should transact by their representatives what they cannot transact by themselves.

The inhabitants of a particular town are much better acquainted with its wants and interests than with those of other places; and are better judges of the capacity of their neighbors than of that of the rest of their countrymen. The members, therefore, of the legislature should not be chosen from the general body of the nation; but it is proper that in every considerable place a representative should be elected by the inhabitants. [361]

[361] See Aristotle, *Politics*, III. chap. vii.

The great advantage of representatives is, their capacity of discussing public affairs. For this the people collectively are extremely unfit, which is one of the chief inconveniences of a democracy.

It is not at all necessary that the representatives who have received a general instruction from their constituents should wait to be directed on each particular affair, as is practiced in the diets of Germany. True it is that by this way of proceeding the speeches of the deputies might with greater propriety be called the voice of the nation; but, on the other hand, this would occasion infinite delays; would give each deputy a power of controlling the assembly; and, on the most urgent and pressing occasions, the wheels of government might be stopped by the caprice of a single person.

When the deputies, as Mr. Sidney well observes, represent a body of people, as in Holland, they ought to be accountable to their constituents; but it is a different thing in England, where they are deputed by boroughs.

All the inhabitants of the several districts ought to have a right of voting at the election of a representative, except such as are in so mean a situation as to be deemed to have no will of their own.

One great fault there was in most of the ancient republics, that the people had a right to active resolutions, such as require some execution, a thing of which they are absolutely incapable. They ought to have no share in the government but for the choosing of representatives, which is within their reach. For though few can tell the exact degree of men's capacities, yet there are none but are capable of knowing in general whether the person they choose is better qualified than most of his neighbors.

Neither ought the representative body to be chosen for the executive part of government, for which it is not so fit; but for the enacting of laws, or to see whether the laws in being are duly executed, a thing suited to their abilities, and which none indeed but themselves can properly perform.

In such a state there are always persons distinguished by their birth, riches, or honors: but were they to be confounded with the common people, and to have only the weight of a single vote like the rest, the common liberty would be their slavery, and they would have no interest in supporting it, as most of the popular resolutions would be against them. The share they have, therefore, in the legislature ought to be proportioned to their other advantages in the state; which happens only when they form a body that has a right to check the licentiousness of the people, as the people have a right to oppose any encroachment of theirs.

The legislative power is therefore committed to the body of the nobles, and to that which represents the people, each having their assemblies and deliberations apart, each their separate views and interests.

Of the three powers above mentioned, the judiciary is in some measure next to nothing: there remain, therefore, only two; and as these have need of a regulating power to moderate them, the part of the legislative body composed of the nobility is extremely proper for this purpose.

The body of the nobility ought to be hereditary. In the first place it is so in its own nature; and in the next there must be a considerable interest to preserve its privileges—privileges that in themselves are obnoxious to popular envy, and of course in a free state are always in danger.

But as a hereditary power might be tempted to pursue its own particular interests, and forget those of the people, it is proper that where a singular advantage may be gained by corrupting the nobility, as in the laws relating to the supplies, they should have no other share in the legislation than the power of rejecting, and not that of resolving.

By the *power of resolving* I mean the right of ordaining by their own authority, or of amending what has been ordained by others. By the *power of rejecting* I would be understood to mean the right of annulling a resolution taken by another; which was the power of the tribunes at Rome. And though the person possessed of the privilege of rejecting may likewise have the right of approving, yet this approbation passes for no more than a declaration that he intends to make no use of his privilege of rejecting, and is derived from that very privilege.

The executive power ought to be in the hands of a monarch, because this branch of government, having need of dispatch, is better administered by one than by many: on the other hand, whatever depends on the legislative power is oftentimes better regulated by many than by a single person.

But if there were no monarch, and the executive power should be committed to a certain number of persons selected from the legislative body, there would be an end then of liberty; by reason the two powers would be united, as the same persons would sometimes possess, and would be always able to possess, a share in both.

Were the legislative body to be a considerable time without meeting, this would likewise put an end to liberty. For of two things one would naturally follow: either that there would be no longer any legislative resolutions, and then the state would fall into anarchy; or that these resolutions would be taken by the executive power, which would render it absolute.

It would be needless for the legislative body to continue always assembled. This would be troublesome to the representatives, and, moreover, would cut out too much work for the executive power, so as to take off its attention to its office, and oblige it to think only of defending its own prerogatives, and the right it has to execute.

Again, were the legislative body to be always assembled, it might happen to be kept up only by filling the places of the deceased members with new representatives; and in that case, if the legislative body were once corrupted, the evil would be past all remedy. When different legislative bodies succeed one another, the people who have a bad opinion of that which is actually sitting may reasonably entertain some hopes of the next: but were it to be always the same body, the people upon seeing it once corrupted would no longer expect any good from its laws; and of course they would either become desperate or fall into a state of indolence.

The legislative body should not meet of itself. For a body is supposed to have no will but when it is met; and besides, were it not to meet unanimously, it would be impossible to determine which was really the legislative body; the part assembled, or the other. And if it had a right to prorogue itself, it might happen never to be prorogued; which would be extremely dangerous, in case it should ever attempt to encroach on the executive power. Besides, there are seasons, some more proper than others, for assembling the legislative body: it is fit, therefore, that the executive power should regulate the time of meeting, as well as the duration of those assemblies, according to the circumstances and exigencies of a state known to itself.

Were the executive power not to have a right of restraining the encroachments of the legislative body, the latter would become despotic; for as it might arrogate to itself what authority it pleased, it would soon destroy all the other powers.

But it is not proper, on the other hand, that the legislative power should have a right to stay the executive. For as the execution has its natural limits, it is useless to confine it; besides, the executive power is generally employed in momentary operations. The power, therefore, of the Roman tribunes was faulty, as it put a stop not only to the legislation, but likewise to the executive part of government; which was attended with infinite mischief.

But if the legislative power in a free state has no right to stay the executive, it has a right and ought to have the means of examining in what manner its laws have been executed; an advantage which this government has over that of Crete and Sparta, where the Cosmi [362] and the Ephori [363] gave no account of their administration.

[362] See *Aristotle*, Republic, II. chap. 10.
[363] *Ibid.* chap. ix.

But whatever may be the issue of that examination, the legislative body ought not to have a power of arraigning the person, nor, of course, the conduct, of him who is entrusted with the executive power. His person should be sacred, because as it is necessary for the good of the state to prevent the legislative body from rendering themselves arbitrary, the moment he is accused or tried there is an end of liberty.

In this case the state would be no longer a monarchy, but a kind of republic, though not a free government. But as the person entrusted with the executive power cannot abuse it without bad counselors, and such as have the laws as ministers, though the laws protect them as subjects, these men may be examined and punished—an advantage which this government has over that of Gnidus, where the law allowed of no such thing as calling the Amymones [364] to an account, even after their administration; [365] and therefore the people could never obtain any satisfaction for the injuries done them.

[364] These were magistrates chosen annually by the people. See Stephen of Byzantium.
[365] It was lawful to accuse the Roman magistrates after the expiration of their several offices. See in Dionysius Halicarnassus, lib. IX, the affair of Genutius the tribune.

Though, in general, the judiciary power ought not to be united with any part of the legislative, yet this is liable to three exceptions, founded on the particular interest of the party accused.

The great are always obnoxious to popular envy; and were they to be judged by the people, they might be in danger from their judges, and would, moreover, be deprived of the privilege which the meanest subject is possessed of in a free state, of being tried by his peers. The nobility, for this reason, ought not to be cited before the ordinary courts of judicature, but before that part of the legislature which is composed of their own body.

It is possible that the law, which is clear-sighted in one sense, and blind in another, might, in some cases, be too severe. But as we have already observed, the national judges are no more than the mouth that pronounces the words of the law, mere passive beings, incapable of moderating either its force or rigor. That part, therefore, of the legislative body, which we have just now observed to be a necessary tribunal on another occasion, is also a necessary tribunal in this; it belongs to its supreme authority to moderate the law in favor of the law itself, by mitigating the sentence.

It might also happen that a subject entrusted with the administration of public affairs may infringe the rights of the people, and be guilty of crimes which the ordinary magistrates either could not or would not punish. But, in general, the legislative power cannot try causes: and much less can it try this particular case, where it represents the party aggrieved, which is the people. It can only, therefore, impeach. But before what court shall it bring its impeachment? Must it go and demean itself before the ordinary tribunals, which are its inferiors, and, being composed, moreover, of men who are chosen from the people as well as itself, will naturally be swayed by the authority of so powerful an accuser? No: in order to preserve the dignity of the people, and the security of the subject, the legislative part which represents the people must bring in its charge before the legislative part which represents the nobility, who have neither the same interests nor the same passions.

Here is an advantage which this government has over most of the ancient republics, where this abuse prevailed, that the people were at the same time both judge and accuser.

The executive power, pursuant of what has been already said, ought to have a share in the legislature by the power of rejecting, otherwise it would soon be stripped of its prerogative. But should the legislative power usurp a share of the executive, the latter would be equally undone.

If the prince were to have a part in the legislature by the power of resolving, liberty would be lost. But as it is necessary he should have a share in the legislature for the support of his own prerogative, this share must consist in the power of rejecting.

The change of government at Rome was owing to this, that neither the senate, who had one part of the executive power, nor the magistrates, who were entrusted with the other, had the right of rejecting, which was entirely lodged in the people.

Here then is the fundamental constitution of the government we are treating of. The legislative body being composed of two parts, they check one another by the mutual privilege of rejecting. They are both restrained by the executive power, as the executive is by the legislative.

These three powers should naturally form a state of repose or inaction. But as there is a necessity for movement in the course of human affairs, they are forced to move, but still in concert.

As the executive power has no other part in the legislative than the privilege of rejecting, it can have no share in the public debates. It is not even necessary that it should propose, because as it may always disapprove of the resolutions that shall be taken, it may likewise reject the decisions on those proposals which were made against its will.

In some ancient commonwealths, where public debates were carried on by the people in a body, it was natural for the executive power to propose and debate in conjunction with the people, otherwise their resolutions must have been attended with a strange confusion.

Were the executive power to determine the raising of public money, otherwise than by giving its consent, liberty would be at an end; because it would become legislative in the most important point of legislation.

If the legislative power was to settle the subsidies, not from year to year, but forever, it would run the risk of losing its liberty, because the executive power would be no longer dependent; and when once it was possessed of such a perpetual right, it would be a matter of indifference whether it held it of itself or of another. The same may be said if it should come to a resolution of entrusting, not an annual, but a perpetual command of the fleets and armies to the executive power.

To prevent the executive power from being able to oppress, it is requisite that the armies with which it is entrusted should consist of the people, and have the same spirit as the people, as was the case at Rome till the time of Marius. To obtain this end, there are only two ways, either that the persons employed in the army should have sufficient property to answer for their conduct to their fellow-subjects, and be enlisted only for a year, as was customary at Rome: or if there should be a standing army, composed chiefly of the most despicable part of the nation, the legislative power should have a right to disband them as soon as it pleased; the soldiers should live in common with the rest of the people; and no separate camp, barracks, or fortress should be suffered.

When once an army is established, it ought not to depend immediately on the legislative, but on the executive, power; and this from the very nature of the thing, its business consisting more in action than in deliberation.

It is natural for mankind to set a higher value upon courage than timidity, on activity than prudence, on strength than counsel. Hence the army will ever despise a senate, and respect their own officers. They will naturally slight the orders sent them by a body of men whom they look upon as cowards, and therefore unworthy to command them. So that as soon as the troops depend entirely on the legislative body, it becomes a military government; and if the contrary has ever happened, it has been owing to some extraordinary circumstances. It is because the army was always kept divided; it is because it was composed of several bodies that depended each on a particular province; it is because the capital towns were strong places, defended by their natural situation, and not garrisoned with regular troops. Holland, for instance, is still safer than Venice; she might drown or starve the revolted troops; for as they are not quartered in towns capable of furnishing them with necessary subsistence, this subsistence is of course precarious.

In perusing the admirable treatise of Tacitus 'On the Manners of the Germans,' [366] we find it is from that nation the English have borrowed the idea of their political government. This beautiful system was invented first in the woods.

[366] *De minoribus rebus principes consultant, de majoribus omnes; ita tamen ut ea quoque quorum penes plebem arbitrium est, apud principes pertractentur.*

As all human things have an end, the state we are speaking of will lose its liberty, will perish. Have not Rome, Sparta, and Carthage perished? It will perish when the legislative power shall be more corrupt than the executive.

It is not my business to examine whether the English actually enjoy this liberty or not. Sufficient it is for my purpose to observe that it is established by their laws; and I inquire no further.

Neither do I pretend by this to undervalue other governments, nor to say that this extreme political liberty ought to give uneasiness to those who have only a moderate share of it. How should I have any such design, I who think that even the highest refinement of reason is not always desirable, and that mankind generally find their account better in mediums than in extremes?

Harrington, in his Oceana, has also inquired into the utmost degree of liberty to which the constitution of a state may be carried. But of him indeed it may be said that for want of knowing the nature of real liberty he busied himself in pursuit of an imaginary one; and that he built a Chalcedon, though he had a Byzantium before his eyes.

7. Of the Monarchies we are acquainted with.

The monarchies we are acquainted with have not, like that we have been speaking of, liberty for their direct view: the only aim is the glory of the subject, of the state, and of the sovereign. But hence there results a spirit of liberty, which in those states is capable of achieving as great things, and of contributing as much perhaps to happiness as liberty itself.

Here the three powers are not distributed and founded on the model of the constitution above-mentioned; they have each a particular distribution, according to which they border more or less on political liberty; and if they did not border upon it, monarchy would degenerate into despotic government.

8. *Why the Ancients had not a clear Idea of Monarchy.*

The ancients had no notion of a government founded on a body of nobles, and much less on a legislative body composed of the representatives of the people. The republics of Greece and Italy were cities that had each their own form of government, and convened their subjects within their walls. Before Rome had swallowed up all the other republics, there was scarcely anywhere a king to be found, no, not in Italy, Gaul, Spain, or Germany; [367] they were all petty states or republics. Even Africa itself was subject to a great commonwealth: and Asia Minor was occupied by Greek colonies. There was, therefore, no instance of deputies of towns or assemblies of the states; one must have gone as far as Persia to find a monarchy.

[367] Nevertheless, during the same epoch there were kings in Macedonia, Syria, Egypt, etc.—*Crévier.*

I am not ignorant that there were confederate republics; in which several towns sent deputies to an assembly. But I affirm there was no monarchy on that model.

The first plan, therefore, of the monarchies we are acquainted with was thus formed. The German nations that conquered the Roman empire were certainly a free people. Of this we may be convinced only by reading Tacitus 'On the Manners of the Germans.' The conquerors spread themselves over all the country; living mostly in the fields, and very little in towns. When they were in Germany, the whole nation was able to assemble. This they could no longer do when dispersed through the conquered provinces. And yet as it was necessary that the nation should deliberate on public affairs, pursuant to their usual method before the conquest, they had recourse to representatives. Such is the origin of the Gothic government amongst us. At first it was mixed with aristocracy and monarchy—a mixture attended with this inconvenience, that the common people were bondmen. The custom afterwards succeeded of granting letters of enfranchisement, and was soon followed by so perfect a harmony between the civil liberty of the people, the privileges of the nobility and clergy, and the prince's prerogative, that I really think there never was in the world a government so well tempered as that of each part of Europe, so long as it lasted. Surprising that the corruption of the government of a conquering nation should have given birth to the best species of constitution that could possibly be imagined by man!

9. *Aristotle's Manner of Thinking.*

Aristotle is greatly puzzled in treating of monarchy. [368] He makes five species; and he does not distinguish them by the form of constitution, but by things merely accidental, as the virtues and vices of the prince; or by things extrinsic, such as tyranny usurped or inherited.

[368] *Politics*, book III. chap. xiv

Among the number of monarchies he ranks the Persian empire and the kingdom of Sparta. But is it not evident that the one was a despotic state and the other a republic?

The ancients, who were strangers to the distribution of the three powers in the government of a single person, could never form a just idea of monarchy.

10. *What other Politicians thought.*

To temper monarchy, Arybas, [369] king of Epirus, [370] found no other remedy than a republic. The Molossi, not knowing how to limit the same power, made two kings, [371] by which means the state was weakened more than the prerogative; they wanted rivals, and they created enemies.

[369] Notwithstanding the fact that Arybas sought to render his monarchy more stable, the kings of Epirus retained their power until overthrown by Paulus Æmilius.—D.
[370] See Justin, book XVII.
[371] Aristotle, *Politics*, book V. chap. viii. Montesquieu seems to have misconstrued Aristotle, since the Molossi never had but one king.—P.

Two kings were tolerable nowhere but at Sparta; here they did not form, but were only a part of the constitution.

11. *Of the Kings of the heroic Times of Greece.*

In the heroic times of Greece, a kind of monarchy arose that was not of long duration. [372] Those who had been inventors of arts, who had fought in their country's cause, who had established societies, or distributed lands among the people, obtained the regal power, and transmitted it to their children. They were kings, priests, and judges. This was one of the five species of monarchy mentioned by Aristotle; [373] and the only one that can give us any idea of the monarchical constitution. But the plan of this constitution is opposite to that of our modern monarchies.

[372] Aristotle, *Politics*. book III. chap. xiv.
[373] Aristotle, *Politics*. book III. chap. xiv.

The three powers were there distributed in such a manner that the people were the legislature, [374] and the king had the executive together with the judiciary power; whereas in modern monarchies the prince is invested with the executive and legislative powers, or at least with part of the legislative, but does not act in a judiciary capacity.

[374] See what Plutarch says in the Life of Theseus. See likewise Thucydides, book I.

In the government of the kings of the heroic times, the three powers were ill-distributed. Hence those monarchies could not long subsist. For as soon as the people got the legislative power into their hands, they might, as they everywhere did, upon the very least caprice, subvert the regal authority.

Among a free people possessed of the legislative power, and enclosed within walls, where everything tending towards oppression appears still more odious, it is the masterpiece of legislation to know where to place properly the judiciary power. But it could not be in worse hands than in those of the person to whom the executive power had been already committed. From that very instant the monarch became terrible. But at the same time as he had no share in the legislature, he could make no defense against it, thus his power was in one sense too great, in another too little.

They had not as yet discovered that the true function of a prince was to appoint judges, and not to sit as judge himself. The opposite policy rendered the government of a single person insupportable. Hence all these kings were banished. The Greeks had no notion of the proper distribution of the three powers in the government of one person; they could see it only in that of many; and this kind of constitution they distinguished by the name of *Polity*. [375]

[375] Aristotle, *Politics*, book IV. chap. viii.

12. *Of the Government of the Kings of Rome, and in what Manner the three Powers were there distributed.*

The government of the kings of Rome had some relation to that of the kings of the heroic times of Greece. Its subversion, like the latter's, was owing to its general defect, though in its own particular nature it was exceedingly good.

In order to give an adequate idea of this government, I shall distinguish that of the first five kings, that of Servius Tullius, and that of Tarquin.

The crown was elective, and under the first five kings the senate had the greatest share in the election.

Upon the king's decease the senate examined whether they should continue the established form of government. If they thought proper to continue it, they named a magistrate [376] taken from their own body, who chose a king; the senate were to approve of the election, the people to confirm it, and the augurs to declare the approbation of the gods. If any of these three conditions was wanting, they were obliged to proceed to another election.

[376] Dionysius Halicarnassus. book II. p. 120, and book IV. pp. 242, 243.

The constitution was a mixture of monarchy, aristocracy, and democracy; and such was the harmony of power that there was no instance of jealousy or dispute in the first reigns. The king commanded the armies, and had the direction of the sacrifices: he had the power of determining [377] civil and criminal [378] causes; he called the senate together, convened the people, laid some affairs before the latter, and regulated the rest with the senate. [379]

[377] See Tanaquil's Discourse on Livy, book I, dec. 1, and the regulations of Servius Tullius in Dionysius Halicarnassus, book IV. p. 229.
[378] See Dionysius Halicarnassus, book II, p. 118, and book III, p. 171.
[379] It was by virtue of a senatus-consultum that Tullius Hostilius ordered Alba to be destroyed.—Dionysius Halicarnassus, book III. pp. 167 and 172.

The authority of the senate was very great. The kings oftentimes pitched upon senators with whom they sat in judgment; and they never laid any affair before the people till it had been previously debated [380] in that august assembly.

[380] Ibid., book IV. p. 276.

The people had the right of choosing [381] magistrates, of consenting to the new laws, and, with the king's permission, of making war and peace; but they had not the judicial power. When Tullius Hostilius referred the trial of Horatius to the people, he had his particular reasons, which may be seen in Dionysius Halicarnassus. [382]

[381] Dionysius Halicarnassus. book II. And yet they could not have the nomination of all offices, since Valerius Publicola made that famous law by which every citizen was forbidden to exercise any employment, unless he had obtained it by the suffrage of the people.
[382] Book III, p. 159.

The constitution altered under [383] Servius Tullius. The senate had no share in his election; he caused himself to be proclaimed by the people; he resigned the power of hearing civil causes, [384] reserving none to himself but those of a criminal nature; he laid all affairs directly before the people, eased them of the taxes, and imposed the whole burden on the patricians. Hence in proportion as he weakened the regal together with the senatorial power, he augmented that of the plebeians. [385]

[383] Dionysius Halicarnassus. book IV.
[384] He divested himself of half the regal power, says Dionysius Halicarnassus, book IV., p. 229.
[385] It was thought that if he had not been prevented by Tarquin he would have established a popular government. —Dionysius Halicarnassus, book IV, p. 243.

Tarquin would neither be chosen by the senate nor by the people; he considered Servius Tullius as a usurper, and seized the crown as his hereditary right. He destroyed most of the senators; those who remained he never consulted; nor did he even so much as summon them to assist at his decisions. [386] Thus his power increased: but the odium of that power received a new addition, by usurping also the authority of the people, against whose consent he enacted several laws. The three powers were by these means re-united in his person; but the people at a critical minute recollected that they were legislators, and there was an end of Tarquin.

[386] Dionysius Halicarnassus. book IV.

13. *General Reflections on the State of Rome after the Expulsion of its Kings.*

It is impossible to be tired of so agreeable a subject as ancient Rome: thus strangers at present leave the modern palaces of that celebrated capital to visit the ruins; and thus the eye, after recreating itself with the view of flowery meads, is pleased with the wild prospect of rocks and mountains.

The patrician families were at all times possessed of great privileges. These distinctions, which were considerable under the kings, became much more important after their expulsion. Hence arose the jealousy of the plebeians, who wanted to reduce them. The contest struck at the constitution, without weakening the government; for it was very indifferent as to what family were the magistrates, provided the magistracy preserved its authority.

An elective monarchy, like that of Rome, necessarily supposes a powerful aristocratic body to support it, without which it changes immediately into tyranny or into a popular state. But a popular state has no need of this distinction of families to maintain itself. To this it was owing that the patricians, who were a necessary part of the constitution under the regal government, became a superfluous branch under the consuls; the people could suppress them without hurting themselves, and change the constitution without corrupting it.

After Servius Tullius had reduced the patricians, it was natural that Rome should fall from the regal hands into those of the people. But the people had no occasion to be afraid of relapsing under a regal power by reducing the patricians.

A state may alter in two different ways, either by the amendment or by the corruption of the constitution. If it has preserved its principles and the constitution changes, this is owing to its amendment; if upon changing the constitution its principles are lost, this is because it has been corrupted.

The government of Rome, after the expulsion of the kings, should naturally have been a democracy. The people had already the legislative power in their hands; it was their unanimous consent that had expelled the Tarquins; and if they had not continued steady to those principles, the Tarquins might easily have been restored. To pretend that their design in expelling them was to render themselves slaves to a few families is quite absurd. The situation therefore of things required that Rome should have formed a democracy, and yet this did not happen. There was a necessity that the power of the principal families should be tempered, and that the laws should have a bias to democracy.

The prosperity of states is frequently greater in the insensible transition from one constitution to another than in either of those constitutions. Then it is that all the springs of government are upon the stretch, that the citizens assert their claims, that friendships or enmities are formed amongst the jarring parties, and that there is a noble emulation between those who defend the ancient and those who are strenuous in promoting the new constitution.

14. *In what Manner the Distribution of the three Powers began to change after the Expulsion of the Kings.*

There were four things that greatly prejudiced the liberty of Rome. The patricians had engrossed to themselves all public employments whatever; an exorbitant power was annexed to the consulate; the people were often insulted; and, in fine, they had scarcely any influence at all left in the public suffrages. These four abuses were redressed by the people.

1st. It was regulated that the plebeians might aspire to some magistracies; and by degrees they were rendered capable of them all, except that of *Inter-rex*.

2nd. The consulate was dissolved into several other magistracies; [387] prætors were created, on whom the power was conferred of trying private causes; quæstors [388] were nominated for determining those of a criminal nature; ædiles were established for the civil administration; treasurers [389] were made for the management of the public money; and, in fine, by the creation of censors the consuls were divested of that part of the legislative power which regulates the morals of the citizens and the transient polity of the different bodies of the state. The chief privileges left them were to preside in the great meetings [390] of the people, to assemble the senate, and to command the armies.

[387] Livy, dec. 1, book VI.
[388] *Quæstores parricidii.*—Pomponius, Leg. 2, ff. *de Orig. Jur.*
[389] Plutarch, Life of Publicola.
[390] *Comitiis centuriatis.*

3rd. The sacred laws appointed tribunes, who had a power of checking the encroachments of the patricians, and prevented not only private but likewise public injuries.

In fine, the plebeians increased their influence in the general assemblies. The people of Rome were divided in three different manners—by centuries, by curiæ, and by tribes; and whenever they gave their votes, they were convened in one of those three ways.

In the first the patricians, the leading men, the rich and the senate, which was very nearly the same thing, had almost the whole authority; in the second they had less; and less still in the third.

The division into centuries was a division rather of estates and fortunes than of persons. The whole people were distributed into a hundred and ninety-three centuries, [391] which had each a single vote. The patricians and leading men composed the first ninety-eight centuries; and the other ninety-five consisted of the remainder of the citizens. In this division therefore the patricians were masters of the suffrages.

[391] See Livy, book I. Dionysius Halicarnassus, book IV. and VII.

In the division into curiæ, [392] the patricians had not the same advantages; some, however, they had, for it was necessary to consult the augurs, who were under the direction of the patricians; and no proposal could be made there to the people unless it had been previously laid before the senate, and approved of by a senatus-consultum. But, in the division into tribes they had nothing to do either with the augurs or with the decrees of the senate; and the patricians were excluded.

[392] Dionysius Halicarnassus, book IX, p. 598.

Now the people endeavored constantly to have those meetings by curiæ which had been customary by centuries, and by tribes, those they used to have before by curiæ; by which means the direction of public affairs soon devolved from the patricians to the plebeians.

Thus when the plebeians obtained the power of trying the patricians—a power which commenced in the affair of Coriolanus, [393] they insisted upon assembling by tribes, [394] and not by centuries; and when the new magistracies [395] of tribunes and ædiles were established in favor of the people, the latter obtained that they should meet by curiæ in order to nominate them; and after their power was quite settled, they gained [396] so far their point as to assemble by tribes to proceed to this nomination.

[393] Dionysius Halicarnassus. book VII.
[394] Contrary to the ancient custom, as may be seen in Dionysius Halicarnassus. bookV, p. 320.
[395] Dionysius Halicarnassus. book V. pp. 410 and 411.
[396] Ibid. book IX. p. 650.

15. *In what Manner Rome, in the flourishing State of that Republic, suddenly lost its Liberty.*

In the heat of the contests between the patricians and the plebeians, the latter insisted upon having fixed laws, to the end that the public judgments should no longer be the effect of capricious will or arbitrary power. The senate, after a great deal of resistance, acquiesced; and decemvirs were nominated to compose those laws. It was thought proper to grant them an extraordinary power, because they were to give laws to parties whose views and interest it was almost impossible to unite. The nomination of all magistrates was suspended; and the decemvirs were chosen in the *comitia* sole administrators of the republic. Thus they found themselves invested with the consular and the tribunition power. By one they had the privilege of assembling the senate, by the other that of convening the people; but they assembled neither senate nor people. Ten men only of the republic had the whole legislative, the whole executive, and the whole judiciary power. Rome saw herself enslaved by as cruel a tyranny as that of Tarquin. When Tarquin trampled on the liberty of that city, she was seized with indignation at the power he had usurped; when the decemvirs exercised every act of oppression, she was astonished at the extraordinary power she had granted.

What a strange system of tyranny—a tyranny carried on by men who had obtained the political and military power, merely from their knowledge in civil affairs, and who at that very juncture stood in need of the courage of those citizens to protect them abroad who so tamely submitted to domestic oppression!

The spectacle of Virginia's death, whom her father immolated to chastity and liberty, put an end to the power of the decemvirs. Every man became free, because every man had been injured; each showed himself a citizen because each had a tie of the parent. The senate and the people resumed a liberty which had been committed to ridiculous tyrants.

No people were so easily moved by public spectacles as the Romans. That of the empurpled body of Lucretia put an end to the regal government. The debtor who appeared in the forum covered with wounds caused an alteration in the republic. The decemvirs owed their expulsion to the tragedy of Virginia. To condemn Manlius, it was necessary to keep the people from seeing the Capitol. Cæsar's bloody garment flung Rome again into slavery.

16. *Of the legislative Power in the Roman Republic.*

There were no rights to contest under the decemvirs: but upon the restoration of liberty, jealousies revived; and so long as the patricians had any privileges left, they were sure to be stripped of them by the plebeians.

The mischief would not have been so great had the plebeians been satisfied with this success; but they also injured the patricians as citizens. When the people assembled by curiæ or centuries, they were composed of senators, patricians, and plebeians; in their disputes the plebeians gained this point, [397] that they alone without patricians or senate should enact the laws called Plebiscita; and the assemblies in which they were made had the name of comitia by tribes. Thus there were cases in which the patricians [398] had no share in the legislative power, but [399] were subject to the legislation of another body of the state. This was the extravagance of liberty. The people, to establish a democracy, acted against the very principles of that government. One would have imagined that so exorbitant a power must have destroyed the authority of the senate. But Rome had admirable institutions. Two of these were especially remarkable: one by which the legislative power of the people was established, and the other by which it was limited.

[397] Dionysius Halicarnassus. book XI. p.725.

[398] By the sacred laws, the plebeians had the power of making the plebiscita by themselves, without admitting the patricians into their assembly.—Dionysius Halicarnassus, book VI, p. 410; and book VII, p. 430.

[399] By the law enacted after the expulsion of the decemvirs, the patricians were made subject to the plebiscita, though they had not a right of voting there. Livy, book III. 55, and Dionysius Halicarnassus, book XI, p. 725. This law was confirmed by that of Publius Philo the dictator, in the year of Rome 416. Livy, book VIII.

The censors, and before them the consuls, modeled [400] and created, as it were, every five years the body of the people; they exercised the legislation on the very part that was possessed of the legislative power. *Tiberius Gracchus*, says Cicero, *caused the freedmen to be admitted into the tribes, not by the force of his eloquence, but by a word, by a gesture; which had he not effected, the republic, whose drooping head we are at present scarcely able to uphold, would not even exist.*

[400] In the year 312 of Rome the consuls performed still the business of surveying the people and their estates, as appears by Dionysius Halicarnassus, book XI.

On the other hand, the senate had the power of rescuing, as it were, the republic out of the hands of the people, by creating a dictator, before whom the sovereign bowed his head, and the most popular laws were silent. [401]

[401] Such as those by which it was allowed to appeal from the decisions of all the magistrates to the people.

17. Of the executive Power in the same Republic.

Jealous as the people were of their legislative power, they had no great uneasiness about the executive. This they left almost entirely to the senate and to the consuls, reserving scarcely anything more to themselves than the right of choosing the magistrates, and of confirming the acts of the senate and of the generals.

Rome, whose passion was to command, whose ambition was to conquer, whose commencement and progress were one continued usurpation, had constantly affairs of the greatest weight upon her hands; her enemies were ever conspiring against her, or she against her enemies.

As she was obliged to behave on the one hand with heroic courage, and on the other with consummate prudence, it was requisite, of course, that the management of affairs should be committed to the senate. Thus the people disputed every branch of the legislative power with the senate, because they were jealous of their liberty; but they had no disputes about the executive, because they were animated with the love of glory.

So great was the share the senate took in the executive power, that, as Polybius [402] informs us, foreign nations imagined that Rome was an aristocracy. The senate disposed of the public money, and farmed out the revenue; they were arbiters of the affairs of their allies; they determined war or peace, and directed in this respect the consuls; they fixed the number of the Roman and of the allied troops, disposed of the provinces and armies to the consuls or prætors, and upon the expiration of the year of command had the power of appointing successors; they decreed triumphs, received and sent embassies: they nominated, rewarded, punished, and were judges of kings, declared them allies of the Roman people, or stripped them of that title.

[402] Book VI.

The consuls levied the troops which they were to carry into the field; had the command of the forces by sea and by land; disposed of the forces of the allies; were invested with the whole power of the republic in the provinces; gave peace to the vanquished nations, imposed conditions on them, or referred them to the senate.

In the earliest times, when the people had some share in the affairs relating to war or peace, they exercised rather their legislative than their executive power. They scarcely did anything else but confirm the acts of the kings, and after their expulsion those of the consuls or senate. So far were they from being the arbiters of war that we have instances of its having been often declared, notwithstanding the opposition of the tribunes. But growing wanton in their prosperity, they increased their executive power. Thus [403] they created the military tribunes, the nomination of whom till then had belonged to the generals; and some time before the first Punic war, they decreed that only their own body should have the right of declaring war. [404]

[403] In the year of Rome 444, Livy, dec. 1, book IX. As the war against Perseus appeared somewhat dangerous, it was ordained by a senatus-consultum that this law should be suspended, and the people agreed to it. Livy, dec. 5, book II.
[404] They extorted it from the senate, says Freinshemius, dec. 2, book VI.

18. *Of the judiciary Power in the Roman Government.*

The judiciary power was given to the people, to the senate, to the magistrates, and to particular judges. We must see in what manner it was distributed; beginning with their civil affairs.

The consuls had the judiciary power [405] after the expulsion of the kings, as the prætors were judges after the consuls. Servius Tullius had divested himself of the power of determining civil causes, which was not resumed by the consuls, except in some [406] very rare cases, for that reason called *extraordinary*. [407] They were satisfied with naming the judges, and establishing the several tribunals. By a discourse of Appius Claudius, in Dionysius Halicarnassus, [408] it appears that as early as the 259th year of Rome this was looked upon as a settled custom among the Romans; and it is not tracing it very high to refer it to Servius Tullius.

[405] There is no manner of doubt but the consuls had the power of trying civil causes before the creation of the prætors. See Livy, dec. 1, book II. Dionysius Halicarnassus, book X, pp. 627, 645.

[406] The tribunes frequently tried causes by themselves only, but nothing rendered them more odious.—Dionysius Halicarnassus, book XI, p. 709.

[407] *Judicia extraordinaria.* See the Institutes, book IV.

[408] Book VI, p. 360.

Every year the prætor made a list [409] of such as he chose for the office of judges during his magistracy. A sufficient number was pitched upon for each cause; a custom very nearly the same as that now practiced in England. And what was extremely favorable to liberty [410] was the prætor's fixing the judges with the consent [411] of the parties. The great number of exceptions that can be made in England amounts pretty nearly to this very custom.

[409] *Album Judicium.*

[410] "Our ancestors," says Cicero, *pro Cluentio,* "would not suffer any man whom the parties had not agreed to, to be judge of the least pecuniary affair, much less of a citizen's reputation."

[411] See in the fragments of the Servilian, Cornelian, and other laws, in what manner these laws appointed judges for the crimes they proposed to punish. They were often pitched upon by choice, sometimes by lot, or, in fine, by lot mixed together with choice.

The judges decided only the questions relating to matter of fact; [412] for example, whether a sum of money had been paid or not, whether an act had been committed or not. But as to questions of law, [413] as these required a certain capacity, they were always carried before the tribunal of the centumvirs. [414]

[412] Seneca, *De Benefic.* lib. II. chap. 7, *in fine.*

[413] See Quintilian, lib. IV, p. 54, in fol. ed., Paris, 1541.

[414] Leg. 2 ff. *de Orig. Jur.* Magistrates who were called decemvirs presided in court, the whole under a prætor's direction.

The kings reserved to themselves the judgment of criminal affairs, and in this were succeeded by the consuls. It was in consequence of this authority that Brutus put his children and all those who were concerned in the Tarquinian conspiracy to death. This was an exorbitant power. The consuls already invested with the military command extended the exercise of it even to civil affairs; and their procedures, being stripped of all forms of justice, were rather exertions of violence than legal judgments.

This gave rise to the Valerian law, by which it was made lawful to appeal to the people from every decision of the consuls that endangered the life of a citizen. The consuls had no longer the power of pronouncing sentence in capital cases against a Roman citizen, without the consent of the people. [415]

[415] "Quoniam de capite civis Romani, injussu populi Romani, non erat permissum consulibus jus dicere."—See Pomponius, Leg. 2, §6, ff. *de Orig. Jur.*

We see in the first conspiracy for the restoration of the Tarquins that the criminals were tried by Brutus the consul; in the second the senate and comitia were assembled to try them. [416]

[416] Dionysius Halicarnassus, book V. p. 322.

The laws distinguished by the name of sacred allowed the plebeians the privilege of choosing tribunes; whence was formed a body whose pretensions at first were immense. It is hard to determine which was greater, the insolence of the plebeians in demanding, or the condescension of the senate in granting. The Valerian law allowed appeals to the people, that is, to the people composed of senators, patricians, and plebeians. The plebeians made a law that appeals should be brought before their own body. A question was soon after started, whether the plebeians had a right to try a patrician; this was the subject of a dispute to which the impeachment of Coriolanus gave rise, and which ended with that affair. When Coriolanus was accused by the tribunes before the people, he insisted, contrary to the spirit of the Valerian law, that as he was a patrician, none but the consuls had the power to try him; on the other hand, the plebeians, also contrary to the spirit of that same law, pretended that none but their body were empowered to be his judges, and accordingly they pronounced sentence upon him.

This was moderated by the law of the Twelve Tables; whereby it was ordained that none but the *great assemblies* of the people [417] should try a citizen in capital cases. Hence the body of the plebeians, or, which amounts to the very same, the comitia by tribes, had no longer any power of hearing criminal causes, except such as were punished with fines. To inflict a capital punishment a law was requisite; but to condemn to a pecuniary mulct, there was occasion only for a plebiscitum.

[417] The comitia by centuries. Thus Manlius Capitolinus was tried in these comitia.— Livy, Dec. 1, book VI. p. 60.

This regulation of the law of the Twelve Tables was extremely prudent. It produced an admirable balance between the body of the plebeians and the senate. For as the full judiciary power of both depended on the greatness of the punishment and the nature of the crime, it was necessary they should both agree.

The Valerian law abolished all the remains of the Roman government in any way relating to that of the kings of the heroic times of Greece. The consuls were divested of the power to punish crimes. Though all crimes are public, yet we must distinguish between those which more nearly concern the mutual intercourse of the citizens and those which more immediately interest the state in the relation it bears to its subjects. The first are called private, the second public. The latter were tried by the people; and in regard to the former, they named by particular commission a quæstor for the prosecution of each crime. The person chosen by the people was frequently one of the magistrates, sometimes a private man. He was called the *quæstor of parricide*, and is mentioned in the law of the Twelve Tables. [418]

[418] Pomponius, in the second Law in the Digest *de Orig. Jur.*

The quæstor nominated the judge of the question, who drew lots for the judges, and regulated the tribunal in which he presided. [419]

[419] See a fragment of Ulpian, who gives another of the Cornelian Law: it is to be met with in the Collation of the Mosaic and Roman Laws, tit. I, de *sicariis et homicidiis*.

Here it is proper to observe what share the senate had in the nomination of the quæstor, that we may see how far the two powers were balanced. Sometimes the senate caused a dictator to be chosen, in order to exercise the office of quæstor; [420] at other times they ordained that the people should be convened by a tribune, with the view of proceeding to the nomination of a quæstor; [421] and, in fine, the people frequently appointed a magistrate to make his report to the senate concerning a particular crime, and to desire them to name a quæstor, as may be seen in the judgment upon Lucius Scipio [422] in Livy. [423]

[420] This took place, especially in regard to crimes committed in Italy, which were subject chiefly to the inspection of the senate. See Livy, Dec. 1, book IX., concerning the conspiracies at Capua.
[421] This was the case in the prosecution for the murder of Posthumius, in the year 340 of Rome. See Livy.
[422] This judgment was passed in the year of Rome 567.
[423] Book VIII.

In the year of Rome 604, some of these commissions were rendered permanent. [424] All criminal causes were gradually divided into different parts; to which they gave the name of *perpetual questions*. Different prætors were created, to each of whom some of those questions were assigned. They had a power conferred upon them for the term of a year, of trying such criminal causes as bore any relation to those questions, and then they were sent to govern their province.

[424] Cicero, in *Bruto*.

At Carthage the senate of the hundred was composed of judges who enjoyed that dignity for life. [425] But at Rome the prætors were annual; and the judges were not even for so long a term, but were nominated for each cause. We have already shown in the sixth chapter of this book how favorable this regulation was to liberty in particular governments.

[425] This is proved from Livy, book XLIII. 46, who says that Hannibal rendered their magistracy annual.

The judges were chosen from the order of senators, till the time of the Gracchi. Tiberius Gracchus caused a law to pass that they should be taken from the equestrian order; a change so very considerable that the tribune boasted of having cut, by one rogation only, the sinews of the senatorial dignity.

It is necessary to observe that the three powers may be very well distributed in regard to the liberty of the constitution, though not so well in respect to the liberty of the subject. At Rome the people had the greatest share of the legislative, a part of the executive, and part of the judiciary power; by which means they had so great a weight in the government as required some other power to balance it. The senate indeed had part of the executive power, and some share of the legislative; [426] but this was not sufficient to counterbalance the weight of the people. It was necessary that they should partake of the judiciary power: and accordingly they had a share when the judges were chosen from among the senators. But when the Gracchi deprived the senators of the judicial power, [427] the senate were no longer able to withstand the people. To favor, therefore, the liberty of the subject, they struck at that of the constitution; but the former perished with the latter.

[426] The senatus-consultums were in force for the space of a year, though not confirmed
   by the people.—Dionysius Halicarnassus. book IX. p. 595; book XI, p. 735.
[427] In the year 630.

Infinite were the mischiefs that thence arose. The constitution was changed at a time when the fire of civil discord had scarcely left any such thing as a constitution. The knights ceased to be that middle order which united the people to the senate; and the chain of the constitution was broken.

There were even particular reasons against transferring the judiciary power to the equestrian order. The constitution of Rome was founded on this principle, that none should be enlisted as soldiers but such as were men of sufficient property to answer for their conduct to the republic. The knights, as persons of the greatest property, formed the cavalry of the legions. But when their dignity increased, they refused to serve any longer in that capacity, and another kind of cavalry was obliged to be raised: thus Marius enlisted all sorts of people into his army, and soon after the republic was lost. [428]

[428] *Capite censos plerosque.*—Sallust, *de bello Jugurth.*

Besides, the knights were the farmers of the revenue; men whose great rapaciousness increased the public calamities. Instead of giving to such as those the judicial power, they ought to have been constantly under the eye of the judges. This we must say in commendation of the ancient French laws, that they have acted towards the officers of the revenue with as great a diffidence as would be observed between enemies. When the judiciary power at Rome was transferred to the publicans, there was then an end of all virtue, polity, laws, and government.

Of this we find a very ingenious description in some fragments of Diodorus Siculus and Dio. *Mutius Scævola,* says Diodorus, [429] *wanted to revive the ancient manners, and the laudable custom of sober and frugal living. For his predecessors having entered into a contract with the farmers of the revenue, who at that time were possessed of the judiciary power at Rome, had infected the province with all manner of corruption. But Scævola made an example of the publicans, and imprisoned those by whom others had been confined.*

[429] Fragment of this author, book XXXVI, in the collection of Constantine
   Porphyrogenitus, of Virtues and Vices.

Dio informs us [430] that Publius Rutilius, his lieutenant, was equally obnoxious to the equestrian order, and that upon his return they accused him of having received some presents, and condemned him to a fine; upon which he instantly made a cession of his goods. His innocence appeared in this, that he was found to be worth a great deal less than what he was charged with having extorted, and he showed a just title to what he possessed: but he would not live any longer in the same city with such profligate wretches.

[430] Fragment of his history, taken from the Extract of Virtues and Vices.

The Italians, says Diodorus again, [431] bought up whole droves of slaves in Sicily, to till their lands and to take care of their cattle; but refused them a necessary subsistence. These wretches were then forced to go and rob on the highways, armed with lances and clubs, covered with beasts' skins, and followed by large mastiffs. Thus the whole province was laid waste, and the inhabitants could not call anything their own but what was secured by fortresses. There was neither proconsul nor prætor that could or would oppose this disorder, or that presumed to punish these slaves, because they belonged to the knights, who at Rome were possessed of the judiciary power. [432] And yet this was one of the causes of the war of the slaves. But I shall add only one word more. A profession deaf and inexorable, that can have no other view than lucre, that was always asking and never granting, that impoverished the rich and increased even the misery of the poor—such a profession, I say, should never have been entrusted with the judiciary power at Rome.

[431] Fragment of the book XXXIV in the Extract of Virtues and Vices.
[432] "Penes quos Romæ tum judicia erant, atque ex equestri ordine solerent sortito judices eligi in causa Prætorum et Proconsulum, quibus post administratam provinciam dies dicta erat."

19. Of the Government of the Roman Provinces.

Such was the distribution of the three powers in Rome. But they were far from being thus distributed in the provinces. Liberty prevailed in the centre and tyranny in the extreme parts.

While Rome extended her dominions no farther than Italy, the people were governed as confederates, and the laws of each republic were preserved. But when she enlarged her conquests, and the senate had no longer an immediate inspection over the provinces, nor the magistrates residing at Rome were any longer capable of governing the empire, they were obliged to send prætors and proconsuls. Then it was that the harmony of the three powers was lost. The persons appointed to that office were entrusted with a power which comprehended that of all the Roman magistracies; nay, even that of the people. [433] They were despotic magistrates, extremely well adapted to the distance of the places to which they were destined. They exercised the three powers; and were, if I may presume to use the expression, the bashaws of the republic.

[433] They made their edicts upon entering the provinces.

We have elsewhere observed that in a commonwealth the same magistrate ought to be possessed of the executive power, as well civil as military. Hence a conquering republic can hardly communicate her government, and rule the conquered state according to her own constitution. And indeed as the magistrate she sends to govern is invested with the executive power, both civil and military, he must also have the legislative: for who is it that could make laws without him? It is necessary, therefore, that the governor she sends be entrusted with the three powers, as was practiced in the Roman provinces.

It is more easy for a monarchy to communicate its government, because the officers it sends have, some the civil executive, and others the military executive power, which does not necessarily imply a despotic authority.

It was a privilege of the utmost consequence to a Roman citizen to have none but the people for his judge. Were it not for this, he would have been subject in the provinces to the arbitrary power of a proconsul or of a proprætor. The city never felt the tyranny which was exercised only on conquered nations.

Thus, in the Roman world, as at Sparta, the freemen enjoyed the highest degree of liberty, while those who were slaves labored under the extremity of servitude.

While the citizens paid taxes, they were raised with great justice and equality. The regulation of Servius Tullius was observed, who had distributed the people into six classes, according to their difference of property, and fixed the several shares of the public imposts in proportion to that which each person had in the government. Hence they bore with the greatness of the tax because of their proportionable greatness of credit, and consoled themselves for the smallness of their credit because of the smallness of the tax.

There was also another thing worthy of admiration, which is, that as Servius Tullius's division into classes was in some measure the fundamental principle of the constitution, it thence followed that an equal levying of the taxes was so connected with this fundamental principle that the one could not be abolished without the other.

But while the city paid the taxes as she pleased, or paid none at all, [434] the provinces were plundered by the knights, who were the farmers of the public revenue. We have already made mention of their oppressive extortions, with which all history abounds.

[434] After the conquest of Macedonia the Romans paid no taxes.

All Asia, says Mithridates, [435] *expects me as her deliverer; so great is the hatred which the rapaciousness of the proconsuls,* [436] *the confiscations made by the officers of the revenue, and the quirks and cavils of judicial proceedings,* [437] *have excited against the Romans.*

[435] Speech taken from Trogus Pompeius, and related by Justin, book XXXVIII.
[436] See the orations against Verres.
[437] It is well known what sort of a tribunal was that of Varus, which provoked the Germans to revolt.

Hence it was that the strength of the provinces did not increase, but rather weakened, the strength of the republic. Hence it was that the provinces looked upon the loss of the liberty of Rome as the epoch of their own freedom.

20. *The End of this Book.*

I should be glad to inquire into the distribution of the three powers, in all the moderate governments we are acquainted with, in order to calculate the degrees of liberty which each may enjoy. But we must not always exhaust a subject, so as to leave no work at all for the reader. My business is not to make people read, but to make them think.

BOOK XII.

OF THE LAWS THAT FORM POLITICAL LIBERTY, IN RELATION TO THE SUBJECT

1. *Idea of this Book.*

It is not sufficient to have treated of political liberty in relation to the constitution; we must examine it likewise in the relation it bears to the subject.

We have observed that in the former case it arises from a certain distribution of the three powers; but in the latter, we must consider it in another light. It consists in security, or in the opinion people have of their security.

The constitution may happen to be free, and the subject not. The subject may be free, and not the constitution. In those cases, the constitution will be free by right, and not in fact; the subject will be free in fact, and not by right.

It is the disposition only of the laws, and even of the fundamental laws, that constitutes liberty in relation to the constitution. But as it regards the subject: manners, customs, or received examples may give rise to it, and particular civil laws may encourage it, as we shall presently observe.

Further, as in most states liberty is more checked or depressed than their constitution requires, it is proper to treat of the particular laws that in each constitution are apt to assist or check the principle of liberty which each state is capable of receiving.

2. *Of the Liberty of the Subject.*

Philosophic liberty consists in the free exercise of the will; or at least, if we must speak agreeably to all systems, in an opinion that we have the free exercise of our will. Political liberty consists in security, or, at least, in the opinion that we enjoy security.

This security is never more dangerously attacked than in public or private accusations. It is, therefore, on the goodness of criminal laws that the liberty of the subject principally depends.

Criminal laws did not receive their full perfection all at once. Even in places where liberty has been most sought after, it has not been always found. Aristotle [438] informs us that at Cumæ the parents of the accuser might be witnesses. So imperfect was the law under the kings of Rome that Servius Tullius pronounced sentence against the children of Ancus Martius, who were charged with having assassinated the king, his father-in-law. [439] Under the first kings of France, Clotarius made a law [440] that nobody should be condemned without being heard; which shows that a contrary custom had prevailed in some particular case or among some barbarous people. It was Charondas that first established penalties against false witnesses. [441] When the subject has no fence to secure his innocence, he has none for his liberty.

[438] *Politics*, book II.
[439] Tarquinius Priscus. See Dionysius Halicarnassus, book IV.
[440] As early as the year 560.
[441] Aristotle, *Politics*, book II. He gave his laws at Thurium in the 84th Olympiad.

The knowledge already acquired in some countries, or that may be hereafter attained in others, concerning the surest rules to be observed in criminal judgments, is more interesting to mankind than any other thing in the world.

Liberty can be founded on the practice of this knowledge only; and supposing a state to have the best laws imaginable in this respect, a person tried under that state, and condemned to be hanged the next day, would have much more liberty than a pasha enjoys in Turkey.

3. *The same Subject continued.*

Those laws which condemn a man to death on the deposition of a single witness are fatal to liberty. In reason there should be two, because a witness who affirms, and the accused who denies, make an equal balance, and a third must incline the scale.

The Greeks [442] and Romans [443] required one voice more to condemn: but our French laws insist upon two. The Greeks pretend that their custom was established by the gods; [444] but this more justly may be said of ours. [445]

[442] See Aristides, Orat. *in Minervam.*
[443] Dionysius Halicarnassus on the judgment of Coriolanus, book VII.
[444] *Minervæ calculus.*
[445] Voltaire declares that it I England, and not France, that is deserving on this high praise; for it is in the former that the juries must agree in order to condemn a man.— Ed.

4. *That Liberty is favored by the Nature and Proportion of Punishments.*

Liberty is in perfection when criminal laws derive each punishment from the particular nature of the crime. There are then no arbitrary decisions; the punishment does not flow from the capriciousness of the legislator, but from the very nature of the thing; and man uses no violence to man.

There are four sorts of crimes. Those of the first species are prejudicial to religion, the second to morals, the third to the public tranquility, and the fourth to the security of the subject. The punishments inflicted for these crimes ought to proceed from the nature of each of these species.

In the class of crimes that concern religion, I rank only those which attack it directly, such as all simple sacrileges. For as to crimes that disturb the exercise of it, they are of the nature of those which prejudice the tranquility or security of the subject, and ought to be referred to those classes.

In order to derive the punishment of simple sacrileges from the nature of the thing, [446] it should consist in depriving people of the advantages conferred by religion in expelling them out of the temples, in a temporary or perpetual exclusion from the society of the faithful, in shunning their presence, in execrations, comminations, and conjurations.

[446] St. Lewis made such severe laws against those who swore that the pope thought himself obliged to admonish him for it. This prince moderated his zeal, and softened his laws.—See his Ordinances.

In things that prejudice the tranquility or security of the state, secret actions are subject to human jurisdiction. But in those which offend the Deity, where there is no public act, there can be no criminal matter, the whole passes between man and God, who knows the measure and time of His vengeance. Now if magistrates, confounding things, should inquire also into hidden sacrileges, this inquisition would be directed to a kind of action that does not at all require it: the liberty of the subject would be subverted by arming the zeal of timorous as well as of presumptuous consciences against him.

The mischief arises from a notion which some people have entertained of revenging the cause of the Deity. But we must honor the Deity and leave him to avenge his own cause. And, indeed, were we to be directed by such a notion, where would be the end of punishments? If human laws are to avenge the cause of an infinite Being, they will be directed by his infinity, and not by the weakness, ignorance, and caprice of man.

An historian [447] of Provence relates a fact which furnishes us with an excellent description of the consequences that may arise in weak capacities from the notion of avenging the Deity's cause. A Jew was accused of having blasphemed against the Virgin Mary; and upon conviction was condemned to be flayed alive. A strange spectacle was then exhibited: gentlemen masked, with knives in their hands, mounted the scaffold, and drove away the executioner, in order to be the avengers themselves of the honor of the blessed Virgin. I do not here choose to anticipate the reflections of the reader.

[447] Father Bougerel.

The second class consists of those crimes which are prejudicial to morals. Such is the violation of public or private continence, that is, of the police directing the manner in which the pleasure annexed to the conjunction of the sexes is to be enjoyed. The punishment of those crimes ought to be also derived from the nature of the thing; the privation of such advantages as society has attached to the purity of morals, fines, shame, necessity of concealment, public infamy, expulsion from home and society, and, in fine, all such punishments as belong to a corrective jurisdiction, are sufficient to repress the temerity of the two sexes. In effect these things are less founded on malice than on carelessness and self-neglect.

We speak here of none but crimes which relate merely to morals, for as to those that are also prejudicial to the public security, such as rapes, they belong to the fourth species.

The crimes of the third class are those which disturb the public tranquility. The punishments ought therefore to be derived from the nature of the thing, and to be in relation to this tranquility; such as imprisonment, exile, and other like chastisements proper for reclaiming turbulent spirits, and obliging them to conform to the established order.

I confine those crimes that injure the public tranquility to things which imply a bare offence against the police; for as to those which by disturbing the public peace attack at the same time the security of the subject, they ought to be ranked in the fourth class.

The punishments inflicted upon the latter crimes are such as are properly distinguished by that name. They are a kind of retaliation, by which the society refuses security to a member who has actually or intentionally deprived another of his security. These punishments are derived from the nature of the thing, founded on reason, and drawn from the very source of good and evil. A man deserves death when he has violated the security of the subject so far as to deprive, or attempt to deprive, another man of his life. This punishment of death is the remedy, as it were, of a sick society. When there is a breach of security with regard to property, there may be some reasons for inflicting a capital punishment: but it would be much better, and perhaps more natural, that crimes committed against the security of property should be punished with the loss of property; and this ought, indeed, to be the case if men's fortunes were common or equal. But as those who have no property of their own are generally the readiest to attack that of others, it has been found necessary, instead of a pecuniary, to substitute a corporal, punishment.

All that I have here advanced is founded in nature, and extremely favorable to the liberty of the subject.

5. *Of certain Accusations that require particular Moderation and Prudence.*

It is an important *maxim*, that we ought to be very circumspect in the prosecution of witchcraft and heresy. The accusation of these two crimes may be vastly injurious to liberty, and productive of infinite oppression, if the legislator knows not how to set bounds to it. For as it does not directly point at a person's actions, but at his character, it grows dangerous in proportion to the ignorance of the people; and then a man is sure to be always in danger, because the most exceptional conduct, the purest morals, and the constant practice of every duty in life are not a sufficient security against the suspicion of his being guilty of the like crimes.

Under Manuel Comnenus, the Protestator [448] was accused of having conspired against the emperor, and of having employed for that purpose some secrets that render men invisible. It is mentioned in the life of this emperor [449] that Aaron was detected, as he was poring over a book of Solomon's, the reading of which was sufficient to conjure up whole legions of devils. Now by supposing a power in witchcraft to rouse the infernal spirits to arms, people look upon a man whom they call a sorcerer as the person in the world most likely to disturb and subvert society; and of course they are disposed to punish him with the utmost severity.

[448] Nicetas, Life of Manuel Comnenus, book IV.
[449] Ibid.

But their indignation increases when witchcraft is supposed to have the power of subverting religion. The history of Constantinople [450] informs us that in consequence of a revelation made to a bishop of a miracle having ceased because of the magic practices of a certain person, both that person and his son were put to death. On how many surprising things did not this single crime depend? That revelations should not be uncommon, that the bishop should be favored with one, that it was real, that there had been a miracle in the case, that this miracle had ceased, that there was a magic art, that magic could subvert religion, that this particular person was a magician, and, in fine, that he had committed that magic act.

[450] Theophylactus, History of the Emperor Maurice, chap. 11.

The Emperor Theodorus Lascarus attributed his illness to witchcraft. Those who were accused of this crime had no other resource left than to handle a red-hot iron without being hurt. Thus among the Greeks a person ought to have been a sorcerer to be able to clear himself of the imputation of witchcraft. Such was the excess of their stupidity that to the most dubious crime in the world they joined the most dubious proofs of innocence.

Under the reign of Philip the Long, the Jews were expelled from France, being accused of having poisoned the springs with their lepers. So absurd an accusation ought to make us doubt all those that are founded on public hatred.

I have not here asserted that heresy ought not to be punished; I said only that we ought to be extremely circumspect in punishing it.

6. Of the Crime against Nature.

God forbid that I should have the least inclination to diminish the public horror against a crime which religion, morality, and civil government equally condemn. It ought to be proscribed, were it only for its communicating to one sex the weaknesses of the other, and for leading people by a scandalous prostitution of their youth to an ignominious old age. What I shall say concerning it will in no way diminish its infamy, being leveled only against the tyranny that may abuse the very horror we ought to have against the vice.

As a natural circumstance of this crime is secrecy, there are frequent instances of its having been punished by legislators upon the deposition of a child. This was opening a very wide door to calumny. *Justinian*, says Procopius, [451] *published a law against this crime; he ordered an inquiry to be made not only against those who were guilty of it, after the enacting of that law, but even before. The deposition of a single witness, sometimes of a child, sometimes of a slave, was sufficient, especially against such as were rich, and against those of the green faction.*

[451] Secret History.

It is very odd that these three crimes, witchcraft, heresy, and that against nature, of which the first might easily be proved not to exist; the second to be susceptible of an infinite number of distinctions, interpretations, and limitations; the third to be often obscure and uncertain—it is very odd, I say, that these three crimes should amongst us be punished with fire.

I may venture to affirm that the crime against nature will never make any great progress in society, unless people are prompted to it by some particular custom, as among the Greeks, where the youths of that country performed all their exercises naked; as amongst us, where domestic education is disused; as amongst the Asiatics, where particular persons have a great number of women whom they despise, while others can have none at all. Let there be no customs preparatory to this crime; let it, like every other violation of morals, be severely proscribed by the civil magistrate; and nature will soon defend or resume her rights. Nature, that fond, that indulgent parent, has strewn her pleasures with a bounteous hand, and while she fills us with delights, she prepares us, by means of our issue, in whom we see ourselves, as it were, reproduced—she prepares us, I say, for future satisfactions of a more exquisite kind than those very delights.

7. Of the Crime of High Treason.

It is determined by the laws of China that whosoever shows any disrespect to the emperor is to be punished with death. As they do not mention in what this disrespect consists, everything may furnish a pretext to take away a man's life, and to exterminate any family whatsoever.

Two persons of that country who were employed to write the court gazette, having inserted some circumstances relating to a certain fact that was not true, it was pretended that to tell a lie in the court gazette was a disrespect shown to the court, in consequence of which they were put to death. [452] A prince of the blood having inadvertently made some mark on a memorial signed with the red pencil by the emperor, it was determined that he had behaved disrespectfully to the sovereign; which occasioned one of the most terrible persecutions against that family that ever was recorded in history. [453]

[452] Father Du Halde, tom. i. p. 43.
[453] Father Parennin in the Edifying Letters.

If the crime of high treason be indeterminate, this alone is sufficient to make the government degenerate into arbitrary power. I shall descant more largely on this subject when I come to treat [454] of the composition of laws.

[454] Book XXIX.

8. Of the Misapplication of the Terms Sacrilege and High Treason.

It is likewise a shocking abuse to give the appellation of high treason to an action that does not deserve it. By an imperial law [455] it was decreed that those who called in question the prince's judgment, or doubted the merit of such as he had chosen for a public office, should be prosecuted as guilty of sacrilege. [456] Surely it was the cabinet council and the prince's favorites who invented that crime. By another law, it was determined that whosoever made any attempt to injure the ministers and officers belonging to the sovereign should be deemed guilty of high treason, as if he had attempted to injure the sovereign himself. [457] This law is owing to two princes [458] remarkable for their weakness—princes who were led by their ministers as flocks by shepherds; princes who were slaves in the palace, children in the council, strangers to the army; princes, in fine, who preserved their authority only by giving it away every day. Some of those favorites conspired against their sovereigns. Nay, they did more, they conspired against the empire—they called in barbarous nations; and when the emperors wanted to stop their progress the state was so enfeebled as to be under a necessity of infringing the law, and of exposing itself to the crime of high treason in order to punish those favorites.

[455] Gratian, Valentinian, and Theodosius. This is the second in the *Code de Crimin. Sacril.*

[456] *Sacrilegii instar est dubitare an is dignus sit quem elegerit imperator.—Code de Crimin. Sacril.* This law has served as a model to that of Roger in the constitution of Naples, tit. 4.
[457] The 5th law, *ad leg. Jul. Majest.*
[458] Arcadius and Honorius.

And yet this is the very law which the judge of Monsieur de Cinq-Mars built upon [459] when endeavoring to prove that the latter was guilty of the crime of high treason for attempting to remove Cardinal Richelieu from the ministry. He says: *Crimes that aim at the persons of ministers are deemed by the imperial constitutions of equal consequence with those which are leveled against the emperor's own person. A minister discharges his duty to his prince and to his country: to attempt, therefore, to remove him, is endeavoring to deprive the former one of his arms,* [460] *and the latter of part of its power.* It is impossible for the meanest tools of power to express themselves in more servile language.

[459] Memoirs of Montresor. tom. i.
[460] Nam ipsi pars corporis nostri sunt—The same law of the Cod., *ad leg. Jul. Majest.*

By another law of Valentinian, Theodosius, and Arcadius, [461] false coiners are declared guilty of high treason. But is not this confounding the ideas of things? Is not the very horror of high treason diminished by giving that name to another crime?

[461] It is the 9th of the Code Theod. *de falsa moneta.*

9. *The same Subject continued.*

Paulinus having written to the Emperor Alexander that "he was preparing to prosecute for high treason a judge who had decided contrary to his edict," the emperor answered, "that under his reign there was no such thing as indirect high treason." [462]

[462] *Etiam ex aliis causis majestatis crimina cessant meo sæculo*—Leg. 1. *eod. ad leg. Jul. Majest.*

Faustinian wrote to the same emperor that as he had sworn by the prince's life never to pardon his slave, he found himself thereby obliged to perpetuate his wrath, lest he should incur the guilt of *læsa majestas.* Upon which the emperor made answer, *Your fears are groundless,* [463] *and you are a stranger to my principles.*

[463] Alienam sectæ meæ solicitudinem concepisti.—Leg. 2, Cod., iii, tit. 4, ad leg. Jul. Majest.

It was determined by a senatus-consultum [464] that whosoever melted down any of the emperor's statues which happened to be rejected should not be deemed guilty of high treason. The Emperors Severus and Antoninus wrote to Pontius [465] that those who sold unconsecrated statues of the emperor should not be charged with high treason. The same princes wrote to Julius Cassianus that if a person in flinging a stone should by chance strike one of the emperor's statues he should not be liable to a prosecution for high treason. [466] The Julian law requires this sort of limitations; for in virtue of this law the crime of high treason was charged not only upon those who melted down the emperor's statues, but likewise on those who committed any such like action, [467] which made it an arbitrary crime. When a number of crimes of *læsa majestas* had been established, they were obliged to distinguish the several sorts. Hence Ulpian, the civilian, after saying that the accusation of *læsa majestas* did not die with the criminal, adds that this does not relate to all the treasonable acts established by the Julian law, [468] but only to that which implies an attempt against the empire, or against the emperor's life.

[464] See the 4th law in ff. *ad leg., Jul. Majest.*
[465] See the 5th law ibid.
[466] Ibid.
[467] *Aliudve quid simile admiserint*—Leg. 6, ff. *ad leg. Jul. Majest.*
[468] In the last law, ff. *ad leg. Jul. de Adulteris.*

10. *The same Subject continued.*

There was a law passed in England under Henry VIII, by which whoever predicted the king's death was declared guilty of high treason. This law was extremely vague; the terror of despotic power is so great that it recoils upon those who exercise it. In this king's last illness, the physicians would not venture to say he was in danger; and surely they acted very right. [469]

[469] See Burnet, History of the Reformation.

11. *Of Thoughts.*

Marsyas dreamed that he had cut Dionysius's throat. [470] Dionysius put him to death, pretending that he would never have dreamed of such a thing by night if he had not thought of it by day. This was a most tyrannical action: for though it had been the subject of his thoughts, yet he had made no attempt [471] towards it. The laws do not take upon them to punish any other than overt acts.

[470] Plutarch's Life of Dionysius.
[471] The thought must be joined with some sort of action.

12. *Of indiscreet Speeches.*

Nothing renders the crime of high treason more arbitrary than declaring people guilty of it for indiscreet speeches. Speech is so subject to interpretation; there is so great a difference between indiscretion and malice; and frequently so little is there of the latter in the freedom of expression, that the law can hardly subject people to a capital punishment for words unless it expressly declares what words they are. [472]

[472] *Si non tale sit delictum in quod vel scriptura legis descendit vel ad exemplum legis vindicandum est*, says Modestinus in the 7th law, in ff. *ad leg. Jul. Majest.*

Words do not constitute an overt act; they remain only in idea. When considered by themselves, they have generally no determinate signification; for this depends on the tone in which they are uttered. It often happens that in repeating the same words they have not the same meaning; this depends on their connection with other things, and sometimes more is signified by silence than by any expression whatever. Since there can be nothing so equivocal and ambiguous as all this, how is it possible to convert it into a crime of high treason? Wherever this law is established, there is an end not only of liberty, but even of its very shadow.

In the manifesto of the late Czarina against the family of the D'Olgoruckys, [473] one of these princes is condemned to death for having uttered some indecent words concerning her person: another, for having maliciously interpreted her imperial laws, and for having offended her sacred person by disrespectful expressions.

[473] In 1740.

Not that I pretend to diminish the just indignation of the public against those who presume to stain the glory of their sovereign; what I mean is that, if despotic princes are willing to moderate their power, a milder chastisement would be more proper on those occasions than the charge of high treason—a thing always terrible even to innocence itself. [474]

[474] *Nec lubricum linguæ ad pœnam facile trahendum est.*—Modestinus, in the 7th law in ff. *ad leg. Jul. Majest.*

Overt acts do not happen every day; they are exposed to the eye of the public; and a false charge with regard to matters of fact may be easily detected. Words carried into action assume the nature of that action. Thus a man who goes into a public market-place to incite the subject to revolt incurs the guilt of high treason, because the words are joined to the action, and partake of its nature. It is not the words that are punished, but an action in which words are employed. They do not become criminal, but when they are annexed to a criminal action: everything is confounded if words are construed into a capital crime, instead of considering them only as a mark of that crime.

The Emperors Theodosius, Arcadius, and Honorius wrote thus to Rufinus, who was *præfectus prætorio*: *Though a man should happen to speak amiss of our person or government, we do not intend to punish him:* [475] *if he has spoken through levity, we must despise him; if through folly, we must pity him; and if he wrongs us, we must forgive him. Therefore, leaving things as they are, you are to inform us accordingly, that we may be able to judge of words by persons, and that we may duly consider whether we ought to punish or overlook them.*

[475] Si id ex levitate processerit, contemnendum est; si ex insania, miseratione dignissimum; si ab injuria, remittendum.—Leg. unica. Cod. *si quis Imperat. maled.*

13. *Of Writings.*

In writings there is something more permanent than in words, but when they are in no way preparative to high treason they cannot amount to that charge.

And yet Augustus and Tiberius subjected satirical writers to the same punishment as for having violated the law of majesty. Augustus, [476] because of some libels that had been written against persons of the first quality; Tiberius, because of those which he suspected to have been written against himself. Nothing was more fatal to Roman liberty. Cremutius Cordus was accused of having called Cassius in his annals the last of the Romans. [477]

[476] Tacitus, *Annal.* book I. This continued under the following reigns. See the first law in the Cod. *de famosis libellis.*
[477] Tacitus, *Annal,* book IV.

Satirical writings are hardly known in despotic governments, where dejection of mind on the one hand, and ignorance on the other, afford neither abilities nor will to write. In democracies they are not hindered, for the very same reason which causes them to be prohibited in monarchies; being generally levelled against men of power and authority, they flatter the malignancy of the people, who are the governing party. In monarchies they are forbidden, but rather as a subject of civil animadversion than as a capital crime. They may amuse the general malevolence, please the malcontents, diminish the envy against public employments, give the people patience to suffer, and make them laugh at their sufferings.

But no government is so averse to satirical writings as the aristocratic. There the magistrates are petty sovereigns, but not great enough to despise affronts. If in a monarchy a satirical stroke is designed against the prince, he is placed on such an eminence that it does not reach him; but an aristocratic lord is pierced to the very heart. Hence the decemvirs, who formed an aristocracy, punished satirical writings with death. [478]

[478] The law of the Twelve Tables.

14. *Breach of Modesty in punishing Crimes.*

There are rules of modesty observed by almost every nation in the world; now it would be very absurd to infringe these rules in the punishment of crimes, the principal view of which ought always to be the establishment of order.

Was it the intent of those Oriental nations who exposed women to elephants trained up for an abominable kind of punishment—was it, I say, their intent to establish one law by the breach of another?

By an ancient custom of the Romans it was not permitted to put girls to death till they were ripe for marriage. Tiberius found an expedient of having them debauched by the executioner before they were brought to the place of punishment: [479] that bloody and subtle tyrant destroyed the morals of the people to preserve their customs.

[479] Suetonius, in *Tiberio.*

When the magistrates of Japan caused women to be exposed naked in the market-places, and obliged them to go upon all fours like beasts, modesty was shocked: [480] but when they wanted to compel a mother—when they wanted to force a son—I cannot proceed; even Nature herself is struck with horror.

[480] Collection of Voyages that contributed to the establishment of the East India Company, tom. v, part II.

15. *Of the Enfranchisement of Slaves in order to accuse their Master.*

Augustus made a law that the slaves of those who conspired against his person should be sold to the public, that they might depose against their master. [481] Nothing ought to be neglected which may contribute to the discovery of a heinous crime; it is natural, therefore, that in a government where there are slaves they should be allowed to inform; but they ought not to be admitted as witnesses.

[481] Dio, in Xiphilinus, lv. 5. Tacitus attributes this law, not to Augustus, but to Tiberius.—P.

Vindex discovered the conspiracy that had been formed in favor of Tarquin; but he was not admitted a witness against the children of Brutus. It was right to give liberty to a person who had rendered so great a service to his country; but it was not given him with a view of enabling him to render this service.

Hence the Emperor Tacitus ordained that slaves should not be admitted as witnesses against their masters, even in the case of high treason: [482] a law which was not inserted in Justinian's compilation.

[482] Flavius Vopiscus in his Life.

16. *Of Calumny with regard to the Crime of High Treason.*

To do justice to the Cæsars, they were not the first devisers of the horrid laws which they enacted. It was Sylla [483] that taught them that calumniators ought not to be punished; but the abuse was soon carried to such excess as to reward them. [484]

[483] Sylla made a law of majesty, which is mentioned in Cicero's Orations, *pro Cluentio*, art. 3; *in Pisonem*, art. 21; 2nd against Verres, art. 5. Familiar Epistles, book III, letter 11. Cæsar and Augustus inserted them in the Julian Laws; others made additions to them.

[484] Et quò quis distinctior accusator, eò magis honores assequebatur, ac veluti sacrosanctus erat.—Tacit.

17. *Of the revealing of Conspiracies.*

If thy brother, the son of thy mother, or thy son, or thy daughter, or the wife of thy bosom, or thy friend, which is as thine own soul, entice thee secretly, saying, Let us go and serve other gods, *thou shalt surely kill him, thou shalt stone him.* [485] This law of Deuteronomy cannot be a civil law among most of the nations known to us, because it would pave the way for all manner of wickedness.

[485] Deut., xiii. 6.

No less severe is the law of several countries which commands the subjects, on pain of death, to disclose conspiracies in which they are not even so much as concerned. When such a law is established in a monarchical government, it is very proper it should be under some restrictions.

It ought not to be applied in its full severity save to the strongest cases of high treason. In those countries it is of the utmost importance not to confound the different degrees of this crime. In Japan, where the laws subvert every idea of human reason, the crime of concealment is applied even to the most ordinary cases.

A certain relation [486] makes mention of two young ladies who were shut up for life in a box thick set with pointed nails, one for having had a love intrigue, and the other for not disclosing it.

[486] Collection of Voyages that contributed to the establishment of the East India Company, book V, part II, p. 423.

18. *How dangerous it is in Republics to be too severe in punishing the Crime of High Treason.*

As soon as a republic has compassed the destruction of those who wanted to subvert it, there should be an end of terrors, punishments, and even of rewards.

Great punishments, and consequently great changes, cannot take place without investing some citizens with an exorbitant power. It is, therefore, more advisable in this case to exceed in lenity than in severity; to banish but few, rather than many; and to leave them their estates, instead of making a vast number of confiscations. Under pretence of avenging the republic's cause, the avengers would establish tyranny. The business is not to destroy the rebel, but the rebellion. They ought to return as quickly as possible into the usual track of government, in which everyone is protected by the laws, and no one injured.

The Greeks set no bounds to the vengeance they took upon tyrants, or of those they suspected of tyranny; they put their children to death, [487] nay, sometimes five of their nearest relatives; [488] and they proscribed an infinite number of families. By such means their republics suffered the most violent shocks: exiles, or the return of the exiled, were always epochs that indicated a change of the constitution.

[487] Dionysius Halicarnassus, Roman Antiquities, book VIII.
[488] *Tyranno occiso quinque ejus proximos cognatione magistratus necato.*—Cicero *De Invent.* lib. II.

The Romans had more sense. When Cassius was put to death for having aimed at tyranny, the question was proposed whether his children should undergo the same fate: but they were preserved. *They*, says Dionysius Halicarnassus, [489] *who wanted to change this law at the end of the Marsian and civil wars, and to exclude from public offices the children of those who had been proscribed by Sylla, are very much to blame.*

[489] Book VIII, p. 547.

We find in the wars of Marius and Sylla to what excess the Romans had gradually carried their barbarity. Such scenes of cruelty it was hoped would never be revived. But under the triumvirs they committed greater acts of oppression, though with some appearance of lenity; and it is provoking to see what sophisms they made use of to cover their inhumanity. Appian has given us [490] the formula of the proscriptions. One would imagine they had no other aim than the good of the republic, with such calmness do they express themselves; such advantages do they point out to the state; such expediency do they show in the means they adopt; such security do they promise to the opulent; such tranquility to the poor; so apprehensive do they seem of endangering the lives of the citizens; so desirous of appeasing the soldiers; such felicity, in fine, do they presage to the commonwealth. [491]

[490] Of the Civil Wars, book IV.
[491] "Quod felix faustumque sit."

Rome was drenched in blood when Lepidus triumphed over Spain: yet, by an unparalleled absurdity, he ordered public rejoicings in that city, upon pain of proscription. [492]

[492] *Sacris et epulis dent hunc diem: qui secus faxit, inter proscriptos esto.*

19. *In what Manner the Use of Liberty is suspended in a Republic.*

In countries where liberty is most esteemed, there are laws by which a single person is deprived of it, in order to preserve it for the whole community. Such are in England what they call Bills of Attainder. [493] These are in relation to those Athenian laws by which a private person was condemned, [494] provided they were made by the unanimous suffrage of six thousand citizens. They are in relation also to those laws which were made at Rome against private citizens, and were called privileges. [495] These were never passed except in the great meetings of the people. But in what manner soever they were enacted, Cicero was for having them abolished, because the force of a law consists in its being made for the whole community. [496] I must own, notwithstanding, that the practice of the freest nation that ever existed induces me to think that there are cases in which a veil should be drawn for a while over liberty, as it was customary to cover the statues of the gods.

[493] It is not sufficient in the courts of justice of that kingdom that the evidence be of such a nature as to satisfy the judges; there must be a legal proof; and the law requires the deposition of two witnesses against the accused. No other proof will do.

Now, if a person who is presumed guilty of high treason should contrive to secrete the witnesses, so as to render it impossible for him to be legally condemned, the government then may bring a bill of attainder against him; that is, they may enact a particular law for that single fact. They proceed then in the same manner as in all other bills brought into parliament; it must pass the two houses, and have the king's consent, otherwise it is not a bill: that is, a sentence of the legislature. The person accused may plead against the hill by counsel, and the members of the house may speak in defense of the bill.

[494] "Legem de singulari aliquo rogato, nisi sex millibus ita visum."—*Ex Andocide de Mysteriis*. This is what they call Ostracism.

[495] De privis hominibus latæ.—*Cicero, de Leg*. lib. III.

[496] Scitum est jussum in omnes.—*Ibid*.

20. *Of Laws favorable to the Liberty of the Subject in a Republic*.

In popular governments it often happens that accusations are carried on in public, and every man is allowed to accuse whomsoever he pleases. This rendered it necessary to establish proper laws, in order to protect the innocence of the subject. At Athens, if an accuser had not the fifth part of the votes on his side, he was obliged to pay a fine of a thousand drachms. Æschines, who accused Ctesiphon, was condemned to pay this fine. [497] At Rome, a false accuser was branded with infamy [498] by marking the letter K [499] on his forehead. Guards were also appointed to watch the accuser, in order to prevent his corrupting either the judges or the witnesses. [500]

[497] See Philostratus, book I.: Lives of the Sophists: Æschines. See likewise Plutarch and Phocius.

[498] By the Remmian law.

[499] This was the initial of an old Latin word which today is written *Calumnia*.—P.

[500] Plutarch, in a treatise entitled, *How a Person May Reap Advantage from his Enemies*.

I have already taken notice of that Athenian and Roman law by which the party accused was allowed to withdraw before judgment was pronounced.

21. *Of the Cruelty of Laws in respect to Debtors in a Republic*.

Great is the superiority which one fellow-subject has already over another, by lending him money, which the latter borrows in order to spend, and, of course, has no longer in his possession. What must be the consequence if the laws of a republic make a further addition to this servitude and subjection?

At Athens and Rome [501] it was at first permitted to sell such debtors as were insolvent. Solon redressed this abuse at Athens [502] by ordaining that no man's body should answer for his civil debts. But the decemvirs [503] did not reform the same custom at Rome; and though they had Solon's regulation before their eyes, yet they did not choose to follow it. This is not the only passage of the law of the Twelve Tables in which the decemvirs show their design of checking the spirit of democracy.

[501] "A great many sold their children to pay their debts."—Plutarch, Life of Solon.

[502] Plutarch, Life of Solon.

[503] It appears from history that this custom was established among the Romans before the Law of the Twelve Tables.—Livy, dec. 1, book II.

Often did those cruel laws against debtors throw the Roman republic into danger. A man covered with wounds made his escape from his creditor's house and appeared in the forum. [504] The people were moved with this spectacle, and other citizens whom their creditors durst no longer confine broke loose from their dungeons. They had promises made them, which were all broken. The people upon this, having withdrawn to the Sacred Mount, obtained, not an abrogation of those laws, but a magistrate to defend them. Thus they quitted a state of anarchy, but were soon in danger of falling into tyranny. Manlius, to render himself popular, was going to set those citizens at liberty who by their inhuman creditors [505] had been reduced to slavery. Manlius's designs were prevented, but without remedying the evil. Particular laws facilitated to debtors the means of paying; [506] and in the year of Rome 428 the consuls proposed a law [507] which deprived creditors of the power of confining their debtors in their own houses. [508] A usurer, by name Papirius, attempted to corrupt the chastity of a young man named Publius, whom he kept in irons. Sextus's crime gave to Rome its political liberty; that of Papirius gave it also the civil.

[504] Dionysius Halicarnassus. Roman Antiquities, book VI.

[505] Plutarch, Life of Furius Camillas.

[506] See what follows in the 24th chapter of the book of laws as relative to the use of money.

[507] One hundred and twenty years after the law of the Twelve Tables: *Eo anno plebi Romanœ, velut aliud initium libertatis factum est, quod necti desierunt.*—Livy, viii. 38.

[508] *Bona debitoris, non corpus obnoxium esset.*—Ibid.

Such was the fate of this city, that new crimes confirmed the liberty which those of a more ancient date had procured it. Appius's attempt upon Virginia flung the people again into that horror against tyrants with which the misfortune of Lucretia had first inspired them. Thirty-seven years after [509] the crime of the infamous Papirius, an action of the like criminal nature [510] was the cause of the people's retiring to the Janiculum, [511] and of giving new vigor to the law made for the safety of debtors.

[509] The year of Rome 465.

[510] That of Plautius who made an attempt upon the body of Veturius.—Valerius Maximus, book VI, art. 9. These two events ought not to be confounded; they are neither the same persons nor the same times.

[511] See a fragment of Dionysius Halicarnassus in the extract of Virtues and Vices; Livy's Epitome, book II., and Freinshemius, book II.

Since that time creditors were oftener prosecuted by debtors for having violated the laws against usury than the latter were sued for refusing to pay them.

22. Of Things that strike at Liberty in Monarchies.

Liberty often has been weakened in monarchies by a thing of the least use in the world to the prince: this is the naming of commissioners to try a private person.

The prince himself derives so very little advantage from those commissioners that it is not worthwhile to change for their sake the common course of things. He is morally sure that he has more of the spirit of probity and justice than his commissioners, who think themselves sufficiently justified by his nomination and orders, by a vague interest of state, and even by their very apprehensions.

Upon the arraigning of a peer under Henry VIII it was customary to try him by a committee of the House of Lords: by which means he put to death as many peers as he pleased.

23. Of Spies in Monarchies.

Should I be asked whether there is any necessity for spies in monarchies, my answer would be that the usual practice of good princes is not to employ them. When a man obeys the laws, he has discharged his duty to his prince. He ought at least to have his own house for an asylum, and the rest of his conduct should be exempt from inquiry. The trade of a spy might perhaps be tolerable, were it practiced by honest men; but the necessary infamy of the person is sufficient to make us judge of the infamy of the thing. A prince ought to act towards his subjects with candor, frankness, and confidence. He that has so much disquiet, suspicion, and fear is an actor embarrassed in playing his part. When he finds that the laws are generally observed and respected, he may judge himself safe. The behavior of the public answers for that of every individual. Let him not be afraid: he cannot imagine how natural it is for his people to love him. And how should they do otherwise than love him, since he is the source of almost all bounties and favors; punishments being generally charged to the account of the laws? He never shows himself to his people but with a serene countenance; they have even a share of his glory, and they are protected by his power. A proof of his being beloved is that his subjects have confidence in him: what the minister refuses, they imagine the prince would have granted. Even under public calamities they do not accuse his person; they are apt to complain of his being misinformed, or beset by corrupt men. *Did the prince but know*, say the people; these words are a kind of invocation, and a proof of the confidence they have in his person.

24. Of Anonymous Letters.

The Tartars are obliged to put their names to their arrows, that the arm may be known which shoots them. When Philip of Macedon was wounded at the siege of a certain town, these words were found on the javelin, *Aster has given this mortal wound to Philip*. [512] If they who accuse a person did it merely to serve the public, they would not carry their complaint to the prince, who may be easily prejudiced, but to the magistrates, who have rules that are formidable only to calumniators. But if they are unwilling to leave the laws open between them and the accused, it is a presumption they have reason to be afraid of them; and the least punishment they ought to suffer is not to be credited. No notice, therefore, should ever be taken of those letters, except in cases that admit not of the delays of the ordinary course of justice, and in which the prince's welfare is concerned. Then it may be imagined that the accuser has made an effort, which has untied his tongue. But in other cases one ought to say, with the Emperor Constantius: *We cannot suspect a person who has wanted an accuser, whilst he did not want an enemy.* [513]

[512] Plutarch's Morals, Comparison of some Roman and Greek Histories, tom. ii, p. 487.
[513] Leg. 6, Cod. Theod. *de famosis libellis.*

25. Of the Manner of governing in Monarchies.

The royal authority is a spring that ought to move with the greatest freedom and ease. The Chinese boast of one of their emperors who governed, they say, like the heavens, that is, by his example.

There are some cases in which a sovereign ought to exert the full extent of his power; and others in which he should reduce it within narrower limits. The sublimity of administration consists in knowing the proper degree of power which should be exerted on different occasions.

The whole felicity of monarchies consists in the opinion which the subjects entertain of the lenity of the government. A weak minister is ever ready to remind us of our slavery. But granting, even, that we are slaves, he should endeavor to conceal our misery from us. All he can say or write is that the prince is uneasy, that he is surprised, and that he will redress all grievances. There is a certain ease in commanding; the prince ought only to encourage, and let the laws menace. [514]

[514] "Nerva," says Tacitus, "increased the ease of government." It is worthy of note that the best editions of Tacitus have *felicitatem imperii,* and not *facilitatem imperii.—* Ed.

26. That in a Monarchy the Prince ought to be of easy Access.

The utility of this maxim will appear from the inconvenience attending the contrary practice. *The Czar Peter 1,* says the Sieur Perry, [515] *has published a new edict, by which he forbids any of his subjects to offer him a petition till after having presented it to two of his officers. In case of refusal of justice they may present him a third, but upon pain of death if they are in the wrong. After this no one ever presumed to offer a petition to the Czar.*

[515] State of Russia, p. 173, Paris, 1717.

27. Of the Manners of a Monarch.

The manners of a prince contribute as much as the laws themselves to liberty; like these he may transform men into brutes, and brutes into men. If he prefers free and generous spirits, he will have subjects; if he likes base, dastardly souls, he will have slaves. Would he know the great art of ruling, let him call honor and virtue to attend his person; and let him encourage personal merit. He may even sometimes cast an eye on talents and abilities. Let him not be afraid of those rivals who are called men of merit; he is their equal when once he loves them. Let him gain the hearts of his people, without subduing their spirits. Let him render himself popular; he ought to be pleased with the affections of the lowest of his subjects, for they too are men. The common people require so very little condescension, that it is fit they should be humored; the infinite distance between the sovereign and them will surely prevent them from giving him any uneasiness. Let him be exorable to supplication, and resolute against demands; let him be sensible, in fine, that his people have his refusals, while his courtiers enjoy his favors.

28. *Of the Regard which Monarchs owe to their Subjects.*

Princes ought to be extremely circumspect with regard to raillery. It pleases with moderation, because it is an introduction to familiarity; but a satirical raillery is less excusable in them than in the meanest of their subjects, for it is they alone that give a mortal wound.

Much less should they offer a public affront to any of their subjects; kings were instituted to pardon and to punish, but never to insult.

When they affront their subjects, their treatment is more cruel than that of the Turk or the Muscovite. The insults of these are a humiliation, not a disgrace; but both must follow from the insolent behavior of monarchs.

Such is the prejudice of the eastern nations that they look upon an affront from the prince as the effect of paternal goodness; and such, on the contrary, is our way of thinking that besides the cruel vexation of being affronted, we despair of ever being able to wipe off the disgrace.

Princes ought to be overjoyed to have subjects to whom honor is dearer than life, an incitement to fidelity as well as to courage.

They should remember the misfortunes that have happened to sovereigns for insulting their subjects: the revenge of Chærea, of the eunuch Narses, of Count Julian, and, in fine, of the Duchess of Montpensier, who, being enraged against Henry III for having published some of her private failings, tormented him during her whole life.

29. *Of the civil Laws proper for mixing some portion of Liberty in a despotic Government.*

Though despotic governments are of their own nature everywhere the same, yet from circumstances—from a religious opinion, from prejudice, from received examples, from a particular turn of mind, from manners or morals—it is possible they may admit of a considerable difference.

It is useful that some particular notions should be established in those governments. Thus in China the prince is considered as the father of his people; and at the commencement of the empire of the Arabs, the prince was their preacher. [516]

[516] The Caliphs.

It is proper there should be some sacred book to serve for a rule, as the Koran among the Arabs, the books of Zoroaster among the Persians, the Veda among the Indians, and the classic books among the Chinese. The religious code supplies the civil and fixes the extent of arbitrary sway.

It is not at all amiss that in dubious cases the judges should consult the ministers of religion. [517] Thus, in Turkey, the Cadis consult the Mollahs. [518] But if it is a capital crime, it may be proper for the particular judge, if such there be, to take the governor's advice, to the end that the civil and ecclesiastical power may be tempered also by the political authority.

[517] History of the Tartars, part III, p. 277, in the remarks.
[518] It is plain here that Montesquieu confounds the Mollahs with the Mufti.—P.

30. *The same Subject continued.*

Nothing but the very excess and rage of despotic power ordained that the father's disgrace should drag after it that of his wife and children. They are wretched enough already without being criminals: besides, the prince ought to leave suppliants or mediators between himself and the accused, to assuage his wrath or to inform his justice.

It is an excellent custom of the Maldivians [519] that when a lord is disgraced he goes every day to pay his court to the king till he is taken again into favor: his presence disarms the prince's indignation.

[519] See Francis Pirard.

In some despotic governments [520] they have a notion that it is trespassing against the respect due to their prince to speak to him in favor of a person in disgrace. These princes seem to use all their endeavors to deprive themselves of the virtue of clemency.

[520] As at present in Persia, according to Sir John Chardin, this custom is very ancient. "They put Cavades," says Procopius, "into the castle of oblivion; there is a law which forbids any one to speak of those who are shut up, or even to mention their name."

Arcadius and Honorius, by a law [521] on which we have already descanted, [522] positively declare that they will show no favor to those who shall presume to petition them in behalf of the guilty. [523] This was a very bad law indeed, since it is bad even under a despotic government.

[521] The fifth law in the Cod. *ad leg. Jul. Majest.*
[522] In the 8th chapter of this book.
[523] Frederick copied this law in the Constitutions of Naples, book I.

The custom of Persia, which permits every man that pleases to leave the kingdom, is excellent; and though the contrary practice derives its origin from despotic power, which has ever considered the subjects as slaves [524] and those who quit the country as fugitives, yet the Persian practice is useful even to a despotic government, because the apprehension of people's withdrawing for debt restrains or moderates the oppressions of pashas and extortioners.

[524] In monarchies there is generally a law which forbids those who are invested with public employments to go out of the kingdom without the prince's leave. This law ought to be established also in republics. But in those that have particular institutions

the prohibition ought to be general, in order to prevent the introduction of foreign manners.

BOOK XIII.

OF THE RELATION WHICH THE LEVYING OF TAXES AND THE GREATNESS OF THE PUBLIC REVENUES BEAR TO LIBERTY

1. *Of the Public Revenues.*

The *public revenues* are a portion that each subject gives of his property, in order to secure or enjoy the remainder.

To fix these revenues in a proper manner, regard should be had both to the necessities of the state and to those of the subject. The real wants of the people ought never to give way to the imaginary wants of the state.

Imaginary wants are those which flow from the passions and the weakness of the governors, from the vain conceit of some extraordinary project, from the inordinate desire of glory, and from a certain impotence of mind incapable of withstanding the impulse of fancy. Often have ministers of a restless disposition imagined that the wants of their own mean and ignoble souls were those of the state.

Nothing requires more wisdom and prudence than the regulation of that portion of which the subject is deprived, and that which he is suffered to retain.

The public revenues should not be measured by the people's abilities to give, but by what they ought to give; and if they are measured by their abilities to give, it should be considered what they are able to give for a constancy.

2. *That it is bad Reasoning to say that the Greatness of Taxes is good in its own Nature.*

There have been instances in particular monarchies of petty states exempt from taxes that have been as miserable as the circumjacent places which groaned under the weight of exactions. The chief reason of this is, that the petty state can hardly have any such thing as industry, arts, or manufactures, because of its being subject to a thousand restraints from the great state by which it is environed. The great state is blessed with industry, manufactures, and arts, and establishes laws by which those several advantages are procured. The petty state becomes, therefore, necessarily poor, let it pay never so few taxes.

And yet some have concluded from the poverty of those petty states that in order to render the people industrious they should be loaded with taxes. But it would be a juster inference, that they ought to pay no taxes at all. None live here but wretches who retire from the neighboring parts to avoid working—wretches who, disheartened by labor, make their whole felicity consist in idleness.

The effect of wealth in a country is to inspire every heart with ambition: that of poverty is to give birth to despair. The former is excited by labor, the latter is soothed by indolence.

Nature is just to all mankind, and repays them for their industry: she renders them industrious by annexing rewards in proportion to their labor. But if an arbitrary prince should attempt to deprive the people of nature's bounty, they would fall into a disrelish of industry; and then indolence and inaction must be their only happiness.

3. Of Taxes in Countries where Part of the People are Villains or Bondmen.

The state of villainage is sometimes established after a conquest. In that case, the bondman or villain that tills the land ought to have a kind of partnership with his master. Nothing but a communication of loss or profit can reconcile those who are doomed to labor to such as are blessed with a state of affluence.

4. Of a Republic in the like Case.

When a republic has reduced a nation to the drudgery of cultivating her lands, she ought never to suffer the free subject to have the power of increasing the tribute of the bondman. This was not permitted at Sparta. Those brave people thought the Helotes [525] would be more industrious in cultivating their lands, and knowing that their servitude was not to increase; they imagined, likewise, that the masters would be better citizens, when they desired no more than what they were accustomed to enjoy.

[525] Plutarch.

5. Of a Monarchy in the like Case.

When the nobles of a monarchical state cause the lands to be cultivated for their own use by a conquered people, they ought never to have the power of increasing the service or tribute. [526] Besides, it is right the prince should be satisfied with his own demesne and the military service. But if he wants to raise taxes on the vassals of his nobility, the lords of the several districts ought to be answerable for the tax, [527] and be obliged to pay it for the vassals, by whom they may be afterwards reimbursed. If this rule be not followed, the lord and the collectors of the public taxes will harass the poor vassal by turns till he perishes with misery or flies into the woods.

[526] This is what induced Charlemagne to make his excellent institution upon this head.
    See the fifth book of the Capitularies, art. 303.
[527] This is the practice in Germany.

6. Of a despotic Government in the like Case.

The foregoing rule is still more indispensably necessary in a despotic government. The lord who is every moment liable to be stripped of his lands and his vassals is not so eager to preserve them.

When Peter I thought proper to follow the custom of Germany, and to demand his taxes in money, he made a very prudent regulation, which is still followed in Russia. The gentleman levies the tax on the peasant, and pays it to the Czar. If the number of peasants diminishes, he pays all the same; if it increases, he pays no more; so that it is his interest not to worry or oppress his vassals.

7. *Of Taxes in Countries where Villainage is not established.*

When the inhabitants of a state are all free subjects, and each man enjoys his property with as much right as the prince his sovereignty, taxes may then be laid either on persons, on lands, on merchandise, on two of these, or on all three together.

In the taxing of persons, it would be an unjust proportion to conform exactly to that of property. At Athens the people were divided into four classes. [528] Those who drew five hundred measures of liquid or dried fruit from their estates paid a talent [529] to the public; those who drew three hundred measures paid half a talent; those who had two hundred measures paid ten minæ; those of the fourth class paid nothing at all. The tax was fair, though it was not proportionable: if it did not follow the measure of people's property, it followed that of their wants. It was judged that every man had an equal share of what was *necessary for nature*, that whatsoever was *necessary for nature* ought not to be taxed; that to this succeeded the useful, which ought to be taxed, but less than the superfluous; and that the largeness of the taxes on what was superfluous prevented superfluity.

[528] Pollux, book VIII. chap. 10, art. 130.
[529] Or 60 minæ.

In the taxing of lands it is customary to make lists or registers, in which the different classes of estates are ranged. But it is very difficult to know these differences, and still more so to find people that are not interested in mistaking them. Here, therefore, are two sorts of injustice, that of the man and that of the thing. But if in general the tax be not exorbitant, and the people continue to have plenty of necessaries, these particular acts of injustice will do no harm. On the contrary, if the people are permitted to enjoy only just what is necessary for subsistence, the least disproportion will be of the greatest consequence.

If some subjects do not pay enough, the mischief is not so great; their convenience and ease turn always to the public advantage; if some private people pay too much, their ruin redounds to the public detriment. If the government proportions its fortune to that of individuals, the ease and convenience of the latter will soon make its fortune rise. The whole depends upon a critical moment: shall the state begin with impoverishing the subjects to enrich itself? Or had it better wait to be enriched by its subjects? Is it more advisable for it to have the former or the latter advantage? Which shall it choose—to begin or to end with opulence?

The duties felt least by the people are those on merchandise, because they are not demanded of them in form. They may be so prudently managed that the people themselves shall hardly know they pay them. For this purpose it is of the utmost consequence that the person who sells the merchandise should pay the duty. He is very sensible that he does not pay it for himself; and the consumer, who pays it in the main, confounds it with the price. Some authors have observed that Nero had abolished the duty of the five-and-twentieth part arising from the sale of slaves; [530] and yet he had only ordained that it should be paid by the seller instead of the purchaser; this regulation, which left the impost entire, seemed nevertheless to suppress it.

[530] *Vectigal quintae et vicesimae venalium manipiorum remissum specie magis, quam vi, quia cum venditor pendere juberetur, in partem pretii emptoribus accrescebat.*— Tacit. *Annal.* lib. XIII.

There are two states in Europe where the imposts are very heavy upon liquors: in one the brewer alone pays the duty, in the other it is levied indiscriminately upon all the consumers; in the first nobody feels the rigor of the impost, in the second it is looked upon as a grievance; in the former the subject is sensible only of the liberty he has of not paying, in the latter he feels only the necessity that compels him to pay.

Further, the obliging the consumers to pay requires a perpetual rummaging and searching into their houses. Now nothing is more contrary than this to liberty; and those who establish these sorts of duties have not surely been so happy as to hit upon the best method of collecting the revenue.

8. *In what Manner the Deception is preserved.*

In order to make the purchaser confound the price of the commodity with the impost, there must be some proportion between the impost and the value of the commodity: for which reason there ought not to be an excessive duty upon merchandise of little value. There are countries in which the duty exceeds seventeen or eighteen times the value of the commodity. In this case the prince removes the disguise: his subjects plainly see they are dealt with in an unreasonable manner, which renders them most exquisitely sensible of their servile condition.

Besides, the prince, to be able to levy a duty so disproportioned to the value of the commodity, must be himself the vendor, and the people must not have it in their power to purchase it elsewhere: a practice subject to a thousand inconveniences.

Smuggling being in this case extremely lucrative, the natural and most reasonable penalty, namely, the confiscation of the merchandise, becomes incapable of putting a stop to it; especially as this very merchandise is intrinsically of inconsiderable value. Recourse must therefore be had to extravagant punishments, such as those inflicted for capital crimes.

All proportion then of penalties is at an end. Persons that cannot really be considered as vicious are punished like the most infamous criminals; which of all things in the world is the most contrary to the spirit of a moderate government.

Again, in proportion as people are tempted to cheat the farmer of the revenues, the more the latter is enriched, and the former impoverished. To put a stop to smuggling, the farmer must be invested with extraordinary means of oppressing, and then the country is ruined.

9. *Of a bad Kind of Impost.*

We shall here, by the way, take notice of an impost laid in particular countries on the different articles of civil contracts. As these are things subject to very nice disquisitions, a vast deal of knowledge is necessary to make any tolerable defense against the farmer of the revenues, who interprets, in that case, the regulations of the prince, and exercises an arbitrary power over people's fortunes. Experience has demonstrated that a duty on the paper on which the deeds are drawn would be of far greater service.

10. *That the Greatness of Taxes depends on the Nature of the Government.*

Taxes ought to be very light in despotic governments: otherwise who would be at the trouble of tilling the land? Besides, how is it possible to pay heavy duties in a government that makes no manner of return to the different contributions of the subject?

The exorbitant power of the prince, and the extreme depression of the people, require that there should not be even a possibility of the least mistake between them. The taxes ought to be so easy to collect, and so clearly settled, as to leave no opportunity for the collectors to increase or diminish them. A portion of the fruits of the earth, a capitation, a duty of so much per cent on merchandise, are the only taxes suitable to that government.

Merchants in despotic countries ought to have a personal safeguard, to which all due respect should be paid. Without this they would be too weak to dispute with the custom-house officers.

11. *Of Confiscations.*

With respect to confiscations, there is one thing very particular that, contrary to the general custom, they are more severe in Europe than in Asia. In Europe not only the merchandise, but even sometimes the ships and carriages, are confiscated; which is never practiced in Asia. This is because in Europe the merchant can have recourse to magistrates, who are able to shelter him from oppression; in Asia the magistrates themselves would be the greatest oppressors. What remedy could a merchant have against a pasha who was determined to confiscate his goods?

The prince, therefore, checks his own power, finding himself under the necessity of acting with some kind of lenity. In Turkey they raise only a single duty for the importation of goods, and afterwards the whole country is open to the merchant. Smuggling is not attended with confiscation or increase of duty. In China [531] they never look into the baggage of those who are not merchants. Defrauding the customs in the territory of the Mogul is not punished with confiscation, but with doubling the duty. The princes of Tartary, who reside in towns, impose scarcely any duty at all on the goods that pass through their country. [532] In Japan, it is true, to cheat the customs is a capital crime; but this is because they have particular reasons for prohibiting all communication with foreigners; hence the fraud [533] is rather a contravention of the laws made for the security of the government than of those of commerce.

[531] Father Du Halde, tom. ii, p. 37.
[532] History of the Tartars, part III, p. 290.
[533] Being willing to trade with foreigners without having any communication with them, they have pitched upon two nations for that purpose—the Dutch for the commerce of Europe, and the Chinese for that of Asia; they confine the factors and sailors in a kind of prison, and lay such a restraint upon them as tires their patience.

12. *Relation between the Weight of Taxes and Liberty.*

It is a general rule that taxes may be heavier in proportion to the liberty of the subject, and that there is a necessity for reducing them in proportion to the increase of slavery. This has always been and always will be the case. It is a rule derived from nature that never varies. We find it in all parts—in England, in Holland, and in every state where liberty gradually declines, till we come to Turkey. Switzerland seems to be an exception to this rule, because they pay no taxes; but the particular reason for that exemption is well known, and even confirms what I have advanced. In those barren mountains provisions are so dear, and the country is so populous, that a Swiss pays four times more to nature than a Turk does to the sultan.

A conquering people, such as were formerly the Athenians and the Romans, may rid themselves of all taxes as they reign over vanquished nations. Then indeed they do not pay in proportion to their liberty, because in this respect they are no longer a people, but a monarch.

But the general rule still holds good. In moderate governments there is an indemnity for the weight of the taxes, which is liberty. In despotic countries [534] there is an equivalent for liberty, which is the lightness of the taxes.

[534] In Russia the taxes are but small; they have been increased since the despotic power of the prince is exercised with more moderation. See the History of the Tartars, part II.

In some monarchies in Europe there are particular provinces [535] which from the very nature of their civil government are in a more flourishing condition than the rest. It is pretended that these provinces are not sufficiently taxed, because through the goodness of their government they are able to be taxed higher; hence the ministers seem constantly to aim at depriving them of this very government, whence a diffusive blessing is derived, which redounds even to the prince's advantage.

[535] The *Pays d'etats*, where the states of the province assemble to deliberate on public affairs.

13. In what Government Taxes are capable of Increase.

Taxes may be increased in most republics, because the citizen, who thinks he is paying himself, cheerfully submits to them, and moreover is generally able to bear their weight, from the nature of the government.

In a monarchy taxes may be increased, because the moderation of the government is capable of procuring opulence: it is a recompense, as it were, granted to the prince for the respect he shows to the laws. In despotic governments they cannot be increased, because there can be no increase of the extremity of slavery.

14. That the Nature of the Taxes is in Relation to the Government.

A capitation is more natural to slavery; a duty on merchandise is more natural to liberty, by reason it has not so direct a relation to the person.

It is natural in a despotic government for the prince not to give money to his soldiers, or to those belonging to his court; but to distribute lands amongst them, and of course that there should be very few taxes. But if the prince gives money, the most natural tax he can raise is a capitation, which can never be considerable. For as it is impossible to make different classes of the contributors, because of the abuses that might arise thence, considering the injustice and violence of the government, they are under an absolute necessity of regulating themselves by the rate of what even the poorest and most wretched are able to contribute.

The natural tax of moderate governments is the duty laid on merchandise. As this is really paid by the consumer, though advanced by the merchant, it is a loan which the latter has already made to the former. Hence the merchant must be considered on the one side as the general debtor of the state, and on the other as the creditor of every individual. He advances to the state the duty which the consumer will sometime or other refund: and he has paid for the consumer the duty which he has advanced for the merchandise. It is therefore obvious that in proportion to the moderation of the government, to the prevalence of the spirit of liberty, and to the security of private fortunes, a merchant has it in his power to advance money to the state, and to pay considerable duties for individuals. In England a merchant lends really to the government fifty or sixty pounds sterling for every tun of wine he imports. Where is the merchant that would dare do any such thing in a country like Turkey? And were he so presumptuous, how could he do it with a crazy or shattered fortune?

15. *Abuse of Liberty.*

To these great advantages of liberty it is owing that liberty itself has been abused. Because a moderate government has been productive of admirable effects, this moderation has been laid aside; because great taxes have been raised, they wanted to carry them to excess; and ungrateful to the hand of liberty, of whom they received this present, they addressed themselves to slavery, who never grants the least favor.

Liberty produces excessive taxes; the effect of excessive taxes is slavery; and slavery produces a diminution of tribute.

Most of the edicts of the eastern monarchs are to exempt every year some province of their empire from paying tribute. [536] The manifestations of their wills are favors. But in Europe the edicts of princes are disagreeable even before they are seen, because they always make mention of their own wants, but not a word of ours.

[536] This is the practice of the emperors of China. The author speaks here of annual exemptions, and not perpetual.—Ed.

From an unpardonable indolence in the ministers of those countries, owing to the nature of the government, and frequently to the climate, the people derive this advantage, that they are not incessantly plagued with new demands. The public expense does not increase, because the ministers do not form new projects: and if some by chance are formed, they are such as are soon executed. The governors of the state do not perpetually torment the people, for they do not perpetually. torment themselves. But it is impossible there should be any fixed rule in our finances, since we always know that we shall have something or other to execute, without ever knowing what it is.

It is no longer customary with us to give the appellation of a great minister to a wise dispenser of the public revenues, but to a person of dexterity and cunning, who is clever at finding out what we call the ways and means.

16. *Of the Conquests of the Mahometans.*

It was this excess of taxes [537] that occasioned the prodigious facility with which the Mahometans carried on their conquests. Instead of a continual series of extortions devised by the subtle avarice of the Greek emperors, the people were subjected to a simple tribute which was paid and collected with ease. Thus they were far happier in obeying a barbarous nation than a corrupt government, in which they suffered every inconvenience of lost liberty, with all the horror of present slavery.

[537] See in history the greatness, the oddity, and even the folly of those taxes. Anastasius invented a tax for breathing, "ut quisque pro haustu æris penderet."

17. *Of the Augmentation of Troops.*

A new distemper has spread itself over Europe, infecting our princes, and inducing them to keep up an exorbitant number of troops. It has its redoublings, and of necessity becomes contagious. For as soon as one prince augments his forces, the rest of course do the same; so that nothing is gained thereby but the public ruin. Each monarch keeps as many armies on foot as if his people were in danger of being exterminated: and they give the name of peace [538] to this general effort of all against all. Thus is Europe ruined to such a degree that were private people to be in the same situation as the three most opulent powers of this part of the globe, they would not have necessary subsistence. We are poor with the riches and commerce of the whole world; and soon, by thus augmenting our troops, we shall be all soldiers, and be reduced to the very same situation as the Tartars. [539]

[538] True it is that this state of effort is the chief support of the balance, because it checks the great powers.
[539] All that is wanting for this is to improve the new invention of the militia established in most parts of Europe, and carry it to the same excess as they do the regular troops.

Great princes, not satisfied with hiring or buying troops of petty states, make it their business on all sides to pay subsidies for alliances, that is, generally to throw away their money.

The consequence of such a situation is the perpetual augmentation of taxes; and the mischief which prevents all future remedy is that they reckon no more upon their revenues, but in waging war against their whole capital. It is no unusual thing to see governments mortgage their funds even in time of peace, and to employ what they call extraordinary means to ruin themselves—means so extraordinary indeed, that such are hardly thought of by the most extravagant young spendthrift.

18. *Of an Exemption from Taxes.*

The maxim of the great eastern empires, of exempting such provinces as have very much suffered from taxes, ought to be extended to monarchical states. There are some, indeed, where this practice is established; yet the country is more oppressed than if no such rule took place; because as the prince levies still neither more nor less, the state becomes bound for the whole. In order to ease a village that pays badly, they load another that pays better; the former is not relieved, and the latter is ruined. The people grow desperate, between the necessity of paying for fear of exactions, and the danger of paying for fear of new burdens.

A well-regulated government ought to set aside, for the first article of its expense, a determinate sum to answer contingent cases. It is with the public as with individuals, who are ruined when they live up exactly to their income.

With regard to an obligation for the whole amongst the inhabitants of the same village, some pretend [540] that it is but reasonable, because there is a possibility of a fraudulent combination on their side: but was it ever heard that, upon mere supposition, we are to establish a thing in itself unjust and ruinous to the state?

[540] See A Treatise on the Roman Finances, chap. 2. Printed at Paris by Briasson, 1740.

19. *Which is more suitable to the Prince and to the People, the farming the Revenues, or managing them by Commission.*

The managing of the revenues by commission is like the conduct of a good father of a family, who collects his own rents himself with economy and order.

By this management of the revenues the prince is at liberty to press or to retard the levy of the taxes, either according to his own wants or to those of his people. By this he saves to the state the immense profits of the farmers, who impoverish it in a thousand ways. By this he prevents the people from being mortified with the sight of sudden fortunes. By this the public money passes through few hands, goes directly to the treasury, and consequently makes a quicker return to the people. By this the prince avoids an infinite number of bad laws extorted from him by the importunate avarice of the farmers, who pretend to offer a present advantage for regulations pernicious to posterity.

As the moneyed man is always the most powerful, the farmer renders himself arbitrary even over the prince himself; he is not the legislator, but he obliges the legislator to give laws.

I acknowledge that it is sometimes of use to farm out a new duty, for there is an art in preventing frauds, which motives of interest suggest to the farmers, but commissioners never think of. Now the manner of levying it being once established by the farmer, it may afterwards be safely entrusted to a commission. In England the management of the Excise and of the Post-office was borrowed from that of the farmers of the revenue.

In republics the revenues of the state are generally managed by commission. The contrary practice was a great defect in the Roman government. [541] In despotic governments the people are infinitely happier where this management is established— witness Persia and China. [542] The unhappiest of all are those where the prince farms out his sea-ports and trading cities. The history of monarchies abounds with mischiefs done by the farmers of the revenue.

[541] Cæsar was obliged to remove the publicans from the province of Asia, and to establish there another kind of regulation, as we learn from Dio; and Tacitus informs us that Macedonia and Achaia, provinces left by Augustus to the people of Rome, and consequently governed pursuant to the ancient plan, obtained to be of the number of those which the emperor governed by his officers.

[542] See Sir John Chardin's Travels through Persia, tom. vi.

Incensed at the oppressive extortions of the publicans, Nero formed a magnanimous but impracticable scheme of abolishing all kinds of imposts. He did not think of managing the revenues by commissioners, but he made four edicts: [543] that the laws enacted against publicans, which had hitherto been kept secret, should be promulgated; that they should exact no claims for above a year backward; that there should be a prætor established to determine their pretensions without any formality; and that the merchants should pay no duty for their vessels. These were the halcyon days of that emperor.

[543] Tacitus, *Annal*, XIII.

20. *Of the Farmers of the Revenues.*

When the lucrative profession of a farmer of the revenue becomes likewise a post of honor, the state is ruined. It may do well enough in despotic governments, where this employment is oftentimes exercised by the governors themselves. But it is by no means proper in a republic, since a custom of the like nature destroyed that of Rome. Nor is it better in monarchies, nothing being more opposite to the spirit of this government. All the other orders of the state are dissatisfied; honor loses its whole value; the gradual and natural means of distinction are no longer respected; and the very principle of the government is subverted.

It is true indeed that scandalous fortunes were raised in former times; but this was one of the calamities of the Fifty Years' War. These riches were then considered as ridiculous; now we admire them.

Every profession has its particular lot. That of the tax-gatherers is wealth; and wealth is its own reward. Glory and honor fall to the share of that nobility who are sensible of no other happiness. Respect and esteem are for those ministers and magistrates whose whole life is a continued series of labor, and who watch day and night over the welfare of the empire.

BOOK XIV.

OF LAWS IN RELATION TO THE NATURE OF THE CLIMATE

1. *General Idea.*

If it be true that the temper of the mind and the passions of the heart are extremely different in different climates, the laws ought to be in relation both to the variety of those passions and to the variety of those tempers.

2. *Of the Difference of Men in different Climates.*

Cold air constringes the extremities of the external fibers of the body; [544] this increases their elasticity, and favors the return of the blood from the extreme parts to the heart. It contracts [545] those very fibers; consequently it increases also their force. On the contrary, warm air relaxes and lengthens the extremes of the fibers; of course it diminishes their force and elasticity.

[544] This appears even in the countenance: in cold weather people look thinner.
[545] We know that it shortens iron.

People are therefore more vigorous in cold climates. Here the action of the heart and the reaction of the extremities of the fibers are better performed, the temperature of the humors is greater, the blood moves more freely towards the heart, and reciprocally the heart has more power. This superiority of strength must produce various effects; for instance, a greater boldness, that is, more courage; a greater sense of superiority, that is, less desire of revenge; a greater opinion of security, that is, more frankness, less suspicion, policy, and cunning. In short, this must be productive of very different tempers. Put a man into a close, warm place, and for the reasons above given he will feel a great faintness. If under this circumstance you propose a bold enterprise to him, I believe you will find him very little disposed towards it; his present weakness will throw him into despondency; he will be afraid of everything, being in a state of total incapacity. The inhabitants of warm countries are, like old men, timorous; the people in cold countries are, like young men, brave. If we reflect on the late wars, [546] which are more recent in our memory, and in which we can better distinguish some particular effects that escape us at a greater distance of time, we shall find that the northern people, transplanted into southern regions, [547] did not perform such exploits as their countrymen who, fighting in their own climate, possessed their full vigor and courage.

[546] Those for the succession to the Spanish monarchy.
[547] For instance, in Spain.

This strength of the fibers in northern nations is the cause that the coarser juices are extracted from their ailments. Hence two things result: one, that the parts of the chyle or lymph are more proper, by reason of their large surface, to be applied to and to nourish the fibers; the other, that they are less proper, from their coarseness, to give a certain subtlety to the nervous juice. Those people have therefore large bodies and but little vivacity.

The nerves that terminate from all parts in the cutis form each a nervous bundle; generally speaking, the whole nerve is not moved, but a very minute part. In warm climates, where the cutis is relaxed, the ends of the nerves are expanded and laid open to the weakest action of the smallest objects. In cold countries the cutis is constringed and the papillæ compressed: the miliary glands are in some measure paralytic; and the sensation does not reach the brain, except when it is very strong and proceeds from the whole nerve at once. Now, imagination, taste, sensibility, and vivacity depend on an infinite number of small sensations.

I have observed the outermost part of a sheep's tongue, where, to the naked eye, it seems covered with papillæ. On these papillæ I have discerned through a microscope small hairs, or a kind of down; between the papillæ were pyramids shaped towards the ends like pincers. Very likely these pyramids are the principal organ of taste.

I caused the half of this tongue to be frozen, and, observing it with the naked eye, I found the papillæ considerably diminished: even some rows of them were sunk into their sheath. The outermost part I examined with the microscope, and perceived no pyramids. In proportion as the frost went off, the papillæ seemed to the naked eye to rise, and with the microscope the miliary glands began to appear.

This observation confirms what I have been saying, that in cold countries the nervous glands are less expanded: they sink deeper into their sheaths, or they are sheltered from the action of external objects; consequently they have not such lively sensations.

In cold countries they have very little sensibility tor pleasure; in temperate countries, they have more; in warm countries, their sensibility is exquisite. As climates are distinguished by degrees of latitude, we might distinguish them also in some measure by those of sensibility. I have been at the opera in England and in Italy, where I have seen the same pieces and the same performers: and yet the same music produces such different effects on the two nations: one is so cold and phlegmatic, and the other so lively and enraptured, that it seems almost inconceivable.

It is the same with regard to pain, which is excited by the laceration of some fiber of the body. The Author of nature has made it an established rule that this pain should be more acute in proportion as the laceration is greater: now it is evident that the large bodies and coarse fibers of the people of the north are less capable of laceration than the delicate fibers of the inhabitants of warm countries; consequently the soul is there less sensible of pain. You must flay a Muscovite alive to make him feel.

From this delicacy of organs peculiar to warm climates it follows that the soul is most sensibly moved by whatever relates to the union of the two sexes: here everything leads to this object.

In northern climates scarcely has the animal part of love a power of making itself felt. In temperate climates, love, attended by a thousand appendages, endeavors to please by things that have at first the appearance, though not the reality, of this passion. In warmer climates it is liked for its own sake, it is the only cause of happiness, it is life itself.

In southern countries a machine of a delicate frame but strong sensibility resigns itself either to a love which rises and is incessantly laid in a seraglio, or to a passion which leaves women in a greater independence, and is consequently exposed to a thousand inquietudes. In northern regions a machine robust and heavy finds pleasure in whatever is apt to throw the spirits into motion, such as hunting, travelling, war, and wine. If we travel towards the north, we meet with people who have few vices, many virtues, and a great share of frankness and sincerity. If we draw near the south, we fancy ourselves entirely removed from the verge of morality; here the strongest passions are productive of all manner of crimes, each man endeavoring, let the means be what they will, to indulge his inordinate desires. In temperate climates we find the inhabitants inconstant in their manners, as well as in their vices and virtues: the climate has not a quality determinate enough to fix them.

The heat of the climate may be so excessive as to deprive the body of all vigor and strength. Then the faintness is communicated to the mind; there is no curiosity, no enterprise, no generosity of sentiment; the inclinations are all passive; indolence constitutes the utmost happiness; scarcely any punishment is so severe as mental employment; and slavery is more supportable than the force and vigor of mind necessary for human conduct.

3. *Contradiction in the Tempers of some Southern Nations.*

The Indians [548] are naturally a pusillanimous people; even the children [549] of Europeans born in India lose the courage peculiar to their own climate. But how shall we reconcile this with their customs and penances so full of barbarity? The men voluntarily undergo the greatest hardships, and the women burn themselves; here we find a very odd compound of fortitude and weakness.

[548] "One hundred European soldiers," says Tavernier, "would without any great difficulty beat a thousand Indian soldiers."
[549] Even the Persians who settle in the Indies contract in the third generation the indolence and cowardice of the Indians. See Bernier on the Mogul, tom. i, p. 182.

Nature, having framed those people of a texture so weak as to fill them with timidity, has formed them at the same time of an imagination so lively that every object makes the strongest impression upon them. That delicacy of organs which renders them apprehensive of death contributes likewise to make them dread a thousand things more than death: the very same sensibility induces them to fly and dare all dangers.

As a good education is more necessary to children than to such as have arrived at maturity of understanding, so the inhabitants of those countries have much greater need than the European nations of a wiser legislator. The greater their sensibility, the more it behooves them to receive proper impressions, to imbibe no prejudices, and to let themselves be directed by reason.

At the time of the Romans the inhabitants of the north of Europe were destitute of arts, education, and almost of laws; and yet the good sense annexed to the gross fibers of those climates enabled them to make an admirable stand against the power of Rome, till the memorable period in which they quitted their woods to subvert that great empire.

4. *Cause of the Immutability of Religion, Manners,*
Customs, and Laws in the Eastern Countries.

If to that delicacy of organs which renders the eastern nations so susceptible of every impression you add likewise a sort of indolence of mind, naturally connected with that of the body, by means of which they grow incapable of any exertion or effort, it is easy to comprehend that when once the soul has received an impression it cannot change it. This is the reason that the laws, manners, and customs, [550] even those which seem quite indifferent, such as their mode of dress, are the same to this very day in eastern countries as they were a thousand years ago.

[550] We find by a fragment of Nicolaus Damascenus, collected by Constantine Porphyrogenitus, that it was an ancient custom in the East to send to strangle a governor who had given any displeasure; it was in the time of the Medes.

5. *That those are bad Legislators who favor the Vices of the Climate, and good Legislators who oppose those Vices.*

The Indians believe that repose and non-existence are the foundation of all things, and the end in which they terminate. Hence they consider entire inaction as the most perfect of all states, and the object of their desires. To the Supreme Being they give the title of immovable. [551] The inhabitants of Siam believe that their utmost happiness [552] consists in not being obliged to animate a machine, or to give motion to a body.

[551] Panamanack: See Kircher.
[552] La Loubiere, Relation of Siam, p. 446.

In those countries where the excess of heat enervates and exhausts the body, rest is so delicious, and motion so painful, that this system of metaphysics seems natural; and Foe, [553] the legislator of the Indies, was directed by his own sensations when he placed mankind in a state extremely passive; but his doctrine arising from the laziness of the climate favored it also in its turn; which has been the source of an infinite deal of mischief.

[553] Foe endeavored to reduce the heart to a mere vacuum: "We have eyes and ears, but perfection consists in neither seeing nor hearing; a mouth, hands, &c., but perfection requires that these members should be inactive." This is taken from the dialogue of a Chinese philosopher, quoted by Father Du Halde, tom. iii.

The legislators of China were more rational when, considering men not in the peaceful state which they are to enjoy hereafter, but in the situation proper for discharging the several duties of life, they made their religion, philosophy, and laws all practical. The more the physical causes incline mankind to inaction, the more the moral causes should estrange them from it.

6. *Of Agriculture in warm Climates.*

Agriculture is the principal labor of man. The more the climate inclines him to shun this labor, the more the religion and laws of the country ought to incite him to it. Thus the Indian laws, which give the lands to the prince, and destroy the spirit of property among the subjects, increase the bad effects of the climate, that is, their natural indolence.

7. *Of Monkery.*

The very same mischiefs result from monkery: it had its rise in the warm countries of the East, where they are less inclined to action than to speculation.

In Asia the number of dervishes or monks seems to increase together with the warmth of the climate. The Indies, where the heat is excessive, are full of them; and the same difference is found in Europe.

In order to surmount the laziness of the climate, the laws ought to endeavor to remove all means of subsisting without labor: but in the southern parts of Europe they act quite the reverse. To those who want to live in a state of indolence, they afford retreats the most proper for a speculative life, and endow them with immense revenues. These men, who live in the midst of plenty which they know not how to enjoy, are in the right to give their superfluities away to the common people. The poor are bereft of property; and these men indemnify them by supporting them in idleness, so as to make them even grow fond of their misery.

8. *An excellent Custom of China.*

The historical relations [554] of China mention a ceremony [555] of opening the ground which the emperor performs every year. The design of this public and solemn act is to excite the people to tillage. [556]

[554] Father Du Halde, History of China, tom. i, p. 72.
[555] Several of the kings of India do the same. La Loubiere, Account of the Kingdom of Siam, p. 69.
[556] Venty, the third emperor of the third dynasty, tilled the lands himself, and made the empress and his wives employ their time in the silkworks in his palace. History of China.

Further, the emperor is every year informed of the husbandman who has distinguished himself most in his profession; and he makes him a mandarin of the eighth order.

Among the ancient Persians [557] the kings quitted their grandeur and pomp on the eighth day of the month, called *Chorrem-ruz*, to eat with the husbandmen. These institutions were admirably calculated for the encouragement of agriculture.

[557] Hyde, Religion of the Persians.

9. *Means of encouraging Industry.*

We shall show, in the nineteenth book, that lazy nations are generally proud. Now the effect might well be turned against the cause, and laziness be destroyed by pride. In the south of Europe, where people have such a high notion of the point of honor, it would be right to give prizes to husbandmen who had excelled in agriculture; or to artists who had made the greatest improvements in their several professions. This practice has succeeded in our days in Ireland, where it has established one of the most considerable linen manufactures in Europe.

10. *Of the Laws in relation to the Sobriety of the People.*

In warm countries the aqueous part of the blood loses itself greatly by perspiration; [558] it must therefore be supplied by a like liquid. Water is there of admirable use; strong liquors would congeal the globules [559] of blood that remain after the transuding of the aqueous humor.

[558] Monsieur Bernier, travelling from Lahore to Cashmere, wrote thus: "My body is a sieve; scarcely have I swallowed a pint of water, but I see it transude like dew out of

all my limbs, even to my fingers' ends. I drink ten pints a day, and it does me no manner of harm."—Bernier, Travels, tom. ii, p. 261.

[559] In the blood there are red globules, fibrous parts, white globules, and water, in which the whole swims.

In cold countries the aqueous part of the blood is very little evacuated by perspiration. They may therefore make use of spirituous liquors, without which the blood would congeal. They are full of humors; consequently strong liquors, which give a motion to the blood, are proper for those countries.

The law of Mahomet, which prohibits the drinking of wine, is therefore fitted to the climate of Arabia: and indeed, before Mahomet's time, water was the common drink of the Arabs. The law [560] which forbade the Carthaginians to drink wine was a law of the climate; and, indeed, the climate of those two countries is pretty nearly the same.

[560] Plato, Book II of Laws; Aristotle, Of the Care of Domestic Affairs; Eusebius, Evangelical Preparation, book XII. chap. 17.

Such a law would be improper for cold countries, where the climate seems to force them to a kind of national intemperance, very different from personal ebriety. Drunkenness predominates throughout the world, in proportion to the coldness and humidity of the climate. Go from the equator to the north pole, and you will find this vice increasing together with the degree of latitude. Go from the equator again to the south pole, and you will find the same vice travelling south, [561] exactly in the same proportion.

[561] This is seen in the Hottentots, and the inhabitants of the most southern part of Chili.

It is very natural that where wine is contrary to the climate, and consequently to health, the excess of it should be more severely punished than in countries where intoxication produces very few bad effects to the person, fewer to the society, and where it does not make people frantic and wild, but only stupid and heavy. Hence those laws [562] which inflicted a double punishment for crimes committed in drunkenness were applicable only to a personal, and not to a national, ebriety. A German drinks through custom, and a Spaniard by choice.

[562] As Pittacus did, according to Aristotle, *Politics*, lib. I. cap iii. He lived in a climate where drunkenness is not a national vice.

In warm countries the relaxing of the fibers produces a great evacuation of the liquids, but the solid parts are less transpired. The fibers, which act but faintly, and have very little elasticity, are not much impaired; and a small quantity of nutritious juice is sufficient to repair them; for which reason they eat very little.

It is the variety of wants in different climates that first occasioned a difference in the manner of living, and this gave rise to a variety of laws. Where people are very communicative there must be particular laws, and others where there is but little communication.

11. *Of the Laws in relation to the Distempers of the Climate.*

Herodotus [563] informs us that the Jewish laws concerning the leprosy were borrowed from the practice of the Egyptians. And, indeed, the same distemper required the same remedies. The Greeks and the primitive Romans were strangers to these laws, as well as to the disease. The climate of Egypt and Palestine rendered them necessary; and the facility with which this disease is spread is sufficient to make us sensible of the wisdom and sagacity of those laws.

[563] Book II.

Even we ourselves have felt the effects of them. The Crusades brought the leprosy amongst us; but the wise regulations made at that time hindered it from infecting the mass of the people.

We find by the law of the Lombards [564] that this disease was spread in Italy before the Crusades, and merited the attention of the legislature. Rotharis ordained that a leper should be expelled from his house, banished to a particular place, and rendered incapable of disposing of his property; because from the very moment he had been turned out of his house he was reckoned dead in the eye of the law. In order to prevent all communication with lepers, they were rendered incapable of civil acts.

[564] Book II. tit. 1, § 3; tit. 18, § 1.

I am apt to think that this disease was brought into Italy by the conquests of the Greek emperors, in whose armies there might be some soldiers from Palestine or Egypt. Be that as it may, the progress of it was stopped till the time of the Crusades.

It is related that Pompey's soldiers returning from Syria brought a distemper home with them not unlike the leprosy. We have no account of any regulation made at that time; but it is highly probable that some such step was taken, since the distemper was checked till the time of the Lombards.

It is now two centuries since a disease unknown to our ancestors was first transplanted from the new world to ours, and came to attack human nature even in the very source of life and pleasure. Most of the principal families in the south of Europe were seen to perish by a distemper that had grown too common to be ignominious, and was considered in no other light than in that of its being fatal. It was the thirst of gold that propagated this disease; the Europeans went continually to America, and always brought back a new leaven of it. [565]

[565] It has been thought that this malady has a still more ancient origin, and that it is probable the Spaniards carried it to America at the start.

Reasons drawn from religion seemed to require that this punishment of guilt should be permitted to continue; but the infection had reached the bosom of matrimony, and given the vicious taint even to guiltless infants.

As it is the business of legislators to watch over the health of the citizens, it would have been a wise part in them to have stopped this communication by laws made on the plan of those of Moses.

The plague is a disease whose infectious progress is much more rapid. Egypt is its principal seat, whence it spreads over the whole globe. Most countries in Europe have made exceedingly good regulations to prevent this infection, and in our times an admirable method has been contrived to stop it; this is by forming a line of troops round the infected country, which cuts off all manner of communication.

The Turks, [566] who have no such regulations, see the Christians escape this infection in the same town, and none but themselves perish; they buy the clothes of the infected, wear them, and proceed in their old way, as if nothing had happened. The doctrine of a rigid fate, which directs their whole conduct, renders the magistrate a quiet spectator; he thinks that everything comes from the hand of God, and that man has nothing more to do than to submit.

[566] Ricaut, State of the Ottoman Empire, p. 284.

12. *Of the Laws against Suicides.*

We do not find in history that the Romans ever killed themselves without a cause; but the English are apt to commit suicide most unaccountably; they destroy themselves even in the bosom of happiness. This action among the Romans was the effect of education, being connected with their principles and customs; among the English it is the consequence of a distemper, [567] being connected with the physical state of the machine, and independent of every other cause.

[567] It may be complicated with the scurvy, which, in some countries especially, renders a man whimsical and unsupportable to himself. See Pirard, Voyages, part II, chap. 21.

In all probability it is a defect of the filtration of the nervous juice: the machine, whose motive faculties are often unexerted, is weary of itself; the soul feels no pain, but a certain uneasiness in existing. Pain is a local sensation, which leads us to the desire of seeing an end of it; the burden of life, which prompts us to the desire of ceasing to exist, is an evil confined to no particular part.

It is evident that the civil laws of some countries may have reasons for branding suicide with infamy: but in England it cannot be punished without punishing the effects of madness.

13. *Effects arising from the Climate of England.*

In a nation so distempered by the climate as to have a disrelish of everything, nay, even of life, it is plain that the government most suitable to the inhabitants is that in which they cannot lay their uneasiness to any single person's charge, and in which, being under the direction rather of the laws than of the prince, it is impossible for them to change the government without subverting the laws themselves.

And if this nation has likewise derived from the climate a certain impatience of temper, which renders them incapable of bearing the same train of things for any long continuance, it is obvious that the government above mentioned is the fittest for them.

This impatience of temper is not very considerable of itself; but it may become so when joined with courage.

It is quite a different thing from levity, which makes people undertake or drop a project without cause; it borders more upon obstinacy, because it proceeds from so lively a sense of misery that it is not weakened even by the habit of suffering.

This temper in a free nation is extremely proper for disconcerting the projects of tyranny, [568] which is always slow and feeble in its commencement, as in the end it is active and lively; which at first only stretches out a hand to assist, and exerts afterwards a multitude of arms to oppress.

[568] Here I take this word for the design of subverting the established power, and especially that of democracy; this is the signification in which it was understood by the Greeks and Romans.

Slavery is ever preceded by sleep. But a people who find no rest in any situation, who continually explore every part, and feel nothing but pain, can hardly be lulled to sleep.

Politics is a smooth file, which cuts gradually, and attains its end by a slow progression. Now the people of whom we have been speaking are incapable of bearing the delays, the details, and the coolness of negotiations: in these they are more unlikely to succeed than any other nation; hence they are apt to lose by treaties what they obtain by their arms.

14. *Other Effects of the Climate.*

Our ancestors, the ancient Germans, lived in a climate where the passions were extremely calm. Their laws decided only in such cases where the injury was visible to the eye, and went no further. And as they judged of the outrages done to men from the greatness of the wound, they acted with no other delicacy in respect to the injuries done to women. The law of the Alemans [569] on this subject is very extraordinary. If a person uncovers a woman's head, he pays a fine of fifty sous; if he uncovers her leg up to the knee, he pays the same; and double from the knee upwards. One would think that the law measured the insults offered to women as we measure a figure in geometry; it did not punish the crime of the imagination, but that of the eye. But upon the migration of a German nation into Spain, the climate soon found a necessity for different laws. The law of the Visigoths inhibited the surgeons to bleed a free woman, except either her father, mother, brother, son, or uncle was present. As the imagination of the people grew warm, so did that of the legislators; the law suspected everything when the people had become suspicious.

[569] Chapter 58, §§ 1, 2.

These laws had, therefore, a particular regard for the two sexes. But in their punishments they seem rather to humor the revengeful temper of private persons than to administer public justice. Thus, in most cases, they reduced both the criminals to be slaves to the offended relatives or to the injured husband; a free-born woman [570] who had yielded to the embraces of a married man was delivered up to his wife to dispose of her as she pleased. They obliged the slaves, [571] if they found their master's wife in adultery, to bind her and carry her to her husband; they even permitted her children [572] to be her accusers, and her slaves to be tortured in order to convict her. Thus their laws were far better adapted to refine, even to excess, a certain point of honor than to form a good civil administration. We must not, therefore, be surprised if Count Julian was of opinion that an affront of that kind ought to be expiated by the ruin of his king and country: we must not be surprised if the Moors, with such a conformity of manners, found it so easy to settle and to maintain themselves in Spain, and to retard the fall of their empire.

[570] Law of the Visigoths, book III. tit. 4, § 9.
[571] Ibid. book III. tit. 4, § 6.
[572] Ibid. book III. tit. 4, § 13.

15. Of the different Confidence which the Laws have in the People, according to the Difference of Climates.

The people of Japan are of so stubborn and perverse a temper that neither their legislators nor magistrates can put any confidence in them: they set nothing before their eyes but judgments, menaces, and chastisements; every step they take is subject to the inquisition of the civil magistrate. Those laws which out of five heads of families establish one as a magistrate over the other four; those laws which punish a family or a whole ward for a single crime; those laws, in fine, which find nobody innocent where one may happen to be guilty, are made with a design to implant in the people a mutual distrust, and to make every man the inspector, witness, and judge of his neighbor's conduct.

On the contrary, the people of India are mild, [573] tender, and compassionate. Hence their legislators repose great confidence in them. They have established [574] very few punishments; these are not severe, nor are they rigorously executed. They have subjected nephews to their uncles, and orphans to their guardians, as in other countries they are subjected to their fathers; they have regulated the succession by the acknowledged merit of the successor. They seem to think that every individual ought to place entire confidence in the good nature of his fellow-subjects. [575]

[573] See Bernier, tom. ii, p. 140.
[574] See in the 14th Collection of the Edifying Letters, p. 403, the principal laws or customs of the inhabitants of the peninsula on this side the Ganges.
[575] See Edifying Letters, IX, p. 378. Great exception has been taken to Montesquieu's abuse upon the effects of climate physically; it is Servan who avers that the weakness attributed to organisms under the equator is erroneous.—Ed.

They enfranchise their slaves without difficulty, they marry them, they treat them as their children. [576] Happy climate which gives birth to innocence, and produces a lenity in the laws!

[576] I had once thought that the lenity of slavery in India had made Diodorus say that there was neither master nor slave in that country; but Diodorus has attributed to the whole continent of India what, according to Strabo, lib. XV., belonged only to a particular nation.

BOOK XV.

IN WHAT MANNER THE LAWS OF CIVIL SLAVERY RELATE TO THE NATURE OF THE CLIMATE

1. *Of civil Slavery.*

Slavery, properly so called, is the establishment of a right which gives to one man such a power over another as renders him absolute master of his life and fortune. The state of slavery is in its own nature bad. It is neither useful to the master nor to the slave; not to the slave, because he can do nothing through a motive of virtue; nor to the master, because by having an unlimited authority over his slaves he insensibly accustoms himself to the want of all moral virtues, and thence becomes fierce, hasty, severe, choleric, voluptuous, and cruel.

In despotic countries, where they are already in a state of political servitude, civil slavery is more tolerable than in other governments. Every one ought to be satisfied in those countries with necessaries and life. Hence the condition of a slave is hardly more burdensome than that of a subject.

But in a monarchical government, where it is of the utmost importance that human nature should not be debased or dispirited, there ought to be no slavery. In democracies, where they are all upon equality; and in aristocracies, where the laws ought to use their utmost endeavors to procure as great an equality as the nature of the government will permit, slavery is contrary to the spirit of the constitution: it only contributes to give a power and luxury to the citizens which they ought not to have. [577]

[577] Montesquieu seems to have forgotten that all the democracies of Greece adopted domestic servitude as the basis of social independence.—Ed.

2. *Origin of the Right of Slavery among the Roman Civilians.*

One would never have imagined that slavery should owe its birth to pity, and that this should have been excited in three different ways. [578]

[578] Justinian, Institutes, book I.

The law of nations to prevent prisoners from being put to death has allowed them to be made slaves. The civil law of the Romans empowered debtors, who were subject to be ill-used by their creditors, to sell themselves. And the law of nature requires that children whom a father in a state of servitude is no longer able to maintain should be reduced to the same state as the father.

These reasons of the civilians are all false. It is false that killing in war is lawful, unless in a case of absolute necessity: but when a man has made another his slave, he cannot be said to have been under a necessity of taking away his life, since he actually did not take it away. War gives no other right over prisoners than to disable them from doing any further harm by securing their persons. All nations [579] concur in detesting the murdering of prisoners in cold blood.

200

[579] Excepting a few cannibals.

Neither is it true that a freeman can sell himself. Sale implies a price; now when a person sells himself, his whole substance immediately devolves to his master; the master, therefore, in that case, gives nothing, and the slave receives nothing. You will say he has a *peculium*. But this peculium goes along with his person. If it is not lawful for a man to kill himself because he robs his country of his person, for the same reason he is not allowed to barter his freedom. The freedom of every citizen constitutes a part of the public liberty, and in a democratic state is even a part of the sovereignty. To sell one's freedom [580] is so repugnant to all reason as can scarcely be supposed in any man. If liberty may be rated with respect to the buyer, it is beyond all price to the seller. The civil law, which authorizes a division of goods among men, cannot be thought to rank among such goods a part of the men who were to make this division. The same law annuls all iniquitous contracts; surely then it affords redress in a contract where the grievance is most enormous.

[580] I mean slavery in a strict sense, as formerly among the Romans, and at present in our colonies.

The third way is birth, which falls with the two former; for if a man could not sell himself, much less could he sell an unborn infant. If a prisoner of war is not to be reduced to slavery, much less are his children.

The lawfulness of putting a malefactor to death arises from this circumstance: the law by which he is punished was made for his security. A murderer, for instance, has enjoyed the benefit of the very law which condemns him; it has been a continual protection to him; he cannot, therefore, object to it. But it is not so with the slave. The law of slavery can never be beneficial to him; it is in all cases against him, without ever being for his advantage; and therefore this law is contrary to the fundamental principle of all societies.

If it be pretended that it has been beneficial to him, as his master has provided for his subsistence, slavery, at this rate, should be limited to those who are incapable of earning their livelihood. But who will take up with such slaves? As to infants, nature, who has supplied their mothers with milk, had provided for their sustenance; and the remainder of their childhood approaches so near the age in which they are most capable of being of service that he who supports them cannot be said to give them an equivalent which can entitle him to be their master.

Nor is slavery less opposed to the civil law than to that of nature. What civil law can restrain a slave from running away, since he is not a member of society, and consequently has no interest in any civil institutions? He can be retained only by a family law, that is, by the master's authority.

3. *Another Origin of the Right of Slavery.*

I would as soon say that the right of slavery proceeds from the contempt of one nation for another, founded on a difference in customs.

Lopez de Gama [581] relates *that the Spaniards found near St. Martha several basketsful of crabs, snails, grasshoppers, and locusts, which proved to be the ordinary provision of the natives. This the conquerors turned to a heavy charge against the conquered.* The author owns that this, with their smoking and trimming their beards in a different manner, gave rise to the law by which the Americans became slaves to the Spaniards.

[581] Biblioth. Ang. tom. xiii, part II, art. 3.

Knowledge humanizes mankind, and reason inclines to mildness; but prejudices eradicate every tender disposition.

4. *Another Origin of the Right of Slavery.*

I would as soon say that religion gives its professors a right to enslave those who dissent from it, in order to render its propagation more easy.

This was the notion that encouraged the ravagers of America in their iniquity. [582] Under the influence of this idea they founded their right of enslaving so many nations; for these robbers, who would absolutely be both robbers and Christians, were superlatively devout.

[582] See Solis, History of the Conquest of Mexico, and Garcilasso de la Vega, History of the Conquest of Peru.

Lewis XII [583] was extremely uneasy at a law by which all the negroes of his colonies were to be made slaves; but it being strongly urged to him as the readiest means for their conversion, he acquiesced without further scruple.

[583] Labat, New Voyage to the Isles of America, vol. iv, p. 114, 1728, 12mo.

5. *Of the Slavery of the Negroes.*

Were I to vindicate our right to make slaves of the negroes, these should be my arguments:—

The Europeans, having extirpated the Americans, were obliged to make slaves of the Africans, for clearing such vast tracts of land.

Sugar would be too dear if the plants which produce it were cultivated by any other than slaves.

These creatures are all over black, and with such a flat nose that they can scarcely be pitied.

It is hardly to be believed that God, who is a wise Being, should place a soul, especially a good soul, in such a black ugly body.

It is so natural to look upon color as the criterion of human nature, that the Asiatics, among whom eunuchs are employed, always deprive the blacks of their resemblance to us by a more opprobrious distinction.

The color of the skin may be determined by that of the hair, which, among the Egyptians, the best philosophers in the world, was of such importance that they put to death all the red-haired men who fell into their hands.

The negroes prefer a glass necklace to that gold which polite nations so highly value. Can there be a greater proof of their wanting common sense?

It is impossible for us to suppose these creatures to be men, because, allowing them to be men, a suspicion would follow that we ourselves are not Christians. [584]

[584] The above arguments form a striking instance of the prejudice under which even a liberal mind can labor.—Ed.

Weak minds exaggerate too much the wrong done to the Africans. For were the case as they state it, would the European powers, who make so many needless conventions among themselves, have failed to enter into a general one, in behalf of humanity and compassion?

6. *The true Origin of the Right of Slavery.*

It is time to inquire into the true origin of the right of slavery. It ought to be founded on the nature of things; let us see if there be any cases where it can be derived thence.

In all despotic governments people make no difficulty in selling themselves; the political slavery in some measure annihilates the civil liberty.

According to Mr. Perry, [585] the Muscovites sell themselves very readily: their reason for it is evident; their liberty is not worth keeping.

[585] Present State of Russia.

At Achim every one is for selling himself. Some of the chief lords [586] have not less than a thousand slaves, all principal merchants, who have a great number of slaves themselves, and these also are not without their slaves. Their masters are their heirs, and put them into trade. In those states, the freemen being overpowered by the government, have no better resource than that of making themselves slaves to the tyrants in office.

[586] Dampier, Voyages, vol. iii.

This is the true and rational origin of that mild law of slavery which obtains in some countries: and mild it ought to be, as founded on the free choice a man makes of a master, for his own benefit; which forms a mutual convention between the two parties.

7. *Another Origin of the Right of Slavery.*

There is another origin of the right of slavery, and even of the most cruel slavery which is to be seen among men.

There are countries where the excess of heat enervates the body, and renders men so slothful and dispirited that nothing but the fear of chastisement can oblige them to perform any laborious duty: slavery is there more reconcilable to reason; and the master being as lazy with respect to his sovereign as his slave is with regard to him, this adds a political to a civil slavery.

Aristotle [587] endeavors to prove that there are natural slaves; but what he says is far from proving it. If there be any such, I believe they are those of whom I have been speaking.

[587] *Politics*, lib. I. chap. i.

But as all men are born equal, slavery must be accounted unnatural, though in some countries it be founded on natural reason; and a wide difference ought to be made between such countries, and those in which even natural reason rejects it, as in Europe, where it has been so happily abolished.

Plutarch, in the 'Life of Numa,' says that in Saturn's time there was neither slave nor master. Christianity has restored that age in our climates.

8. *Inutility of Slavery among us.*

Natural slavery, then, is to be limited to some particular parts of the world. In all other countries, even the most servile drudgeries may be performed by freemen.

Experience verifies my assertion. Before Christianity had abolished civil slavery in Europe, working in the mines was judged too toilsome for any but slaves or malefactors: at present there are men employed in them who are known to live comfortably. [588] The magistrates have, by some small privileges, encouraged this profession: to an increase of labor they have joined an increase of gain; and have gone so far as to make those people better pleased with their condition than with any other which they could have embraced.

[588] As may be seen in the mines of Hartz, in Lower Saxony, and in those of Hungary.

No labor is so heavy but it may be brought to a level with the workman's strength, when regulated by equity, and not by avarice. The violent fatigues which slaves are made to undergo in other parts may be supplied by a skilful use of ingenious machines. The Turkish mines in the Bannat of Temeswær, though richer than those of Hungary, did not yield so much; because the working of them depended entirely on the strength of their slaves.

I know not whether this article be dictated by my understanding or by my heart. Possibly there is not that climate upon earth where the most laborious services might not with proper encouragement be performed by freemen. Bad laws having made lazy men, they have been reduced to slavery because of their laziness.

9. *Several Kinds of Slavery.*

Slavery is of two kinds, real and personal. The real annexes the slave to the land, which Tacitus makes [589] the condition of slaves among the Germans. They were not employed in the family: a stated tribute of corn, cattle, or other movables, paid to their master, was the whole of their servitude. And such a servitude still continues in Hungary, Bohemia, and several parts of Lower Germany.

[589] *De Moribus Germanorum.*

Personal slavery consists in domestic services, and relates more to the master's person.

The worst degree of slavery is when it is at once both real and personal, as that of the Helotes among the Lacedæmonians. They underwent the fatigues of the field, and suffered all manner of insults at home. This helotism is contrary to the nature of things. Real slavery is to be found only among nations remarkable for their simplicity of life:

[590] all family business being done by the wives and children. Personal slavery is peculiar to voluptuous nations; luxury requiring the service of slaves in the house. But helotism joins in the same person the slavery established by voluptuous nations and that of the most simple.

[590] Tacitus, *De Moribus Germanorum,* says the master is not to be distinguished from the slave by any delicacy of living.

10. *Regulations necessary in respect to Slavery.*

But of whatsoever kind the slavery be, the civil laws should endeavor on the one hand to abolish the abuses of it, and on the other to guard against its dangers.

11. *Abuses of Slavery.*

In Mahometan states, [591] not only the life and goods of female slaves, but also what is called their virtue or honor, are at their master's disposal. One of the misfortunes of those countries is that the greatest part of the nation are born only to be subservient to the pleasures of the other. This servitude is alleviated by the laziness in which such slaves spend their days; which is an additional disadvantage to the state.

[591] Sir John Chardin, Travels to Persia.

It is this indolence which renders the eastern seraglios so delightful to those very persons whom they were made to confine. [592] People who dread nothing but labor may imagine themselves happy in those places of indolence and ease. But this shows how contrary they are to the very intent of the institution of slavery.

[592] Sir John Chardin, vol. ii, in his description of the market of Izagour.

Reason requires that the master's power should not extend to what does not appertain to his service: slavery should be calculated for utility, and not for pleasure. The laws of chastity arise from those of nature, and ought in all nations to be respected.

If a law which preserves the chastity of slaves be good in those states where an arbitrary power bears down all before it, how much more will it be so in monarchies, and how much more still in republics?

The law of the Lombards [593] has a regulation which ought to be adopted by all governments. "If a master debauches his slave's wife, the slave and his wife shall be restored to their freedom." An admirable expedient, which, without severity, lays a powerful restraint on the incontinence of masters!

[593] Lib. I. tit. 32, § 5.

The Romans seem to have erred on this head. They allowed an unlimited scope to the master's lusts, and, in some measure, denied their slaves the privilege of marrying. It is true, they were the lowest part of the nation; yet there should have been some care taken of their morals, especially as in prohibiting their marriage they corrupted the morals of the citizens.

12. *Danger from the Multitude of Slaves.*

The multitude of slaves has different effects in different governments. It is no grievance in a despotic state, where the political servitude of the whole body takes away the sense of civil slavery. Those who are called freedmen in reality are little more so than they who do not come within that class; and as the latter, in quality of eunuchs, freedmen, or slaves, have generally the management of all affairs, the condition of a freedman and that of a slave are very nearly allied. This makes it therefore almost a matter of indifference whether in such states the slaves be few or numerous.

But in moderate governments it is a point of the highest importance that there should not be a great number of slaves. The political liberty of those states adds to the value of civil liberty; and he who is deprived of the latter is also bereft of the former. He sees the happiness of a society, of which he is not so much as a member; he sees the security of others fenced by laws, himself without any protection. He perceives that his master has a soul, capable of enlarging itself: while his own labors under a continual depression. Nothing more assimilates a man to a beast than living among freedmen, himself a slave. Such people as these are natural enemies of society; and their number must be dangerous.

It is not therefore to be wondered at that moderate governments have been so frequently disturbed by the revolts of slaves, and that this so seldom happens in despotic states. [594]

[594] The revolt of the Mamelukes was a different case; this was a body of the militia who usurped the empire.

13. *Of armed Slaves.*

The danger of arming slaves is not so great in monarchies as in republics. In the former, a warlike people and a body of nobility are a sufficient check upon these armed slaves; whereas the pacific members of a republic would have a hard task to quell a set of men who, having offensive weapons in their hands, would find themselves a match for the citizens.

The Goths, who conquered Spain, spread themselves over the country, and soon became very weak. They made three important regulations: they abolished an ancient custom which prohibited intermarriages with the Romans; [595] they enacted that all the freedmen [596] belonging to the Fiscus should serve in war, under penalty of being reduced to slavery; and they ordained that each Goth should arm and bring into the field the tenth part of his slaves. [597] This was but a small proportion: besides, these slaves thus carried to the field did not form a separate body; they were in the army, and might be said to continue in the family.

[595] Law of the Visigoths, lib. III, tit. 1, § 1.
[596] Ibid. lib. V, tit. 7, § 20.
[597] Ibid. IX, tit. 2, § 9.

14. *The same Subject continued.*

When a whole nation is of a martial temper, the slaves in arms are less to be feared.

By a law of the Alemans, a slave who had committed a clandestine theft [598] was liable to the same punishment as a freedman in the like case; but if he was found guilty of an open robbery, [599] he was only bound to restore the things so taken. Among the Alemans, courage and intrepidity extenuated the guilt of an action. They employed their slaves in their wars. Most republics have been attentive to dispirit their slaves; but the Alemans, relying on themselves and being always armed, were so far from fearing theirs that they were rather for augmenting their courage; they were the instruments either of their depredations or of their glory.

[598] Law of the Alemans, chap. v, § 3.
[599] Ibid. § 5, *per virtutem.*

15. *Precautions to be used in Moderate Governments.*

Lenity and humane treatment may prevent the dangers to be apprehended from the multitude of slaves in a moderate government. Men grow reconciled to everything, and even to servitude, if not aggravated by the severity of the master. The Athenians treated their slaves with great lenity; and this secured that state from the commotions raised by the slaves among the austere Lacedæmonians.

It does not appear that the primitive Romans met with any trouble from their slaves. Those civil broils which have been compared to the Punic wars were the consequence of their having divested themselves of all humanity towards their slaves. [600]

[600] "Sicily," says Florus, "suffered more in the Servile than in the Punic war."—Lib. III.

A frugal and laborious people generally treat their slaves more kindly than those who are above labor. The primitive Romans used to live, work, and eat with their slaves; in short, they behaved towards them with justice and humanity. The greatest punishment they made them suffer was to make them pass before their neighbors with a forked piece of wood on their backs. Their manners were sufficient to secure the fidelity of their slaves; so that there was no necessity for laws.

But when the Romans aggrandized themselves; when their slaves were no longer the companions of their labor, but the instruments of their luxury and pride; as they then wanted morals, they had need of laws. It was even necessary for these laws to be of the most terrible kind, in order to establish the safety of those cruel masters who lived with their slaves as in the midst of enemies.

They made the Sillanian Senatus-Consultum, and other laws, [601] which decreed that when a master was murdered all the slaves under the same roof, or in any place so near the house as to be within the hearing of a man's voice, should, without distinction, be condemned to die. Those who in this case sheltered a slave, in order to save him, were punished as murderers; [602] he whom his master [603] ordered to kill him, and who obeyed, was reputed guilty; even he who did not hinder him from killing himself was liable to be punished. [604] If a master was murdered on a journey, they put to death those who were with him and those who fled. [605] All these laws operated even against persons whose innocence was proved; the intent of them was to inspire their slaves with a prodigious respect for their master. They were not dependent on the civil government, but on a fault or imperfection of the civil government. They were not derived from the equity of civil laws, since they were contrary to the principle of those laws. They were properly founded on the principles of war, with this difference, that the enemies were in the bosom of the state. The Sillanian Senatus-Consultum was derived from the law of nations, which requires that a society, however imperfect, should be preserved.

[601] See the whole title of the *Senat. Cons. Sillan.* in ff.

[602] Leg. siquis, § 12, ff. *de Senat. Cons. Sillan.*

[603] When Antony commanded Eros to kill him, it was the same as commanding him to kill himself; because, if he had obeyed, he would have been punished as the murderer of his master.

[604] Leg. 1, § 22, ff. *de Senat. Cons. Sillan.*

[605] Leg. 1, § 31, ff. ibid.

It is a misfortune in government when the magistrates thus find themselves under the necessity of making cruel laws; because they have rendered obedience difficult, they are obliged to increase the penalty of disobedience, or to suspect the slave's fidelity. A prudent legislator foresees the ill consequences of rendering the legislature terrible. The slaves amongst the Romans could have no confidence in the laws; and therefore the laws could have none in them.

16. *Regulations between Masters and Slaves.*

The magistrates ought to take care that the slave has his food and raiment; and this should be regulated by law.

The laws ought to provide that care be taken of them in sickness and old age. Claudius [606] decreed that the slaves who in sickness had been abandoned by their masters should, in case they recovered, be emancipated. This law insured their liberty; but should not there have been some care also taken to preserve their lives?

[606] Xiphilin, In *Claudio.*

When the law permitted a master to take away the life of his slave, he was invested with a power which he ought to exercise as judge, and not as master; it was necessary, therefore, that the law should ordain those formalities which remove the suspicion of an act of violence.

When fathers, at Rome, were no longer permitted to put their children to death, the magistrates ordained the punishment which the father would have inflicted. [607] A like custom between the master and his slaves would be highly reasonable in a country where masters have the power of life and death.

[607] See law 3, in Cod., *de patriâ potestate*, by the Emperor Alexander.

The law of Moses was extremely severe. If a man struck his servant so that he died under his hand, he was to be punished; but, if he survived a day or two, no punishment ensued, because he was his money. [608] Strange that a civil institution should thus relax the law of nature!

[608] Lev. xxi. 20.

By a law of the Greeks, [609] a slave too severely treated by his master might insist upon being sold to another. In later times there was a law of the same nature at Rome. [610] A master displeased with his slave, and a slave with his master, ought to be separated.

[609] Plutarch On Superstition.
[610] See the constitution of Antoninus Pius, *Institutes*, lib. I, tit. 7.

When a citizen uses the slave of another ill, the latter ought to have the liberty of complaining before the judge. The laws of Plato, [611] and of most nations, took away from slaves the right of natural defense. It was necessary then that they should give them a civil defense.

[611] Lib. IX.

At Sparta slaves could have no justice against either insults or injuries. So excessive was their misery, that they were not only the slaves of a citizen, but also of the public; they belonged to all, as well as to one. At Rome, when they considered the injury done to a slave, they had regard only to the interest of the master. [612] In the breach of the Aquilian law they confounded a wound given to a beast and that given to a slave; they regarded only the diminution of their value. At Athens, [613] he who had abused the slave of another was punished severely, and sometimes even with death. The law of Athens was very reasonable in not adding the loss of security to that of liberty.

[612] This was frequently the spirit of the laws of those nations who came out of Germany, as may be seen by their codes.
[613] Demosthenes, *Orat. contra Midian*, p. 610, Edition of Frankfort, 1604.

17. *Of Enfranchisements.*

It is easy to perceive that many slaves in a republican government create a necessity of making many free. The evil is, if they have too great a number of slaves they cannot keep them in due bounds; if they have too many freedmen, they cannot live, and must become a burden to the republic: besides, it may be as much in danger from the multitude of freedmen as from that of slaves. It is necessary, therefore, that the law should have an eye to these two inconveniences.

The several laws and decrees of the senate made at Rome, both for and against slaves, sometimes to limit, and at other times to facilitate, their enfranchisement, plainly show the embarrassment in which they found themselves in this respect. There were even times in which they durst not make laws. When, under Nero, [614] they demanded of the senate permission for the masters to reduce again to slavery the ungrateful freedmen, the emperor declared that it was their duty to decide the affairs of individuals, and to make no general decree.

[614] Tacitus, Annals, lib. XIII.

Much less can I determine what ought to be the regulations of a good republic in such an affair; this depends on too many circumstances. Let us, however, make some reflections.

A considerable number of freedmen ought not suddenly to be made by a general law. We known that among the Volsinienses [615] the freedmen, becoming masters of the suffrages, enacted an abominable law, which gave them the right of lying the first night with the young women married to the free-born.

[615] Freinshemius, Supplement, dec. 2, lib. V.

There are several ways of insensibly introducing new citizens into a republic. The laws may favor the acquiring a *peculium*, and put slaves into a condition of buying their liberty: they may prescribe a term to servitude, like those of Moses, which limited that of the Hebrew slaves to six years. [616] It is easy to enfranchise every year a certain number of those slaves who, by their age, health, or industry, are capable of getting a subsistence. The evil may be even cured in its root, as a great number of slaves are connected with the several employments which are given them; to divide among the free-born a part of these employments, for example, commerce or navigation, is diminishing the number of slaves.

[616] Exod. xxi.

When there are many freedmen, it is necessary that the civil laws should determine what they owe to their patron, or that these duties should be fixed by the contract of enfranchisement.

It is certain that their condition should be more favored in the civil than in the political state; because, even in a popular government, the power ought not to fall into the hands of the vulgar.

At Rome, where they had so many freedmen, the political laws with regard to them were admirable. They gave them very little, and excluded them almost from nothing: they had even a share in the legislature, but the resolutions they were capable of taking were almost of no weight. They might bear a part in the public offices, and even in the dignity of the priesthood; [617] but this privilege was in some sort rendered useless by the disadvantages they had to encounter in the elections. They had a right to enter into the army; but they were to be registered in a certain class of the census before they could be soldiers. Nothing hindered the [618] freedmen from being united by marriage with the families of the free-born; but they were not permitted to mix with those of the senator. In short, their children were free-born, though they were not so themselves.

[617] Tacitus, Annals, lib. III.
[618] Augustus's speech in Dio, lib. LVI.

18. *Of Freedmen and Eunuchs.*

Thus in a republican government it is frequently of advantage that the situation of the freedmen be but little below that of the free-born, and that the laws be calculated to remove a dislike of their condition. But in a despotic government, where luxury and arbitrary power prevail, they have nothing to do in this respect; the freedmen generally finding themselves above the free-born. They rule in the court of the prince, and in the palaces of the great; and as they study the foibles and not the virtues of their master, they lead him entirely by the former, not by the latter. Such were the freedmen of Rome in the times of the emperors.

When the principal slaves are eunuchs, let never so many privileges be granted them, they can hardly be regarded as freedmen. For as they are incapable of having a family of their own, they are naturally attached to that of another: and it is only by a kind of fiction that they are considered as citizens.

And yet there are countries where the magistracy is entirely in their hands. "In Tonquin," [619] says Dampier, [620] "all the mandarins, civil and military, are eunuchs." They have no families, and though they are naturally avaricious, the master or the prince benefits in the end by this very passion.

[619] It was formerly the same in China. The two Mahometan Arabs who travelled thither in the ninth century use the word eunuch whenever they speak of a governor of the city.

[620] Volume iii.

Dampier tells us, too, that in this country the eunuchs cannot live without women, and therefore marry. The law which permits their marriage may be founded partly on their respect for these eunuchs, and partly on their contempt of the fair sex.

Thus they are trusted with the magistracy, because they have no family; and permitted to marry, because they are magistrates.

Then it is that the sense which remains would fain supply that which they have lost; and the enterprises of despair become a kind of enjoyment. So, in Milton, that spirit who has nothing left but desires, enraged at his degradation, would make use of his impotency itself.

We see in the history of China a great number of laws to deprive eunuchs of all civil and military employments; but they always returned to them again. It seems as if the eunuchs of the east were a necessary evil.

BOOK XVI.

HOW THE LAWS OF DOMESTIC SLAVERY BEAR
A RELATION TO THE NATURE OF THE CLIMATE

1. *Of domestic Servitude.*

Slaves are established for the family; but they are not a part of it. Thus I distinguish their servitude from that which the women in some countries suffer, and which I shall properly call domestic servitude.

2. *That in the Countries of the South there is a natural Inequality between the two Sexes.*

Women, in hot climates, are marriageable at eight, nine, or ten years of age; [621] thus, in those countries, infancy and marriage generally go together. They are old at twenty: their reason therefore never accompanies their beauty. When beauty demands the empire, the want of reason forbids the claim; when reason is obtained, beauty is no more. These women ought then to be in a state of dependence; for reason cannot procure in old age that empire which even youth and beauty could not give. It is therefore extremely natural that in these places a man, when no law opposes it, should leave one wife to take another, and that polygamy should be introduced.

[621] "Mahomet married Cadhisja at five, and took her to his bed at eight years old. In the hot countries of Arabia and the Indies, girls are marriageable at eight years of age, and are brought to bed the year after."—Prideaux, Life of Mahomet. We see women in the kingdom of Algiers pregnant at nine, ten, and eleven years of age.— Laugier de Tassis, History of the Kingdom of Algiers, p. 61.

In temperate climates, where the charms of women are best preserved, where they arrive later at maturity, and have children at a more advanced season of life, the old age of their husbands in some degree follows theirs; and as they have more reason and knowledge at the time of marriage, if it be only on account of their having continued longer in life, it must naturally introduce a kind of equality between the two sexes; and, in consequence of this, the law of having only one wife.

In cold countries the almost necessary custom of drinking strong liquors establishes intemperance amongst men. Women, who in this respect have a natural restraint, because they are always on the defensive, have therefore the advantage of reason over them.

Nature, which has distinguished men by their reason and bodily strength, has set no other bounds to their power than those of this strength and reason. It has given charms to women, and ordained that their ascendancy over man shall end with these charms: but in hot countries, these are found only at the beginning, and never in the progress of life.

Thus the law which permits only one wife is physically conformable to the climate of Europe, and not to that of Asia. This is the reason why Mahomedanism was so easily established in Asia, and with such difficulty extended in Europe; why Christianity is maintained in Europe, and has been destroyed in Asia; and, in fine, why the Mahometans have made such progress in China, and the Christians so little. Human reasons, however, are subordinate to that Supreme Cause who does whatever He pleases, and renders everything subservient to His will.

Some particular reasons induced Valentinian [622] to permit polygamy in the empire. That law, so improper for our climates, was abrogated by Theodosius, Arcadius, and Honorius. [623]

[622] See Jornandes, *de Regno et Tempor. Success.*, and the ecclesiastic historians.
[623] See Law 7 of the Code *de Judæis et Cælicolis*, and Nov. 18, chap. v.

3. *That a Plurality of Wives greatly depends on the Means of supporting them.*

Though in countries where polygamy is once established the number of wives is principally determined by the opulence of the husband, yet it cannot be said that opulence established polygamy in those states, since poverty may produce the same effect, as I shall prove when I come to speak of the savages.

Polygamy, in powerful nations, is less a luxury in itself than the occasion of great luxury. In hot climates they have few wants, and it costs little to maintain a wife and children; [624] they may therefore have a great number of wives.

[624] In Ceylon a man may live on ten sols a month; they eat nothing there but rice and fish. Collection of Voyages made to Establish the East India Company.

4. *That the Law of Polygamy is an affair that depends on Calculation.*

According to the calculations made in several parts of Europe, there are here born more boys than girls; [625] on the contrary, by the accounts we have of Asia, there are there born more girls than boys. [626] The law which in Europe allows only one wife, and that in Asia which permits many, have therefore a certain relation to the climate.

[625] Dr. Arbuthnot finds that in England the number of boys exceeds that of girls; but people have been to blame to conclude that the case is the same in all climates.
[626] See Kempfer, who relates that upon numbering the people of Meaco there were found 182,072 males, and 223,573 females.

In the cold climates of Asia there are born, as in Europe, more males than females; and hence, say the Lamas, [627] is derived the reason of that law which amongst them permits a woman to have many husbands. [628]

[627] Father Du Halde, History of China, vol. iv.
[628] Albuzeir-el-hassen, one of the Mahometan Arabs who, in the ninth century, went into India and China, thought this custom a prostitution. And indeed nothing could be more contrary to the ideas of a Mahometan.

But it is difficult for me to believe that there are many countries where the disproportion can be great enough for any exigency to justify the introducing either the law in favor of many wives or that of many husbands. This would only imply that a majority of women, or even a majority of men, is more conformable to nature in certain countries than in others.

I confess that if what history tells us be true, that at Bantam there are ten women to one man, [629] this must be a case particularly favorable to polygamy.

[629] Collection of Voyages that Contributed to the Establishment of the East India Company, vol. i.

In all this I only give their reasons, but do not justify their customs.

5. *The Reason of a Law of Malabar.*

In the tribe of the Naires, on the coast of Malabar, the men can have only one wife, while a woman, on the contrary, may have many husbands. [630] The origin of this custom is not I believe difficult to discover. The Naires are the tribe of nobles, who are the soldiers of all those nations. In Europe soldiers are forbidden to marry; in Malabar, where the climate requires greater indulgence, they are satisfied with rendering marriage as little burdensome to them as possible: they give one wife amongst many men, which consequently diminishes the attachment to a family, and the cares of housekeeping, and leaves them in the free possession of a military spirit.

[630] See Francis Pirard, chap. xxvii. Edifying Letters, coll. iii, x, on the Malleami on the coast of Malabar. This is considered as an abuse of the military profession, as a woman, says Pirard, of the tribe of the Bramins never would marry many husbands.

6. *Of Polygamy considered in itself.*

With regard to polygamy in general, independently of the circumstances which may render it tolerable, it is not of the least service to mankind, nor to either of the two sexes, whether it be that which abuses or that which is abused. Neither is it of service to the children; for one of its greatest inconveniences is, that the father and mother cannot have the same affection for their offspring; a father cannot love twenty children with the same tenderness as a mother can love two. It is much worse when a wife has many husbands; for then paternal love only is held by this opinion, that a father may believe, if he will, or that others may believe, that certain children belong to him.

They say that the Emperor of Morocco has women of all colors, white, black, and tawny, in his seraglio. But the wretch has scarcely need of a single color.

Besides, the possession of so many wives does not always prevent their entertaining desires for those of others; [631] it is with lust as with avarice, whose thirst increases by the acquisition of treasure.

[631] This is the reason why women in the East are so carefully concealed.

In the reign of Justinian, many philosophers, displeased with the constraint of Christianity, retired into Persia. What struck them the most, says Agathias, [632] was that polygamy was permitted amongst men who did not even abstain from adultery.

[632] Life and Actions of Justinian, p. 403.

May I not say that a plurality of wives leads to that passion which nature disallows? for one depravation always draws on another. I remember that in the revolution which happened at Constantinople, when Sultan Achmet was deposed, history says that the people, having plundered the Kiaya's house, found not a single woman; they tell us that at Algiers, [633] in the greatest part of their seraglios, they have none at all.

[633] Laugier de Tassis, History of Algiers.

7. Of an Equality of Treatment in case of many Wives.

From the law which permitted a plurality of wives followed that of an equal behavior to each. Mahomet, who allowed of four, would have everything, as provisions, dress, and conjugal duty, equally divided between them. This law is also in force in the Maldivian isles, [634] where they are at liberty to marry three wives.

[634] See Pirard, chap. xii.

The law of Moses [635] even declares that if anyone has married his son to a slave, and this son should afterwards espouse a free woman, her food, her raiment, and her duty of marriage shall he not diminish. They might give more to the new wife, but the first was not to have less than she had before.

[635] Exod. xxi. 10, 11.

8. Of the Separation of Women from Men.

The prodigious number of wives possessed by those who live in rich and voluptuous countries is a consequence of the law of polygamy. Their separation from men, and their close confinement, naturally follow from the greatness of this number. Domestic order renders this necessary; thus an insolvent debtor seeks to conceal himself from the pursuit of his creditors. There are climates where the impulses of nature have such force that morality has almost none. If a man be left with a woman, the temptation and the fall will be the same thing; the attack certain, the resistance none. In these countries, instead of precepts, they have recourse to bolts and bars.

One of the Chinese classic authors considers the man as a prodigy of virtue who, finding a woman alone in a distant apartment, can forbear making use of force. [636]

[636] "It is an admirable touch-stone, to find by oneself a treasure, and to know the right owner; or to see a beautiful woman in a lonely apartment; or to hear the cries of an enemy, who must perish without our assistance."—Translation of a Chinese piece of morality, which may be seen in Du Halde, vol. iii, p. 151.

9. Of the Connection between domestic and political Government.

In a republic the condition of citizens is moderate, equal, mild, and agreeable; everything partakes of the benefit of public liberty. An empire over the women cannot, among them, be so well exerted; and where the climate demands this empire, it is most agreeable to a monarchical government. This is one of the reasons why it has ever been difficult to establish a popular government in the East.

On the contrary, the slavery of women is perfectly conformable to the genius of a despotic government, which delights in treating all with severity. Thus at all times have we seen in Asia domestic slavery and despotic government walk hand in hand with an equal pace.

In a government which requires, above all things, that a particular regard be paid to its tranquility, and where the extreme subordination calls for peace, it is absolutely necessary to shut up the women; for their intrigues would prove fatal to their husbands. A government which has not time to examine into the conduct of its subjects views them with a suspicious eye, only because they appear and suffer themselves to be known.

Let us only suppose that the levity of mind, the indiscretions, the tastes and caprices of our women, attended by their passions of a higher and a lower kind, with all their active fire, and in that full liberty with which they appear amongst us, were conveyed into an eastern government, where would be the father of a family who could enjoy a moment's repose? The men would be everywhere suspected, everywhere enemies; the state would be overturned, and the kingdom overflowed with rivers of blood.

10. *The Principle on which the Morals of the East are founded.*

In the case of a multiplicity of wives, the more a family ceases to be united, the more ought the laws to reunite its detached parts in a common centre; and the greater the diversity of interests, the more necessary is it for the laws to bring them back to a common interest.

This is more particularly done by confinement. The women should not only be separated from the men by the walls of the house, but they ought also to be separated in the same enclosure, in such a manner that each may have a distinct household in the same family. Hence each derives all that relates to the practice of morality, modesty, chastity, reserve, silence, peace, dependence, respect, and love; and, in short, a general direction of her thoughts to that which, in its own nature, is a thing of the greatest importance, a single and entire attachment to her family.

Women have naturally so many duties to fulfill—duties which are peculiarly theirs, that they cannot be sufficiently excluded from everything capable of inspiring other ideas; from everything that goes by the name of amusements; and from everything which we call business.

We find the manners more pure in the several parts of the East, in proportion as the confinement of women is more strictly observed. In great kingdoms there are necessarily great lords. The greater their wealth, the more enlarged is their ability of keeping their wives in an exact confinement, and of preventing them from entering again into society. Hence it proceeds that in the empires of Turkey, Persia, of the Mogul, China, and Japan, the manners of their wives are admirable.

But the case is not the same in India, where a multitude of islands and the situation of the land have divided the country into an infinite number of petty states, which from causes that we have not here room to mention are rendered despotic.

There are none there but wretches, some pillaging and others pillaged. Their grandees have very moderate fortunes, and those whom they call rich have only a bare subsistence. The confinement of their women cannot therefore be very strict; nor can they make use of any great precautions to keep them within due bounds; hence it proceeds that the corruption of their manners is scarcely to be conceived.

We may there see to what an extreme the vices of a climate indulged in full liberty will carry licentiousness. It is there that nature has a force and modesty a weakness, which exceeds all comprehension. At Patan [637] the wanton desires of the women are so outrageous, that the men are obliged to make use of a certain apparel to shelter them from their designs. [638] According to Mr. Smith, [639] things are not better conducted in the petty kingdoms of Guinea. In these countries the two sexes lose even those laws which properly belong to each.

[637] Collection of Voyages for the establishment of the East India Company, vol. ii, p. 2.

[638] In the Maldivian isles the fathers marry their daughters at ten and eleven years of age, because it is a great sin, say they, to suffer them to endure the want of a husband. See Pirard, chap. xii. At Bantam, as soon as a girl is twelve or thirteen years old, she must be married, if they would not have her lead a debauched life. Collection of Voyages for the establishment of the East India Company, p. 348.

[639] Voyage to Guinea, part II. "When the women happen to meet with a man, they lay hold of him, and threaten to make a complaint to their husbands if he slight their addresses. They steal into a man's bed, and wake him; and if he refuses to comply with their desires, they threaten to suffer themselves to be caught *in flagranti*."

11. *Of domestic Slavery independently of Polygamy.*

It is not only a plurality of wives which in certain places of the East requires their confinement, but also the climate itself. Those who consider the horrible crimes, the treachery, the dark villainies, the poisonings, the assassinations, which the liberty of women has occasioned at Goa and in the Portuguese settlements in the Indies, where religion permits only one wife; and who compare them with the innocence and purity of manners of the women of Turkey, Persia, Hindostan, China, and Japan, will clearly see that it is frequently as necessary to separate them from the men, when they have but one, as when they have many.

These are things which ought to be decided by the climate. What purpose would it answer to shut up women in our northern countries, where their manners are naturally good; where all their passions are calm; and where love rules over the heart with so regular and gentle an empire that the least degree of prudence is sufficient to conduct it?

It is a happiness to live in those climates which permit such freedom of converse, where that sex which has most charms seems to embellish society, and where wives, reserving themselves for the pleasures of one, contribute to the amusement of all.

12. *Of natural Modesty.*

All nations are equally agreed in fixing contempt and ignominy on the incontinence of women. Nature has dictated this to all. She has established the attack, and she has established too the resistance; and having implanted desires in both, she has given to the one boldness, and to the other shame. To individuals she has granted a long succession of years to attend to their preservation: but to continue the species, she has granted only a moment.

It is then far from being true that to be incontinent is to follow the laws of nature; on the contrary, it is a violation of these laws, which can be observed only by behaving with modesty and discretion.

Besides, it is natural for intelligent beings to feel their imperfections. Nature has, therefore, fixed shame in our minds—a shame of our imperfections.

When, therefore, the physical power of certain climates violates the natural law of the two sexes, and that of intelligent beings, it belongs to the legislature to make civil laws, with a view to opposing the nature of the climate and re-establishing the primitive laws.

13. Of Jealousy.

With respect to nations, we ought to distinguish between the passion of jealousy and a jealousy arising from customs, manners, and laws. The one is a hot raging fever; the other, cold, but sometimes terrible, may be joined with indifference and contempt.

The one, an abuse of love, derives its source from love itself. The other depends only on manners, on the customs of a nation, on the laws of the country, and sometimes even on religion. [640]

[640] Mahomet desired his followers to watch their wives; a certain Iman, when he was dying, said the same thing; and Confucius preached the same doctrine.

It is generally the effect of the physical power of the climate; and, at the same time, the remedy of this physical power.

14. Of the Eastern Manner of domestic Government.

Wives are changed so often in the East that they cannot have the power of domestic government. This care is, therefore, committed to the eunuchs, whom they entrust with their keys and the management of their families. "In Persia," says Sir John Chardin, "married women are furnished with clothes as they want them, after the manner of children." Thus that care which seems so well to become them, that care which everywhere else is the first of their concern, does not at all regard them.

15. Of Divorce and Repudiation.

There is this difference between a divorce and a repudiation, that the former is made by mutual consent, arising from a mutual antipathy; while the latter is formed by the will, and for the advantage of one of the two parties, independently of the will and advantage of the other.

The necessity there is sometimes for women to repudiate, and the difficulty there always is in doing it, render that law very tyrannical which gives this right to men without granting it to women. A husband is the master of the house; he has a thousand ways of confining his wife to her duty, or of bringing her back to it; so that in his hands it seems as if repudiation could be only a fresh abuse of power. But a wife who repudiates only makes use of a dreadful kind of remedy. It is always a great misfortune for her to go in search of a second husband, when she has lost the most part of her attractions with another. One of the advantages attending the charms of youth in the female sex is that in an advanced age the husband is led to complacency and love by the remembrance of past pleasures.

It is then a general rule that in all countries where the laws have given to men the power of repudiating, they ought also to grant it to women. Nay, in climates where women live in domestic slavery, one would think that the law ought to favor women with the right of repudiation, and husbands only with that of divorce.

When wives are confined in a seraglio, the husband ought not to repudiate on account of an opposition of manners; it is the husband's fault if their manners are incompatible.

Repudiation on account of the barrenness of the woman ought never to take place except where there is only one wife: [641] when there are many, this is of no importance to the husband.

[641] It does not follow hence that repudiation on account of sterility should be permitted amongst Christians.

A law of the Maldivians permitted them to take again a wife whom they had repudiated. [642] A law of Mexico [643] forbade their being reunited under pain of death. The law of Mexico was more rational than that of the Maldivians: at the time even of the dissolution, it attended to the perpetuity of marriage; instead of this, the law of the Maldivians seemed equally to sport with marriage and repudiation.

[642] They took them again preferably to any other, because in this case there was less expense.—Pirard, Travels.
[643] Solis, History of the Conquest of Mexico, p. 499.

The law of Mexico admitted only of divorce. This was a particular reason for their not permitting those who were voluntarily separated to be ever reunited. Repudiation seems chiefly to proceed from a hastiness of temper, and from the dictates of passion; while divorce appears to be an affair of deliberation.

Divorces are frequently of great political use: but as to the civil utility, they are established only for the advantage of the husband and wife, and are not always favorable to their children.

16. Of Repudiation and Divorce amongst the Romans.

Romulus permitted a husband to repudiate his wife, if she had committed adultery, prepared poison, or procured false keys. He did not grant to women the right of repudiating their husbands. Plutarch [644] calls this a law extremely severe.

[644] Life of Romulus.

As the Athenian law [645] gave the power of repudiation to the wife as well as to the husband, and as this right was obtained by the women among the primitive Romans, notwithstanding the law of Romulus, it is evident that this institution was one of those which the deputies of Rome brought from Athens, and which were inserted in the laws of the Twelve Tables.

[645] This was a law of Solon.

Cicero says that the reasons of repudiation sprang from the law of the Twelve Tables. [646] We cannot then doubt but that this law increased the number of the reasons for repudiation established by Romulus.

[646] Mimam res suas sibi habere jussit, ex duodecim tabulis causam addidit.—Philipp, ii.

The power of divorce was also an appointment, or at least a consequence, of the law of the Twelve Tables. For from the moment that the wife or the husband had separately the right of repudiation, there was a much stronger reason for their having the power of quitting each other by mutual consent.

The law did not require that they should lay open the causes of divorce [647] In the nature of the thing, the reasons for repudiation should be given, while those for a divorce are unnecessary; because, whatever causes the law may admit as sufficient to break a marriage, a mutual antipathy must be stronger than them all.

[647] Justinian altered this, Nov. 117, chap. x.

The following fact, mentioned by Dionysius Halicarnassus, [648] Valerius Maximus, [649] and Aulus Gellius, [650] does not appear to me to have the least degree of probability: though they had at Rome, say they, the power of repudiating a wife, yet they had so much respect for the auspices that nobody for the space of five hundred and twenty years ever made [651] use of this right, till Carvilius Ruga repudiated his, because of her sterility. We need only be sensible of the nature of the human mind to perceive how very extraordinary it must be for a law to grant such right to a whole nation, and yet for nobody to make use of it. Coriolanus, setting out on his exile, advised his [652] wife to marry a man more happy than himself. We have just been seeing that the law of the Twelve Tables and the manners of the Romans greatly extended the law of Romulus. But to what purpose were these extensions if they never made use of a power to repudiate? Besides, if the citizens had such a respect for the auspices that they would never repudiate, how came the legislators of Rome to have less than they? And how came the laws incessantly to corrupt their manners?

[648] Lib. II.
[649] Lib. II. chap. iv.
[650] Lib. IV. chap. iii. 8.
[651] According to Dionysius Halicarnassus and Valerius Maximus; and five hundred and twenty-three, according to Aulus Gellius. Neither did they agree in placing this under the same consuls.
[652] See the Speech of Veturia in Dionysius Halicarnassus, viii.

All that is surprising in the fact in question will soon disappear, only by comparing two passages in Plutarch. The regal law [653] permitted a husband to repudiate in the three cases already mentioned, and "it enjoined," says Plutarch, [654] "that he who repudiated in any other case should be obliged to give the half of his substance to his wife, and that the other half should be consecrated to Ceres." They might then repudiate in all cases, if they were but willing to submit to the penalty. Nobody had done this before Carvilius Ruga, [655] who, as Plutarch says in another place, [656] "put away his wife for her sterility two hundred and thirty years after Romulus." That is, she was repudiated seventy-one years before the law of the Twelve Tables, which extended both the power and causes of repudiation.

[653] Plutarch, Life of Romulus.
[654] Ibid.
[655] Indeed sterility is not a cause mentioned by the law of Romulus: but to all appearance he was not subject to a confiscation of his effects, since he followed the orders of the censors.
[656] In his comparison between Theseus and Romulus.

The authors I have cited say that Carvilius Ruga loved his wife, but that the censors made him take an oath to put her away, because of her barrenness, to the end that he might give children to the republic; and that this rendered him odious to the people. We must know the genius and temper of the Romans before we can discover the true cause of the hatred they had conceived against Carvilius. He did not fall into disgrace with the people for repudiating his wife; this was an affair that did not at all concern them. But Carvilius had taken an oath to the censors, that by reason of the sterility of his wife he would repudiate her to give children to the republic. This was a yoke which the people saw the censors were going to put upon them. I shall discover, in the prosecution of this work, [657] the repugnance which they always felt to regulations of the like kind. But whence can such a contradiction between those authors arise? It is because Plutarch examined into a fact, and the others have recounted a prodigy.

[657] Book XXIII, chap. iii.

BOOK XVII.

HOW THE LAWS OF POLITICAL SERVITUDE BEAR A RELATION TO THE NATURE OF THE CLIMATE

1. *Of political Servitude.*

Political servitude does not less depend on the nature of the climate than that which is civil and domestic; and this we shall now demonstrate.

2. *The Difference between Nations in point of Courage.*

We have already observed that great heat enervates the strength and courage of men, and that in cold climates they have a certain vigor of body and mind, which renders them patient and intrepid, and qualifies them for arduous enterprises. This remark holds good, not only between different nations, but even in the different parts of the same country. In the north of China [658] people are more courageous than those in the south; and those in the south of Korea [659] have less bravery than those in the north.

[658] Father Du Halde, vol. i, p. 112.

[659] The Chinese books make mention of this. Ibid.

We ought not, then, to be astonished that the effeminacy of the people in hot climates has almost always rendered them slaves; and that the bravery of those in cold climates has enabled them to maintain their liberties. This is an effect which springs from a natural cause.

This has also been found true in America; the despotic empires of Mexico and Peru were near the Line, and almost all the little free nations were, and are still, near the Poles.

3. Of the Climate of Asia.

The relations of travelers [660] inform us "that the vast continent of the north of Asia, which extends from forty degrees or thereabouts to the Pole, and from the frontiers of Muscovy even to the eastern ocean, is in an extremely cold climate; that this immense tract of land is divided by a chain of mountains which run from west to east, leaving Siberia on the north, and Great Tartary on the south; that the climate of Siberia is so cold that, excepting a few places, it is unsusceptible of cultivation; and that, though the Russians have settlements all along the Irtis, they cultivate nothing; that this country produces only some little firs and shrubs; that the natives of the country are divided into wretched hordes or tribes, like those of Canada; that the reason of this cold proceeds, on the one hand, from the height of the land, and on the other from the mountains, which, in proportion as they run from south to north, are leveled in such a manner that the north wind everywhere blows without opposition; that this wind, which renders Nova Zembla uninhabitable, blowing in Siberia makes it a barren waste; that in Europe, on the contrary, the mountains of Norway and Lapland are admirable bulwarks, which cover the northern countries from the wind; so that at Stockholm, which is about fifty-nine degrees latitude, the earth produces plants, fruits, and corn; and that about Abo, which is sixty-one degrees, and even to sixty-three and sixty-four, there are mines of silver, and the land is fruitful enough."

[660] See Travels to the North, vol. viii; the History of the Tartars; and Father Du Halde, vol. iv.

We see also in these relations "that Great Tartary, situated to the south of Siberia, is also exceedingly cold; that the country will not admit of cultivation; that nothing can be found but pasturage for flocks and herds; that trees will not grow there, but only brambles, as in Iceland; that there are, near China and India, some countries where there grows a kind of millet, but that neither corn nor rice will ripen; that there is scarcely a place in Chinese Tartary at forty-three, forty-four, and forty-five degrees where it does not freeze seven or eight months in the year, so that it is as cold as Iceland, though it might be imagined, from its situation, to be as hot as the south of France; that there are no cities, except four or five towards the eastern ocean, and some which the Chinese, for political reasons, have built near China; that in the rest of Great Tartary there are only a few situated in Buchar, Turkestan, and Cathay; that the reason of this extreme cold proceeds from the nature of the nitrous earth, full of saltpetre and sand, and more particularly from the height of the land. Father Verbiest found that a certain place, eighty leagues north of the great wall, towards the source of Kavamhuran, exceeded the height of the sea near Pekin three thousand geometrical paces; that this height [661] is the cause that though almost all the great rivers of Asia have their source in this country, there is, however, so great a want of water that it can be inhabited only near the rivers and lakes."

[661] Tartary is, then, a kind of flat mountain.

These facts being laid down, I reason thus: Asia has properly no temperate zone, as the places situated in a very cold climate immediately touch upon those which are exceedingly hot, that is, Turkey, Persia, India, China, Korea, and Japan.

In Europe, on the contrary, the temperate zone is very extensive, though situated in climates widely different from each other; there being no affinity between the climates of Spain and Italy and those of Norway and Sweden. But as the climate grows insensibly cold upon our advancing from south to north, nearly in proportion to the latitude of each country, it thence follows that each resembles the country joining it; that there is no very extraordinary difference between them, and that, as I have just said, the temperate zone is very extensive.

Hence it comes that in Asia, the strong nations are opposed to the weak; the warlike, brave, and active people touch immediately upon those who are indolent, effeminate, and timorous; the one must, therefore, conquer, and the other be conquered. In Europe, on the contrary, strong nations are opposed to the strong; and those who join each other have nearly the same courage. This is the grand reason of the weakness of Asia, and of the strength of Europe; of the liberty of Europe, and of the slavery of Asia: a cause that I do not recollect ever to have seen remarked. Hence it proceeds that liberty in Asia never increases; whilst in Europe it is enlarged or diminished, according to particular circumstances.

The Russian nobility have indeed been reduced to slavery by the ambition of one of their princes; but they have always discovered those marks of impatience and discontent which are never to be seen in the southern climates. Have they not been able for a short time to establish an aristocratic government? Another of the northern kingdoms has lost its laws; but we may trust to the climate that they are not lost in such a manner as never to be recovered.

4. *The Consequences resulting from this.*

What we have now said is perfectly conformable to history. Asia has been subdued thirteen times; eleven by the northern nations, and twice by those of the south. In the early ages it was conquered three times by the Scythians; afterwards it was subdued once by the Medes, and once by the Persians; again by the Greeks, the Arabs, the Moguls, the Turks, the Tartars, the Persians, and the Afghans. I mention only the Upper Asia, and say nothing of the invasions made in the rest of the south of that part of the world which has most frequently suffered prodigious revolutions.

In Europe, on the contrary, since the establishment of the Greek and Phoenician colonies, we know but of four great changes; the first caused by the conquest of the Romans; the second by the inundation of barbarians, who destroyed those very Romans; the third by the victories of Charlemagne; and the last by the invasions of the Normans. And if this be rightly examined, we shall find, even in these changes, a general strength diffused through all the parts of Europe. We know the difficulty which the Romans met with in conquering Europe, and the ease and facility with which they invaded Asia. We are sensible of the difficulties the northern nations had to encounter in overturning the

Roman empire; of the wars and labors of Charlemagne; and of the several enterprises of the Normans. The destroyers were incessantly destroyed.

5. *That when the People in the North of Asia and those of the North of Europe made Conquests, the Effects of the Conquest were not the same.*

The nations in the north of Europe conquered as freemen; the people in the north of Asia conquered as slaves, and subdued as others only to gratify the ambition of a master.

The reason is that the people of Tartary, the natural conquerors of Asia, are themselves enslaved. They are incessantly making conquests in the south of Asia, where they form empires: but that part of the nation which continues in the country finds that it is subject to a great master, who, being despotic in the south, will likewise be so in the north, and exercising an arbitrary power over the vanquished subjects, pretends to the same over the conquerors. This is at present most conspicuous in that vast country called Chinese Tartary, which is governed by the emperor, with a power almost as despotic as that of China itself, and which he every day extends by his conquests.

We may likewise see in the history of China that the emperors [662] sent Chinese colonies into Tartary. These Chinese have become Tartars, and the mortal enemies of China; but this does not prevent their carrying into Tartary the spirit of the Chinese government.

[662] As Vouty V, emperor of the fifth dynasty.

A part of the Tartars who were conquerors have very often been themselves expelled; when they have carried into their deserts that servile spirit which they had acquired in the climate of slavery. The history of China furnishes us with strong proofs of this assertion, as does also our ancient history. [663]

[663] The Scythians thrice conquered Asia, and thrice were driven thence. Justin, lib. II.

Hence it follows that the genius of the Getic or Tartarian nation has always resembled that of the empires of Asia. The people in these are governed by the cudgel; the inhabitants of Tartary by whips. The spirit of Europe has ever been contrary to these manners; and in all ages, what the people of Asia have called punishment those of Europe have deemed the most outrageous abuse. [664]

[664] This is in no way contrary to what I shall say in book XXVIII. chap. xx. concerning the manner of thinking among the German nations in respect to the cudgel; let the instrument be what it will, the power or action of beating was always considered by them as an affront.

The Tartars who destroyed the Grecian empire established in the conquered countries slavery and despotic power: the Goths, after subduing the Roman empire, founded monarchy and liberty.

I do not know whether the famous Rudbeck, who in his 'Atlantica' has bestowed such praises on Scandinavia, has made mention of that great prerogative which ought to set this people above all the nations upon earth; namely, this country's having been the source of the liberties of Europe—that is, of almost all the freedom which at present subsists amongst mankind.

Jornadez the Goth called the north of Europe the forge of the human race. [665] I should rather call it the forge where those weapons were framed which broke the chains of southern nations. In the north were formed those valiant people who sallied forth and deserted their countries to destroy tyrants and slaves, and to teach men that, nature having made them equal, reason could not render them dependent, except where it was necessary to their happiness.

[665] "Humani generis officinam."

6. *A new physical Cause of the Slavery of Asia, and of the Liberty of Europe.*

In Asia they have always had great empires; in Europe these could never subsist. Asia has larger plains; it is cut out into much more extensive divisions by mountains and seas; and as it lies more to the south, its springs are more easily dried up; the mountains are less covered with snow; and the rivers, being not so large, form more contracted barriers. [666]

[666] The waters lose themselves or evaporate before or after their streams are united.

Power in Asia ought, then, to be always despotic; for if their slavery was not severe they would soon make a division inconsistent with the nature of the country.

In Europe the natural division forms many nations of a moderate extent, in which the ruling by laws is not incompatible with the maintenance of the state: on the contrary, it is so favorable to it, that without this the state would fall into decay, and become a prey to its neighbors.

It is this which has formed a genius for liberty that renders every part extremely difficult to be subdued and subjected to a foreign power, otherwise than by the laws and the advantage of commerce.

On the contrary, there reigns in Asia a servile spirit, which they have never been able to shake off, and it is impossible to find in all the histories of that country a single passage which discovers a freedom of spirit; we shall never see anything there but the excess of slavery.

7. *Of Africa and America.*

This is what I had to say of Asia and Europe. Africa is in a climate like that of the south of Asia, and is in the same servitude. America, [667] being lately destroyed and repeopled by the nations of Europe and Africa, can now scarcely display its genuine spirit; but what we know of its ancient history is very conformable to our principles.

[667] The petty barbarous nations of America are called by the Spaniards *Indios Bravos* and are much more difficult to subdue than the great empires of Mexico and Peru.

8. *Of the Capital of the Empire.*

One of the consequences of what we have been mentioning is, that it is of the utmost importance to a great prince to make a proper choice of the seat of his empire. He who places it to the southward will be in danger of losing the north; but he who fixes it on the north may easily preserve the south. I do not speak of particular cases. In mechanics there are frictions by which the effects of the theory are frequently changed or retarded; and policy has also its frictions.

BOOK XVIII.

OF LAWS IN THE RELATION THEY BEAR TO THE NATURE OF THE SOIL

1. *How the Nature of the Soil has an Influence on the Laws.*

The goodness of the land, in any country, naturally establishes subjection and dependence. The husbandmen, who compose the principal part of the people, are not very jealous of their liberty; they are too busy and too intent on their own private affairs. A country which overflows with wealth is afraid of pillage, afraid of an army. "Who is there that forms this goodly party?" said Cicero to Atticus; [668] "are they the men of commerce and husbandry? Let us not imagine that these are averse to monarchy—these to whom all governments are equal, as soon as they bestow tranquility."

[668] Lib. XVII.

Thus monarchy is more frequently found in fruitful countries, and a republican government in those which are not so; and this is sometimes a sufficient compensation for the inconveniences they suffer by the sterility of the land.

The barrenness of the Attic soil established there a democracy; and the fertility of that of Lacedæmonia an aristocratic constitution. For in those times Greece was averse to the government of a single person, and aristocracy bore the nearest resemblance to that government.

Plutarch says [669] that the Cilonian sedition having been appeased at Athens, the city fell into its ancient dissensions, and was divided into as many parties as there were kinds of land in Attica. The men who inhabited the eminences would, by all means, have a popular government; those of the flat, open country demanded a government composed of the chiefs; and they who were near the sea desired a mixture of both.

[669] Life of Solon.

2. *The same Subject continued.*

These fertile provinces are always of a level surface, where the inhabitants are unable to dispute against a stronger power; they are then obliged to submit; and when they have once submitted, the spirit of liberty cannot return; the wealth of the country is a pledge of their fidelity. But in mountainous districts, as they have but little, they may preserve what they have. The liberty they enjoy, or, in other words, the government they are under, is the only blessing worthy of their defense. It reigns, therefore, more in mountainous and rugged countries than in those which nature seems to have most favored.

The mountaineers preserve a more moderate government, because they are not so liable to be conquered. They defend themselves easily, and are attacked with difficulty; ammunition and provisions are collected and carried against them with great expense, for the country furnishes none. It is, then, a more arduous, a more dangerous, enterprise to make war against them; and all the laws that can be enacted for the safety of the people are there of least use.

3. *What Countries are best cultivated.*

Countries are not cultivated in proportion to their fertility, but to their liberty; and if we make an imaginary division of the earth, we shall be astonished to see in most ages deserts in the most fruitful parts, and great nations in those where nature seems to refuse everything.

It is natural for a people to leave a bad soil to seek a better, and not to leave a good soil to go in search of worse. Most invasions have, therefore, been made in countries which nature seems to have formed for happiness; and as nothing is more nearly allied than desolation and invasion, the best provinces are most frequently depopulated, while the frightful countries of the north continue always inhabited, from their being almost uninhabitable.

We find by what historians tell us of the passage of the people of Scandinavia along the banks of the Danube that this was not a conquest, but only a migration into desert countries.

These happy climates must therefore have been depopulated by other migrations, though we know not the tragic scenes that happened. "It appears by many monuments of antiquity," says Aristotle, [670] "that the Sardinians were a Grecian colony. They were formerly very rich; and Aristeus, so famed for his love of agriculture, was their law-giver. But they have since fallen to decay; for the Carthaginians, becoming their masters, destroyed everything proper tor the nourishment of man, and forbade the cultivation of the lands on pain of death." Sardinia was not recovered in the time of Aristotle, nor is it to this day.

[670] Or he who wrote the book *De Mirabilibus.*

The most temperate parts of Persia, Turkey, Muscovy, and Poland have not been able to recover perfectly from the devastations of the Tartars.

4. *New Effects of the Fertility and Barrenness of Countries.*

The barrenness of the earth renders men industrious, sober, inured to hardship, courageous, and fit for war; they are obliged to procure by labor what the earth refuses to bestow spontaneously. The fertility of a country gives ease, effeminacy, and a certain fondness for the preservation of life. It has been remarked that the German troops raised in those places where the peasants are rich, as, for instance, in Saxony, are not so good as the others. Military laws may provide against this inconvenience by a more severe discipline.

5. *Of the Inhabitants of Islands.*

The inhabitants of islands have a higher relish for liberty than those of the continent. Islands are commonly of small extent; [671] one part of the people cannot be so easily employed to oppress the other; the sea separates them from great empires; tyranny cannot so well support itself within a small compass: conquerors are stopped by the sea; and the islanders, being without the reach of their arms, more easily preserve their own laws.

[671] Japan is an exception to this, by its great extent as well as by its slavery.

6. *Of Countries raised by the Industry of Man.*

Those countries which the industry of man has rendered habitable, and which stand in need of the same industry to provide for their subsistence, require a mild and moderate government. There are principally three of this species: the two fine provinces of Kiang-nan and Tsekiang in China; Egypt, and Holland.

The ancient emperors of China were not conquerors. The first thing they did to aggrandize themselves was what gave the highest proof of their wisdom. They raised from beneath the waters two of the finest provinces of the empire; these owe their existence to the labor of man. And it is the inexpressible fertility of these two provinces which has given Europe such ideas of the felicity of that vast country. But a continual and necessary care to preserve from destruction so considerable a part of the empire demanded rather the manners of a wise than of a voluptuous nation, rather the lawful authority of a monarch than the tyrannic sway of a despotic prince. Power was, therefore, necessarily moderated in that country, as it was formerly in Egypt, and as it is now in Holland, which nature has made to attend to herself, and not to be abandoned to negligence or caprice.

Thus, in spite of the climate of China, where they are naturally led to a servile obedience; in spite of the apprehensions which follow too great an extent of empire, the first legislators of this country were obliged to make excellent laws, and the government was frequently obliged to follow them.

7. *Of human Industry.*

Mankind by their industry, and by the influence of good laws, have rendered the earth more proper for their abode. We see rivers flow where there have been lakes and marshes: this is a benefit which nature has not bestowed; but it is a benefit maintained and supplied by nature. When the Persians [672] were masters of Asia, they permitted those who conveyed a spring to any place which had not been watered before to enjoy the benefit for five generations; and as a number of rivulets flowed from Mount Taurus, they spared no expense in directing the course of their streams. At this day, without knowing how they came thither, they are found in the fields and gardens.

[672] Polybius, lib. X.

Thus, as destructive nations produce evils more durable than themselves, the actions of an industrious people are the source of blessings which last when they are no more.

8. *The general Relation of Laws.*

The laws have a very great relation to the manner in which the several nations procure their subsistence. There should be a code of laws of a much larger extent for a nation attached to trade and navigation than for people who are content with cultivating the earth. There should be a much greater for the latter than for those who subsist by their flocks and herds. There must be a still greater for these than for such as live by hunting.

9. *Of the Soil of America.*

The cause of there being such a number of savage nations in America is the fertility of the earth, which spontaneously produces many fruits capable of affording them nourishment. If the women cultivate a spot of land around their cottages, the maize grows up presently; and hunting and fishing put the men in a state of complete abundance. Besides, black cattle, as cows, buffaloes, &c., thrive there better than carnivorous beasts. The latter have always reigned in Africa.

We should not, I believe, have all these advantages in Europe if the land was left uncultivated; it would scarcely produce anything besides forests of oaks and other barren trees.

10. *Of Population in the Relation it bears to the Manner of procuring Subsistence.*

Let us see in what proportion countries are peopled where the inhabitants do not cultivate the earth. As the produce of uncultivated land is to that of land improved by culture, so the number of savages in one country is to that of husbandmen in another: and when the people who cultivate the land cultivate also the arts, this is also in such proportions as would require a minute detail.

They can scarcely form a great nation. If they are herdsmen and shepherds, they have need of an extensive country to furnish subsistence for a small number; if they live by hunting, their number must be still less, and in order to find the means of life they must constitute a very small nation.

Their country commonly abounds with forests, which, as the inhabitants have not the art of draining off the waters, are filled with bogs; here each troop canton themselves, and form a petty nation.

11. *Of savage and barbarous Nations.*

There is this difference between savage and barbarous nations: the former are dispersed clans, which for some particular reason cannot be joined in a body; and the latter are commonly small nations, capable of being united. The savages are generally hunters; the barbarians are herdsmen and shepherds.

This appears plain in the north of Asia. The people of Siberia cannot live in bodies, because they are unable to find subsistence; the Tartars may live in bodies for some time, because their herds and flocks may for a time be reassembled. All the clans may then be reunited, and this is effected when one chief has subdued many others; after which they may do two things—either separate, or set out with a design to make a great conquest in some southern empire.

12. *Of the Law of Nations among People who do not cultivate the Earth.*

As these people do not live in circumscribed territories, many causes of strife arise between them; they quarrel about waste land as we about inheritances. Thus they find frequent occasions for war, in disputes in relation either to their hunting, their fishing, the pasture for their cattle, or the violent seizing of their slaves; and as they are not possessed of landed property, they have many things to regulate by the law of nations, and but few to decide by the civil law.

13. *Of the Civil Laws of those Nations who do not cultivate the Earth.*

The division of lands is what principally increases the civil code. Among nations where they have not made this division there are very few civil laws.

The institutions of these people may be called manners rather than *laws*.

Among such nations as these the old men, who remember things past, have great authority; they cannot there be distinguished by wealth, but by wisdom and valor.

These people wander and disperse themselves in pasture grounds or in forests. Marriage cannot there have the security which it has among us, where it is fixed by the habitation, and where the wife continues in one house; they may then more easily change their wives, possess many, and sometimes mix indifferently like brutes.

Nations of herdsmen and shepherds cannot leave their cattle, which are their subsistence; neither can they separate themselves from their wives, who look after them. All this ought, then, to go together, especially as living generally in a flat open country, where there are few places of considerable strength, their wives, their children, their flocks, may become the prey of their enemies.

The laws regulate the division of plunder, and give, like our Salic laws, a particular attention to theft.

14. *Of the political State of the People who do not cultivate the Land.*

These people enjoy great liberty; for as they do not cultivate the earth, they are not fixed: they are wanderers and vagabonds; and if a chief should deprive them of their liberty, they would immediately go and seek it under another, or retire into the woods, and there live with their families. The liberty of the man is so great among these people that it necessarily draws after it that of the citizen.

15. *Of People who know the Use of Money.*

Aristippus, being cast away, swam and got safely to the next shore, where, beholding geometrical figures traced in the sand, he was seized with a transport of joy, judging that he was among Greeks, and not in a nation of barbarians.

Should you ever happen to be cast by some adventure among an unknown people; upon seeing a piece of money you may be assured that you have arrived in a civilized country.

The culture of lands requires the use of money. This culture supposes many inventions and many degrees of knowledge; and we always see ingenuity, the arts, and a sense of want making their progress with an equal pace. All this conduces to the establishment of a sign of value.

Torrents and eruptions have made the discovery that metals are contained in the bowels of the earth. [673] When once they have been separated, they have easily been applied to their proper use.

[673] It is thus that Diodorus tells us the shepherds found gold in the Pyrenean mountains. Aristotle concurs in this idea, but Strabo treats it as a fable.—Ed.

16. Of Civil Laws among People who know not the Use of Money.

When a people have not the use of money, they are seldom acquainted with any other injustice than that which arises from violence; and the weak, by uniting, defend themselves from its effects. They have nothing there but political regulations. But where money is established, they are subject to that injustice which proceeds from craft—an injustice that may be exercised in a thousand ways. Hence they are forced to have good civil laws, which spring up with the new practices of iniquity.

In countries where they have no specie, the robber takes only bare movables, which have no mutual resemblance. But where they make use of money, the robber takes the signs, and these always resemble each other. In the former nothing can be concealed, because the robber takes along with him the proofs of his conviction; but in the latter it is quite the contrary.

17. Of political Laws among Nations who have not the Use of Money.

The greatest security of the liberties of a people who do not cultivate the earth is their not knowing the use of money. What is gained by hunting, fishing, or keeping herds of cattle cannot be assembled in such great quantity, nor be sufficiently preserved, for one man to find himself in a condition to corrupt many others: but when, instead of this, a man has a sign of riches, he may obtain a large quantity of these signs, and distribute them as he pleases.

The people who have no money have but few wants; and these are supplied with ease, and in an equal manner. Equality is then unavoidable; and hence it proceeds that their chiefs are not despotic.

If what travelers tell us be true, the constitution of a nation of Lewisiana, called the Natches, is an exception to this. Their chief disposes of the goods of all his subjects, and obliges them to work and toil, according to his pleasure. [674] He has a power like that of the grand signior, and they cannot even refuse him their heads. When the presumptive heir enters the world, they devote all the sucking children to his service during his life. One would imagine that this is the great Sesostris. He is treated in his cottage with as much ceremony as an emperor of Japan or China.

[674] Edifying Letters, coll. XX.

18. *Of the Power of Superstition.*

The prejudices of superstition are superior to all others, and have the strongest influence on the human mind. Thus, though the savage nations have naturally no knowledge of despotic tyranny, still they feel the weight of it. They adore the sun; and if their chief had not imagined that he was the brother of this glorious luminary, they would have thought him a wretch like themselves.

19. *Of the Liberty of the Arabs and the Servitude of the Tartars.*

The Arabs and Tartars are nations of herdsmen and shepherds. The Arabs find themselves in that situation of which we have been speaking, and are therefore free; whilst the Tartars (the most singular people on earth) are involved in a political slavery. [675] I have already given reasons for this [676] and shall now assign some others.

[675] When a khan is proclaimed, all the people cry that his word shall be as a sword.
[676] Book XVII. chap. 5.

They have no towns, no forests, and but few marshes; their rivers are generally frozen, and they dwell in a level country of an immense extent. They have pasture for their herds and flocks, and consequently property; but they have no kind of retreat, or place of safety. A khan is no sooner overcome than they cut off his head; his children are treated in the same manner, [677] and all his subjects belong to the conqueror. These are not condemned to a civil slavery, for in that case they would be a burden to a simple people, who have no lands to cultivate, and no need of any domestic service. They therefore add to the bulk of the nation; but instead of civil servitude, a political slavery must naturally be introduced among them.

[677] We ought not therefore to be astonished at Mahomet, the son of Miriveis, who, upon taking Ispahan, put all the princes of the blood to the sword.

It is apparent that in a country where the several clans make continual war, and are perpetually conquering each other; in a country where, by the death of the chief, the body politic of the vanquished clan is always destroyed, the nation in general can enjoy but little freedom; for there is not a single party that must not have been often subdued.

A conquered people may preserve some degree of liberty when, by the strength of their situation, they are in a state that will admit of capitulating after their defeat. But the Tartars, always defenseless, being once overcome, can never be able to obtain conditions.

I have said, in chapter 2, that the inhabitants of cultivated plains are seldom free. Circumstances have occurred to put the Tartars, who dwell in uncultivated plains, in the same situation.

20. *Of the Law of Nations as practiced by the Tartars.*

The Tartars appear to be mild and humane among themselves; and yet they are most cruel conquerors: when they take cities they put the inhabitants to the sword, and imagine that they act humanely if they only sell the people, or distribute them among their soldiers.

They have destroyed Asia, from India even to the Mediterranean; and all the country which forms the east of Persia they have rendered a desert.

The law of nations is owing, I think, to the following cause. These people having no towns, all their wars are carried on with eagerness and impetuosity. They fight whenever they hope to conquer; and when they have no such hope, they join the stronger army. With such customs, it is contrary to the law of nations that a city incapable of repelling their attack should stop their progress. They regard not cities as an association of inhabitants, but as places made to bid defiance to their power. They besiege them without military skill, and expose themselves greatly in the attack; and therefore revenge themselves on all those who have spilled their blood.

21. *The Civil Law of the Tartars.*

Father Du Halde says that amongst the Tartars the youngest of the males is always the heir, by reason that as soon as the elder brothers are capable of leading a pastoral life they leave the house with a certain number of cattle, given them by their father, and build a new habitation. The last of the males, who continues at home with the father, is then his natural heir.

I have heard that a like custom was also observed in some small districts of England; and we find it still in Brittany, in the duchy of Rohan, where it obtains with regard to ignoble tenures. This is doubtless a pastoral law conveyed thither by some of the people of Britain, or established by some German nation. By Cæsar and Tacitus we are informed that the latter cultivated but little land.

22. *Of a Civil Law of the German Nations.*

I shall here explain how that particular passage of the Salic law which is commonly distinguished by the term "the Salic law" relates to the institutions of a people who do not cultivate the earth, or at least who cultivate it but very little.

The Salic law ordains [678] that, when a man has left children behind him, the males shall succeed to the Salic land in preference to the females.

[678] Tit. 62.

To understand the nature of those Salic lands, there needs no more than to search into the usages or customs of the Franks with regard to lands before they left Germany.

Mr. Echard has very plainly proved that the word Salic is derived from Sala, which signifies a house; and therefore that the Salic land was the land belonging to the house. I shall proceed further, and examine into the nature of the house, and of the land belonging to the house, among the Germans.

"They dwell not in towns," says Tacitus, "nor can they bear to have their habitations contiguous to those of others; every one leaves a space or small piece of ground about his house, which is enclosed." [679] Tacitus is very exact in this account, for many laws of the Barbarian codes have different decrees against those who threw down this enclosure, as well as against such as broke into the house. [680]

[679] "Nullas Germanorum populis urbes habitari satis notum est, ne pati quidem inter se junctas sedes; colunt discreti, ut nemus placuit. Vicos locant, non in nostrum morem connexis et cohærentibus ædificiis: suam quisque domum spatio circumdat."—*De Moribus Germanorum.*
[680] The Law of the Alemans, chap. 10, and the Law of the Bavarians, tit. 10, §§ 1, 2.

We learn from Tacitus and Cæsar that the lands cultivated by the Germans were given them only for the space of a year, after which they again became public. They had no other patrimony but the house and a piece of land within the enclosure that surrounded it. [681] It was this particular patrimony which belonged to the males. And, indeed, how could it belong to the daughters? They were to pass into another habitation.

[681] This enclosure is called *Cortis* in the charters.

The Salic land was then within that enclosure which belonged to a German house; this was the only property they had. The Franks, after their conquests, acquired new possessions, and continued to call them Salic lands.

When the Franks lived in Germany their wealth consisted of slaves, flocks, horses, arms, &c. The habitation and the small portion of land adjoining it were naturally given to the male children who were to dwell there. But afterwards, when the Franks had by conquest acquired large tracts of land, they thought it hard that the daughters and their children should be incapable of enjoying any part of them. Hence it was that they introduced a custom of permitting the father to settle the estate after his death upon his daughter, and her children. They silenced the law; and it appears that these settlements were frequent, since they were entered in the formularies. [682]

[682] See Marculfus, lib. II. form. 10, 12. Appendix to Marculfus, form. 49, and the ancient formularies of *Sirmondus*, form. 22.

Among these formularies I find one of a singular nature. [683] A grandfather ordained by will that his grandchildren should share his inheritance with his sons and daughters. What then became of the Salic law? In those times either it would not be observed, or the continual use of nominating the daughters to an inheritance had made them consider their ability to succeed as a case authorized by custom.

[683] Form. 55, in Lindembrock's collection.

The Salic law had not in view a preference of one sex to the other, much less had it a regard to the perpetuity of a family, a name, or the transmission of land. These things did not enter into the heads of the Germans; it was purely an economical law, which made the house and the land dependent thereon to the males who should dwell in it, and to whom it consequently was of most service.

We need here only transcribe the title of the Allodial Lands of the Salic law; that famous text of which so many have talked, and which so few have read.

"1. If a man dies without issue, his father or mother shall succeed him. 2. If he has neither father nor mother, his brother or sister shall succeed him. 3. If he has neither brother nor sister, the sister of his mother shall succeed him. 4. If his mother has no sister, the sister of his father shall succeed him. 5. If his father has no sister, the nearest relative by the male side shall succeed. 6. Not any part of the Salic land shall pass to the females; but it shall belong to the males; that is, the male children shall succeed their father." [684]

[684] De terra vero Salica in mulierem nulla portio hereditatis transit, sed hoc virilis sexus acquirit, hoc est filii in ipsa hereditate succedunt.—Tit. 68, § 6.

It is plain that the first five articles relate to the inheritance of a man who dies without issue; and the sixth to the succession of him who has children.

When a man dies without children, the law ordains that neither of the two sexes shall have the preference to the other, except in certain cases. In the first two degrees of succession, the advantages of the males and females were the same; in the third and fourth, the females had the preference; and the males in the fifth.

Tacitus points out the source of these extravagances. "The sister's children," says he, "are as dear to their uncle as to their own father. There are men who regard this degree of kindred as more strict, and even more holy. They prefer it when they receive hostages." [685] Hence it proceeds that our earliest historians speak in such strong terms of the love of the kings of the Franks for their sisters and their sisters' children. [686] And, indeed, if the children of the sister were considered in her brother's house as his own children, it was natural for these to regard their aunt as their mother.

[685] Sororum filiis idem apud avunculum quam apud patrem honor. Quidam sanctiorem arctioremque hunc nexum sanguinis arbitrantur, et in accipiendis obsidibus magis exigunt, tanquam ii et animum firmius et domum latius teneant—De Moribus Germanorum.

[686] See, in Gregory of Tours, lib. VIII. chap. 18, 20 and lib. XI, 16, 20, the rage of Gontram at Leovigild's ill-treatment of Ingunda, his niece, which Childebert her brother took up arms to revenge.

The sister of the mother was preferred to the father's sister; this is explained by other texts of the Salic law. When a woman became a widow, [687] she fell under the guardianship of her husband's relatives; the law preferred to this guardianship the relatives by the females before those by the males. Indeed, a woman who entered into a family joining herself with those of her own sex, became more united to her relatives by the female than by the male. Moreover, when a man killed another, and had not wherewithal to pay the pecuniary penalty, the law permitted him to deliver up his substance, and his relatives were to supply the deficiency. [688] After the father, mother, and brother, the sister of the mother was to pay, as if this tie had something in it most tender: now the degree of kindred which imposes the burdens ought also to confer the advantages.

[687] Salic Law, tit. 47.
[688] Ibid., tit. 61, § 1.

The Salic law enjoins that after the father's sister, the succession should be held by the nearest relative male; but if this relative was beyond the fifth degree, he should not inherit. Thus a female of the fifth degree might inherit to the prejudice of a male of the sixth; and this may be seen in the law of the Ripuarian Franks (a faithful interpreter of the Salic law), under the title of *Allodial Lands*, where it closely adheres to the Salic law on the same subject. [689]

[689] Et deinceps usque ad quintum genuculum qui proximus fuerit in hereditatem succedat.—Tit. 56, § 6.

If the father left issue, the Salic law would have the daughters excluded from the inheritance of the Salic land, and determined that it should belong to the male children.

It would be easy for me to prove that the Salic law did not absolutely exclude the daughters from the possession of the Salic land, but only in the case where they were debarred by their brothers. This appears from the letter of the Salic law; which, after having said that the women shall possess none of the Salic land, but only the males, interprets and restrains itself by adding, "that is, the son shall succeed to the inheritance of the father."

2. The text of the Salic law is cleared up by the law of the Ripuarian Franks, which has also a title on allodial lands very conformable to that of the Salic law. [690]

[690] Tit. 56.

3. The laws of these barbarous nations who all sprang from Germany interpret each other, more particularly as they all have nearly the same spirit. The Saxon law enjoined the father and mother to leave their inheritance to their son, and not to their daughter; but if there were none but daughters, they were to have the whole inheritance. [691]

[691] Tit. 7, § 1: Pater aut mater defuncti, filio non filiæ hereditatem relinquant;" § 4, "qui defunctus, non filios, sed filias reliquerit, ad eas omnis hereditas pertineat.

4. We have two ancient formularies [692] that state the case in which, according to the Salic law, the daughters were excluded by the males; that is, when they stood in competition with their brother.

[692] In Marculfus, lib. II, form. 12, and in the Appendix to Marculfus, form. 49.

5. Another formulary [693] proves that the daughter succeeded to the prejudice of the grandson; she was therefore excluded only by the son.

[693] Lindembrock's collection, form. 55.

6. If daughters had been generally debarred by the Salic law from the inheritance of land, it would be impossible to explain the histories, formularies, and charters which are continually mentioning the lands and possessions of the females under the first race.

People have been wrong in asserting that the Salic lands were fiefs. [694] 1. This head is distinguished by the title of allodial lands. 2. Fiefs at first were not hereditary, 3.

If the Salic lands had been fiefs, how could Marculfus treat that custom as impious which excluded the women from inheriting, when the males themselves did not succeed to fiefs? 4. The charters which have been cited to prove that the Salic lands were fiefs only show that they were freeholds. 5. Fiefs were not established till after the conquest, and the Salic customs existed long before the Franks left Germany. 6. It was not the Salic law that formed the establishment of fiefs, by setting bounds to the succession of females; but it was the establishment of fiefs that prescribed limits to the succession of females, and to the regulations of the Salic law.

[694] Ducange, Pithou, &c.

After what has been said, one would not imagine that the perpetual succession of males to the crown of France should have taken its rise from the Salic law. And yet this is a point indubitably certain. I prove it from the several codes of the barbarous nations. The Salic law, [695] and the law of the Burgundians, [696] debarred the daughters from the right of succeeding to the land in conjunction with their brothers; neither did they succeed to the crown. The law of the Visigoths, [697] on the contrary, permitted the daughters to inherit the land with the brothers: [698] and the women were capable of inheriting the crown. [699] Among these people the regulations of the civil law had an effect on the political.

[695] Tit. 62.
[696] Tit. 1, § 3; tit. 16, § 1; tit. 51.
[697] Lib. IV, tit. 2, § 1.
[698] Among the Ostrogoths, the crown twice devolved to the males by means of females; the first time to Athalaricus, through Amalasuntha, and the second to Theodat, through Amalafreda. Not but that the females of that nation might have held the crown in their own right; for Amalasuntha reigned after the death of Athalaricus; nay, even after the election of Theodat, and in conjunction with that prince. See Amalasuntha's and Theodat's letters, in Cassiodorus, x.
[699] The German nations, says Tacitus had common customs, as well as those which were peculiar to each.

This was not the only case in which the political law of the Franks gave way to the civil. By the Salic law, all the brothers succeeded equally to the land, and this was also decreed by a law of the Burgundians. Thus, in the kingdom of the Franks, and in that of the Burgundians, all the brothers succeeded to the crown, if we except a few murders and usurpations which took place amongst the Burgundians.

23. Of the regal Ornaments among the Franks.

A people who do not cultivate the land have no idea of luxury. We may see, in Tacitus, the admirable simplicity of the German nations: they had no artificial elegances of dress; their ornaments were derived from nature. If the family of their chief was to be distinguished by any sign, it was no other than that which nature bestowed. The kings of the Franks, of the Burgundians, and the Visigoths wore their long hair for a diadem.

24. Of the Marriages of the Kings of the Franks.

I have already mentioned that with people who do not cultivate the earth, marriages are less fixed than with others, and that they generally take many wives. "Of all the barbarous nations the Germans were almost the only people who were satisfied with one wife, [700] if we except," says Tacitus, "some persons who, not from a dissoluteness of manners, but because of their nobility, had many." [701]

[700] Prope soli Barbarorum singulis uxoribus contenti stint.—*De Moribus Germanorum.*
[701] Exceptis admodum paucis qui non libidine, sed ob nobilitatem, plurimis nuptiis ambiuntur.—*Ibid.*

This explains the reason why the kings of the first race had so great a number of wives. These marriages were less a proof of incontinence than a consequence of dignity: and it would have wounded them in a tender point to have deprived them of such a prerogative. [702] This also explains the reason why the example of the kings was not followed by the subjects.

[702] See Fredegarius, Chronicle of the year 628.

25. Childeric.

"The laws of matrimony amongst the Germans," says Tacitus, "are strictly observed. Vice is not there a subject of ridicule. To corrupt or be corrupted is not called fashion, or the custom of the age: [703] there are few examples in this populous nation of the violation of conjugal faith." [704]

[703] "Severa matrimonia —— nemo illic vitia ridet, nec corrumpere et corrumpi sæculum vocatur."—*De Moribus Germanorum.*
[704] "Paucissima in tam numerosa gente adulteria."—*Ibid.*

This was the reason of the expulsion of Childeric: he shocked their rigid virtue, which conquest had not had time to corrupt.

26. Of the Time when the Kings of the Franks became of age.

Barbarians who do not cultivate the earth have, strictly speaking, no jurisdiction, and are, as we have already remembered, rather governed by the law of nations than by civil institutions. They are, therefore, always armed. Thus Tacitus tells us "that the Germans undertook no affairs either of a public or private nature unarmed." [705] They gave their vote by the sound of their arms. [706] As soon as they could carry them, they were presented to the assembly; [707] they put a javelin into their hands; [708] and from that moment they were out of their minority: they had been a part of the family, now they became a part of the republic. [709]

[705] "Nihil neque publicæ neque privatæ rei nisi armati agunt."—*Ibid.*, 13.

[706] "Si displicuit sententia, fremitu aspernantur; sin placuit, frameas concutiunt."— *Ibid.*, 11.

[707] "Sed arma sumere non ante cuiquam moris, quam civitas suffecturum probaverit."—*Ibid.*, 13.

[708] "Tum in ipso concilia vel principum aliquis, vel pater, vel propinquus, scuto, frameâque juvenem ornant.

[709] "Hæc apud illos toga, hic primus juventæ honos; ante hoc domus pars videntur, mox reipublicæ."

"The eagles," said the king of the Ostrogoths, [710] "cease to feed their young ones as soon as their wings and talons are formed; the latter have no need of assistance when they are able themselves to seize their prey: it would be a disgrace if the young people in our armies were thought to be of an age unfit for managing their estates or regulating the conduct of their lives. It is virtue that constitutes full age among the Goths."

[710] Theodoric in *Cassiodorus*, lib. I. ep. 38.

Childebert II was fifteen years old when Gontram, his uncle, declared that he was of age, and capable of governing by himself. [711] We find in the Ripuarian laws that the age of fifteen, the ability of bearing arms, and majority, went together. It is there said [712] "that if a Ripuarian dies, or is killed, and leaves a son behind him, that son can neither prosecute, nor be prosecuted, till he has completely attained the age of fifteen; and then he may either answer for himself or choose a champion." It was necessary that his mind should be sufficiently formed to be able to defend himself in court; and that his body should have all the strength that was proper for his defense in single combat. Among the Burgundians, [713] who also made use of this combat in their judiciary proceedings, they were of age at fifteen.

[711] He was scarcely five years old, says Gregory of Tours, lib. V. chap. 1, when he succeeded to his father, in the year 575. Gontram declared him of age in the year 585; he was, therefore, at that time no more than fifteen.

[712] Tit. 81.

[713] Tit. 87.

Agathias tells us that the arms of the Franks were light: they might, therefore, be of age at fifteen. In succeeding times the arms they made use of were heavy, and they were already greatly so in the time of Charlemagne, as appears by our capitularies and romances. Those who had fiefs, [714] and were consequently obliged to do military service, were not then of age till they were twenty-one years old. [715]

[714] There was no change in the time with regard to the common people.

[715] St. Lewis was not of age till twenty-one; this was altered by an edict of Charles V in the year 1374.

27. *The same Subject continued.*

We have seen that the Germans did not appear in their assemblies before they were of age; they were a part of the family, but not of the republic. This was the reason that the children of Clodomir, king of Orleans, and conqueror of Burgundy, were not proclaimed kings, because they were of too tender an age to be present at the assembly. They were not yet kings, but they had a right to the regal dignity as soon as they were able to bear arms; and in the meantime, Clotildis, their grandmother, governed the state. [716] But their uncles Clotarius and Childebert assassinated them, and divided their kingdom. This was the cause that in the following ages princes in their minority were proclaimed kings immediately after the death of their fathers. Thus Duke Gondovald saved Childebert II from the cruelty of Chilperic, and caused him to be proclaimed king when he was only five years old. [717]

[716] It appears from Gregory of Tours, lib. III, that she chose two natives of Burgundy, which had been conquered by Clodomir, to raise them to the see of Tours, which also belonged to Clodomir.

[717] Gregory of Tours, lib. V. chap. i.: "Vix lustro ætatis uno jam peracto qui die Dominicæ Natalis regnare cœpit."

But even in this change they followed the original spirit of the nation; for the public acts did not pass in the name of the young monarch. So that the Franks had a double administration: the one which concerned the person of the infant king, and the other which regarded the kingdom; and in the fiefs there was a difference between the guardianship and the civil administration.

28. *Of Adoption among the Germans.*

As the Germans became of age by the wielding of arms, so they were adopted by the same sign. Thus Gontram, willing to declare his nephew Childebert of age and to adopt him for his son, made use of these words: "I have put this javelin into thy hands as a token that I have given thee all my kingdom." [718] Then, turning towards the assembly, he added, "You see that my son Childebert is grown a man; obey him." Theodoric, king of the Ostrogoths, intending to adopt the king of the Heruli, wrote to him thus: [719] "It is a noble custom of ours to be adopted by arms; for men of courage alone deserve to be our children. Such is the efficacy of this act, that whoever is the object of it had rather die than submit to anything ignominious. Therefore, in compliance with the national usage, and because you are a man of courage, we adopt you for our son by these bucklers, these swords, these horses, which we send you as a present."

[718] See Gregory of Tours. lib. VII. chap. 23.
[719] In *Cassiodorus*, lib. IV. ep. 2.

29. *Of the sanguinary Temper of the Kings of the Franks.*

Clovis was not the only prince amongst the Franks who had invaded Gaul. Many of his relatives had penetrated into this country with particular tribes; but as he had met with much greater success, and could grant considerable settlements to such as followed him, the Franks flocked to him from all parts, so that the other chiefs found themselves too weak to resist him. He formed a design of exterminating his whole race, and he succeeded. [720] He feared, says Gregory of Tours, [721] lest the Franks should choose another chief. His children and successors followed this practice to the utmost of their power. Thus the brother, the uncle, the nephew, and, what is still worse, the father or the son, were perpetually conspiring against their whole family. The law continually divided the monarchy; while fear, ambition, and cruelty wanted to reunite it.

[720] Gregory of Tours, lib. II.
[721] Ibid.

30. *Of the national Assemblies of the Franks.*

It has been remarked above that nations who do not cultivate the land enjoy great liberty.

This was the case of the Germans. Tacitus says that they gave their kings, or chiefs, a very moderate degree of power; [722] and Cæsar adds further that in times of peace they had no common magistrates; but their princes administered justice in each village. [723] Thus, as Gregory of Tours [724] sufficiently proves, the Franks in Germany had no king.

[722] "Nec Regibus libera aut infinita potestas. Cæterum neque animadvertere, neque vincire, neque verberare, &c."—*De Moribus Germanorum.*
[723] "In pace nullus est communis magistratus, sed principes regionum atque pagorum inter suos jus dicunt."—*De Bello Gall.* lib. VI.
[724] Lib. II.

"The princes," says Tacitus, "deliberate on matters of no great concern; while affairs of importance are submitted to the whole nation, but in such a manner that these very affairs which are under the cognizance of the people are at the same time laid before the princes." [725] This custom was observed by them after their conquests, as may be seen in all their records. [726]

[725] "De minoribus principes consultant, de majoribus omnes; ita tamen ut ea quorum penes plebem arbitrium est, apud principes pertractentur."—*De Moribus Germanorum*, 11.
[726] "Lex consensu Populi fit et constitutione Regis."—Capitularies of Charles the Bald, year 864, art. 6.

Tacitus says that capital crimes might be carried before the assembly. [727] It was the same after the conquest, when the great vassals were tried before that body.

[727] "Licet apud Concilium accusare et discrimen capitis intendere."—*De Moribus Germanorum.*

31. *Of the Authority of the Clergy under the first Race.*

The priests of barbarous nations are commonly invested with power, because they have both that authority which is due to them from their religious character, and that influence which among such a people is the offspring of superstition. Thus we see in Tacitus that priests were held in great veneration by the Germans, and that they presided in the assemblies of the people. [728] They alone were permitted [729] to chastise, to bind, to smite; which they did, not by order of the prince, or as his ministers of justice, but as by an inspiration of that Deity ever supposed to be present with those who made war.

[728] "Silentium per sacerdotes, quibus et coercendi jus est, imperatur."—*Ibid.*
[729] "Nec Regibus libera aut infinita potestas. Cæterum neque animadvertere, neque vincire, neque verberare, nisi sacerdotibus est permissum, non quasi in poenam, nec Ducis jussu, sed velut Deo imperante, quem adesse, bellatoribus credunt."—*Ibid.*

We ought not, therefore, to be astonished when, from the very beginning of the first race, we meet with bishops the dispensers of justice, [730] when we see them appear in the assemblies of the nation; when they have such a prodigious influence on the minds of sovereigns; and when they acquire so large a share of property. [731]

[730] See the Constitutions of Clotarius, year 560, art. 6.
[731] The last ten chapters of this book, reunited in Books XXVIII., XXX., and XXXI., form a complete treatise upon the origin and early ages of the French monarchy, and they should be thus read to be understood.—Ed.

BOOK XIX.

OF LAWS IN RELATION TO THE PRINCIPLES WHICH FORM THE GENERAL SPIRIT, MORALS, AND CUSTOMS OF A NATION

1. *Of the Subject of this Book.*

This subject is very extensive. In that crowd of ideas which presents itself to my mind, I shall be more attentive to the order of things than to the things themselves. I shall be obliged to wander to the right and to the left, that I may investigate and discover the truth.

2. *That it is necessary People's Minds should be prepared for the Reception of the best Laws.*

Nothing could appear more insupportable to the Germans than the tribunal of Varus. [732] That which Justinian [733] erected amongst the Lazi, to proceed against the murderers of their king, appeared to them as an affair most horrid and barbarous. Mithridates, [734] haranguing against the Romans, reproached them more particularly for their law proceedings. [735] The Parthians could not bear with one of their kings who, having been educated at Rome, rendered himself affable and easy of access to all. [736] Liberty itself has appeared intolerable to those nations who have not been accustomed to enjoy it. Thus pure air is sometimes disagreeable to such as have lived in a fenny country.

[732] They cut out the tongues of the advocates, and cried, "Viper, don't hiss."—Tacitus.
[733] Agathias, lib. IV.
[734] Justin, lib. XXXVIII.
[735] "Calumnias litium"—Justin, lib. XXXVIII.
[736] "Prompti aditus, nova comitas, ignotæ Parthis virtutes, nova vitia."—Tacitus.

Balbi, a Venetian, being at Pegu, was introduced to the king. [737] When the monarch was informed that they had no king at Venice, he burst into such a fit of laughter that he was seized with a cough, and with difficulty could speak to his courtiers. What legislator could propose a popular government to a people like this?

[737] He has described this interview, which happened in 1596, in the Collection of Voyages for the establishment of an India Company, vol. iii, part I, p. 33.

3. Of Tyranny.

There are two sorts of tyranny: one real, which arises from oppression; the other is seated in opinion, and is sure to be felt whenever those who govern establish things shocking to the existing ideas of a nation.

Dio [738] tells us that Augustus was desirous of being called Romulus; but having been informed that the people feared that he would cause himself to be crowned king, he changed his design. The old Romans were averse to a king, because they could not suffer any man to enjoy such power; these would not have a king, because they could not bear his manners. For though Cæsar, the Triumvirs, and Augustus were really invested with regal power, they had preserved all the outward appearance of equality, while their private lives were a kind of contrast to the pomp and luxury of foreign monarchs; so that when the Romans were resolved to have no king, this only signified that they would preserve their customs, and not imitate those of the African and eastern nations.

[738] Book LIV. 532.

The same writer informs us that the Romans were exasperated against Augustus for making certain laws which were too severe; but as soon as he had recalled Pylades the comedian, whom the jarring of different factions had driven out of the city, the discontent ceased. A people of this stamp have a more lively sense of tyranny when a player is banished than when they are deprived of their laws.

4. Of the general Spirit of Mankind.

Mankind are influenced by various causes: by the climate, by the religion, by the laws, by the maxims of government, by precedents, morals, and customs; whence is formed a general spirit of nations.

In proportion as, in every country, any one of these causes acts with more force, the others in the same degree are weakened. Nature and the climate rule almost alone over the savages; customs govern the Chinese; the laws tyrannize in Japan; morals had formerly all their influence at Sparta; maxims of government, and the ancient simplicity of manners, once prevailed at Rome.

5. *How far we should be attentive lest the general Spirit of a Nation be changed.*

Should there happen to be a country whose inhabitants were of a social temper, open-hearted, cheerful, endowed with taste and a facility in communicating their thoughts; who were sprightly and agreeable; sometimes imprudent, often indiscreet; and besides had courage, generosity, frankness, and a certain notion of honor, no one ought to endeavor to restrain their manners by laws, unless he would lay a constraint on their virtues. If in general the character be good, the little foibles that may be found in it are of small importance.

They might lay a restraint upon women, enact laws to reform their manners and to reduce their luxury, but who knows but that by these means they might lose that peculiar taste which would be the source of the wealth of the nation, and that politeness which would render the country frequented by strangers?

It is the business of the legislature to follow the spirit of the nation, when it is not contrary to the principles of government; for we do nothing so well as when we act with freedom, and follow the bent of our natural genius.

If an air of pedantry be given to a nation that is naturally gay, the state will gain no advantage from it, either at home or abroad. Leave it to do frivolous things in the most serious manner, and with gaiety the things most serious.

6. *That Everything ought not to be corrected.*

Let them but leave us as we are, said a gentleman of a nation which had a very great resemblance to that we have been describing, and nature will repair whatever is amiss. She has given us a vivacity capable of offending, and hurrying us beyond the bounds of respect: this same vivacity is corrected by the politeness it procures, inspiring us with a taste of the world, and, above all, for the conversation of the fair sex.

Let them leave us as we are; our indiscretions joined to our good nature would make the laws which should constrain our sociability not at all proper for us.

7. *Of the Athenians and Lacedæmonians.*

The Athenians, this gentleman adds, were a nation that had some relation to ours. They mingled gaiety with business; a stroke of raillery was as agreeable in the senate as in the theatre. This vivacity, which discovered itself in their councils, went along with them in the execution of their resolves. The characteristic of the Spartans was gravity, seriousness, severity, and silence. It would have been as difficult to bring over an Athenian by teasing as it would a Spartan by diverting him.

8. *Effects of a sociable Temper.*

The more communicative a people are, the more easily they change their habits, because each is in a greater degree a spectacle to the other and the singularities of individuals are better observed. The climate which influences one nation to take pleasure in being communicative, makes it also delight in change, and that which makes it delight in change forms its taste.

The society of the fair sex spoils the manners and forms the taste; the desire of giving greater pleasure than others establishes the embellishments of dress; and the desire of pleasing others more than ourselves gives rise to fashions. Thus fashion is a subject of importance; by encouraging a trifling turn of mind, it continually increases the branches of its commerce. [739]

[739] Fable of the Bees.

9. *Of the Vanity and Pride of Nations.*

Vanity is as advantageous to a government as pride is dangerous. To be convinced of this we need only represent, on the one hand, the numberless benefits which result from vanity, as industry, the arts, fashions, politeness, and taste; on the other, the infinite evils which spring from the pride of certain nations, as laziness, poverty, a total neglect of everything—in fine, the destruction of the nations which have happened to fall under their government, as well as of their own. Laziness is the effect of pride; [740] labor, a consequence of vanity. The pride of a Spaniard leads him to decline labor; the vanity of a Frenchman to work better than others.

[740] The people who follow the khan of Malacamber, those of Carnataca and Coromandel, are proud and indolent; they consume little, because they are miserably poor; while the subjects of the Mogul and the people of Hindostan employ themselves, and enjoy the conveniences of life, like the Europeans.—Collection of Voyages for the Establishment of an India Company, vol. i, p. 54.

All lazy nations are grave; for those who do not labor regard themselves as the sovereigns of those who do.

If we search among all nations, we shall find that for the most part gravity, pride, and indolence go hand in hand.

The people of Achim [741] are proud and lazy; those who have no slaves, hire one, if it be only to carry a quart of rice a hundred paces; they would be dishonored if they carried it themselves.

[741] See Dampier, vol. iii.

In many places people let their nails grow, that all may see they do not work.

Women in the Indies [742] believe it shameful for them to learn to read: this is, they say, the business of their slaves, who sing their spiritual songs in the temples of their pagods. In one tribe they do not spin; in another they make nothing but baskets and mats; they are not even to pound rice; and in others they must not go to fetch water. These rules are established by pride, and the same passion makes them followed. There is no necessity for mentioning that the moral qualities, according as they are blended with others, are productive of different effects; thus pride, joined to a vast ambition and notions of grandeur, produced such effects among the Romans as are known to all the world.

[742] Edifying Letters, coll. XII, p. 80.

10. *Of the Character of the Spaniards and Chinese.*

The characters of the several nations are formed of virtues and vices, of good and bad qualities. From the happy mixture of these, great advantages result, and frequently where it would be least expected; there are others whence great evils arise—evils which one would not suspect.

The Spaniards have been in all ages famous for their honesty. Justin [743] mentions their fidelity in keeping whatever was entrusted to their care; they have frequently suffered death rather than reveal a secret. They have still the same fidelity for which they were formerly distinguished. All the nations who trade at Cadiz trust their fortunes to the Spaniards, and have never yet repented it. But this admirable quality, joined to their indolence, forms a mixture whence such effects result as to them are most pernicious. The rest of the European nations carry on in their very sight all the commerce of their monarchy.

[743] Lib. XLIII.

The character of the Chinese is formed of another mixture, directly opposite to that of the Spaniards; the precariousness of their subsistence [744] inspires them with a prodigious activity, and such an excessive desire of gain, that no trading nation can confide in them. [745] This acknowledged infidelity has secured them the possession of the trade to Japan. No European merchant has ever dared to undertake it in their name, how easy soever it might be for them to do it from their maritime provinces in the north.

[744] By the nature of the soil and climate.
[745] Father Du Halde, vol. ii.

11. *A Reflection.*

I have said nothing here with a view to lessen that infinite distance which must ever be between virtue and vice. God forbid that I should be guilty of such an attempt! I would only make my readers comprehend that all political are not all moral vices; and that all moral are not political vices; and that those who make laws which shock the general spirit of a nation ought not to be ignorant of this.

12. *Of Customs and Manners in a despotic State.*

It is a capital maxim that the manners and customs of a despotic empire ought never to be changed; for nothing would more speedily produce a revolution. The reason is that in these states there are no laws, that is, none that can be properly called so; there are only manners and customs; and if you overturn these you overturn all.

Laws are established, manners are inspired; these proceed from a general spirit, those from a particular institution: now it is as dangerous, nay more so, to subvert the general spirit as to change a particular institution.

There is less communication in a country where each, either as superior or inferior, exercises or is oppressed by arbitrary power, than there is in those where liberty reigns in every station. They do not, therefore, so often change their manners and behavior. Fixed and established customs have a near resemblance to laws. Thus it is here necessary that a prince or a legislator should less oppose the manners and customs of the people than in any other country upon earth.

Their women are commonly confined, and have no influence in society. In other countries, where they have intercourse with men, their desire of pleasing, and the desire men also have of giving them pleasure, produce a continual change of customs. The two sexes spoil each other; they both lose their distinctive and essential quality; what was naturally fixed becomes quite unsettled, and their customs and behavior alter every day.

13. *Of the Behavior of the Chinese.*

But China is the place where the customs of the country can never be changed. Besides their women being absolutely separated from the men, their customs, like their morals, are taught in the schools. A man of letters may be known by his easy address. [746] These things being once taught by precept, and inculcated by grave doctors, become fixed, like the principles of morality, and are never changed.

[746] Father Du Halde.

14. *What are the natural Means of changing the Manners and Customs of a Nation.*

We have said that the laws were the particular and precise institutions of a legislator, and manners and customs the institutions of a nation in general. Hence it follows that when these manners and customs are to be changed, it ought not to be done by laws; this would have too much the air of tyranny: it would be better to change them by introducing other manners and other customs.

Thus when a prince would make great alterations in his kingdom, he should reform by law what is established by law, and change by custom what is settled by custom; for it is very bad policy to change by law what ought to be changed by custom.

The law which obliged the Muscovites to cut off their beards and to shorten their clothes, and the rigor with which Peter I made them crop, even to their knees, the long cloaks of those who entered into the cities, were instances of tyranny. There are means that may be made use of to prevent crimes; these are punishments: there are those for changing our customs; these are examples.

The facility and ease with which that nation has been polished plainly shows that this prince had a worse opinion of his people than they deserved; and that they were not brutes, though he was pleased to call them so. The violent measures which he employed were needless; he would have attained his end as well by milder methods.

He himself experienced the facility of bringing about these alterations. The women were shut up, and in some measure slaves; he called them to court; he sent them silks and fine stuffs, and made them dress like the German ladies. This sex immediately relished a manner of life which so greatly flattered their taste, their vanity, and their passions; and by their means it was relished by the men.

What rendered the change the more easy was that their manners at that time were foreign to the climate, and had been introduced among them by conquest and by a mixture of nations. Peter I, in giving the manners and customs of Europe to a European nation, found a facility which he did not himself expect. The empire of the climate is the first, the most powerful, of all empires. He had then no occasion for laws to change the manners and customs of his country; it would have been sufficient to have introduced other manners and other customs.

Nations are in general very tenacious of their customs; to take them away by violence is to render them unhappy: we should not therefore change them, but engage the people to make the change themselves.

All punishment which is not derived from necessity is tyrannical. The law is not a mere act of power; things in their own nature indifferent are not within its province.

15. *The Influence of domestic Government on the political.*

This alteration in the manners of women will doubtless have a great influence on the government of Muscovy. One naturally follows the other: the despotic power of the prince is connected with the servitude of women; the liberty of women with the spirit of monarchy.

16. *How some Legislators have confounded the Principles which govern Mankind.*

Manners and customs are those habits which are not established by legislators, either because they were not able or were not willing to establish them.

There is this difference between laws and manners, that the laws are most adapted to regulate the actions of the subject, and manners to regulate the actions of the man. There is this difference between manners and customs, that the former principally relate to the interior conduct, the latter to the exterior.

These things have been sometimes confounded. [747] Lycurgus made the same code for the laws, manners, and customs, and the legislators of China have done the same.

[747] Moses made the same code for laws and religion. The old Romans confounded the ancient customs with the laws.

We ought not to be surprised that the legislators of China and Sparta should confound the laws, manners, and customs; the reason is, their manners represent their laws, and their customs their manners.

The principal object which the legislators of China had in view was to make their subjects live in peace and tranquility. They would have people filled with a veneration for one another, that each should be every moment sensible of his dependence on society, and of the obligations he owed to his fellow-citizens. They therefore gave rules of the most extensive civility.

Thus the inhabitants of the villages of China [748] practice amongst themselves the same ceremonies as those observed by persons of an exalted station; a very proper method of inspiring mild and gentle dispositions, of maintaining peace and good order, and of banishing all the vices which spring from an asperity of temper. In effect, would not the freeing them from the rules of civility be to search out a method for them to indulge their own humors?

[748] See Father Du Halde.

Civility is in this respect of more value than politeness. Politeness flatters the vices of others, and civility prevents ours from being brought to light. It is a barrier which men have placed within themselves to prevent the corruption of each other.

Lycurgus, whose institutions were severe, had no regard to civility; in forming the external behavior he had a view to that warlike spirit with which he would fain inspire his people. A people who were in a continual state of discipline and instruction, and who were endued with equal simplicity and rigor, atoned by their virtues for their want of complaisance.

17. Of the peculiar Quality of the Chinese Government.

The legislators of China went further. [749] They confounded their religion, laws, manners, and customs; all these were morality, all these were virtue. The precepts relating to these four points were what they called rites; and it was in the exact observance of these that the Chinese government triumphed. They spent their whole youth in learning them, their whole life in the practice. They were taught by their men of letters, they were inculcated by the magistrates; and as they included all the ordinary actions of life, when they found the means of making them strictly observed, China was well governed.

[749] See the classic books from which Father Du Halde gives us some excellent extracts.

Two things have contributed to the ease with which these rites are engraved on the hearts and minds of the Chinese; one, the difficulty of writing, which during the greatest part of their lives wholly employs their attention, [750] because it is necessary to prepare them to read and understand the books in which they are comprised; the other, that the ritual precepts having nothing in them that is spiritual, but being merely rules of common practice, are more adapted to convince and strike the mind than things merely intellectual.

[750] It is this which has established emulation, which has banished laziness, and cultivated a love of learning.

Those princes who, instead of ruling by these rites, governed by the force of punishments, wanted to accomplish that by punishments which it is not in their power to produce, that is, to give habits of morality. By punishments, a subject is very justly cut off from society, who, having lost the purity of his manners, violates the laws; but if all the world were to lose their moral habits, would these reestablish them? Punishments may be justly inflicted to put a stop to many of the consequences of the general evil, but they will not remove the evil itself. Thus when the principles of the Chinese government were discarded, and morality was banished, the state fell into anarchy, and revolutions succeeded.

18. *A Consequence drawn from the preceding Chapter.*

Hence it follows that the laws of China are not destroyed by conquest. Their customs, manners, laws, and religion being the same thing, they cannot change all these at once; and as it will happen that either the conqueror or the conquered must change, in China it has always been the conqueror. For the manners of the conquering nation not being their customs, nor their customs their laws, nor their laws their religion, it has been more easy for them to conform by degrees to the vanquished people than the latter to them.

There still follows hence a very unhappy consequence, which is that it is almost impossible for Christianity ever to be established in China. [751] The vows of virginity, the assembling of women in churches, their necessary communication with the ministers of religion, their participation in the sacraments, auricular confession, extreme unction, the marriage of only one wife—all these overturn the manners and customs of the country, and with the same blow strike at their religion and laws.

[751] See the reasons given by the Chinese magistrates in their decrees for proscribing the Christian religion. Edifying Letters, coll. XVII.

The Christian religion, by the establishment of charity, by a public worship, by a participation of the same sacraments, seems to demand that all should be united; while the rites of China seem to ordain that all should be separated.

And as we have seen that this separation [752] depends, in general, on the spirit of despotism, this will show us the reason why monarchies, and indeed all moderate governments, are more consistent with the Christian religion. [753]

[752] See book IV. chap. 3, and book XIX. chap. 13.
[753] See book XXIV. chap 3.

19. *How this Union of Religion, Laws, Manners, and*
Customs among the Chinese was effected.

The principal object of government which the Chinese legislators had in view was the peace and tranquility of the empire; and subordination appeared to them as the most proper means to maintain it. Filled with this idea, they believed it their duty to inspire a respect for parents, and therefore exerted all their power to effect it. They established an infinite number of rites and ceremonies to do them honor when living, and after their death. It was impossible for them to pay such honors to deceased parents without being led to reverence the living. The ceremonies at the death of a father were more nearly related to religion; those for a living parent had a greater relation to the laws, manners, and customs: however, these were only parts of the same code; but this code was very extensive.

A veneration for their parents was necessarily connected with a suitable respect for all who represented them; such as old men, masters, magistrates, and the sovereign. This respect for parents supposed a return of love towards children, and consequently the same return from old men to the young, from magistrates to those who were under their jurisdiction, and from the emperor to his subjects. This formed the rites, and these rites the general spirit of the nation.

We shall now show the relation which things in appearance the most indifferent may bear to the fundamental constitution of China. This empire is formed on the plan of a government of a family. If you diminish the paternal authority, or even if you retrench the ceremonies which express your respect for it, you weaken the reverence due to magistrates, who are considered as fathers; nor would the magistrates have the same care of the people, whom they ought to look upon as their children; and that tender relation which subsists between the prince and his subjects would insensibly be lost. Retrench but one of these habits and you overturn the state. It is a thing in itself very indifferent whether the daughter-in-law rises every morning to pay such and such duties to her mother-in-law; but if we consider that these exterior habits incessantly revive an idea necessary to be imprinted on all minds—an idea that forms the ruling spirit of the empire—we shall see that it is necessary that such or such a particular action be performed.

20. *Explanation of a Paradox relating to the Chinese.*

It is very remarkable that the Chinese, whose lives are guided by rites, are nevertheless the greatest cheats upon earth. This appears chiefly in their trade, which, in spite of its natural tendency, has never been able to make them honest. He who buys of them ought to carry with him his own weights; [754] every merchant having three sorts, the one heavy for buying, another light for selling, and another of the true standard for those who are upon their guard. It is possible, I believe, to explain this contradiction.

[754] Lange, Journal in 1721 and 1722; in Voyages to the North, vol. viii, p. 363.

The legislators of China had two objects in view: they were desirous that the people should be submissive and peaceful, and that they should also be laborious and industrious. By the nature of the soil and climate, their subsistence is very precarious; nor can it be in any other way secured than by industry and labor.

When everyone obeys, and everyone is employed, the state is in a happy situation. It is necessity, and perhaps the nature of the climate, that has given to the Chinese an inconceivable greediness for gain, and laws have never been made to restrain it. Everything has been forbidden when acquired by acts of violence; everything permitted when obtained by artifice or labor. Let us not then compare the morals of China with those of Europe. Everyone in China is obliged to be attentive to what will be for his advantage; if the cheat has been watchful over his own interest, he who is the dupe ought to be attentive to his. At Sparta they were permitted to steal; in China they are suffered to deceive.

21. *How the Laws ought to have a Relation to Manners and Customs.*

It is only singular institutions which thus confound laws, manners, and customs—things naturally distinct and separate; but though they are in themselves different, there is nevertheless a great relation between them.

Solon being asked if the laws he had given to the Athenians were the best, he replied, "I have given them the best they were able to bear" [755]—a fine expression, that ought to be perfectly understood by all legislators! When Divine Wisdom said to the Jews, "I have given you precepts which are not good," this signified that they had only a relative goodness; which is the sponge that wipes out all the difficulties in the law of Moses.

[755] Plutarch, Life of Solon, 9.

22. *The same Subject continued.*

When a people have pure and regular manners, their laws become simple and natural. Plato [756] says that Rhadamanthus, who governed a nation extremely religious, finished every process with extraordinary despatch, administering only the oath on each accusation. "But," says the same Plato, [757] "when a people are not religious we should never have recourse to an oath, except he who swears is entirely disinterested, as in the case of a judge and a witness."

[756] Of Laws, lib. XII.
[757] Ibid., XII.

23. *How the Laws are founded on the Manners of a People.*

At the time when the manners of the Romans were pure, they had no particular law against the embezzlement of the public money. When this crime began to appear, it was thought so infamous, that to be condemned to restore [758] what they had taken was considered as a sufficient disgrace: for a proof of this, see the sentence of L. Scipio. [759]

[758] "In simplum."
[759] Livy, lib. XXXVIII.

24. *The same Subject continued.*

The laws which gave the right of tutelage to the mother were most attentive to the preservation of the infant's person; those which granted it to the next heir were most attentive to the preservation of the state. When the manners of a people are corrupted, it is much better to give the tutelage to the mother. Among those whose laws confide in the manners of the subjects, the guardianship is granted either to the next heir or to the mother, and sometimes to both.

If we reflect on the Roman laws, we shall find that the spirit of these was conformable to what I have advanced. At the time when the laws of the Twelve Tables were made, the manners of the Romans were most admirable. The guardianship was given to the nearest relative of the infant, from a consideration that he ought to have the trouble of the tutelage who might enjoy the advantage of possessing the inheritance. They did not imagine the life of the heir in danger though it was put into a person's hands who would reap a benefit by his death. But when the manners of Rome were changed, her legislators altered their conduct. "If, in the pupillary substitution," say Gaius [760] and Justinian, [761] "the testator is afraid that the substitute will lay any snares for the pupil, he may leave the vulgar substitution open, [762] and put the pupillary into a part of the testament, which cannot be opened till after a certain time." These fears and precautions were unknown to the primitive Romans.

[760] *Institutes*, lib. tit. 2, 6, § 2. Ozel's compilation, Leyden, 1658.
[761] *Institutes*, lib. II., *de pupil. substit.* § 3.
[762] The form of the vulgar substitution ran thus: "If such a one is unwilling to take the inheritance, I substitute in his stead," &c.; the pupillary substitution: "If such a one dies before he arrives at the age of puberty, I substitute," &c.

25. *The same Subject continued.*

The Roman law gave the liberty of making presents before marriage; after the marriage they were not allowed. This was founded on the manners of the Romans, who were led to marriage only by frugality, simplicity, and modesty; but might suffer themselves to be seduced by domestic cares, by complacency, and the constant tenor of conjugal felicity.

A law of the Visigoths [763] forbade the man giving more to the woman he was to marry than the tenth part of his substance, and his giving her anything during the first year of their marriage. This also took its rise from the manners of the country. The legislators were willing to put a stop to that Spanish ostentation which only led them to display an excessive liberality in acts of magnificence.

[763] Lib. III, tit. 5, § 5.

The Romans by their laws put a stop to some of the inconveniences which arose from the most durable empire in the world—that of virtue; the Spaniards, by theirs, would prevent the bad effects of a tyranny the most frail and transitory—that of beauty.

26. *The same Subject continued.*

The law of Theodosius and Valentinian [764] drew the causes of repudiation from the ancient manners and customs of the Romans. [765] It placed in the number of these causes the behavior of the husband who beat his wife [766] in a manner that disgraced the character of a free-born woman. This cause was omitted in the following laws: [767] for their manners, in this respect, had undergone a change, the eastern customs having banished those of Europe. The first eunuch of the empress, wife to Justinian II, threatened, says the historian, to chastise her in the same manner as children are punished at school. Nothing but established manners, or those which they were seeking to establish, could raise even an idea of this kind.

[764] Leg. 8, Cod., *de Repudiis*.
[765] And the law of the Twelve Tables. See Cicero, Philippic.

[766] "Si verberibus quæ ingenuis aliena sunt, afficientem probaverit."
[767] In Nov. 117, chap. xiv.

We have seen how the laws follow the manners of a people; let us now observe how the manners follow the laws.

27. How the Laws contribute to form the Manners, Customs, and Character of a Nation.

The customs of an enslaved people are a part of their servitude, those of a free people are a part of their liberty.

I have spoken in the eleventh book [768] of a free people, and have given the principles of their constitution: let us now see the effects which follow from this liberty, the character it is capable of forming, and the customs which naturally result from it.

[768] Chapter 6.

I do not deny that the climate may have produced a great part of the laws, manners, and customs of this nation; but I maintain that its manners and customs have a close connection with its laws.

As there are in this state two visible powers—the legislative and executive, and as every citizen has a will of his own, and may at pleasure assert his independence, most men have a greater fondness for one of these powers than for the other, and the multitude have commonly neither equity nor sense enough to show an equal affection to both.

And as the executive power, by disposing of all employments, may give great hopes, and no fears, every man who obtains any favor from it is ready to espouse its cause; while it is liable to be attacked by those who have nothing to hope from it.

All the passions being unrestrained, hatred, envy, jealousy, and an ambitious desire of riches and honors, appears in their extent; were it otherwise, the state would be in the condition of a man weakened by sickness, who is without passions because he is without strength.

The hatred which arises between the two parties will always subsist, because it will always be impotent.

These parties being composed of freemen, if the one becomes too powerful for the other, as a consequence of liberty, this other is depressed; while the citizens take the weaker side with the same readiness as the hands lend their assistance to remove the infirmities and disorders of the body.

Every individual is independent, and being commonly led by caprice and humour, frequently changes parties; he abandons one where he left all his friends, to unite himself to another in which he finds all his enemies: so that in this nation it frequently happens that the people forget the laws of friendship, as well as those of hatred.

The sovereign is here in the same case with a private person; and against the ordinary maxims of prudence is frequently obliged to give his confidence to those who have most offended him, and to disgrace the men who have best served him: he does that by necessity which other princes do by choice.

As we are afraid of being deprived of the blessing we already enjoy, and which may be disguised and misrepresented to us; and as fear always enlarges objects, the people are uneasy under such a situation, and believe themselves in danger, even in those moments when they are most secure.

As those who with the greatest warmth oppose the executive power dare not avow the self-interested motives of their opposition, so much the more do they increase the terrors of the people, who can never be certain whether they are in danger or not. But even this contributes to make them avoid the real dangers, to which they may, in the end, be exposed.

But the legislative body having the confidence of the people, and being more enlightened than they, may calm their uneasiness, and make them recover from the bad impressions they have entertained.

This is the great advantage which this government has over the ancient democracies, in which the people had an immediate power; for when they were moved and agitated by the orators, these agitations always produced their effect.

But when an impression of terror has no certain object, it produces only clamor and abuse; it has, however, this good effect, that it puts all the springs of government into motion, and fixes the attention of every citizen. But if it arises from a violation of the fundamental laws, it is sullen, cruel, and produces the most dreadful catastrophes.

Soon we should see a frightful calm, during which everyone would unite against that power which had violated the laws.

If, when the uneasiness proceeds from no certain object, some foreign power should threaten the state, or put its prosperity or its glory in danger, the little interests of party would then yield to the more strong and binding, and there would be a perfect coalition in favor of the executive power.

But if the disputes were occasioned by a violation of the fundamental laws, and a foreign power should appear, there would be a revolution that would neither alter the constitution nor the form of government. For a revolution formed by liberty becomes a confirmation of liberty.

A free nation may have a deliverer: a nation enslaved can have only another oppressor.

For whoever is able to dethrone an absolute prince has a power sufficient to become absolute himself.

As the enjoyment of liberty, and even its support and preservation, consists in every man's being allowed to speak his thoughts, and to lay open his sentiments, a citizen in this state will say or write whatever the laws do not expressly forbid to be said or written.

A people like this, being always in a ferment, are more easily conducted by their passions than by reason, which never produces any great effect in the mind of man; it is therefore easy for those who govern to make them undertake enterprises contrary to their true interest.

This nation is passionately fond of liberty, because this liberty is real; and it is possible for it, in its defense, to sacrifice its wealth, its ease, its interest, and to support the burden of the heaviest taxes, even such as a despotic prince durst not lay upon his subjects.

But as the people have a certain knowledge of the necessity of submitting to those taxes, they pay them from the well-founded hope of their discontinuance; their burdens are heavy, but they do not feel their weight; whilst in other states the uneasiness is infinitely greater than the evil.

This nation must therefore have a fixed and certain credit, because it borrows of itself and pays itself. It is possible for it to undertake things above its natural strength, and employ against its enemies immense sums of fictitious riches, which the credit and nature of the government may render real.

To preserve its liberty, it borrows of its subjects: and the subjects, seeing that its credit would be lost if ever it were conquered, have a new motive to make fresh efforts in defense of its liberty.

This nation, inhabiting an island, is not fond of conquering, because it would be weakened by distant conquests—especially as the soil of the island is good, for it has then no need of enriching itself by war; and as no citizen is subject to another, each sets a greater value on his own liberty than on the glory of one or any number of citizens.

Military men are there regarded as belonging to a profession which may be useful but is often dangerous, and as men whose very services are burdensome to the nation: civil qualifications are therefore more esteemed than the military.

This nation, which liberty and the laws render easy, on being freed from pernicious prejudices, has become a trading people; and as it has some of those primitive materials of trade out of which are manufactured such things as from the artist's hand receive a considerable value, it has made settlements proper to procure the enjoyment of this gift of heaven in its fullest extent.

As this nation is situated towards the north, and has many superfluous commodities, it must want also a great amount of merchandise which its climate will not produce: it has therefore entered into a great and necessary intercourse with the southern nations; and making choice of those states whom it is willing to favor with an advantageous commerce, it enters into such treaties with the nation it has chosen as are reciprocally useful to both.

In a state where, on the one hand, the opulence is extreme, and on the other the taxes are excessive, they are hardly able to live on a small fortune without industry. Many, therefore, under a pretence of travelling, or of health, retire from among them, and go in search of plenty, even to the countries of slavery.

A trading nation has a prodigious number of little particular interests; it may then injure or be injured in an infinite number of ways. Thus it becomes immoderately jealous, and is more afflicted at the prosperity of others than it rejoices at its own.

And its laws, otherwise mild and easy, may be so rigid with respect to the trade and navigation carried on with it, that it may seem to trade only with enemies.

If this nation sends colonies abroad, it must rather be to extend its commerce than its dominion.

As men are fond of introducing into other places what they have established among themselves, they have given the people of the colonies their own form of government; and this government carrying prosperity along with it, they have raised great nations in the forests they were sent to inhabit.

Having formerly subdued a neighboring nation, which by its situation, the goodness of its ports, and the nature of its products, inspires it with jealousy, though it has given this nation its own laws, yet it holds it in great dependence: the subjects there are free and the state itself in slavery.

The conquered state has an excellent civil government, but is oppressed by the law of nations. Laws are imposed by one country on the other, and these are such as render its prosperity precarious and dependent on the will of a master.

The ruling nation inhabiting a large island, and being in possession of a great trade, has with extraordinary ease grown powerful at sea; and as the preservation of its liberties requires that it should have neither strongholds nor fortresses nor land forces, it has occasion for a formidable navy to defend it against invasions; a navy which must be superior to that of all other powers, who, employing their treasures in wars on land, have not sufficient for those at sea.

The empire of the sea has always given those who have enjoyed it a natural pride; because, thinking themselves capable of extending their insults wherever they please, they imagine that their power is as boundless as the ocean.

This nation has a great influence in the affairs of its neighbors; for as its power is not employed in conquests, its friendship is more courted, and its resentment more dreaded, than could naturally be expected from the inconstancy of its government, and its domestic divisions.

Thus it is the fate of the executive power to be almost always disturbed at home and respected abroad.

Should this nation on some occasions become the centre of the negotiations of Europe, probity and good faith would be carried to a greater height than in other places; because the ministers being frequently obliged to justify their conduct before a popular council, their negotiations could not be secret; and they would be forced to be, in this respect, a little more honest.

Besides, as they would in some sort be answerable for the events which an irregular conduct might produce, the surest, the safest way for them would be to take the straightest path.

If the nobles were formerly possessed of an immoderate power, and the monarch had found the means of abasing them by raising the people, the point of extreme servitude must have been that between humbling the nobility and that in which the people began to feel their power.

Thus this nation, having been formerly subject to an arbitrary power, on many occasions preserves the style of it, in such a manner as to let us frequently see upon the foundation of a free government the form of an absolute monarchy.

With regard to religion, as in this state every subject has a free will, and must consequently be either conducted by the light of his own mind or by the caprice of fancy, it necessarily follows that everyone must either look upon all religion with indifference, by which means they are led to embrace the established religion, or they must be zealous for religion in general, by which means the number of sects is increased.

It is not impossible but that in this nation there may be men of no religion, who would not, however, bear to be obliged to change that which they would choose, if they cared to choose any; for they would immediately perceive that their lives and fortunes are not more peculiarly theirs than their manner of thinking, and that whoever would deprive them of the one might even with better reason take away the other.

If, among the different religions, there is one that has been attempted to be established by methods of slavery, it must there be odious; because as we judge of things by the appendages we join with them, it could never present itself to the mind in conjunction with the idea of liberty.

The laws against those who profess this religion could not, however, be of the sanguinary kind; for liberty can never inflict such punishments; but they may be so rigorous as to do all the mischief that can be done in cold blood.

It is possible that a thousand circumstances might concur to give the clergy so little credit, that other citizens may have more. Therefore, instead of a separation, they have chosen rather to support the same burdens as the laity, and in this respect to make only one body with them; but as they always seek to conciliate the respect of the people, they distinguish themselves by a more retired life, a conduct more reserved, and a greater purity of manners.

The clergy not being able to protect religion, nor to be protected by it, only seek to persuade; their pens therefore furnish us with excellent works in proof of a revelation and of the providence of the Supreme Being.

Yet the state prevents the sitting of their assemblies, and does not suffer them to correct their own abuses; it chooses thus, through a caprice of liberty, rather to leave their reformation imperfect than to suffer the clergy to be the reformers.

Those dignities which make a fundamental part of the constitution are more fixed than elsewhere; but, on the other hand, the great in this country of liberty are nearer upon a level with the people; their ranks are more separated, and their persons more confounded.

As those who govern have a power which, in some measure, has need of fresh vigor every day, they have a greater regard for such as are useful to them than for those who only contribute to their amusement: we see, therefore, fewer courtiers, flatterers, and parasites; in short, fewer of all those who make their own advantage of the folly of the great.

Men are less esteemed for frivolous talents and attainments than for essential qualities; and of this kind there are but two, riches and personal merit.

They enjoy a solid luxury, founded, not on the refinements of vanity, but on that of real wants; they ask nothing of nature but what nature can bestow.

The rich enjoy a great superfluity of fortune, and yet have no relish for frivolous amusements; thus, many having more wealth than opportunities of expense, employ it in a fantastic manner: in this nation they have more judgment than taste.

As they are always employed about their own interest, they have not that politeness which is founded on indolence; and they really have not leisure to attain it.

The era of Roman politeness is the same as that of the establishment of arbitrary power. An absolute government produces indolence, and this gives birth to politeness.

The more people there are in a nation who require circumspect behaviour, and care not to displease, the more there is of politeness. But it is rather the politeness of morals than that of manners which ought to distinguish us from barbarous nations.

In a country where every man has, in some sort, a share in the administration of the government, the women ought scarcely to live with the men. They are therefore modest, that is, timid; and this timidity constitutes their virtue: whilst the men without a taste for gallantry plunge themselves into a debauchery, which leaves them at leisure, and in the enjoyment of their full liberty.

Their laws not being made for one individual more than another, each considers himself a monarch; and, indeed, the men of this nation are rather confederates than fellow-subjects.

As the climate has given many persons a restless spirit and extended views, in a country where the constitution gives every man a share in its government and political interests, conversation generally turns upon politics: and we see men spend their lives in the calculation of events which, considering the nature of things and the caprices of fortune, or rather of men, can scarcely be thought subject to the rules of calculation.

In a free nation it is very often a matter of indifference whether individuals reason well or ill; it is sufficient that they do reason: hence springs that liberty which is a security from the effects of these reasonings.

But in a despotic government, it is equally pernicious whether they reason well or ill; their reasoning is alone sufficient to shock the principle of that government.

Many people who have no desire of pleasing abandon themselves to their own particular humor; and most of those who have wit and ingenuity are ingenious in tormenting themselves: filled with contempt or disgust for all things, they are unhappy amidst all the blessings that can possibly contribute to promote their felicity.

As no subject fears another, the whole nation is proud; for the pride of kings is founded only on their independence.

Free nations are haughty; others may more properly be called vain.

But as these men who are naturally so proud live much by themselves, they are commonly bashful when they appear among strangers; and we frequently see them behave for a considerable time with an odd mixture of pride and ill-placed shame.

The character of the nation is more particularly discovered in their literary performances, in which we find the men of thought and deep meditation.

As society gives us a sense of the ridicule of mankind, retirement renders us more fit to reflect on the folly of vice. Their satirical writings are sharp and severe, and we find among them many Juvenals, without discovering one Horace.

In monarchies extremely absolute, historians betray the truth, because they are not at liberty to speak it; in states remarkably free, they betray the truth, because of their liberty itself; which always produces divisions, every one becoming as great a slave to the prejudices of his faction as he could be in a despotic state.

Their poets have more frequently an original rudeness of invention than that particular kind of delicacy which springs from taste; we there find something which approaches nearer to the bold strength of a Michael Angelo than to the softer graces of a Raphael.

BOOK XX. [769]

[769] This book was the beginning of the second part of 'The Spirit of Laws' in all the editions published during the life of the author.—Ed.

OF LAWS IN RELATION TO COMMERCE, CONSIDERED IN ITS NATURE AND DISTINCTIONS

1. *Of Commerce.*

The following subjects deserve to be treated in a more extensive manner than the nature of this work will permit. Fain would I glide down a gentle river, but I am carried away by a torrent.

Commerce is a cure for the most destructive prejudices; for it is almost a general rule that wherever we find agreeable manners, there commerce flourishes; and that wherever there is commerce, there we meet with agreeable manners.

Let us not be astonished, then, if our manners are now less savage than formerly. Commerce has everywhere diffused a knowledge of the manners of all nations: these are compared one with another, and from this comparison arise the greatest advantages.

Commercial laws, it may be said, improve manners tor the same reason that they destroy them. They corrupt the purest morals. [770] This was the subject of Plato's complaints; and we every day see that they polish and refine the most barbarous.

[770] Cæsar said of the Gauls that they were spoiled by the neighborhood and commerce of Marseilles; insomuch that they who formerly always conquered the Germans had now become inferior to them.—War of the Gauls, lib. VI.

2. Of the Spirit of Commerce.

Peace is the natural effect of trade. Two nations who traffic with each other become reciprocally dependent; for if one has an interest in buying, the other has an interest in selling: and thus their union is founded on their mutual necessities.

But if the spirit of commerce unites nations, it does not in the same manner unite individuals. We see that in countries [771] where the people move only by the spirit of commerce, they make a traffic of all the humane, all the moral virtues; the most trifling things, those which humanity would demand, are there done, or there given, only for money.

[771] Holland.

The spirit of trade produces in the mind of a man a certain sense of exact justice, opposite, on the one hand, to robbery, and on the other to those moral virtues which forbid our always adhering rigidly to the rules of private interest, and suffer us to neglect this for the advantage of others.

The total privation of trade, on the contrary, produces robbery, which Aristotle ranks in the number of means of acquiring; yet it is not at all inconsistent with certain moral virtues. Hospitality, for instance, is most rare in trading countries, while it is found in the most admirable perfection among nations of vagabonds.

It is a sacrilege, says Tacitus, for a German to shut his door against any man whomsoever, whether known or unknown. He who has behaved with hospitality to a stranger goes to show him another house where this hospitality is also practised; and he is there received with the same humanity. [772] But when the Germans had founded kingdoms, hospitality had become burdensome. This appears by two laws of the code of the Burgundians; [773] one of which inflicted a penalty on every barbarian who presumed to show a stranger the house of a Roman; and the other decreed that whoever received a stranger should be indemnified by the inhabitants, every one being obliged to pay his proper proportion.

[772] Et qui modo hospes fuerat, monstrator hospitii.—*De Moribus Germanorum. Vide* Cæsar, *De Bello Gall.* lib. VI.
[773] Tit. 38.

3. Of the Poverty of the People.

There are two sorts of poor; those who are rendered such by the severity of government: these are, indeed, incapable of performing almost any great action, because their indigence is a consequence of their slavery. Others are poor, only because they either despise or know not the conveniences of life; and these are capable of accomplishing great things, because their poverty constitutes a part of their liberty.

4. *Of Commerce in different Governments.*

Trade has some relation to forms of government. In a monarchy, it is generally founded on luxury; and though it be also founded on real wants, yet the principal view with which it is carried on is to procure everything that can contribute to the pride, the pleasure, and the capricious whims of the nation. In republics, it is commonly founded on economy. Their merchants, having an eye to all the nations of the earth, bring from one what is wanted by another. It is thus that the republics of Tyre, Carthage, Athens, Marseilles, Florence, Venice, and Holland engaged in commerce.

This kind of traffic has a natural relation to a republican government: to monarchies it is only occasional. For as it is founded on the practice of gaining little, and even less than other nations, and of remedying this by gaining incessantly, it can hardly be carried on by a people swallowed up in luxury, who spend much, and see nothing but objects of grandeur.

Cicero was of this opinion, when he so justly said, "*I do not like that the same people should be at once both the lords and factors of the whole earth.*" [774] For this would, indeed, be to suppose that every individual in the state, and the whole state collectively, had their heads constantly filled with grand views, and at the same time with small ones; which is a contradiction.

[774] "Nolo eundem populum imperatorem et portitorem esse terrarium."

Not but that the most noble enterprises are completed also in those states which subsist by economical commerce: they have even an intrepidity not to be found in monarchies. And the reason is this:

One branch of commerce leads to another, the small to the moderate, the moderate to the great; thus he who has gratified his desire of gaining a little raises himself to a situation in which he is not less desirous of gaining a great deal.

Besides, the grand enterprises of merchants are always necessarily connected with the affairs of the public. But, in monarchies, these public affairs give as much distrust to the merchants as in free states they appear to give safety. Great enterprises, therefore, in commerce are not for monarchical, but for republican, governments.

In short, an opinion of greater certainty, as to the possession of property in these states, makes them undertake everything. They flatter themselves with the hopes of receiving great advantages from the smiles of fortune; and thinking themselves sure of what they have already acquired, they boldly expose it in order to acquire more; risking nothing, but as the means of obtaining.

I do not pretend to say that any monarchy is entirely excluded from an economical commerce; but of its own nature it has less tendency towards it: neither do I mean that the republics with which we are acquainted are absolutely deprived of the commerce of luxury; but it is less connected with their constitution.

With regard to a despotic state, there is no occasion to mention it. A general rule: A nation in slavery labors more to preserve than to acquire; a free nation, more to acquire than to preserve.

5. *Of Nations that have entered into an economical Commerce.*

Marseilles, a necessary retreat in the midst of a tempestuous sea; Marseilles, a harbor which all the winds, the shelves of the sea, the disposition of the coasts, point out for a landing-place, became frequented by mariners; while the sterility of the adjacent country determined the citizens to an economical commerce. [775] It was necessary that they should be laborious to supply what nature had refused; that they should be just, in order to live among barbarous nations, from whom they were to derive their prosperity; that they should be moderate, to the end that they might always taste the sweets of a tranquil government; in fine, that they should be frugal in their manners, to enable them to subsist by trade—a trade the more certain as it was less advantageous.

[775] Justin, lib. XLIII. chap. 3.

We everywhere see violence and oppression give birth to a commerce founded on economy, while men are constrained to take refuge in marshes, in isles, in the shallows of the sea, and even on rocks themselves. Thus it was that Tyre, Venice, and the cities of Holland were founded. Fugitives found there a place of safety. It was necessary that they should subsist; they drew, therefore, their subsistence from all parts of the world.

6. *Some Effects of an extensive Navigation.*

It sometimes happens that a nation, when engaged in an economical commerce, having need of the merchandise of one country, which serves as a capital or stock for procuring the commodities of another, is satisfied with making very little profit, and frequently none at all, in trading with the former, in expectation of gaining greatly by the latter. Thus, when the Dutch were almost the only nation that carried on the trade from the south to the north of Europe; the French wines which they imported to the north were in some measure only a capital or stock for conducting their commerce in that part of the world.

It is a known fact that there are some kinds of merchandise in Holland which, though imported from afar, sell for very little more than they cost upon the spot. They account for it thus: a captain who has occasion to ballast his ship will load it with marble; if he wants wood for stowage, he will buy it; and, provided he loses nothing by the bargain, he will think himself a gainer. Thus it is that Holland has its quarries and its forests.

Further, it may happen so that not only a commerce which brings in nothing shall be useful, but even a losing trade shall be beneficial. I have heard it affirmed in Holland that the whale fishery in general does not answer the expense; but it must be observed that the persons employed in building the ships, as also those who furnish the rigging and provisions, are jointly concerned in the fishery. Should they happen to lose in the voyage, they have had a profit in fitting out the vessel. This commerce, in short, is a kind of lottery, and everyone is allured with the hopes of a prize. Mankind are generally fond of gaming; and even the most prudent have no aversion to it, when the disagreeable circumstances attending it, such as dissipation, anxiety, passion, loss of time, and even of life and fortune, are concealed from their view.

7. *The Spirit of England with respect to Commerce.*

The tariff or customs of England are very unsettled with respect to other nations; they are changed, in some measure, with every parliament, either by taking off particular duties, or by imposing new ones. They endeavor by these means still to preserve their independence. Supremely jealous with respect to trade, they bind themselves but little by treaties, and depend only on their own laws.

Other nations have made the interests of commerce yield to those of politics; the English, on the contrary, have ever made their political interests give way to those of commerce.

They know better than any other people upon earth how to value, at the same time, these three great advantages—religion, commerce, and liberty.

8. *In what Manner economical Commerce has been sometimes restrained.*

In several kingdoms laws have been made extremely proper to humble the states that have entered into economical commerce. They have forbidden their importing any merchandise, except the product of their respective countries; and have permitted them to traffic only in vessels built in the kingdom to which they brought their commodities.

It is necessary that the kingdom which imposes these laws should itself be able easily to engage in commerce; otherwise it will, at least, be an equal sufferer. It is much more advantageous to trade with a commercial nation, whose profits are moderate, and who are rendered in some sort dependent by the affairs of commerce; with a nation whose larger views and whose extended trade enables them to dispose of their superfluous merchandise; with a wealthy nation, who can take off many of their commodities, and make them a quicker return in specie; with a nation under a kind of necessity to be faithful, pacific from principle, and that seeks to gain, and not to conquer: it is much better, I say, to trade with such a notion than with others, their constant rivals, who will never grant such great advantages.

9. *Of the Prohibition of Commerce.*

It is a true maxim that one nation should never exclude another from trading with it, except for very great reasons. The Japanese trade only with two nations, the Chinese and the Dutch. The Chinese [776] gain a thousand per cent upon sugars, and sometimes as much by the goods they take in exchange. The Dutch make nearly the same profits. Every nation that acts upon Japanese principles must necessarily be deceived; for it is competition which sets a just value on merchandise, and establishes the relation between them.

[776] Father Du Halde, vol. ii, p. 170.

Much less ought a state to lay itself under an obligation of selling its manufactures only to a single nation, under a pretence of their taking all at a certain price. The Poles, in this manner, dispose of their corn to the city of Danzig; and several Indian princes have made a like contract for their spices with the Dutch. [777] These agreements are proper only for a poor nation, whose inhabitants are satisfied to forego the hopes of enriching themselves, provided they can be secure of a certain subsistence; or for nations whose slavery consists either in renouncing the use of those things which nature has given them, or in being obliged to submit to a disadvantageous commerce.

[777] This was first established by the Portuguese.—Pirard, Voyages, chap. xv. part II.

10. *An Institution adapted to economical Commerce.*

In states that carry on an economical commerce, they have luckily established banks, which by their credit have formed a new species of wealth: but it would be quite wrong to introduce them into governments whose commerce is founded only on luxury. The erecting of banks in countries governed by an absolute monarch supposes money on the one side, and on the other power: that is, on the one hand, the means of procuring everything, without any power; and on the other, the power, without any means of procuring at all. In a government of this kind, none but the prince ever had, or can have, a treasure; and wherever there is one, it no sooner becomes great than it becomes the treasure of the prince.

For the same reason, all associations of merchants, in order to carry on a particular commerce, are seldom proper in absolute governments. The design of these companies is to give to the wealth of private persons the weight of public riches. But in those governments this weight can be found only in the prince. Nay, they are not even always proper in states engaged in economical commerce; for, if the trade be not so great as to surpass the management of particular persons, it is much better to leave it open than, by exclusive privileges, to restrain the liberty of commerce.

11. *The same Subject continued.*

A free port may be established in the dominions of states whose commerce is economical. That economy in the government which always attends the frugality of individuals is, if I may so express myself, the soul of its economical commerce. The loss it sustains with respect to customs it can repair by drawing from the wealth and industry of the republic. But in a monarchy a step of this kind must be opposite to reason; for it could have no other effect than to ease luxury of the weight of taxes. This would be depriving itself of the only advantage that luxury can procure, and of the only curb which, in a constitution like this, it is capable of receiving.

12. *Of the Freedom of Commerce.*

The freedom of commerce is not a power granted to the merchants to do what they please: this would be more properly its slavery. The constraint of the merchant is not the constraint of commerce. It is in the freest countries that the merchant finds innumerable obstacles; and he is never less crossed by laws than in a country of slaves.

England prohibits the exportation of her wool; coals must be brought by sea to the capital; no horses, except geldings, are allowed to be exported; and the vessels of her colonies trading to Europe must take in water in England. [778] The English constrain the merchant, but it is in favor of commerce.

[778] Acts of Navigation, 1660. It is only in time of war that the merchants of Boston and Philadelphia send their vessels directly to the Mediterranean.

13. *What it is that destroys this Liberty.*

Wherever commerce subsists, customs are established. Commerce is the exportation and importation of merchandise, with a view to the advantage of the state: customs are a certain right over this same exportation and importation, founded also on the advantage of the state. Hence it becomes necessary that the state should be neutral between its customs and its commerce, that neither of these two interfere with each other, and then the inhabitants enjoy a free commerce.

The farming of the customs destroys commerce by its injustice and vexations, as well as by the excess of the imposts: but independent of this, it destroys it even more by the difficulties that arise from it, and by the formalities it exacts. In England, where the customs are managed by the king's officers, business is negotiated with a singular dexterity: one word of writing accomplishes the greatest affairs. The merchant needs not lose an infinite deal of time; he has no occasion for a particular commissioner, either to obviate all the difficulties of the farmers, or to submit to them.

14. *The Laws of Commerce concerning the Confiscation of Merchandise.*

The Magna Charta of England forbids the seizing and confiscating, in case of war, the effects of foreign merchants, except by way of reprisals. It is an honor to the English nation that they have made this one of the articles of their liberty.

In the late war between Spain and England, the former made a law which punished with death those who brought English merchandise into the dominions of Spain; and the same penalty on those who carried Spanish merchandise into England. [779] An ordinance like this cannot, I believe, find a precedent in any laws but those of Japan. It equally shocks humanity, the spirit of commerce, and the harmony which ought to subsist in the proportion of penalties; it confounds all our ideas, making that a crime against the state which is only a violation of civil polity.

[779] Published in Cadiz in March, 1740.

15. *Of seizing the Persons of Merchants.*

Solon made a law that the Athenians should no longer seize the body for civil debts. [780] This law he received from Egypt. It had been made by Boccoris, and renewed by Sesostris. [781]

[780] Plutarch, Against Lending Upon Usury.
[781] Diodorus, Book I, part II, chap. iii.

This law is extremely good with respect to the generality of civil affairs; but there is sufficient reason for its not being observed in those of commerce. [782] For as merchants are obliged to entrust large sums, frequently for a very short time, and to pay money as well as to receive it, there is a necessity that the debtor should constantly fulfill his engagements at the time prefixed; and hence it becomes necessary to lay a constraint on his person.

[782] The Greek legislators were to blame in preventing the arms and plough of any man from being taken in pledge, and yet permitting the taking of the man himself.— Diodorus, book I. part II. chap. iii.

In affairs relating to common civil contracts, the law ought not to permit the seizure of the person; because the liberty of one citizen is of greater importance to the public than the ease or prosperity of another. But in conventions derived from commerce, the law ought to consider the public prosperity as of greater importance than the liberty of a citizen; which, however, does not hinder the restrictions and limitations that humanity and good policy demand.

16. *An excellent Law.*

Admirable is that law of Geneva which excludes from the magistracy, and even from the admittance into the great council, the children of those who have lived or died insolvent, except they have discharged their father's debts. It has this effect: it creates a confidence in the merchants, in the magistrates, and in the city itself. There the credit of the individual has still all the weight of public credit.

17. *A Law of Rhodes.*

[783] The inhabitants of Rhodes went further. Sextus Empiricus observes that among those people a son could not be excused from paying his father's debts by renouncing the succession. This law of Rhodes was calculated for a republic founded on commerce. Now I am inclined to think that reasons drawn from commerce itself should make this limitation, that the debts contracted by the father since the son's entering into commerce should not affect the estate or property acquired by the latter. A merchant ought always to know his obligations, and to square his conduct by his circumstances and present fortune.

[783] Hypotiposes, book I. chap. 14.

18. *Of the Judges of Commerce.*

Xenophon, in his book of Revenues, [784] would have rewards given to those overseers of commerce who dispatched the causes brought before them with the greatest expedition. He was sensible of the need of our modern jurisdiction of a consul.

[784] *De Proventibus*, III.

The affairs of commerce are but little susceptible of formalities. They are the actions of a day, and are every day followed by others of the same nature. Hence it becomes necessary that every day they should be decided. It is otherwise with those actions of life which have a principal influence on futurity, but rarely happen. We seldom marry more than once; deeds and wills are not the work of every day; we are but once of age.

Plato [785] says that in a city where there is no maritime commerce there ought not to be above half the number of civil laws: this is very true. Commerce brings into the same country different kinds of people; it introduces also a great number of contracts and species of wealth, with various ways of acquiring it.

[785] On Laws, book VIII.

Thus in a trading city there are fewer judges, and more laws.

19. *That a Prince ought not to engage himself in Commerce.*

Theophilus, [786] seeing a vessel laden with merchandise for his wife Theodora, ordered it to be burned. *I am emperor*, said he, *and you make me the master of a galley. By what means shall these poor men gain a livelihood if we take their trade out of their hands?* He might have added. Who shall set bounds to us if we monopolize all ourselves? Who shall oblige us to fulfill our engagements? Our courtiers will follow our example; they will be more greedy and more unjust than we: the people have some confidence in our justice, they will have none in our opulence: all these numerous duties, the cause of their wants, are certain proofs of ours.

[786] Zonaras.

20. *The same Subject continued.*

When the Portuguese and Castilians bore sway in the East Indies, commerce had such opulent branches that their princes did not fail to seize them. This ruined their settlements in those parts of the world.

The viceroy of Goa granted exclusive privileges to particular persons. The people had no confidence in these men; and the commerce declined, by the perpetual change of those to whom it was entrusted; nobody took care to improve it, or to leave it entire to his successor. In short, the profit centered in a few hands, and was not sufficiently extended.

21. *Of the Commerce of the Nobility in a Monarchy.*

In a monarchical government, it is contrary to the spirit of commerce that any of the nobility should be merchants. *This*, said the Emperors Honorius and Theodosius, [787] *would be pernicious to cities; and would remove the facility of buying and selling between the merchants and the plebeians.*

[787] Leg., *Nobiliores*, Cod. *de Comm*, et leg. *ult. de rescind, vendit.*

It is contrary to the spirit of monarchy to admit the nobility into commerce. The custom of suffering the nobility of England to trade is one of those things which has there mostly contributed to weaken the monarchical government.

22. *A singular Reflection.*

Persons struck with the practice of some states imagine that in France they ought to make laws to engage the nobility to enter into commerce. But these laws would be the means of destroying the nobility, without being of any advantage to trade. The practice of this country is extremely wise; merchants are not nobles, though they may become so. They have the hopes of obtaining a degree of nobility, unattended with its actual inconveniences. There is no surer way of being advanced above their profession than to manage it well, or with success; the consequence of which is generally an affluent fortune.

Laws which oblige everyone to continue in his profession, and to devolve it upon his children, neither are nor can be of use in any but despotic kingdoms; where nobody either can or ought to have emulation. [788]

[788] This is actually very often the case in such governments.

Let none say that everyone will succeed better in his profession when he cannot change it for another: I say that a person will succeed best when those who have excelled hope to rise to another.

The possibility of purchasing honor with gold encourages many merchants to put themselves in circumstances by which they may attain it. I do not take it upon me to examine the justice of thus bartering for money the price of virtue. There are governments where this may be very useful.

In France the dignity of the long robe, which places those who wear it between the great nobility and the people, and without having such shining honors as the former, has all their privileges; a dignity which, while this body, the depositary of the laws, is encircled with glory, leaves the private members in a mediocrity of fortune; a dignity in which there are no other means of distinction but by a superior capacity and virtue, yet which still leaves in view one much more illustrious: the warlike nobility, likewise, who conceive that, whatever degree of wealth they are possessed of, they may still increase their fortunes; who are ashamed of augmenting, if they begin not with dissipating, their estates; who always serve their prince with their whole capital stock, and when that is sunk make room for others, who follow their example; who take the field that they may never be reproached with not having been there; who, when they can no longer hope for riches, live in expectation of honors; and when they have not obtained the latter, enjoy the consolation of having acquired glory: all these things together have necessarily contributed to augment the grandeur of this kingdom; and if for two or three centuries it has been incessantly increasing in power, this must be attributed not to Fortune, who was never famed for constancy, but to the goodness of its laws.

23. *To what Nations Commerce is prejudicial.*

Riches consist either in lands or in movable effects. The soil of every country is commonly possessed by the natives. The laws of most states render foreigners unwilling to purchase their lands; and nothing but the presence of the owner improves them: this kind of riches, therefore, belongs to every state in particular; but movable effects, as money, notes, bills of exchange, stocks in companies, vessels, and, in fine, all merchandise, belong to the whole world in general; in this respect, it is composed of but one single state, of which all the societies upon earth are members. The people who possess more of these movable effects than any other on the globe are the most opulent. Some states have an immense quantity acquired by their commodities, by the labor of their mechanics, by their industry, by their discoveries, and even by chance. The avarice of nations makes them quarrel for the movables of the whole universe. If we could find a state so unhappy as to be deprived of the effects of other countries, and at the same time of almost all its own, the proprietors of the lands would be only planters to foreigners. This state, wanting all, could acquire nothing; therefore, it would be much better for the inhabitants not to have the least commerce with any nation upon earth, for commerce in these circumstances must necessarily lead them to poverty.

A country that constantly exports fewer manufactures or commodities than it receives will soon find the balance sinking; it will receive less and less, until, falling into extreme poverty, it will receive nothing at all.

In trading countries the specie, which suddenly vanishes, quickly returns; because those nations that have received it are its debtors. But it never returns into those states of which we have just been speaking, because those who have received it owe them nothing.

Poland will serve us for an example. It has scarcely any of those things which we call the movable effects of the universe, except corn, the produce of its lands. Some of the lords possess entire provinces; they oppress the husbandmen, in order to have greater quantities of corn, which they send to strangers, to procure the superfluous demands of luxury. If Poland had no foreign trade, its inhabitants would be happier. The grandees, who would have only their corn, would give it to their peasants for subsistence; as their too extensive estates would become burdensome, they would divide them among their peasants; everyone would find skins or wool in their herds or flocks, so that they would no longer be at an immense expense in providing clothes; the great, who are ever fond of luxury, not being able to find it but in their own country, would encourage the labor of the poor. This nation, I affirm, would then become more flourishing, at least if it did not become barbarous; and this the laws might easily prevent.

Let us next consider Japan. The vast quantity of what they receive is the cause of the vast quantity of merchandise they send abroad. Things are thus in as nice an equilibrium as if the importation and exportation were but small. Besides, this kind of exuberance in the state is productive of a thousand advantages; there is a greater consumption, a greater quantity of those things on which the arts are exercised; more men employed, and more numerous means of acquiring power; exigencies may also happen that require a speedy assistance, which so opulent a state can better afford than any other. It is difficult for a country to avoid having superfluities; but it is the nature of commerce to render the superfluous useful, and the useful necessary. The state will be, therefore, able to afford necessaries to a much greater number of subjects.

Let us say, then, that it is not those nations who have need of nothing that must lose by trade; it is those who have need of everything. It is not such people as have a sufficiency within themselves, but those who are most in want, that will find an advantage in putting a stop to all commercial intercourse.

BOOK XXI.

OF LAWS IN RELATION TO COMMERCE, CONSIDERED IN THE REVOLUTIONS IT HAS MET WITH IN THE WORLD

1. *Some general Considerations.*

Though commerce be subject to great revolutions, yet it is possible that certain physical causes, as the quality of the soil, or the climate, may fix its nature forever.

We at present carry on the trade of the Indies merely by means of the silver which we send thither. The Romans carried annually thither about fifty millions of sesterces; [789] and this silver, as ours is at present, was exchanged for merchandise, which was brought to the west. Every nation that ever traded to the Indies has constantly carried bullion and brought merchandise in return. [790]

[789] Pliny, lib. VI. chap. xxiii.
[790] See Pausanias, *Laconia*, sine III. chap. xii.

It is nature itself that produces this effect. The Indians have their hearts adapted to their manner of living. Our luxury cannot be theirs; nor theirs our wants. Their climate demands and permits hardly anything which comes from ours. They go in a great measure naked; such clothes as they have the country itself furnishes; and their religion, which is deeply rooted, gives them an aversion for those things that serve for our nourishment. They want, therefore, nothing but our bullion to serve as the medium of value; and for this they give us merchandise in return, with which the frugality of the people and the nature of the country furnish them in great abundance. Those ancient authors who have mentioned the Indies describe them just as we now find them, as to their policy, customs, and manners. [791] The Indies have ever been the same Indies they are at present; and in every period of time those who traded with that country carried specie thither and brought none in return.

[791] See Pliny, book VI. chap. 19, and Strabo, book XV.

2. *Of the People of Africa.*

The greatest part of the people on the coast of Africa are savages and barbarians. The principal reason, I believe, of this is, because the small countries capable of being inhabited are separated from each other by large and almost uninhabitable tracts of land. They are without industry or arts. They have gold in abundance, which they receive immediately from the hand of nature. Every civilised state is therefore in a condition to traffic with them to advantage, by raising their esteem for things of no value, and receiving a very high price in return

3. *That the Wants of the People in the South are different from those of the North.*

In Europe there is a kind of balance between the southern and northern nations. The first have every convenience of life, and few of its wants: the last have many wants, and few conveniences. To one nature has given much, and demands but little; to the other she has given but little, and demands a great deal. The equilibrium is maintained by the laziness of the southern nations, and by the industry and activity which she has given to those in the north. The latter are obliged to undergo excessive labor, without which they would want everything, and degenerate into barbarians. This has neutralised slavery to the people of the south: as they can easily dispense with riches, they can more easily dispense with liberty. But the people of the north have need of liberty, for this can best procure them the means of satisfying all those wants which they have received from nature. The people of the north, then, are in a forced state, if they are not either free or barbarians. Almost all the people of the south are, in some measure, in a state of violence, if they are not slaves.

4. *The principal Difference between the Commerce of the Ancients and the Moderns.*

The world has found itself, from time to time, in different situations; by which the face of commerce has been altered. The trade of Europe is, at present, carried on principally from the north to the south; and the difference of climate is the cause that the several nations have great occasion for the merchandise of each other. For example, the liquors of the south, which are carried to the north, form a commerce little known to the ancients. Thus the burden of vessels, which was formerly computed by measures of corn, is at present determined by tuns of liquor.

The ancient commerce, so far as it is known to us, was carried on from one port in the Mediterranean to another; and was almost wholly confined to the south. Now the people of the same climate, having nearly the same things of their own, have not the same need of trading among themselves as with those of a different climate. The commerce of Europe was therefore formerly less extended than at present.

This does not at all contradict what I have said of our commerce to the Indies: for here the prodigious difference of climate destroys all relation between their wants and ours.

5. *Other Differences.*

Commerce is sometimes destroyed by conquerors, sometimes cramped by monarchs; it traverses the earth, flies from the places where it is oppressed, and stays where it has liberty to breath: it reigns at present where nothing was formerly to be seen but deserts, seas, and rocks; and where it once reigned now there are only deserts.

To see Colchis in its present situation, which is no more than a vast forest, where the people are every day diminishing, and only defend their liberty to sell themselves by piecemeal to the Turks and Persians, one could never imagine that this country had ever, in the time of the Romans, been full of cities, where commerce convened all the nations of the world. We find no monument of these facts in the country itself; there are no traces of them, except in Pliny [792] and Strabo. [793]

[792] Lib. VI.
[793] Lib. XI.

The history of commerce is that of the communication of people. Their numerous defeats, and the flux and reflux of populations and devastations, here form the most extraordinary events.

6. Of the Commerce of the Ancients.

The immense treasures of Semiramis, [794] which could not be acquired in a day, give us reason to believe that the Assyrians themselves had pillaged other rich nations, as other nations afterwards pillaged them.

[794] Diodorus, lib. II.

The effect of commerce is riches; the consequence of riches, luxury; and that of luxury the perfection of arts. We find that the arts were carried to great perfection in the time of Semiramis; [795] which is a sufficient indication that a considerable commerce was then established.

[795] Ibid.

In the empires of Asia there was a great commerce of luxury. The history of luxury would make a fine part of that of commerce. The luxury of the Persians was that of the Medes, as the luxury of the Medes was that of the Assyrians.

Great revolutions have happened in Asia. The northeast parts of Persia, viz., Hyrcania, Margiana, Bactria, &c., were formerly full of flourishing cities, [796] which are now no more; and the north of this empire, [797] that is, the isthmus which separates the Caspian and the Euxine Seas, was covered with cities and nations, which are now destroyed.

[796] Pliny, lib. VI. chap. 16, and Strabo, lib. XI.
[797] Strabo, lib. XI.

Eratosthenes and Aristobulus [798] learned from Patroclus [799] that the merchandise of India passed by the Oxus into the sea of Pontus. Marcus Varro [800] tells us that at the time when Pompey commanded against Mithridates, they were informed that people went in seven days from India to the country of the Bactrians, and to the river Icarus, which falls into the Oxus; that by this method they were able to bring the merchandise of India across the Caspian Sea, and to enter the mouth of Cyrus; whence it was only five days' passage to the Phasis, a river that discharges itself into the Euxine Sea. There is no doubt but it was by the nations inhabiting these several countries that the great empires of the Assyrians, Medes, and Persians had communication with the most distant parts of the east and west.

[798] Ibid.

[799] The authority of Patroclus is of great weight, as appears from a passage in Strabo, lib. II.

[800] Pliny, lib. VI. chap. 17. See also Strabo, lib. XI, upon the passage by which the merchandise was conveyed from the Phasis to the Cyrus.

An entire stop is now put to this communication. All these countries have been laid waste by the Tartars, [801] and are still infested by this destructive nation. The Oxus no longer runs into the Caspian Sea; the Tartars, for some private reasons, have changed its course, and it now loses itself in the barren sands. [802]

[801] There must have been very great changes in that country since the time of Ptolemy, who gives us an account of so many rivers that empty themselves into the east side of the Caspian Sea. In the Czar's chart we find only the river of Astrabat: in that of M. Bathalsi there is none at all.

[802] See Jenkinson's account of this, in the Collection of Voyages to the North, vol. iv.

The Jaxartes, which was formerly a barrier between the polite and barbarous nations, has had its course turned in the same manner by the Tartars, and it no longer empties itself into the sea. [803]

[803] I am disposed to think that hence Lake Aral was formed.

Seleucus Nicator formed the project of joining the Euxine to the Caspian Sea. [804] This project, which would have greatly facilitated the commerce of those days, vanished at his death. [805] We are not certain it could have been executed in the isthmus which separates the two seas. This country is at present very little known; it is depopulated, and full of forests; however, water is not wanting, for an infinite number of rivers roll into it from Mount Caucasus; but as this mountain forms the north of the isthmus, and extends like two arms [806] towards the south, it would have been a grand obstacle to such an enterprise, especially in those times, when they had not the art of making sluices.

[804] Claudius Cæsar, in Pliny, lib. VI. chap. 11.
[805] He was slain by Ptolemy Ceraunus.
[806] See Strabo, lib. XI.

It may be imagined that Seleucus would have joined the two seas in the very place where Peter I has since joined them; that is, in that neck of land where the Tanais approaches the Volga; but the north of the Caspian Sea was not then discovered.

While the empires of Asia enjoyed the commerce of luxury, the Tyrians had the commerce of economy, which they extended throughout the world. Bochard has employed the first book of his Canaan in enumerating all the colonies which they sent into all the countries bordering upon the sea; they passed the pillars of Hercules, and made establishments on the coasts of the ocean. [807]

[808] They founded Tartessus, and made a settlement at Cadiz.

In those times their pilots were obliged to follow the coasts, which were, if I may so express myself, their compass. Voyages were long and painful. The laborious voyage of

Ulysses has been the fruitful subject of the finest poem in the world, next to that which alone has the preference.

The little knowledge which the greatest part of the world had of those who were far distant from them favored the nations engaged in the economical commerce. They managed trade with as much obscurity as they pleased; they had all the advantages which the most intelligent nations could take over the most ignorant.

The Egyptians—a people who by their religion and their manners were averse to all communication with strangers—had scarcely at that time any foreign trade. They enjoyed a fruitful soil and great plenty. Their country was the Japan of those times; it possessed everything within itself.

So little jealous were these people of commerce, that they left that of the Red Sea to all the petty nations that had any harbors in it. Here they suffered the Idumeans, the Syrians and the Jews to have fleets. Solomon employed in this navigation the Tyrians, who knew those seas. [809]

[809] I Kings, 9. II Chron., 8.

Josephus [810] says that this nation, being entirely employed in agriculture, knew little of navigation: the Jews, therefore, traded only occasionally in the Red Sea. They took from the Idumeans Eloth and Eziongeber, from whom they received this commerce; they lost these two cities, and with them lost this commerce.

[810] Against Appian.

It was not so with the Phoenicians: theirs was not a commerce of luxury; nor was their trade owing to conquest; their frugality, their abilities, their industry, their perils, and the hardships they suffered, rendered them necessary to all the nations of the world.

Before Alexander, the people bordering on the Red Sea traded only in this sea, and in that of Africa. The astonishment which filled the globe at the discovery of the Indian Sea, under that conqueror, is a sufficient proof of this. I have observed [811] that bullion was always carried to the Indies, and never any brought thence; now the Jewish fleets, which brought gold and silver by the way of the Red Sea, returned from Africa, and not from the Indies. [812]

[811] Chapter 1 of this book.
[812] The proportion between gold and silver, as settled in Europe, may sometimes render it profitable to take gold instead of silver into the East Indies; but the advantage is very trifling.

Besides, this navigation was made on the eastern coast of Africa; for the state of navigation at that time is a convincing proof that they did not sail to a very distant shore.

I am not ignorant that the fleets of Solomon and Jehoshaphat returned only every three years; but I do not see that the time taken up in the voyage is any proof of the greatness of the distance.

Pliny and Strabo inform us that the junks of India and the Red Sea were twenty days in performing a voyage which a Greek or Roman vessel would accomplish in seven. [813] In this proportion, a voyage of one year, made by the fleets of Greece or Rome, would take very nearly three when performed by those of Solomon. Two ships of unequal swiftness do not perform their voyage in a time proportionate to their swiftness. Slowness is frequently the cause of much greater slowness. When it becomes necessary to follow the coast, and to be incessantly in a different position, when they must wait for a fair wind to get out of a gulf, and for another to proceed, a good sailor takes the advantage of every favorable moment, while the other still continues in a difficult situation, and waits many days for another change.

[813] See Pliny, lib. VI. 22, and Strabo, lib. XV.

The slowness of the Indian vessels, which in an equal time could make but the third of the way of those of the Greeks and Romans, may be explained by what we every day see in our modern navigation. The Indian vessels, which were built with a kind of sea-rushes, drew less water than those of Greece and Rome, which were of wood and joined with iron.

We may compare these Indian vessels to those at present made use of in ports of little depth of water. Such are those of Venice, and even of all Italy in general. [814] of the Baltic, and of the province of Holland. [815] Their ships, which ought to be able to go in and out of port, are built round and broad at the bottom; while those of other nations, who have good harbors, are formed to sink deep into the water. This mechanism renders these last-mentioned vessels able to sail much nearer the wind; while the first can hardly sail, except the wind be nearly in the poop. A ship that sinks deep into the water sails towards the same side with almost every wind; this proceeds from the resistance which the vessel, while driven by the wind, meets with from the water, from which it receives a strong support; and from the length of the vessel which presents its side to the wind, while, from the form of the helm, the prow is turned to the point proposed; so that she can sail very near the wind, or, in other words, very near the point whence the wind blows. But when the hull is round and broad at the bottom, and consequently draws little water, it no longer finds this steady support; the wind drives the vessel, which is incapable of resistance, and can run them but with a small variation from the point opposite to the wind. Whence it follows that broad-bottomed vessels are longer in performing voyages.

[814] They are mostly shallow; but Sicily has excellent ports.
[815] I say the province of Holland; for the ports of Zealand are deep enough.

1. They lose much time in waiting for the wind, especially if they are obliged frequently to change their course, 2. They sail much slower, because not having a proper support from a depth of water, they cannot carry so much sail. If this be the case at a time when the arts are everywhere known, at a time when art corrects the defects of nature, and even of art itself; if at this time, I say, we find this difference, how great must that have been in the navigation of the ancients?

I cannot yet leave this subject. The Indian vessels were small, and those of the Greeks and Romans, if we except those machines built for ostentation, much less than ours. Now, the smaller the vessel the greater danger it encounters from foul weather. A tempest that would swallow up a small vessel would only make a large one roll. The more one body surpasses another in size, the more its surface is relatively small. Whence it follows that in a small ship there is a less proportion, that is, a greater difference in respect to the surface of the vessel, compared with the weight or lading she can carry, than in a large one. We know that it is a pretty general practice to make the weight of the lading equal to that of half the water the vessel could contain. Suppose a vessel will contain eight hundred tons, her lading then must be four hundred; and that of a vessel which would hold but four hundred tons of water would be two hundred tons. Thus the largeness of the first ship will be to the weight she carries as 8 to 4, and that of the second as 4 to 2. Let us suppose, then, that the surface of the greater is to the surface of the smaller as 8 to 6; the surface of the latter will be to her weight as 6 to 2, [816] while the surface of the former will be to her weight only as 8 to 4. Therefore as the winds and waves act only upon the surface, the large vessel will, by her weight, resist their impetuosity much more than the small.

[816] That is, to compare magnitudes of the same kind, the action or pressure of the fluid upon the ship will be to the resistance of the same ship as, &c.

7. Of the Commerce of the Greeks.

The first Greeks were all pirates. Minos, who enjoyed the empire of the sea, was only more successful, perhaps, than others in piracy; for his maritime dominion extended no farther than round his own isle. But when the Greeks became a great people, the Athenians obtained the real dominion of the sea; because this trading and victorious nation gave laws to the most potent monarch of that time, [817] and humbled the maritime powers of Syria, of the isle of Cyprus, and Phoenicia.

[817] The King of Persia.

But this Athenian lordship of the sea deserves to be more particularly mentioned. *Athens*, says Xenophon, [818] *rules the sea; but as the country of Attica is joined to the continent, it is ravaged by enemies while the Athenians are engaged in distant expeditions. Their leaders suffer their lands to be destroyed, and secure their wealth by sending it to some island. The populace, who are not possessed of lands, have no uneasiness. But if the Athenians inhabited an island, and, besides this, enjoyed the empire of the sea, they would, so long as they were possessed of these advantages, be able to annoy others, and at the same time to be out of all danger of being annoyed.* One would imagine that Xenophon was speaking of England.

[818] On the Athenian Republic.

The Athenians, a people whose heads were filled with ambitious projects; the Athenians, who augmented their jealousy instead of increasing their influence; who were more attentive to extend their maritime empire than to enjoy it; whose political government was such that the common people distributed the public revenues among themselves, while the rich were in a state of oppression; the Athenians, I say, did not carry on so extensive a commerce as might be expected from the produce of their mines, from the multitude of their slaves, from the number of their seamen, from their influence over the cities of Greece, and, above all, from the excellent institutions of Solon. Their trade was almost wholly confined to Greece and to the Euxine Sea, whence they drew their subsistence.

Corinth was admirably situated; it separated two seas, and opened and shut the Peloponnesus; it was the key of Greece, and a city of the greatest importance, at a time when the people of Greece were a world, and the cities of Greece nations. Its trade was more extensive than that of Athens, having a port to receive the merchandise of Asia, and another those of Italy; for the great difficulties which attended the doubling Cape Malea, where the meeting of opposite winds causes shipwrecks, [819] induced everyone to go to Corinth, and they could even convey their vessels over land from one sea to the other. Never was there a city in which the works of art were carried to so high a degree of perfection. But here religion finished the corruption which their opulence began. They erected a temple to Venus, in which more than a thousand courtesans were consecrated to that deity; from this seminary came the greatest part of those celebrated beauties whose history Athenæus has presumed to commit to writing.

[819] See Strabo, lib. VIII.

It seems that in Homer's time the opulence of Greece centered in Rhodes, Corinth, and Orchomenus; *Jupiter*, he says, *loved the Rhodians, and made them a very wealthy nation.* [820] On Corinth he bestows the epithet of rich. [821] In like manner, when he speaks of cities that have plenty of gold, he mentions Orchomenus, to which he joins Thebes in Egypt. Rhodes and Corinth preserved their power; but Orchomenus lost hers. The situation of Orchomenus in the neighborhood of the Hellespont, the Propontis, and the Euxine Sea makes us naturally imagine that she was indebted for her opulence to a trade along that maritime coast, which had given rise to the fable of the golden fleece; and, indeed, the name of *Minyeios* has been given to Orchomenus as well as to the Argonauts. [822] But these seas becoming afterwards more frequented, the Greeks planted along the coasts a greater number of colonies, which traded with the barbarous nations, and at the same time preserved an intercourse with their mother country. In consequence of this, Orchomenus began to decline, till at length it was lost in the crowd of the other cities of Greece.

[820] Iliad, lib. II.
[821] Ibid.
[822] Strabo, lib. IX, p. 914.

Before Homer's time the Greeks had scarcely any trade but among themselves, and with a few barbarous nations; in proportion, however, as they formed new colonies, they extended their dominion. Greece was a large peninsula, the capes of which seemed to have kept off the seas, while its gulfs opened on all sides to receive them. If we cast an eye on Greece, we shall find, in a pretty compact country, a considerable extent of sea-coast. Her innumerable colonies formed an immense circle round her; and there she beheld, in some measure, the whole civilized world. Did she penetrate into Sicily and Italy, she formed new nations. Did she navigate towards the sea of Pontus, the coast of Asia Minor, or that of Africa, she acted in the same manner. Her cities increased in prosperity in proportion as they happened to have new people in their neighborhood. And what was extremely beautiful, she was surrounded on every side with a prodigious number of islands, drawn, as it were, in a line of circumvallation.

What a source of prosperity must Greece have found in those games with which she entertained, in some measure, the whole globe; in those temples, to which all the kings of the earth sent their offerings; in those festivals, at which such a concourse of people used to assemble from all parts; in those oracles, to which the attention of all mankind was directed; and, in short, in that exquisite taste for the polite arts, which she carried to such a height that to expect ever to surpass her would be only betraying our ignorance!

8. *Of Alexander: his Conquests.*

Four great events happened in the reign of Alexander which entirely changed the face of commerce: the taking of Tyre, the conquest of Egypt, that likewise of the Indies, and the discovery of the sea which lies south of that country.

The empire of Persia extended to the Indus. [823] Darius, long before Alexander, had sent some vessels, which sailed down this river, and passed even into the Red Sea. [824] How then were the Greeks the first who traded with the Indies by the south? Had not the Persians done this before? Did they make no advantage of seas which were so near them, of the very seas that washed their coasts? Alexander, it is true, conquered the Indies; but was it necessary for him to conquer a country in order to trade with it? This is what I shall now examine.

[823] Strabo, lib. XV.
[824] Herodotus, *Melpomene.*

Ariana, [825] which extended from the Persian Gulf as far as the Indus, and from the South Sea to the mountains of Paropamisus, depended indeed, in some measure, on the empire of Persia; but in the southern part it was barren, scorched, rude, and uncultivated. [826] Tradition relates [827] that the armies of Semiramis and Cyrus perished in these deserts; and Alexander, who caused his fleet to follow him, could not avoid losing in this place a great part of his army. The Persians left the whole coast to the Ichthyophagi, [828] the Oritæ, and other barbarous nations. Besides, the Persians were no great sailors, [829] and their very religion debarred them from entertaining any such notion as that of a maritime commerce. The voyage undertaken by Darius's direction upon the Indus and the Indian Sea proceeded rather from the capriciousness of a prince vainly ambitious of showing his power than from any settled regular project. It was attended with no consequence either to the advantage of commerce or of navigation. They emerged from their ignorance only to plunge into it again.

[825] Strabo, lib. XV.
[826] Pliny says, "Ariana region ambusta fervoribus, desertisque circumdata." (Nat. Hist. VI. chap. xxiii.)—Ed.
[827] Strabo, lib. XV.
[828] Pliny, lib. VI. chap. 33, Strabo, lib. XV.
[829] They sailed not upon the rivers, lest they should defile the elements (Hyde, Religion of the Persians.) Even to this day they have no maritime commerce. Those who take to the sea are treated by them as Atheists.

Besides, it was a received opinion [830] before the expedition of Alexander that the southern parts of India were uninhabitable. [831] This proceeded from a tradition that Semiramis [832] had brought back thence only twenty men, and Cyrus but seven.

[830] Strabo, lib. XV.

[831] Herodotus, *Melpomene*, says that Darius conquered the Indies; this must be understood only to mean Ariana; and even this was only an ideal conquest.
[832] Strabo, lib. XV.

Alexander entered by the north. His design was to march towards the east; but having found a part of the south full of great nations, cities, and rivers, he attempted to conquer it, and succeeded.

He then formed a design of uniting the Indies to the western nations by a maritime commerce, as he had already united them by the colonies he had established by land.

He ordered a fleet to be built on the Hydaspes, then fell down that river, entered the Indus, and sailed even to its mouth. He left his army and his fleet at Patala, went himself with a few vessels to view the sea, and marked the places where he would have ports to be opened and arsenals erected. Upon his return from Patala he separated the fleet, and took the route by land, for the mutual support of fleet and army. The fleet followed the coast from the Indus along the banks of the country of the Oritæ, of the Ichthyophagi, of Carmania and Persia. He caused wells to be dug, built cities, and would not suffer the Ichthyophagi to live on fish, [833] being desirous of having the borders of the sea inhabited by civilized nations. Nearchus and Onesecritus wrote a journal of this voyage, which was performed in ten months. They arrived at Susa, where they found Alexander, who gave an entertainment to his whole army.

[833] This cannot be understood of all the Ichthyophagi, who inhabited a coast of ten thousand furlongs in extent. How was it possible for Alexander to have maintained them? How could he command their submission? This can be only understood of some particular tribes. Nearchus, in his book *Rerum Indicarum*, says that at the extremity of this coast, on the side of Persia, he had found some people who were less Ichthyophagi than the others. I should think that Alexander's prohibition related to these people, or to some other tribe still more bordering on Persia.

This prince had founded Alexandria, with a view of securing his conquest of Egypt; this was a key to open it, in the very place where the kings his predecessors had a key to shut it; [834] and he had not the least thought of a commerce of which the discovery of the Indian Sea could alone give him the idea.

[834] Alexandria was founded on a flat shore, called Rhacotis, where, in ancient times, the kings had kept a garrison to prevent all strangers, and more particularly the Greeks, from entering the country.—Pliny, lib. VI. chap. 10; Strabo, lib. XVIII.

It even seems that after his discovery he had no new design in regard to Alexandria. He had, indeed, a general scheme of opening a trade between the East Indies and the western parts of his empire; but as for the project of conducting this commerce through Egypt, his knowledge was too imperfect to be able to form any such design. It is true he had seen the Indus, he had seen the Nile, but he knew nothing of the Arabian seas between the two rivers. Scarcely had he returned from India when he fitted out new fleets, and navigated on the Euleus, [835] the Tigris, the Euphrates, and the ocean; he removed the cataracts, with which the Persians had encumbered those rivers; and he discovered that the Persian Gulf was a branch of the main sea. But as he went to view this sea [836] in the same manner as he had done in respect to that of India; as he caused a port to be opened for a thousand ships, and arsenals to be erected at Babylon; as he sent five hundred talents into Phoenicia and Syria, to draw mariners into this service whom he intended to distribute in the colonies along the coast; in fine, as he caused immense works to be erected on the Euphrates, and the other rivers of Assyria, there could be no doubt but he designed to carry on the commerce of India by the way of Babylon and the Persian Gulf.

[835] Arrian, *de expedit. Alexandri*, lib. VII.
[836] Ibid.

There are some who pretend that Alexander wanted to subdue Arabia, [837] and had formed a design to make it the seat of his empire: but how could he have pitched upon a place with which he was entirely unacquainted? [838] Besides, of all countries, this would have been the most inconvenient to him; for it would have separated him from the rest of his empire. The Caliphs, who made distant conquests, soon withdrew from Arabia to reside elsewhere.

[837] Strabo, lib. VI, towards the end.
[838] Seeing Babylon overflowed, he looked upon the neighboring country of Arabia as an island.—Aristobulus, in Strabo, lib. XVI.

9. Of the Commerce of the Grecian Kings after the Death of Alexander.

At the time when Alexander made the conquest of Egypt, they had but a very imperfect idea of the Red Sea, and none at all of the ocean, which, joining this sea, on one side washes the coast of Africa, and on the other that of Arabia; nay, they thought it impossible to sail round the peninsula of Arabia. They who attempted it on each side had relinquished their design. "How is it possible," said they, [839] "to navigate to the southern coast of Arabia, when Cambyses' army, which traversed it on the north side, almost entirely perished; and the forces which Ptolemy, the son of Lagus, sent to the assistance of Seleucus Nicator at Babylon, underwent incredible hardships, and, upon account of the heat, could march only in the night?"

[839] See *Rerum Indicarum*.

The Persians were entire strangers to navigation. When they had subdued Egypt, they introduced the same spirit into that country as prevailed in Persia: hence, so great was the supineness of the Persians in this respect, that the Grecian kings found them quite strangers, not only to the commerce of the Tyrians, Idumeans, and the Jews on the ocean, but even to the navigation of the Red Sea. I am apt to think that the destruction of the first Tyre by Nebuchadnezzar, together with the subversion of several petty nations and towns bordering on the Red Sea, had obliterated all their former knowledge of commerce.

Egypt, at the time of the Persian monarchy, did not front the Red Sea; it contained only that long narrow neck of land which the Nile covers with its inundations, and is enclosed on both sides by a chain of mountains. [840] They were, therefore, under the necessity of making a second discovery of the ocean and the Red Sea; and this discovery engaged the curiosity of the Grecian monarchs.

[840] Strabo, lib. XVI.

They ascended the Nile, and hunted after elephants in the countries situated between that river and the sea; by this progression they traced the sea-coast; and as the discoveries were made by the Greeks, the names are all Grecian, and the temples are consecrated to Greek divinities. [841]

[841] Ibid.

The Greeks settled in Egypt were able to command a most extensive commerce; they were masters of all the harbors on the Red Sea; Tyre, the rival of every trading nation, was no more; they were not constrained by the ancient superstitions [842] on the country; in short, Egypt had become the centre of the world.

[842] These gave them an aversion to strangers.

The kings of Syria left the commerce of the south to those of Egypt, and attached themselves only to the northern trade, which was carried on by means of the Oxus and the Caspian Sea. They then imagined that this sea was part of the northern ocean; and Alexander, [843] some time before his death, had fitted out a fleet [844] in order to discover whether it communicated with the ocean by the Euxine Sea, or some other eastern sea towards India. After him, Seleucus and Antiochus applied themselves to make discoveries in it, with particular attention; and with this view they scoured it with their fleets. [845] That part which Seleucus surveyed was called the Seleucidian Sea; that which Antiochus discovered received the name of the Sea of Antiochus. Attentive to the projects they might have formed on that side, they neglected the seas on the south; whether it was that the Ptolemies, by means of their fleets on the Red Sea, had already become the masters of it, or that they discovered an invincible aversion in the Persians against engaging in maritime affairs. The southern coasts of Persia supplied them with no seamen; there had been none in those parts, except towards the latter end of Alexander's reign. But the Egyptian kings, being masters of the Isle of Cyprus, of Phoenicia, and of a great number of towns on the coast of Asia Minor, were possessed of all sorts of conveniences for undertaking maritime expeditions. They had no occasion to force; they had only to follow the genius and bent of their subjects.

[843] Pliny, lib. II. chap. 67, and lib. VI. chap. 9, 12; Strabo, lib. XI.; Arrian, *de expedit. Alexandri*, lib. III, p 74, and lib V, p. 104.
[844] Arrian, *de expedit. Alexandri*, lib. VII.
[845] Pliny, lib. II. chap. 67.

I am surprised, I confess, at the obstinacy with which the ancients believed that the Caspian Sea was a part of the ocean. The expeditions of Alexander, of the kings of Syria, of the Parthians and the Romans, could not make them change their sentiments; notwithstanding these nations described the Caspian Sea with wonderful exactness: but men are generally tenacious of their errors. When only the south of this sea was known, it was at first taken for the ocean; in proportion as they advanced along the banks of the northern coast, instead of imagining it a great lake, they still believed it to be the ocean, that here made a sort of bay: surveying the coast, their discoveries never went eastward beyond the Jaxartes, nor westward farther than the extremity of Albania. The sea towards the north was shallow, and of course very unfit for navigation. [846] Hence it was that they always looked upon this as the ocean.

[846] See the Czar's Chart.

The land army of Alexander had been in the east only as far as the Hypanis, which is the last of those rivers that fall into the Indus: thus the first trade which the Greeks carried on with the Indies was confined to a very small part of the country. Seleucus Nicator penetrated as far as the Ganges, and thereby discovered the sea into which this river falls, that is to say, the Bay of Bengal. [847] The moderns discover countries by voyages at sea; the ancients discovered seas by conquests at land.

[847] Pliny, lib. VI. chap. 17.

Strabo, [848] notwithstanding the testimony of Apollodorus, seems to doubt whether the Grecian kings of Bactria proceeded farther than Seleucus and Alexander. [849] Were it even true that they went no farther to the east than Seleucus, yet they went farther towards the south; they discovered Siger, and the ports on the coast of Malabar, which gave rise to the navigation I am going to mention. [850]

[848] Lib. XV.
[849] Apollonius Adrumatinus in Strabo, lib. II.
[850] The Macedonians of Bactria, India, and Ariana, having separated themselves from Syria, formed a great state.

Pliny informs us that the navigation of the Indies was successively carried on in three different ways. [851] At first they sailed from the Cape of Siagre to the island of Patalena, which is at the mouth of the Indus. This we find was the course that Alexander's fleet steered to the Indies. They took afterwards a shorter and more certain course, by sailing from the same cape or promontory to Siger: [852] this can be no other than the kingdom of Siger mentioned by Strabo, [853] and discovered by the Grecian kings of Bactria. Pliny, by saying that this way was shorter than the other, can mean only that the voyage was made in less time: for, as Siger was discovered by the kings of Bactria, it must have been farther than the Indus: by this passage they must therefore have avoided the winding of certain coasts, and taken advantage of particular winds. The merchants at last took a third way; they sailed to Canes, or Ocelis, ports situated at the entrance of the Red Sea; whence by a west wind they arrived at Muziris, the first staple town of the Indies, and thence to the other ports. Here we see that instead of sailing to the mouth of the Red Sea as far as Siagre, by coasting Arabia Felix to the north-east, they steered directly from west to east, from one side to the other, by means of the monsoons, whose regular course they discovered by sailing in these latitudes. The ancients never lost sight of the coasts, except when they took advantage of these and the trade-winds, which were to them a kind of compass. [854]

[851] Lib. VI. chap. 23.
[852] Pliny, lib. VI. chap. 23.
[853] Lib. XI. *Sigertidis regnum.*

[854] The monsoons blow part of the year from one quarter, and part from another; the trade winds blow the whole year round from the same quarter.

Pliny [855] says that they set sail for the Indies in the middle of summer and returned towards the end of December, or in the beginning of January. This is entirely conformable to our naval journals. In that part of the Indian Ocean which is between the Peninsula of Africa, and that on this side the Ganges, there are two monsoons; the first, during which the winds blow from west to east, begins in the month of August or September; and the second, during which the wind is in the east, begins in January. Thus we set sail from Africa for Malabar at the season of the year that Ptolemy's fleet used to put to sea thence; and we return too at the same time as they.

[855] Lib. VI. chap. 23.

Alexander's fleet was seven months in sailing from Patala to Susa. It set out in the month of July, that is, at a season when no ship dare now put to sea to return from the Indies. Between these two monsoons there is an interval during which the winds vary; when a north wind, meeting with the common winds, raises, especially near the coasts, the most terrible tempests. These continue during the months of June, July, and August. Alexander's fleet, therefore, setting sail from Patala in the month of July, must have been exposed to many storms, and the voyage must have been long, because they sailed against the monsoon.

Pliny says that they set out for the Indies at the end of summer; thus they spent the time proper for taking advantage of the monsoon in their passage from Alexandria to the Red Sea.

Observe here, I pray, how navigation has, little by little, arrived at perfection. Darius's fleet was two years and a half in falling down the Indus and going to the Red Sea. [856] Afterwards the fleet of Alexander, [857] descending the Indus, arrived at Susa, in ten months, having sailed three months on the Indus, and seven on the Indian Ocean; at last the passage from the coast of Malabar to the Red Sea was made in forty days. [858]

[856] Herodotus, *Melpomene.*
[857] Pliny, lib. VI. chap. 23.
[858] Pliny, lib. VI. cap 23.

Strabo, [859] who accounts for their ignorance of the countries between the Hypanis and the Ganges, says there were very few of those who sailed from Egypt to the Indies that ever proceeded so far as the Ganges. Their fleets, in fact, never went thither: they sailed with the western monsoons from the mouth of the Red Sea to the coast of Malabar. They cast anchor in the ports along that coast, and never attempted to get round the peninsula on this side the Ganges by Cape Comorin and the coast of Coromandel. The plan of navigation laid down by the kings of Egypt and the Romans was to set out and return the same year. [860]

[859] Lib. XV.
[860] Pliny, lib. VI. chap. 23.

Thus it is demonstrable that the commerce of the Greeks and Romans to the Indies was much less extensive than ours. We know immense countries, which to them were entirely unknown; we traffic with all the Indian nations; we even manage their trade and carry on their commerce. But this commerce of the ancients was carried on with far greater facility than ours. And if the moderns were to trade only with the coast of Guzerat and Malabar, and, without seeking for the southern isles, were satisfied with what these islanders brought them, they would certainly prefer the way of Egypt to that of the Cape of Good Hope. Strabo informs us [861] that they traded thus with the people of Taprobane.

[861] Lib. XV.

10. Of the Circuit of Africa.

We find from history that before the discovery of the mariner's compass four attempts were made to sail round the coast of Africa. The Phoenicians sent by Necho [862] and Eudoxus, [863] flying from the wrath of Ptolemy Lathyrus, set out from the Red Sea, and succeeded. Sataspes [864] sent by Xerxes, and Hanno by the Carthaginians, set out from the Pillars of Hercules, and failed in the attempt.

[862] He was desirous of conquering it.—Herodotus, lib. IV.
[863] Pliny, lib. II. chap. 67; Pomponius Mela, lib. III. chap. 9.
[864] Herodotus, *Melpomene.*

The capital point in surrounding Africa was to discover and double the Cape of Good Hope. Those who set out from the Red Sea found this cape nearer by half than it would have been in setting out from the Mediterranean. The shore from the Red Sea is not so shallow as that from the cape to Hercules' Pillars. [865] The discovery of the cape by Hercules' Pillars was owing to the invention of the compass, which permitted them to leave the coast of Africa, and to launch out into the vast ocean, in order to sail towards the island of St. Helena, or towards the coast of Brazil. [866] It was, therefore, possible for them to sail from the Red Sea into the Mediterranean, but not to set out from the Mediterranean to return by the Red Sea.

[865] Add to this what I shall say in chapter 11 of this book on the navigation of Hanno.
[866] In the months of October, November, December, and January the wind in the Atlantic Ocean is found to blow north-east; our ships therefore either cross the line, and to avoid the wind, which is there generally east, they direct their course to the south: or else they enter into the torrid zone, in those places where the wind is west.

Thus, without making this grand circuit, after which they could hardly hope to return, it was most natural to trade to the east of Africa by the Red Sea, and to the western coast by Hercules' Pillars.

The Grecian kings of Egypt discovered at first, in the Red Sea, that part of the coast of Africa which extends from the bottom of the gulf, where stands the town of Heroum, as far as Dira, that is, to the strait now known by the name of Babelmandel. Thence to the promontory of Aromatia, situate at the entrance of the Red Sea, [867] the coast had never been surveyed by navigators: and this is evident from what Artemidorus tells us, [868] that they were acquainted with the places on that coast, but knew not their distances: the reason of which is, they successively gained a knowledge of those ports by land, without sailing from one to the other.

[867] The sea to which we give this name was called by the ancients the Gulf of Arabia; the name of Red Sea they gave to that part of the ocean which borders on this gulf.
[868] Strabo, lib. XVI.

Beyond this promontory, at which the coast along the ocean commenced, they knew nothing, as we learn from Eratosthenes and Artemidorus. [869]

[869] Strabo, lib. XVI. Artemidorus settled the borders of the known coast at the place called Austricornu; and Eratosthenes, Cinnamomiferam.

Such was the knowledge they had of the coasts of Africa in Strabo's time, that is, in the reign of Augustus. But after the prince's decease, the Romans found out the two capes Raptum and Prassum, of which Strabo makes no mention, because they had not as yet been discovered. It is plain that both those names are of Roman origin.

Ptolemy, the geographer, flourished under Adrian and Antoninus Pius; and the author of the Periplus of the Red Sea, whoever he was, lived a little after. Yet the former limits known Africa to Cape Prassum, [870] which is in about the 14th degree of south latitude; while the author of the Periplus [871] confines it to Cape Raptum, which is nearly in the tenth degree of the same latitude. In all likelihood the latter took his limit from a place then frequented, and Ptolemy his from a place with which there was no longer any communication.

[870] Lib. I. chap. 7; lib. IV. chap. 9; table 4 of Africa.
[871] This Periplus is attributed to Arrian.

What confirms me in this notion is that the people about Cape Prassum were Anthropophagi. [872] Ptolemy takes notice [873] of a great number of places between the port or emporium Aromatum and Cape Raptum, but leaves an entire blank between Capes Raptum and Prassum. The great profits of the East India trade must have occasioned a neglect of that of Africa. In fine, the Romans never had any settled navigation; they had discovered these several ports by land expeditions, and by means of ships driven on that coast; and as at present we are well acquainted with the maritime parts of Africa, but know very little of the inland country, the ancients, on the contrary, had a very good knowledge of the inland parts, but were almost strangers to the coasts. [874]

[872] Ptolemy, lib. IV. chap. 9.
[873] Lib. IV. chap. 7, 8.
[874] See what exact descriptions Strabo and Ptolemy have given us of the different parts of Africa. Their knowledge was owing to the several wars which the two most powerful nations in the world had waged with the people of Africa, to the alliances they had contracted, and to the trade they had carried on with those countries.

I said that the Phoenicians sent by Necho and Eudoxus under Ptolemy Lathyrus had made the circuit of Africa; but at the time of Ptolemy, the geographer, those two voyages must have been looked upon as fabulous, since he places after [875] the *Sinus Magnus*, which I apprehend to be the Gulf of Siam, an unknown country, extending from Asia to Africa, and terminating at Cape Prassum, so that the Indian Ocean would have been no more than a lake. The ancients who discovered the Indies towards the north, advancing eastward, placed this unknown country to the south.

[875] Lib.VII. chap. 3.

11. *Of Carthage and Marseilles.*

The law of nations which prevailed at Carthage was very extraordinary: all strangers who traded to Sardinia and towards Hercules' Pillars this haughty republic sentenced to be drowned. Her civil polity was equally surprising; she forbade the Sardinians to cultivate their lands, upon pain of death. She increased her power by her riches, and afterwards her riches by her power. Being mistress of the coasts of Africa, which are washed by the Mediterranean, she extended herself along the ocean. Hanno, by order of the senate of Carthage, distributed thirty thousand Carthaginians from Hercules' Pillars as far as Cerne. This place, he says, is as distant from Hercules' Pillars as the latter from Carthage. This situation is extremely remarkable. It lets us see that Hanno limited his settlements to the 25th degree of north latitude; that is, to two or three degrees south of the Canaries.

Hanno being at Cerne undertook another voyage, with a view of making further discoveries towards the south. He took but little notice of the continent. He followed the coast for twenty-six days, when he was obliged to return for want of provisions. The Carthaginians, it seems, made no use of this second enterprise. Scylax says [876] that the sea is not navigable beyond Cerne, because it is shallow, full of mud and sea-weeds: [877] and, in fact, there are many of these in those latitudes. [878] The Carthaginian merchants mentioned by Scylax might find obstacles which Hanno, who had sixty vessels of fifty oars each, had surmounted. Difficulties are at most but relative; besides, we ought not to confound an enterprise in which bravery and resolution must be exerted with things that require no extraordinary conduct.

[876] See his *Periplus*, under the article on Carthage.
[877] See Herodotus, *Melpomene*, on the obstacles which Sataspes encountered.
[878] See the charts and relations in the first volume of Collection of Voyages that Contributed to the Establishment of the East India Company, part I, p. 201. This weed covers the surface of the water in such a manner as to be scarcely perceived, and ships can only pass through it with a stiff gale.

The relation of Hanno's voyage is a fine fragment of antiquity. It was written by the very man that performed it.

His recital is not mingled with ostentation. Great commanders write their actions with simplicity; because they receive more glory from facts than from words.

The style is agreeable to the subject; he deals not in the marvelous. All he says of the climate, of the soil, the behavior, the manners of the inhabitants, correspond with what is every day seen on this coast of Africa; one would imagine it the journal of a modern sailor.

He observed from his fleet that in the day-time there was a prodigious silence on the continent, that in the night he heard the sound of various musical instruments, and that fires might then be everywhere seen, some larger than others. [879] Our relations are conformable to this; it has been discovered that in the day the savages retire into the forests to avoid the heat of the sun, that they light up great fires in the night to disperse the beasts of prey, and that they are passionately fond of music and dancing.

[879] Pliny tells us the same thing, speaking of Mount Atlas: "Noctibus micare crebris ignibus, tibiarum cantu timpanorumque sonitu strepere, neminem interdiu cerni."

The same writer describes a volcano with all the phenomena of Vesuvius; and relates that he captured two hairy women, who chose to die rather than follow the Carthaginians, and whose skins he carried to Carthage. This has been found not void of probability.

This narration is so much the more valuable as it is a monument of Punic antiquity; and hence alone it has been regarded as fabulous. For the Romans retained their hatred of the Carthaginians, even after they had destroyed them. But it was victory alone that decided whether we ought to say the *Punic* or the *Roman* faith.

Some moderns [880] have imbibed these prejudices. What has become, say they, of the cities described by Hanno, of which even in Pliny's time there remained no vestiges? But it would have been a wonder indeed if any such vestiges had remained. Was it a Corinth or Athens that Hanno built on those coasts? He left Carthaginian families in such places as were most commodious for trade, and secured them as well as his hurry would permit against savages and wild beasts. The calamities of the Carthaginians put a period to the navigation of Africa; these families must necessarily then either perish or become savages. Besides, were the ruins of these cities even still in being, who is it that would venture into the woods and marshes to make the discovery? We find, however, in Scylax and Polybius that the Carthaginians had considerable settlements on those coasts. These are the vestiges of the cities of Hanno; there are no others, for the same reason that there are no others of Carthage itself.

[881] Mr. Dodwell. See his Dissertation on Hanno's *Periplus*.

The Carthaginians were in the high road to wealth; and had they gone so far as four degrees of north latitude, and fifteen of longitude, they would have discovered the Gold Coast. They would then have had a trade of much greater importance than that which is carried on at present on that coast, at a time when America seems to have degraded the riches of all other countries. They would there have found treasures of which they could never have been deprived by the Romans.

Very surprising things have been said of the riches of Spain. If we may believe Aristotle, [882] the Phoenicians who arrived at Tartessus found so much silver there that their ships could not hold it all; and they made of this metal their meanest utensils. The Carthaginians, according to Diodorus, [883] found so much gold and silver in the Pyrenean mountains, that they adorned the anchors of their ships with it. But no foundation can be built on such popular reports. Let us therefore examine the facts themselves.

[882] Of Wonderful Things.
[883] Diodorus speaks of the Phoenicians in this relation, and not of the Carthaginians.—Ed.

We find in a fragment of Polybius, cited by Strabo, [884] that the silver mines at the source of the river Bætis, in which forty thousand men were employed, produced to the Romans twenty-five thousand drachmas a day, that is, about five million livres a year, at fifty livres to the mark. The mountains that contained these mines were called the Silver Mountains: [885] which shows they were the Potosi of those times. At present, the mines of Hanover do not employ a fourth part of the workmen, and yet they yield more. But as the Romans had not many copper mines, and but few of silver; and as the Greeks knew none but the Attic mines, which were of little value, they might well be astonished at their abundance.

[884] Lib III.
[885] *Mons Argentarius.*

In the war that broke out for the succession of Spain, a man called the Marquis of Rhodes, of whom it was said that he was ruined in gold mines and enriched in hospitals, [886] proposed to the court of France to open the Pyrenean mines. He alleged the example of the Tyrians, the Carthaginians, and the Romans. He was permitted to search, but sought in vain; he still alleged, and found nothing.

[887] He had some share in their management.

The Carthaginians, being masters of the gold and silver trade, were willing to be so of the lead and pewter. These metals were carried by land from the ports of Gaul upon the ocean to those of the Mediterranean. The Carthaginians were desirous of receiving them at the first hand; they sent Himilco to make a settlement in the isles called Cassiterides, [888] which are imagined to be those of Scilly.

[889] See Festus Avienus.

These voyages from Bætica into England have made some persons imagine that the Carthaginians knew the compass: but it is very certain that they followed the coasts. There needs no other proof than Himilco's being four months in sailing from the mouth of the Bætis to England; besides, the famous piece of history of the Carthaginian [890] pilot who, being followed by a Roman vessel, ran aground, that he might not show her the way to England, [891] plainly intimates that those vessels were very near the shore when they fell in with each other.

[890] Strabo, lib. III, towards the end.
[891] He was rewarded by the senate of Carthage.

The ancients might have performed voyages that would make one imagine they had the compass, though they had not. If a pilot was far from land, and during his voyage had such serene weather that in the night he could always see a polar star [892] and in the day the rising and setting of the sun, it is certain he might regulate his course as well as we do now by the compass: but this must be a fortuitous case, and not a regular method of navigation.

[892] Montesquieu has been found fault with in this construction, as though he were giving the impression that there was more than one North Star.—Ed.

We see in the treaty which put an end to the first Punic war that Carthage was principally attentive to preserve the empire of the sea, and Rome that of the land. Hanno, [893] in his negotiation with the Romans, declared that they should not be suffered even to wash their hands in the sea of Sicily; they were not permitted to sail beyond the *promontorium pulchrum*; they were forbidden to trade in Sicily, Sardinia, and Africa, except at Carthage: [894] an exception that proves there was no design to favor them in their trade with that city.

[893] Freinshemius, Supplement to Livy, 2nd Decad.
[894] In the parts subject to the Carthaginians.

In early times there had been very great wars between Carthage and Marseilles [895] on the subject of fishing. After the peace they entered jointly into economical commerce. Marseilles at length grew jealous, especially as, being equal to her rival in industry, she had become inferior to her in power. This is the motive of her great fidelity to the Romans. The war between the latter and the Carthaginians in Spain was a source of riches to Marseilles, which had now become their magazine. The ruin of Carthage and Corinth still increased the glory of Marseilles, and had it not been for the civil wars, in which this republic ought on no account to have engaged, she would have been happy under the protection of the Romans, who were not the least jealous of her commerce.

[895] Justin, lib. XLIII. chap. 5.

12. *The Isle of Delos. Mithridates.*

Upon the destruction of Corinth by the Romans, the merchants retired to Delos, an island which from religious considerations was looked upon as a place of safety: [896] besides, it was extremely well situated for the commerce of Italy and Asia, which, since the reduction of Africa and the weakening of Greece, had grown more important.

[896] See Strabo, lib. X.

From the earliest times the Greeks, as we have already observed, sent colonies to Propontis and to the Euxine Sea—colonies which retained their laws and liberties under the Persians. Alexander, having undertaken his expedition against the barbarians only, did not molest these people. [897] Neither does it appear that the kings of Pontus, who were masters of many of those colonies, ever deprived them of their own civil government. [898]

[897] He confirmed the liberty of the city of Amisus, an Athenian colony which had enjoyed a popular government, even under the kings of Persia. Lucullus having taken

Sinone and Amisus, restored them to their liberty, and recalled the inhabitants, who had fled on board their ships.

[898] See what Appian writes concerning the Phanagoreans, the Amisians, and the Synopians, in his treatise Of the War against Mithridates.

The power of those kings increased as soon as they subdued those cities. [899] Mithridates found himself able to hire troops on every side; to repair his frequent losses; to have a multitude of workmen, ships, and military machines; to procure himself allies; to bribe those of the Romans, and even the Romans themselves; to keep the barbarians of Asia and Europe in his pay; [900] to continue the war for many years, and of course to discipline his troops, he found himself able to train them to arms, to instruct them in the military art of the Romans, [901] and to form considerable bodies out of their deserters; in a word, he found himself able to sustain great losses, and to be frequently defeated, without being ruined; [902] neither would he have been ruined if the voluptuous and barbarous king had not destroyed, in his prosperous days, what had been done by the great prince in times of adversity.

[899] See Appian, in regard to the immense treasures which Mithridates employed in his wars, those which he had buried, those which he frequently lost by the treachery of his own people, and those which were found after his death.
[900] See Appian Of the War against Mithridates.
[901] Ibid.
[902] He lost at one time 170,000 men, yet he soon recruited his armies.

Thus it was that when the Romans had arrived at their highest pitch of grandeur, and seemed to have nothing to apprehend but from the ambition of their own subjects, Mithridates once more ventured to contest the mighty point, which the overthrow of Philip, of Antiochus, and of Perseus had already decided. Never was there a more destructive war: the two contending parties, being possessed of great power, and receiving alternate advantages, the inhabitants of Greece and of Asia fell a sacrifice in the quarrel, either as foes, or as friends of Mithridates. Delos was involved in the general fatality, and commerce failed on every side: which was a necessary consequence, the people themselves being destroyed.

The Romans, in pursuance of a system of which I have spoken elsewhere, [903] acting as destroyers, that they might not appear as conquerors, demolished Carthage and Corinth; a practice by which they would have ruined themselves had they not subdued the world. When the kings of Pontus became masters of the Greek colonies on the Euxine Sea, they took care not to destroy what was to be the foundation of their own grandeur.

[903] In the Considerations on the Causes of the Rise and Declension of the Roman Grandeur.

13. Of the Genius of the Romans as to Maritime Affairs.

The Romans laid no stress on anything but their land forces, who were disciplined to stand firm, to fight on one spot, and there bravely to die. They could not like the practice of seamen, who first offer to fight, then fly, then return, constantly avoid danger, often make use of stratagem, and seldom of force. This was not suitable to the genius of the Greeks [904] much less to that of the Romans.

[904] As Plato has observed. lib. IV of Laws.

They destined therefore to the sea only those citizens who were not considerable enough to have a place in their legions. [905] Their marines were commonly freedmen.

[905] Polybius, lib. V.

At this time we have neither the same esteem for land forces nor the same contempt for those of the sea. In the former, art has decreased; [906] in the latter, it has augmented: [907] now things are generally esteemed in proportion to the degree of ability requisite to discharge them.

[906] See the Considerations on the Causes of the Rise and Declension of the Roman Grandeur.
[907] Ibid.

14. *Of the Genius of the Romans with respect to Commerce.*

The Romans were never distinguished by a jealousy for trade. They attacked Carthage as a rival, not as a commercial nation. They favored trading cities that were not subject to them. Thus they increased the power of Marseilles by the cession of a large territory. They were vastly afraid of barbarians, but had not the least apprehension from a trading people. Their genius, their glory, their military education, and the very form of their government estranged them from commerce.

In the city, they were employed only about war, elections, factions, and law-suits; in the country, about agriculture; and as for the provinces, a severe and tyrannical government was incompatible with commerce.

But their political constitution was not more opposed to trade than their law of nations. *The people,* says Pomponius, the civilian, [908] *with whom we have neither friendship, nor hospitality nor alliance, are not our enemies; however, if anything belonging to us falls into their hands, they are the proprietors of it; freemen become their slaves; and they are upon the same terms with respect to us.*

[908] Leg. 5, ff. *de Captivis.*

Their civil law was not less oppressive. The law of Constantine, [909] after having stigmatized as bastards the children of a mean rank who had been married to those of a superior station, confounds women who retail merchandise with slaves, with the mistresses of taverns, with actresses, with the daughters of those who keep public stews, or who had been condemned to fight in the amphitheatre; this had its origin in the ancient institutions of the Romans.

[909] *Quæ mercimoniis publicè præfuit*—Leg. V. cod. *de natural. liberis.*

I am not ignorant that men prepossessed with these two ideas (that commerce is of the greatest service to a state, and that the Romans had the best-regulated government in the world) have believed that these people greatly honored and encouraged commerce; but the truth is, they seldom troubled their heads about it.

15. Of the Commerce of the Romans with the Barbarians.

The Romans having erected a vast empire in Europe, Asia, and Africa, the weakness of the people and the tyranny of their laws united all the parts of this immense body. The Roman policy was then to avoid all communication with those nations whom they had not subdued: the fear of carrying to them the art of conquering made them neglect the art of enriching themselves. They made laws to hinder all commerce with barbarians. "Let nobody," said Valens and Gratian, [910] "send wine, oil, or other liquors to the barbarians, though it be only for them to taste." "Let no one carry gold to them," add Gratian, Valentinian, and Theodosius; [911] "rather, if they have any, let our subjects deprive them of it by stratagem." The exportation of iron was prohibited on pain of death.

[910] Leg. ad barbaricum. cod. *quæ res exportari non debeant.*
[911] Leg. 2, cod. *de commerc. et mercator.*

Domitian, a prince of great timidity, ordered the vines in Gaul to be pulled up, [912] from fear, no doubt, lest their wines should draw thither the barbarians. Probus and Julian, who had no such fears, gave orders for their being planted again.

[912] Leg. 2 *quæ res exportari non debeant*, and Procopius, War of the Persians, book I.

I am sensible that upon the declension of the Roman empire the barbarians obliged the Romans to establish staple towns, and to trade with them. [913] But even this is a proof that the minds of the Romans were averse to commerce. [914]

[913] See the Chronicles of Eusebius and Cedrenus
[914] See the Considerations on the Causes of the Rise and Declension of the Roman Grandeur.

16. Of the Commerce of the Romans with Arabia and the Indies.

The trade to Arabia Felix, and that to the Indies, were the two branches, and almost the only ones, of their foreign commerce. The Arabians were possessed of immense riches, which they found in their seas and forests; and as they sold much and purchased little, they drew to themselves the gold and silver of the Romans. [915] Augustus, [916] being well apprised of that opulence, resolved they should be either his friends or his enemies. With this view he sent Ælius Gallus from Egypt into Arabia. This commander found the people indolent, peaceable, and unskilled in war. He fought battles, laid sieges to towns, and lost but seven of his men by the sword; but the perfidy of his guides, long marches, the climate, want of provisions, distempers, and ill-conduct, caused the ruin of his army.

[915] Pliny, lib. VI. chap. 28, and Strabo, lib. XVI.

[916] Ibid.

He was therefore obliged to be content with trading to Arabia, in the same manner as other nations; that is, with giving them gold and silver in exchange for their commodities. The Europeans trade with them still in the same manner; the caravans of Aleppo and the royal vessel of Suez carry thither immense sums. [917]

[917] The caravans of Aleppo and Suez carry thither annually to the value of about two millions of livres, and as much more clandestinely; the royal vessel of Suez carries thither also two millions.

Nature had formed the Arabs for commerce, not for war; but when those quiet people came to be near neighbors to the Parthians and the Romans, they acted as auxiliaries to both nations. Ælius Gallus found them a trading people; Mahomet happened to find them trained to war; he inspired them with enthusiasm, which led them to glory and conquest.

The commerce of the Romans to the Indies was very considerable. Strabo [918] had been informed in Egypt that they employed in this navigation one hundred and twenty vessels; this commerce was carried on entirely with bullion. They sent thither annually fifty millions of sesterces. Pliny [919] says that the merchandise brought thence was sold at Rome at cent. per cent profit. He speaks, I believe, too generally; if this trade had been so vastly profitable, everybody would have been willing to engage in it, and then it would have been at an end.

[918] Lib. II, p. 81.
[919] Lib. VI. chap. 23.

It will admit of a question, whether the trade to Arabia and the Indies was of any advantage to the Romans. They were obliged to export their bullion thither, though they had not, like us, the resource of America, which supplies what we send away. I am persuaded that one of the reasons of their increasing the value of their specie by establishing base coin was the scarcity of silver, owing to the continual exportation of it to the Indies: and though the commodities of this country were sold at Rome at the rate of cent. per cent, this profit of the Romans, being obtained from the Romans themselves, could not enrich the empire.

It may be alleged, on the other hand, that this commerce increased the Roman navigation, and of course their power; that new merchandise augmented their inland trade, gave encouragement to the arts, and employment to the industrious; that the number of subjects multiplied in proportion to the new means of support; that this new commerce was productive of luxury, which I have proved to be as favorable to a monarchical government as fatal to a commonwealth; that this establishment was of the same date as the fall of their republic; that the luxury of Rome had become necessary; and that it was extremely proper that a city which had accumulated all the wealth of the universe should refund it by its luxury.

Strabo says [920] that the Romans carried on a far more extensive commerce with the Indies than the kings of Egypt; but it is very extraordinary that those people who were so little acquainted with commerce should have paid more attention to that of India than the Egyptian kings, whose dominions lay so conveniently for it. The reason of this must be explained.

[920] He says, book 12, that the Romans employed a hundred and twenty ships in that trade; and, in book 17, that the Grecian kings scarcely employed twenty.

After the death of Alexander, the kings of Egypt established a maritime commerce with the Indies; while the kings of Syria, who were possessed of the more eastern provinces, and consequently of the Indies, maintained that commerce of which we have taken notice in the sixth chapter, which was carried on partly by land, and partly by rivers, and had been further facilitated by means of the Macedonian colonies; insomuch that Europe had communication with the Indies both by Egypt and by Syria. The dismembering of the latter kingdom, whence was formed that of Bactriana, did not prove in any way prejudicial to this commerce. Marinus the Tyrian, quoted by Ptolemy, [921] mentions the discoveries made in India by means of some Macedonian merchants, who found out new roads, which had been unknown to kings in their military expeditions. We find in Ptolemy [922] that they went from Peter's tower [923] as far as Sera; and the discovery made by mercantile people of so distant a mart, situated in the north-east part of China, was a kind of prodigy. Hence, under the kings of Syria and Bactriana, merchandise was conveyed to the west from the southern parts of India, by the river Indus, the Oxus, and the Caspian Sea; while those of the more eastern and northern parts were transported from Sera, Peter's tower, and other staples, as far as the Euphrates. Those merchants directed their route nearly by the fortieth degree of north latitude, through countries situated to the west of China, more civilized at that time than at present, because they had not as yet been infested by the Tartars.

[921] Lib. I, chap. 2.
[922] Lib. I, chap. 13.
[923] Our best maps place Peter's tower in the hundredth degree of longitude, and about the fortieth of latitude.

Now while the Syrian empire was extending its trade to such a distance by land, Egypt did not greatly enlarge its maritime commerce.

The Parthians soon after appeared, and founded their empire; and when Egypt fell under the power of the Romans, this empire was at its height, and had received its whole extension.

The Romans and Parthians were two rival nations, that fought not for dominion but for their very existence. Between the two empires deserts were formed and armies were always stationed on the frontiers; so that instead of there being any commerce, there was not so much as communication between them. Ambition, jealousy, religion, national antipathy, and difference of manners completed the separation. Thus the trade from east to west, which had formerly so many channels, was reduced to one; and Alexandria becoming the only staple, the trade to this city was immensely enlarged.

We shall say but one word of their inland trade. Its principal branch was the corn brought to Rome for the subsistence of the people; but this was rather a political affair than a point of commerce. On this account the sailors were favored with some privileges, because the safety of the empire depended on their vigilance. [924]

[924] Suetonius, *Life of Claudius*; Leg. 8. Cod. Theodosis. *de Naviculariis.*

17. *Of Commerce after the Destruction of the Western Empire.*

After the invasion of the Roman empire one effect of the general calamity was the destruction of commerce. The barbarous nations at first regarded it only as an opportunity for robbery; and when they had subdued the Romans, they honored it no more than agriculture, and the other professions of a conquered people.

Soon was the commerce of Europe almost entirely lost. The nobility, who had everywhere the direction of affairs, were in no pain about it.

The laws of the Visigoths [925] permitted private people to occupy half the beds of great rivers, provided the other half remained free for nets and boats. There must have been very little trade in countries conquered by these barbarians.

[925] Lib. VIII, tit. 4, § 9.

In those times were established the ridiculous rights of escheatage and shipwrecks. These men thought that, as strangers were not united to them by any civil law, they owed them on the one hand no kind of justice, and on the other no sort of pity.

In the narrow bounds which nature had originally prescribed to the people of the north, all were strangers to them: and in their poverty they regarded all only as contributing to their riches. Being established, before their conquest, on the coasts of a sea of very little breadth, and full of rocks, from these very rocks they drew their subsistence.

But the Romans, who made laws for all the world, had established the most humane ones with regard to shipwrecks. [926] They suppressed the rapine of those who inhabited the coasts, and what was more still, the rapacity of their treasuries. [927]

[926] Toto titulo, ff. *de incend, ruin. et naufrag.*; Cod. *de naufragiis*; Leg. 3, ff. ad leg. Cornel, *de sicariis.*
[927] Leg. 1, Cod. *de naufragiis.*

18. *A particular Regulation.*

The law of the Visigoths made, however, one regulation in favor of commerce. [928] It ordained that foreign merchants should be judged, in the differences that arose among themselves, by the laws and by judges of their own nation. This was founded on an established custom among all mixed people, that every man should live under his own law—a custom of which I shall speak more at large in another place.

[928] Lib II, tit. 3, § 2.

19. *Of Commerce after the Decay of the Roman Power in the East.*

The Mahomedans appeared, conquered, extended, and dispersed themselves. Egypt had particular sovereigns; these carried on the commerce of India, and being possessed of the merchandise of this country, drew to themselves the riches of all other nations. The sultans of Egypt were the most powerful princes of those times. History informs us with what a constant and well-regulated force they stopped the ardor, the fire, and the impetuosity of the crusades.

20. *How Commerce broke through the Barbarism of Europe.*

Aristotle's philosophy being carried to the west, pleased the subtle geniuses who were the virtuosi of those times of ignorance. The schoolmen were infatuated with it, and borrowed from that philosopher [929] a great many notions on lending upon interest, whereas its source might have been easily traced in the gospel; in short, they condemned it absolutely and in all cases. Hence commerce, which was the profession only of mean persons, became that of knaves; for whenever a thing is forbidden, which nature permits or necessity requires, those who do it are looked upon as dishonest.

[929] See Aristotle, *Politics*, lib. I. chap. 9, 10.

Commerce was transferred to a nation covered with infamy, and soon ranked with the most shameful usury, with monopolies, with the levying of subsidies, and with all the dishonest means of acquiring wealth.

The Jews, enriched by their exactions, were pillaged by the tyranny of princes; which pleased indeed, but did not ease, the people. [930]

[930] See in *Marca Hispanica*, the constitutions of Aragon, in the years 1228 and 1231; and in Brussel, the agreement, in the year 1206, between the King, the Countess of Champagne, and Guy of Dampierre.

What passed in England may serve to give us an idea of what was done in other countries. King John [931] having imprisoned the Jews, in order to obtain their wealth, there were few who had not at least one of their eyes plucked out. Thus did that king administer justice. A certain Jew, who had a tooth pulled out every day for seven days successively, gave ten thousand marks of silver for the eighth. Henry III extorted from Aaron, a Jew at York, fourteen thousand marks of silver, and ten thousand for the queen, in those times they did by violence what is now done in Poland with some semblance of moderation. As princes could not dive into the purses of their subjects because of their privileges, they put the Jews to the torture, who were not considered as citizens.

[931] Stow, Survey of London, book III, p. 54.

At last a custom was introduced of confiscating the effects of those Jews who embraced Christianity. This ridiculous custom is known only by the law which suppressed it. [932] The most vain and trifling reasons were given in justification of that proceeding; it was alleged that it was proper to try them, in order to be certain that they had entirely shaken off the slavery of the devil. But it is evident that this confiscation was a species of the right of amortization, to recompense the prince, or the lords, for the taxes levied on the Jews, which ceased on their embracing Christianity. [933] In those times, men, like lands, were regarded as property. I cannot help remarking, by the way, how this nation has been sported with from one age to another: at one time, their effects were confiscated when they were willing to become Christians; and at another, if they refused to turn Christians, they were ordered to be burned.

[932] The edict passed at Baville, 4th of April, 1392.

[933] In France the Jews were slaves in mortmain, and the lords their successors. Mr. Brussel mentions an agreement made in the year 1206, between the King and Thibaut, Count of Champagne, by which it was agreed that the Jews of the one should not lend in the lands of the other.

In the meantime, commerce was seen to arise from the bosom of vexation and despair. The Jews, proscribed by turns from every country, found out the way of saving their effects. Thus they rendered their retreats for ever fixed; for though princes might have been willing to get rid of their persons, yet they did not choose to get rid of their money.

The Jews invented letters of exchange; [934] commerce, by this method, became capable of eluding violence, and of maintaining everywhere its ground; the richest merchant having none but invisible effects, which he could convey imperceptibly wherever he pleased.

[934] It is known that under Philip Augustus and Philip the Long, the Jews who were chased from France took refuge in Lombardy, and that there they gave to foreign merchants and travelers secret letters, drawn upon those to whom they had entrusted their effects in France, which were accepted.

The Theologians were obliged to limit their principles; and commerce, which they had before connected by main force with knavery, reentered, if I may so express myself, the bosom of probity.

Thus we owe to the speculations of the schoolmen all the misfortunes which accompanied the destruction of commerce; [935] and to the avarice of princes, the establishment of a practice which puts it in some measure out of their power.

[935] See 83rd novel of the Emperor Leo, which revokes the law of Basil his father. This law of Basil is in Hermenopulus, under the name of Leo, lib. III, tit. 7, § 27.

From this time it became necessary that princes should govern with more prudence than they themselves could ever have imagined; for great exertions of authority were, in the event, found to be impolitic; and from experience it is manifest that nothing but the goodness and lenity of a government can make it flourish.

We begin to be cured of Machiavelism, and recover from it every day. More moderation has become necessary in the councils of princes. What would formerly have been called a master-stroke in politics would be now, independent of the horror it might occasion, the greatest imprudence.

Happy is it for men that they are in a situation in which, though their passions prompt them to be wicked, it is, nevertheless, to their interest to be humane and virtuous.

21. *The Discovery of two new Worlds, and in what Manner Europe is affected by it.*

The compass opened, if I may so express myself, the universe. Asia and Africa were found, of which only some borders were known; and America, of which we knew nothing.

The Portuguese, sailing on the Atlantic Ocean, discovered the most southern point of Africa; they saw a vast sea, which carried them to the East Indies. Their danger upon this sea, the discovery of Mozambique, Melinda, and Calicut, have been sung by Camoens, whose poems make us feel something of the charms of the Odyssey and the magnificence of the Æneid.

The Venetians had hitherto carried on the trade of the Indies through the Turkish dominions, and pursued it in the midst of oppressions and discouragements. By the discovery of the Cape of Good Hope, and those which were made some time after, Italy was no longer the centre of the trading world; it was, if I may be permitted the expression, only a corner of the universe, and is so still. The commerce even of the Levant depending now on that of the great trading nations to both the Indies, Italy even in that branch can no longer be considered as a principal.

The Portuguese traded to the Indies in right of conquest. The constraining laws which the Dutch at present impose on the commerce of the little Indian princes had been established before by the Portuguese. [936]

[936] See the account of Pirard, part II, chap. 15.

The fortune of the house of Austria was prodigious. Charles V succeeded to the possession of Burgundy, Castile, and Aragon; he arrived afterwards at the imperial dignity; and to procure him a new kind of grandeur, the globe extended itself, and there was seen a new world paying him obeisance.

Christopher Columbus discovered America; and though Spain sent thither only a force so small that the least prince in Europe could have sent the same, yet it subdued two vast empires, and other great states.

While the Spaniards discovered and conquered the west, the Portuguese pushed their conquests and discoveries in the east. These two nations met each other; they had recourse to Pope Alexander VI, who made the celebrated line of partition, and determined the great suit.

But the other nations of Europe would not suffer them quietly to enjoy their shares. The Dutch chased the Portuguese from almost all their settlements in the East Indies; and several other nations planted colonies in America.

The Spaniards considered these newly-discovered countries as the subject of conquest; while others, more refined in their views, found them to be the proper subjects of commerce, and upon this principle directed their proceedings. Hence several nations have conducted themselves with so much wisdom that they have given a kind of sovereignty to companies of merchants, who, governing these far-distant countries only with a view to trade, have made a great accessory power without embarrassing the principal state.

The colonies they have formed are under a kind of dependence, of which there are but very few instances in all the colonies of the ancients; whether we consider them as holdings of the state itself, or of some trading company established in the state.

The design of these colonies is to trade on more advantageous conditions than could otherwise be done with the neighboring people, with whom all advantages are reciprocal. It has been established that the metropolis, [937] or mother country, alone shall trade in the colonies, and that from very good reason; because the design of the settlement was the extension of commerce, not the foundation of a city or of a new empire.

[937] This, in the language of the ancients, is the state which founded the colony.

Thus it is still a fundamental law of Europe that all commerce with a foreign colony shall be regarded as a mere monopoly, punishable by the laws of the country; and in this case we are not to be directed by the laws and precedents of the ancients, which are not at all applicable. [938]

[938] Except the Carthaginians, as we see by the treaty which put an end to the first Punic war.

It is likewise acknowledged that a commerce established between the mother countries does not include a permission to trade in the colonies; for these always continue in a state of prohibition.

The disadvantage of a colony that loses the liberty of commerce is visibly compensated by the protection of the mother country, who defends it by her arms, or supports it by her laws.

Hence follows a third law of Europe, that when a foreign commerce with a colony is prohibited, it is not lawful to trade in those seas, except in such cases as are excepted by treaty. Nations who are, with respect to the whole globe, what individuals are in a state, are governed like the latter by the laws of nature, and by particular laws of their own making. One nation may resign to another the sea, as well as the land. The Carthaginians forbade the Romans to sail beyond certain limits, [939] as the Greeks had obliged the King of Persia to keep as far distant from the sea-coast as a horse could gallop. [940]

[939] Polybius, lib. III.
[940] The King of Persia obliged himself by treaty not to sail with any vessel of war beyond the Cyanean rocks and the Chelidonean isles.—Plutarch, Life of Cimon.

The great distance of our colonies is not an inconvenience that affects their safety; for if the mother country, on whom they depend for their defense, is remote, no less remote are those nations who rival the mother country, and by whom they may be afraid of being conquered.

Besides, this distance is the cause that those who are established there cannot conform to the manner of living in a climate so different from their own; they are obliged therefore to draw from the mother country all the conveniences of life. The Carthaginians, [941] to render the Sardinians and Corsicans more dependent, forbade their planting, sowing, or doing anything of the kind, under pain of death; so that they supplied them with necessaries from Africa.

[941] Aristotle, Of Wonderful Things; Livy, lib. VII. dec. 2.

The Europeans have compassed the same thing, without having recourse to such severe laws. Our colonies in the Caribbean islands are under an admirable regulation in this respect; the subject of their commerce is what we neither have nor can produce; and they want what is the subject of ours.

A consequence of the discovery of America was the connecting Asia and Africa with Europe; it furnished materials for a trade with that vast part of Asia known by the name of the East Indies. Silver, that metal so useful as the medium of commerce, became now as merchandise the basis of the greatest commerce in the world. In fine, the navigation to Africa became necessary in order to furnish us with men to labor in the mines, and to cultivate the lands of America.

Europe has arrived at so high a degree of power that nothing in history can be compared with it, whether we consider the immensity of its expenses, the grandeur of its engagements, the number of its troops, and the regular payments even of those that are least serviceable, and which are kept only for ostentation.

Father Du Halde says [942] that the interior trade of China is much greater than that of all Europe. That might be, if our foreign trade did not augment our inland commerce. Europe carries on the trade and navigation of the other three parts of the world; as France, England, and Holland do nearly that of Europe.

[942] Tom. ii, p. 170.

22. Of the Riches which Spain drew from America.

If Europe has derived so many advantages from the American trade, it seems natural to imagine that Spain must have derived much greater. [943] She drew from the newly-discovered world so prodigious a quantity of gold and silver, that all we had before could not be compared with it.

[943] This has been already shown in a small treatise written by the author about twenty years ago; which has been almost entirely incorporated in the present work.

But (what one could never have expected) this great kingdom was everywhere baffled by its misfortunes. Philip II, who succeeded Charles V, was obliged to make the celebrated bankruptcy known to all the world. There never was a prince who suffered more from the murmurs, the insolence, and the revolt of troops constantly ill-paid.

From that time the monarchy of Spain has been incessantly declining. This has been owing to an interior and physical defect in the nature of those riches, which renders them vain—a defect which increases every day.

Gold and silver are either a fictitious or a representative wealth. The representative signs of wealth are extremely durable, and, in their own nature, but little subject to decay. But the more they are multiplied, the more they lose their value, because the fewer are the things which they represent.

The Spaniards, after the conquest of Mexico and Peru, abandoned their natural riches, in pursuit of a representative wealth which daily degraded itself. Gold and silver were extremely scarce in Europe, and Spain becoming all of a sudden mistress of a prodigious quantity of these metals, conceived hopes to which she had never before aspired. The wealth she found in the conquered countries, great as it was, did not, however, equal that of their mines. The Indians concealed part of it; and besides, these people, who made no other use of gold and silver than to give magnificence to the temples of their gods and to the palaces of their kings, sought not for it with an avarice like ours. In short, they had not the secret of drawing these metals from every mine; but only from those in which the separation might be made with fire: they were strangers to the manner of making use of mercury, and perhaps to mercury itself.

However, it was not long before the specie of Europe was doubled; this appeared from the price of commodities, which everywhere was doubled.

The Spaniards raked into the mines, scooped out mountains, invented machines to draw out water, to break the ore, and separate it; and as they sported with the lives of the Indians, they forced them to labor without mercy. The specie of Europe soon doubled, and the profit of Spain diminished in the same proportion; they had every year the same quantity of metal, which had become by one-half less precious.

In double the time the specie still doubled, and the profit still diminished another half.

It diminished even more than half: let us see in what manner.

To extract the gold from the mines, to give it the requisite preparations, and to import it into Europe, must be attended with some certain expense. I will suppose this to be as 1 to 64. When the specie was once doubled, and consequently became by one-half less precious, the expense was as 2 to 64. Thus the galoons which brought to Spain the same quantity of gold, brought a thing which really was of less value by one-half, though the expenses attending it had been twice as high.

If we proceed doubling and doubling, we shall find in this progression the cause of the impotency of the wealth of Spain.

It is about two hundred years since they have worked their Indian mines. I suppose the quantity of specie at present in the trading world is to that before the discovery of the Indies as 32 is to 1; that is, it has been doubled five times: in two hundred years more the same quantity will be to that before the discovery as 64 is to 1; that is, it will be doubled once more. Now, at present, fifty quintals of ore yield four, five, and six ounces of gold; [944] and when it yields only two, the miner receives no more from it than his expenses. In two hundred years, when the miner will extract only four, this too will only defray his charges. There will then be but little profit to be drawn from the gold mines. The same reasoning will hold good of silver, except that the working of the silver mines is a little more advantageous than those of gold.

[944] See Frezier, Voyages.

But, if mines should be discovered so fruitful as to give a much greater profit, the more fruitful they may be, the sooner the profit will cease.

The Portuguese in Brazil have found mines of gold so rich [945] that they must necessarily very soon make a considerable diminution in the profits of those of Spain, as well as in their

[945] According to Lord Anson, Europe receives every year from Brazil two millions sterling in gold, which is found in sand at the foot of the mountains, or in the beds of rivers. When I wrote the little treatise mentioned in the first note of this chapter, the returns from Brazil were far from being so considerable an item as they are at present.

I have frequently heard people deplore the blindness of the court of France, who repulsed Christopher Columbus, when he made the proposal of discovering the Indies. [946] Indeed they did, though perhaps without design, an act of the greatest wisdom. Spain has behaved like the foolish king who desired that everything he touched might be converted into gold, and who was obliged to beg of the gods to put an end to his misery.

[946] Voltaire deplores the insufficiency of Montesquieu's knowledge upon finance and commerce, saying that these principles were not then discovered, or, at least, had not been developed in his time.——Ed.

The companies and banks established in many nations have put a finishing stroke to the lowering of gold and silver as a sign of representation of riches; for by new fictions they have multiplied in such a manner the signs of wealth, that gold and silver having this office only in part have become less precious.

Thus public credit serves instead of mines, and diminishes the profit which the Spaniards drew from theirs.

True it is that the Dutch trade to the East Indies has increased, in some measure, the value of the Spanish merchandise: [947] for as they carry bullion, and give it in exchange for the merchandise of the East, they ease the Spaniards of part of a commodity which in Europe abounds too much.

[947] Voltaire holds that the Spaniards had no manufactures of their own, and that they were obliged to draw such supplies from abroad.——Ed.

And this trade, in which Spain seems to be only indirectly concerned, is as advantageous to that nation as to those who are directly employed in carrying it on.

From what has been said we may form a judgment of the last order of the council of Spain, which prohibits the making use of gold and silver in gildings, and other superfluities; a decree as ridiculous as it would be for the states of Holland to prohibit the consumption of spices.

My reasoning does not hold good against all mines; those of Germany and Hungary, which produce little more than the expense of working them, are extremely useful. They are found in the principal state; they employ many thousand men, who there consume their superfluous commodities, and they are properly a manufacture of the country.

The mines of Germany and Hungary promote the culture of land; the working of those of Mexico and Peru destroys it.

The Indies and Spain are two powers under the same master; but the Indies are the principal, while Spain is only an accessory, it is in vain for politics to attempt to bring back the principal to the accessory; the Indies will always draw Spain to themselves.

Of the merchandise, to the value of about fifty millions of livres, annually sent to the Indies, Spain furnishes only two millions and a half: the Indies trade for fifty millions, the Spaniards for two and a half.

That must be a bad kind of riches which depends on accident, and not on the industry of a nation, on the number of its inhabitants, and on the cultivation of its lands. The king of Spain, who receives great sums from his custom-house at Cadiz, is in this respect only a rich individual in a state extremely poor. Everything passes between strangers and himself, while his subjects have scarcely any share in it; this commerce is independent both of the good and bad fortune of his kingdom.

Were some provinces of Castile able to give him a sum equal to that of the custom-house of Cadiz, his power would be much greater; his riches would be the effect of the wealth of the country; these provinces would animate all the others, and they would be altogether more capable of supporting their respective charges; instead of a great treasury he would have a great people.

23. A Problem.

It is not for me to decide the question whether, if Spain be not herself able to carry on the trade of the Indies, it would not be better to leave it open to strangers. I will only say that it is for their advantage to load this commerce with as few obstacles as politics will permit. When the merchandise which several nations send to the Indies is very dear, the inhabitants of that country give a great deal of their commodities, which are gold and silver, for very little of those of foreigners; the contrary to this happens when they are at a low price, it would perhaps be of use that these nations should undersell each other, to the end that the merchandise carried to the Indies might be always cheap. These are principles which deserve to be examined, without separating them, however, from other considerations: the safety of the Indies, the advantages of only one custom-house, the danger of making great alterations, and the foreseen inconveniences, which are often less dangerous than those which cannot be foreseen.

BOOK XXII.

OF LAWS IN RELATION TO THE USE OF MONEY

1. The Reason of the Use of Money.

People who have little merchandise, as savages, and among civilized nations those who have only two or three species, trade by exchange. Thus the caravans of Moors that go to Timbuctoo, in the heart of Africa, have no need of money, for they exchange their salt for gold. The Moor puts his salt in a heap, and the Negro his dust in another; if there is not gold enough, the Moor takes away some of his salt, or the Negro adds more gold, till both parties are agreed.

But when a nation traffics with a great variety of merchandise, money becomes necessary; because a metal easily carried from place to place saves the great expenses which people would be obliged to be at if they always proceeded by exchange.

As all nations have reciprocal wants, it frequently happens that one is desirous of a large quantity of the other's merchandise, when the latter will have very little of theirs, though with respect to another nation the case is directly opposite. But when nations have money, and proceed by buying and selling, those who take most merchandise pay the balance in specie. And there is this difference, that, in the case of buying, the trade carried on is in proportion to the wants of the nation that has the greatest demands; while in bartering, the trade is only according to the wants of the nation whose demands are the fewest; without which the latter would be under an impossibility of balancing its accounts.

2. *Of the Nature of Money.*

Money is a sign which represents the value of all merchandise. Metal is taken for this sign, as being durable, [948] because it is consumed but little by use; and because, without being destroyed, it is capable of many divisions. A precious metal has been chosen as a sign, as being most portable. A metal is most proper for a common measure, because it can be easily reduced to the same standard. Every state fixes upon it a particular impression, to the end that the form may correspond with the standard and the weight, and that both may be known by inspection only.

[948] The salt made use of for this purpose in Abyssinia has this defect, that it is continually wasting away.

The Athenians, not having the use of metals, made use of oxen, [949] and the Romans of sheep; but one ox is not the same as another ox in the manner that one piece of metal may be the same as another.

[949] Herodotus, in *Clio*, tells us that the Lydians found out the art of coining money; the Greeks learned it from them: the Athenian coin had the impression of their ancient ox. I have seen one of those pieces in the Earl of Pembroke's cabinet.

A specie is the sign of the value of merchandise, paper is the sign of the value of specie; and when it is of the right sort, it represents this value in such a manner that as to the effects produced by it there is not the least difference.

In the same manner, as money is the sign and representative of a thing, everything is a sign and representative of money; and the state is in a prosperous condition when on the one hand money perfectly represents all things, and on the other all things perfectly represent money, and are reciprocally the sign of each other; that is, when they have such a relative value that we may have the one as soon as we have the other. This never happens in any other than a moderate government, nor does it always happen there; for example, if the laws favor the dishonest debtor, his effects are no longer a representative or sign of money. With regard to a despotic government, it would be a prodigy did things there represent their sign. Tyranny and distrust make every one bury their specie; [950] things therefore are not there the representative of money.

[950] It is an ancient custom in Algiers for the father of a family to have a treasure concealed in the earth.—Laugier de Tassis, History of the Kingdom of Algiers.

Legislators have sometimes had the art not only to make things in their own nature the representative of specie, but to convert them even into specie, like the current coin. Cæsar, when he was dictator, permitted debtors to give their lands in payment to their creditors, at the price they were worth before the civil war. [951] Tiberius ordered that those who desired specie should have it from the public treasury on binding over their land to double the value [952] Under Cæsar the lands were the money which paid all debts; under Tiberius ten thousand sesterces in land became as current money equal to five thousand sesterces in silver. The Magna Charta of England provides against the seizing of the lands or revenues of a debtor, when his movable or personal goods are sufficient to pay, and he is willing to give them up to his creditors; thus all the goods of an Englishman represent money.

[951] Cæsar on the Civil War, book III.
[952] Tacitus, lib. VI.

The laws of the Germans constituted money a satisfaction for the injuries that were committed, and for the sufferings due to guilt. But as there was but very little specie in the country, they again constituted this money to be paid in goods or chattels. This we find appointed in a Saxon law, with certain regulations suitable to the ease and convenience of the several ranks of people. At first the law declared the value of a sou in cattle; [953] the sou of two tremises answered to an ox of twelve months, or to a ewe with her lamb; that of three tremises was worth an ox of sixteen months. With these people money became cattle, goods, and merchandise, and these again became money.

[953] The Laws of the Saxons, chap. 18.

Money is not only a sign of things; it is also a sign and representative of money, as we shall see in the chapter on exchange.

3. Of ideal Money.

There is both real and ideal money. Civilized nations generally make use of ideal money only, because they have converted their real money into ideal. At first their real money was some metal of a certain weight and standard, but soon dishonesty or want made them retrench a part of the metal from every piece of money, to which they left the same name; for example, from a livre at a pound weight they took half the silver, and still continued to call it a livre; the piece which was the twentieth part of a pound of silver they continued to call a sou, though it is no more the twentieth part of this pound of silver. By this method the livre is an ideal livre, and the sou an ideal sou. Thus of the other subdivisions; and so far may this be carried that what we call a livre shall be only a small part of the original livre or pound, which renders it still more ideal. It may even happen that we have no piece of money of the precise value of a livre, nor any piece exactly with a sou, then the livre and the sou will be purely ideal. They may give to any piece of money the denomination of as many livres and as many sous as they please, the variation may be continual, because it is as easy to give another name to a thing as it is difficult to change the thing itself.

To take away the source of this abuse, it would be an excellent law for all countries who are desirous of making commerce flourish to ordain that none but real money should be current, and to prevent any methods from being taken to render it ideal.

Nothing ought to be so exempt from variation as that which is the common measure of all. Trade is in its own nature extremely uncertain; and it is a great evil to add a new uncertainty to that which is founded on the nature of the thing.

4. *Of the Quantity of Gold and Silver.*

While civilized nations are the mistresses of the world, gold and silver, whether they draw it from among themselves, or fetch it from the mines, must increase every day. On the contrary, it diminishes when barbarous nations prevail. We know how great was the scarcity of these metals when the Goths and Vandals on the one side, and on the other the Saracens and Tartars, broke in like a torrent on the civilized world.

5. *The same Subject continued.*

The bullion drawn from the American mines, imported into Europe, and thence sent to the East, has greatly promoted the navigation of the European nations; for it is merchandise which Europe receives in exchange from America, and which she sends in exchange to the Indies. A prodigious quantity of gold and silver is therefore an advantage, when we consider these metals as merchandise; but it is otherwise when we consider them as a sign, because their abundance gives an alloy to their quality as a sign, which is chiefly founded on their scarcity.

Before the first Punic war, [954] copper was to silver as 960 to 1; [955] it is at present nearly as 73 1/2 to 1. When the proportion shall be as it was formerly, silver will better perform its office as a sign.

[954] See chapter 12 of this book.
[955] Supposing a mark of eight ounces of silver to be worth forty-nine livres, and copper twenty sols per pound.

6. *The Reason why Interest was lowered one-half after the Conquest of the Indies.*

Garcilasso informs us [956] that in Spain after the conquest of the Indies the interest, which was at ten per cent, fell to five. This was a necessary consequence. A great quantity of specie being all of a sudden brought into Europe, much fewer persons had need of money. The price of all things increased, while the value of money diminished; the proportion was then broken, and all the old debts were discharged. We may recollect the time of the System, [957] when everything was at a high price except specie. Those who had money after the conquest of the Indies were obliged to lower the price or hire of their merchandise, that is, in other words, their interest.

[956] History of the Civil Wars of the Spaniards in the West Indies.
[957] In France, Law's project was called by this name.

From this time they were unable to bring interest to its ancient standard, because the quantity of specie brought to Europe has been annually increasing. Besides, as the public funds of some states, founded on riches procured by commerce, gave but a very small interest, it became necessary for the contracts of individuals to be regulated by these. In short, the course of exchange having rendered the conveying of specie from one country to another remarkably easy, money cannot be scarce in a place where they may be so readily supplied with it by those who have it in plenty.

7. How the Price of Things is fixed in the Variation of the Sign of Riches.

Money is the price of merchandise or manufactures. But how shall we fix this price? or, in other words, by what piece of money is everything to be represented?

If we compare the mass of gold and silver in the whole world with the quantity of merchandise therein contained, it is certain that every commodity or merchandise in particular may be compared to a certain portion of the entire mass of gold and silver. As the total of the one is to the total of the other, so part of the one will be to part of the other. Let us suppose that there is only one commodity or merchandise in the world, or only one to be purchased, and that this is divisible like money; a part of this merchandise will answer to a part of the mass of gold and silver; the half of the total of the one to the half of the total of the other; the tenth, the hundredth, the thousandth part of the one, to the tenth, the hundredth, the thousandth part of the other. But as that which constitutes property among mankind is not all at once in trade, and as the metals or money which are the sign of property are not all in trade at the same time, the price is fixed in the compound ratio of the total of things with the total of signs, and that of the total of things in trade with the total of signs in trade also; and as the things which are not in trade to-day may be in trade to-morrow, and the signs not now in trade may enter into trade at the same time, the establishment of the price of things fundamentally depends on the proportion of the total of things to the total of signs.

Thus the prince or the magistrate can no more ascertain the value of merchandise than he can establish by a decree that the relation 1 has to 10 is equal to that of 1 to 20. Julian's lowering the price of provisions at Antioch was the cause of a most terrible famine. [958]

[958] Socrates, History of the Church, lib. II.

8. The same Subject continued.

The Negroes on the coast of Africa have a sign of value without money. It is a sign merely ideal, founded on the degree of esteem which they fix in their minds for all merchandise, in proportion to the need they have of it. A certain commodity or merchandise is worth three macoutes; another, six macoutes; another, ten macoutes; that is, as if they said simply three, six, and ten. The price is formed by a comparison of all merchandise with each other. They have therefore no particular money; but each kind of merchandise is money to the other.

Let us for a moment transfer to ourselves this manner of valuing things, and join it with ours: all the merchandise and goods in the world, or else all the merchandise or manufactures of a state, particularly considered as separate from all others, would be worth a certain number of macoutes; and, dividing the money of this state into as many parts as there are macoutes, one part of this division of money will be the sign of a macoute.

If we suppose the quantity of specie in a state doubled, it will be necessary to double the specie in the macoute; but if in doubling the specie you double also the macoute, the proportion will remain the same as before the doubling of either.

If, since the discovery of the Indies, gold and silver have increased in Europe in the proportion of 1 to 20, the price of provisions and merchandise must have been enhanced in the proportion of 1 to 20. But if, on the other hand, the quantity of merchandise has increased as 1 to 2—it necessarily follows that the price of this merchandise and provisions, having been raised in proportion of 1 to 20, and fallen in proportion of 1 to 2—it necessarily follows, I say, that the proportion is only as 1 to 10.

The quantity of goods and merchandise increases by an augmentation of commerce, the augmentation of commerce by an augmentation of the specie which successively arrives, and by new communications with freshly-discovered countries and seas, which furnish us with new commodities and new merchandise.

9. Of the relative Scarcity of Gold and Silver.

Besides the positive plenty and scarcity of gold and silver, there is still a relative abundance and a relative scarcity of one of these metals compared with the other.

The avaricious hoard up their gold and silver, for as they do not care to spend, they are fond of signs that are not subject to decay. They prefer gold to silver, because as they are always afraid of losing, they can best conceal that which takes up the least room. Gold therefore disappears when there is plenty of silver, by reason that everyone has some to conceal; it appears again when silver is scarce, because they are obliged to draw it from its confinement.

It is then a rule that gold is common when silver is scarce, and gold is scarce when silver is common. This lets us see the difference between their relative and their real abundance and scarcity, of which I shall presently speak more at large.

10. Of Exchange.

The relative abundance and scarcity of specie in different countries forms what is called the course of exchange.

Exchange is a fixing of the actual and momentary value of money.

Silver as a metal has value like all other merchandise, and an additional value as it is capable of becoming the sign of other merchandise. If it were no more than mere merchandise, it would lose much of its value.

Silver, as money, has a value, which the prince in some respects can fix, and in others cannot.

1. The prince establishes a proportion between a quantity of silver as metal, and the same quantity as money, 2. He fixes the proportion between the several metals made use of as money. 3. He establishes the weight and standard of every piece of money. In fine, 4, he gives to every piece that ideal value of which I have spoken. I shall call the value of money in these four respects its positive value, because it may be fixed by law.

The coin of every state has, besides this, a relative value, as it is compared with the money of other countries. This relative value is established by the exchange, and greatly depends on its positive value. It is fixed by the general opinion of the merchants, never by the decrees of the prince; because it is subject to incessant variations, and depends on a thousand accidents.

The several nations, in fixing this relative value, are chiefly guided by that which has the greatest quantity of specie. If she has as much specie as all the others together, it is then most proper for the others to regulate theirs by her standard: and the regulation between all the others will pretty nearly agree with the regulation made with this principal nation.

In the actual state of the globe, Holland is the nation we are speaking of. [959] Let us examine the course of exchange with relation to her.

[959] The Dutch regulate the exchange for almost all Europe, by a kind of determination among themselves in a manner most agreeable to their own interests. In point of fact, however, if the Dutch undertook to regulate exchange for all Europe, it would be done in a manner most advantageous to themselves, which would not be permitted; and experience further contradicts Montesquieu's statement.—Ed.

They have in Holland a piece of money called a florin, worth twenty sous, or forty half-sous or gros. But, to render our ideas as simple as possible, let us imagine that they have not any such piece of money in Holland as a florin, and that they have no other but the gros: a man who should have a thousand florins should have forty thousand gros; and so of the rest. Now the exchange with Holland is determined by our knowing how many gros every piece of money in other countries is worth; and as the French commonly reckon by a crown of three livres, the exchange makes it necessary for them to know how many gros are contained in a crown of three livres. If the course of exchange is at fifty-four, a crown of three livres will be worth fifty-four gros; if it is at sixty, it will be worth sixty gros. If silver is scarce in France, a crown of three livres will be worth more gros; if plentiful, it will be worth less.

This scarcity or plenty, whence results the mutability of the course of exchange, is not the real, but a relative, scarcity or plenty. For example, when France has greater occasion for funds in Holland than the Dutch of having funds in France, specie is said to be common in France and scarce in Holland: and *vice versa*.

Let us suppose that the course of exchange with Holland is at fifty-four. If France and Holland composed only one city, they would act as we do when we give change for a crown: the Frenchman would take three livres out of his pocket, and the Dutchman fifty-four gros from his. But as there is some distance between Paris and Amsterdam, it is necessary that he who for a crown of three livres gives me fifty-four gros, which he has in Holland, should give me a bill of exchange for fifty-four gros payable in Holland. The fifty-four gros is not the thing in question, but a bill for that sum. Thus, in order to judge of the scarcity or plenty of specie, [960] we must know if there are in France more bills of fifty-four gros drawn upon Holland than there are crowns drawn upon France. If there are more bills from Holland than there are from France, specie is scarce in France, and common in Holland; it then becomes necessary that the exchange should rise, and that they give for my crown more than fifty-four gros; otherwise I will not part with it; and *vice versa*.

[960] There is much specie in a place when there is more specie than paper; there is little, when there is more paper than specie.

Thus the various turns in the course of exchange form an account of debtor and creditor, which must be frequently settled, and which the state in debt can no more discharge by exchange than an individual can pay a debt by giving change for a piece of silver.

We will suppose that there are but three states in the world, France, Spain, and Holland; that several individuals in Spain are indebted to France, to the value of one hundred thousand marks of silver; and that several individuals of France owe in Spain one hundred and ten thousand marks: now, if some circumstance both in Spain and France should cause each to withdraw his specie, what will then be the course of exchange? These two nations will reciprocally acquit each other of a hundred thousand marks; but France will still owe ten thousand marks in Spain, and the Spaniards will still have bills upon France, to the value of ten thousand marks; while France will have none at all upon Spain.

But if Holland was in a contrary situation with respect to France, and in order to balance the account must pay her ten thousand marks, the French would have two ways of paying the Spaniards: either by giving their creditors in Spain bills for ten thousand marks upon their debtors in Holland, or else by sending specie to the value of ten thousand marks to Spain.

Hence it follows that when a state has occasion to remit a sum of money to another country, it is indifferent, in the nature of the thing, whether specie be conveyed thither or they take bills of exchange. The advantage or disadvantage of these two methods solely depends on actual circumstances. We must inquire which will yield most gros in Holland-money carried thither in specie, or a bill upon Holland for the like sum. [961]

[961] With the expenses of carriage and insurance deducted.

When money of the same standard and weight in France yields money of the same standard and weight in Holland, we say that the exchange is at par. In the actual state of specie [962] the par is nearly at fifty-four gros to the crown. When the exchange is above fifty-four gros, we say it is high; when beneath, we say it is low.

[962] In 1744.

In order to know the loss and gain of a state in a particular situation of exchange, it must be considered as debtor and creditor, as buyer and seller. When the exchange is below par, it loses as a debtor, and gains as a creditor; it loses as a buyer and gains as a seller. It is obvious it loses as debtor; suppose, for example, France owes Holland a certain number of gros, the fewer gros there are in a crown the more crowns she has to pay. On the contrary, if France is creditor for a certain number of gros, the less number of gros there are in a crown the more crowns she will receive. The state loses also as buyer, for there must be the same number of gros to purchase the same quantity of merchandise; and while the exchange is low, every French crown is worth fewer gros. For the same reason the state gains as a seller. I sell my merchandise in Holland for a certain number of gros; I receive then more crowns in France, when for every fifty gros I receive a crown, than I should do if I received only the same crown for every fifty-four. The contrary to this takes place in the other state. If the Dutch are indebted a certain number of crowns to France, they will gain; if this money is owing to them, they will lose; if they sell, they lose; and if they buy, they gain.

It is proper to pursue this somewhat further. When the exchange is below par; for example, if it be at fifty instead of fifty-four, it should follow that France, on sending bills of exchange to Holland for fifty-four thousand crowns, could buy merchandise only to the value of fifty thousand; and that on the other hand, the Dutch sending the value of fifty thousands crowns to France might buy fifty-four thousand, which makes a difference of 8/54, that is, a loss to France of more than one-seventh; so that France would be obliged to send to Holland one-seventh more in specie or merchandise than she would do were the exchange at par. And as the mischief must constantly increase, because a debt of this kind would bring the exchange still lower, France would in the end be ruined. It seems, I say, as if this should certainly follow; and yet it does not, because of the principle which I have elsewhere established; [963] which is that states constantly lean towards a balance, in order to preserve their independency. Thus they borrow only in proportion to their ability to pay, and measure their buying by what they sell; and taking the example from above, if the exchange falls in France from fifty-four to fifty, the Dutch who buy merchandise in France to the value of a thousand crowns, for which they used to pay fifty-four thousand gros, would now pay only fifty thousand, if the French would consent to it. But the merchandise of France will rise insensibly, and the profit will be shared between the French and the Dutch; for when a merchant can gain, he easily shares his profit; there arises then a communication of profit between the French and the Dutch. In the same manner the French, who bought merchandise of Holland for fifty-four thousand gros, and who, when the exchange was at fifty-four, paid for them a thousand crowns, will be obliged to add one-seventh more in French crowns to buy the same merchandise. But the French merchant, being sensible of the loss he suffers, will take up less of the merchandise of Holland. The French and the Dutch merchant will then both be losers, the state will insensibly fall into a balance, and the lowering of the exchange will not be attended with all those inconveniences which we had reason to fear.

[963] See book XX. chap. 21.

A merchant may send his stock into a foreign country when the exchange is below par without injuring his fortune, because, when it returns, he recovers what he had lost; but a prince who sends only specie into a foreign country which never can return, is always a loser.

When the merchants have great dealings in any country, the exchange there infallibly rises. This proceeds from their entering into many engagements, buying great quantities of merchandise, and drawing upon foreign countries to pay for them.

A prince may amass great wealth in his dominions, and yet specie may be really scarce, and relatively common; for instance, if the state is indebted for much merchandise to a foreign country, the exchange will be low, though specie be scarce.

The exchange of all places constantly tends to a certain proportion, and that in the very nature of things. If the course of exchange from Ireland to England is below par, and that of England to Holland is also under par, that of Ireland to Holland will be still lower; that is, in the compound ratio of that of Ireland to England, and that of England to Holland; for a Dutch merchant who can have his specie indirectly from Ireland, by way of England, will not choose to pay dearer by having it in the direct way. This, I say, ought naturally to be the case; but, however, it is not exactly so. There are always circumstances which vary these things; and the different profit of drawing by one place, or of drawing by another, constitutes the particular art and dexterity of the bankers, which does not belong to the present subject.

When a state raises its specie, for instance, when it gives the name of six livres, or two crowns, to what was before called three livres, or one crown, this new denomination, which adds nothing real to the crown, ought not to procure a single gros more by the exchange. We ought only to have for the two new crowns the same number of gros which we before received for the old one. If this does not happen, it must not be imputed as an effect of the regulation itself, but to the novelty and suddenness of the affair. The exchange adheres to what is already established, and is not altered till after a certain time.

When a state, instead of only raising the specie by a law, calls it in, in order to diminish its size, it frequently happens that during the time taken up in passing again through the mint there are two kinds of money—the large, which is the old, and the small, which is the new; and as the large is cried down as not to be received as money, and bills of exchange must consequently be paid in the new, one would imagine then that the exchange should be regulated by the new. If, for example, in France, the ancient crown of three livres, being worth in Holland sixty gros, was reduced one-half, the new crown ought to be valued only at thirty. On the other hand, it seems as if the exchange ought to be regulated by the old coin; because the banker who has specie, and receives bills, is obliged to carry the old coin to the mint in order to change it for the new, by which he must be a loser. The exchange then ought to be fixed between the value of the old coin and that of the new. The value of the old is decreased, if we may call it so, both because there is already some of the new in trade, and because the bankers cannot keep up to the rigor of the law, having an interest in letting loose the old coin from their chests, and being sometimes obliged to make payments with it. Again, the value of the new specie must rise, because the banker having this finds himself in a situation in which, as we shall immediately prove, he will reap great advantage by procuring the old. The exchange should then be fixed, as I have already said, between the new and the old coin. For then the bankers find it to their interest to send the old out of the kingdom, because by this method they procure the same advantage as they could receive from a regular exchange of the old specie, that is, a great many gros in Holland; and in return, a regular exchange a little lower, between the old and the new specie, which would bring many crowns to France.

Suppose that three livres of the old coin yield by the actual exchange forty-five gros, and that by sending this same crown to Holland they receive sixty, but with a bill of forty-five gros, they procure a crown of three livres in France, which being sent in the old specie to Holland, still yields sixty gros; thus all the old specie would be sent out of the kingdom, and the bankers would run away with the whole profit.

To remedy this, new measures must be taken. The state which coined the new specie would itself be obliged to send great quantities of the old to the nation which regulates the exchange, and, by thus gaining credit there, raise the exchange pretty nearly to as many gros for a crown of three livres out of the country. I say to nearly the same, for while the profits are small the bankers will not be tempted to send it abroad, because of the expense of carriage and the danger of confiscation.

It is fit that we should give a very clear idea of this. Mr. Bernard, or any other banker employed by the state, proposes bills upon Holland, and gives them at one, two, or three gros higher than the actual exchange; he has made a provision in a foreign country, by means of the old specie, which he has continually been sending thither; and thus he has raised the exchange to the point we have just mentioned. In the meantime, by disposing of his bills, he seizes on all the new specie, and obliges the other bankers, who have payments to make, to carry their old specie to the mint; and, as he insensibly obtains all the specie, he obliges the other bankers to give him bills of exchange at a very high price. By this means his profit in the end compensates in a great measure for the loss he suffered at the beginning.

It is evident that during these transactions, the state must be in a dangerous crisis. Specie must become extremely scarce—1, because much the greatest part is cried down;

2, because a part will be sent into foreign countries; 3, because everyone will lay it up, as not being willing to give that profit to the prince which he hopes to receive himself. It is dangerous to do it slowly; and dangerous also to do it in too much haste. If the supposed gain be immoderate, the inconveniences increase in proportion.

We see, from what has been already said, that when the exchange is lower than the specie, a profit may be made by sending it abroad; for the same reason, when it is higher than the specie, there is profit in causing it to return.

But there is a case in which profit may be made by sending the specie out of the kingdom, when the exchange is at par; that is, by sending it into a foreign country to be coined over again. When it returns, an advantage may be made of it, whether it be circulated in the country or paid for foreign bills.

If a company has been erected in a state with an immense number of shares, and these shares have in a few months risen twenty or twenty-five times above the original purchase value; if, again, the same state established a bank, whose bills were to perform the office of money, while the legal value of these bills was prodigious, in order to answer to the legal value of the shares (this is Mr. Law's System), it would follow, from the nature of things, that these shares and these bills would vanish in the same manner as they arose. Stocks cannot suddenly be raised twenty or twenty-five times above their original value without giving a number of people the means of procuring immense riches in paper: everyone would endeavor to make his fortune; and as the exchange offers the most easy way of removing it from home, or conveying it whither one pleases, people would incessantly remit a part of their effects to the nation that regulates the exchange. A continual process of remittances into a foreign country must lower the exchange. Let us suppose that at the time of the System, in proportion to the standard and weight of the silver coin, the exchange was fixed at forty gros to the crown; when a vast quantity of paper became money, they were unwilling to give more than thirty-nine gros for a crown, and afterwards thirty-eight, thirty-seven, &c. This proceeded so far, that after a while they would give but eight gros, and at last there was no exchange at all.

The exchange ought in this case to have regulated the proportion between the specie and the paper of France. I suppose that, by the weight and standard of the silver, the crown of three livres in silver was worth forty gros, and that the exchange being made in paper, the crown of three livres in paper was worth only eight gros, the difference was four-fifths. The crown of three livres in paper was then worth four-fifths less than the crown of three livres in silver.

11. *Of the Proceedings of the Romans with respect to Money.*

How great soever the exertion of authority had been in our times, with respect to the specie of France, during the administration of two successive ministers, still it was vastly exceeded by the Romans; not at the time when corruption had crept into their republic, nor when they were in a state of anarchy, but when they were as much by their wisdom as their courage in the full vigor of the constitution, after having conquered the cities of Italy, and at the very time that they disputed for empire with the Carthaginians.

And here I am pleased that I have an opportunity of examining more closely into this matter, that no example may be taken from what can never justly be called one.

In the first Punic war the as, [964] which ought to be twelve ounces of copper, weighed only two, and in the second it was no more than one. This retrenchment answers to what we now call the raising of coin. To take half the silver from a crown of six livres, in order to make two crowns, or to raise it to the value of twelve livres, is precisely the same thing.

[964] Pliny, Natural History, lib. XXXIII, art. 13.

They have left us no monument of the manner in which the Romans conducted this affair in the first Punic war; but what they did in the second is a proof of the most consummate wisdom. The republic found herself under an impossibility of paying her debts: the as weighed two ounces of copper, and the denarius, valued at ten ases, weighed twenty ounces of copper. The republic, being willing to gain half on her creditors, made the as of an ounce of copper, [965] and by this means paid the value of a denarius with ten ounces. This proceeding must have given a great shock to the state; they were obliged therefore to break the force of it as well as they could. It was in itself unjust, and it was necessary to render it as little so as possible. They had in view the deliverance of the republic with respect to the citizens; they were not therefore obliged to direct their view to the deliverance of the citizens with respect to each other. This made a second step necessary. It was ordained that the denarius, which hitherto contained but ten ases, should contain sixteen. The result of this double operation was, that while the creditors of the republic lost one-half, [966] those of individuals lost only a fifth; [967] the price of merchandise was increased only a fifth; the real change of the money was only a fifth. The other consequences are obvious.

[965] Ibid.
[966] They received ten ounces of copper for twenty.
[967] They received sixteen ounces of copper for twenty.

The Romans then conducted themselves with greater prudence than we, who in our transactions involved both the public treasure and the fortunes of individuals. But this is not all: their business was carried on amidst more favorable circumstances than ours.

12. *The Circumstances in which the Romans changed the Value of the Specie.*

There was formerly very little gold and silver in Italy. This country has few or no mines of gold or silver. When Rome was taken by the Gauls, they found only a thousand-weight of gold [968] And yet the Romans had sacked many powerful cities, and brought home their wealth. For a long time they made use of none but copper money; and it was not till after the peace with Pyrrhus that they had silver enough to coin money: [969] they made denarii of this metal of the value of ten ases, [970] or ten pounds of copper. At that time the proportion of silver was to that of copper as 1 to 960. For as the Roman denarius was valued at ten ases, or ten pounds of copper, it was worth one hundred and twenty ounces of copper; and as the same denarius was valued only at one-eighth of an ounce of silver, [971] this produced the above proportion.

[968] Pliny, lib. XXXIII, art. 5.
[969] Freinshemius, dec. 2, lib. V.
[970] Freinshemius, lib. V. dec. 2.. They struck also, says the same author, half denarii, called quinarii; and quarters, called sesterces.
[971] An eighth, according to Budæus; according to other authors, a seventh.

When Rome became mistress of that part of Italy which is nearest to Greece and Sicily, by degrees she found herself between two rich nations—the Greeks and the Carthaginians. Silver increased at Rome; and as the proportion of 1 to 960 between silver and copper could be no longer supported, she made several regulations with respect to money, which to us are unknown. However, at the beginning of the second Punic war, the Roman denarius was worth no more than twenty ounces of copper; [972] and thus the proportion between silver and copper was no longer but as 1 to 160. The reduction was very considerable, since the republic gained five-sixths upon all copper money. But she did only what was necessary in the nature of things, by establishing the proportion between the metals made use of as money.

[972] Pliny, Natural History, lib. XXXIII, art. 13.

The peace which terminated the first Punic war left the Romans masters of Sicily. They soon entered Sardinia; afterwards they began to know Spain; and thus the quantity of silver increased at Rome. They took measures to reduce the denarius from twenty ounces to sixteen, [973] which had the effect of putting a nearer proportion between the silver and copper; thus the proportion, which was before as 1 to 160, was now made as 1 to 128.

[973] Ibid.

If we examine into the conduct of the Romans, we shall never find them so great as in choosing a proper conjuncture for performing any extraordinary operation.

13. *Proceedings with respect to Money in the Time of the Emperors.*

In the changes made in the specie during the time of the republic, they proceeded by diminishing it: in its wants, the state entrusted the knowledge to the people, and did not pretend to deceive them. Under the emperors, they proceeded by way of alloy. These princes, reduced to despair even by their liberalities, found themselves obliged to degrade the specie; an indirect method, which diminished the evil without seeming to touch it. They withheld a part of the gift and yet concealed the hand that did it; and, without speaking of the diminution of the pay, or of the gratuity, it was found diminished.

We even still see in cabinets a kind of medals which are called plated, and are only pieces of copper covered with a thin plate of silver. [974] This money is mentioned in a fragment of the 77th book of Dio. [975]

[974] See Father Joubert, Science of Medals, p. 59, Paris, 1739.
[975] Extract of Virtues and Vices.

Didius Julian first began to debase it. We find that the coin of Caracalla [976] had an alloy of more than half; that of Alexander Severus of two-thirds; [977] the debasing still increased, till in the time of Gallienus nothing was to be seen but copper silvered over. [978]

[976] See Savote, part II, chap. 12, and *Le Journal des Savants* of the 28th of July, 1681, on a discovery of fifty thousand medals.
[977] See Savote, ibid.
[978] Ibid.

It is evident that such violent proceedings could not take place in the present age; a prince might deceive himself, but he could deceive nobody else. The exchange has taught the banker to draw a comparison between all the money in the world, and to establish its just value. The standard of money can be no longer a secret. Were the prince to begin to alloy his silver, everybody else would continue it, and do it for him; the specie of the true standard would go abroad first, and nothing would be sent back but base metal. If, like the Roman Emperors, he debased the silver without debasing the gold, the gold would suddenly disappear, and he would be reduced to his bad silver. The exchange, as I have said in the preceding book, [979] has deprived princes of the opportunity of showing great exertions of authority, or at least has rendered them ineffectual.

[979] Chapter 16.

14. *How the Exchange is a Constraint on despotic Power.*

Russia would have descended from its despotic power, but could not. The establishment of commerce depended on that of the exchange, and the transactions were inconsistent with all its laws.

In 1745 the Czarina [980] made a law to expel the Jews, because they remitted into foreign countries the specie of those who were banished into Siberia, as well as that of the foreigners entertained in her service. As all the subjects of the empire are slaves, they can neither go abroad themselves nor send away their effects without permission. The exchange which gives them the means of remitting their specie from one country to another is therefore entirely incompatible with the laws of Russia.

[980] Elizabeth, daughter of Peter I.—Ed.

Commerce itself is inconsistent with the Russian laws. The people are composed only of slaves employed in agriculture, and of slaves called ecclesiastics or gentlemen, who are the lords of those slaves; there is then nobody left for the third estate, which ought to be composed of mechanics and merchants.

15. *The Practice of some Countries in Italy.*

They have made laws in some part of Italy to prevent subjects from selling their lands in order to remove their specie into foreign countries. These laws may be good, when the riches of a state are so connected with the country itself that there would be great difficulty in transferring them to another. But since, by the course of exchange, riches are in some degree independent of any particular state, and since they may with so much ease be conveyed from one country to another, that must be a bad law which will not permit persons for their own interest to dispose of their lands, while they can dispose of their money. It is a bad law, because it gives an advantage to movable effects, in prejudice to the land; because it deters strangers from settling in the country; and, in short, because it may be eluded.

16. *The Assistance a State may derive from Bankers.*

The banker's business is to change, not to lend, money. [981] If the prince makes use of them to change his specie, as he never does it but in great affairs, the least profit he can give for the remittance becomes considerable; and if they demand large profits, we may be certain that there is a fault in the administration. On the contrary, when they are employed to advance specie, their art consists in procuring the greatest profit for the use of it, without being liable to be charged with usury.

[981] The mistake here is apparent, bankers and money-changers being by no means identical.—Ed.

17. *Of Public Debts.*

Some have imagined that it was for the advantage of a state to be indebted to itself: they thought that this multiplied riches by increasing the circulation.

Those who are of this opinion have, I believe, confounded a circulating paper which represents money, or a circulating paper which is the sign of the profits that a company has or will make by commerce, with a paper which represents a debt. The first two are extremely advantageous to the state: the last can never be so; and all that we can expect from it is that individuals have a good security from the government for their money. But let us see the inconveniences which result from it.

1. If foreigners possess much paper which represents a debt, they annually draw out of the nation a considerable sum for interest.

2. In a nation that is thus perpetually in debt, the exchange must be very low.

3. The taxes raised for the payment of the interest of the debt are an injury to the manufactures, by raising the price of the artificer's labor.

4. It takes the true revenue of the state from those who have activity and industry, to convey it to the indolent; that is, it gives facilities for labor to those who do not work, and clogs with difficulties those who do work.

These are its inconveniences: I know of no advantages. Ten persons have each a yearly income of a thousand crowns, either in land or trade; this raises to the nation, at five per cent, a capital of two hundred thousand crowns. If these ten persons employed one-half of their income, that is, five thousand crowns, in paying the interest of a hundred thousand crowns, which they had borrowed of others, that still would be only to the state as two hundred thousand crowns; that is, in the language of the algebraists, 200,000 crowns -100,000 crowns + 100,000 crowns = 200,000.

People are thrown perhaps into this error by reflecting that the paper which represents the debt of a nation is the sign of riches; for none but a rich state can support such paper without falling into decay. And if it does not fall, it is a proof that the state has other riches besides. They say that it is not an evil, because there are resources against it; and that it is an advantage, since these resources surpass the evil.

18. *Of the Payment of Public Debts.*

It is necessary that there should be a proportion between the state as creditor and the state as debtor. The state may be a creditor to infinity, but it can only be a debtor to a certain degree, and when it surpasses that degree the title of creditor vanishes.

If the credit of the state has never received the least blemish, it may do what has been so happily practiced in one of the kingdoms of Europe; [982] that is, it may require a great quantity of specie, and offer to reimburse every individual, at least if they will not reduce their interest. When the state borrows, the individuals fix the interest; when it pays, the interest for the future is fixed by the state.

[982] England.

It is not sufficient to reduce the interest: it is necessary to erect a sinking-fund from the advantage of the reduction, in order to pay every year a part of the capital: a proceeding so happy that its success increases every day.

When the credit of the state is not entire, there is a new reason for endeavoring to form a sinking-fund, because this fund being once established will soon procure the public confidence.

1. If the state is a republic, the government of which is in its own nature consistent with its entering into projects of a long duration, the capital of the sinking-fund may be inconsiderable; but it is necessary in a monarchy for the capital to be much greater.

2. The regulations ought to be so ordered that all the subjects of the state may support the weight of the establishment of these funds, because they have all the weight of the establishment of the debt; thus the creditor of the state, by the sums he contributes, pays himself.

3. There are four classes of men who pay the debts of the state: the proprietors of the land, those engaged in trade, the laborers and artificers, and, in fine, the annuitants either of the state or of private people. Of these four classes the last, in a case of necessity one would imagine, ought least to be spared, because it is a class entirely passive, while the state is supported by the active vigor of the other three. But as it cannot be higher taxed, without destroying the public confidence, of which the state in general and these three classes in particular have the utmost need; as a breach in the public faith cannot be made on a certain number of subjects without seeming to be made on all; as the class of creditors is always the most exposed to the projects of ministers, and always in their eye, and under their immediate inspection, the state is obliged to give them a singular protection, that the part which is indebted may never have the least advantage over that which is the creditor.

19. *Of lending upon Interest.*

Specie is the sign of value. It is evident that he who has occasion for this sign ought to pay for the use of it, as well as for everything else that he has occasion for. All the difference is that other things may be either hired or bought; while money, which is the price of things, can only be hired, and not bought. [983]

[983] We do not speak here of gold and silver considered as a merchandise.

318

To lend money without interest is certainly an action laudable and extremely good; but it is obvious that it is only a counsel of religion, and not a civil law.

In order that trade may be successfully carried on, it is necessary that a price be fixed on the use of specie; but this should be very inconsiderable. If it be too high, the merchant who sees that it will cost him more in interest than he can gain by commerce will undertake nothing; if there is no consideration to be paid for the use of specie, nobody will lend it; and here too the merchant will undertake nothing.

I am mistaken when I say nobody will lend; the affairs of society will ever make it necessary. Usury will be established, but with all the disorders with which it has been constantly attended.

The laws of Mahomet confound usury with lending upon interest. Usury increases in Mahometan countries in proportion to the severity of the prohibition. The lender indemnifies himself for the danger he undergoes of suffering the penalty.

In those eastern countries, the greater part of the people are secure in nothing; there is hardly any proportion between the actual possession of a sum and the hopes of receiving it again after having lent it: usury, then, must be raised in proportion to the danger of insolvency.

20. *Of Maritime Usury.*

The greatness of maritime usury is founded on two things: the danger of the sea, which makes it proper that those who expose their specie should not do it without considerable advantage, and the ease with which the borrower, by means of commerce, speedily accomplishes a variety of great affairs. But usury, with respect to landmen, not being founded on either of these two reasons, is either prohibited by the legislators, or, what is more rational, reduced to proper bounds.

21. *Of Lending by Contract, and the State of Usury among the Romans.*

Besides the loans made for the advantage of commerce, there is still a kind of lending by a civil contract, whence results interest or usury.

As the people of Rome increased every day in power, the magistrates sought to insinuate themselves in their favor by enacting such laws as were most agreeable to them. They retrenched capitals; they first lowered, and at length prohibited, interest; they took away the power of confining the debtor's body; in fine, the abolition of debts was contended for whenever a tribune was disposed to render himself popular.

These continual changes, whether made by the laws or by the plebiscita, naturalized usury at Rome; for the creditors, seeing the people their debtor, their legislator, and their judge, had no longer any confidence in their agreements: the people, like a debtor who has lost his credit, could only tempt them to lend by allowing an exorbitant interest, [984] especially as the laws applied a remedy to the evil only from time to time, while the complaints of the people were continual, and constantly intimidated the creditors. This was the cause that all honest means of borrowing and lending were abolished at Rome, and that the most monstrous usury established itself in that city, notwithstanding the strict prohibition and severity of the law. [985] This evil was a consequence of the severity of the laws against usury. Laws excessively good are the source of excessive evil. The borrower found himself under the necessity of paying for the interest of the money, and for the danger the creditor underwent of suffering the penalty of the law.

[984] Cicero assures us that in his day money was lent at Rome at thirty-four per cent., and forty-eight per cent. in the country.—Ed.
[985] Tacitus, Annals, vi. 16.

22. *The same Subject continued.*

The primitive Romans had not any laws to regulate the rate of usury. [986] In the contests which arose on this subject between the plebeians and the patricians, even in the sedition on the Mons Sacer, nothing was alleged, on the one hand, but justice, and on the other, the severity of contracts. [987]

[986] Usury and interest among the Romans signified the same thing.
[987] See Dionysius Halicarnassus, who has described it so well.

They then only followed private agreements, which, I believe, were most commonly at twelve per cent per annum. My reason is, that in the ancient language of the Romans, interest at six per cent was called half-usury, and interest at three per cent, quarter-usury. [988] Total usury must, therefore, have been interest at twelve per cent.

[988] *Usuræ semisses, trientes, quadrantes.* See the several titles of the digests and codes on usury, and especially the 17th law, with the note, ff. *de Usuris.*

But if it be asked how such great interest could be established among a people almost without commerce, I answer that this people, being very often obliged to go to war without pay, were under a frequent necessity of borrowing: and as they incessantly made happy expeditions, they were commonly well able to pay. This is visible from the recital of the contests which arose on this subject; they did not then disagree concerning the avarice of creditors, but said that those who complained might have been able to pay, had they lived in a more regular manner. [989]

[989] See Appius's speech on this subject, in Dionysius Halicarnassus.

They then made laws which had only an influence on the present situation of affairs: they ordained, for instance, that those who enrolled themselves for the war they were engaged in should not be molested by their creditors; that those who were in prison should be set at liberty; that the most indigent should be sent into the colonies; and sometimes they opened the public treasury. The people, being eased of their present burdens, became appeased; and as they required nothing for the future, the senate was far from providing against it.

At the time when the senate maintained the cause of usury with so much constancy, the Romans were distinguished by an extreme love of frugality, poverty, and moderation: but the constitution was such that the principal citizens alone supported all the expenses of government, while the common people paid nothing. How, then, was it possible to deprive the former of the liberty of pursuing their debtors, and at the same time to oblige them to execute their offices, and to support the republic amidst its most pressing necessities?

Tacitus says that the law of the Twelve Tables fixed the interest at one per cent. [990] It is evident that he was mistaken, and that he took another law, of which I am going to speak, for the law of the Twelve Tables. If this had been regulated in the law of the Twelve Tables, why did they not make use of its authority in the disputes which afterwards arose between the creditors and debtors? We find no vestige of this law upon lending at interest; and let us have ever so little knowledge of the history of Rome, we shall see that a law like this could not be the work of the decemvirs.

[990] *Annal,* lib. VI.

The Licinian law, made eighty-five years after that of the Twelve Tables, [991] was one of those temporary regulations of which we have spoken. It ordained that what had been paid for interest should be deducted from the principal, and the rest discharged by three equal payments.

[991] In the year of Rome 388.—Livy, vi. 25.

In the year of Rome 398, the tribunes Duellius and Menenius caused a law to be passed which reduced the interest to one per cent per annum. [992] it is this law which Tacitus confounds with that of the Twelve Tables, [993] and this was the first ever made by the Romans to fix the rate of interest. Ten years after, [994] this usury was reduced one-half, [995] and in the end entirely abolished; [996] and if we may believe some authors whom Livy had read, this was under the consulate of C. Martius Rutilius and Q. Servilius, in the year of Rome 413. [997]

[992] *Unciaria usura.*—Tit. Liv. lib. VII. See the Defence of the Spirit of Laws, article "Usury."
[993] *Annal,* lib. VI.
[994] Under the consulate of L. Manlius Torquatus and C. Plautius, according to Livy, lib. VII. This is the law mentioned by Tacitus, *Annal,* lib. VI.
[995] *Semiunciaria usura.*
[996] As Tacitus says. *Annal,* lib. VI.
[997] This law was passed at the instance of M. Genucius, tribune of the people.—Tit. Liv. lib. VII., towards the end.

It fared with this law as with all those in which the legislator carries things to excess: an infinite number of ways were found to elude it. They enacted, therefore, many others to confirm, correct, and temper it. Sometimes they quitted the laws to follow the common practice; at others, the common practice to follow the laws; but in this case, custom easily prevailed. [998] When a man wanted to borrow, he found an obstacle in the very law made in his favor; this law must be evaded by the person it was made to succor, and by the person condemned. Sempronius Asellus, the prætor, having permitted the debtors to act in conformity to the laws, [999] was slain by the creditors for attempting to revive the memory of a severity that could no longer be supported. [1000]

[998] *Verteri jam more foenus receptum erat.*—Appian. On the Civil War, lib. I.

[999] *Permisit eos legibus agere.*—Appian on the Civil War, lib. I.; and the Epitome of Livy, lib. LXIV.
[1000] In the year of Rome 663.

I quit the city, in order to cast an eye on the provinces.

I have somewhere else observed that the Roman provinces were exhausted by a severe and arbitrary government. [1001] But this is not all; they were also ruined by a most shocking usury.

[1001] Book XI. chap. 19.

Cicero takes notice that the inhabitants of Salamis wanted to borrow a sum of money at Rome, but could not, because of the Gabinian law. [1002] We must, therefore, inquire into the nature of this law.

[1002] Letters to Atticus, lib. V. ep. 21.

As soon as lending upon interest was forbidden at Rome, they contrived all sort of means to elude the law; [1003] and as their allies, [1004] and the Latins, were not subject to the civil laws of the Romans, they employed a Latin, or an ally, to lend his name, and personate the creditor. The law, therefore, had only subjected the creditors to a matter of form, and the public were not relieved.

[1003] Livy.
[1004] Ibid.

The people complained of this artifice; and Marius Sempronius, tribune of the people, by the authority of the senate, caused a plebiscitum to be enacted to this purport, that in regard to loans the laws prohibiting usury between Roman citizens should equally take place between a citizen and an ally, or a citizen and a Latin. [1005]

[1005] In the year 559 of Rome.—See Livy.

At that time they gave the name of allies to the people of Italy properly so called, which extended as far as the Arno and the Rubicon, and was not governed in the form of a Roman province.

It is an observation of Tacitus [1006] that new frauds were constantly committed, whenever any laws were passed for the preventing of usury. Finding themselves debarred from lending or borrowing in the name of an ally, they soon contrived to borrow of some inhabitant of the provinces.

[1006] *Annal,* lib. VI.

To remedy this abuse they were obliged to enact a new law; and Gabinius [1007] upon the passing of that famous law, which was intended to prevent the corruption of suffrages, must naturally have reflected that the best way to attain his end was to discourage the lending upon interest: these were two objects naturally connected; for usury always increased at the time of elections, [1008] because they stood in need of money to bribe the voters. It is plain that the Gabinian law had extended the Senatus Consultum of Marcus Sempronius to the provinces, since the people of Salamis could not borrow money at Rome because of that very law. Brutus, under fictitious names, lent them some money [1009] at four per cent a month, [1010] and obtained for that purpose two Senatus Consulta; in the former of which it was expressly mentioned that this loan should not be considered as an evasion of the law, [1011] and that the governor of Sicily should determine according to the stipulations mentioned in the bond of the Salaminians.

[1007] In the year 615 of Rome.
[1008] See Cicero to Atticus, lib. IV. ep. 15, 16.
[1009] Cicero to Atticus, lib. VI. ep. 10.
[1010] Pompey having lent 600 talents to King Ariobarzanes, made that prince pay him thirty Attic talents every thirty days.—*Cic. ad Att*. lib. III. ep. 21, lib. VI. ep. 11.
[1011] "Ut neque Salaminiis, neque cui eis dedisset, fraudi esset."—Ibid.

As lending upon interest was forbidden by the Gabinian law between provincials and Roman citizens, and the latter at that time had all the money of the globe in their hands, there was a necessity for tempting them with the bait of extravagant interest, to the end that the avaricious might thus lose sight of the danger of losing their money. And as they were men of great power in Rome, who awed the magistrates and overruled the laws, they were emboldened to lend, and to extort great usury. Hence the provinces were successively ravaged by everyone who had any credit in Rome: and as each governor, at entering upon his province, published his edict [1012] wherein he fixed the rate of interest in what manner he pleased, the legislature played into the hands of avarice, and the latter served the mean purposes of the legislator.

[1012] Cicero's edict fixed it to one per cent a month, with interest upon interest at the expiration of the year. With regard to the farmers of the republic, he engaged them to grant a respite to their debtors; if the latter did not pay at the time fixed, he awarded the interest mentioned in the bond.—*Cic. ad Att*., lib. VI. ep. 1.

But the public business must be carried on; and wherever a total inaction obtains, the state is undone. On some occasions the towns, the corporate bodies and societies, as well as private people, were under the necessity of borrowing—a necessity but too urgent, were it only to repair the ravages of armies, the rapacity of magistrates, the extortions of collectors, and the corrupt practices daily introduced; for never was there at one period so much poverty and opulence. The senate, being possessed of the executive power, granted, through necessity, and oftentimes through favor, a permission of borrowing from Roman citizens, so as to enact decrees for that particular purpose. But even these decrees were discredited by the law; for they might give occasion to the people's insisting upon new rates of interest, which would augment the danger of losing the capital, while they made a further extension of usury. [1013] I shall ever repeat it, that mankind are governed not by extremes, but by principles of moderation.

[1013] See what Lucretius says, in the 21st letter to Atticus, lib. V. There was even a general Senatus Consultum, to fix the rate of interest at one per cent per month. See the same letter.

He pays least, says Ulpian, who pays latest. [1014] This decides the question whether interest be lawful; that is, whether the creditor can sell time, and the debtor buy it.

[1014] Leg. 12, ff. *de verb. signif.*

BOOK XXIII.

OF LAWS IN THE RELATION THEY BEAR TO THE NUMBER OF INHABITANTS

1. *Of Men and Animals with respect to the Multiplication of their Species.*

> Delight of human kind, [1015] and gods above;
> Parent of Rome, propitious Queen of Love;
> *　　　*　　　*　　　*　　　*　　　*
> For when the rising spring adorns the mead,
> And a new scene of nature stands display'd;
> When teeming buds, and cheerful greens appear,
> And western gales unlock the lazy year;
> The joyous birds thy welcome first express,
> Whose native songs thy genial fire confess:
> Then savage beasts bound o'er their slighted food,
> Struck with thy darts, and tempt the raging flood:
> All nature is thy gift, earth, air, and sea;
> Of all that breathes the various progeny,
> Stung with delight, is goaded on by thee.
> O'er barren mountains, o'er the flow'ry plain,
> The leafy forest, and the liquid main,
> Extends thy uncontroll'd and boundless reign.
> Thro' all the living regions thou dost move,
> And scatter'st where thou go'st the kindly seeds of love.

[1015] Dryden, Lucr.

The females of brutes have an almost constant fecundity. But in the human species, the manner of thinking, the character, the passions, the humor, the caprice, the idea of preserving beauty, the pain of child-bearing, and the fatigue of a too numerous family, obstruct propagation in a thousand different ways.

2. *Of Marriage.*

The natural obligation of the father to provide for his children has established marriage, which makes known the person who ought to fulfill this obligation. The people [1016] mentioned by Pomponius Mela [1017] had no other way of discovering him but by resemblance.

[1016] The Garamantes.
[1017] Lib. I. chap. 8.

Among civilized nations, the father is that person on whom the laws, by the ceremony of marriage, have fixed this duty, because they find in him the man they want. [1018]

[1018] *Pater est quem nuptiæ demonstrant.*

Among brutes this is an obligation which the mother can generally perform; but it is much more extensive among men. Their children indeed have reason; but this comes only by slow degrees. It is not sufficient to nourish them; we must also direct them: they can already live; but they cannot govern themselves.

Illicit conjunctions contribute but little to the propagation of the species. The father, who is under a natural obligation to nourish and educate his children, is not then fixed; and the mother, with whom the obligation remains, finds a thousand obstacles from shame, remorse, the constraint of her sex, and the rigor of laws; and besides, she generally wants the means.

Women who have submitted to public prostitution cannot have the convenience of educating their children: the trouble of education is incompatible with their station; and they are so corrupt that they can have no protection from the law.

It follows from all this that public continence is naturally connected with the propagation of the species.

3. Of the Condition of Children.

It is a dictate of reason that when there is a marriage, children should follow the station or condition of the father; and that when there is not, they can belong to the mother only. [1019]

[1019] For this reason, among nations that have slaves, the child almost always follows the station or condition of the mother.

4. Of Families.

It is almost everywhere a custom for the wife to pass into the family of the husband. The contrary is without any inconvenience established at Formosa, [1020] where the husband enters into the family of the wife.

[1020] Father Du Halde, tom. i, p. 165.

This law, which fixes the family in a succession of persons of the same sex, greatly contributes, independently of the first motives, to the propagation of the human species. The family is a kind of property: a man who has children of a sex which does not perpetuate it is never satisfied if he has not those who can render it perpetual.

Names, whereby men acquire an idea of a thing which one would imagine ought not to perish, are extremely proper to inspire every family with a desire of extending its duration. There are people among whom names distinguish families: there are others where they only distinguish persons: the latter have not the same advantage as the former.

5. *Of the several Orders of lawful Wives.*

Laws and religion sometimes establish many kinds of civil conjunctions; and this is the case among the Mahometans, where there are several orders of wives, the children of whom are distinguished by being born in the house, by civil contracts, or even by the slavery of the mother, and the subsequent acknowledgment of the father.

It would be contrary to reason that the law should stigmatize the children for what it approved in the father. All these children ought, therefore, to succeed, at least if some particular reason does not oppose it, as in Japan, where none inherit but the children of the wife given by the emperor. Their policy demands that the gifts of the emperor should not be too much divided, because they subject them to a kind of service, like that of our ancient fiefs.

There are countries where a wife of the second rank enjoys nearly the same honors in a family as in our part of the world are granted to an only consort: there the children of concubines are deemed to belong to the first or principal wife. Thus it is also established in China. Filial respect, [1021] and the ceremony of deep mourning, are not due to the natural mother, but to her appointed by the law.

[1021] Father Du Halde, tom. ii, p. 129.

By means of this fiction they have no bastard children; and where such a fiction does not take place, it is obvious that a law to legitimatize the children of concubines must be considered as an act of violence, as the bulk of the nation would be stigmatized by such a decree. Neither is there any regulation in those countries with regard to children born in adultery. The recluse lives of women, the locks, the enclosures, and the eunuchs render all infidelity to their husbands so difficult, that the law judges it impossible. Besides, the same sword would exterminate the mother and the child.

6. *Of Bastards in different Governments.*

They have therefore no such thing as bastards where polygamy is permitted; this disgrace is known only in countries in which a man is allowed to marry but one wife. Here they were obliged to stamp a mark of infamy upon concubinage, and consequently they were under a necessity of stigmatizing the issue of such unlawful conjunctions.

In republics, where it is necessary that there should be the purest morals, bastards ought to be more degraded than in monarchies.

The laws made against them at Rome were perhaps too severe; but as the ancient institutions laid all the citizens under a necessity of marrying, and as marriages were also softened by the permission to repudiate or make a divorce, nothing but an extreme corruption of manners could lead them to concubinage.

It is observable that as the quality of a citizen was a very considerable thing in a democratic government, where it carried with it the sovereign power, they frequently made laws in respect to the state of bastards, which had less relation to the thing itself and to the honesty of marriage than to the particular constitution of the republic. Thus the people have sometimes admitted bastards into the number of citizens, in order to increase their power in opposition to the great. [1022] Thus the Athenians excluded bastards from the privilege of being citizens, that they might possess a greater share of the corn sent them by the King of Egypt. In fine, Aristotle informs us that in many cities where there was not a sufficient number of citizens, their bastards succeeded to their possessions; and that when there was a proper number, they did not inherit. [1023]

[1022] Aristotle, *Politics*, lib. VI. chap. 4.
[1023] *Ibid.*, lib. III. chap. 3.

7. Of the Father's Consent to Marriage.

The consent of fathers is founded on their authority, that is, on the right of property. It is also founded on their love, on their reason, and on the uncertainty of that of their children, whom youth confines in a state of ignorance and passion in a state of ebriety.

In the small republics, or singular institutions already mentioned, they might have laws which gave to magistrates that right of inspection over the marriages of the children of citizens which nature had already given to fathers. The love of the public might there equal or surpass all other love. Thus Plato would have marriages regulated by the magistrates: this the Lacedæmonian magistrates performed.

But in common institutions, fathers have the disposal of their children in marriage: their prudence in this respect is always supposed to be superior to that of a stranger. Nature gives to fathers a desire of procuring successors to their children, when they have almost lost the desire of enjoyment themselves. In the several degrees of progenitor, they see themselves insensibly advancing to a kind of immortality. But what must be done, if oppression and avarice arise to such a height as to usurp all the authority of fathers? Let us hear what Thomas Gage says in regard to the conduct of the Spaniards in the West Indies. [1024]

[1024] Thomas Gage, A New Survey of the West Indies, p. 345, 3rd ed.

According to the number of the sons and daughters that are marriageable, the father's tribute is raised and increased, until they provide husbands and wives for their sons and daughters, who, as soon as they are married, are charged with tribute; which, that it may increase, they will suffer none above fifteen years of age to live unmarried. Nay, the set time of marriage appointed for the Indians is at fourteen years for the man, and thirteen for the woman; alleging that they are sooner ripe for the fruit of wedlock, and sooner ripe in knowledge and malice, and strength for work and service, than any other people. Nay, sometimes they force those to marry who are scarcely twelve and thirteen years of age, if they find them well-limbed and strong in body, explaining a point of one of the canons, which alloweth fourteen and fifteen years. NISI MALITIA SUPPLEAT ÆTATEM.

He saw a list of these taken. It was, says he, a most shameful affair. Thus in an action which ought to be the most free, the Indians are the greatest slaves.

8. The same Subject continued.

In England the law is frequently abused by the daughters marrying according to their own fancy without consulting their parents. This custom is, I am apt to imagine, more tolerated there than anywhere else from a consideration that as the laws have not established a monastic celibacy, the daughters have no other state to choose but that of marriage, and this they cannot refuse. In France, on the contrary, young women have always the resource of celibacy; and therefore the law which ordains that they shall wait for the consent of their fathers may be more agreeable. In this light the custom of Italy and Spain must be less rational; convents are there established, and yet they may marry without the consent of their fathers.

9. *Of young Women.*

Young women who are conducted by marriage alone to liberty and pleasure, who have a mind which dares not think, a heart which dares not feel, eyes which dare not see, ears which dare not hear, who appear only to show themselves silly, condemned without intermission to trifles and precepts, have sufficient inducements to lead them on to marriage: it is the young men that want to be encouraged.

10. *What it is that determines Marriage.*

Wherever a place is found in which two persons can live commodiously, there they enter into marriage. Nature has a sufficient propensity to it, when unrestrained by the difficulty of subsistence.

A rising people increase and multiply extremely. This is, because with them it would be a great inconvenience to live in celibacy; and none to have many children. The contrary of which is the case when a nation is formed.

11. *Of the Severity of Government.*

Men who have absolutely nothing, such as beggars, have many children. This proceeds from their being in the case of a rising people: it costs the father nothing to give his heart to his offspring, who even in their infancy are the instruments of this art. These people multiply in a rich or superstitious country, because they do not support the burden of society, but are themselves the burden. But men who are poor, only because they live under a severe government; who regard their fields less as the source of their subsistence than as a cause of vexation; these men, I say, have few children: they have not even subsistence for themselves. How then can they think of dividing it? They are unable to take care of their own persons when they are sick. How then can they attend to the wants of creatures whose infancy is a continual sickness?

It is pretended by some who are apt to talk of things which they have never examined that the greater the poverty of the subjects, the more numerous their families: that the more they are loaded with taxes, the more industriously they endeavor to put themselves in a station in which they will be able to pay them: two sophisms, which have always destroyed and will forever be the destruction of monarchies.

The severity of government may be carried to such an extreme as to make the natural sentiments destructive of the natural sentiments themselves. Would the women of America have refused to bear children had their masters been less cruel? [1025]

[1025] A New Survey of the West Indies, by Thomas Gage, p. 97, 3rd edit.

328

12. *Of the Number of Males and Females in different Countries.*

I have already observed that there are born in Europe rather more boys than girls. [1026] It has been remarked that in Japan there are born rather more girls than boys: [1027] all things compared, there must be more fruitful women in Japan than in Europe, and consequently it must be more populous.

[1026] Book XVI. Chap. 4.
[1027] See Kempfer, who gives a computation of the people of Meaco.

We are informed that at Bantam there are ten girls to one boy. [1028] A disproportion like this must cause the number of families there to be to the number of those of other climates as 1 to 5 1/2 which is a prodigious difference. Their families may be much larger indeed; but there must be few men in circumstances sufficient to provide for so large a family.

[1028] Collection of Voyages that Contributed to the Establishment of the East India Company, vol. i, p. 347.

13. *Of Seaport Towns.*

In seaport towns, where men expose themselves to a thousand dangers, and go abroad to live or die in distant climates, there are fewer men than women: and yet we see more children there than in other places. This proceeds from the greater ease with which they procure the means of subsistence. Perhaps even the oily parts of fish are more proper to furnish that matter which contributes to generation. This may be one of the causes of the infinite number of people in Japan [1029] and China, [1030] where they live almost wholly on fish. [1031] If this be the case, certain monastic rules, which oblige the monks to live on fish, must be contrary to the spirit of the legislator himself.

[1029] Japan is composed of a number of isles, where there are many banks, and the sea is there extremely full of fish.
[1030] China abounds in rivers.
[1031] See Father Du Halde, tom. ii, pp. 139, 142.

14. *Of the Productions of the Earth which require a greater or less Number of Men.*

Pasture-lands are but little peopled, because they find employment only for a few. Corn-lands employ a great many men, and vineyards infinitely more.

It has been a frequent complaint in England [1032] that the increase of pasture-land diminished the inhabitants; and it has been observed in France that the prodigious number of vineyards is one of the great causes of the multitude of people.

[1032] The greatest number of the proprietors of land, says Bishop Burnet, finding more profit in selling their wool than their corn, enclosed their estates; the commons, ready to perish with hunger, rose up in arms; they insisted on a division of the lands; the young king even wrote on this subject. And proclamations were made against those who enclosed their lands.—Abridgment of the History of the Reformation.

Those countries where coal-pits furnish a proper substance for fuel have this advantage over others, that not having the same occasion for forests, the lands may be cultivated.

In countries productive of rice, they are at vast pains in watering the land: a great number of men must therefore be employed. Besides, there is less land required to furnish subsistence for a family than in those which produce other kinds of grain. In fine, the land which is elsewhere employed in raising cattle serves immediately for the subsistence of man; and the labor which in other places is performed by cattle is there performed by men; so that the culture of the soil becomes to man an immense manufacture.

15. Of the Number of Inhabitants with relation to the Arts.

When there is an agrarian law, and the lands are equally divided, the country may be extremely well peopled, though there are but few arts; because every citizen receives from the cultivation of his land whatever is necessary for his subsistence, and all the citizens together consume all the fruits of the earth. Thus it was in some republics.

In our present situation, in which lands are unequally distributed, they produce much more than those who cultivate them are able to consume; if the arts, therefore, should be neglected, and nothing minded but agriculture, the country could not be peopled. Those who cultivate, or employ others to cultivate, having corn to spare, nothing would engage them to work the following year; the fruits of the earth would not be consumed by the indolent; for these would have nothing with which they could purchase them. It is necessary, then, that the arts should be established, in order that the produce of the land may be consumed by the laborer and the artificer. In a word, it is now proper that many should cultivate much more than is necessary for their own use. For this purpose they must have a desire of enjoying superfluities; and these they can receive only from the artificer.

The machines designed to abridge art are not always useful. If a piece of workmanship is of a moderate price, such as is equally agreeable to the maker and the buyer, those machines which would render the manufacture more simple, or, in other words, diminish the number of workmen, would be pernicious. And if water-mills were not everywhere established, I should not have believed them so useful as is pretended, because they have deprived an infinite multitude of their employment, a vast number of persons of the use of water, and great part of the land of its fertility.

16. The Concern of the Legislator in the Propagation of the Species.

Regulations on the number of citizens depend greatly on circumstances. There are countries in which nature does all; the legislator then has nothing to do. What need is there of inducing men by laws to propagation when a fruitful climate yields a sufficient number of inhabitants? Sometimes the climate is more favorable than the soil; the people multiply, and are destroyed by famine: this is the case of China. Hence a father sells his daughters and exposes his children. In Tonquin, [1033] the same causes produce the same effects; so we need not, like the Arabian travelers mentioned by Renaudot, search for the origin of this in their sentiments on the metempsychosis. [1034]

[1033] Dampier, Voyages, vol. ii, p. 41.
[1034] Ibid., p. 167.

For the same reason, the religion of the Isle of Formosa does not suffer the women to bring their children into the world till they are thirty-five years of age: [1035] the priestess, before this age, by bruising the belly procures abortion.

[1035] See the Collection of Voyages that Contributed to the Establishment of the East India Company, vol. i, part I, pp. 182, 188.

17. Of Greece and the Number of its Inhabitants.

That effect which in certain countries of the East springs from physical causes was produced in Greece by the nature of the government. The Greeks were a great nation, composed of cities, each of which had a distinct government and separate laws. They had no more the spirit of conquest and ambition than those of Switzerland, Holland, and Germany have at this day. In every republic the legislator had in view the happiness of the citizens at home, and their power abroad, lest it should prove inferior to that of the neighboring cities. [1036] Thus, with the enjoyment of a small territory and great happiness, it was easy for the number of the citizens to increase to such a degree as to become burdensome. This obliged them incessantly to send out colonies, [1037] and, as the Swiss do now, to let their men out to war. Nothing was neglected that could hinder the too great multiplication of children.

[1036] In valor, discipline, and military exercises.
[1037] The Gauls, who were in the same circumstances, acted in the same manner.

They had among them republics, whose constitution was very remarkable. The nations they had subdued were obliged to provide subsistence for the citizens. The Lacedæmonians were fed by the Helotes, the Cretans by the Periecians, and the Thessalians by the Penestes. They were obliged to have only a certain number of freemen, that their slaves might be able to furnish them with subsistence. It is a received maxim in our days, that it is necessary to limit the number of regular troops: now the Lacedæmonians were an army maintained by the peasants: it was proper, therefore, that this army should be limited; without this the freemen, who had all the advantages of society, would increase beyond number, and the laborers be overloaded.

The politics of the Greeks were particularly employed in regulating the number of citizens. Plato fixes them at five thousand and forty, [1038] and he would have them stop or encourage propagation, as was most convenient, by honors, shame, and the advice of the old men; he would even regulate the number of marriages in such a manner that the republic might be recruited without being overcharged. [1039]

[1038] Republic. lib. V.
[1039] Republic. lib. V.

If the laws of a country, says Aristotle, forbid the exposing of children, the number of those brought forth ought to be limited. [1040] If they have more than the number prescribed by law, he advises to make the women miscarry before the fetus be formed. [1041]

[1040] *Politics*, lib. VII. chap. 16.
[1041] Ibid.

The same author mentions the infamous means made use of by the Cretans to prevent their having too great a number of children—a proceeding too indecent to repeat.

There are places, says Aristotle again [1042] where the laws give the privilege of being citizens to strangers, or to bastards, or to those whose mothers only are citizens; but as soon as they have a sufficient number of people this privilege ceases. The savages of Canada burn their prisoners; but when they have empty cottages to give them, they receive them into their nation.

[1042] Ibid., lib. III. chap. 5.

Sir William Petty, in his calculations, supposes that a man in England is worth what he would sell for at Algiers. [1043] This can be true only with respect to England. There are countries where a man is worth nothing; there are others where he is worth less than nothing.

[1043] Sixty pounds sterling.

18. *Of the State and Number of People before the Romans.*

Italy, Sicily, Asia Minor, Gaul, and Germany were nearly in the same state as Greece; full of small nations that abounded with inhabitants, they had no need of laws to increase their number.

19. *Of the Depopulation of the Globe.*

All these little republics were swallowed up in a large one, and the globe insensibly became depopulated: in order to be convinced of this, we need only consider the state of Italy and Greece before and after the victories of the Romans.

You will ask me, says Livy, [1044] *where the Volsci could find soldiers to support the war, after having been so often defeated. There must have been formerly an infinite number of people in those countries, which at present would be little better than a desert, were it not for a few soldiers and Roman slaves.*

[1044] Lib. VI.

The Oracles have ceased, says Plutarch, *because the places where they spoke are destroyed. At present we can scarcely find in Greece three thousand men fit to bear arms.*

I shall not describe, says Strabo, [1045] *Epirus and the adjacent places, because these countries are entirely deserted. This depopulation, which began long ago, still continues; so that the Roman soldiers encamp in the houses they have abandoned.* We find the cause of this in Polybius, who says that Paulus Æmilius, after his victory, destroyed seventy cities of Epirus, and carried away a hundred and fifty thousand slaves.

332

[1045] Lib. VII, p. 496.

20. *That the Romans were under the Necessity of making Laws to encourage the Propagation of the Species.*

The Romans, by destroying others, were themselves destroyed: incessantly in action, in the heat of battle, and in the most violent attempts, they wore out like a weapon kept constantly in use.

I shall not here speak of the attention with which they applied themselves to procure citizens in the room of those they lost, [1046] of the associations they entered into, the privileges they bestowed, and of that immense nursery of citizens, their slaves. I shall mention what they did to recruit the number, not of their citizens, but of their men; and as these were the people in the world who knew best how to adapt their laws to their projects, an examination of their conduct in this respect cannot be a matter of indifference.

[1046] I have treated of this in the Considerations on the Causes of the Rise and Declension of the Roman Grandeur.

21. *Of the Laws of the Romans relating to the Propagation of the Species.*

The ancient laws of Rome endeavored greatly to incite the citizens to marriage. The senate and the people made frequent regulations on this subject, as Augustus says in his speech related by Dio. [1047]

[1047] Lib. LVI.

Dionysius Halicarnassus [1048] cannot believe that after the death of three hundred and five of the Fabii, exterminated by the Veientes, there remained no more of this family than one single child; because the ancient law, which obliged every citizen to marry and to educate all his children, was still in force. [1049]

[1048] Lib. II.
[1049] In the year of Rome 277.

Independently of the laws, the censors had a particular eye upon marriages, and according to the exigencies of the republic engaged them to it by shame and by punishments. [1050]

[1050] See what was done in this respect in Livy, lib. XLV; the Epitome of Livy, lib. LIX; Aulus Gellius, lib. I. chap. 6; Valerius Maximus, lib. II. cap 19.

The corruption of manners that began to take place contributed vastly to disgust the citizens with marriage, which was painful to those who had no taste for the pleasures of innocence. This is the purport of that speech which Metellus Numidicus, when he was censor, made to the people: [1051] *If it were possible for us to do without wives, we should deliver ourselves from this evil: but as nature has ordained that we cannot live very happily with them, nor subsist without them, we ought to have more regard to our own preservation than to transient gratifications.*

[1051] It is in Aulus Gellius, lib. I. chap. 6.

The corruption of manners destroyed the censorship, which was itself established to destroy the corruption of manners: for when this depravation became general, the censor lost his power. [1052]

[1052] See what I have said in Book V. chap. 19.

Civil discords, triumvirates, and proscriptions weakened Rome more than any war she had hitherto engaged in. They left but few citizens, [1053] and the greatest part of them unmarried. To remedy this last evil, Cæsar and Augustus re-established the censorship, and would even be censors themselves. [1054] Cæsar gave rewards to those who had many children. [1055] All women under forty-five years of age who had neither husband nor children were forbidden to wear jewels or to ride in litters; [1056] an excellent method thus to attack celibacy by the power of vanity. The laws of Augustus were more pressing; [1057] he imposed new penalties on such as were not married, [1058] and increased the rewards both of those who were married and of those who had children. Tacitus calls these Julian laws; [1059] to all appearance they were founded on the ancient regulations made by the senate, the people, and the censors.

[1053] Cæsar, after the Civil War, having made a survey of the Roman citizens, found there were no more than one hundred and fifty thousand heads of families.—Florus, Epitome of Livy, dec. 17.
[1054] See Dio, lib. XLIII., and Xiphilinus in *August.*
[1055] Dio, lib. XLIII.; Suetonius, Life of Cæsar, chap. 20; Appian, On the Civil War, lib. II.
[1056] Eusebius, Chronicle.
[1057] Dio, lib. LIV.
[1058] In the year of Rome 736.
[1059] *Julias rogationes.—Annal*, lib. III.

The law of Augustus met with innumerable obstacles, and thirty-four years after it had been made the Roman knights insisted on its being abolished. [1060] He placed on one side such as were married, and on the other side those who were not: these last appeared by far the greatest number; upon which the citizens were astonished and confounded. Augustus, with the gravity of the ancient censors, addressed them in this manner: [1061]

[1060] In the year of Rome 762.—Dio, lib. LVI.
[1061] I have abridged this speech, which is of tedious length; it is to be found in Dio, lib. LVI.

While sickness and war snatch away so many citizens, what must become of this state if marriages are no longer contracted? The city does not consist of houses, of porticos, of public places, but of inhabitants. You do not see men like those mentioned in Fable starting out of the earth to take care of your affairs. Your celibacy is not owing to the desire of living alone; for none of you eats or sleeps by himself. You only seek to enjoy your irregularities undisturbed. Do you cite the example of the Vestal Virgins? If you preserve not the laws of chastity, you ought to be punished like them. You are equally bad citizens, whether your example has an influence on the rest of the world, or whether it be disregarded. My only view is the perpetuity of the republic. I have increased the penalties of those who have disobeyed; and with respect to rewards, they are such as I do not know whether virtue has ever received greater. For less will a thousand men expose life itself; and yet will not these engage you to take a wife and provide for children?

He made a law, which was called after his name, Julia and Papia Poppæa, from the names of the consuls for part of that year. [1062] The greatness of the evil appeared even in their being elected: Dio tells us that they were not married, and that they had no children. [1063]

[1062] Marcus Papius Mutilus and Q. Poppæus Sabinus.—Dio, lib. LVI.
[1063] Ibid.

This decree of Augustus was properly a code of laws, and a systematic body of all the regulations that could be made on this subject. The Julian laws were incorporated in it, and received greater strength. [1064] It was so extensive in its use, and had an influence on so many things, that it formed the finest part of the civil law of the Romans.

[1064] Ulpian, Fragment, tit. 14, distinguishes very rightly between the Julian and the Papian law.

We find parts of it dispersed in the precious fragments of Ulpian, [1065] in the Laws of the Digest, collected from authors who wrote on the Papian laws, in the historians and others who have cited them, in the Theodosian code which abolished them, and in the works of the fathers, who have censured them, without doubt from a laudable zeal for the things of the other life, but with very little knowledge of the affairs of this.

[1065] James Godfrey has made a collection of these.

These laws had many heads, [1066] of which we know thirty-five. But to return to my subject as speedily as possible, I shall begin with that head which Aulus Gellius informs us was the seventh, and relates to the honors and rewards granted by that law. [1067]

[1066] The 35th is cited in the 19th law ff. *de ritu nuptiarum.*
[1067] Lib. II. chap. 15.

The Romans, who for the most part sprang from the cities of the Latins, which were Lacedæmonian colonies, [1068] and had received a part of their laws even from those cities, [1069] had, like the Lacedæmonians, such veneration for old age as to give it all honor and precedence. When the republic wanted citizens, she granted to marriage and to the number of children the privileges which had been given to age. [1070] She granted some to marriage alone, independent of the children which might spring from it: this was called the right of husbands. She gave others to those who had any children, and larger still to those who had three children. These three things must not be confounded. These last had those privileges which married men constantly enjoyed; as, for example, a particular place in the theatre; [1071] they had those which could only be enjoyed by men who had children, and which none could deprive them of but such as had a greater number.

[1068] Dionysius Halicarnassus.
[1069] The deputies of Rome, who were sent to search into the laws of Greece, went to Athens, and to the cities of Italy.
[1070] Aulus Gellius, lib. II. chap. 15.
[1071] Suetonius, *Life of Augustus*, chap. 44.

These privileges were very extensive. The married men who had the most children were always preferred, whether in the pursuit or in the exercise of honors, [1072] The consul who had the most numerous offspring was the first who received the fasces; [1073] he had his choice of the provinces: [1074] the senator who had most children had his name written first in the catalogue of senators, and was the first in giving his opinion in the senate. [1075] They might even stand sooner than ordinary for an office, because every child gave a dispensation of a year. [1076] If an inhabitant of Rome had three children, he was exempted from all troublesome offices. [1077] The freeborn women who had three children, and the freedwomen who had four, passed out of that perpetual tutelage [1078] in which they had been held by the ancient laws of Rome. [1079]

[1072] Tacitus, lib. II: "Ut numerus liberorum in candidatis præpolleret, quod lex jubebat."
[1073] Aulus Gellius, lib. II. chap. 15.
[1074] Tacitus, *Annal,* lib. XV.
[1075] See Law 6, § 5, *De Decurion.*
[1076] See Law 2, ff. *de minorib.*
[1077] Law 1st and 2nd, ff. *de vacatione et excusat. munerum.*
[1078] Ulpian, Fragment., tit. 29, § 3.
[1079] Plutarch, Life of Numa.

As they had rewards, they had also penalties. [1080] Those who were not married could receive no advantage from the will of any person that was not a relative; [1081] and those who, being married, had no children, could receive only half. [1082] The Romans, says Plutarch, marry only to *be* heirs, and not to *have* them. [1083]

[1080] See the Ulpian, Fragment., tit. 14, 15, 16, 17, 18, which compose one of the most valuable pieces of the ancient civil law of the Romans.
[1081] Sozomenus, lib. I. chap. 9. They could receive from their relatives.—Ulpian, Fragment., tit. 16, § i.
[1082] Sozomenus, lib. I. chap. 9; and Leg. unic., Cod. Theod. *de infirm, poenis cælib. et orbit.*
[1083] Moral Works, Of the Love of Fathers towards their Children.

The advantages which a man and his wife might receive from each other by will were limited by law. [1084] If they had children of each other, they might receive the whole; if not, they could receive only a tenth part of the succession on the account of marriage; and if they had any children by a former venter, as many tenths as they had children.

[1084] See a more particular account of this in Ulpian. Fragment., tit. 15, 16.

If a husband absented himself from his wife on any other cause than the affairs of the republic, he could not inherit from her. [1085]

[1085] Ibid., tit. 16, § 1.

The law gave to a surviving husband or wife two years to marry again, [1086] and a year and a half in case of a divorce. The fathers who would not suffer their children to marry, or refused to give their daughters a portion, were obliged to do it by the magistrates. [1087]

[1086] Ibid., tit. 14. It seems the first Julian laws allowed three years.—Speech of Augustus, in Dio, lib. LVI; Suetonius, Life of Augustus, chap. 34. Other Julian laws granted but one year: the Papian law gave two.—Ulpian, Fragment., tit. 14. These laws were not agreeable to the people; Augustus, therefore, softened or strengthened them as they were more or less disposed to comply with them.
[1087] This was the 35th head of the Papian law.—Leg. 19, ff.*de ritu nuptiarum*.

They were not allowed to betroth when the marriage was to be deferred for more than two years: [1088] and as they could not marry a girl till she was twelve years old, they could not be betrothed to her till she was ten. The law would not suffer them to trifle to no purpose; [1089] and under a pretence of being betrothed, to enjoy the privileges of married men.

[1088] See Dio, lib. LIV, year 736; Suetonius, in *Octavio*, chap. 34.
[1089] Dio, lib. LIV; and in the same Dio, the speech of Augustus, lib. LVI.

It was contrary to law for a man of sixty to marry a woman of fifty. [1090] As they had given great privileges to married men, the law would not suffer them to enter into useless marriages. For the same reason, the Calvisian Senatus Consultum declared the marriage of a woman above fifty with a man less than sixty to be unequal: [1091] so that a woman of fifty years of age could not marry without incurring the penalties of these laws. Tiberius added to the rigor of the Papian law, [1092] and prohibited men of sixty from marrying women under fifty; so that a man of sixty could not marry in any case whatsoever, without incurring the penalty. But Claudius abrogated this law made under Tiberius. [1093]

[1090] Ulpian, Fragment., tit. 16, and Leg. 27, Cod. *de nuptiis*.
[1091] Ulpian, Fragment., tit. 16, § 3.
[1092] See Suetonius, *Life of Claudius*, chap. 23.
[1093] Ibid., *Life of Claudius*, chap. 23, and Ulpian, Fragment., tit. 16, § 3.

All these regulations were more conformable to the climate of Italy than to that of the North, where a man of sixty years of age has still a considerable degree of strength, and where women of fifty are not always past child-bearing.

That they might not be unnecessarily limited in the choice they were to make, Augustus permitted all the freeborn citizens who were not senators [1094] to marry freedwomen. [1095] The Papian law forbade the senators marrying freedwomen, [1096] or those who had been brought up to the stage; and from the time of Ulpian, [1097] free-born persons were forbidden to marry women who had led a disorderly life, who had played in the theatre, or who had been condemned by a public sentence. This must have been established by a decree of the senate. During the time of the republic they had never made laws like these, because the censors corrected this kind of disorder as soon as it arose, or else prevented its rising.

[1094] Dio, lib. LIV; Ulpian, Fragment., tit. 13.
[1095] Augustus's speech, in Dio, lib. LVI.
[1096] Ulpian, Fragment., chap. 13, and the Leg. 44. ff. *de ritu nuptiarum.*
[1097] Ulpian, Fragment., tit. 13 and 16.

Constantine made a law [1098] in which he comprehended, in the prohibition of the Papian law, not only the senators, but even such as had a considerable rank in the state, without mentioning persons in an inferior station: this constituted the law of those times. These marriages were therefore no longer forbidden, except to the free-born comprehended in the law of Constantine. Justinian, however, abrogated the law of Constantine, [1099] and permitted all sorts of persons to contract these marriages; and thus we have acquired so fatal a liberty.

[1098] See Law 1, cod. *de nat. lib.*
[1099] Novell. 117.

It is evident that the penalties inflicted on such as married contrary to the prohibition of the law were the same as those inflicted on persons who did not marry. These marriages did not give them any civil advantage; [1100] for the dowry [1101] was confiscated after the death of the wife. [1102]

[1100] Law 37. § 7, ff. *de operib. libertorum*, § 7; Ulpian, Fragment., tit. 16, § 2.
[1101] Ulpian, Fragment., tit. 16, § 2.
[1102] See book XXVI. chap. 13.

Augustus having adjudged the succession and legacies of those whom these laws had declared incapable, to the public treasury, [1103] they had the appearance rather of fiscal than of political and civil laws. The disgust they had already conceived at a burden which appeared too heavy was increased by their seeing themselves a continual prey to the avidity of the treasury. On this account, it became necessary, under Tiberius, that these laws should be softened; [1104] that Nero should lessen the rewards given out of the treasury to the informers; [1105] that Trajan should put a stop to their plundering; [1106] that Severus should also moderate these laws; [1107] and that the civilians should consider them as odious, and in all their decisions deviate from the literal rigor.

[1103] Except in certain cases. See the Ulpian, Fragment., tit. 18, and the only law in Cod. *de Caduc. tollend.*

[1104] *Relatum de moderanda Papiâ Poppœâ.*—Tacitus, *Annal*, lib. III. p. 117.

[1105] He reduced them to the fourth part.—Suetonius, *Life of Nero*, chap. 10.

[1106] See Pliny, Panegyric.

[1107] Severus extended even to twenty-five years for the males, and to twenty for the females, the time fixed by the Papian law, as we see by comparing Ulpian, Fragment., tit. 16, with what Tertullian says, *Apol.*, chap. 4.

Besides, the emperors enervated these laws [1108] by the privileges they granted of the rights of husbands, of children, and of three children. More than this, they gave particular persons a dispensation from the penalties of these laws. [1109] But the regulations established for the public utility seemed incapable of admitting an alleviation.

[1108] P. Scipio, the censor, complains, in his speech to the people, of the abuses which were already introduced, that they received the same privileges for adopted as for natural children.—Aulus Gellius, lib. V. chap. 19.

[1109] See the 31st Law, ff. *de ritu nuptiarum.*

It was highly reasonable that they should grant the rights of children to the vestals, [1110] whom religion retained in a necessary virginity: they gave, in the same manner, the privilege of married men to soldiers, [1111] because they could not marry. It was customary to exempt the emperors from the constraint of certain civil laws. Thus Augustus was freed from the constraint of the law which limited the power of enfranchising, [1112] and of that which set bounds to the right of bequeathing by testament. [1113] These were only particular cases; but, at last, dispensations were given without discretion, and the rule itself became no more than an exception.

[1110] Augustus in the Papian law gave them the privilege of mothers. See Dio, lib. LXVI. Numa had granted them the ancient privilege of women who had three children, that is, of having no guardian.—Plutarch, Life of Numa.

[1111] This was granted them by Claudius.—Dio, lib. LX.

[1112] Leg. apud eum, ff. *de manumissionib.* § 1.

[1113] Dio, lib. LV.

The sects of philosophers had already introduced in the empire a disposition that estranged them from business—a disposition which could not gain ground in the time of the republic, [1114] when everybody was employed in the arts of war and peace. Hence arose an idea of perfection, as connected with a life of speculation; hence an estrangement from the cares and embarrassments of a family. The Christian religion coming after this philosophy fixed, if I may make use of the expression, the ideas which that had only prepared.

[1114] See, in Cicero, Offices, his sentiments on the spirit of speculation.

Christianity stamped its character on jurisprudence; for empire has ever a connection with the priesthood. This is visible from the Theodosian code, which is only a collection of the decrees of the Christian emperors.

A panegyrist of Constantine [1115] said to that emperor, *Your laws were made only to correct vice and to regulate manners: you have stripped the ancient laws of that artifice which seemed to have no other aim than to lay snares for simplicity.*

[1115] Nazarius, in *panegyrico Constantini*, year 321.

It is certain that the alterations made by Constantine took their rise either from sentiments relating to the establishment of Christianity, or from ideas conceived of its perfection. From the first proceeded those laws which gave such authority to bishops, and which have been the foundation of the ecclesiastical jurisdiction; hence those laws which weakened paternal authority [1116] by depriving the father of his property in the possessions of his children. To extend a new religion, they were obliged to take away the dependence of children, who are always least attached to what is already established.

[1116] See Laws 1, 2, 3, in the Theodosian code *de bonis maternis, maternique generis,* &c., and the only law in the same code. *de bonis quæ filiis famil. acquiruntur.*

The laws made with a view to Christian perfection were more particularly those by which the penalties of the Papian laws were abolished; the unmarried were equally exempted from them, with those who, being married, had no children.

These laws were established, says an ecclesiastical historian, [1117] *as if the multiplication of human species was an effect of our care; instead of being sensible that the number is increased or diminished according to the order of Providence.*

[1117] Sozomenus, p. 29.

Principles of religion have had an extraordinary influence on the propagation of the human species. Sometimes they have promoted it, as among the Jews, the Mahometans, the Gaurs, and the Chinese; at others they have put a damp to it, as was the case of the Romans upon their conversion to Christianity.

They everywhere incessantly preached continency; a virtue the more perfect because in its own nature it can be practiced but by very few.

Constantine had not taken away the decimal laws which granted a greater extent to the donations between man and wife, in proportion to the number of their children. Theodosius, the younger, abrogated even these laws. [1118]

[1118] Leg. 2, 3, Cod. Theod. *de jur. liber.*

Justinian declared all those marriages valid which had been prohibited by the Papian laws. [1119] These laws required people to marry again: Justinian granted privileges to those who did not marry again. [1120]

[1119] Leg. Sancimus, Cod. *de nuptiis.*
[1120] Novell. 127, chap. iii; Novell. 118, chap. v.

By the ancient institutions, the natural right which everyone had to marry and beget children could not be taken away. Thus when they received a legacy, [1121] on condition of not marrying, or when a patron made his freedman swear [1122] that he would neither marry nor beget children, the Papian law annulled both the condition and the oath. [1123] The clauses *on continuing in widowhood* established among us contradict the ancient law, and descend from the constitutions of the emperors, founded on ideas of perfection.

[1121] Leg. 54 ff. *de condit. et demonst.*
[1122] Leg. 5, § 4, *de jure patronatus.*
[1123] Paul, Sentences, Lib. III. tit. 4, § 15.

There is no law that contains an express abrogation of the privileges and honors which the Romans had granted to marriages, and to a number of children. But where celibacy had the pre-eminence, marriage could not be held in honor; and since they could oblige the officers of the public revenue to renounce so many advantages by the abolition of the penalties, it is easy to perceive that with yet greater ease they might put a stop to the rewards.

The same spiritual reason which had permitted celibacy soon imposed it even as necessary. God forbid that I should here speak against celibacy as adopted by religion; but who can be silent when it is built on libertinism; when the two sexes, corrupting each other even by the natural sensations themselves, fly from a union which ought to make them better, to live in that which always renders them worse?

It is a rule drawn from nature, that the more the number of marriages is diminished, the more corrupt are those who have entered into that state; the fewer married men, the less fidelity is there in marriage; as when there are more thieves, more thefts are committed.

22. Of the Exposing of Children.

The Roman policy was very good in respect to the exposing of children. Romulus, says Dionysius Halicarnassus, [1124] laid the citizens under an obligation to educate all their male children, and the eldest of their daughters. If the infants were deformed and monstrous, he permitted the exposing them, after having shown them to five of their nearest neighbors.

[1124] Antiquities of Rome, lib. II.

Romulus did not suffer them to kill any infants under three years old: [1125] by which means he reconciled the law that gave to fathers the right over their children of life and death with that which prohibited their being exposed.

[1125] Ibid.

We find also in Dionysius Halicarnassus [1126] that the law which obliged the citizens to marry, and to educate all their children, was in force in the 277th year of Rome; we see that custom had restrained the law of Romulus which permitted them to expose their younger daughters.

[1126] Lib. IX.

We have no knowledge of what the law of the Twelve Tables (made in the year of Rome 301) appointed with respect to the exposing of children, except from a passage of Cicero, [1127] who, speaking of the office of tribune of the people, says that soon after its birth, like the monstrous infant of the law of the Twelve Tables, it was stifled; the infant that was not monstrous was therefore preserved, and the law of the Twelve Tables made no alteration in the preceding institutions.

[1127] Lib. III. *de legib.*

The Germans, says Tacitus, [1128] *never expose their children; among them the best manners have more force than in other places the best laws.* The Romans had therefore laws against this custom, and yet they did not follow them. We find no Roman law that permitted the exposing of children; [1129] this was, without doubt, an abuse introduced towards the decline of the republic, when luxury robbed them of their freedom, when wealth divided was called poverty, when the father believed that all was lost which he gave to his family, and when this family was distinct from his property.

[1128] *De Moribus Germanorum.*
[1129] There is no title on this subject in the Digest; the title of the Code says nothing of it, any more than the Novels.

23. *Of the State of the World after the Destruction of the Romans.*

The regulations made by the Romans to increase the number of their citizens had their effect while the republic, in the full vigor of her constitution, had nothing to repair but the losses she sustained by her courage, by her intrepidity, by her firmness, her love of glory and of virtue. But soon the wisest laws could not re-establish what a dying republic, what a general anarchy, what a military government, what a rigid empire, what a proud despotic power, what a feeble monarchy, what a stupid, weak, and superstitious court had successively pulled down. It might, indeed, be said that they conquered the world only to weaken it, and to deliver it up defenseless to barbarians. The Gothic nations, the Getes, the Saracens and Tartars by turns harassed them; and soon the barbarians had none to destroy but barbarians. Thus, in fabulous times, after the inundations and the deluge, there arose out of the earth armed men, who exterminated one another.

24. *The Changes which happened in Europe with regard to the Number of the Inhabitants.*

In the state Europe was in one would not imagine it possible for it to be retrieved, especially when under Charlemagne it formed only one vast empire. But by the nature of government at that time it became divided into an infinite number of petty sovereignties, and as the lord or sovereign, who resided in his village or city, was neither great, rich, powerful, nor even safe but by the number of his subjects, every one employed himself with a singular attention to make his little country flourish. This succeeded in such a manner that notwithstanding the irregularities of government, the want of that knowledge which has since been acquired in commerce, and the numerous wars and disorders incessantly arising, most countries of Europe were better peopled in those clays than they are even at present.

I have not time to treat fully of this subject, but I shall cite the prodigious armies engaged in the Crusades, composed of men of all countries. Puffendorf says that in the reign of Charles IX there were in France twenty millions of men. [1130]

[1130] Introduction to the History of Europe, chap. v. of France. This is obviously a numerical blunder, since, according to the Census of 1751, and France was never so populous as at that time, she did not possess twenty millions.—Voltaire.

It is the perpetual reunion of many little states that has produced this diminution. Formerly, every village of France was a capital; there is at present only one large one. Every part of the state was a centre of power; at present all has a relation to one centre, and this centre is in some measure the state itself.

25. *The same Subject continued.*

Europe, it is true, has for these two ages past greatly increased its navigation; this has both procured and deprived it of inhabitants. Holland sends every year a great number of mariners to the Indies, of whom not above two-thirds return; the rest either perish or settle in the Indies. The same thing must happen to every other nation concerned in that trade.

We must not judge of Europe as of a particular state engaged alone in an extensive navigation. This state would increase in people, because all the neighboring nations would endeavor to have a share in this commerce, and mariners would arrive from all parts. Europe, separated from the rest of the world by religion, [1131] by vast seas and deserts, cannot be repaired in this manner.

[1131] Mahomedan countries surround it almost on every side.

26. *Consequences.*

From all this we may conclude that Europe is at present in a condition to require laws to be made in favor of the propagation of the human species. The politics of the ancient Greeks incessantly complain of the inconveniences attending a republic, from the excessive number of citizens; but the politics of this age call upon us to take proper means to increase ours.

27. *Of the Law made in France to encourage the Propagation of the Species.*

Lewis XIV appointed particular pensions to those who had ten children, and much larger to such as had twelve. [1132] But it is not sufficient to reward prodigies. In order to communicate a general spirit, which leads to the propagation of the species, it is necessary for us to establish, like the Romans, general rewards, or general penalties.

[1132] The edict of 1666 in favor of marriages.

28. *By what means we may remedy a Depopulation.*

When a state is depopulated by particular accidents, by wars, pestilence, or famine, there are still resources left. The men who remain may preserve the spirit of industry; they may seek to repair their misfortunes, and calamity itself may make them become more industrious. This evil is almost incurable when the depopulation is prepared beforehand by interior vice and a bad government. When this is the case, men perish with an insensible and habitual disease; born in misery and weakness, in violence or under the influence of a wicked administration, they see themselves destroyed, and frequently without perceiving the cause of their destruction. Of this we have a melancholy proof in the countries desolated by despotic power, or by the excessive advantages of the clergy over the laity.

In vain shall we wait for the succor of children yet unborn to re-establish a state thus depopulated. There is not time for this; men in their solitude are without courage or industry. With land sufficient to nourish a nation, they have scarcely enough to nourish a family. The common people have not even a property in the miseries of the country, that is, in the fallows with which it abounds. The clergy, the prince, the cities, the great men, and some of the principal citizens insensibly become proprietors of all the land which lies uncultivated; the families who are ruined have left their fields, and the laboring man is destitute.

In this situation they should take the same measures throughout the whole extent of the empire which the Romans took in a part of theirs; they should practice in their distress what these observed in the midst of plenty; that is, they should distribute land to all the families who are in want, and procure them materials for clearing and cultivating it. This distribution ought to be continued so long as there is a man to receive it, and in such a manner as not to lose a moment that can be industriously employed.

29. *Of Hospitals.*

A man is not poor because he has nothing, but because he does not work. The man who without any degree of wealth has an employment is as much at his ease as he who without labor has an income of a hundred crowns a year. He who has no substance, and yet has a trade, is not poorer than he who, possessing ten acres of land, is obliged to cultivate it for his subsistence. The mechanic who gives his art as an inheritance to his children has left them a fortune, which is multiplied in proportion to their number. It is not so with him who, having ten acres of land, divides it among his children.

In trading countries, where many men have no other subsistence but from the arts, the state is frequently obliged to supply the necessities of the aged, the sick, and the orphan. A well-regulated government draws this support from the arts themselves. It gives to some such employment as they are capable of performing; others are taught to work, and this teaching of itself becomes an employment.

The alms given to a naked man in the street do not fulfill the obligations of the state, which owes to every citizen a certain subsistence, a proper nourishment, convenient clothing, and a kind of life not incompatible with health.

Aurungzebe, being asked why he did not build hospitals, said, "I will make my empire so rich that there shall be no need of hospitals." [1133] He ought to have said, "I will begin by rendering my empire rich, and then I will build hospitals."

[1133] See Sir John Chardin, Travels through Persia, vol. viii.

The riches of the state suppose great industry. Amidst the numerous branches of trade it is impossible but that some must suffer, and consequently the mechanics must be in a momentary necessity.

Whenever this happens, the state is obliged to lend them a ready assistance, whether it be to prevent the sufferings of the people, or to avoid a rebellion. In this case hospitals, or some equivalent regulations, are necessary to prevent this misery.

But when the nation is poor, private poverty springs from the general calamity, and is, if I may so express myself, the general calamity itself. All the hospitals in the world cannot cure this private poverty; on the contrary, the spirit of indolence, which it constantly inspires, increases the general, and consequently the private, misery.

Henry VIII, [1134] resolving to reform the Church of England, ruined the monks, of themselves a lazy set of people, that encouraged laziness in others, because, as they practiced hospitality, an infinite number of idle persons, gentlemen and citizens, spent their lives in running from convent to convent. He demolished even the hospitals, in which the lower people found subsistence, as the gentlemen did theirs in the monasteries. Since these changes, the spirit of trade and industry has been established in England.

[1134] See Burnet, History of the Reformation.

At Rome, the hospitals place every one at his ease except those who labor, except those who are industrious, except those who have land, except those who are engaged in trade.

I have observed that wealthy nations have need of hospitals, because fortune subjects them to a thousand accidents; but it is plain that transient assistances are much better than perpetual foundations. The evil is momentary; it is necessary, therefore, that the succor should be of the same nature, and that it be applied to particular accidents.

BOOK XXIV.

OF LAWS IN RELATION TO RELIGION CONSIDERED IN ITSELF, AND IN ITS DOCTRINES

1. *Of Religion in General.*

As amidst several degrees of darkness we may form a judgment of those which are the least thick, and among precipices which are the least deep, so we may search among false religions for those that are most conformable to the welfare of society; for those which, though they have not the effect of leading men to the felicity of another life, may contribute most to their happiness in this.

I shall examine, therefore, the several religions of the world, in relation only to the good they produce in civil society, whether I speak of that which has its root in heaven, or of those which spring from the earth.

As in this work I am not a divine but a political writer, I may here advance things which are not otherwise true than as they correspond with a worldly manner of thinking, not as considered in their relation to truths of a more sublime nature.

With regard to the true religion, a person of the least degree of impartiality must see that I have never pretended to make its interests submit to those of a political nature, but rather to unite them; now, in order to unite, it is necessary that we should know them.

The Christian religion, which ordains that men should love each other, would, without doubt, have every nation blest with the best civil, the best political laws; because these, next to this religion, are the greatest good that men can give and receive.

2. *A Paradox of M. Bayle's.*

M. Bayle has pretended to prove [1135] that it is better to be an Atheist than an Idolater; that is, in other words, that it is less dangerous to have no religion at all than a bad one. *I had rather*, said he, *it should be said of me that I had no existence than that I am a villain.* This is only a sophism founded on this, that it is of no importance to the human race to believe that a certain man exists, whereas it is extremely useful for them to believe the existence of a God. From the idea of his non-existence immediately follows that of our independence; or, if we cannot conceive this idea, that of disobedience. To say that religion is not a restraining motive, because it does not always restrain, is equally absurd as to say that the civil laws are not a restraining motive. It is a false way of reasoning against religion to collect, in a large work, a long detail of the evils it has produced if we do not give at the same time an enumeration of the advantages which have flowed from it. Were I to relate all the evils that have arisen in the world from civil laws, from monarchy, and from republican government, I might tell of frightful things. Were it of no advantage for subjects to have religion, it would still be of some, if princes had it, and if they whitened with foam the only rein which can restrain those who fear not human laws.

[1135] Thoughts on the Comet.

A prince who loves and fears religion is a lion, who stoops to the hand that strokes, or to the voice that appeases him. He who fears and hates religion is like the savage beast that growls and bites the chain which prevents his flying on the passenger. He who has no religion at all is that terrible animal who perceives his liberty only when he tears in pieces and when he devours.

The question is not to know whether it would be better that a certain man or a certain people had no religion than to abuse what they have, but to know what is the least evil, that religion be sometimes abused, or that there be no such restraint as religion on mankind.

To diminish the horror of Atheism, they lay too much to the charge of idolatry. It is far from being true that when the ancients raised altars to a particular vice, they intended to show that they loved the vice; this signified, on the contrary, that they hated it. When the Lacedæmonians erected a temple to Fear, it was not to show that this warlike nation desired that he would in the midst of battle possess the hearts of the Lacedæmonians. They had deities to whom they prayed not to inspire them with guilt; and others whom they besought to shield them from it.

3. That a moderate Government is most agreeable to the Christian Religion, and a despotic Government to the Mahometan.

The Christian religion is a stranger to mere despotic power. The mildness so frequently recommended in the Gospel is incompatible with the despotic rage with which a prince punishes his subjects, and exercises himself in cruelty.

As this religion forbids the plurality of wives, its princes are less confined, less concealed from their subjects, and consequently have more humanity: they are more disposed to be directed by laws, and more capable of perceiving that they cannot do whatever they please.

While the Mahometan princes incessantly give or receive death, the religion of the Christians renders their princes less timid, and consequently less cruel. The prince confides in his subjects, and the subjects in the prince. How admirable the religion which, while it only seems to have in view the felicity of the other life, continues the happiness of this!

It is the Christian religion that, in spite of the extent of the empire and the influence of the climate, has hindered despotic power from being established in Ethiopia, and has carried into the heart of Africa the manners and laws of Europe.

The heir to the empire of Ethiopia [1136] enjoys a principality and gives to other subjects an example of love and obedience. Not far thence may we see the Mahometan shutting up the children of the King of Sennar, at whose death the council sends to murder them, in favor of the prince who mounts the throne.

[1136] Description of Ethiopia, by M. Ponce, Physician. Edifying Letters.

Let us set before our eyes, on the one hand, the continual massacres of the kings and generals of the Greeks and Romans, and, on the other, the destruction of people and cities by those famous conquerors Timur Beg and Jenghiz Khan, who ravaged Asia, and we shall see that we owe to Christianity, in government, a certain political law; and in war, a certain law of nations—benefits which human nature can never sufficiently acknowledge.

It is owing to this law of nations that among us victory leaves these great advantages to the conquered, life, liberty, laws, wealth, and always religion, when the conqueror is not blind to his own interest.

We may truly say that the people of Europe are not at present more disunited than the people and the armies, or even the armies among themselves were, under the Roman empire when it had become a despotic and military government. On the one hand, the armies engaged in war against each other, and, on the other, they pillaged the cities, and divided or confiscated the lands.

4. Consequences from the Character of the Christian Religion, and that of the Mahometan.

From the characters of the Christian and Mahometan religions, we ought, without any further examination, to embrace the one and reject the other: for it is much easier to prove that religion ought to humanize the manners of men than that any particular religion is true.

It is a misfortune to human nature when religion is given by a conqueror. The Mahometan religion, which speaks only by the sword, acts still upon men with that destructive spirit with which it was founded.

The history of Sabbaco, [1137] one of the pastoral kings of Egypt, is very extraordinary. The tutelar god of Thebes, appearing to him in a dream, ordered him to put to death all the priests of Egypt. He judged that the gods were displeased at his being on the throne, since they commanded him to commit an action contrary to their ordinary pleasure; and therefore he retired into Ethiopia.

[1137] See Diodorus, lib. II.

5. That the Catholic Religion is most agreeable to a Monarchy, and the Protestant to a Republic.

When a religion is introduced and fixed in a state, it is commonly such as is most suitable to the plan of government there established; for those who receive it, and those who are the cause of its being received, have scarcely any other idea of policy than that of the state in which they were born.

When the Christian religion, two centuries ago, became unhappily divided into Catholic and Protestant, the people of the north embraced the Protestant, and those of the south adhered still to the Catholic.

The reason is plain: the people of the north have, and will forever have, a spirit of liberty and independence, which the people of the south have not; and therefore a religion which has no visible head is more agreeable to the independence of the climate than that which has one.

In the countries themselves where the Protestant religion became established, the revolutions were made pursuant to the several plans of political government. Luther having great princes on his side would never have been able to make them relish an ecclesiastical authority that had no exterior pre-eminence; while Calvin, having to do with people who lived under republican governments, or with obscure citizens in monarchies, might very well avoid establishing dignities and preferments.

Each of these two religions was believed to be perfect; the Calvinist judging his most conformable to what Christ had said, and the Lutheran to what the Apostles had practiced.

6. Another of M. Bayle's Paradoxes.

M. Bayle, after having abused all religions, endeavors to sully Christianity: he boldly asserts that true Christians cannot form a government of any duration. Why not? Citizens of this profession being infinitely enlightened with respect to the various duties of life, and having the warmest zeal to fulfill them, must be perfectly sensible of the rights of natural defense. The more they believe themselves indebted to religion, the more they would think due to their country. The principles of Christianity, deeply engraved on the heart, would be infinitely more powerful than the false honor of monarchies, than the humane virtues of republics, or the servile fear of despotic states.

It is astonishing that this great man should not be able to distinguish between the orders for the establishment of Christianity and Christianity itself; and that he should be liable to be charged with not knowing the spirit of his own religion. When the legislator, instead of laws, has given counsels, this is because he knew that if these counsels were ordained as laws they would be contrary to the spirit of the laws themselves.

7. Of the Laws of Perfection in Religion.

Human laws, made to direct the will, ought to give precepts, and not counsels; religion, made to influence the heart, should give many counsels, and few precepts.

When, for instance, it gives rules, not for what is good, but for what is better; not to direct to what is right, but to what is perfect, it is expedient that these should be counsels, and not laws: for perfection can have no relation to the universality of men or things. Besides, if these were laws, there would be a necessity for an infinite number of others, to make people observe the first. Celibacy was advised by Christianity; when they made it a law in respect to a certain order of men, it became necessary to make new ones every day, in order to oblige those men to observe it. [1138] The legislator wearied himself, and he wearied society, to make men execute by precept what those who love perfection would have executed as counsel.

[1138] Dupin, Ecclesiastical Library of the Sixth Century, vol. v.

8. Of the Connection between the moral Laws and those of Religion.

In a country so unfortunate as to have a religion that God has not revealed, it is necessary for it to be agreeable to morality; because even a false religion is the best security we can have of the probity of men.

The principal points of religion of the inhabitants of Pegu [1139] are, not to commit murder, not to steal, to avoid uncleanliness, not to give the least uneasiness to their neighbor, but to do him, on the contrary, all the good in their power. With these rules they think they should be saved in any religion whatsoever. Hence it proceeds that those people, though poor and proud, behave with gentleness and compassion to the unhappy.

[1139] Collection of Voyages that Contributed to the Establishment of the East India Company, vol. iii, part I, p. 63.

9. Of the Essenes.

The Essenes [1140] made a vow to observe justice to mankind, to do no ill to any person, upon whatsoever account, to keep faith with all the world, to hate injustice, to command with modesty, always to side with truth, and to fly from all unlawful gain.

[1140] Prideaux, History of the Jews.

10. Of the Sect of Stoics.

The several sects of philosophy among the ancients were a species of religion. Never were any principles more worthy of human nature, and more proper to form the good man, than those of the Stoics; and if I could for a moment cease to think that I am a Christian, I should not be able to hinder myself from ranking the destruction of the sect of Zeno among the misfortunes that have befallen the human race.

It carried to excess only those things in which there is true greatness—the contempt of pleasure and of pain.

It was this sect alone that made citizens; this alone that made great men; this alone great emperors.

Laying aside for a moment revealed truths, let us search through all nature, and we shall not find a nobler object than the Antoninuses; even Julian himself—Julian (a commendation thus wrested from me will not render me an accomplice of his apostasy)—no, there has not been a prince since his reign more worthy to govern mankind.

While the Stoics looked upon riches, human grandeur, grief, disquietudes, and pleasures as vanity, they were entirely employed in laboring for the happiness of mankind, and in exercising the duties of society. It seems as if they regarded that sacred spirit, which they believed to dwell within them, as a kind of favorable providence watchful over the human race.

Born for society, they all believed that it was their destiny to labor for it; with so much the less fatigue, their rewards were all within themselves. Happy by their philosophy alone, it seemed as if only the happiness of others could increase theirs.

11. *Of Contemplation.*

Men being made to preserve, to nourish, to clothe themselves, and do all the actions of society, religion ought not to give them too contemplative a life. [1141]

[1141] This is the inconvenience of the doctrine of Foe and Laockium.

The Mahomedans become speculative by habit; they pray five times a day, and each time they are obliged to cast behind them everything which has any concern with this world: this forms them for speculation. Add to this that indifference for all things which is inspired by the doctrine of unalterable fate.

If other causes besides these concur to disengage their affections; for instance, if the severity of the government, if the laws concerning the property of land, give them a precarious spirit—all is lost.

The religion of the Gaurs formerly rendered Persia a flourishing kingdom; it corrected the bad effects of despotic power. The same empire is now destroyed by the Mahometan religion.

12. *Of Penances.*

Penances ought to be joined with the idea of labor, not with that of idleness; with the idea of good, not with that of supereminence; with the idea of frugality, not with that of avarice.

13. *Of inexpiable Crimes.*

It appears from a. passage of the books of the pontiffs, quoted by Cicero, [1142] that they had among the Romans inexpiable crimes: [1143] and it is on this that Zozymus founds the narration so proper to blacken the motives of Constantine's conversion; and Julian, that bitter raillery on this conversion in his Cæsars.

[1142] Lib. II. of Laws.

[1143] *Sacrum commissum, quod neque expiari poterit, impie commissum est; quod expiari poterit publici sacerdotes expianto.*

The Pagan religion indeed, which prohibited only some of the grosser crimes, and which stopped the hand but meddled not with the heart, might have crimes that were inexpiable; but a religion which bridles all the passions; which is not more jealous of actions than of thoughts and desires; which holds us not by a few chains but by an infinite number of threads; which, leaving human justice aside, establishes another kind of justice; which is so ordered as to lead us continually from repentance to love, and from love to repentance; which puts between the judge and the criminal a greater mediator, between the just and the mediator a great judge—a religion like this ought not to have inexpiable crimes. But while it gives fear and hope to all, it makes us sufficiently sensible that though there is no crime in its own nature inexpiable, yet a whole criminal life may be so; that it is extremely dangerous to affront mercy by new crimes and new expiations; that an uneasiness on account of ancient debts, from which we are never entirely free, ought to make us afraid of contracting new ones, of filling up the measure, and going even to that point where paternal goodness is limited.

14. *In what Manner Religion has an Influence on Civil Laws.*

As both religion and the civil laws ought to have a peculiar tendency to render men good citizens, it is evident that when one of these deviates from this end, the tendency of the other ought to be strengthened. The less severity there is in religion, the more there ought to be in the civil laws.

Thus the reigning religion of Japan having few doctrines, and proposing neither future rewards nor punishments, the laws to supply these defects have been made with the spirit of severity, and are executed with an extraordinary punctuality.

When the doctrine of necessity is established by religion, the penalties of the laws ought to be more severe, and the magistrate more vigilant; to the end that men who would otherwise become abandoned might be determined by these motives; but it is quite otherwise where religion has established the doctrine of liberty.

From the inactivity of the soul springs the Mahometan doctrine of predestination, and from this doctrine of predestination springs the inactivity of the soul. This, they say, is in the decrees of God; they must therefore indulge their repose. In a case like this, the magistrate ought to waken by the laws those who are lulled asleep by religion.

When religion condemns things which the civil laws ought to permit, there is danger lest the civil laws, on the other hand, should permit what religion ought to condemn. Either of these is a constant proof of a want of true ideas of that harmony and proportion which ought to subsist between both.

Thus the Tartars under Jenghiz Khan, [1144] among whom it was a sin and even a capital crime to put a knife in the fire, to lean against a whip, to strike a horse with his bridle, to break one bone with another, did not believe it to be any sin to break their word, to seize upon another man's goods, to do an injury to a person, or to commit murder. In a word, laws which render that necessary which is only indifferent have this inconvenience, that they make those things indifferent which are absolutely necessary.

[1144] See the account of John Duplan Carpin, sent to Tartary by Pope Innocent IV in the year 1246.

The people of Formosa believe [1145] that there is a kind of hell, but it is to punish those who at certain seasons have not gone naked, who have dressed in calico and not in silk, who have presumed to look for oysters, or who have undertaken any business without consulting the song of birds; while drunkenness and debauchery are not regarded as crimes. They believe even that the debauches of their children are agreeable to their gods.

[1145] Collection of Voyages that Contributed to the Establishment of the East India Company, vol. v, part I, p. 192.

When religion absolves the mind by a thing merely accidental, it loses its greatest influence on mankind. The people of India believe that the waters of the Ganges have a sanctifying virtue. [1146] Those who die on its banks are imagined to be exempted from the torments of the other life, and to be entitled to dwell in a region full of delights; and for this reason the ashes of the dead are sent from the most distant places to be thrown into this river. Little then does it signify whether they had lived virtuously or not, so they be but thrown into the Ganges.

[1146] Edifying Letters, coll. xv.

The idea of a place of rewards has a necessary connection with the idea of the abodes of misery; and when they hope for the former without fearing the latter, the civil laws have no longer any influence. Men who think themselves sure of the rewards of the other life are above the power of the legislator; they look upon death with too much contempt. How shall the man be restrained by laws who believes that the greatest pain the magistrate can inflict will end in a moment to begin his happiness?

15. *How false Religions are sometimes corrected by the Civil Laws.*

Simplicity, superstition, or a respect for antiquity have sometimes established mysteries or ceremonies shocking to modesty: of this the world has furnished numerous examples. Aristotle says [1147] that in this case the law permits the fathers of families to repair to the temple to celebrate these mysteries for their wives and children. How admirable the civil law which in spite of religion preserves the manners untainted!

[1147] *Politics*, lib. VII. chap. 17.

Augustus [1148] excluded the youth of either sex from assisting at any nocturnal ceremony, unless accompanied by a more aged relative; and when he revived the *Lupercalia*, he would not allow the young men to run naked.

[1148] Suetonius, *Life of Augustus*, chap. 31.

16. *How the Laws of Religion correct the Inconveniences of a political Constitution.*

On the other hand, religion may support a state when the laws themselves are incapable of doing it.

Thus when a kingdom is frequently agitated by civil wars, religion may do much by obliging one part of the state to remain always quiet. Among the Greeks, the Eleans, as priests of Apollo, lived always in peace. In Japan, [1149] the city of Meaco enjoys a constant peace, as being a holy city. Religion supports this regulation, and that empire, which seems to be alone upon earth, and which neither has nor will have any dependence on foreigners, has always in its own bosom a trade which war cannot ruin.

[1149] Collection of Voyages that Contributed to the Establishment of the East India Company, vol. iv, p. 127.

In kingdoms where wars are not entered upon by a general consent, and where the laws have not pointed out any means either of terminating or preventing them, religion establishes times of peace, or cessation from hostilities, that the people may be able to sow their corn and perform those other labors which are absolutely necessary for the subsistence of the state.

Every year all hostility ceases between the Arabian tribes for four months: the least disturbance would then be an impiety. [1150] In former times, when every lord in France declared war or peace, religion granted a truce, which was to take place at certain seasons.

[1150] See Prideaux, Life of Mahomet, p. 64.

17. *The same Subject continued.*

When a state has many causes for hatred, religion ought to produce many ways of reconciliation. The Arabs, a people addicted to robbery, are frequently guilty of doing injury and injustice. Mahomet enacted this law: [1151] "If any one forgives the blood of his brother, [1152] he may pursue the malefactor for damages and interest; but he who shall injure the wicked, after having received satisfaction, shall, in the day of judgment, suffer the most grievous torments."

[1151] Koran, book I., chapter "Of the Cow."
[1152] On renouncing the law of retaliation.

The Germans inherited the hatred and enmity of their near relatives: but these were not eternal. Homicide was expiated by giving a certain number of cattle, and all the family received satisfaction: a thing extremely useful, says Tacitus, because enmities are most dangerous among a free people. [1153] I believe, indeed, that their ministers of religion, who were held by them in so much credit, were concerned in these reconciliations.

[1153] *De Moribus Germanorum.*

Among the inhabitants of Malacca, [1154] where no form of reconciliation is established, he who has committed murder, certain of being assassinated by the relatives or friends of the deceased, abandons himself to fury, and wounds or kills all he meets.

[1154] Collection of Voyages that Contributed to the Establishment of the East India Company, vol. vii, p. 303. See also Memoirs of the Count de Forbin, and what he says of the people of Macassar.

18. *How the Laws of Religion have the Effect of Civil Laws.*

The first Greeks were small nations, frequently dispersed, pirates at sea, unjust on land, without government and without laws. The mighty actions of Hercules and Theseus let us see the state of that rising people. What could religion do more to inspire them with horror against murder? It declared that the man who had been murdered was enraged against the assassin, that he would possess his mind with terror and trouble, and oblige him to yield to him the places he had frequented when alive. [1155] They could not touch the criminal, nor converse with him, without being defiled: [1156] the murderer was to be expelled from the city, and an expiation made for the crime. [1157]

[1155] Plato, of Laws, lib. IX.
[1156] Tragedy of Œdipus Coloneus.
[1157] Plato, Laws, ix.

19. *That it is not so much the Truth or Falsity of a Doctrine which renders it useful or pernicious to Men in civil Government, as the Use or Abuse of it.*

The most true and holy doctrines may be attended with the very worst consequences when they are not connected with the principles of society: and on the contrary, doctrines the most false may be attended with excellent consequences when contrived so as to be connected with these principles.

The religion of Confucius disowns the immortality of the soul: and the sect of Zeno did not believe it. These two sects have drawn from their bad principles consequences, not just indeed, but most admirable as to their influence on society. Those of the religion of Tao, and of Foe, [1158] believe the immortality of the soul; but from this sacred doctrine they draw the most frightful consequences.

[1158] A Chinese philosopher reasons thus against the doctrine of Foe: "It is said in a book of that sect, that the body is our dwelling-place and the soul the immortal guest which lodges there; but if the bodies of our relatives are only a lodging, it is natural to regard them with the same contempt we should feel for a structure of earth and dirt. Is not this endeavoring to tear from the heart the virtue of love to one's own parents? This leads us even to neglect the care of the body, and to refuse it the compassion and affection so necessary for its preservation; hence the disciples of Foe kill themselves by thousands."—Work of an ancient Chinese philosopher, in the Collection of Father Du Halde, vol. iii, p. 52.

The doctrine of the immortality of the soul falsely understood has, almost in every part of the globe and in every age, engaged women, slaves, subjects, friends, to murder themselves, that they might go and serve in the other world the object of their respect or love in this. Thus it was in the West Indies; thus it was among the Danes; [1159] thus it is at present in Japan, [1160] in Macassar, [1161] and many other places.

[1159] See Tho. Bartholin, Antiquities of the Danes.
[1160] An Account of Japan, in the Collection of Voyages that Contributed to the Establishment of the East India company.
[1161] Forbin, Memoirs.

These customs do not so directly proceed from the doctrine of the immortality of the soul as from that of the resurrection of the body, whence they have drawn this consequence, that after death the same individual will have the same wants, the same sentiments, the same passions. In this point of view, the doctrine of the immortality of the soul has a prodigious effect on mankind; because the idea of only a simple change of habitation is more within the reach of the human understanding, and more adapted to flatter the heart, than the idea of a new modification.

It is not enough for religion to establish a doctrine; it must also direct its influence. This the Christian religion performs in the most admirable manner, particularly with regard to the doctrines of which we have been speaking. It makes us hope for a state which is the object of our belief; not for a state which we have already experienced or known: thus every article, even the resurrection of the body, leads us to spiritual ideas.

20. *The same Subject continued.*

The sacred books [1162] of the ancient Persians say, *If you would be holy instruct your children, because all the good actions which they perform will be imputed to you.* They advise them to marry betimes, because children at the day of judgment will be as a bridge, over which those who have none cannot pass. These doctrines were false, but extremely useful.

[1162] Hyde, Religion of the Persians.

21. *Of the Metempsychosis.*

The doctrine of the immortality of the soul is divided into three branches—that of pure immortality, that of a simple change of habitation, and that of a metempsychosis, that is, the system of the Christians, that of the Scythians, and that of the Indians. We have just been speaking of the first two, and I shall say of the last that as it has been well or ill explained, it has had good or bad effects. As it inspires men with a certain horror against bloodshed, very few murders are committed in the Indies; and though they seldom punish with death, yet they enjoy a perfect tranquility.

On the other hand, women burn themselves at the death of their husbands; thus it is only the innocent who suffer a violent death.

22. *That it is dangerous for Religion to inspire an Aversion for Things in themselves indifferent.*

A kind of honor established in the Indies by the prejudices of religion has made the several tribes conceive an aversion against each other. This honor is founded entirely on religion; these family distinctions form no civil distinctions; there are Indians who would think themselves dishonored by eating with their king.

These sorts of distinctions are connected with a certain aversion for other men, very different from those sentiments which naturally arise from difference of rank; which among us comprehends a love for inferiors.

The laws of religion should never inspire an aversion to anything but vice, and above all they should never estrange man from a love and tenderness for his own species.

The Mahometan and Indian religions embrace an infinite number of people; the Indians hate the Mahometans, because they eat cows; the Mahometans detest the Indians because they eat hogs.

23. *Of Festivals.*

When religion appoints a cessation from labor it ought to have a greater regard to the necessities of mankind than to the grandeur of the being it designs to honor.

Athens was subject to great inconveniences from the excessive number of its festivals. [1163] These powerful people, to whose decision all the cities of Greece came to submit their quarrels, could not have time to dispatch such a multiplicity of affairs.

[1163] Xenophon, On the Republic of Athens, 3, § 8.

When Constantine ordained that the people should rest on the Sabbath, he made this decree for the cities, [1164] and not for the inhabitants of the open country; he was sensible that labor in the cities was useful, but in the fields necessary.

[1164] Leg. 3. cod. *de Feriis*. This law was doubtless made only for the Pagans.

For the same reason, in a country supported by commerce, the number of festivals ought to be relative to this very commerce. Protestant and Catholic countries are situated in such a manner that there is more need of labor in the former than in the latter; [1165] the suppression of festivals is therefore more suitable to Protestant than to Catholic countries.

[1165] The Catholics lie more toward the south, and the Protestants towards the north.

Dampier observes that the diversions of different nations vary greatly, according to the climate. [1166] As hot climates produce a quantity of delicate fruits, the barbarians easily find necessaries, and therefore spend much time in diversions. The Indians of colder countries have not so much leisure, being obliged to fish and hunt continually; hence they have less music, dancing and festivals. If a new religion should be established among these people, it ought to have regard to this in the institution of festivals.

[1166] Dampier, Voyages, ii.

24. *Of the local Laws of Religion.*

There are many local laws in various religions; and when Montezuma with so much obstinacy insisted that the religion of the Spaniards was good for their country, and his for Mexico, he did not assert an absurdity; because, in fact, legislators could never help having a regard to what nature had established before them.

The opinion of the metempsychosis is adapted to the climate of the Indies. An excessive heat burns up all the country: [1167] they can breed but very few cattle; they are always in danger of wanting them for tillage; their black cattle multiply but indifferently; [1168] and they are subject to many distempers. A law of religion which preserves them is therefore more suitable to the policy of the country.

[1167] See Bernier, Travels, vol. ii, p. 137.
[1168] Edifying Letters, Coll. 12, p. 95.

While the meadows are scorched, rice and pulse, by the assistance of water, are brought to perfection; a law of religion which permits only this kind of nourishment must therefore be extremely useful to men in those climates.

The flesh of cattle in that country is insipid [1169] but the milk and butter which they receive from them serve for a part of their subsistence; therefore the law which prohibits the eating and killing of cows is in the Indies not unreasonable.

[1169] Bernier, Travels, vol. ii, p. 137.

Athens contained a prodigious multitude of people, but its territory was barren. It was therefore a religious maxim with this people that those who offered some small presents to the gods honored them more than those who sacrificed an ox. [1170]

[1170] Euripides, in *Athenæus*, lib. II.

25. *The Inconvenience of transplanting a Religion from one Country to another.*

It follows hence that there are frequently many inconveniences attending the transplanting a religion from one country to any other.

"*The hog,*" says M. de Boulainvilliers, [1171] "*must be very scarce in Arabia, where there are almost no woods, and hardly anything fit for the nourishment of these animals; besides, the saltness of the water and food renders the people most susceptible of cutaneous disorders.*" This local law could not be good in other countries, [1172] where the hog is almost a universal, and in some sort a necessary, nourishment.

[1171] Life of Mahomet.
[1172] As in China.

I shall here make a reflection. Sanctorius has observed that pork transpires but little, [1173] and that this kind of meat greatly binders the transpiration of other food; he has found that this diminution amounts to a third. [1174] Besides, it is known that the want of transpiration forms or increases the disorders of the skin. The feeding on pork ought rather to be prohibited in climates where the people are subject to these disorders, as in Palestine, Arabia, Egypt, and Libya.

[1173] *Medicina Statica*, § 3, aphor. 23.
[1174] Ibid.

26. *The same Subject continued.*

Sir John Chardin says [1175] that there is not a navigable river in Persia, except the Kur, which is at the extremity of the empire. The ancient law of the Gaurs which prohibited sailing on rivers was not therefore attended with any inconvenience in this country, though it would have ruined the trade of another.

[1175] Travels into Persia, vol. ii.

Frequent bathings are extremely useful in hot climates. On this account they are ordained in the Mahometan law and in the Indian religion. In the Indies it is a most meritorious act to pray to God in the running stream; [1176] but how could these things be performed in other climates?

[1176] Bernier, Travels, vol. ii.

When a religion adapted to the climate of one country clashes too much with the climate of another it cannot be there established; and whenever it has been introduced it has been afterwards discarded, it seems to all human appearance as if the climate had prescribed the bounds of the Christian and the Mahometan religions.

It follows hence, that it is almost always proper for a religion to have particular doctrines, and a general worship. In laws concerning the practice of religious worship there ought to be but few particulars; for instance, they should command mortification in general and not a certain kind of mortification. Christianity is full of good sense; abstinence is of divine institution; but a particular kind of abstinence is ordained by human authority and therefore may be changed.

BOOK XXV.

OF LAWS IN RELATION TO THE ESTABLISHMENT
OF RELIGION AND ITS EXTERNAL POLITY

1. *Of Religious Sentiments.*

The pious man and the atheist always talk of religion; the one speaks of what he loves, and the other of what he fears.

2. *Of the Motives of Attachment to different Religions.*

The different religions of the world do not give to those who profess them equal motives of attachment; this depends greatly on the manner in which they agree with the turn of thought and perceptions of mankind.

We are extremely addicted to idolatry, and yet have no great inclination for the religion of idolaters; we are not very fond of spiritual ideas, and yet are most attached to those religions which teach us to adore a spiritual being. This proceeds from the satisfaction we find in ourselves at having been so intelligent as to choose a religion which raises the deity from that baseness in which he had been placed by others. We look upon idolatry as the religion of an ignorant people, and the religion which has a spiritual being for its object as that of the most enlightened nations.

When with a doctrine that gives us the idea of a spiritual supreme being we can still join those of a sensible nature and admit them into our worship, we contract a greater attachment to religion; because those motives which we have just mentioned are added to our natural inclinations for the objects of sense. Thus the Catholics, who have more of this kind of worship than the Protestants, are more attached to their religion than the Protestants are to theirs, and more zealous for its propagation.

When the people of Ephesus were informed that the fathers of the council had declared they might call the Virgin Mary the Mother of God, they were transported with joy, they kissed the hands of the bishops, they embraced their knees, and the whole city resounded with acclamations. [1177]

[1177] St. Cyril's Letter.

When an intellectual religion superadds a choice made by the deity, and a preference for those who profess it over those who do not, this greatly attaches us to religion. The Mahometans would not be such good Mussulmans if, on the one hand, there were not idolatrous nations who make them imagine themselves the champions of the unity of God; and on the other Christians, to make them believe that they are the objects of his preference.

A religion burdened with many ceremonies [1178] attaches us to it more strongly than that which has a fewer number. We have an extreme propensity to things in which we are continually employed: witness the obstinate prejudices of the Mahometans and the Jews, [1179] and the readiness with which barbarous and savage nations change their religion, who, as they are employed entirely in hunting or war, have but few religious ceremonies.

[1178] This does not contradict what I have said in the last chapter of the preceding book: I here speak of the motives of attachment of religion, and there of the means of rendering it more general.

[1179] This has been remarked over all the world. See, as to the Turks, the Missions of the Levant; the Collection of Voyages that Contributed to the Establishment of the East India Company, vol. iii, part I, p. 201 on the Moors of Batavia; and Father Labat on the Mahometan Negroes, &c.

Men are extremely inclined to the passions of hope and fear; a religion, therefore, that had neither a heaven nor a hell could hardly please them. This is proved by the ease with which foreign religions have been established in Japan, and the zeal and fondness with which they were received. [1180]

[1180] The Christian and the Indian religions: these have a hell and a paradise, which the religion of Sintos has not.

In order to raise an attachment to religion it is necessary that it should inculcate pure morals. Men who are knaves by retail are extremely honest in the gross; they love morality. And were I not treating of so grave a subject I should say that this appears remarkably evident in our theatres: we are sure of pleasing the people by sentiments avowed by morality; we are sure of shocking them by those it disapproves.

When external worship is attended with great magnificence, it flatters our minds and strongly attaches us to religion. The riches of temples and those of the clergy greatly affect us. Thus even the misery of the people is a motive that renders them fond of a religion which has served as a pretext to those who were the cause of their misery.

3. Of Temples.

Almost all civilized nations dwell in houses; hence naturally arose the idea of building a house for God in which they might adore and seek him, amidst all their hopes and fears.

And, indeed, nothing is more comfortable to mankind than a place in which they may find the deity peculiarly present, and where they may assemble together to confess their weakness and tell their griefs.

But this natural idea never occurred to any but such as cultivated the land; those who have no houses for themselves were never known to build temples.

This was the cause that made Jenghiz Khan discover such a prodigious contempt for mosques. [1181] This prince examined the Mahometans; [1182] he approved of all their doctrines, except that of the necessity of going to Mecca; he could not comprehend why God might not be everywhere adored. As the Tartars did not dwell in houses, they could have no idea of temples.

[1181] Entering the mosque of Bochara, he took the Koran, and threw it under his horse's feet.—History of the Tartars, part III, p. 273.

[1182] Ibid., p. 342.

Those people who have no temples have but a small attachment to their own religion. This is the reason why the Tartars have in all times given so great a toleration; [1183] why the barbarous nations, who conquered the Roman empire did not hesitate a moment to embrace Christianity; why the savages of America have so little fondness for their own religion; why, since our missionaries have built churches in Paraguay, the natives of that country have become so zealous for ours.

[1183] This disposition of mind has been communicated to the Japanese, who, as it may be easily proved, derive their origin from the Tartars.

As the deity is the refuge of the unhappy, and none are more unhappy than criminals, men have been naturally led to think temples an asylum for those wretches. [1184] This idea appeared still more natural to the Greeks, where murderers, chased from their city and the presence of men, seemed to have no houses but the temples, nor other protectors than the gods.

[1184] See Chardin, Persia, vol. ii. 31, edit. of 1735.

At first these were only designed for involuntary homicides; but when the people made them a sanctuary for those who had committed great crimes they fell into a gross contradiction. If they had offended men, they had much greater reason to believe they had offended the gods.

These asylums multiplied in Greece. The temples, says Tacitus, [1185] were filled with insolvent debtors and wicked slaves; the magistrate found it difficult to exercise his office; the people protected the crimes of men as the ceremonies of the gods; at length the senate was obliged to retrench a great number of them.

[1185] *Annal*, lib. II.

The laws of Moses were perfectly wise. The man who involuntarily killed another was innocent; but he was obliged to be taken away from before the eyes of the relatives of the deceased. Moses therefore appointed an asylum for such unfortunate people. [1186]The perpetrators of great crimes deserved not a place of safety, and they had none: [1187] the Jews had only a portable tabernacle, which continually changed its place; this excluded the idea of a sanctuary. It is true that they had afterwards a temple; but the criminals who would resort thither from all parts might disturb the divine service. If persons who had committed manslaughter had been driven out of the country, as was customary among the Greeks, they had reason to fear that they would worship strange gods. All these considerations made them establish cities of safety, where they might stay till the death of the high-priest.

[1186] Numb.xxxv.
[1187] Ibid.

4. *Of the Ministers of Religion.*

The first men, says Porphyry, [1188] sacrificed only vegetables. In a worship so simple, every one might be priest in his own family.

[1188] *De Abstinentia animal*, II. 5.

The natural desire of pleasing the deity multiplied ceremonies. Hence it followed, that men employed in agriculture became incapable of observing them all and of filling up the number.

Particular places were consecrated to the gods; it then became necessary that they should have ministers to take care of them; in the same manner as every citizen took care of his house and domestic affairs. Hence the people who have no priests are commonly barbarians; such were formerly the Pedalians, [1189] and such are still the Wolgusky. [1190]

[1189] Lilius Giraldus, p. 726.
[1190] A people of Siberia. See the account given by Mr. Everard Ysbrant Ides, in the Collection of Travels to the North, vol. viii.

Men consecrated to the deity ought to be honored, especially among people who have formed an idea of a personal purity necessary to approach the places most agreeable to the gods, and for the performance of particular ceremonies.

The worship of the gods requiring a continual application, most nations were led to consider the clergy as a separate body. Thus, among the Egyptians, the Jews, and the Persians, [1191] they consecrated to the deity certain families who performed and perpetuated the service. There have been even religions which have not only estranged ecclesiastics from business, but have also taken away the embarrassments of a family; and this is the practice of the principal branch of Christianity.

[1191] Mr. Hyde.

I shall not here treat of the consequences of the law of celibacy: it is evident that it may become hurtful in proportion as the body of the clergy may be too numerous; and, in consequence of this, that of the laity too small.

By the nature of the human understanding we love in religion everything which carries the idea of difficulty; as in point of morality we have a speculative fondness for everything which bears the character of severity. Celibacy has been most agreeable to those nations to whom it seemed least adapted, and with whom it might be attended with the most fatal consequences. In the southern countries of Europe, where, by the nature of the climate, the law of celibacy is more difficult to observe, it has been retained; in those of the north, where the passions are less lively, it has been banished. Further, in countries where there are but few inhabitants it has been admitted; in those that are vastly populous it has been rejected. It is obvious that these reflections relate only to the too great extension of celibacy, and not to celibacy itself.

5. Of the Bounds which the Laws ought to prescribe to the Riches of the Clergy.

As particular families may be extinct, their wealth cannot be a perpetual inheritance. The clergy is a family which cannot be extinct; wealth is therefore fixed to it forever, and cannot go out of it.

Particular families may increase; it is necessary then that their wealth should also increase. The clergy is a family which ought not to increase; their wealth ought then to be limited.

We have retained the regulations of the Levitical laws as to the possessions of the clergy, except those relating to the bounds of these possessions; indeed, among us we must ever be ignorant of the limit beyond which any religious community can no longer be permitted to acquire.

These endless acquisitions appear to the people so unreasonable that he who should speak in their defense would be regarded as an idiot.

The civil laws find sometimes many difficulties in altering established abuses, because they are connected with things worthy of respect; in this case an indirect proceeding would be a greater proof of the wisdom of the legislator than another which struck directly at the thing itself. Instead of prohibiting the acquisitions of the clergy, we should seek to give them a distaste for them; to leave them the right and to take away the deed.

In some countries of Europe, a respect for the privileges of the nobility has established in their favor a right of indemnity over immovable goods acquired in mortmain. The interest of the prince has in the same case made him exact a right of amortization. In Castile, where no such right prevails, the clergy have seized upon everything. In Aragon, where there is some right of amortization, they have obtained less; in France, where this right and that of indemnity are established, they have acquired less still; and it may be said that the prosperity of this kingdom is in a great measure owing to the exercise of these two rights. If possible, then, increase these rights, and put a stop to the mortmain.

Render the ancient and necessary patrimony of the clergy sacred and inviolable, let it be fixed and eternal like that body itself, but let new inheritances be out of their power.

Permit them to break the rule when the rule has become an abuse; suffer the abuse when it enters into the rule.

They still remember in Rome a certain memorial sent thither on some disputes with the clergy, in which was this maxim: *The clergy ought to contribute to the expenses of the state, let the Old Testament say what it will.* They concluded from this passage that the author of this memorial was better versed in the language of the tax-gatherers than in that of religion.

6. Of Monasteries.

The least degree of common sense will let us see that bodies designed for a perpetual continuance should not be allowed to sell their funds for life, nor to borrow for life; unless we want them to be heirs to all those who have no relatives and to those who do not choose to have any. These men play against the people, but they hold the bank themselves.

7. *Of the Luxury of Superstition.*

Those are guilty of impiety towards the gods, says Plato, [1192] *who deny their existence; or who, while they believe it, maintain that they do not interfere with what is done below; or, in fine, who think that they can easily appease them by sacrifices: three opinions equally pernicious.* Plato has here said all that the clearest light of nature has ever been able to say in point of religion. The magnificence of external worship has a principal connection with the institution of the state. In good republics, they have curbed not only the luxury of vanity, but even that of superstition. They have introduced frugal laws into religion. Of this number are many of the laws of Solon; many of those of Plato on funerals, adopted by Cicero; and, in fine, some of the laws of Numa on sacrifices. [1193]

[1192] Of Laws, book X.
[1193] *Rogum vino ne respergito*—Law of the Twelve Tables.

Birds, says Cicero, [1194] and paintings begun and finished in a day are gifts the most divine. We offer common things, says a Spartan, [1195] that we may always have it in our power to honor the gods.

[1194] Cicero derives these appropriate words from Plato (Laws, book XII).—Ed.
[1195] Plutarch attributes this beautiful idea to Lycurgus.—Ed.

The desire of man to pay his worship to the deity is very different from the magnificence of this worship. Let us not offer our treasures to him if we are not proud of showing that we esteem what he would have us despise.
What must the gods think of the gifts of the impious, said the admirable Plato, *when a good man would blush to receive presents from a villain?*
Religion ought not, under the pretence of gifts, to draw from the people what the necessity of the state has left them; but as Plato says, [1196] *The chaste and the pious ought to offer gifts which resemble themselves.*

[1196] On Laws, book II.

Nor is it proper for religion to encourage expensive funerals. What is there more natural than to take away the difference of fortune in a circumstance and in the very moment which equals all fortunes?

8. *Of the Pontificate.*

When religion has many ministers it is natural for them to have a chief and for a sovereign pontiff to be established. In monarchies, where the several orders of the state cannot be kept too distinct, and where all powers ought not to be lodged in the same person, it is proper that the pontificate be distinct from the empire. The same necessity is not to be met with in a despotic government, the nature of which is to unite all the different powers in the same person. But in this case it may happen that the prince may regard religion as he does the laws themselves, as dependent on his own will. To prevent this inconvenience, there ought to be monuments of religion, for instance, sacred books which fix and establish it. The King of Persia is the chief of the religion; but this religion is regulated by the Koran. The Emperor of China is the sovereign pontiff; but there are books in the hands of everybody to which he himself must conform. In vain a certain emperor attempted to abolish them; they triumphed over tyranny.

9. Of Toleration in point of Religion.

We are here politicians, and not divines; but the divines themselves must allow, that there is a great difference between tolerating and approving a religion.

When the legislator has believed it a duty to permit the exercise of many religions, it is necessary that he should enforce also a toleration among these religions themselves. It is a principle that every religion which is persecuted becomes itself persecuting; for as soon as by some accidental turn it arises from persecution, it attacks the religion which persecuted it; not as religion, but as tyranny.

It is necessary, then, that the laws require from the several religions, not only that they shall not embroil the state, but that they shall not raise disturbances among themselves. A citizen does not fulfill the laws by not disturbing the government; it is requisite that he should not trouble any citizen whomsoever.

10. The same Subject continued.

As there are scarcely any but persecuting religions that have an extraordinary zeal for being established in other places (because a religion that can tolerate others seldom thinks of its own propagation), it must therefore be a very good civil law, when the state is already satisfied with the established religion, not to suffer the establishment of another. [1197]

[1197] I do not mean to speak in this chapter of the Christian religion; for, as I have elsewhere observed, the Christian religion is our chief blessing. See the end of the preceding chapter, and the Defense of the Spirit of Laws, part II.

This is then a fundamental principle of the political laws in regard to religion; that when the state is at liberty to receive or to reject a new religion it ought to be rejected; when it is received it ought to be tolerated.

11. Of changing a Religion.

A prince who undertakes to destroy or to change the established religion of his kingdom must greatly expose himself. If his government be despotic, he runs a much greater risk of seeing a revolution arise from such a proceeding, than from any tyranny whatsoever, and a revolution is not an uncommon thing in such states. The reason of this is that a state cannot change its religion, manners and customs in an instant, and with the same rapidity as the prince publishes the ordinance which establishes a new religion.

Besides, the ancient religion is connected with the constitution of the kingdom and the new one is not; the former agrees with the climate and very often the new one is opposed to it. Moreover, the citizens become disgusted with their laws, and look upon the government already established with contempt; they conceive a jealousy against the two religions, instead of a firm belief in one; in a word, these innovations give to the state, at least for some time, both bad citizens and bad believers.

12. *Of penal Laws.*

Penal laws ought to be avoided in respect to religion: they imprint fear, it is true; but as religion has also penal laws which inspire the same passion, the one is effaced by the other, and between these two different kinds of fear the mind becomes hardened.

The threatenings of religion are so terrible, and its promises so great, that when they actuate the mind, whatever efforts the magistrate may use to oblige us to renounce it, he seems to leave us nothing when he deprives us of the exercise of our religion, and to bereave us of nothing when we are allowed to profess it.

It is not, therefore, by filling the soul with the idea of this great object, by hastening her approach to that critical moment in which it ought to be of the highest importance, that religion can be most successfully attacked: a more certain way is to tempt her by favors, by the conveniences of life, by hopes of fortune; not by that which revives, but by that which extinguishes the sense of her duty; not by that which shocks her, but by that which throws her into indifference at the time when other passions actuate the mind, and those which religion inspires are hushed into silence. As a general rule in changing a religion the invitations should be much stronger than the penalties.

The temper of the human mind has appeared even in the nature of punishments. If we take a survey of the persecutions in Japan, [1198] we shall find that they were more shocked at cruel torments than at long sufferings, which rather weary than affright, which are the more difficult to surmount, from their appearing less difficult.

[1198] In the Collection of Voyages that Contributed to the Establishment of the East India Company, vol. v.

In a word, history sufficiently informs us that penal laws have never had any other effect than to destroy.

13. *A most humble Remonstrance to the Inquisitors of Spain and Portugal.*

A Jewess of ten years of age, who was burned at Lisbon at the last *auto-da-fé*, gave occasion to the following little piece, the most idle, I believe, that ever was written. When we attempt to prove things so evident we are sure never to convince.

The author declares, that though a Jew he has a respect for the Christian religion; and that he should be glad to take away from the princes who are not Christians, a plausible pretence for persecuting this religion.

"You complain," says he to the Inquisitors, "that the Emperor of Japan caused all the Christians in his dominions to be burned by a slow fire. But he will answer, we treat you who do not believe like us, as you yourselves treat those who do not believe like you; you can only complain of your weakness, which has hindered you from exterminating us, and which has enabled us to exterminate you.

"But it must be confessed that you are much more cruel than this emperor. You put us to death who believe only what you believe, because we do not believe *all* that you believe. We follow a religion which you yourselves know to have been formerly dear to God. We think that God loves it still, and you think that he loves it no more: and because you judge thus, you make those suffer by sword and fire who hold an error so pardonable as to believe that God still loves what he once loved. [1199]

[1199] The source of the blindness of the Jews is their not perceiving that the economy of the Gospel is in the order of the decrees of God and that it is in this light a consequence of his immutability.

"If you are cruel to us, you are much more so to our children; you cause them to be burned because they follow the inspirations given them by those whom the law of nature and the laws of all nations teach them to regard as gods.

"You deprive yourselves of the advantage you have over the Mahometans, with respect to the manner in which their religion was established. When they boast of the number of their believers, you tell them that they have obtained them by violence, and that they have extended their religion by the sword; why then do you establish yours by fire?

"When you would bring us over to you, we object to a source from which you glory to have descended. You reply to us, that though your religion is new, it is divine; and you prove it from its growing amidst the persecutions of Pagans, and when watered by the blood of your martyrs; but at present you play the part of the Diocletians, and make us take yours.

"We conjure you, not by the mighty God whom both you and we serve, but by that Christ, who, you tell us, took upon him a human form, to propose himself as an example for you to follow; we conjure you to behave to us as he himself would behave were he upon earth. You would have us become Christians, and you will not be so yourselves.

"But if you will not be Christians, be at least men; treat us as you would, if having only the weak light of justice which nature bestows, you had not a religion to conduct, and a revelation to enlighten you.

"If heaven has had so great a love for you as to make you see the truth, you have received a singular favor; but is it for children who have received the inheritance of their father, to hate those who have not?

"If you have this truth, hide it not from us by the manner in which you propose it. The characteristic of truth is its triumph over hearts and minds, and not that impotency which you confess when you would force us to receive it by tortures.

"If you were wise, you would not put us to death for no other reason than because we are unwilling to deceive you. If your Christ is the son of God, we hope he will reward us for being so unwilling to profane his mysteries; and we believe that the God whom both you and we serve will not punish us for having suffered death for a religion which he formerly gave us, only because we believe that he still continues to give it.

"You live in an age in which the light of nature shines more brightly than it has ever done; in which philosophy has enlightened human understanding; in which the morality of your gospel has been better known; in which the respective rights of mankind with regard to each other and the empire which one conscience has over another are best understood. If you do not therefore shake off your ancient prejudices, which, whilst unregarded, mingle with your passions, it must be confessed that you are incorrigible, incapable of any degree of light or instruction; and a nation must be very unhappy that gives authority to such men.

"Would you have us frankly tell you our thoughts? You consider us rather as your enemies than as the enemies of your religion; for if you loved your religion you would not suffer it to be corrupted by such gross ignorance.

"It is necessary that we should warn you of one thing; that is, if any one in times to come shall dare to assert that in the age in which we live, the people of Europe were civilized, you will be cited to prove that they were barbarians; and the idea they will have of you will be such as will dishonor your age and spread hatred over all your contemporaries."

14. *Why the Christian Religion is so odious in Japan.*

We have already mentioned the perverse temper of the people of Japan. [1200] The magistrates considered the firmness which Christianity inspires, when they attempted to make the people renounce their faith, as in itself most dangerous; they fancied that it increased their obstinacy. The law of Japan punishes severely the least disobedience. The people were ordered to renounce the Christian religion; they did not renounce it; this was disobedience; the magistrates punished this crime; and the continuance in disobedience seemed to deserve another punishment.

[1200] Book VI. chap. 24.

Punishments among the Japanese are considered as the revenge of an insult done to the prince; the songs of triumph sung by our martyrs appeared as an outrage against him: the title of martyr provoked the magistrates; in their opinion it signified rebel; they did all in their power to prevent their obtaining it. Then it was that their minds were exasperated, and a horrid struggle was seen between the tribunals that condemned and the accused who suffered; between the civil laws and those of religion.

15. *Of the Propagation of Religion.*

All the people of the East, except the Mahometans, believe all religions in themselves indifferent. They fear the establishment of another religion no otherwise than as a change in government. Among the Japanese, where there are many sects, and where the state has had for so long a time an ecclesiastical superior, they never dispute on religion. [1201] It is the same with the people of Siam. [1202] The Calmucks [1203] do more; they make it a point of conscience to tolerate every species of religion; at Calicut it is a maxim of the state that every religion is good. [1204]

[1201] See Kempfer.
[1202] Forbin, Memoirs.
[1203] History of the Tartars, part V.
[1204] Pirard, Travels.

But it does not follow hence, that a religion brought from a far distant country, and quite different in climate, laws, manners, and customs, will have all the success to which its holiness might entitle it. This is more particularly true in great despotic empires: here strangers are tolerated at first, because there is no attention given to what does not seem to strike at the authority of the prince. As they are extremely ignorant, a European may render himself agreeable by the knowledge he communicates: this is very well in the beginning. But as soon as he has any success, when disputes arise and when men who have some interest become informed of it, as their empire, by its very nature, above all things requires tranquility, and as the least disturbance may overturn it, they proscribe the new religion and those who preach, it: disputes between the preachers breaking out, they begin to entertain a distaste for a religion on which even those who propose it are not agreed.

BOOK XXVI.

OF LAWS IN RELATION TO THE ORDER
OF THINGS WHICH THEY DETERMINE

1. *Idea of this Book.*

Men are governed by several kinds of laws; by the law of nature; by the divine law, which is that of religion; by ecclesiastical, otherwise called canon law, which is that of religious polity; by the law of nations, which may be considered as the civil law of the whole globe, in which sense every nation is a citizen; by the general political law, which relates to that human wisdom whence all societies derive their origin; by the particular political law, the object of which is each society; by the law of conquest founded on this, that one nation has been willing and able, or has had a right to offer violence to another; by the civil law of every society, by which a citizen may defend his possessions and his life against the attacks of any other citizen; in fine, by domestic law, which proceeds from a society's being divided into several families, all which have need of a particular government.

There are therefore different orders of laws, and the sublimity of human reason consists in perfectly knowing to which of these orders the things that are to be determined ought to have a principal relation, and not to throw into confusion those principles which should govern mankind.

2. *Of Laws divine and human.*

We ought not to decide by divine laws what should be decided by human laws; nor determine by human what should be determined by divine laws.

These two sorts of laws differ in their origin, in their object, and in their nature.

It is universally acknowledged, that human laws are, in their own nature, different from those of religion; this is an important principle: but this principle is itself subject to others, which must be inquired into.

1. It is in the nature of human laws to be subject to all the accidents which can happen, and to vary in proportion as the will of man changes; on the contrary, by the nature of the laws of religion, they are never to vary. Human laws appoint for some good; those of religion for the best: good may have another object, because there are many kinds of good; but the best is but one; it cannot therefore change. We may alter laws, because they are reputed no more than good; but the institutions of religion are always supposed to be the best.

2. There are kingdoms in which the laws are of no value as they depend only on the capricious and fickle humor of the sovereign. If in these kingdoms the laws of religion

were of the same nature as the human institutions, the laws of religion too would be of no value. It is however, necessary to the society that it should have something fixed; and it is religion that has this stability.

3. The influence of religion proceeds from its being believed; that of human laws from their being feared. Antiquity accords with religion, because we have frequently a firmer belief in things in proportion to their distance; for we have no ideas annexed to them drawn from those times which can contradict them. Human laws, on the contrary, receive advantage from their novelty, which implies the actual and particular attention of the legislator to put them in execution.

3. *Of civil Laws contrary to the Law of Nature.*

If a slave, says Plato, defends himself, and kills a freeman, he ought to be treated as a parricide. [1205] This is a civil law which punishes self-defense, though dictated by nature.

[1205] Lib. IX. on Laws.

The law of Henry VIII which condemned a man without being confronted by witnesses was contrary to self-defense. In order to pass sentence of condemnation, it is necessary that the witnesses should know whether the man against whom they make their deposition is he whom they accuse, and that this man be at liberty to say, "I am not the person you mean."

The law passed during the same reign, which condemned every woman, who, having carried on a criminal commerce did not declare it to the king before she married him, violated the regard due to natural modesty. It is as unreasonable to oblige a woman to make this declaration, as to oblige a man not to attempt the defense of his own life.

The law of Henry II which condemned the woman to death who lost her child, in case she did not make known her pregnancy to the magistrate, was not less contrary to self-defense. It would have been sufficient to oblige her to inform one of her nearest relatives, who might watch over the preservation of the infant.

What other information could she give in this situation, so torturing to natural modesty? Education has heightened the notion of preserving that modesty; and in those critical moments scarcely has she any idea remaining of the loss of life.

There has been much talk of a law in England which permitted girls seven years old to choose a husband. [1206] This law was shocking in two ways; it had no regard to the time when nature gives maturity to the understanding, nor to that in which she gives maturity to the body.

[1206] M. Bayle, in his Criticism on the History of Calvinism, speaks of this law, p. 263.

Among the Romans, a father might oblige his daughter to repudiate her husband, though he himself had consented to the marriage. [1207] But it is contrary to nature for a divorce to be in the power of a third person.

[1207] See Law 5. Cod. *de repudiis et judicio de moribus sublato.*

A divorce can be agreeable to nature only when it is by consent of the two parties, or at least of one of them; but when neither consents it is a monstrous separation. In short, the power of divorce can be given only to those who feel the inconveniences of marriage, and who are sensible of the moment when it is for their interest to make them cease.

4. *The same Subject continued.*

Gundebald, King of Burgundy, decreed that if the wife or son of a person guilty of robbery did not reveal the crime, they were to become slaves. [1208] This was contrary to nature: a wife to inform against her husband! a son to accuse his father! To avenge one criminal action, they ordained another still more criminal.

[1208] Law of the Burgundians, tit. 47.

The law of Recessuinthus permits the children of the adulteress, or those of her husband, to accuse her, and to put the slaves of the house to the torture. [1209] How iniquitous the law which, to preserve a purity of morals overturns nature, the origin, the source of all morality!

[1209] In the Code of the Visigoths, lib. III, tit. 4, § 13.

With pleasure we behold in our theatres a young hero [1210] express as much horror against the discovery of his mother-in-law's guilt, as against the guilt itself. In his surprise, though accused, judged, condemned, proscribed, and covered with infamy, he scarcely dares to reflect on the abominable blood whence Phædra sprang; he abandons the most tender object, all that is most dear, all that lies nearest his heart, all that can fill him with rage, to deliver himself up to the unmerited vengeance of the gods. It is nature's voice, the sweetest of all sounds, that inspires us with this pleasure.

[1210] Hippolyte, see the *Phèdre* of Racine, act. IV. sc. 2.—Ed.

5. *Cases in which we may judge by the Principles of the civil Law in limiting the Principles of the Law of Nature.*

An Athenian law obliged children to provide for their fathers when fallen into poverty; [1211] it excepted those who were born of a courtesan, [1212] those whose chastity had been infamously prostituted by their father, and those to whom he had not given any means of gaining a livelihood [1213]

[1211] Under pain of infamy, another under pain of imprisonment.
[1212] Plutarch, Life of Solon.
[1213] Plutarch, Life of Solon, and Gallienus, in *Exhort. ad Art.*, chap. 8.

The law considered that, in the first case, the father being uncertain, he had rendered the natural obligation precarious; that in the second, he had sullied the life he had given, and done the greatest injury he could do to his children in depriving them of their reputation; that in the third, he had rendered insupportable a life which had no means of subsistence. The law suspended the natural obligation of children because the father had violated his; it looked upon the father and the son as no more than two citizens, and determined in respect to them only from civil and political views; ever considering that a good republic ought to have a particular regard to manners. I am apt to think that Solon's law was a wise regulation in the first two cases, whether that in which nature has left the son in ignorance with regard to his father, or that in which she even seems to ordain he should not own him; but it cannot be approved with respect to the third, where the father had only violated a civil institution.

6. *That the Order of succession or Inheritance depends on the Principles of political or civil Law, and not on those of the Law of Nature.*

The Voconian law ordained that no woman should be left heiress to an estate, not even if she had an only child. Never was there a law, says St. Augustine, more unjust. [1214] A formula of Marculfus treats that custom as impious which deprives daughters of the right of succeeding to the estate of their fathers. [1215] Justinian gives the appellation of barbarous to the right which the males had formerly of succeeding in prejudice to the daughters. [1216] These notions proceeded from their having considered the right of children to succeed to their father's possessions as a consequence of the law of nature; which it is not.

[1214] *De Civitate Dei*, lib. IV.
[1215] Lib. II. chap. 12.
[1216] Novell. 21.

The law of nature ordains that fathers shall provide for their children; but it does not oblige them to make them their heirs. The division of property, the laws of this division, and the succession after the death of the person who has had this division can be regulated only by the community, and consequently by political or civil laws.

True it is that a political or civil order frequently demands that children should succeed to their father's estate; but it does not always make this necessary.

There may be some reasons given why the laws of our fiefs appoint that the eldest of the males, or the nearest relatives of the male side, should have all, and the females nothing, and why, by the laws of the Lombards, [1217] the sisters, the natural children, the other relatives; and, in their default, the treasury might share the inheritance with the daughters.

[1217] Lib. II, tit. 14, § 6, 7, and 8.

It was regulated in some of the dynasties of China that the brothers of the emperor should succeed to the throne, and that the children should not. If they were willing that the prince should have a certain degree of experience, if they feared his being too young, and if it had become necessary to prevent eunuchs from placing children successively on the throne, they might very justly establish a like order of succession, and when some writers have treated these brothers as usurpers, they have judged only by ideas received from the laws of their own countries. [1218]

[1218] Father Du Halde on the Second Dynasty.

According to the custom of Numidia, [1219] Desalces, brother of Gala, succeeded to the kingdom; not Massinissa, his son. And even to this day, among the Arabs in Barbary, where each village has its chief, they adhere to this ancient custom, by choosing the uncle, or some other relative to succeed. [1220]

[1219] Livy, Decad. 3, lib. VI.
[1220] Shaw, Travels, vol. i, p. 402.

There are monarchies merely elective; and since it is evident that the order of succession ought to be derived from the political or civil laws, it is for these to decide in what cases it is agreeable to reason that the succession be granted to children, and in what cases it ought to be given to others.

In countries where polygamy is established, the prince has many children; and the number of them is much greater in some of these countries than in others. There are states [1221] where it is impossible for the people to maintain the children of the king; they might therefore make it a law that the crown shall devolve, not on the king's children, but on those of his sister.

[1221] See the Collection of Voyages that Contributed to the Establishment of the East India Company, vol. iv, part I, p. 114. And Mr. Smith, Voyage to Guinea, part II, p. 150, concerning the kingdom of Judia.

A prodigious number of children would expose the state to the most dreadful civil wars. The order of succession which gives the crown to the children of the sister, the number of whom is not larger than those of a prince who has only one wife, must prevent these inconveniences.

There are people among whom reasons of state, or some maxims of religion, have made it necessary that the crown should be always fixed in a certain family: hence, in India, proceeds the jealousy of their tribes, [1222] and the fear of losing the descent; they have there conceived that never to want princes of the blood royal, they ought to take the children of the eldest sister of the king.

[1222] See Edifying Letters, coll. xiv, and the Voyages that Contributed to the Establishment of the East India Company, vol. iii, part II, p. 644.

A general maxim: it is an obligation of the law of nature to provide for our children; but to make them our successors is an obligation of the civil or political law. Hence are derived the different regulations with respect to bastards in the different countries of the world; these are according to the civil or political laws of each country.

7. That we ought not to decide by the Precepts of Religion what belongs only to the Law of Nature.

The Abassines have a most severe lent of fifty days, which weakens them to such a degree that for a long time they are incapable of business: the Turks do not fail to attack them after their lent. [1223] Religion ought, in favor of the natural right of self-defense, to set bounds to these customs.

[1223] Collection of Voyages that Contributed to the Establishment of the East India Company, vol. iv, part I, pp. 35, 103.

The Jews were obliged to keep the Sabbath; but it was an instance of great stupidity in this nation not to defend themselves when their enemies chose to attack them on this day. [1224]

[1224] As they did when Pompey besieged the Temple. Dio, XXXVII.—Ed.

Cambyses, laying siege to Pelusium, set in the first rank a great number of those animals which the Egyptians regarded as sacred; the consequence was that the soldiers of the garrison durst not molest them. Who does not see that self-defense is a duty superior to every precept?

8. *That we ought not to regulate by the Principles of the canon Law Things which should be regulated by those of the civil Law.*

By the civil law of the Romans, [1225] he who took a thing privately from a sacred place was punished only for the guilt of theft; by the canon law, he was punished for the crime of sacrilege. [1226] The canon law takes cognizance of the place; the civil laws of the fact. But to attend only to the place is neither to reflect on the nature and definition of a theft, nor on the nature and definition of sacrilege.

[1225] Leg. ff. *ad. leg. Juliam peculatus.*
[1226] Chap. quisquis 17, quæstione 4. *Cujas*, Observat., lib. XIII. 19, tom. iii.

As the husband may demand a separation by reason of the infidelity of his wife, the wife might formerly demand it on account of the infidelity of the husband. [1227] This custom, contrary to a regulation made in the Roman laws, [1228] was introduced into the ecclesiastic court, [1229] where nothing was regarded but the maxims of canon law; and indeed, if we consider marriage as a thing merely spiritual, and as relating only to the things of another life, the violation is in both cases the same, but the political and civil laws of almost all nations have, with reason, made a distinction between them. They have required from the women a degree of reserve and continency which they have not exacted from the men, because in women, a violation of chastity supposes a renunciation of all virtue; because women, by violating the laws of marriage, quit the state of their natural dependence; because nature has marked the infidelity of women with certain signs; and, in fine, because the children of the wife born in adultery necessarily belong and are an expense to the husband, while the children produced by the adultery of the husband are not the wife's, nor are an expense to the wife.

[1227] Beaumanoir, Ancient Customs of Beauvoisis, chap. xviii.
[1228] Law of the first code. *ad. leg. Jul. de adulteriis.*
[1229] At present they do not take cognizance of these things in France.

9. *That Things which ought to be regulated by the Principles of civil Law can seldom be regulated by those of Religion.*

The laws of religion have a greater sublimity; the civil laws a greater extent.

The laws of perfection drawn from religion have more in view the goodness of the person that observes them than of the society in which they are observed; the civil laws, on the contrary, have more in view the moral goodness of men in general than that of individuals.

Thus, venerable as those ideas are which immediately spring from religion, they ought not always to serve as a first principle to the civil laws; because these have another, the general welfare of society.

The Romans made regulations among themselves to preserve the morals of their women; these were political institutions. Upon the establishment of monarchy, they made civil laws on this head, and formed them on the principles of their civil government. When the Christian religion became predominant, the new laws that were then made had less relation to the general rectitude of morals than to the holiness of marriage; they had less regard to the union of the two sexes in a civil than in a spiritual state.

At first, by the Roman law, a husband, who brought back his wife into his house after she had been found guilty of adultery, was punished as an accomplice in her debauch. [1230] Justinian, from other principles, ordained that during the space of two years he might go and take her again out of the monastery. [1231]

[1230] Leg. 11, § ult., ff. *ad. leg. Jul. de adulteriis.*
[1231] Nov. 134. Col. 9, chap. x, tit. 170.

Formerly, when a woman, whose husband was gone to war, heard no longer any tidings of him, she might easily marry again, because she had in her hands the power of making a divorce. The law of Constantine obliged the woman to wait four years, after which she might send the bill of divorce to the general; and, if her husband returned, he could not then charge her with adultery. [1232] But Justinian decreed that, let the time be never so long after the departure of her husband, she should not marry unless, by the deposition and oath of the general, she could prove the death of her husband. [1233] Justinian had in view the indissolubility of marriage; but we may safely say that he had it too much in view. He demanded a positive proof when a negative one was sufficient; he required a thing extremely difficult to give, an account of the fate of a man at a great distance, and exposed to so many accidents; he presumed a crime, that is, a desertion of the husband, when it was so natural to presume his death. He injured the commonwealth by obliging women to live out of marriage; he injured individuals by exposing them to a thousand dangers.

[1232] Leg. 7, *de repudiis, et judicio de morib. sublato.*
[1233] Auth. hodie quantiscumque. cod. *de repudiis.*

The law of Justinian, which ranked among the causes of divorce the consent of the husband and wife to enter into a monastery, was entirely opposite to the principles of the civil laws. [1234] It is natural that the causes of divorce should have their origin in certain impediments which could not be foreseen before marriage; but this desire of preserving chastity might be foreseen, since it is in ourselves. This law favors inconstancy in a state which is by its very nature perpetual; it shook the fundamental principle of divorce, which permits the dissolution of one marriage only from the hope of another. In short, if we view it in a religious light, it is no more than giving victims to God without a sacrifice.

[1234] Auth. quod hodie. cod. *de repudiis.*

10. *In what Case we ought to follow the civil Law which permits, and not the Law of Religion which forbids.*

When a religion which prohibits polygamy is introduced into a country where it is permitted, we cannot believe (speaking only as a politician) that the laws of the country ought to suffer a man who has many wives to embrace this religion; unless the magistrate or the husband should indemnify them, by restoring them in some way or other to their civil state. Without this their condition would be deplorable; no sooner would they obey the laws than they would find themselves deprived of the greatest advantages of society.

11. *That human Courts of Justice should not be regulated by the Maxims of those Tribunals which relate to the Other Life.*

The tribunal of the inquisition, formed by the Christian monks on the idea of the tribunal of penitence, is contrary to all good policy. It has everywhere met with a general dislike, and must have sunk under the oppositions it met with, if those who were resolved to establish it had not drawn advantages even from these oppositions.

This tribunal is insupportable in all governments. In monarchies, it only makes informers and traitors; in republics, it only forms dishonest men; in a despotic state, it is as destructive as the government itself.

12. *The same Subject continued.*

It is one abuse of this tribunal that, of two persons accused of the same crime, he who denies is condemned to die; and he who confesses avoids the punishment. This has its source in monastic ideas, where he who denies seems in a state of impenitence and damnation; and he who confesses, in a state of repentance and salvation. But a distinction of this kind can have no relation to human tribunals. Human justice, which sees only the actions, has but one compact with men, namely, that of innocence; divine justice, which sees the thoughts, has two, that of innocence and repentance.

13. *In what Cases, with regard to Marriage, we ought to follow the Laws of Religion; and in what Cases we should follow the civil Laws.*

It has happened in all ages and countries, that religion has been blended with marriages. When certain things have been considered as impure or unlawful, and had nevertheless become necessary, they were obliged to call in religion to legitimate in the one case, and to reprove in others.

On the other hand, as marriage is of all human actions that in which society is most interested, it became proper that this should be regulated by the civil laws.

Everything which relates to the nature of marriage, its form, the manner of contracting it, the fruitfulness it occasions, which has made all nations consider it as the object of a particular benediction, a benediction which, not being always annexed to it, is supposed to depend on certain superior graces; all this is within the resort of religion.

The consequences of this union with regard to property, the reciprocal advantages, everything which has a relation to the new family, to that from which it sprang, and to that which is expected to arise; all this relates to the civil laws.

As one of the great objects of marriage is to take away that uncertainty which attends unlawful conjunctions, religion here stamps its seal, and the civil laws join theirs to it, to the end that it may be as authentic as possible. Thus, besides the conditions required by religion to make a marriage valid, the civil laws may still exact others.

The civil laws receive this power from their being additional obligations, and not contradictory ones. The law of religion insists upon certain ceremonies, the civil laws on the consent of fathers; in this case, they demand something more than that of religion, but they demand nothing contrary to it.

It follows hence, that the religious law must decide whether the bond be indissoluble or not; for if the laws of religion had made the bond indissoluble, and the civil laws had declared it might be broken, they would be contradictory to each other.

Sometimes the regulations made by the civil laws with respect to marriage are not absolutely necessary; such are those established by the laws, which, instead of annulling the marriage, only punish those who contract it.

Among the Romans, the Papian law declared those marriages illegal which had been prohibited, and yet only subjected them to a penalty; [1235] but a Senatus Consultum, made at the instance of the Emperor Marcus Antoninus, declared them void; there then no longer subsisted any such thing as a marriage, wife, dowry, or husband. [1236] The civil laws determine according to circumstances: sometimes they are most attentive to repair the evil; at others, to prevent it.

[1235] See what has been said on this subject, in book XXIII. chap. 21, in the relation they bear to the number of inhabitants.
[1236] See Leg. 16, ff. *de ritu nuptiarum*, and Leg. 3, § 1; also Dig. *de donationibus inter virum et uxorem.*

14. *In what instances Marriages between Relatives shall be regulated by the Laws of Nature: and in what instances by the civil Laws.*

With regard to the prohibition of marriage between relatives, it is a thing extremely delicate to fix exactly the point at which the laws of nature stop and where the civil laws begin. For this purpose we must establish some principles.

The marriage of the son with the mother confounds the state of things: the son ought to have an unlimited respect for his mother, the wife an unlimited respect for her husband; therefore the marriage of the mother to her son would subvert the natural state of both.

Besides, nature has forwarded in women the time in which they are able to have children, but has retarded it in men; and, for the same reason, women sooner lose this ability and men later. If the marriage between the mother and the son were permitted, it would almost always be the case that when the husband was capable of entering into the views of nature, the wife would be incapable.

The marriage between the father and the daughter is contrary to nature, as well as the other; but it is not less contrary, because it has not these two obstacles. Thus the Tartars, who may marry their daughters, [1237] never marry their mothers, as we see in the accounts we have of that nation. [1238]

[1237] This law is very ancient among them. Attila, says Priscus, in his embassy stopped in a certain place to marry Esca his daughter. *A thing permitted*, he adds, *by the laws of the Scythians*, p. 22.
[1238] History of the Tartars, part III, p. 236.

It has ever been the natural duty of fathers to watch over the chastity of their children. Entrusted with the care of their education, they are obliged to preserve the body in the greatest perfection, and the mind from the least corruption; to encourage whatever has a tendency to inspire them with virtuous desires, and to nourish a becoming tenderness. Fathers, always employed in preserving the morals of their children, must have a natural aversion to everything that can render them corrupt. Marriage, you will say, is not a corruption; but before marriage they must speak, they must make their persons beloved, they must seduce; it is this seduction which ought to inspire us with horror.

There should be therefore an insurmountable barrier between those who ought to give the education, and those who are to receive it, in order to prevent every kind of corruption, even though the motive be lawful. Why do fathers so carefully deprive those who are to marry their daughters of their company and familiarity?

The horror that arises against the incest of the brother with the sister should proceed from the same source. The desire of fathers and mothers to preserve the morals of their children and families untainted is sufficient to inspire their offspring with a detestation of everything that can lead to the union of the two sexes.

The prohibition of marriage between cousins-german has the same origin. In the early ages, that is, in the times of innocence, in the ages when luxury was unknown, it was customary for children [1239] upon their marriage not to remove from their parents, but settle in the same house; as a small habitation was at that time sufficient for a large family; the children of two brothers, or cousins-german, [1240] were considered both by others and themselves as brothers. The estrangement then between the brothers and sisters as to marriage subsisted also between the cousins-german. [1241] These principles are so strong and no natural that they have had their influence almost over all the earth, independently of any communication. It was not the Romans who taught the inhabitants of Formosa [1242] that the marriage of relatives of the fourth degree was incestuous; it was not the Romans that communicated this sentiment to the Arabs; [1243] it was not they who taught it to the inhabitants of the Maldivian islands. [1244]

[1239] It was thus among the ancient Romans.
[1240] Among the Romans they had the same name; the cousins-german were called brothers.
[1241] It was thus at Rome in the first ages, till the people made a law to permit them; they were willing to favor a man extremely popular, who had married his cousin-german. Plutarch's treatise entitled Questions Concerning the Affairs of the Romans.
[1242] Collection of Voyages to the Indies, vol. v, part 1. An account of the state of the isle of Formosa.

[1243] Koran, chapter on Women.
[1244] See Francis Pirard.

But if some nations have not rejected marriages between fathers and children, sisters and brothers, we have seen in the first book, that intelligent beings do not always follow the law of nature. Who could have imagined it! Religious ideas have frequently made men fall into these mistakes. If the Assyrians and the Persians married their mothers, the first were influenced by a religious respect for Semiramis, and the second did it because the religion of Zoroaster gave a preference to these marriages. [1245] If the Egyptians married their sisters, it proceeded from the wildness of the Egyptian religion, which consecrated these marriages in honor of Isis. As the spirit of religion leads us to attempt whatever is great and difficult, we cannot infer that a thing is natural from its being consecrated by a false religion.

[1245] They were considered as more honorable. See Philo, *de specialibus legib. quæ pertinet ad præcepta decalogi.* Paris, 1640, p. 778.

The principle which informs us that marriages between fathers and children, between brothers and sisters, are prohibited in order to preserve natural modesty in families will help us to the discovery of those marriages that are forbidden by the law of nature, and of those which can be so only by the civil law.

As children dwell, or are supposed to dwell in their father's house, and consequently the son-in-law with the mother-in-law, the father-in-law with the daughter-in-law, or wife's daughter, the marriage between them is forbidden by the law of nature, in this case the resemblance has the same effect as the reality, because it springs from the same cause; the civil law neither can, nor ought to permit these marriages.

There are nations, as we have already observed, among whom cousins-german are considered as brothers, because they commonly dwell in the same house; there are others where this custom is not known. Among the first the marriage of cousins-german ought to be regarded as contrary to nature; not so among the others.

But the laws of nature cannot be local. Therefore, when these marriages are forbidden or permitted, they are, according to the circumstances, permitted or forbidden by a civil law.

It is not a necessary custom for the brother-in-law and the sister-in-law to dwell in the same house. The marriage between them is not then prohibited to preserve chastity in the family; and the law which forbids or permits it is not a law of nature, but a civil law, regulated by circumstances and dependent on the customs of each country: these are cases in which the laws depend on the morals, or customs of the inhabitants.

The civil laws forbid marriages when by the customs received in a certain country they are found to be in the same circumstances as those forbidden by the law of nature; and they permit them when this is not the case. The prohibitions of the laws of nature are invariable, because the thing on which they depend is invariable; the father, the mother and the children necessarily dwell in the same house. But the prohibitions of the civil laws are accidental because they depend on an accidental circumstance, cousins-german and others dwelling in the house by accident.

This explains why the laws of Moses, those of the Egyptians, [1246] and of many other nations permitted the marriage of the brother-in-law with the sister-in-law; whilst these very marriages were disallowed by other nations.

[1246] See Law 8, Cod. *de incestis et inutilibus nuptiis.*

In the Indies they have a very natural reason for admitting this sort of marriages. The uncle is there considered as the father and is obliged to maintain and educate his nephew as if he were his own child; this proceeds from the disposition of this people, which is good-natured and full of humanity. This law or this custom has produced another; if a husband has lost his wife, he does not fail to marry her sister: [1247] which is extremely natural, for his new consort becomes the mother of her sister's children, and not a cruel stepmother.

[1247] Edifying Letters, 4th, p. 403.

15. *That we should not regulate by the Principles of political Law those Things which depend on the Principles of civil Law.*

As men have given up their natural independence to live under political laws, they have given up the natural community of goods to live under civil laws.

By the first, they acquired liberty; by the second, property. We should not decide by the laws of liberty, which, as we have already said, is only the government of the community, what ought to be decided by the laws concerning property. It is a paralogism to say that the good of the individual should give way to that of the public; this can never take place, except when the government of the community, or, in other words, the liberty of the subject is concerned; this does not affect such cases as relate to private property, because the public good consists in every one's having his property, which was given him by the civil laws, invariably preserved.

Cicero maintains that the Agrarian laws were unjust; because the community was established with no other view than that every one might be able to preserve his property.

Let us, therefore, lay down a certain maxim, that whenever the public good happens to be the matter in question, it is not for the advantage of the public to deprive an individual of his property, or even to retrench the least part of it by a law, or a political regulation. In this case we should follow the rigor of the civil law, which is the *Palladium* of property.

Thus when the public has occasion for the estate of an individual, it ought never to act by the rigor of political law; it is here that the civil law ought to triumph, which, with the eyes of a mother, regards every individual as the whole community.

If the political magistrate would erect a public edifice, or make a new road, he must indemnify those who are injured by it; the public is in this respect like an individual who treats with an individual. It is fully enough that it can oblige a citizen to sell his inheritance, and that it can strip him of this great privilege which he holds from the civil law, the not being forced to alienate his possessions.

After the nations which subverted the Roman empire had abused their very conquests, the spirit of liberty called them back to that of equity. They exercised the most barbarous laws with moderation: and if any one should doubt the truth of this, he need only read Beaumanoir's admirable work on jurisprudence, written in the twelfth century.

They mended the highways in his time as we do at present. He says, that when a highway could not be repaired, they made a new one as near the old as possible; but indemnified the proprietors at the expense of those who reaped any advantage from the road. [1248] They determined at that time by the civil law; in our days, we determine by the law of politics.

[1248] "The lord appointed collectors to receive the toll from the peasant, the gentlemen were obliged to contribute by the count, and the clergy to the bishop."—Beaumanoir, chap. xxii.

16. *That we ought not to decide by the Rules of the civil Law when it is proper to decide by those of the political Law.*

Most difficulties on this subject may be easily solved by not confounding the rules derived from property with those which spring from liberty.

Is the demesne of a state or government alienable, or is it not? This question ought to be decided by the political law, and not by the civil. It ought not to be decided by the civil law, because it is as necessary that there should be demesnes for the subsistence of a state, as that the state should have civil laws to regulate the disposal of property.

If then they alienate the demesne, the state will be forced to make a new fund for another. But this expedient overturns the political government, because, by the nature of the thing, for every demesne that shall be established, the subject will always be obliged to pay more, and the sovereign to receive less; in a word, the demesne is necessary, and the alienation is not.

The order of succession is, in monarchies, founded on the welfare of the state; this makes it necessary that such an order should be fixed to avoid the misfortunes, which I have said must arise in a despotic kingdom, where all is uncertain, because all is arbitrary.

The order of succession is not fixed for the sake of the reigning family; but because it is the interest of the state that it should have a reigning family. The law which regulates the succession of individuals is a civil law, whose view is the interest of individuals; that which regulates the succession to monarchy is a political law, which has in view the welfare and preservation of the kingdom.

It follows hence, that when the political law has established an order of succession in government, and this order is at an end, it is absurd to reclaim the succession in virtue of the civil law of any nation whatsoever. One particular society does not make laws for another society. The civil laws of the Romans are no more applicable than any other civil laws. They themselves did not make use of them when they proceeded against kings; and the maxims by which they judged kings are so abominable that they ought never to be revived.

It follows also hence, that when the political law has obliged a family to renounce the succession, it is absurd to insist upon the restitutions drawn from the civil law. Restitutions are in the law, and may be good against those who live in the law: but they are not proper for such as have been raised up for the law, and who live for the law.

It is ridiculous to pretend to decide the rights of kingdoms, of nations, and of the whole globe by the same maxims on which (to make use of an expression of Cicero) [1249] we should determine the right of a gutter between individuals.

[1249] Lib. I. of Laws.

17. *The same Subject continued.*

Ostracism ought to be examined by the rules of politics, and not by those of the civil law; and so far is this custom from rendering a popular government odious, that it is, on the contrary, extremely well adapted to prove its lenity. We should be sensible of this ourselves, if, while banishment is always considered among us as a penalty, we are able to separate the idea of ostracism from that of punishment.

Aristotle [1250] tells us, it is universally allowed, that this practice has something in it both humane and popular. If in those times and places where this sentence was executed they found nothing in it that appeared odious; is it for us who see things at such a distance to think otherwise than the accuser, the judges and the accused themselves?

[1250] Repub. lib. III. cap 13.

And if we consider that this judgment of the people loaded the person with glory on whom it was passed; that when at Athens it fell upon a man without merit, [1251] from that very moment they ceased to use it; [1252] we shall find that numbers of people have obtained a false idea of it; for it was an admirable law that could prevent the ill consequences which the glory of a citizen might produce by loading him with new glory.

[1251] Hyperbolus. See Plutarch, Life of Aristides.
[1252] It was found opposite to the spirit of the legislator.

18. *That it is necessary to inquire whether the Laws*
which seem contradictory are of the same Class.

At Rome the husband was permitted to lend his wife to another. Plutarch tells us this in express terms. [1253] We know that Cato lent his wife to Hortensius, [1254] and Cato was not a man to violate the laws of his country.

[1253] Plutarch in his comparison between Lycurgus and Numa.
[1254] Plutarch, Life of Cato.

On the other hand, a husband who suffered his wife to be debauched, who did not bring her to justice, or who took her again after her condemnation was punished. [1255] These laws seem to contradict each other, and yet are not contradictory. The law which permitted a Roman to lend his wife was visibly a Lacedæmonian institution, established with a view of giving the republic children of a good species, if I may be allowed the term; the other had in view the preservation of morals. The first was a law of politics, the second a civil law.

[1255] Leg. 11 § ult., ff. *ad. leg. Jul. de adulteriis.*

19. *That we should not decide those Things by the civil Law which ought to be decided by domestic Laws.*

The law of the Visigoths enjoins that the slaves of the house shall be obliged to bind the man and woman they surprise in adultery, and to present them to the husband and to the judge: [1256] a terrible law, which puts into the hands of such mean persons, the care of public, domestic, and private vengeance!

[1256] Law of the Visigoths, Lib. III, tit. 4, § 6.

This law can be nowhere proper but in the seraglios of the East, where the slave who has the charge of the enclosure is deemed an accomplice upon the discovery of the least infidelity. He seizes the criminals, not so much with a view to bring them to justice, as to do justice to himself, and to obtain a scrutiny into the circumstances of the action, in order to remove the suspicion of his negligence.

But, in countries where women are not guarded, it is ridiculous to subject those who govern the family to the inquisition of their slaves.

This inquisition may, in certain cases, be at the most a particular domestic regulation, but never a civil law.

20. *That we ought not to decide by the Principles of the civil Laws those Things which belong to the Law of Nations.*

Liberty consists principally in not being forced to do a thing, where the laws do not oblige: people are in this state only as they are governed by civil laws; and because they live under those civil laws, they are free.

It follows hence, that princes who live not among themselves under civil laws are not free; they are governed by force; they may continually force, or be forced. Hence it follows that treaties made by force are as obligatory as those made by free consent. When we, who live under civil laws, are, contrary to law, constrained to enter into a contract, we may, by the assistance of the law, recover from the effects of violence: but a prince, who is always in that state in which he forces, or is forced, cannot complain of a treaty which he has been compelled to sign. This would be to complain of his natural state; it would seem as if he would be a prince with respect to other princes, and as if other princes should be subjects with respect to him; that is, it would be contrary to the nature of things.

21. *That we should not decide by political Laws Things which belong to the Law of Nations.*

Political laws demand that every man be subject to the natural and civil courts of the country where he resides, and to the censure of the sovereign.

The law of nations requires that princes shall send ambassadors; and a reason drawn from the nature of things does not permit these ambassadors to depend either on the sovereign to whom they are sent, or on his tribunals. They are the voice of the prince who sends them, and this voice ought to be free; no obstacle should hinder the execution of their office: they may frequently offend, because they speak for a man entirely independent; they might be wrongfully accused, if they were liable to be punished for crimes: if they could be arrested for debts, these might be forged. Thus a prince, who has naturally a bold and enterprising spirit, would speak by the mouth of a man who had everything to fear. We must then be guided, with respect to ambassadors, by reasons drawn from the law of nations, and not by those derived from political law. But if they make an ill use of their representative character, a stop may be put to it by sending them back. They may even be accused before their master, who becomes either their judge or their accomplice.

22. *The unhappy State of the Inca Athualpa.*

The principles we have just been establishing were cruelly violated by the Spaniards. The Inca Athualpa [1257] could not be tried by the law of nations: they tried him by political and civil laws; they accused him for putting to death some of his own subjects, for having many wives &c., and to fill up the measure of their stupidity, they condemned him, not by the political and civil laws of his own country, but by the political and civil laws of theirs.

[1257] See *Garcilaso de la Vega*, p. 108.

23. *That when, by some Circumstance, the political Law becomes destructive to the State, we ought to decide by such a political Law as will preserve it, which sometimes becomes a Law of Nations.*

When that political law which has established in the kingdom a certain order of succession becomes destructive to the body politic for whose sake it was established, there is not the least room to doubt but another political law may be made to change this order; and so far would this law be from opposing the first that it would in the main be entirely conformable to it, since both would depend on this principle, that THE SAFETY OF THE PEOPLE IS THE SUPREME LAW.

I have said [1258] that a great state becoming accessory to another is itself weakened, and even weakens the principal. We know that it is for the interest of the state to have the supreme magistrate within itself, that the public revenues be well administered, and that its specie be not sent abroad to enrich another country. It is of importance that he who is to govern has not imbibed foreign maxims; these are less agreeable than those already established. Besides, men have an extravagant fondness for their own laws and customs: these constitute the happiness of every community; and, as we learn from the histories of all nations, are rarely changed without violent commotions and a great effusion of blood.

[1258] See book. V. chap. 14; book VIII. chap. 16; 17, 18, 19, and 20, book IX. chap. 4-7; and book X. chap. 9, 10.

It follows hence, that if a great state has for its heir the possessor of a great state, the former may reasonably exclude him, because a change in the order of succession must be of service to both countries. Thus a law of Russia, made in the beginning of the reign of Elizabeth, most wisely excluded from the possession of the crown every heir who possessed another monarchy; thus the law of Portugal disqualifies every stranger who lays claim to the crown by right of blood.

But if a nation may exclude, it may with greater reason be allowed a right to oblige a prince to renounce. If the people fear that a certain marriage will be attended with such consequences as shall rob the nation of its independence, or dismember some of its provinces, it may very justly oblige the contractors and their descendants to renounce all right over them; while he who renounces, and those to whose prejudice he renounces, have the less reason to complain, as the state might originally have made a law to exclude them.

24. *That the Regulations of the Police are of a different Class from other civil Laws.*

There are criminals whom the magistrate punishes, there are others whom he reproves. The former are subject to the power of the law, the latter to his authority: those are cut off from society; these they oblige to live according to the rules of society.

In the exercise of the *Police*, it is rather the magistrate who punishes, than the law; in the sentence passed on crimes, it is rather the law which punishes, than the magistrate. The business of the *Police* consists in affairs which arise every instant, and are commonly of a trifling nature: there is then but little need of formalities. The actions of the Police are quick; they are exercised over things which return every day: it would be therefore improper for it to inflict severe punishments. It is continually employed about minute particulars; great examples are therefore not designed for its purpose. It is governed rather by regulations than laws; those who are subject to its jurisdiction are incessantly under the eye of the magistrate: it is therefore his fault if they fall into excess. Thus we ought not to confound a flagrant violation of the laws, with a simple breach of the *Police*; these things are of a different order.

Hence it follows, that the laws of an Italian republic, [1259] where bearing fire-arms is punished as a capital crime and where it is not more fatal to make an ill use of them than to carry them, is not agreeable to the nature of things.

[1259] Venice.

It follows, moreover, that the applauded action of that emperor who caused a baker to be impaled whom he found guilty of a fraud, was the action of a sultan who knew not how to be just without committing an outrage on justice.

25. *That we should not follow the general Disposition of the civil Law, in things which ought to be subject to particular Rules drawn from their own Nature.*

Is it a good law that all civil obligations passed between sailors in a ship in the course of a voyage should be null? Francis Pirard tells us [1260] that, in his time, it was not observed by the Portuguese, though it was by the French. Men who are together only for a short time, who have no wants, since they are provided for by the prince; who have only one object in view, that of their voyage; who are no longer in society, but are only the inhabitants of a ship, ought not to contract obligations that were never introduced but to support the burden of civil society.

[1260] Chap. xiv. p. 12.

In the same spirit was the law of the Rhodians, made at a time when they always followed the coasts; it ordained that those who during a tempest stayed in a vessel should have ship and cargo, and those who quitted it should have nothing.

BOOK XXVII.

1. *Of the Origin and Revolutions of the Roman Laws on Successions.*

This affair derives its establishment from the most distant antiquity, and to penetrate to its foundation, permit me to search among the first laws of the Romans for what, I believe, nobody yet has been so happy as to discover.

We know that Romulus [1261] divided the land of his little kingdom among his subjects; it seems to me that hence the laws of Rome on successions were derived.

[1261] Dionysius Halicarnassus, lib. II. c. 3. Plutarch's comparison between Numa and Lycurgus.

The law of the division of lands made it necessary that the property of one family should not pass into another: hence it followed that there were but two orders of heirs established by law, the children and all the descendants that lived under the power of the father, whom they called *sui hæredes*, or his natural heirs; and, in their default, the nearest relatives on the male side, whom they called *agnati*. [1262]

[1262] *Ast si intestato moritur cui suus hæres nec extabit, agnatus proximus familiam habeto.* Fragment of the law of the Twelve Tables in Ulpian, the last title.

It followed likewise, that the relatives on the female side, whom they called *cognati*, ought not to succeed; they would have conveyed the estate into another family, which was not allowed.

Thence also it followed that the children ought not to succeed to the mother, nor the mother to her children; for this might carry the estate of one family into another. Thus we see them excluded by the law of the Twelve Tables: [1263] it called none to the succession but the *agnati*, and there was no agnation between the son and the mother.

[1263] See the Frag. Of Ulpian, § 8, tit. 26. *Institutes*, tit. 3, *In præmio ad S.C. Tertullianum.*

But it was indifferent whether the *suus hæres*, or, in default of such, the nearest by agnation, was male or female; because, as the relatives on the mother's side could not succeed, though a woman who was an heiress should happen to marry, yet the estate always returned into the family whence it came. On this account, the law of the Twelve Tables does not distinguish, whether the person who succeeded was male or female. [1264]

[1264] Paulus, lib. IV. Sentences, tit. 8, § 3.

This was the cause that, though the grandchildren by the son succeeded to the grandfather, the grandchildren by the daughter did not succeed; for, to prevent the estate from passing into another family, the *agnati* were preferred to them. Hence the daughter, and not her children, succeeded to the father. [1265]

[1265] *Institutes*, tit. lib. III.

Thus among the primitive Romans, the women succeeded, when this was agreeable to the law of the division of lands, and they did not succeed, when this might suffer by it.

Such were the laws of succession among the primitive Romans; and as these had a natural dependence on the constitution, and were derived from the division of lands, it is easy to perceive that they had not a foreign origin, and were not of the number of those brought into the republic by the deputies sent into the cities of Greece.

Dionysius Halicarnassus tells us [1266] that Servius Tullius, finding the laws of Romulus and Numa on the division of lands abolished, restored them, and made new ones to give the old a greater weight. We cannot therefore doubt but that the laws we have been speaking of, made in consequence of this division, were the work of these three Roman legislators.

[1266] Lib. IV, p. 276.

The order of succession having been established in consequence of a political law, no citizen was allowed to break in upon it by his private will; that is, in the first ages of Rome he had not the power of making a testament. Yet it would have been hard to deprive him, in his last moments, of the friendly commerce of kind and beneficent actions.

They therefore found a method of reconciling, in this respect; the laws with the desires of the individual. He was permitted to dispose of his substance in an assembly of the people; and thus every testament was; in some sort; an act of the legislative power.

The law of the Twelve Tables permitted the person who made his will to choose which citizen he pleased for his heir. The reason that induced the Roman laws so strictly to restrain the number of those who might succeed *ab intestato* was the law of the division of lands; and the reason why they extended so widely the power of the testator was that, as the father might sell his children, [1267] he might with greater reason deprive them of his substance. These were therefore different effects, since they flowed from different principles; and such is, in this respect, the spirit of the Roman laws.

[1267] Dionysius Halicarnassus proves, by a law of Numa, that the law which permitted a father to sell his son three times was made by Romulus, and not by the Decemvirs. —Lib. II.

The ancient laws of Athens did not suffer a citizen to make a will. Solon permitted it, with an exception to those who had children; [1268] and the legislators of Rome, filled with the idea of paternal power, allowed the making a will even to the prejudice of their children. It must be confessed that the ancient laws of Athens were more consistent than those of Rome. The indefinite permission of making a will which had been granted to the Romans, ruined little by little the political regulation on the division of lands; it was the principal thing that introduced the fatal difference between riches and poverty: many shares were united in the same person; some citizens had too much, and a multitude of others had nothing. Thus the people being continually deprived of their shares were incessantly calling out for a new distribution of lands. They demanded it in an age when the frugality, the parsimony and the poverty of the Romans were their distinguishing characteristics; as well as at a time when their luxury had become still more astonishing.

[1268] See Plutarch, Life of Solon.

Testaments being properly a law made in the assembly of the people, those who were in the army were thereby deprived of a testamentary power. The people therefore gave the soldiers the privilege of making before their companions [1269] the dispositions which should have been made before them. [1270]

[1269] This testament, called *in procinctu*, was different from that which they styled military, which was established only by the constitutions of the emperors. Leg. 1, ff. *de militari testamento*. This was one of the artifices by which they cajoled the soldiers.
[1270] This testament was not in writing, and it was without formality, *sine librâ et tabulis*, as Cicero says, *De Oratore*, lib. I.

The great assembly of the people met but twice a year; besides, both the people and the affairs brought before them were increased; they therefore judged it convenient to permit all the citizens to make their will before some Roman citizens of ripe age, who were to represent the body of the people; [1271] they took five citizens, [1272] in whose presence the inheritor purchased his family, that is, his inheritance, of the testator; [1273] another citizen brought a pair of scales to weigh the value; for the Romans, as yet, had no money. [1274]

[1271] *Institutes*, lib. II, tit. 10, § 1. Aulus Gellius, lib. XV. chap. 27. They called this form of testament *per æs et libram*.
[1272] Ulpian, tit. 10, § 2.
[1273] Theophilus, *Institutes*, lib. II, tit. 10.
[1274] Livy, lib. IV, *nondum argentum signatum erat*. He speaks of the time of the siege of Veii.

To all appearance these five citizens were to represent the five classes of the people; and they set no value on the sixth, as being composed of men who had no property.

We ought not to say, with Justinian, that these scales were merely imaginary; they became, indeed, imaginary in time, but were not so originally. Most of the laws, which afterwards regulated wills, were built on the reality of these scales: we find sufficient proof of this in the fragments of Ulpian. [1275] The deaf, the dumb, the prodigal, could not make a will: the deaf, because he could not hear the words of the buyer of the inheritance; the dumb, because he could not pronounce the terms of nomination; the prodigal, because as he was excluded from the management of all affairs, he could not sell his inheritance. I omit any further examples.

[1275] Tit. 20, § 13.

Wills being made in the assembly of the people were rather the acts of political than of civil laws, a public rather than a private right; whence it followed that the father, while his son was under his authority, could not give him leave to make a will.

Among most nations, wills are not subject to greater formalities than ordinary contracts; because both the one and the other are only expressions of the will of him who makes the contract, and both are equally a private right. But among the Romans, where testaments were derived from the public law, they were attended with much greater formalities than other affairs; [1276] and this is still the case in those provinces of France which are governed by the Roman law.

[1276] *Institutes*, lib. II, tit. 10, § 1.

Testaments being, as I have said, a law of the people, they ought to be made with the force of a command, and in such terms as are called *direct and imperative.* [1277] Hence a rule was formed, that they could neither give nor transmit an inheritance without making use of the imperative words: whence it followed, that they might very justly in certain cases make a substitution; [1278] and ordain, that the inheritance should pass to another heir; but that they could never make a fiduciary bequest, [1279] that is, charge any one in terms of entreaty to restore an inheritance, or a part of it, to another.

[1277] Let Titus be my heir.
[1278] Vulgar, pupillary, and exemplary.
[1279] Augustus, for particular reasons, first began to authorize the fiduciary bequest, which, in the Roman law, was called *fidei commissum. Institutes*, ii, tit. 23, *in præmio.*

When the father neither instituted his son his heir, nor disinherited him, the will was annulled; but it was valid, though he did not disinherit his daughter, nor institute her his heiress. The reason is plain: when he neither instituted nor disinherited his son, he did an injury to his grandson, who might have succeeded *ab intestato* to his father; but in neither instituting nor disinheriting his daughter, he did no injury to his daughter's children, who could not succeed *ab intestato* to their mother, because they were neither *sui hæredes*, nor *agnati.* [1280]

[1280] *Ad liberos matris intestatæ hæredit as*, leg. 12 Tab., *non pertinebat, quia, fœminæ suos hæredes non habent.* Ulpian, Fragment., tit. 26, § 7.

The laws of the ancient Romans concerning successions, being formed with the same spirit which dictated the division of lands, did not sufficiently restrain the riches of women; thus a door was left open to luxury, which is always inseparable from this sort of opulence. Between the second and third Punic war, they began to perceive the evil and made the Voconian law; [1281] but as they were induced to this by the most important considerations; as but few monuments have reached us that take notice of this law, and as it has hitherto been spoken of in a most confused manner, I shall endeavor to clear it up.

[1281] It was proposed by Quintus Voconius, tribune of the people, in the year 585 of Rome, 169 B.C. See Cicero, Second Oration against Verres. In the Epitome of Livy, lib. XLI we should read Voconius, instead of Voluminus.

Cicero has preserved a fragment, which forbids the instituting a woman an heiress, whether she was married or unmarried. [1282]

[1282] *Sanxit . . . . . ne quis hæredem virginem neve mulierem faceret.*—Cicero, Second Oration against Verres, 107.

The Epitome of Livy, where he speaks of this law, says no more: [1283] it appears from Cicero [1284] and St. Augustine [1285] that the daughter, though an only child, was comprehended in the prohibition.

[1283] *Legem tulit, ne quis hæredem mulierem institueret*—Lib. IV.
[1284] Second Oration against Verres.
[1285] Of City of God, lib. III.

Cato, the elder, contributed all in his power to get this law passed. [1286] Aulus Gellius cites a fragment of a speech, [1287] which he made on this occasion. By preventing the succession of women, his intent was to take away the source of luxury; as by undertaking the defense of the Oppian law, he intended to put a stop to luxury itself.

[1286] Epitome of Livy, lib. XL.
[1287] Lib. XXVII. chap. 6.

In the Institutes of Justinian [1288] and Theophilus, [1289] mention is made of a chapter of the Voconian law which limits the power of bequeathing. In reading these authors, everybody would imagine that this chapter was made to prevent the inheritance from being so exhausted by legacies as to render it unworthy of the heir's acceptance. But this was not the spirit of the Voconian law. We have just seen that they had in view the hindering women from inheriting an estate. The article of this law, which set bounds to the power of bequeathing entered into this view: for if people had been possessed of the liberty to bequeath as much as they pleased, the women might have received as legacies what they could not receive by succession.

[1288] Institutes, lib. III, tit. 22
[1289] Ibid.

The Voconian law was made to hinder the women from growing too wealthy; for this end it was necessary to deprive them of large inheritances, and not of such as were incapable of supporting luxury. The law fixed a certain sum to be given to the women whom it deprived of the succession. Cicero, [1290] from whom we have this particular, does not tell us what was the sum; but by Dio we are informed it was a hundred thousand sesterces. [1291]

[1290] "Nemo censuit plus Fadiæ dandum, quam posset ad cam lege Voconia pervenire." *De finibus boni et mali*, lib. VI.
[1291] "Cum lege Voconia mulieribus prohiberetur, ne qua majorem centum millibus nummum hæreditatem posset adire." Lib. LXVI.

The Voconian law was made to regulate opulence, not to lay a restraint upon poverty; hence Cicero [1292] informs us that it related only to those whose names were registered in the censors' books.

[1292] *Qui census esset.* Second Oration against Verres.

This furnished a pretence for eluding the law: it is well known that the Romans were extremely fond of set forms; and we have already taken notice that it was the spirit of the republic to follow the letter of the law. There were fathers who would not give in their names to be enrolled by the censors, because they would have it in their power to leave the succession to a daughter: and the prætors determined that this was no violation of the Voconian law since it was not contrary to the letter of it.

One Anius Asellus had appointed his daughter his sole heir and executrix. He had a right to make this disposition, says Cicero; [1293] he was not restrained by the Voconian law, since he was not included in the census. Verres, during the time of his prætorship, had deprived Anius' daughter of the succession; and Cicero maintains that Verres had been bribed, otherwise he would not have annulled a disposition which all the other prætors had confirmed.

[1293] *Census non erat.* Ibid.

What kind of citizens then must those have been, who were not registered in the census in which all the freemen of Rome were included? According to the institution of Servius Tullius, mentioned by Dionysius of Halicarnassus, [1294] every citizen not enrolled in the census became a slave; even Cicero himself observes [1295] that such a man forfeited his liberty, and the same thing is affirmed by Zonaras. There must have been therefore a difference between not being in the census according to the spirit of the Voconian law, and not being in it according to the spirit of Servius Tullius' institutions.

[1294] Lib. IV.
[1295] In *Oratione pro Cæcina.*

They whose names were not registered in the first five classes, [1296] in which the inhabitants ranked in proportion to their fortunes, were not comprised in the census according to the spirit of the Voconian law: they who were not enrolled in one of these six classes, or who were not ranked by the censors among such as were called *ærarii*, were not included in the census according to the spirit of Servius' institutions. Such was the force of nature, that to elude the Voconian law fathers submitted to the disgrace of being confounded in the sixth class with the *proletarii* and *capite censi*, or perhaps to have their names entered in the *Cærites tabulæ.* [1297]

[1296] These five classes were so considerable, that authors sometimes mention no more than five.
[1297] *In Cæritum tabulas referri; ærarius fieri.*

We have elsewhere observed that the Roman laws did not admit of fiduciary bequests. The hopes of evading the Voconian law were the cause of their being introduced: they instituted an heir qualified by the law, and they begged he would resign the succession to a person whom the law had excluded; this new method of disposition was productive of very different effects. Some resigned the inheritance; and the conduct of Sextus Peduccus on an occasion of this nature was very remarkable. [1298] A considerable succession was left him, and nobody living knew that he was desired to resign it to another, when he waited upon the widow of the testator and made over to her the whole fortune belonging to her late husband.

[1298] Cicero, *de finib. boni et mali*, lib. II.

Others kept possession of the inheritance; and here the example of P. Sextilius Rufus is also famous, having been made use of by Cicero in his disputations against the Epicureans. [1299] "In my younger days," says he, "I was desired by Sextilius to accompany him to his friends, in order to know whether he ought to restore the inheritance of Quintus Fadius Gallus to his daughter Fadia. There were several young people present, with others of more maturity and judgment; and not one of them was of opinion that he should give more to Fadia than the lady was entitled to by the Voconian law. In consequence of this, Sextilius kept possession of a fine estate, of which he would not have retained a single sestertius had he preferred justice to utility. It is possible, added he, that you would have resigned the inheritance; nay it is possible that Epicurus himself would have resigned it; but you would not have acted according to your own principles." Here I shall pause a little to reflect.

[1299] Ibid.

It is a misfortune inherent in humanity that legislators should be sometimes obliged to enact laws repugnant to the dictates of nature: such was the Voconian law. The reason is, the legislature considers the society rather than the citizen, and the citizen rather than the man. The law sacrificed both the citizen and the man, and directed its views to the prosperity of the republic. Suppose a person made a fiduciary bequest in favor of his daughter; the law paid no regard to the sentiments of nature in the father, nor to the filial piety of the daughter; all it had an eye to was the person to whom the bequest was made in trust, and who on such occasion found himself in a terrible dilemma. If he restored the estate, he was a bad citizen; if he kept it, he was a bad man. None but good-natured people thought of eluding the law; and they could pitch upon none but honest men to help them to elude it; for a trust of this kind requires a triumph over avarice and inordinate pleasure, which none but honest men are likely to obtain. Perhaps in this light to look upon them as bad citizens would have savored too much of severity. It is not impossible but that the legislator carried his point in a great measure, since his law was of such a nature as obliged none but honest men to elude it.

At the time when the Voconian law was passed, the Romans still preserved some remains of their ancient purity of manners. Their conscience was sometimes engaged in favor of the law; and they were made to swear they would observe it: [1300] so that honesty in some measure was set in opposition against itself. But latterly their morals were corrupted to such a degree that the fiduciary bequests must have had less efficacy to elude the Voconian law, than that very legislator had to enforce its observance.

[1300] Sextilius said he had sworn to observe it.—Cicero, *de finibus boni et mali*, lib. II.

The civil wars were the destruction of an infinite number of citizens. Under Augustus, Rome was almost deserted; it was necessary to re-people it. They made the Papian laws, which omitted nothing that could encourage the citizens to marry and procreate children. [1301] One of the principal means was to increase, in favor of those who gave in to the views of the law, the hopes of being heirs, and to diminish the expectations of those who refused; and as the Voconian law had rendered women incapable of succeeding, the Papian law, in certain cases, dispensed with this prohibition. [1302]

[1301] See what has been said in book XXIII. chap. 21.
[1302] The same difference occurs in several regulations of the Papian law. See Ulpian, Fragment, §§ 4, 5, 6.

Women, [1303] especially those who had children, were rendered capable of receiving in virtue of the will of their husbands; they even might, when they had children, receive in virtue of the will of strangers. All this was in direct opposition to the regulations of the Voconian law: and yet it is remarkable that the spirit of this law was not entirely abandoned. For example, the Papian law, which permitted a man who had one child [1304] to receive an entire inheritance by the will of a stranger, granted the same favor to the wife only when she had three children. [1305]

[1303] See Ulpian, Fragment., tit. 15, § 16.
[1304] *Quod tibi filiolus, vel filia nascitur ex me, Jura Parentis habes; propter me scriberis hæres.*—Juvenal, Sat. 9.
[1305] See Law 9, Cod. Theod. *De bonis proscriptorum*, and Dio, lib. V. See Ulpian, Fragment., tit. ult., § 6, and tit. 29, § 3.

It must be remarked that the Papian law did not render the women who had three children capable of succeeding except in virtue of the will of strangers; and that with respect to the succession of relatives, it left the ancient laws, and particularly the Voconian, in all their force. [1306] But this did not long subsist.

[1306] Ulpian, Fragment., tit. 16, § 1. Sozomenus, lib. I. chap. 9.

Rome, corrupted by the riches of every nation, had changed her manners; the putting a stop to the luxury of women was no longer minded. Aulus Gellius, who lived under Adrian, [1307] tells us, that in his time the Voconian law was almost abolished; it was buried under the opulence of the city. Thus we find in the sentences of Paulus, [1308] who lived under Niger, and in the fragments of Ulpian, [1309] who was in the time of Alexander Severus, that the sisters on the father's side might succeed, and that none but the relatives of a more distant degree were in the case of those prohibited by the Voconian law.

[1307] Lib. XX. chap. 1.
[1308] Lib. IV, tit. 8, § 3.
[1309] Tit. 26, § 6.

The ancient laws of Rome began to be thought severe. The prætors were no longer moved except by reasons of equity, moderation, and decorum.

We have seen, that by the ancient laws of Rome mothers had no share in the inheritance of their children. The Voconian law afforded a new reason for their exclusion. But the Emperor Claudius gave the mother the succession of her children as a consolation for her loss. The Tertullian senatus consultum, made under Adrian, [1310] gave it them when they had three children if free women, or four if they were freedwomen. It is evident, that this decree of the senate was only an extension of the Papian law, which in the same case had granted to women the inheritance left them by strangers. At length Justinian favored them with the succession independently of the number of their children. [1311]

[1310] That is, the Emperor Pius who changed his name to that of Adrian by adoption.
[1311] Lib.. 2, Cod. *de jure liberorum. Institutes*, tit. 3, § 4, *de senatus consult.*

The same causes which had debilitated the law against the succession of women subverted that, by degrees, which had limited the succession of the relatives on the woman's side.

These laws were extremely conformable to the spirit of a good republic, where they ought to have such an influence as to prevent this sex from rendering either the possession, or the expectation of wealth, an instrument of luxury. On the contrary, the luxury of a monarchy rendering marriage expensive and costly, it ought to be there encouraged, both by the riches which women may bestow, and by the hope of the inheritances it is in their power to procure. Thus when monarchy was established at Rome, the whole system of successions was changed. The prætors called the relatives of the woman's side in default of those of the male side; though by the ancient laws, the relatives on the woman's side were never called. The Orphitian senatus consultum called children to the succession of their mother; and the Emperors Valentinian, Theodosius, and Arcadius called the grandchildren by the daughter to the succession of the grandfather. [1312] In short, the Emperor Justinian [1313] left not the least vestige of the ancient right of successions: he established three orders of heirs, the descendants, the ascendants, and the collaterals, without any distinction between the males and females; between the relatives on the woman's side, and those on the male side; and abrogated all laws of this kind, which were still in force: he believed that he followed nature, even in deviating from what he called the embarrassments of the ancient jurisprudence.

[1312] Leg. 9, Cod. *de suis et legitimis.*
[1313] Lib. XIV. Cod, *de suis et legitimis hæredibus*, et Nov. 118, 127.

BOOK XXVIII.

OF THE ORIGIN AND REVOLUTIONS OF THE CIVIL LAWS AMONG THE FRENCH [1314]

[1314] In a private letter Montesquieu, speaking of this book, says that it cost him so much labor that his hair turned grey on account of it.—Ed.

1. *Different Character of the Laws of the several People of Germany.*

After the Franks had quitted their own country, they made a compilation of the Salic laws with the assistance of the sages of their own nation. [1315] The tribe of the Ripuarian Franks having joined itself under Clovis [1316] to that of the Salians preserved its own customs; and Theodoric, [1317] King of Austrasia, ordered them to be reduced to writing. He collected likewise the customs of those Bavarians and Germans, who were dependent on his kingdom. [1318] For Germany having been weakened by the migration of such a multitude of people, the Franks, after conquering all before them, made a retrograde march and extended their dominion into the forests of their ancestors. Very likely the Thuringian code was given by the same Theodoric, since the Thuringians were also his subjects. [1319] As the Frisians were subdued by Charles Martel and Pepin, their law cannot be prior to those princes. [1320] Charlemagne, the first that reduced the Saxons, gave them the law still extant; and we need only read these last two codes to be convinced they came from the hands of conquerors. As soon as the Visigoths, the Burgundians, and the Lombards had founded their respective kingdoms, they reduced their laws to writing, not with an intent of obliging the vanquished nations to conform to their customs, but with a design of following them themselves.

[1315] See the prologue to the Salic Law. Mr. Leibnitz says, in his treatise of the origin of the Franks, that this law was made before the reign of *Clovis*: but it could not be before the Franks had quitted Germany, for at that time they did not understand the Latin tongue.
[1316] See Gregory of Tours.
[1317] See the prologue to the Law of the Bavarians, and that to the Salic Law.
[1318] Ibid.
[1319] Lex Angliorum Werinorum, hoc est Thuringorum.
[1320] They did not know how to write.

There is an admirable simplicity in the Salic and Ripuarian laws, as well as in those of the Alemans, Bavarians, Thuringians, and Frisians. They breathe an original coarseness and a spirit which no change or corruption of manners had weakened. They received but very few alterations, because all those people, except the Franks, remained in Germany. Even the Franks themselves laid there the foundation of a great part of their empire, so that they had none but German laws. The same cannot be said of the laws of the Visigoths, of the Lombards and Burgundians; their character considerably altered from the great change which happened in the character of those people after they had settled in their new habitations.

The kingdom of the Burgundians did not last long enough to admit of great changes in the laws of the conquering nation. Gundebald and Sigismond, who collected their customs, were almost the last of their kings. The laws of the Lombards received additions rather than changes. The laws of Rotharis were followed by those of Grimoaldus, Luitprandus, Rachis, and Astulphus, but did not assume a new form. It was not so with the laws of the Visigoths; [1321] their kings new-moulded them, and had them also new-moulded by the clergy.

[1321] They were made by Euric, and amended by Leovigildus. See Isidorus's chronicle. Chaindasuinthus and Recessuinthus reformed them. Egigas ordered the code now extant to be made, and commissioned bishops for that purpose; nevertheless the laws of Chaindasuinthus and Recessuinthus were preserved, as appears by the sixth council of Toledo.

The kings indeed of the first race struck out of the Salic and Ripuarian laws whatever was absolutely inconsistent with Christianity, but left the main part untouched. [1322] This cannot be said of the laws of the Visigoths.

[1322] See the prologue to the Law of the Bavarians.

The laws of the Burgundians, and especially those of the Visigoths, admitted of corporal punishments; these were not tolerated by the Salic and Ripuarian laws; [1323] they preserved their character much better.

[1323] We find only a few in Childebert's decree.

The Burgundians and Visigoths, whose provinces were greatly exposed, endeavored to conciliate the affections of the ancient inhabitants, and to give them the most impartial civil laws; [1324] but as the Kings of the Franks had established their power, they had no such considerations. [1325]

[1324] See the prologue to the Code of the Burgundians, and the code itself, especially tit. 12, § 5, and tit. 38. See also Gregory of Tours, book II. chap. 33, and the code of the Visigoths.
[1325] See lower down, chapter 3.

The Saxons, who lived under the dominion of the Franks, were of an intractable temper, and prone to revolt. Hence we find in their laws the severities of a conqueror, [1326] which are not to be met with in the other codes of the laws of the barbarians.

[1326] See chap. ii. §§ 8 and 9, and chap. iv. §§ 2 and 7.

We see the spirit of the German laws in the pecuniary punishments, and the spirit of a conqueror in those of an afflictive nature.
The crimes they commit in their own country are subject to corporal punishment; and the spirit of the German laws is followed only in the punishment of crimes committed beyond the extent of their own territory.

They are plainly told that their crimes shall meet with no mercy, and they are refused even the asylum of churches.

The bishops had an immense authority at the court of the Visigoth Kings, the most important affairs being debated in councils. All the maxims, principles and views of the present inquisition are owing to the code of the Visigoths; and the monks have only copied against the Jews the laws formerly enacted by bishops.

In other respects the laws of Gundebald for the Burgundians seem pretty judicious; and those of Rotharis, and of the other Lombard princes, are still more so. But the laws of the Visigoths, those for instance of Recessuinthus, Chaindasuinthus, and Egigas are puerile, ridiculous and foolish; they attain not their end; they are stuffed with rhetoric and void of sense, frivolous in the substance and bombastic in the style.

2. *That the Laws of the Barbarians were all personal.*

It is a distinguishing character of these laws of the barbarians that they were not confined to a certain district; the Frank was tried by the law of the Franks, the Aleman by that of the Alemans, the Burgundian by that of the Burgundians, and the Roman by the Roman law; nay, so far were the conquerors in those days from reducing their laws to a uniform system or body, that they did not even think of becoming legislators to the people they had conquered.

The original of this I find in the manners of the Germans. These people were parted asunder by marshes, lakes, and forests; and Cæsar observes [1327] they were fond of such separations. Their dread of the Romans brought about their reunion; and yet each individual among these mixed people was still to be tried by the established customs of his own nation. Each tribe apart was free and independent; and when they came to be intermixed, the independence still continued; the country was common, the government peculiar; the territory the same, and the nations different. The spirit of personal laws prevailed therefore among those people before ever they set out from their own homes, and they carried it with them into the conquered provinces.

[1327] *De Bello Gallico*, lib. VI.

We find this custom established in the formulas of Marculfus, [1328] in the codes of the laws of the barbarians, but chiefly in the law of the Ripuarians [1329] and the decrees of the kings of the first race, [1330] whence the capitularies on that subject in the second race were derived. [1331] The children followed the laws of their father, [1332] the wife that of her husband, [1333] the widow came back to her own original law, [1334] and the freedman was under that of his patron. [1335] Besides, every man could make choice of what laws he pleased; but the constitution of Lotharius I [1336] required that this choice should be made public.

[1328] Lib. I, formul. 8.
[1329] Chapter 31.
[1330] That of Clotarius in the year 560, in the edition of the Capitularies of Balusius, vol. i, art. 4, ib. *in fine.*
[1331] Capitularies added to the Law of the Lombards, Lib. I, tit. 25, chap. 71, lib. II, tit. 41, chap. 7, and tit. 56, chap. 1, 2.
[1332] Ibid.

[1333] Ibid., lib. VI, tit. 7, chap. 1.
[1334] Ibid., chap. 2.
[1335] Ibid., lib. II, tit. 35, chap. 2.
[1336] In the Law of the Lombards, lib. II, tit. 57.

3. *Capital Difference between the Salic Laws and those of the Visigoths and Burgundians.*

We have already observed that the laws of the Burgundians and Visigoths were impartial; but it was otherwise with regard to the Salic law, for it established between the Franks and Romans the most mortifying distinctions. When a Frank, a barbarian, or one living under the Salic law happened to be killed, a composition of 200 sols was to be paid to his relatives; [1337] only 100 upon the killing of a Roman proprietor, [1338] and no more than forty-five for a Roman tributary. The composition for the murder of one of the king's vassals, if a Frank, was 600 sols; [1339] if a Roman, though the king's guest, [1340] only 300. [1341] The Salic law made therefore a cruel distinction between the Frank and Roman lord, and the Frank and Roman commoner.

[1337] Salic Law, tit. 44, § 1.
[1338]"Qui res in pago ubi remanet proprias habet."—Salic Law., tit. 44, §§ 15, 7.
[1339] "Qui in truste dominica est."—Ibid. tit. 41, § 4.
[1340] "Si Romanus homo conviva regis fuerit."—Ibid., § 6.
[1341] The principal Romans followed the court, as may be seen by the lives of several bishops, who were there educated; there were hardly any but Romans that knew how to write.

Further, if a number of people were got together to assault a Frank in his house, [1342] and he happened to be killed, the Salic law ordained a composition of 600 sols; but if a Roman or a freedman was assaulted, only one-half that composition. [1343] By the same law, [1344] if a Roman put a Frank in irons, he was liable to a composition of 30 sols; but if a Frank had thus used a Roman, he paid only 15. A Frank, stripped by a Roman, was entitled to the composition of 62 1/2 sols, and a Roman stripped by a Frank received only 30. Such unequal treatment must needs have been very grievous to a Roman.

[1342] Salic Law, tit. 45.
[1343] Lidus whose condition was better than that of a bondman.—Law of the Alemans, chap. 95.
[1344] Tit. 35, §§ 3, 4.

And yet a celebrated author [1345] forms a system of *the establishment of the Franks in Gaul,* on a supposition that they were the best friends of the Romans. The Franks then, the best friends of the Romans, they who did, and they who suffered from the Romans such an infinite deal of mischief! [1346] The Franks, the friends of the Romans, they who, after subduing them by their arms, oppressed them in cold blood by their laws! They were exactly the friends of the Romans as the Tartars who conquered China were the friends of the Chinese. If some Catholic bishops thought fit to make use of the Franks in destroying the Arian Kings, does it follow that they had a desire of living under those barbarous people? And can we hence conclude that the Franks had any particular regard for the Romans? I should draw quite different consequences; the less the Franks had to fear from the Romans, the less indulgence they showed them.

[1345] The Abbé du Bos.
[1346] Witness the expedition of Arbogastes, in Gregory of Tours, History, lib. II.

The Abbé du Bos has consulted but indifferent authorities for his history, such as poets and orators; works of parade and ostentation are improper foundations for building systems.

4. *In what manner the Roman Law came to be lost in the Country subject to the Franks, and preserved in that subject to the Goths and Burgundians.*

What has been above said will throw some light upon other things, which have hitherto been involved in great obscurity.

The country at this day called France was under the first race governed by the Roman law, or the Theodosian code, and by the different laws of the Barbarians, [1347] who settled in those parts.

[1347] The Franks, the Visigoths, and Burgundians.

In the country subject to the Franks, the Salic law was established for the Franks, and the Theodosian code [1348] for the Romans. In that subject to the Visigoths, a compilation of the Theodosian code, made by order of Alaric, [1349] regulated disputes among the Romans; and the national customs, which Euric caused to be reduced to writing, [1350] determined those among the Visigoths. But how comes it, some will say, that the Salic laws gained almost a general authority in the country of the Franks, and the Roman law gradually declined; whilst in the jurisdiction of the Visigoths the Roman law spread itself, and obtained at last a general sway?

[1348] It was finished in 438.
[1349] The 20th year of the reign of this prince, and published two years after by Anian, as appears from the preface to that code.
[1350] The year 504 of the Spanish era, the Chronicle of Isidorus.

My answer is that the Roman law came to be disused among the Franks because of the great advantages accruing from being a Frank, a Barbarian, [1351] or a person living under the Salic law; every one, in that case, readily quitting the Roman to live under the Salic law. The clergy alone retained it, [1352] as a change would be of no advantage to them. The difference of conditions and ranks consisted only in the largeness of the composition, as I shall show in another place. Now particular laws [1353] allowed the clergy as favorable compositions as those of the Franks, for which reason they retained the Roman law. This law brought no hardships upon them; and in other respects it was most proper for them, as it was the work of Christian emperors.

[1351] Francum, aut Barbarum, aut hominem qui Salica lege vivit.—Salic Law, tit. 45, § 1.

[1352] *According to the Roman law under which the church lives*, as is said in the law of the Ripuarians, tit. 58, § 1. See also the numberless authorities on this head pronounced by Ducange, under the words *Lex Romana*.

[1353] See the Capitularies added to the Salic law in Lindembrock, at the end of that law, and the different codes of the laws of the Barbarians concerning the privileges of ecclesiastics in this respect. See also the letter of Charlemagne to his son Pepin, King of Italy, in the year 807, in the edition of Baluzius, tom. i, 462, where it is said, that an ecclesiastic should receive a triple compensation; and the Collection of the Capitularies, lib. V, art. 302, tom. i. Edition of Baluzius.

On the other hand, in the patrimony of the Visigoths, as the Visigoth law [1354] gave no civil advantages to the Visigoths over the Romans, the latter had no reason to discontinue living under their own law in order to embrace another. They retained therefore their own laws without adopting those of the Visigoths.

[1354] See that law.

This is still further confirmed in proportion as we proceed in our inquiry. The law of Gundebald was extremely impartial, not favoring the Burgundians more than the Romans. It appears by the preamble to that law that it was made for the Burgundians, and to regulate the disputes which might arise between them and the Romans; and in the latter case the judges were equally divided of a side. This was necessary for particular reasons, drawn from the political regulations of those times. [1355] The Roman law was continued in Burgundy, in order to regulate the disputes of Romans among themselves. The latter had no inducement to quit their own law, as in the country of the Franks; and rather as the Salic law was not established in Burgundy, as appears by the famous letter which Agobard wrote to Lewis the Pious.

[1355] Of this I shall speak in another place, book. XXX. Chap. 6-9.

Agobard [1356] desired that prince to establish the Salic law in Burgundy; consequently it had not been established there at that time. Thus the Roman law did, and still does subsist in so many provinces, which formerly depended on this kingdom.

[1356] Agobard, *Opera*.

The Roman and Gothic laws continued likewise in the country of the establishment of the Goths, where the Salic law was never received. When Pepin and Charles Martel expelled the Saracens, the towns and provinces which submitted to these princes petitioned for a continuance of their own laws and obtained it; [1357] this, in spite of the usages of those times, when all laws were personal, soon made the Roman law to be considered as a real and territorial law in those countries.

[1357] See Gervais of Tilbury, in Duchesne's Collection, iii, p. 366. And a chronicle of the year 759, produced by Catel, Hist. of Languedoc. And the uncertain author of the Life of Lewis the Debonnaire, upon the demand made by the people of Septimania, at the assembly in Carisiaco, in Duchesne's Collection, ii, p. 316.

This appears by the edict of Charles the Bald, given at Pistes in the year 864, which distinguishes the countries where causes were decided by the Roman law from where it was otherwise. [1358]

[1358] *In illa terra in qua judicia secundum legem Romanam terminantur, secundum ipsam legem judicetur; et in illa terra in qua, &c.*, Art. 16. See also art. 20.

The edict of Pistes shows two things; one, that there were countries where causes were decided by the Roman law, and others where they were not; and the other, that those countries where the Roman law obtained were precisely the same where it is still followed at this very day, as appears by the said edict: [1359] thus the distinction of the provinces of France *under custom* and those *under written law* was already established at the time of the edict of Pistes.

[1359] See arts. 12 and 16 of the edict of Pistes *in Cavilono, in Narbona,* &c.

I have observed that in the beginning of the monarchy all laws were personal; and thus when the edict of Pistes distinguishes the countries of the Roman law from those which were otherwise, the meaning is that, in countries which were not of the Roman law, such a multitude of people had chosen to live under some or other of the laws of the Barbarians that there were scarcely any who would be subject to the Roman law; and that in the countries of the Roman law there were few who would choose to live under the laws of the Barbarians.

I am not ignorant that what is here advanced will be reckoned new; but if the things which I assert be true, surely they are very ancient. After all, what great matter is it, whether they come from me, from the Valesiuses, or from the Bignons?

5. *The same Subject continued.*

The law of Gundebald subsisted a long time among the Burgundians, in conjunction with the Roman law; it was still in use under Lewis the Pious, as Agobard's letter plainly evinces. In like manner, though the edict of Pistes calls the country occupied by the Visigoths the country of the Roman law, yet the law of the Visigoths was always in force there; as appears by the synod of Troyes held under Lewis the Stammerer, in the year 878, that is, fourteen years after the edict of Pistes.

In process of time the Gothic and Burgundian laws fell into disuse even in their own country, which was owing to those general causes that everywhere suppressed the personal laws of the Barbarians.

6. *How the Roman Law kept its Ground in the Demesne of the Lombards.*

The facts all coincide with my principles. The law of the Lombards was impartial, and the Romans were under no temptation to quit their own for it. The motive which prevailed with the Romans under the Franks to make choice of the Salic law did not take place in Italy; hence the Roman law maintained itself there, together with that of the Lombards.

It even fell out that the latter gave way to the Roman institutes, and ceased to be the law of the ruling nation; and though it continued to be that of the principal nobility, yet the greatest part of the cities formed themselves into republics, and the nobility moldered away of themselves, or were destroyed. [1360] The citizens of the new republics had no inclination to adopt a law which established the custom of judiciary combats, and whose institutions retained much of the customs and usages of chivalry. As the clergy of those days, a clergy even then so powerful in Italy, lived almost all under the Roman law, the number of those who followed the institutions of the Lombards must have daily diminished.

[1360] See what Machiavelli says of the ruin of the ancient nobility of Florence.

Besides, the institutions of the Lombards had not that extent, that majesty of the Roman law, by which Italy was reminded of her universal dominion. The institutions of the Lombards and the Roman law could be then of no other use than to furnish out statutes for those cities that were erected into republics. Now which could better furnish them, the institutions of the Lombards that determined on some particular cases, or the Roman law which embraced them all?

7. *How the Roman Law came to be lost in Spain.*

Things happened otherwise in Spain. The law of the Visigoths prevailed, and the Roman law was lost. Chaindasuinthus [1361] and Recessuinthus proscribed the Roman laws, [1362] and even forbade citing them in their courts of judicature. Recessuinthus was likewise author of the law which took off the prohibition of marriage between the Goths and Romans. [1363] It is evident that these two laws had the same spirit; this king wanted to remove the principal causes of separation which subsisted between the Goths and the Romans. Now it was thought that nothing made a wider separation than the prohibition of intermarriages, and the liberty of living under different institutions.

[1361] He began to reign in the year 642.
[1362] *We will no longer be harassed either by foreign or by the Roman laws.*—Law of the Visigoths, ii, tit. 1, §§ 9, 10.
[1363] *Ut tam Gotho Romanam, quam Romano Gotham matrimonia liceat sociari.*—Law of the Visigoths, iii, tit. 1, 1.

But though the kings of the Visigoths had proscribed the Roman law, it still subsisted in the demesnes they possessed in South Gaul. [1364] These countries being distant from the centre of the monarchy lived in a state of great independence. We see from the history of Vamba, who ascended the throne in 672, that the natives of the country had become the prevailing party. [1365] Hence the Roman law had greater authority and the Gothic less. The Spanish laws neither suited their manners nor their actual situation; the people might likewise be obstinately attached to the Roman law, because they had annexed to it the idea of liberty. Besides, the laws of Chaindasuinthus and of Recessuinthus contained most severe regulations against the Jews; but these Jews had a vast deal of power in South Gaul. The author of the history of King Vamba calls these provinces the brothel of the Jews. When the Saracens invaded these provinces, it was by invitation; and who could have invited them but the Jews or the Romans? The Goths were the first that were oppressed, because they were the ruling nation. We see in Procopius, that during their calamities they withdrew out of Narbonne Gaul into Spain. [1366] Doubtless, under this misfortune; they took refuge in those provinces of Spain which still held out; and the number of those who in South Gaul lived under the law of the Visigoths was thereby greatly diminished.

[1364] See Liv. VI. 19, 26.

[1365] The revolt of these provinces was a general defection, as appears by the sentence in the sequel of the history. Paulus and his adherents were Romans; they were even favored by the bishops. Vamba durst not put to death the rebels whom he had quelled. The author of the history calls Narbonne Gaul the nursery of treason.

[1366] "Gothi, qui cladi superfuerant, ex Gallia cum uxoribus liberique egressi, in Hispanian ad Teudim jam palam tyrannum se receperunt."—*De Bello Gothorum*, lib. I. chap. 13.

8. *A false Capitulary.*

Did not that wretched compiler Benedictus Levita attempt to transform this Visigoth establishment, which prohibited the use of Roman law, into a capitulary [1367] ascribed since to Charlemagne? He made of this particular institution a general one, as if he intended to exterminate the Roman law throughout the universe.

[1367] Capitularies, lib. VI, chap. 269, year 1613, edition of Baluzius, p. 1021.

9. *In what manner the Codes of Barbarian Laws and the Capitularies came to be lost.*

The Salic, the Ripuarian, Burgundian, and Visigoth laws came, by degrees, to be disused among the French in the following manner:

As fiefs became hereditary, and arrière-fiefs extended, many usages were introduced, to which these laws were no longer applicable. Their spirit indeed was continued, which was to regulate most disputes by fines. But as the value of money was, doubtless, subject to change, the fines were also changed; and we see several charters, [1368] where the lords fixed the fines, that were payable in their petty courts. Thus the spirit of the law was followed, without adhering to the law itself.

[1368] M. de la Thaumassière has collected many of them. See, for instance, chapters 41, 46, and others.

Besides, as France was divided into a number of petty lordships, which acknowledged rather a feudal than a political dependence, it was very difficult for only one law to be authorized. And, indeed, it would be impossible to see it observed. The custom no longer prevailed of sending extraordinary officers [1369] into the provinces to inspect the administration of justice and political affairs; it appears, even by the charters, that when new fiefs were established our kings divested themselves of the right of sending those officers. Thus, when almost everything had become a fief, these officers could not be employed; there was no longer a common law because no one could enforce the observance of it.

[1369] *Missi Dominici.*

The Salic, Burgundian, and Visigoth laws were, therefore, extremely neglected at the end of the second race; and at the beginning of the third, they were scarcely ever mentioned.

Under the first and second race, the nation was often assembled; that is, the lords and bishops; the commons were not yet thought of. In these assemblies, attempts were made to regulate the clergy, a body which formed itself, if I may so speak, under the conquerors, and established its privileges. The laws made in these assemblies are what we call the Capitularies. Hence four things ensued: the feudal laws were established and a great part of the church revenues was administered by those laws; the clergy effected a wider separation, and neglected those decrees of reformation where they themselves were not the only reformers; [1370] a collection was made of the canons of councils and of the decretals of popes; [1371] and these the clergy received, as coming from a purer source. Ever since the erection of the grand fiefs, our kings, as we have already observed, had no longer any deputies in the provinces to enforce the observance of their laws; and hence it is that, under the third race, we find no more mention made of Capitularies.

[1370] Let not the bishops, says Charles the Bald, in the Capitulary of 844, art. 8, under pretence of the authority of making canons, oppose this constitution, or neglect the observance of it. It seems he already foresaw the fall thereof.

[1371] In the collection of canons a vast number of the decretals of the popes were inserted; they were very few in the ancient collection. Dionysius Exiguus put a great many into his; but that of Isidorus Mercator was stuffed with genuine and spurious decretals. The old collection obtained in France till Charlemagne. This prince received from the hand of Pope Adrian I the collection of Dionysius Exiguus, and caused it to be accepted. The collection of Isidorus Mercator appeared in France about the reign of Charlemagne; people grew passionately fond of it: to this succeeded what we now call *the course of canon law*.

10. *The same Subject continued.*

Several capitularies were added to the law of the Lombards, as well as to the Salic and Bavarian laws. The reason of this has been a matter of inquiry; but it must be sought for in the thing itself. There were several sorts of capitularies. Some had relation to political government, others to economical, most of them to ecclesiastical polity, and some few to civil government. Those of the last species were added to the civil law, that is, to the personal laws of each nation; for which reason it is said in the Capitularies that there is nothing stipulated therein contrary to the Roman law. [1372] In effect, those capitularies regarding economical, ecclesiastical, or political government had no relation to that law; and those concerning civil government had reference only to the laws of the barbarous people, which were explained, amended, enlarged, or abridged. But the adding of these capitularies to the personal laws occasioned, I imagine, the neglect of the very body of the Capitularies themselves; in times of ignorance, the abridgment of a work often causes the loss of the work itself.

[1372] See the edict of Pistes, art. 20.

11. *Other Causes of the Disuse of the Codes of Barbarian Laws, as well as of the Roman Law, and of the Capitularies.*

When the German nations subdued the Roman empire, they learned the use of writing; and, in imitation of the Romans, they wrote down their own usages, and digested them into codes. [1373] The unhappy reigns which followed that of Charlemagne, the invasions of the Normans and the civil wars, plunged the conquering nations again into the darkness out of which they had emerged, so that reading and writing were quite neglected. Hence it is, that in France and Germany the written laws of the Barbarians, as well as the Roman law and the Capitularies fell into oblivion. The use of writing was better preserved in Italy, where reigned the Popes and the Greek Emperors, and where there were flourishing cities, which enjoyed almost the only commerce in those days. To this neighborhood of Italy it was owing that the Roman law was preserved in the provinces of Gaul, formerly subject to the Goths and Burgundians; and so much the more, as this law was there a territorial institution, and a kind of privilege. It is probable that the disuse of the Visigoth laws in Spain proceeded from the want of writing, and by the loss of so many laws, customs were everywhere established.

[1373] This is expressly set down in some preambles to these codes: we even find in the laws of the Saxons and Frisians different regulations, according to the different districts. To these usages were added some particular regulations suitable to the exigency of circumstances; such were the severe laws against the Saxons.

Personal laws fell to the ground. Compositions, and what they call *Freda*, [1374] were regulated more by custom than by the text of these laws. Thus, as in the establishment of the monarchy, they had passed from German customs to written laws; some ages after, they came back from written laws to unwritten customs.

[1374] Of this I shall speak elsewhere (chap. xiv. book XXX.).

12. *Of local Customs.*

Revolution of the Laws of barbarous Nations, as well as of the Roman Law. By several memorials it appears, that there were local customs, as early as the first and second race. We find mention made of the "custom of the place," [1375] of the "ancient usage," [1376] of "custom," [1377] of "laws," [1378] and of "customs." It has been the opinion of some authors that what went by the name of customs were the laws of the barbarous nations, and what had the appellation of law were the Roman institutes. This cannot possibly be. King Pepin ordained [1379] that wherever there should happen to be no law, custom should be complied with; but that it should never be preferred to the law. Now, to pretend that the Roman law was preferred to the codes of the laws of the Barbarians is subverting all memorials of antiquity, and especially those codes of Barbarian laws, which constantly affirm the contrary.

[1375] Preface to Marculfus, *Formulæ.*
[1376] Law of the Lombards, book II, tit. 58, § 3.
[1377] Ibid., tit. 41, § 6.

[1378] Life of St. Leger.
[1379] Law of the Lombards, book II, tit. 41, sec. 6.

So far were the laws of the barbarous nations from being those customs, that it was these very laws, as personal institutions, which introduced them. The Salic law, for instance, was a personal law; but generally, or almost generally, in places inhabited by the Salian Franks, this Salic law, how personal soever, became, in respect to those Salian Franks, a territorial institution, and was personal only in regard to those Franks who lived elsewhere. Now if several Burgundians, Alemans, or even Romans should happen to have frequent disputes, in a place where the Salic law was territorial, they must have been determined by the laws of those people; and a great number of decisions agreeable to some of those laws must have introduced new customs into the country. This explains the constitution of Pepin. It was natural that those customs should affect even the Franks who lived on the spot, in cases not decided by the Salic law; but it was not natural that they should prevail over the Salic law itself.

Thus there were in each place an established law and received customs which served as a supplement to that law when they did not contradict it.

They might even happen to supply a law that was in no way territorial; and to continue the same example, if a Burgundian was judged by the law of his own nation, in a place where the Salic law was territorial, and the case happened not to be explicitly mentioned in the very text of this law, there is no manner of doubt but that judgment would have been passed upon him according to the custom of the place.

In the reign of King Pepin, the customs then established had not the same force as the laws; but it was not long before the laws gave way to the customs. And as new regulations are generally remedies that imply a present evil, it may well be imagined that as early as Pepin's time, they began to prefer the customs to the established laws.

What has been said sufficiently explains the manner in which the Roman law began so very early to become territorial, as may be seen in the edict of Pistes; and how the Gothic law continued still in force, as appears by the synod of Troyes above-mentioned. [1380] The Roman had become the general personal law, and the Gothic the particular personal law; consequently the Roman law was territorial. But how came it, some will ask, that the personal laws of the Barbarians fell everywhere into disuse, while the Roman law was continued as a territorial institution in the Visigoth and Burgundian provinces? I answer that even the Roman law had very nearly the same fate as the other personal institutions; otherwise we would still have the Theodosian code in those provinces where the Roman law was territorial, whereas we have the institutes of Justinian. Those provinces retained scarcely anything more than the name of the country under the Roman, or written law, than the natural affection which people have for their own institutions, especially when they consider them as privileges, and a few regulations of the Roman law which were not yet forgotten. This was, however, sufficient to produce such an effect that, when Justinian's compilation appeared, it was received in the provinces of the Gothic and Burgundian demesne as a written law, whereas it was admitted only as written reason in the ancient demesne of the Franks.

[1380] See chapter 5.

13. *Difference between the Salic law, or that of the Salian Franks, and that of the Ripuarian Franks and other barbarous Nations.*

The Salic law did not allow of the custom of negative proofs; that is, if a person brought a demand or charge against another, he was obliged by the Salic law to prove it, and it was not sufficient for the second to deny it, which is agreeable to the laws of almost all nations.

The law of the Ripuarian Franks had quite a different spirit; [1381] it was contented with negative proofs, and the person) against whom a demand or accusation was brought, might clear himself, in most cases, by swearing, in conjunction with a certain number of witnesses, that he had not committed the crime laid to his charge. The number of witnesses who were obliged to swear [1382] increased in proportion to the importance of the affair; sometimes it amounted to seventy-two. [1383] The laws of the Alemans, Bavarians, Thuringians, Frisians, Saxons, Lombards, and Burgundians were formed on the same plan as those of the Ripuarian.

[1381] This relates to what Tacitus says, that the Germans had general and particular customs.
[1382] Law of the Ripuarians, tit. 6, 7, 8, and others.
[1383] Ibid., tit. 11, 12, 17.

I observed that the Salic law did not allow of negative proofs. There was one case, however, in which they were allowed: [1384] but even then they were not admitted alone, and without the concurrence of positive proofs. The plaintiff caused witnesses to be heard, [1385] in order to ground his action, the defendant produced also witnesses on his side, and the judge was to come at the truth by comparing those testimonies. [1386] This practice was vastly different from that of the Ripuarian, and other barbarous laws, where it was customary for the party accused to clear himself by swearing he was not guilty, and by making his relatives also swear that he had told the truth. These laws could be suitable only to a people remarkable for their natural simplicity and candor; we shall see presently that the legislators were obliged to take proper methods to prevent their being abused.

[1384] It was when an accusation was brought against an Antrustio, that is, the king's vassal, who was supposed to be possessed of a greater degree of liberty. See *Pactus legis Salicæ*, tit. 76.
[1385] See 76th Tit. of the Pactus legis *Salicæ*.
[1386] According to the practice now followed in England.

14. *Another Difference.*

The Salic law did not admit of the trial by combat, though it had been received by the laws of the Ripuarians [1387] and of almost all the barbarous nations. [1388] To me it seems that the law of combat was a natural consequence and a remedy of the law which established negative proofs. When an action was brought, and it appeared that the defendant was going to elude it by an oath, what other remedy was left to a military man, [1389] who saw himself upon the point of being confounded, than to demand satisfaction for the injury done to him: and even for the attempt of perjury? The Salic law, which did not allow the custom of negative proofs, neither admitted nor had any need of the trial by combat; but the laws of the Ripuarians [1390] and of the other barbarous nations [1391] who had adopted the practice of negative proofs, were obliged to establish the trial by combat.

[1387] Tit. 32; tit. 57, § 2; tit. 59, § 4.
[1388] See the following note.
[1389] This spirit appears in the Law of Ripuarians, tit. 59, § 4, and tit. 67, § 5, and in the Capitulary of Lewis the Debonnaire, added to the law of the Ripuarians in the year 803, art. 22.
[1390] See that law.
[1391] The law of the Frisians, Lombards, Bavarians, Saxons, Thuringians, and Burgundians.

Whoever will please to examine the two famous regulations of Gundebald, King of Burgundy, concerning this subject will find they are derived from the very nature of the thing. [1392] It was necessary, according to the language of the Barbarian laws, to rescue the oath out of the hands of a person who was going to abuse it.

[1392] In the Law of the Burgundians, tit. 8, §§ 1 and 2, on criminal affairs; and tit. 45, which extends also to civil affairs. See also the law of the Thuringians, tit. 1, § 31; tit. 7, § 6; and tit. 8; and the law of the Alemans, tit. 89; the law of the Bavarians, tit. 8, chap. ii, § 6, and chap. iii, § 1, and tit. 9, chap. iv, § 4; the law of the Frisians, tit. 2, § 3, and tit. 14, § 4; the law of the Lombards, book I, tit. 32, § 3, and tit. 35, § 1, and book II, tit. 35, § 2.

Among the Lombards, the law of Rotharis admits of cases in which a man who had made his defense by oath should not be suffered to undergo the hardship of a duel. This custom spread itself further: [1393] we shall presently see the mischiefs that arose from it, and how they were obliged to return to the ancient practice.

[1393] See chap. xviii, towards the end.

15. A Reflection.

I do not pretend to deny that in the changes made in the code of the Barbarian laws, in the regulations added to that code, and in the body of the Capitularies, it is possible to find some passages where the trial by combat is not a consequence of the negative proof. Particular circumstances might, in the course of many ages, give rise to particular laws. I speak only of the general spirit of the laws of the Germans, of their nature and origin; I speak of the ancient customs of those people that were either hinted at or established by those laws; and this is the only matter in question.

16. *Of the Ordeal or Trial by boiling Water, established by the Salic Law.*

The Salic law [1394] allowed of the ordeal, or trial by boiling water; and as this trial was excessively cruel, the law found an expedient to soften its rigor. [1395] It permitted the person, who had been summoned to make the trial with boiling water, to ransom his hand, with the consent of the adverse party. The accuser, for a particular sum determined by the law, might be satisfied with the oath of a few witnesses, declaring that the accused had not committed the crime. This was a particular case, in which the Salic law admitted of the negative proof.

[1394] As also some other laws of the Barbarians.
[1395] Tit. 56.

This trial was a thing privately agreed upon, which the law permitted only, but did not ordain. The law gave a particular indemnity to the accuser, who would allow the accused to make his defense by a negative proof: the plaintiff was at liberty to be satisfied with the oath of the defendant, as he was at liberty to forgive him the injury.

The law contrived a middle course, [1396] that before sentence passed, both parties, the one through fear of a terrible trial, the other for the sake of a small indemnity, should terminate their disputes, and put an end to their animosities. It is plain, that when once this negative proof was completed, nothing more was requisite; and, therefore, that the practice of legal duels could not be a consequence of this particular regulation of the Salic law.

[1396] Ibid. tit. 56.

17. *Particular Notions of our Ancestors.*

It is astonishing that our ancestors should thus rest the honor, fortune and life of the subject, on things that depended less on reason than on hazard, and that they should incessantly make use of proofs incapable of convicting, and that had no manner of connection either with innocence or guilt.

The Germans, who had never been subdued, [1397] enjoyed an excessive independence. Different families waged war with each other [1398] to obtain satisfaction for murders, robberies or affronts. This custom was moderated by subjecting these hostilities to rules; it was ordained that they should be no longer committed but by the direction and under the eye of the magistrate. [1399] This was far preferable to a general license of annoying each other.

[1397] This appears by what Tacitus says, *Omnibus idem habitus.*—De Moribus Germanorum, 4.
[1398] Velleius Paterculus, lib. II. chap. 118, says that the Germans decided all their disputes by the sword.
[1399] See the codes of Barbarian laws, and in respect to less ancient times, Beaumanoir, Ancient Custom of Beauvoisis.

As the Turks in their civil wars look upon the first victory as a decision of heaven in favor of the victor, so the inhabitants of Germany in their private quarrels considered the event of a combat as a decree of Providence, ever attentive to punish the criminal or the usurper.

Tacitus informs us that when one German nation intended to declare war against another, they looked out for a prisoner who was to fight with one of their people, and by the event they judged of the success of the war. A nation who believed that public quarrels could be determined by a single combat might very well think that it was proper also for deciding the disputes of individuals.

Gundebald, King of Burgundy, gave the greatest sanction to the custom of legal duels. [1400] The reason he assigns for this law is mentioned in his edict, *It is*, says he, *in order to prevent our subjects from attesting by oath what is uncertain, and perjuring themselves about what is certain.* Thus, while the clergy declared that an impious law which permitted combats, [1401] the Burgundian Kings looked upon that as a sacrilegious law which authorized the taking of an oath.

[1400] Law of the Burgundians, chap. xlv.
[1401] See the works of Agobard.

The trial by combat had some reason for it, founded on experience. In a military nation, cowardice supposes other vices; it is an argument of a person's having deviated from the principles of his education, of his being insensible of honor, and of having refused to be directed by those maxims which govern other men; it shows that he neither fears their contempt, nor sets any value upon their esteem. Men of any tolerable extraction seldom want either the dexterity requisite to co-operate with strength, or the strength necessary to concur with courage; for as they set a value upon honor, they are practiced in matters without which this honor cannot be obtained. Besides, in a military nation, where strength, courage and prowess are esteemed, crimes really odious are those which arise from fraud, artifice, and cunning, that is, from cowardice.

With regard to the trial by fire, after the party accused had put his hand on a hot iron, or in boiling water, they wrapped the hand in a bag and sealed it up; if after three days there appeared no mark, he was acquitted, Is it not plain, that among people inured to the handling of arms, the impression made on a rough or callous skin by the hot iron or by boiling water could not be so great as to be seen three days afterwards? And if there appeared any mark, it showed that the person who had undergone the trial was an effeminate fellow. Our peasants are not afraid to handle hot iron with their callous hands; and, with regard to the women, the hands of those who worked hard might be very well able to resist hot iron. The ladies did not want champions to defend their cause; and in a nation where there was no luxury, there was no middle state. [1402]

[1402] See Beaumanoir, Ancient Customs of Beauvoisis, chap. 61. See also the Law of the Angli, chap. xiv, where the trial by boiling water is only a subsidiary proof.

By the law of the Thuringians [1403] a woman accused of adultery was condemned to the trial by boiling water only when there was no champion to defend her; and the law of the Ripuarians admits of this trial [1404] only when a person had no witnesses to appear in justification. Now a woman that could not prevail upon any one relative to defend her cause, or a man that could not produce one single witness to attest his honesty, was, from those very circumstances, sufficiently convicted.

[1403] Tit. 14.
[1404] Chap. xxxi, § 5.

I conclude, therefore, that under the circumstances of time in which the trial by combat and the trial by hot iron and boiling water obtained, there was such an agreement between those laws and the manners of the people, that the laws were rather unjust in themselves than productive of injustice, that the effects were more innocent than the cause, that they were more contrary to equity than prejudicial to its rights, more unreasonable than tyrannical.

18. *In what manner the Custom of judicial Combats gained Ground.*

From Agobard's letter to Lewis the Debonnaire, it might be inferred that the custom of judicial combats was not established among the Franks; for having represented to that prince the abuses of the law of Gundebald, he desires that private disputes should be decided in Burgundy by the law of the Franks. [1405] But as it is well known from other quarters that the trial by combat prevailed at that time in France, this has been the cause of some perplexity. However, the difficulty may be solved by what I have said; the law of the Salian Franks did not allow of this kind of trial and that of the Ripuarian Franks did. [1406]

[1405] *Si placeret Domino mostro ut eos transferred ad legem Francorum.*
[1406] See this law, tit. 59, § 4, and tit. 67, § 5.

But, notwithstanding the clamors of the clergy, the custom of judicial combats gained ground continually in France; and I shall presently make it appear that the clergy themselves were in a great measure the occasion of it.

It is the law of the Lombards that furnishes us with this proof. "*There has been long since a detestable custom introduced*," says the preamble to the constitution of Otho II: [1407] "this is, that if the title to an estate was said to be false, the person who claimed under that title made oath upon the Gospel that it was genuine; and without any preceding judgment he took possession of the estate; so that they who would perjure themselves were sure of gaining their point." The Emperor Otho I having caused himself to be crowned at Rome [1408] at the very time that a council was there under Pope John XII, all the lords of Italy represented to that prince the necessity of enacting a law to reform this horrible abuse. [1409] The Pope and the Emperor were of opinion that the affair should be referred to the council which was to be shortly held at Ravenna. [1410] There the lords made the same demands, and redoubled their complaints; but the affair was put off once more, under pretence of the absence of particular persons. When Otho II and Conrad, King of Burgundy, arrived in Italy, [1411] they had a conference at Verona [1412] with the Italian lords, [1413] and at their repeated solicitations, the Emperor, with their unanimous consent, made a law, that whenever there happened any disputes about inheritances, while one of the parties insisted upon the legality of his title and the other maintained its being false, the affair should be decided by combat; that the same rule should be observed in contests relating to fiefs; and that the clergy should be subject to the same law, but should fight by their champions. Here we see that the nobility insisted on the trial by combat because of the inconvenience of the proof introduced by the clergy; that notwithstanding the clamors of the nobility, the notoriousness of the abuse which called out loudly for redress, and the authority of Otho who came into Italy to speak and act as master, still the clergy held out in two councils; in fine, that the joint concurrence of the nobility and princes having obliged the clergy to submit, the custom of judicial combats must have been considered as a privilege of the nobility, as a barrier against injustice and as a security of property, and from that very moment this custom must have gained ground. And this was effected at a time when the power of the Emperors was great, and that of the popes inconsiderable; at a time when the Othos came to revive the dignity of the empire in Italy.

[1407] Law of the Lombards, book II, tit. 55, chap. xxxiv.
[1408] The year 962.
[1409] *Ab Italiæ proceribus est proclamatum, ut imperator sanctus mutatâ lege, facinus indignum destrueret.*—Law of the Lombards, book II, tit. 55, chap. xxxiv.
[1410] It was held in the year 967, in the presence of Pope John XIII and of the Emperor Otho I.
[1411] Otho II's uncle, son to Rodolphus, and King of Transjurian Burgundy.
[1412] In the year 988.
[1413] Cum in hoc ab omnibus imperials aures pulsarentur.—Law of the Lombards, book II, tit. 55, chap. xxxiv.

I shall make one reflection which will corroborate what has been above said, namely, that the institution of negative proofs entailed that of judicial combats. The abuse complained of to the Otho was, that a person who was charged with having a false title to an estate, defended himself by a negative proof, declaring upon the Gospels it was not false. What was done to reform the abuse of a law which had been mutilated? The custom of combat was revived.

I hastened to speak of the constitution of Otho II, in order to give a clear idea of the disputes between the clergy and the laity of those times. There had been indeed a constitution of Lotharius I [1414] of an earlier date, a sovereign who, upon the same complaints and disputes, being desirous of securing the just possession of property, had ordained that the notary should make oath that the deed or title was not forged; and if the notary should happen to die, the witnesses should be sworn who had signed it. The evil, however, still continued, till they were obliged at length to have recourse to the remedy above-mentioned.

[1414] In the law of the Lombards., book II. tit. 55 § 33. In the copy that Muratori made use of it is attributed to the Emperor Guido.

Before that time I find that, in the general assemblies held by Charlemagne, the nation represented to him [1415] that in the actual state of things it was extremely difficult for either the accuser or the accused to avoid perjuring themselves, and that for this reason it was much better to revive the judicial combat, which was accordingly done.

[1415] In the law of the Lombards, book II. tit. 55. § 23.

The usage of judicial combats gained ground among the Burgundians, and that of an oath was limited. Theodoric, King of Italy, suppressed the single combat among the Ostrogoths; [1416] and the laws of Chaindasuinthus and Recessuinthus seemed as if they would abolish the very idea of it. But these laws were so little respected in Narbonne Gaul, that they looked upon the legal duel as a privilege of the Goths. [1417]

[1416] Cassiodorus, iii. 23, 24.

[1417] In palatio quoque, Bera comes Barcinonensis, cum impeteretur a quodam vocato Sunila, et infidelitatis argueretur, cum eodem secundum legem propriam, utpote quia uterque Gothus erat, equestri prælio congressus est et victus.—The anonymous author of the life of Lewis the Debonnaire.

The Lombards who conquered Italy after the Ostrogoths had been destroyed by the Greeks, introduced the custom of judicial combat into that country, but their first laws gave a check to it. [1418] Charlemagne, [1419] Lewis the Debonnaire, and the Othos made divers general constitutions, which we find inserted in the laws of the Lombards and added to the Salic laws, whereby the practice of legal duels, at first in criminal, and afterwards in civil cases, obtained a greater extent. They knew not what to do. The negative proof by oath had its inconveniences; that of legal duels had its inconveniences also; hence they often changed, according as the one or the other affected them most.

[1418] See in the Law of the Lombards, book I, tit. 4, and tit. 9, § 23, and book II, tit. 35 §§ 4 and 5, and tit. 55 §§ 1,2,3. The regulations of Rotharis; and in § 15, that of Luitprandus.

[1419] Ibid., book II, tit. 55, § 23.

On the one hand, the clergy were pleased to see that in all secular affairs people were obliged to have recourse to the altar, [1420] and, on the other, a haughty nobility were fond of maintaining their rights by the sword.

[1420] The judicial oaths were made at that time in the churches, and during the first race of our kings there was a chapel set apart in the royal palace for the affairs that were to be thus decided. See Marculfus, Formulæ book I. chap. 38. The Law of the Ripuarians, tit. 59, § 4, tit. 65, § 5. The History of Gregory of Tours; and the Capitulary of the year 803, added to the Salic Law.

I would not have it inferred that it was the clergy who introduced the custom so much complained of by the nobility. This custom was derived from the spirit of the Barbarian laws, and from the establishment of negative proofs. But a practice that contributed to the impunity of such a number of criminals, having given some people reason to think it was proper to make use of the sanctity of the churches in order to strike terror into the guilty, and to intimidate perjurers, the clergy maintained this usage and the practice which attended it: for in other respects they were absolutely averse to negative proofs. We find in Beaumanoir [1421] that this kind of proof was never allowed in ecclesiastic courts, which contributed greatly, without doubt, to its suppression, and to weaken in this respect the regulation of the codes of the Barbarian laws.

[1421] Chapter 39, P. 212.

This will convince us more strongly of the connection between the usage of negative proofs and that of judicial combats, of which I have said so much. The lay tribunals admitted of both, and both were rejected by the ecclesiastic courts.

In choosing the trial by duel the nation followed its military spirit; for while this was established as a divine decision, the trials by the cross, by cold or boiling waters, which had been also regarded in the same lights, were abolished.

Charlemagne ordained that, if any difference should arise between his children, it should be terminated by the judgment of the cross. Lewis the Debonnaire [1422] limited this judgment to ecclesiastic affairs; his son Lotharius abolished it in all cases; nay, he suppressed even the trial by cold water. [1423]

[1422] We find his Constitutions inserted in the Law of the Lombards, and at the end of the Salic Laws.
[1423] In a constitution inserted in the Law of the Lombards, book. II, tit. 55, § 31.

I do not pretend to say that, at a time when so few usages were universally received, these trials were not revived in some churches, especially as they are mentioned in a charter of Philip Augustus, [1424] but I affirm that they were very seldom practiced. Beaumanoir, [1425] who lived at the time of St. Lewis and a little after, enumerating the different kinds of trial, mentions that of judicial combat, but not a word of the others.

[1424] In the year 1200.
[1425] Ancient Custom of Beauvoisis, chap. 39.

19. *A new Reason of the Disuse of the Salic and Roman Laws, as also of the Capitularies.*

I have already mentioned the reasons that had destroyed the authority of the Salic and Roman laws, as also of the Capitularies; here I shall add that the principal cause was the great extension given to judiciary combats.

As the Salic laws did not admit of this custom, they became in some measure useless, and fell into oblivion, In like manner the Roman laws, which also rejected this custom, were laid aside; their whole attention was then taken up in establishing the law of judicial combats, and in forming a proper digest of the several cases that might happen on those occasions. The regulations of the Capitularies became likewise of no manner of service. Thus it is that such a number of laws lost all their authority, without our being able to tell the precise time in which it was lost; they fell into oblivion, and we cannot find any others that were substituted in their place.

Such a nation had no need of written laws; hence its written laws might very easily fall into disuse.

If there happened to be any disputes between two parties, they had only to order a single combat. For this no great knowledge or abilities were requisite.

All civil and criminal actions are reduced to facts. It is upon these facts they fought; and not only the substance of the affair, but likewise the incidents and imparlances were decided by combat, as Beaumanoir observes, who produces several instances [1426]

[1426] Chap. 61. pp. 309, 310.

I find that, towards the commencement of the third race, the jurisprudence of those times related entirely to precedents; everything was regulated by the point of honor. If the judge was not obeyed, he insisted upon satisfaction from the person that contemned his authority. At Bourges, if the provost had summoned a person and he refused to come, his way of proceeding was to tell him, *I sent for thee, and thou didst not think it worth thy while to come; I demand therefore satisfaction for this thy contempt.* Upon which they fought. [1427] Lewis the Fat reformed this custom. [1428]

[1427] Charter of Lewis the Fat in the year 1145, in the Collection of Ordinances.
[1428] Ibid.

The custom of legal duels prevailed at Orleans, even in all demands of debt. [1429] Lewis the Young declared that this custom should take place only when the demand exceeded five sous. This ordinance was a local law; for in St. Lewis' time it was sufficient that the value was more than twelve deniers. [1430] Beaumanoir [1431] had heard a gentleman of the law affirm that formerly there had been a bad custom in France of hiring a champion for a certain time to fight their battles in all causes. This shows that the custom of judiciary combat must have prevailed at that time to a wonderful extent.

[1429] Charter of Lewis the Young, in 1168, in the Collection of Ordinances.
[1430] See Beaumanoir, chap. 63, p. 325.
[1431] See the Ancient Custom of Beauvoisis, chap. 28, p. 203.

20. *Origin of the Point of Honor.*

We meet with inexplicable enigmas in the codes of laws of the Barbarians. The law of the Frisians [1432] allows only half a sou in composition to a person that had been beaten with a stick, and yet for ever so small a wound it allows more. By the Salic law, if a freeman gave three blows with a stick to another freeman, he paid three sous; if he drew blood, he was punished as if he had wounded him with steel, and he paid fifteen sous: thus the punishment was proportioned to the greatness of the wound. The law of the Lombards established different compositions for one, two, three, four blows, and so on. [1433] At present, a single blow is equivalent to a hundred thousand.

[1432] Additio sapientium Willemari, tit. 5.
[1433] Book I, tit. 6, § 3.

The constitution of Charlemagne, inserted in the law of the Lombards, ordains that those who were allowed the trial by combat should fight with bastons. [1434] Perhaps this was out of regard to the clergy; or probably, as the usage of legal duels gained ground, they wanted to render them less sanguinary. The capitulary of Lewis the Debonnaire allows the liberty of choosing to fight either with the sword or baston. [1435] In process of time none but bondmen fought with the baston. [1436]

[1434] Book ii, tit. 5, § 23.
[1435] Added to the Salic law in 819.
[1436] See Beaumanoir, 64, p. 323.

Here I see the first rise and formation of the particular articles of our point of honor. The accuser began by declaring in the presence of the judge that such a person had committed such an action, and the accused made answer that he lied, [1437] upon which the judge gave orders for the duel. It became then an established rule that whenever a person had the lie given him, it was incumbent on him to fight.

[1437] Ibid., p. 329.

Upon a man's declaring that he would fight, [1438] he could not afterwards depart from his word; if he did, he was condemned to a penalty. Hence this rule ensued, that whenever a person had engaged his word, honor forbade him to recall it.

[1438] See Beaumanoir, 3, p. 25 and 329.

Gentlemen fought one another on horseback, and armed at all points; [1439] villains fought on foot and with bastons. [1440] Hence it followed that the baston was looked upon as the instrument of insults and affronts, [1441] because to strike a man with it was treating him like a villain.

[1439] See in regard to the arms of the combatants, Beaumanoir, chap. 61, p. 308, and chap. 64, p. 328.
[1440] Ibid., chap. 74, p. 328. See also the Charters of St. Aubin of Anjou, quoted by Galland, p. 263.
[1441] Among the Romans, it was not infamous to be beaten with a stick, lege ictus fustium. De iis qui notantur infamia.

None but villains fought with their faces uncovered, [1442] so that none but they could receive a blow on the face. Therefore, a box on the ear became an injury that must be expiated with blood, because the person who received it had been treated as a villain.

[1442] They had only the baston and buckler.—Beaumanoir, chap. 64, p. 328.

The several people of Germany were no less sensible than we of the point of honor; nay, they were more so. Thus the most distant relatives took a very considerable share to themselves in every affront, and on this all their codes are founded. The law of the Lombards ordains [1443] that whosoever goes attended with servants to beat a man unawares, in order to load him with shame and to render him ridiculous, should pay half the composition which he would owe if he had killed him; [1444] and if through the same motive he tied or bound him, he would pay three-quarters of the same composition.

[1443] Book I, tit. 6, § 1.
[1444] Ibid.; § 2.

Let us then conclude that our forefathers were extremely sensible of affronts; but that affronts of a particular kind, such as being struck with a certain instrument on a certain part of the body, and in a certain manner, were as yet unknown to them. All this was included in the affront of being beaten, and in this case the amount of violence determined the magnitude of the outrage.

21. *A new Reflection upon the Point of Honor among the Germans.*

It was a great infamy, says Tacitus, [1445] *among the Germans for a person to leave his buckler behind him in battle; for which reason many after a misfortune of this kind have destroyed themselves.* Thus the ancient Salic law [1446] allows a composition of fifteen sous to any person that had been injuriously reproached with having left his buckler behind him.

[1445] *De Moribus Germanorum.*
[1446] In the *Pactus legis Salicæ.*

When Charlemagne amended the Salic law, [1447] he allowed in this case no more than three sous in composition. As this prince cannot be suspected of having had a design to enervate the military discipline, it is manifest that such an alteration was due to a change of weapons, and that from this change of weapons a great number of usages derive their origin.

[1447] We have both the ancient law and that which was amended by this prince.

22. *Of the Manners in relation to judicial Combats.*

Our connections with the fair sex are founded on the pleasure of enjoyment; on the happiness of loving and being loved; and likewise on the ambition of pleasing the ladies, because they are the best judges of some of those things which constitute personal merit. This general desire of pleasing produces gallantry, which is not love itself, but the delicate, the volatile, the perpetual simulation of love.

According to the different circumstances of every country and age, love inclines more to one of those three things than to the other two. Now I maintain that the prevailing spirit at the time of our judicial combats must have been that of gallantry.

I find in the law of the Lombards, [1448] that if one of the two champions was found to have any magic herbs about him, the judge ordered them to be taken from him, and obliged him to swear he had no more. This law could be founded only on the vulgar opinion; it was fear, the alleged inventor of much that made them imagine this kind of prestige. As in single combats the champions were armed at all points, and as with heavy arms, both of the offensive and defensive kind, those of a particular temper and strength gave immense advantages, the notion of some champions having enchanted arms must certainly have turned the brains of a great many people.

[1448] Book II, tit. 55, § 11.

Hence arose the marvelous system of chivalry. The minds of all sorts of people quickly imbibed these extravagant ideas, In romances are found knights-errant, necromancers, and fairies, winged or intelligent horses, invisible or invulnerable men, magicians who concerned themselves in the birth and education of great personages, enchanted and disenchanted palaces, a new world in the midst of the old one, the usual course of nature being left only to the lower class of mankind.

Knights-errant ever in armor, in a part of the world abounding in castles, forts, and robbers, placed all their glory in punishing injustice, and in protecting weakness. Hence our romances are full of gallantry founded on the idea of love joined to that of strength and protection.

Such was the origin of gallantry, when they formed the notion of an extraordinary race of men who at the sight of a virtuous and beautiful lady in distress were inclined to expose themselves to all hazards for her sake, and to endeavor to please her in the common actions of life.

Our romances of chivalry flattered this desire of pleasing, and communicated to a part of Europe that spirit of gallantry which we may venture to affirm was very little known to the ancients.

The prodigious luxury of that immense city of Rome encouraged sensuous pleasures. The tranquility of the plains of Greece gave rise to the description of the sentiments of love. [1449] The idea of knights-errant, protectors of the virtue and beauty of the fair sex, led to that of gallantry.

[1449] See the Greek romances of the middle age.

This spirit was continued by the custom of tournaments, which, uniting the rights of valor and love, added still a considerable importance to gallantry.

23. *Of the Code of Laws on judicial Combats.*

Some perhaps will have a curiosity to see this abominable custom of judiciary combat reduced to principles and to find the groundwork of such an extraordinary code of laws. Men, though reasonable in the main, reduce their very prejudices to rule. Nothing was more contrary to good sense, than those combats, and yet when once this point was laid down, a kind of prudential management was used in carrying it into execution.

In order to be thoroughly acquainted with the jurisprudence of those times, it is necessary to read with attention the regulations of St. Lewis, who made such great changes in the judiciary order. Défontaines was contemporary with that prince; Beaumanoir wrote after him, [1450] and the rest lived since his time. We must, therefore, look for the ancient practice in the amendments that have been made of it.

[1450] In the year 1283.

24. *Rules established in the judicial Combat.*

When there happened to be several accusers, they were obliged to agree among themselves that the action might be carried on by a single prosecutor; and, if they could not agree, the person before whom the action was brought, appointed one of them to prosecute the quarrel. [1451]

[1451] Beaumanoir, chap. 6, pp. 40, 41.

When a gentleman challenged a villain, he was obliged to present himself on foot with buckler and baston; but if he came on horseback and armed like a gentleman, they took his horse and his arms from him and, stripping him to his shirt, they compelled him to fight in that condition with the villain. [1452]

[1452] Ibid., chap. 64, p. 328.

Before the combat the magistrates ordered three bans to be published. By the first the relatives of the parties were commanded to retire; by the second the people were warned to be silent; and the third prohibited the giving of any assistance to either of the parties, under severe penalties, nay, even on pain of death if by this assistance either of the combatants should happen to be vanquished. [1453]

[1453] Ibid., chap. 64. p. 330.

The officers belonging to the civil magistrate [1454] guarded the list or enclosure where the battle was fought; and in case either of the parties declared himself desirous of peace, they took particular notice of the actual state in which they mutually stood at that very moment, to the end that they might be restored to the same situation in case they did not come to an understanding. [1455]

[1454] Ibid.
[1455] Ibid.

When the pledges were received either for a crime or for false judgment, the parties could not make up the matter without the consent of the lord; and when one of the parties was overcome, there could be no accommodation without the permission of the count, which had some analogy to our letters of grace. [1456]

[1456] The great vassals had particular privileges.

But if it happened to be a capital crime, and the lord, corrupted by presents, consented to an accommodation, he was obliged to pay a fine of sixty livres, and the right he had of punishing the malefactor devolved upon the count. [1457]

[1457] Beaumanoir, chap. 64, p. 330, says he lost his jurisdiction: these words in the authors of those days have not a general signification, but a signification limited to the affair in question. Défontaines, chap. 21, art. 29.

There were a great many people incapable either of offering, or of accepting battle. But liberty was given them, on cause being shown, to choose a champion; and that he might have a stronger interest in defending the party in whose behalf he appeared, his hand was cut off if he lost the battle. [1458]

[1458] This custom, which we meet with in the Capitularies, was still subsisting at the time of Beaumanoir. See chap. 61, p. 315.

When capital laws were made in the last century against duels, perhaps it would have been sufficient to have deprived a warrior of his military capacity by the loss of his hand;

nothing in general being a greater mortification to mankind than to survive the loss of their character.

When, in capital cases, the duel was fought by champions, the parties were placed where they could not behold the battle; each was bound with the cord that was to be used at his execution in case his champion was overcome. [1459] The person overcome in battle did not always lose the point contested; if, for instance, they fought on an imparlance, he lost only the imparlance. [1460]

[1459] Beaumanoir, chap. 64, p. 330.
[1460] Ibid., chap. 61, p. 309.

25. Of the Bounds prescribed to the Custom of judicial Combats.

When pledges of battle had been received upon a civil affair of small importance, the lord obliged the parties to withdraw them.

If a fact was notorious; for instance, if a man had been assassinated in the open marketplace, then there was neither a trial by witnesses, nor by combat; the judge gave his decision from the notoriety of the fact. [1461]

[1461] Ibid., p. 308; chap. 43, p. 239.

When the court of a lord had often determined after the same manner, and the usage was thus known, [1462] the lord refused to grant the parties the privilege of dueling, to the end that the usages might not be altered by the different success of the combats.

[1462] Beaumanoir, chap. 61, p. 314. See also Défontaines, chap. 22, art. 24.

They were not allowed to insist upon dueling but for themselves, for someone belonging to their family, or for their liege lord. [1463]

[1463] Beaumanoir, 63, p. 322.

When the accused had been acquitted, another relative could not insist on fighting him; otherwise disputes would never be terminated. [1464]

[1464] Ibid.

If a person appeared again in public whose relatives, upon a supposition of his being murdered, wanted to revenge his death, there was then no room for a combat; the same may be said if by a notorious absence the fact was proved to be impossible. [1465]

[1465] Ibid.

If a man who had been mortally wounded had exculpated before his death the person accused and named another, they did not proceed to a duel; but if he had mentioned nobody his declaration was looked upon as a forgiveness on his death-bed; the prosecution was continued, and even among gentlemen they could make war against each other. [1466]

[1466] Ibid., p. 323.

When there was a conflict, and one of the relatives had given or received pledges of battle, the right of contest ceased; for then it was thought that the parties wanted to pursue the ordinary course of justice; therefore he that would have continued the contest would have been sentenced to make good all the losses.

Thus the practice of judiciary combat had this advantage, that it was apt to change a general into an individual quarrel, to restore the courts of judicature to their authority, and to bring back into the civil state those who were no longer governed but by the law of nations.

As there are an infinite number of wise things that are managed in a very foolish manner; so there are many foolish things that are very wisely conducted.

When a man who was challenged with a crime visibly showed that it had been committed by the challenger himself, there could be then no pledges of battle; for there is no criminal but would prefer a duel of uncertain event to a certain punishment. [1467]

[1467] Ibid., chap. 63, p. 324.

There were no duels in affairs decided by arbiters, [1468] nor by ecclesiastical courts, nor in cases relating to women's dowries.

[1468] Ibid., p. 325.

A woman, says Beaumanoir, *cannot fight*. if a woman challenged a person without naming her champion, the pledges of battle were not accepted. It was also requisite that a woman should be authorized by her baron, that is, by her husband, to challenge; but she might be challenged without this authority. [1469]

[1469] Ibid.

If either the challenger or the person challenged were under fifteen years of age, there could be no combat. [1470] They might order it, indeed, in disputes relating to orphans when their guardians or trustees were willing to run the risk of this procedure.

[1471] Ibid., chap. 63. p. 323. See also what I have said in book

The cases in which a bondman was allowed to fight are, I think, as follows. He was allowed to fight another bondman; to fight a freedman, or even a gentleman, in case he were challenged; but if he himself challenged, the other might refuse to fight; and even the bondman's lord had a right to take him out of the court. [1472] The bondman might by his lord's charter or by usage fight with any freeman; [1473] and the church claimed this right for her bondmen [1474] as a mark of respect due to her by the laity. [1475]

[1472] Ibid., p. 327.
[1473] Défontaines, 22, art. 7.
[1474] Habeant bellandi et testificandi licentiam.—Charter of Lewis the Fat, in the year 1118.

[1475] Ibid.

26. *On the judiciary Combat between one of the Parties and one of the Witnesses.*

Beaumanoir informs us [1476] that a person who saw a witness going to swear against him might elude the other by telling the judges that his adversary produced a false and slandering witness; and if the witness was willing to maintain the quarrel, he gave pledges of battle. The inquiry was no longer the question; for if the witness was overcome, it was decided that the adversary had produced a false witness, and he lost his cause.

[1476] Chapter 61, p. 315.

It was necessary that the second witness should not be heard; for if he had made his attestation, the affair would have been decided by the deposition of two witnesses. But by staying the second, the deposition of the first witness became void.

The second witness being thus rejected, the party was not allowed to produce any others, but he lost his cause; in case, however, there had been no pledges of battle, he might produce other witnesses.

Beaumanoir observes [1477] that the witness might say to the party he appeared for, before he made his deposition: *I do not care to fight for your quarrel, nor to enter into any debate; but if you are willing to stand by me, I am ready to tell the truth.* The party was then obliged to fight for the witness, and if he happened to be overcome, he did not lose his cause, [1478] but the witness was rejected.

[1477] Chapter 6, p. 39, 40.
[1478] But if the battle was fought by champions, the champion that was overcome had his hand cut off.

This, I believe, was a modification of the ancient custom; and what makes me think so is that we find this usage of challenging the witnesses established in the laws of the Bavarians [1479] and Burgundians [1480] without any restriction.

[1479] Tit. 16, § 7.
[1480] Tit. 45.

I have already made mention of the constitution of Gundebald, against which Agobard [1481] and St. Avitus [1482] made such loud complaints. *When the accused,* says this prince, *produces witnesses to swear that he has not committed the crime, the accuser may challenge one of the witnesses to a combat; for it is very just that the person who has offered to swear, and has declared that he was certain of the truth, should make no difficulty of maintaining it by combat.* Thus the witnesses were deprived by this king of every kind of subterfuge to avoid the judiciary combat.

[1481] Letter to Lewis the Debonnaire.
[1482] Life of St. Avitus.

27. *Of the judicial Combat between one of the Parties and one of the Lords' Peers.*

Appeal of false Judgment. As the nature of judicial combats was to terminate the affair forever, and was incompatible with a new judgment and new prosecutions, [1483] an appeal, such as is established by the Roman and Canon laws, that is, to a superior court in order to rejudge the proceedings of an inferior, was a thing unknown in France.

[1483] Beaumanoir, chap. 2, p. 22.

This is a form of proceeding to which a warlike nation, governed solely by the point of honor, was quite a stranger; and agreeably to this very spirit, the same methods were used against the judges as were allowed against the parties. [1484]

[1484] Ibid., chap. 61, p. 312, and chap. 67, p. 338.

An appeal among the people of this nation was a challenge to fight with arms, a challenge to be decided by blood; and not that invitation to a paper quarrel, the knowledge of which was reserved for succeeding ages.

Thus St. Lewis, in his Institutions, [1485] says that an appeal includes both felony and iniquity. Thus Beaumanoir tells us that if a vassal wanted to make his complaint of an outrage committed against him by his lord, [1486] he was first obliged to announce that he quitted his fief; after which he appealed to his lord paramount, and offered pledges of battle, In like manner the lord renounced the homage of his vassal, if he challenged him before the count.

[1485] Book II. chap. 15.
[1486] Beaumanoir, chap. 61, pp. 310 and 311, and chap. 67, p. 337.

For a vassal to challenge his lord of false judgment was as much as to say to him that his sentence was unjust and malicious; now to utter such words against his lord was in some measure committing the crime of felony.

Hence, instead of bringing a challenge of false judgment against the lord who appointed and directed the court, they challenged the peers of whom the court itself was formed, by which means they avoided the crime of felony, for they insulted only their peers, with whom they could always account for the affront.

It was a very dangerous thing to challenge the peers of false judgment. [1487] If the party waited till judgment was pronounced, he was obliged to fight them all when they offered to make good their judgment. [1488] If the appeal was made before all the judges had given their opinion, he was obliged to fight all who had agreed in their judgment. To avoid this danger, it was usual to petition the lord to direct that each peer should give his opinion aloud; [1489] and when the first had pronounced, and the second was going to do the same, the party told him that he was a liar, a knave and a slanderer, and then he had to fight only with that peer.

[1487] Ibid., 61, p. 313.
[1488] Ibid., p. 314.
[1489] Ibid.

Défontaines [1490] would have it that, before a challenge was made of false judgment, it was customary to let three judges pronounce; and he does not say that it was necessary to fight them all three; much less that there was any obligation to fight all those who had declared themselves of the same opinion. These differences arose from this, that in those times there were few usages exactly in all parts the same; Beaumanoir gives an account of what passed in the county of Clermont; and Défontaines of what was practiced in Vermandois.

[1490] Chapter 22, art. 1, 10, and 11, he says only that each of them was allowed a small
    fine.

When one of the peers or a vassal had declared that he would maintain the judgment, the judge ordered pledges of battle to be given, and likewise took security of the challenger that he would maintain his case. [1491] But the peer who was challenged gave no security, because he was the lord's vassal, and was obliged to defend the challenge, or to pay the lord a fine of sixty livres.

[1491] Beaumanoir, chap. 61, p. 314.

If he who challenged did not prove that the judgment was bad, [1492] he paid the lord a fine of sixty livres, the same fine to the peer whom he had challenged, and as much to every one of those who had openly consented to the judgment. [1493]

[1492] Ibid. Défontaines, chap. 22, art. 9.
[1493] Ibid.

When a person, strongly suspected of a capital crime, had been taken and condemned, he could make no appeal of false judgment: [1494] for he would always appeal either to prolong his life, or to get an absolute discharge.

[1494] Beaumanoir, chap. 61, p. 316, and Défontaines, chap. 22, art. 21.

If a person said that the judgment was false and bad and did not offer to prove it so, that is, to fight, he was condemned to a fine of ten sous if a gentleman, and to five sous if a bondman, for the injurious expressions he had uttered. [1495]

[1495] Beaumanoir, chap. 61, p. 314.

The judges or peers who were overcome forfeited neither life nor limbs, [1496] but the person who challenged them was punished with death, if it happened to be a capital crime. [1497]

[1496] Défontaines, chap. 22, art. 7.
[1497] See Défontaines, chap. 21, arts. 11 and 12, and following, who distinguishes the
    cases in which the appellant of false judgment loses his life, the point contested, or
    only the imparlance.

This manner of challenging the vassals with false judgment was to avoid challenging the lord himself. But if the lord had no peers, [1498] or had not a sufficient number, he might at his own expense borrow peers of his lord paramount; [1499] but these peers were not obliged to pronounce judgment if they did not like it; they might declare that they were come only to give their opinion: in that particular case, the lord himself judged and pronounced sentence as judge; [1500] and if an appeal of false judgment was made against him, it was his business to answer to the challenge.

[1498] Beaumanoir, chap. 62, p. 322. Défontaines, chap. 22, art. 3.
[1499] The count was not obliged to lend any. Beaumanoir, chap. 67, p. 337.
[1500] Nobody can pass judgment in his court. Says Beaumanoir, chap 67, pp. 336, 337.

If the lord happened to be so very poor as not to be able to hire peers of his paramount, [1501] or if he neglected to ask for them, or the paramount refused to give them, then, as the lord could not judge by himself, and as nobody was obliged to plead before a tribunal where judgment could not be given, the affair was brought before the lord paramount.

[1501] Ibid., chap. 62, p. 322.

This, I believe, was one of the principal causes of the separation between the jurisdiction and the fief, whence arose the maxim of the French lawyers, *The fief is one thing, and the jurisdiction is another*. For as there were a vast number of peers who had no subordinate vassals under them, they were incapable of holding their court; all affairs were then brought before their lord paramount, and they lost the privilege of pronouncing judgment, because they had neither power nor will to claim it.

All the judges who had been at the judgment were obliged to be present when it was pronounced, that they might follow one another, and say aye to the person who, wanting to make an appeal of false judgment, asked them whether they followed; [1502] for Défontaines says, [1503] *that it is an affair of courtesy and loyalty, and there is no such thing as evasion or delay*. Hence, I imagine, arose the custom still followed in England of obliging the jury to be all unanimous in their verdict in cases relating to life and death.

[1502] Défontaines, chap. 21, arts. 27 and 28.
[1503] Ibid., art. 28.

Judgment was therefore given, according to the opinion of the majority; and if there was an equal division, sentence was pronounced, in criminal cases, in favor of the accused; in cases of debt, in favor of the debtor; and in cases of inheritance, in favor of the defendant.

Défontaines observes [1504] that a peer could not excuse himself by saying that he would not sit in court if there were only four, [1505] or if the whole number, or at least the wisest part, were not present. This is just as if he were to say, in the heat of an engagement, that he would not assist his lord because he had not all his vassals with him. But it was the lord's business to cause his court to be respected, and to choose the bravest and most knowing of his tenants. This I mention, in order to show the duty of vassals, which was to fight, and to give judgment: and such, indeed, was this duty, that to give judgment was all the same as to fight.

[1504] Chapter 21, art. 37.
[1505] This number at least was necessary. Défontaines, chap. 21, art. 36.

It was lawful for a lord, who went to law with his vassal in his own court, and was cast, to challenge one of his tenants with false judgment. But as the latter owed a respect to his lord for the fealty he had vowed, and the lord, on the other hand, owed benevolence to his vassal for the fealty accepted, it was customary to make a distinction between the lord's affirming in general that the judgment was false and unjust, [1506] and imputing personal prevarications to his tenant. [1507] In the former case he affronted his own court, and in some measure himself, so that there was no room for pledges of battle. But there was room in the latter, because he attacked his vassal's honor; and the person overcome was deprived of life and property, in order to maintain the public tranquility.

[1506] Beaumanoir, chap. 67, p. 337.
[1507] Ibid.

This distinction, which was necessary in that particular case, had afterwards a greater extent. Beaumanoir says that when the challenger of false judgment attacked one of the peers by personal imputation, battle ensued; but if he attacked only the judgment, the peer challenged was at liberty to determine the dispute either by battle or by law. [1508] But as the prevailing spirit in Beaumanoir's time was to restrain the usage of judicial combats, and as this liberty, which had been granted to the peer challenged, of defending the judgment by combat or not is equally contrary to the ideas of honor established in those days, and to the obligation the vassal lay under of defending his lord's jurisdiction, I am apt to think that this distinction of Beaumanoir's was a novelty in French jurisprudence.

[1508] Ibid., pp. 337, 338.

I would not have it thought that all appeals of false judgment were decided by battle; it fared with this appeal as with all others. The reader may recollect the exceptions mentioned in the 25th chapter. Here it was the business of the superior court to examine whether it was proper to withdraw the pledges of battle or not.

There could be no appeal of false judgment against the king's court, because, as there was no one equal to the king, no one could challenge him; and as the king had no superior, none could appeal from his court.

This fundamental regulation, which was necessary as a political law, diminished also as a civil law the abuses of the judicial proceedings of those times. When a lord was afraid that his court would be challenged with false judgment, or perceived that they were determined to challenge, if the interests of justice required that it should not be challenged, he might demand from the king's court men whose judgment could not be set aside. [1509] Thus King Philip, says Défontaines, [1509] sent his whole council to judge an affair in the court of the Abbot of Corbey.

[1510] Défontaines, 22, art. 14.
[1510] Ibid.

But if the lord could not have judges from the king, he might remove his court into the king's, if he held immediately of him; and if there were intermediate lords, he had recourse to his suzerain, removing from one lord to another till he came to the sovereign.

Thus, notwithstanding they had in those days neither the practice nor even the idea of our modern appeals, yet they had recourse to the king, who was the source whence all those rivers flowed, and the sea into which they returned.

28. *Of the Appeal of Default of Justice.*

The appeal of default of justice was, when the court of a particular lord deferred, evaded, or refused to do justice to the parties.

During the time of our princes of the second race, though the count had several officers under him, their person was subordinate, but not their jurisdiction. These officers in their court days, assizes, or *placita*, gave judgment in the last resort as the count himself; all the difference consisted in the division of the jurisdiction. For instance, the count had the power of condemning to death, of judging of liberty, and of the restitution of goods, which the *centenarii* had not. [1511]

[1511] Third capitulary of the year 812, art. 3, edition of Baluzius, p. 497, and of Charles the Bald, added to the law of the Lombards, book II, art. 3.

For the same reason there were greater cases which were reserved to the king; namely, those which directly concerned the political order of the state. [1512] Such were the disputes between bishops, abbots, counts, and other grandees, which were determined by the king together with the great vassals. [1513]

[1512] Third capitulary of the year 812, art. 2, edition of Baluzius, p. 497.
[1513] *Cum fidelibus.*—Capitulary of Lewis the Debonnaire, edition of Baluzius, p. 667.

What some authors have advanced, namely, that an appeal lay from the count to the king's commissary, or Missus Dominicus, is not well-grounded. The count and the Missus had an equal jurisdiction, independent of each other. [1514] The whole difference was that the Missus held his Placita, or assizes, four months in the year, [1515] and the count the other eight.

[1514] See the Capitulary of Charles the Bald, added to the law of the Lombards, book II, art. 3.
[1515] Third capitulary of the year 812, art. 8.

If a person, who had been condemned at an assize, demanded to have his cause tried over again, and was afterwards cast, he paid a fine of fifteen sous, or received fifteen blows from the judges who had decided the affair. [1516]

[1516] Placitum.

When the counts, or the king's commissaries did not find themselves able to bring the great lords to reason, they made them give bail or security [1517] that they would appear in the king's court: this was to try the cause, and not to rejudge it. I find in the capitulary of Metz [1518] a law by which the appeal of false judgment to the king's court is established, and all other kinds of appeal are proscribed and punished.

[1517] This appears by the formulas, charters, and the capitularies.
[1518] In the year 757, edition of Baluzius, p. 180, arts. 9 and 10, and the Synod *apud Vernas*, in the year 755, art. 29, edition of Baluzius, p. 175. These two capitularies were made under King Pepin.

If they refused to submit to the judgment of the sheriffs [1519] and made no complaint, they were imprisoned till they had submitted, but if they complained, they were conducted under a proper guard before the king, and the affair was examined in his court.

[1519] The officers under the count, Scabini.

There could be hardly any room then for an appeal of default of justice. For instead of its being usual in those days to complain that the counts and others who had a right of holding assizes were not exact in discharging this duty, [1520] it was a general complaint that they were too exact. Hence we find such numbers of ordinances, by which the counts and all other officers of justice are forbidden to hold their assizes above thrice a year. It was not so necessary to chastise their indolence, as to check their activity.

[1520] See the Law of the Lombards, ii, tit. 52, art. 22.

But, after an infinite number of petty lordships had been formed, and different degrees of vassalage established, the neglect of certain vassals in holding their courts gave rise to this kind of appeal; [1521] especially as very considerable profits accrued to the lord paramount from the several fines.

[1521] There are instances of appeals of default of justice as early as the time of Philip Augustus.

As the custom of judicial combats gained every day more ground, there were places, cases, and times, in which it was difficult to assemble the peers, and consequently in which justice was delayed. The appeal of default of justice was therefore introduced, an appeal that has been often a remarkable era in our history; because most of the wars of those days were imputed to a violation of the political law; as the cause, or at least the pretence, of our modern wars is the infringement of the laws of nations.

Beaumanoir says [1522] that, in case of default of justice, battle was not allowed: the reasons are these: 1. They could not challenge the lord himself, because of the respect due to his person; neither could they challenge the lord's peers, because the case was clear, and they had only to reckon the days of the summons, or of the other delays; there had been no judgment passed, consequently there could be no appeal of false judgment: in fine, the crime of the peers offended the lord as well as the party, and it was against rule that there should be battle between the lord and his peers.

[1522] Chapter 61, p. 315.

But as the default was proved by witnesses before the superior court, [1523] the witnesses might be challenged, and then neither the lord nor his court were offended.

[1523] Ibid.

In case the default was owing to the lord's tenants or peers, who had delayed to administer justice, or had avoided giving judgment after past delays, then these peers were appealed of default of justice before the paramount; and if they were cast, they paid a fine to their lord. [1524] The latter could not give them any assistance; on the contrary, he seized their fief, till they had each paid a fine of sixty livres.

[1524] Défontaines, chap. 21, art. 24.

2. When the default was owing to the lord, which was the case whenever there happened not to be a sufficient number of peers in his court to pass judgment, or when he had not assembled his tenants or appointed somebody in his place to assemble them, an appeal might be made of the default before the lord paramount; but then the party and not the lord was summoned, because of the respect due to the latter. [1525]

[1525] Ibid., art. 32.

The lord demanded to be tried before the paramount, and if he was acquitted of the default, the cause was remanded to him, and he was likewise paid a fine of sixty livres. [1526] But if the default was proved, the penalty inflicted on him was to lose the trial of the cause, [1527] which was to be then determined in the superior court. And, indeed, the complaint of default was made with no other view.

[1526] Beaumanoir, 61, p. 312.
[1527] Défontaines, 21, art. 1, 29.

3. If the lord was sued in his own court, [1528] which never happened but upon disputes in relation to the fief, after letting all the delays pass, the lord himself was summoned before the peers in the sovereign's name, [1529] whose permission was necessary on that occasion. The peers did not make the summons in their own name, because they could not summon their lord, but they could summon for their lord. [1530]

[1528] This was the case in the famous difference between the Lord of Nesle and Joan, Countess of Flanders, during the reign of Lewis VIII. He called upon her to have it tried within forty days, and thereupon challenged her at the king's court with default of justice. She answered that she would have it tried by her peers in Flanders. The king's court determined that it should not be sent there and that the countess should be cited.
[1529] Défontaines, 21, art. 34.
[1530] Ibid., chap. 21, art. 9.

Sometimes the appeal of default of justice was followed by an appeal of false judgment, when the lord had caused judgment to be passed, notwithstanding the default. [1531]

[1531] Beaumanoir, 61, p. 311.

The vassal who had wrongfully challenged his lord of default of justice was sentenced to pay a fine according to his lord's pleasure. [1532]

[1532] Beaumanoir, chap. 61, p. 312. But he that was neither tenant nor vassal to the lord paid only a fine of sixty livres.—Ibid.

The inhabitants of Gaunt had challenged the Earl of Flanders of default of justice before the king, for having delayed to give judgment in his own court. [1533] Upon examination it was found that he had used fewer delays than even the custom of the country allowed. They were therefore remanded to him; upon which their effects to the value of sixty thousand livres were seized. They returned to the king's court in order to have the fine moderated; but it was decided that the earl might insist upon the fine, and even upon more if he pleased. Beaumanoir was present at those judgments.

[1533] Ibid., chap. 61, p. 318.

4. In other disputes which the lord might have with his vassal, in respect to the person or honor of the latter, or to property that did not belong to the fief, there was no room for a challenge of default of justice; because the cause was not tried in the lord's court, but in that of the paramount: vassals, says Défontaines, [1534] having no power to give judgment on the person of their lord.

[1534] Chapter 21, art. 35.

I have been at some trouble to give a clear idea of those things, which are so obscure and confused in ancient authors that to disentangle them from the chaos in which they were involved may be reckoned a new discovery.

29. *Epoch of the Reign of St. Lewis.*

St. Lewis abolished the judicial combats in all the courts of his demesne, as appears by the ordinance he published thereupon, [1535] and by the Institutions. [1536]

[1535] In the year 1260.
[1536] Book I., chap. 2, 7, and book II. chap. 10, 11.

But he did not suppress them in the courts of his barons, except in the case of challenge of false judgment. [1537]

[1537] As appears everywhere in the Institutions, &c., and Beaumanoir, 61, p. 309.

A vassal could not challenge the court of his lord of false judgment, without demanding a judicial combat against the judges who pronounced sentence. But St. Lewis introduced the practice of challenging of false judgment without fighting, a change that may be reckoned a kind of revolution. [1538]

[1538] Institutions, book I. chap. 6, and book II. chap. 15.

He declared [1539] that there should be no challenge of false judgment in the lordships of his demesnes, because it was a crime of felony. In reality, if it was a kind of felony against the lord, by a much stronger reason it was felony against the king. But he consented that they might demand an amendment [1540] of the judgments passed in his courts; not because they were false or iniquitous, but because they did some prejudice. [1541] On the contrary, he ordained that they should be obliged to make a challenge of false judgment against the courts of the barons, [1542] in case of any complaint.

[1539] Ibid., book II. chap. 15.
[1540] Ibid., book I. chap. 78, and book II. chap. 15.
[1541] Ibid., book I. chap. 78.
[1542] Ibid., book II. chap. 15.

It was not allowed by the Institutions, as we have already observed, to bring a challenge of false judgment against the courts in the king's demesnes. They were obliged to demand an amendment before the same court; and in case the bailiff refused the amendment demanded, the king gave leave to make an appeal to his court; [1543] or rather, interpreting the Institutions by themselves, to present him a request or petition. [1544]

[1543] Ibid., book I. chap. 78.
[1544] Ibid., book II. chap. 15.

With regard to the courts of the lords, St. Lewis, by permitting them to be challenged of false judgment, would have the cause brought before the royal tribunal, [1545] or that of the lord paramount, not to be decided by duel [1546] but by witnesses, pursuant to a certain form of proceeding, the rules of which he laid down in the Institutions. [1547]

[1545] But if they wanted to appeal without falsifying the judgment, the appeal was not admitted.—*Institutions*, book II. chap. 15.
[1546] Ibid., book I. chap. 6, 67; and book II. chap. 15; and Beaumanoir, chap. 11, p. 58.
[1547] Book I. chap. 1-3.

Thus, whether they could falsify the judgment, as in the court of the barons; or whether they could not falsify, as in the court of his demesnes, he ordained that they might appeal without the hazard of a duel.

Défontaines [1548] gives us the first two examples he ever saw, in which they proceeded thus without a legal duel: one, in a cause tried at the court of St. Quentin, which belonged to the king's demesne; and the other, in the court of Ponthieu, where the count, who was present, opposed the ancient jurisprudence: but these two causes were decided by law.

[1548] Chapter 22, arts. 16, 17.

Here, perhaps, it will be asked why St. Lewis ordained for the courts of his barons a different form of proceeding from that which he had established in the courts of his demesne? The reason is this: when St. Lewis made the regulation for the courts of his demesnes, he was not checked or limited in his views: but he had measures to keep with the lords who enjoyed this ancient prerogative, that causes should not be removed from their courts, unless the party was willing to expose himself to the dangers of an appeal of false judgment. St. Lewis preserved the usage of this appeal; but he ordained that it should be made without a judicial combat; that is, in order to make the change less felt, he suppressed the thing, and continued the terms.

This regulation was not universally received in the courts of the lords. Beaumanoir says [1549] that in his time there were two ways of trying causes; one according to the king's establishment, and the other pursuant to the ancient practice; that the lords were at liberty to follow which way they pleased; but when they had pitched upon one in any cause, they could not afterwards have recourse to the other. He adds, [1550] that the Count of Clermont followed the new practice, while his vassals kept to the old one; but that it was in his power to reestablish the ancient practice whenever he pleased, otherwise he would have less authority than his vassals.

[1549] Chapter 61, p. 309.
[1550] Ibid.

It is proper here to observe that France was at that time divided into the country of the king's demesne, and that which was called the country of the barons, or the baronies; and, to make use of the terms of St. Lewis' Institutions, into the country under obedience to the king, and the country out of his obedience. [1551] When the king made ordinances for the country of his demesne, he employed his own single authority. But when he published any ordinances that concerned also the country of his barons, these were made in concert with them, [1552] or sealed and subscribed by them: otherwise the barons received or refused them, according as they seemed conducive to the good of their baronies. The rear-vassals were upon the same terms with the great-vassals. Now the Institutions were not made with the consent of the lords, though they regulated matters which to them were of great importance: but they were received only by those who believed they would redound to their advantage. Robert, son of St. Lewis, received them in his county of Clermont; yet his vassals did not think proper to conform to this practice.

[1551] See Beaumanoir, Défontaines, and the Institutions, book. II. chap. 10, 11, 15, and others.
[1552] See the ordinances at the beginning of the third race, in the collection of Laurière, especially those of Philip Augustus, on ecclesiastic jurisdiction; that of Lewis VIII concerning the Jews; and the charters related by Mr. Brussel; particularly that of St. Lewis, on the release and recovery of lands, and the feodal majority of young women, tom. ii, book III, p. 35, and *ibid.*, the ordinance of Philip Augustus, p. 7.

30. *Observation on Appeals.*

I apprehend that appeals, which were challenges to a combat, must have been made immediately on the spot. "If the party leaves the court without appealing," says Beaumanoir, [1553] "he loses his appeal, and the judgment stands good." This continued still in force, even after all the restrictions of judicial combat. [1554]

[1553] Chapter 63, p. 327: chapter 61, p. 312.
[1554] See the Institutions of St. Lewis, book II. chap. 15, and the Ordinance of Charles VII in the year 1453.

31. *The same Subject continued.*

The villain could not bring a challenge of false judgment against the court of his lord. This we learn from Défontaines, [1555] and he is confirmed moreover by the Institutions. [1556] Hence Défontaines says, [1557] *between the lord and his villain there is no other judge but God.*

[1555] Chapter 21, arts. 21, 22.
[1556] Book I. chap 136.
[1557] Chapter 2, art. 8.

It was the custom of judicial combats that deprived the villains of the privilege of challenging their lord's court of false judgment. And so true is this, that those villains [1558] who by charter or custom had a right to fight had also the privilege of challenging their lord's court of false judgment, even though the peers who tried them were gentlemen; [1559] and Défontaines proposes expedients to gentlemen in order to avoid the scandal of fighting with a villain by whom they had been challenged of false judgment. [1560]

[1558] Défontaines, chap. 22, art. 7. This article, and the 21st of the 22nd chapter of the same author, have been hitherto very badly explained. Défontaines does not oppose the judgment of the lord to that of the gentleman, because it was the same thing; but he opposes the common villain to him who had the privilege of fighting.
[1559] Gentlemen may always be appointed judges. Défontaines, chap. 21, art. 48.
[1560] Chap. 22, art. 14.

As the practice of judicial combats began to decline, and the usage of new appeals to be introduced, it was reckoned unfair that freemen should have a remedy against the injustice of the courts of their lords, and the villains should not; hence the parliament received their appeals all the same as those of freemen.

32. *The same Subject continued.*

When a challenge of false judgment was brought against the lord's court, the lord appeared in person before his paramount to defend the judgment of his court. In like manner, in the appeal of default of justice, the party summoned before the lord paramount brought his lord along with him, to the end that if the default was not proved, he might recover his jurisdiction. [1561]

[1561] Défontaines, chap. 21, art. 33.

In process of time as the practice observed in these two particular cases became general, by the introduction of all sorts of appeals, it seemed very extraordinary that the lord should be obliged to spend his whole life in strange tribunals, and for other people's affairs. Philip of Valois ordained [1562] that none but the bailiffs should be summoned; and when the usage of appeals became still more frequent, the parties were obliged to defend the appeal: the deed of the judge became that of the party. [1563]

[1562] In the year 1332.
[1563] See the situation of things in Boutillier's time, who lived in the year 1402.— *Somme Rurale*, book I, pp. 19, 20.

I took notice that in the appeal of default of justice, [1564] the lord lost only the privilege of having the cause tried in his own court. But if the lord himself was sued as party, [1565] which became a very common practice, [1566] he paid a fine of sixty livres to the king, or to the paramount, before whom the appeal was brought. Thence arose the usage, after appeals had been generally received, of making the fine payable to the lord upon the reversal of the sentence of his judge; a usage which lasted a long time, and was confirmed by the ordinance of Rousillon, but fell, at length, to the ground through its own absurdity.

[1564] See chapter 30.
[1565] Beaumanoir, chap. 61, pp. 312 and 318.
[1566] Ibid.

33. *The same Subject continued.*

In the practice of judicial combats, the person who had challenged one of the judges of false judgment might lose his cause by the combat, but could not possibly gain it. [1567] And, indeed, the party who had a judgment in his favor ought not to have been deprived of it by another man's act. The appellant, therefore, who had gained the battle was obliged to fight likewise against the adverse party: not in order to know whether the judgment was good or bad (for this judgment was out of the case, being reversed by the combat), but to determine whether the demand was just or not; and it was on this new point they fought. Thence proceeds our manner of pronouncing decrees, *The court annuls the appeal; the court annuls the appeal and the judgment against which the appeal was brought.* In effect, when the person who had made the challenge of false judgment happened to be overcome, the appeal was reversed: when he proved victorious, both the judgment and the appeal were reversed; then they were obliged to proceed to a new judgment.

[1567] Défontaines, chap. 21, art. 14.

This is so far true that, when the cause was tried by inquests, this manner of pronouncing did not take place: witness what M. de la Roche Flavin says, [1568] namely, that the chamber of inquiry could not use this form at the beginning of its existence.

[1568] Of the Parliaments of France, book XII. chap. 16.

34. *In what Manner the Proceedings at Law became secret.*

Duels had introduced a public form of proceeding, so that both the attack and the defense were equally known. *The witnesses*, says Beaumanoir, [1569] *ought to give their testimony in open court.*

[1569] Chapter 61, p. 315.

Boutillier's commentator says he had learned of ancient practitioners, and from some old manuscript law books, that criminal processes were anciently carried on in public, and in a form not very different from the public judgments of the Romans. This was owing to their not knowing how to write; a thing in those days very common. The usage of writing fixes the ideas, and keeps the secret; but when this usage is laid aside, nothing but the notoriety of the proceeding is capable of fixing those ideas.

And as uncertainty might easily arise in respect to what had been adjudicated by vassals, or pleaded before them, they could, therefore, refresh their memory [1570] every time they held a court by what were called proceedings on record. [1571] In that case, it was not allowed to challenge the witnesses to combat; for then there would be no end of disputes.

[1570] As Beaumanoir says, chapter 39, p. 209.
[1571] They proved by witnesses what had been already done, said, or decreed in court.

In process of time a private form of proceeding was introduced. Everything before had been public; everything now became secret; the interrogatories, the informations, the re-examinations, the confronting of witnesses, the opinion of the attorney-general; and this is the present practice. The first form of proceeding was suitable to the government of that time, as the new form was proper to the government since established.

Boutillier's commentator fixes the epoch of this change to the ordinance in the year 1539. I am apt to believe that the change was made insensibly, and passed from one lordship to another, in proportion as the lords renounced the ancient form of judging, and that derived from the Institutions of St. Lewis was improved. And indeed, Beaumanoir says [1572] that witnesses were publicly heard only in cases in which it was allowed to give pledges of battle: in others they were heard in secret, and their depositions were reduced to writing. The proceedings became, therefore, secret, when they ceased to give pledges of battle.

[1572] Chapter 39, p. 218.

35. *Of the Costs.*

In former times no one was condemned in the lay courts of France to the payment of costs. [1573] The party cast was sufficiently punished by pecuniary fines to the lord and his peers. From the manner of proceeding by judicial combat it followed, that the party condemned and deprived of life and fortune was punished as much as he could be: and in the other cases of the judicial combat, there were fines sometimes fixed, and sometimes dependent on the disposition of the lord, which were sufficient to make people dread the consequences of suits. The same may be said of causes that were not decided by combat. As the lord had the chief profits, so he was also at the chief expense, either to assemble his peers, or to enable them to proceed to judgment. Besides, as disputes were generally determined at the same place, and almost always at the same time, without that infinite multitude of writings which afterwards followed, there was no necessity of allowing costs to the parties.

[1573] Défontaines in his counsel, chapter 22, arts. 3, 8; and Beaumanoir, 33. Institutions, book I. chap. 90.

The custom of appeals naturally introduced that of giving costs. Thus Défontaines says, [1574] that when they appealed by written law, that is, when they followed the new laws of St. Lewis, they gave costs; but that in the ordinary practice, which did not permit them to appeal without falsifying the judgment, no costs were allowed. They obtained only a fine, and the possession for a year and a day of the thing contested, if the cause was remanded to the lord.

[1574] Chapter 22, art. 8.

But when the number of appeals increased from the new facility of appealing; [1575] when by the frequent usage of those appeals from one court to another, the parties were continually removed from the place of their residence; when the new method of procedure multiplied and prolonged the suits; when the art of eluding the very justest demands became refined; when the parties at law knew how to fly only in order to be followed; when plaints were ruinous and defense easy; when the arguments were lost in whole volumes of words and writings; when the kingdom was filled with limbs of the law, who were strangers to justice; when knavery found encouragement at the very place where it did not find protection; then it was necessary to deter litigious people by the fear of costs. They were obliged to pay costs for the judgment and for the means they had employed to elude it. Charles the Fair made a general ordinance on that subject. [1576]

[1575] At present when they are so inclined to appeal, says Boutillier—*Somme Rurale*, book I, tit. 3, p. 16, Paris, 1621.
[1576] In the year 1324.

36. *Of the public Prosecutor.*

As by the Salic, Ripuarian, and other barbarous laws, crimes were punished with pecuniary fines; they had not in those days, as we have at present, a public officer who had the care of criminal prosecutions. And, indeed, the issue of all causes being reduced to the reparation of injuries, every prosecution was in some measure civil, and might be managed by any one. On the other hand, the Roman law had popular forms for the prosecution of crimes which were inconsistent with the functions of a public prosecutor.

The custom of judicial combats was no less opposite to this idea; for who is it that would choose to be a public prosecutor and to make himself every man's champion against all the world?

I find in the collection of formulas, inserted by Muratori in the laws of the Lombards, that under our princes of the second race there was an advocate for the public prosecutor. [1577] But whoever pleases to read the entire collection of these formulas will find that there was a total difference between such officers and those we now call the public prosecutor, our attorneys-general, our king's solicitors, or our solicitors for the nobility. The former were rather agents to the public for the management of political and domestic affairs, than for the civil. And, indeed, we did not find in those formulas that they were entrusted with criminal prosecutions, or with causes relating to minors, to churches, or to the condition of any one.

[1577] *Advocatus de parte publicâ.*

I said that the establishment of a public prosecutor was repugnant to the usage of judicial combats. I find, notwithstanding, in one of those formulas, an advocate for the public prosecutor, who had the liberty to fight. Muratori has placed it just after the constitution of Henry I, for which it was made. [1578] In this constitution it is said, "That if any man kills his father, his brother, or any of his other relatives, he shall lose their succession, which shall pass to the other relatives, and his own property shall go to the exchequer." Now it was in suing for the estate which had devolved to the exchequer, that the advocate for the public prosecutor, by whom its rights were defended, had the privilege of fighting: this case fell within the general rule.

[1578] See this constitution and this formula, in the second volume of the Historians of Italy, p. 175.

We see in those formulas the advocate for the public prosecutor proceeding against a person who had taken a robber, but had not brought him before the count; [1579] against another who had raised an insurrection or tumult against the count; [1580] against another who had saved a man's life whom the count had ordered to be put to death; [1581] against the advocate of some churches, whom the count had commanded to bring a robber before him, but had not obeyed; [1582] against another who had revealed the king's secret to strangers; [1583] against another, who with open violence had attacked the emperor's commissary; [1584] against another who had been guilty of contempt to the emperor's rescripts, and he was prosecuted either by the emperor's advocate or by the emperor himself; [1585] against another who refused to accept of the prince's coin;

[1586] in fine, this advocate sued for things which by the law were adjudged to the exchequer. [1587]

[1579] Collection of Muratori, p. 104. on the 88th law of Charlemagne, book I, tit. 26, § 78.
[1580] Another formula, Ibid., p. 87.
[1581] Ibid., p. 104.
[1582] Ibid., p. 95.
[1583] Ibid., p. 88.
[1584] Ibid., p. 98.
[1585] Ibid., p. 132.
[1586] Ibid.
[1587] Ibid., p. 137.

But in criminal causes, we never meet with the advocate for the public prosecutor; not even where duels are used; [1588] not even in the case of incendiaries; [1589] not even when the judge is killed on his bench; [1590] not even in causes relating to the conditions of persons, [1591] to liberty and slavery. [1592]

[1588] Ibid., p. 147.
[1589] Ibid.
[1590] Ibid., p. 168.
[1591] Ibid., p. 134.
[1592] Ibid., p. 107.

These formulas are made, not only for the laws of the Lombards, but likewise for the capitularies added to them, so that we have no reason to doubt of their giving us the practice observed with regard to this subject under our princes of the second race.

It is obvious that these advocates for a public prosecutor must have ended with our second race of kings, in the same manner as the king's commissioners in the provinces; because there was no longer a general law nor general exchequer, and because there were no longer any counts in the provinces to hold the assizes, and, of course, there were no more of those officers whose principal function was to support the authority of the counts.

As the usage of combats became more frequent under the third race, it did not allow of any such thing as a public prosecutor. Hence Boutillier, in his *Somme Rurale*, speaking of the officers of justice, takes notice only of the bailiffs, the peers and sergeants. See the Institutions [1593] and Beaumanoir [1594] concerning the manner in which prosecutions were managed in those days.

[1593] Book I, chap. 1; and book II, chap. 11, 13.
[1594] Chapters 1, 61.

I find in the laws of James II, King of Majorca, [1595] a creation of the office of king's attorney-general, with the very same functions as are exercised at present by the officers of that name among us. [1596] It is manifest that this office was not instituted till we had changed the form of our judiciary proceedings.

[1595] See these laws in the Lives of the Saints, of the month of June, iii, p. 26.

[1596] *Qui continue nostrum sacram curiam sequi teneatur, instituatur qui facta et causas in ipsa curia promoveat atque prosequatur.*

37. *In what Manner the Institutions of St. Lewis fell into Oblivion.*

It was the fate of the Institutions that their origin, progress, and decline were comprised within a very short period.

I shall make a few reflections upon this subject. The code we have now under the name of St. Lewis' Institutions was never designed as a law for the whole kingdom, though such a design is mentioned in the preface. The compilation is a general code, which determines all points relating to civil affairs, to the disposal of property by will or otherwise, the dowries and privileges of women, and emoluments and privileges of fiefs, with the affairs in relation to the police, &c. Now, to give a general body of civil laws, at a time when each city, town, or village, had its customs, was attempting to subvert in one moment all the particular laws then in force in every part of the kingdom. To reduce all the particular customs to a general one would be a very inconsiderate thing, even at present when our princes find everywhere the most passive obedience. But if it be true that we ought not to change when the inconveniences are equal to the advantages, much less should we change when the advantages are small and the inconveniences immense. Now, if we attentively consider the situation which the kingdom was in at that time, when every lord was puffed up with the notion of his sovereignty and power, we shall find that to attempt a general alteration of the received laws and customs must be a thing that could never enter into the heads of those who were then in the administration.

What I have been saying proves likewise that this code of institutions was not confirmed in parliament by the barons and magistrates of the kingdom, as is mentioned in a manuscript of the town-hall of Amiens, quoted by M. Ducange. [1597] We find in other manuscripts that this code was given by St. Lewis in the year 1270, before he set out for Tunis. But this fact is not truer than the other; for St. Lewis set out upon that expedition in 1269, as M. Ducange observes: whence he concludes that this code might have been published in his absence. But this I say is impossible. How can St. Lewis be imagined to have pitched upon the time of his absence for transacting an affair which would have been a sowing of troubles, and might have produced not only changes, but revolutions? An enterprise of that kind had need, more than any other, of being closely pursued, and could not be the work of a feeble regency, composed moreover of lords, whose interest it was that it should not succeed. These were Mathieu, Abbot of St. Denis, Simon of Clermont, Count of Nesle, and, in case of death, Philip, Bishop of Evreux, and Jean, Count of Ponthieu. We have seen above [1598] that the Count of Ponthieu opposed the execution of a new judiciary order in his lordship.

[1597] Preface to the Institutions.
[1598] Chapter 29.

Thirdly, I affirm it to be very probable that the code now extant is quite a different thing from St. Lewis' Institutions, It cites the Institutions; therefore it is a comment upon the Institutions, and not the institutions themselves. Besides, Beaumanoir, who frequently makes mention of St. Lewis' Institutions, quotes only some particular laws of that prince, and not this compilation. Défontaines, [1599] who wrote in that prince's reign, makes mention of the first two times that his Institutions on judicial proceedings were put in execution, as of a thing long since elapsed. The institutions of St. Lewis were prior, therefore, to the compilation I am now speaking of, which from their rigor, and their adopting the erroneous prefaces inserted by some ignorant persons in that work, could not have been published before the last year of St. Lewis or even not till after his death.

[1599] See above, chapter 29.

38. *The same Subject continued.*

What is this compilation then which goes at present under the name of St. Lewis' Institutions? What is this obscure, confused, and ambiguous code, where the French law is continually mixed with the Roman, where a legislator speaks and yet we see a civilian, where we find a complete digest of all cases and points of the civil law? To understand this thoroughly, we must transfer ourselves in imagination to those times.

St. Lewis, seeing the abuses in the jurisprudence of his time, endeavored to give the people a dislike to it. With this view he made several regulations for the court of his demesnes, and for those of his barons. And such was his success that Beaumanoir, who wrote a little after the death of that prince, informs us [1600] that the manner of trying causes which had been established by St. Lewis obtained in a great number of the courts of the barons.

[1600] Chapter 61, p. 309.

Thus this prince attained his end, though his regulations for the courts of the lords were not designed as a general law for the kingdom, but as a model which every one might follow, and would even find his advantage in it. He removed the bad practice by showing them a better. When it appeared that his courts, and those of some lords, had chosen a form of proceeding more natural, more reasonable, more conformable to morality, to religion, to the public tranquility, and to the security of person and property, this form was soon adopted, and the other rejected.

To allure when it is rash to constrain, to win by pleasing means when it is improper to exert authority, shows the man of abilities. Reason has a natural, and even a tyrannical sway; it meets with resistance, but this very resistance constitutes its triumph; for after a short struggle it commands an entire submission.

St. Lewis, in order to give a distaste of the French jurisprudence, caused the books of the Roman law to be translated; by which means they were made known to the lawyers of those times. Défontaines, who is the oldest law writer we have, made great use of those Roman laws. [1601] His work is, in some measure, a result from the ancient French jurisprudence, of the laws or Institutions of St. Lewis, and of the Roman law. Beaumanoir made very little use of the latter; but he reconciled the ancient French laws to the regulations of St. Lewis.

[1601] He says himself, in his prologue, *Nus luy en prit onques mais cette chose dont j'ay.*

I have a notion, therefore, that the law book known by the name of the Institutions was compiled by some bailiffs, with the same design as that of the authors of those two

Works, and especially of Défontaines. The title of this work mentions that it is written according to the usage of Paris, Orleans, and the court of Barony; and the preamble says that it treats of the usage of the whole kingdom, of Anjou and of the court of Barony. It is plain that this work was made for Paris, Orleans and Anjou, as the works of Beaumanoir and Défontaines were framed for the counties of Clermont and Vermandois; and as it appears from Beaumanoir that divers laws of St. Lewis had been received in the courts of Barony, the compiler was in the right to say that his work related also to those courts. [1602]

[1602] Nothing so vague as the title and prologue. At first they are the customs of Paris, Orleans, and the court of Barony; then they are the customs of all the lay courts of the kingdom, and of the provostships of France; at length, they are the customs of the whole kingdom, Anjou, and the court of Barony.

It is manifest that the person who composed this work compiled the customs of the country together with the laws and Institutions of St. Lewis. This is a very valuable work, because it contains the ancient customs of Anjou, the Institutions of St. Lewis, as they were then in use; and, in fine, the whole practice of the ancient French law.

The difference between this work and those of Défontaines and Beaumanoir is its speaking in imperative terms as a legislator; and this might be right, since it was a medley of written customs and laws.

There was an intrinsic defect in this compilation; it formed an amphibious code, in which the French and Roman laws were mixed, and where things were joined that were in no relation, but often contradictory to each other.

I am not ignorant that the French courts of vassals or peers; the judgments without power of appealing to another tribunal; the manner of pronouncing sentence by these words *I condemn* or *I absolve*, [1603] had some conformity to the popular judgments of the Romans. But they made very little use of that ancient jurisprudence; they rather chose that which was afterwards introduced by the emperor, in order to regulate, limit, correct, and extend the French jurisprudence.

[1603] Institutions, book II. chap. 15,

39. *The same Subject continued.*

The judiciary forms introduced by St. Lewis fell into disuse. This prince had not so much in view the thing itself, that is, the best manner of trying causes, as the best manner of supplying the ancient practice of trial. The principal intent was to give a disrelish of the ancient jurisprudence, and the next to form a new one. But when the inconveniences of the latter appeared, another soon succeeded.

The Institutions of St. Lewis did not, therefore, so much change the French jurisprudence as they afforded the means of changing it; they opened new tribunals, or rather ways to come at them. And when once the public had easy access to the superior courts, the judgments which before constituted only the usages of a particular lordship formed a universal digest. By means of the Institutions, they had obtained general decisions, which were entirely wanting in the kingdom; when the building was finished, they let the scaffold fall to the ground.

Thus the Institutions produced effects which could hardly be expected from a masterpiece of legislation. To prepare great changes whole ages are sometimes requisite; the events ripen, and the revolutions follow.

The parliament judged in the last resort of almost all the affairs of the kingdom. Before, [1604] it took cognizance only of disputes between the dukes, counts, barons, bishops, abbots, or between the king and his vassals, [1605] rather in the relation they bore to the political than to the civil order. They were soon obliged to render it permanent, whereas it used to be held only a few times in a year: and, in fine, a great number were created; in order to be sufficient for the decision of all manner of causes.

[1604] See *Du Tillet* on the court of peers. See also Laroche, Flavin, book I. chap. 3., Budeus and Paulus Æmilius.
[1605] Other causes were decided by the ordinary tribunals.

No sooner had the parliament become a fixed body, than they began to compile its decrees. Jean de Monluc, in the reign of Philip the Fair, made a collection which at present is known by the name of the Olim registers. [1606]

[1606] See the President Henault's excellent abridgment of the history of France in the year 1313.

40. *In what Manner the judiciary Forms were borrowed from the Decretals.*

But how comes it, some will ask, that when the Institutions were laid aside, the judicial forms of the canon law should be preferred to those of the Roman? It was because they had constantly before their eyes the ecclesiastic courts, which followed the forms of the canon law, and they knew of no court that followed those of the Roman law. Besides, the limits of the spiritual and temporal jurisdiction were at that time very little understood; there were people who sued indifferently [1607] and causes that were tried indifferently, in either court. [1608] It seems [1609] as if the temporal jurisdiction reserved no other cases exclusively to itself than the judgment of feudal matters, [1610] and of such crimes committed by laymen as did not relate to religion. For [1611] if on the account of conventions and contracts, they had occasion to sue in a temporal court, the parties might of their own accord proceed before the spiritual tribunals; and as the latter had not a power to oblige the temporal court to execute the sentence, they commanded submission by means of excommunications. Under those circumstances, when they wanted to change the course of proceedings in the temporal court, they took that of the spiritual tribunals, because they knew it; but did not meddle with that of the Roman law, by reason they were strangers to it: for in point of practice people know only what is really practiced.

[1607] Beaumanoir, chap. 11, p. 58.
[1608] Widows, croises, &c.—Ibid.
[1609] See the whole eleventh chapter of Beaumanoir, chap. 11. p. 58.
[1610] The spiritual tribunals had even laid hold of these, under the pretext of the oath, as may be seen by the famous Concordat between Philip Augustus, the clergy, and the barons, which is to be found in the ordinances of Laurière.
[1611] Beaumanoir, chap. 11, p. 60.

41. *Flux and Reflux of the ecclesiastic and temporal Jurisdiction.*

The civil power being in the hands of an infinite number of lords, it was an easy matter for the ecclesiastic jurisdiction to gain daily a greater extent. But as the ecclesiastic courts weakened those of the lords, and contributed thereby to give strength to the royal jurisdiction, the latter gradually checked the jurisdiction of the clergy. The parliament, which in its form of proceedings had adopted whatever was good and useful in the spiritual courts, soon perceived nothing else but the abuses which had crept into those tribunals; and as the royal jurisdiction gained ground every day, it grew every day more capable of correcting those abuses. And, indeed, they were intolerable; without enumerating them I shall refer the reader to Beaumanoir, to Boutillier and to the ordinances of our kings. [1612] I shall mention only two in which the public interest was more directly concerned. These abuses we know by the decrees that reformed them; they had been introduced in the times of the darkest ignorance, and upon the breaking out of the first gleam of light, they vanished. From the silence of the clergy it may be presumed that they forwarded this reformation: which, considering the nature of the human mind, deserves commendation. Every man that died without bequeathing a part of his estate to the church, which was called dying *without confession*, was deprived of the sacrament and of Christian burial. If he died intestate, his relatives were obliged to prevail upon the bishop that he would, jointly with them, name proper arbiters to determine what sum the deceased ought to have given, in case he had made a will. People could not lie together the first night of their nuptials, or even the two following nights, without having previously purchased leave; these, indeed, were the best three nights to choose; for as to the others, they were not worth much. All this was redressed by the parliament: we find in the glossary of the French law, [1613] by Ragau, the decree which it published against the Bishop of Amiens. [1614]

[1612] See Boutillier, *Somme Rurale*, tit. 9, what persons are incapable of suing in a temporal court; and Beaumanoir, 11, p. 56, and the regulations of Philip Augustus upon this subject; as also the regulation between Philip Augustus, the clergy, and the barons.
[1613] In the word *testamentary Executors*.
[1614] March 19, 1409.

I return to the beginning of my chapter. Whenever we observe in any age or government the different bodies of the state endeavoring to increase their authority, and to take particular advantages of each other, we should be often mistaken were we to consider their encroachments as an evident mark of their corruption. Through a fatality inseparable from human nature, moderation in great men is very rare: and as it is always much easier to push on force in the direction in which it moves than to stop its movement, so in the superior class of the people, it is less difficult, perhaps, to find men extremely virtuous, than extremely prudent.

The human mind feels such an exquisite pleasure in the exercise of power; even those who are lovers of virtue are so excessively fond of themselves that there is no man so happy as not still to have reason to mistrust his honest intentions; and, indeed, our actions depend on so many things that it is infinitely easier to do good, than to do it well.

42. *The Revival of the Roman Law, and the Result thereof. Change of Tribunals.*

Upon the discovery of Justinian's digest towards the year 1137, the Roman law seemed to rise out of its ashes. Schools were then established in Italy, where it was publicly taught; they had already the Justinian code and the *Novellæ*. I mentioned before that this code had been so favorably received in that country as to eclipse the law of the Lombards.

The Italian doctors brought the law of Justinian into France, where they had only the Theodosian code; [1615] because Justinian's laws were not made till after the settlement of the Barbarians in Gaul. [1616] This law met with some opposition: but it stood its ground notwithstanding the excommunications of the popes, who supported their own canons. [1617] St Lewis endeavored to bring it into repute by the translations of Justinian's works, made according to his orders, which are still in manuscript in our libraries; and I have already observed that they made great use of them in compiling the Institutions. Philip the Fair ordered the Laws of Justinian to be taught only as written reason in those provinces of France that were governed by customs; and they were adopted as a law in those provinces where the Roman law had been received. [1618]

[1615] In Italy they followed Justinian's code; hence Pope John VIII, in his constitution published after the Synod of Troyes, makes mention of this code, not because it was known in France, but because he knew it himself, and his constitution was general.
[1616] This emperor's code was published towards the year 530.
[1617] Decretals, v. tit. *de privilegiis,* capite, *super specula.*
[1618] By a charter in the year 1312, in favor of the university of Orleans, quoted by *Du Tillet.*

I have already noticed that the manner of proceeding by judicial combat required very little knowledge in the judges; disputes were decided according to the usage of each place, and to a few simple customs received by tradition. In Beaumanoir's time there were two different ways of administering justice; [1619] in some places they tried by peers, [1620] in others by bailiffs: in following the former way, the peers gave judgment according to the practice of their court; in the latter, it was the *prud'hommes,* or old men, who pointed out this same practice to the bailiffs. [1621] This whole proceeding required neither learning, capacity, nor study. But when the dark code of the Institutions made its appearance; when the Roman law was translated and taught in public schools; when a certain art of procedure and jurisprudence began to be formed; when practitioners and civilians were seen to rise, the peers and the *prud'hommes* were no longer capable of judging: the peers began to withdraw from the lords' tribunals; and the lords were very little inclined to assemble them; especially as the new form of trial, instead of being a solemn proceeding, agreeable to the nobility and interesting to a warlike people, had become a course of pleading which they neither understood, nor cared to learn. The custom of trying by peers began to be less used; [1622] that of trying, by bailiffs to be more so; the bailiffs did not give judgment themselves, [1623] they summed up the evidence and pronounced the judgment of the *prud'hommes*; but the latter being no longer capable of judging, the bailiffs themselves gave judgment.

[1619] Ancient Custom of Beauvoisis, chap. 1, "Of the Office of Bailiffs."

444

[1620] Among the common people the burghers were tried by burghers, as the feudatory tenants were tried by one another. See La Thaumassière, chap. 19.

[1621] Thus all requests began with these words: "*My lord judge, it is customary that in your court,*" &c, as appears from the formula quoted by Boutillier, *Somme Rurale*, book IV, tit. xxi.

[1622] The change was insensible: we meet with trials by peers, even in Boutillier's time, who lived in the year 1402, which is the date of his will: He gives this formula, book I. tit. 21, *Sire Juge, en ma justice haute, moyenne et basse, qui j'ai en tel lieu, cour, plaids,* baillis, homes, *feodaux et sergens.* Yet nothing but feodal matters were tried any longer by the peers. Ibid., book I, tit. i, p. 16.

[1623] As appears by the formula of the letters which their lord used to give them, quoted by Boutillier, *Somme Rurale*, book. I, tit. xiv, which is proved likewise by Beaumanoir, Ancient Custom of Beauvoisis, 1, of the bailiffs: they only directed the proceedings. *The bailiff is obliged in the presence of the peers to take down the words of those who plead, and to ask the parties whether they are willing to have judgment given according to the reasons alleged; and if they say, yes, my lord; the bailiff ought to oblige the peers to give judgment.* See also the Institutions of St. Lewis, book I. chap. 105, and book II. chap. 15. Li Juge si ne doit pas faire le jugement.

This was effected so much the easier, as they had before their eyes the practice of the ecclesiastic courts; the canon and new civil law both concurred alike to abolish the peers.

Thus fell the usage hitherto constantly observed in the French monarchy, that judgment should not be pronounced by a single person, as may be seen in the Salic laws, the capitularies, and in the first law-writers under the third race. [1624] The contrary abuse which obtains only in local jurisdictions has been moderated, and in some measure redressed, by introducing in many places a judge's deputy, whom he consults, and who represents the ancient prud'hommes by the obligation the judge is under of taking two graduates in cases that deserve a corporal punishment; and, in fine, it has become of no effect by the extreme facility of appeals.

[1624] Beaumanoir, chap. 67, p. 336, and chap. 61, pp. 315 and 316. The Institutions, book II. chap. 15.

43. The same Subject continued.

Thus there was no law to prohibit the lords from holding their courts themselves; none to abolish the functions of their peers; none to ordain the creation of bailiffs; none to give them the power of judging. All this was effected insensibly, and by the very necessity of the thing. The knowledge of the Roman law, the decrees of the courts, the new digest of the customs, required a study of which the nobility and illiterate people were incapable.

The only ordinance we have upon this subject is that which obliged the lords to choose their bailiffs from among the laity. [1625] It is a mistake to look upon this as a law of their creation; for it says no such thing. Besides, the intention of the legislator is determined by the reasons assigned in the ordinance: *to the end that the bailiffs may be punished for their prevarications, it is necessary they be taken from the order of the laity.* [1626] The immunities of the clergy in those days are very well known.

[1625] It was published in the year 1287.

[1626] *Ut si ibi delinquent, superiors sui possint animadvertere in eosdem.*

We must not imagine that the privileges which the nobility formerly enjoyed, and of which they are now divested, were taken from them as usurpations; no, many of those privileges were lost through neglect, and others were given up because, as various changes had been introduced in the course of so many ages, they were inconsistent with those changes.

44. *Of the Proof by Witnesses.*

The judges, who had no other rule to go by than the usages, inquired very often by witnesses into every cause that was brought before them.

The usage of judicial combats beginning to decline, they made their inquests in writing. But a verbal proof committed to writing is never more than a verbal proof; so that this only increased the expenses of law proceedings. Regulations were then made which rendered most of those inquests useless; [1627] public registers were established, which ascertained most facts, as nobility, age, legitimacy, and marriage. Writing is a witness very hard to corrupt; the customs were therefore reduced to writing. All this is very reasonable; it is much easier to go and see in the baptismal register whether Peter is the son of Paul than to prove this fact by a tedious inquest. When there are a number of usages in a country, it is much easier to write them all down in a code, than to oblige individuals to prove every usage. At length the famous ordinance was made which prohibited the admitting of the proof by witnesses for a debt exceeding an hundred livres, except there was the beginning of a proof in writing.

[1627] See in what manner age and parentage were proved.—Institutions, book I. chap. 71, 72.

45. *Of the Customs of France.*

France, as we have already observed, was governed by written customs, and the particular usages of each lordship constituted the civil law. Every lordship had its civil law, according to Beaumanoir, [1628] and so particular a law, that this author, who is looked upon as a luminary; and a very great luminary of those times; says he does not believe that throughout the whole kingdom there were two lordships entirely governed by the same law.

[1628] Prologue to the Ancient Custom of Beauvoisis.

This prodigious diversity had a twofold origin. With regard to the first, the reader may recollect what has been already said concerning it in the chapter of local customs: [1629] and as to the second, we meet with it in the different events of legal duels, it being natural that a continual series of fortuitous cases must have been productive of new usages.

[1629] Chapter 12.

These customs were preserved in the memory of old men, but insensibly laws or written customs were formed.

1. At the commencement of the third race, the kings gave not only particular charters, but likewise general ones, in the manner above explained; such are the institutions of Philip Augustus and those made by St. Lewis. In like manner the great vassals, in concurrence with the lords who held under them, granted certain charters or establishments, according to particular circumstances at the assizes of their duchies or counties; such were the assize of Godfrey, Count of Brittany, on the division of the nobles; the customs of Normandy, granted by Duke Ralph; the customs of Champagne, given by King Theobald; the laws of Simon, Count of Montfort, and others. This produced some written laws, and even more general ones than those they had before.

2. At the beginning of the third race, almost all the common people were bondmen; but there were several reasons which afterwards determined the kings and lords to enfranchise them.

The lords by enfranchising their bondmen gave them property; it was necessary therefore to give them civil laws, in order to regulate the disposal of that property. But by enfranchising their bondmen, they likewise deprived themselves of their property; there was a necessity, therefore, of regulating the rights which they reserved to themselves, as an equivalent for that property. Both these things were regulated by the charters of enfranchisement; those charters formed a part of our customs, and this part was reduced to writing. [1630]

[1630] See the Collection of Ordinances, by Laurière.

3. Under the reign of St. Lewis, and of the succeeding princes, some able practitioners, such as Défontaines, Beaumanoir, and others, committed the customs of their bailiwicks to writing. Their design was rather to give the course of judicial proceedings, than the usages of their time in respect to the disposal of property. But the whole is there, and though these particular authors have no authority but what they derive from the truth and notoriety of the things they speak of, yet there is no manner of doubt but that they contributed greatly to the restoration of our ancient French jurisprudence. Such was in those days our common law.

We have come now to the grand epoch. Charles VII and his successors caused the different local customs throughout the kingdom to be reduced to writing, and prescribed set forms to be observed to their digesting. Now, as this digesting was made through all the provinces, and as people came from each lordship to declare in the general assembly of the province the written or unwritten usages of each place, endeavors were made to render the customs more general, as much as possible, without injuring the interests of individuals, which were carefully preserved. [1631] Thus our customs were characterized in a threefold manner; they were committed to writing, they were made more general, and they received the stamp of the royal authority.

[1631] This was observed at the digesting of the customs of Berry and of Paris. See La Thaumassière, chap. 3.

Many of these customs having been digested anew, several changes were made either in suppressing whatever was incompatible with the actual practice of the law, or in adding several things drawn from this practice.

Though the common law is considered among us as in some measure opposite to the Roman, insomuch that these two laws divide the different territories, it is, notwithstanding, true that several regulations of the Roman law entered into our customs, especially when they made the new digests, at a time not very distant from ours, when this law was the principal study of those who were designed for civil employments, at a time when it was not usual for people to boast of not knowing what it was their duty to know, and of knowing what they ought not to know, at a time when a quickness of understanding was made more subservient to learning than pretending to a profession, and when a continual pursuit of amusements was not even the characteristic of women.

I should have been more diffuse at the end of this book, and, entering into the several details, should have traced all the insensible changes which from the opening of appeals have formed the great corpus of our French jurisprudence. But this would have been engrafting one large work upon another. I am like that antiquarian [1632] who set out from his own country, arrived in Egypt, cast an eye on the pyramids and returned home.

[1632] In the Spectator.

BOOK XXIX.

OF THE MANNER OF COMPOSING LAWS

1. *Of the Spirit of a Legislator.*

I say it, and methinks I have undertaken this work with no other view than to prove it, the spirit of a legislator ought to be that of moderation; political, like moral good, lying always between two extremes. [1633] Let us produce an example.

[1633] Aristotle, *Politics*, I.

The set forms of justice are necessary to liberty, but the number of them might be so great as to be contrary to the end of the very laws that established them; processes would have no end; property would be uncertain; the goods of one of the parties would be adjudged to the other without examining, or they would both be ruined by examining too much.

The citizens would lose their liberty and security, the accusers would no longer have any means to convict, nor the accused to justify themselves.

2. *The same Subject continued.*

Cecilius, in Aulus Gellius, [1634] speaking of the law of the Twelve Tables which permitted the creditor to cut the insolvent debtor into pieces, justifies it even by its cruelty, which hindered people from borrowing beyond their ability of paying. [1635] Shall then the cruelest laws be the best? Shall goodness consist in excess, and all the relations of things be destroyed?

[1634] Book XXII. chap. 1.

[1635] Cecilius says that he never saw nor read of an instance in which this punishment had been inflicted; but it is likely that no such punishment was ever established: the opinion of some civilians, that the law of the Twelve Tables meant only the division of the money arising from the sale of the debtor, seems very probable.

3. *That the Laws which seem to deviate from the Views of the Legislator are frequently agreeable to them.*

The law of Solon which declared those persons infamous who espoused no side in an insurrection seemed very extraordinary; but we ought to consider the circumstances in which Greece was at that time. It was divided into very small states; and there was reason to apprehend lest in a republic torn by intestine divisions the soberest part should keep retired, in consequence of which things might be carried to extremity.

In the seditions raised in those petty states the bulk of the citizens either made or engaged in the quarrel. In our large monarchies parties are formed by a few, and the people choose to live quietly, In the latter case it is natural to call back the seditious to the bulk of the citizens, and not these to the seditious; in the other it is necessary to oblige the small number of prudent people to enter among the seditious; it is thus the fermentation of one liquor may be stopped by a single drop of another.

4. *Of the Laws contrary to the Views of the Legislator.*

There are laws so little understood by the legislator as to be contrary to the very end he proposed. Those who made this regulation among the French, that when one of the two competitors died the benefice should devolve to the survivor, had in view, without doubt, the extinction of quarrels; but the very reverse falls out; we see the clergy at variance every day, and like English mastiffs worrying one another to death.

5. *The same Subject continued.*

The law I am going to speak of is to be found in this oath preserved by Æschines: [1636] *I swear that I will never destroy a town of the Amphictyones, and that I will not divert the course of its running waters; if any nation shall presume to do such a thing, I will declare war against them and will destroy their towns.* The last article of this law, which seems to confirm the first, is really contrary to it. Amphictyon is willing that the Greek towns should never be destroyed, and yet his law paves the way for their destruction. In order to establish a proper law of nations among the Greeks, they ought to have been accustomed early to think it a barbarous thing to destroy a Greek town; consequently they ought not even to ruin the destroyers. Amphictyon's law was just, but it was not prudent; this appears even from the abuse made of it. Did not Philip assume the power of demolishing towns, under the pretence of their having infringed the laws of the Greeks? Amphictyon might have inflicted other punishments; he might have ordained, for example, that a certain number of the magistrates of the destroying town, or of the chiefs of the infringing army, should be punished with death; that the destroying nation should cease for a while to enjoy the privileges of the Greeks; that they should pay a fine till the town was rebuilt. The law ought, above all things, to aim at the reparation of damages.

[1636] *De Falsa legatione.*

6. *The Laws which appear the same have not always the same Effect.*

Cæsar made a law to prohibit people from keeping above sixty sesterces in their houses. [1637] This law was considered at Rome as extremely proper for reconciling the debtors to their creditors, because, by obliging the rich to lend to the poor, they enabled the latter to pay their debts. A law of the same nature made in France at the time of the System proved extremely fatal, because it was enacted under a most frightful situation. After depriving people of all possible means of laying out their money, they stripped them even of the last resource of keeping it at home, which was the same as taking it from them by open violence. Cæsar's law was intended to make the money circulate; the French minister's design was to draw all the money into one hand. The former gave either lands or mortgages on private people for the money; the latter proposed in lieu of money nothing but effects which were of no value, and could have none by their very nature, because the law compelled people to accept of them.

[1637] Dio, lib. XLI.

7. *The same Subject continued.*

Necessity of composing Laws in a proper Manner. The law of ostracism was established at Athens, at Argos, [1638] and at Syracuse. At Syracuse it was productive of a thousand mischiefs, because it was imprudently enacted. The principal citizens banished one another by holding the leaf of a fig-tree in their hands, [1639] so that those who had any kind of merit withdrew from public affairs. [1640] At Athens, where the legislator was sensible of the proper extent and limits of his law, ostracism proved an admirable regulation. They never condemned more than one person at a time; and such a number of suffrages were requisite for passing this sentence that it was extremely difficult for them to banish a person whose absence was not necessary to the state. [1641]

[1638] Aristotle, *Republic*, lib. V. chap. 3.
[1639] Plutarch and Diodorus of Sicily say it was an olive leaf. See Diod. XI.—Ed.
[1640] Plutarch, Life of Dionysius.
[1641] *Vide* book XXVI. chap. 17, p. 163, *ante.*

The power of banishing was exercised only every fifth year: and indeed, as the ostracism was designed against none but great personages who threatened the state with danger, it ought not to have been the transaction of every day.

8. *That Laws which appear the same were not always made through the same Motive.*

In France they have received most of the Roman laws on substitutions, but through quite a different motive from the Romans. Among the latter the inheritance was accompanied with certain sacrifices [1642] which were to be performed by the inheritor and were regulated by the pontifical law; hence it was that they reckoned it a dishonor to die without heirs, that they made slaves their heirs, and that they devised substitutions. Of this we have a very strong proof in the vulgar substitution, which was the first invented, and took place only when the heir appointed did not accept of the inheritance. Its view was not to perpetuate the estate in a family of the same name, but to find somebody that would accept of it.

[1642] When the inheritance was too much encumbered they eluded the pontifical law by certain sales, whence come the words *sine sacris hæreditas*.

9. *That the Greek and Roman Laws punished Suicide, but not through the same Motive.*

A man, says Plato, who has killed one nearly related to him, that is, himself, not by an order of the magistrate, not to avoid ignominy, but through pusillanimity shall be punished. [1643] The Roman law punished this action when it was not committed through pusillanimity, through weariness of life, through impatience in pain, but from a criminal despair. The Roman law acquitted where the Greek condemned, and condemned where the other acquitted.

[1643] Book IX. of Laws.

Plato's law was formed upon the Lacedæmonian institutions, where the orders of the magistrate were absolute, where shame was the greatest of miseries, and pusillanimity the greatest of crimes. The Romans had no longer those refined ideas; theirs was only a fiscal law.

During the time of the republic, there was no law at Rome against suicides; this action is always considered by their historians in a favorable light, and we never meet with any punishment inflicted upon those who committed it.

Under the first emperors, the great families of Rome were continually destroyed by criminal prosecutions. The custom was then introduced of preventing judgment by a voluntary death. In this they found a great advantage: they had an honorable interment, and their wills were executed, because there was no law against suicides. [1644] But when the emperors became as avaricious as cruel, they deprived those who destroyed themselves of the means of preserving their estates by rendering it criminal for a person to make away with himself through a criminal remorse.

[1644] *Eorum qui de se statuebant humabantur corpora, manebant testamenta pretium festinandi*. Tacit.

What I have been saying of the motive of the emperors is so true, that they consented that the estates of suicides should not be confiscated when the crime for which they killed themselves was not punished with confiscation. [1645]

[1645] Rescript of the Emperor Pius in the 3rd Law, §§ 1, 2, ff. *de bonis eorum qui ante sententiam mortem sibi consciverunt*.

10. *That Laws which seem contrary proceed sometimes from the same Spirit.*

In our time we give summons to people in their own houses; but this was not permitted among the Romans. [1646]

[1646] Leg. 18, ff. *de in jus vocando.*

A summons was a violent action, [1647] and a kind of warrant for seizing the body; [1648] hence it was no more allowed to summon a person in his own house than it is now allowed to arrest a person in his own house for debt.

[1647] See the Law of the Twelve Tables.
[1648] *Rapit in jus.*—Horace, Satire 9. Hence they could not summon those to whom a particular respect was due.

Both the Roman and our laws admit of this principle alike, that every man ought to have his own house for an asylum, where he should suffer no violence. [1649]

[1649] See Leg. 18, ff. *de in jus vocando.*

11. *How to compare two different Systems of Laws.*

In France the punishment for false witnesses is capital; in England it is not. Now, to be able to judge which of these two laws is the best, we must add that in France the rack is used for criminals, but not in England; that in France the accused is not allowed to produce his witnesses, and that they very seldom admit of what are called justifying circumstances in favor of the prisoner; in England they allow of witnesses on both sides. These three French laws form a close and well-connected system; and so do the three English laws. The law of England, which does not allow of the racking of criminals, has but very little hope of drawing from the accused a confession of his crime; for this reason it invites witnesses from all parts, and does not venture to discourage them by the fear of a capital punishment. The French law, which has one resource more, is not afraid of intimidating the witnesses; on the contrary, reason requires they should be intimidated; it listens only to the witnesses on one side, which are those produced by the attorney-general, and the fate of the accused depends entirely on their testimony. [1650] But in England they admit of witnesses on both sides, and the affair is discussed in some measure between them; consequently false witness is there less dangerous, the accused having a remedy against the false witness which he has not in France. Wherefore, to determine which of those systems is most agreeable to reason, we must take them each as a whole and compare them in their entirety.

[1650] By the ancient French law, witnesses were heard on both sides; hence we find in the Institutions of St. Lewis, book. I. chap. 7, that there was only a pecuniary punishment against false witnesses.

12. *That Laws which appear the same are sometimes really different.*

The Greek and Roman laws inflicted the same punishment on the receiver as on the thief; [1651] the French law does the same. The former acted rationally, but the latter does not. Among the Greeks and Romans the thief was condemned to a pecuniary punishment, which ought also to be inflicted on the receiver; for every man that contributes in what shape soever to a damage is obliged to repair it. But as the punishment of theft is capital with us, the receiver cannot be punished like the thief without carrying things to excess. A receiver may act innocently on a thousand occasions: the thief is always culpable; one hinders the conviction of a crime, the other commits it; in one the whole is passive, the other is active; the thief must surmount more obstacles, and his soul must be more hardened against the laws.

[1651] Leg. 1, ff. *de Receptatoribus.*

The civilians have gone further; they look upon the receiver as more odious than the thief, [1652] for were it not for the receiver the theft, say they, could not be long concealed. But this again might be right when there was only a pecuniary punishment; the affair in question was a damage done, and the receiver was generally better able to repair it; but when the punishment became capital, they ought to have been directed by other principles.

[1652] Ibid.

13. *That we must not separate Laws from the End for which they were made: of the Roman Laws on Theft.*

When a thief was caught in the act, this was called by the Romans a manifest theft; when he was not detected till some time afterwards, it was a non-manifest theft.

The law of the Twelve Tables ordained that a manifest thief should be whipped with rods and condemned to slavery if he had attained the age of puberty; or only whipped if he was not of ripe age; but as for the non-manifest thief, he was only condemned to a fine of double the value of what he had stolen.

When the Porcian laws abolished the custom of whipping the citizens with rods, and of reducing them to slavery, the manifest thief was condemned to a payment of fourfold, and they still continued to condemn the non-manifest thief to a payment of double. [1653]

[1653] See what Favorinus says in Aulus Gellius, book XX. chap. 1.

It seems very odd that these laws should make such a difference in the quality of those two crimes, and in the punishments they inflicted. And, indeed, whether the thief was detected either before or after he had carried the stolen goods to the place intended, this was a circumstance which did not alter the nature of the crime. I do not at all question that the whole theory of the Roman laws in relation to theft was borrowed from the Lacedæmonian institutions. Lycurgus, with a view of rendering the citizens dexterous and cunning, ordained that children should be practiced in thieving, and that those who were caught in the act should be severely whipped. This occasioned among the Greeks, and afterwards among the Romans, a great difference between a manifest and a non-manifest theft. [1654]

[1654] Compare what Plutarch says in the Lycurgus with the laws of the Digest, title de Furtis; and the Institutes, book IV, tit. 1, §§ 1, 2, 3.

Among the Romans, a slave who had been guilty of stealing was thrown from the Tarpeian rock. Here the Lacedæmonian institutions were out of the question; the laws of Lycurgus in relation to theft were not made for slaves; to deviate from them in this respect was in reality conforming to them.

At Rome, when a person of unripe age happened to be caught in the act, the prætor ordered him to be whipped with rods according to his pleasure, as was practiced at Sparta. All this had a more remote origin. The Lacedæmonians had derived these usages from the Cretans; and Plato, [1655] who wants to prove that the Cretan institutions were designed for war, cites the following, namely, the power of bearing pain in individual combats, and in thefts which have to be concealed.

[1655] Of Laws, book I.

As the civil laws depend on the political institutions, because they are made for the same society, whenever there is a design of adopting the civil law of another nation, it would be proper to examine beforehand whether they have both the same institutions and the same political law.

Thus when the Cretan laws on theft were adopted by the Lacedæmonians, as their constitution and government were adopted at the same time, these laws were equally reasonable in both nations. But when they were carried from Lacedæmon to Rome, as they did not find there the same constitution, they were always thought strange, and had no manner of connection with the other civil laws of the Romans.

14. *That we must not separate the Laws from the Circumstances in which they were made.*

It was decreed by a law at Athens that when the city was besieged, all the useless people should be put to death. [1656] This was an abominable political law, in consequence of an abominable law of nations. Among the Greeks, the inhabitants of a town taken lost their civil liberty and were sold as slaves. The taking of a town implied its entire destruction, which is the source not only of those obstinate defenses, and of those unnatural actions, but likewise of those shocking laws which they sometimes enacted.

[1656] Inutilis ætas occidatur.—*Syrian., in Hermog.*

The Roman laws ordained that physicians should be punished for neglect or unskilfulness. [1657] In those cases, if the physician was a person of any fortune or rank, he was only condemned to deportation, but if he was of a low condition he was put to death. By our institutions it is otherwise. The Roman laws were not made under the same circumstances as ours: at Rome every ignorant pretender intermeddled with physic; but among us, physicians are obliged to go through a regular course of study, and to take their degrees, for which reason they are supposed to understand their profession.

[1657] The Cornelian law *de Sicariis*, Institutes, lib. IV, tit. 3, *de lege Aquilia*, § 7.

15. *That sometimes it is proper the Law should amend itself.*

The law of the Twelve Tables allowed people to kill a night-thief as well as a day-thief, [1658] if upon being pursued he attempted to make a defense; but it required that the person who killed the thief should cry out and call his fellow-citizens. This is indeed what those laws, which permit people to do justice to themselves, ought always to require. It is the cry of innocence which in the very moment of the action calls in witnesses and appeals to judges. The people ought to take cognizance of the action, and at the very instant of its being done; an instant when everything speaks, even air, countenance, passions, silence; and when every word either condemns or absolves. A law which may become so opposed to the security and liberty of the citizens ought to be executed in their presence. [1659]

[1658] See the 4th law, ff. *ad leg. Aquil.*
[1659] Ibid.; see the decree of Tassillon added to the law of the Bavarians, *de popularib. Legib.* art. 4.

16. *Things to be observed in the composing of Laws.*

They who have a genius sufficient to enable them to give laws to their own, or to another nation, ought to be particularly attentive to the manner of forming them.

The style ought to be concise. The laws of the Twelve Tables are a model of conciseness; the very children used to learn them by heart. [1670] Justinian's *Novellæ* were so very diffuse that they were obliged to abridge them. [1671]

[1670] Ut carmen necessarium.—Cicero, *De Legib.* 2. Aristotle avers that before the art of writing was discovered, the laws were composed in verse and frequently sung, to prevent them being forgotten.—Ed.
[1671] It is the work of Irnerius.

The style should also be plain and simple, a direct expression being better understood than an indirect one. There is no majesty at all in the laws of the lower empire; princes are made to speak like rhetoricians. When the style of laws is inflated, they are looked upon only as a work of parade and ostentation.

It is an essential article that the words of the laws should excite in everybody the same ideas. Cardinal Richelieu [1672] agreed that a minister might be accused before the king, but he would have the accuser punished if the facts he proved were not matters of moment. This was enough to hinder people from telling any truth whatsoever against the minister, because a matter of moment is entirely relative, and what may be of moment to one is not so to another.

[1672] Testament. Polit.

The law of Honorius punished with death any person that purchased a freedman as a slave, or that gave him molestation. [1673] He should not have made use of so vague an expression; the molestation given a man depends entirely on the degree of his sensibility.

[1673] Aut qualibet manumissione donatum inquietare voluerit. Appendix to the Theodosian code in the first volume of Father Sirmond's works, p. 737.

When the law has to impose a penalty, it should avoid as much as possible the estimating it in money. The value of money changes from a thousand causes, and the same denomination continues without the same thing. Everyone knows the story of that impudent fellow at Rome [1674] who used to give those he met a box on the ear, and afterwards tendered them the five-and-twenty pence of the law of the Twelve Tables.

[1674] Aulus Gellius, book. XX. chap. 1.

When the law has once fixed the idea of things, it should never return to vague expressions. The ordinance of Lewis XIV [1675] concerning criminal matters, after an exact enumeration of the causes in which the king is immediately concerned, adds these words, *and those which in all times have been subject to the determination of the king's judges*; this again renders arbitrary what had just been fixed.

[1675] We find in the verbal process of this ordinance the motives that determined him.

Charles VII says [1676] he has been informed that the parties appeal three, four, and six months after judgment, contrary to the custom of the kingdom in a country where custom prevailed; he therefore ordains that they shall appeal forthwith, unless there happens to be some fraud or deceit on the part of the attorney, [1677] or unless there be a great or evident cause to discharge the appeal. The end of this law destroys the beginning, and it destroys it so effectually, that they used afterwards to appeal during the space of thirty years. [1678]

[1676] In his ordinance of Montel-les-Tours, in the year 1453.
[1677] They might punish the attorney, without there being any necessity of disturbing the public order.
[1678] The ordinance of the year 1667 has made some regulations upon this head.

The law of the Lombards does not allow a woman that has taken a religious habit, [1679] though she has made no vow, to marry; because, says this law, *if a spouse who has been contracted to a woman only by a ring cannot without guilt be married to another, for a much stronger reason the spouse of God or of the blessed Virgin.* Now, I say, that in laws the arguments should be drawn from one reality to another, and not from reality to figure, or from figure to reality.

[1679] Book II, tit. 37.

A law enacted by Constantine [1680] ordains that the single testimony of a bishop should be sufficient without listening to any other witnesses. This prince took a very short method; he judged of affairs by persons, and of persons by dignities.

[1680] In Father Sirmond's appendix to the Theodosian code, tom. i.

The laws ought not to be subtle; they are designed for people of common understanding, not as an art of logic, but as the plain reason of a father of a family.

When there is no necessity for exceptions and limitations in a law, it is much better to omit them: details of that kind throw people into new details.

No alteration should be made in a law without sufficient reason. Justinian ordained that a husband might be repudiated and yet the wife not lose her portion, if for the space of two years he had been incapable of consummating the marriage. [1681] He altered his law afterwards, and allowed the poor wretch three years. [1682] But in a case of that nature two years are as good as three, and three are not worth more than two.

[1681] Leg. 1, Cod. *de Repudiis.*
[1682] See the authentic *Sed Hodie*, in the Cod. *de Repudiis.*

When a legislator condescends to give the reason of his law it ought to be worthy of its majesty. A Roman law decrees that a blind man is incapable to plead, because he cannot see the ornaments of the magistracy. [1683] So bad a reason must have been given on purpose, when such a number of good reasons were at hand.

[1683] Leg. 1, ff. *de Postulando.*

Paul, the jurist, says [1684] that a child grows perfect in the seventh month, and that the ratio of Pythagoras' numbers seems to prove it. It is very extraordinary that they should judge of those things by the ratio of Pythagoras' numbers.

[1684] In his Sentences, book IV. tit. 9.

Some French lawyers have asserted that when the king made an acquisition of a new country, the churches became subject to the *Regale*, because the king's crown is round. I shall not examine here into the king's rights, or whether in this case the reason of the civil or ecclesiastic law ought to submit to that of the law of politics; I shall only say that those august rights ought to be defended by grave maxims. Was there ever such a thing known as the real rights of a dignity founded on the figure of that dignity's sign?

Davila says [1685] that Charles IX was declared of age in the parliament of Rouen at the commencement of his fourteenth year, because the laws require every moment of the time to be reckoned, in cases relating to the restitution and administration of a ward's estate; whereas it considers the year commenced as a year complete, when the case is concerning the acquisition of honors. [1686] I am very far from censuring a regulation which has been hitherto attended with no inconvenience; I shall only notice that the reason alleged is not the true one; [1687] it is false, that the government of a nation is only an honor.

[1685] *Della guerra civile di Francia*, p. 96.
[1686] See Dupuy, *Traité de la Majorité de nos rois*, p. 364, edit. 1655.—Ed.
[1687] The Chancellor de l'Hôpital.—Ibid.

In point of presumption, that of the law is far preferable to that of the man. The French law considers every act of a merchant during the ten days preceding his bankruptcy as fraudulent: [1688] this is the presumption of the law. The Roman law inflicted punishments on the husband who kept his wife after she had been guilty of adultery, unless he was induced to do it through fear of the event of a lawsuit, or through contempt of his own shame; this is the presumption of the man. The judge must have presumed the motives of the husband's conduct, and must have determined a very obscure and ambiguous point; when the law presumes, it gives a fixed rule to the judge.

[1688] It was made in the month of November, 1702.

Plato's law, [1689] as I have observed already, required that a punishment should be inflicted on the person who killed himself not with a design of avoiding shame, but through pusillanimity. This law was so far defective that in the only case in which it was impossible to draw from the criminal an acknowledgment of the motive upon which he had acted, it required the judge to determine concerning these motives.

[1689] Laws, IX. of Laws.

As useless laws debilitate such as are necessary, so those that may be easily eluded weaken the legislation. Every law ought to have its effect, and no one should be suffered to deviate from it by a particular exception.

The Falcidian law ordained among the Romans, that the heir should always have the fourth part of the inheritance; another law suffered the testator to prohibit the heir from retaining this fourth part. [1690] This is making a jest of the laws. The Falcidian law became useless: for if the testator had a mind to favor his heir, the latter had no need of the Falcidian law; and if he did not intend to favor him, he forbad him to make use of it.

[1690] It is the authentic *Sed cum testator*.

Care should be taken that the laws be worded in such a manner as not to be contrary to the very nature of things. In the proscription of the Prince of Orange, Philip II promises to any man that will kill the prince to give him, or his heirs, five-and-twenty thousand crowns, together with the title of nobility; and this upon the word of a king, and as a servant of God. To promise nobility for such an action! to ordain such an action in the quality of a servant of God! This is equally subversive of the ideas of honor, morality, and religion.

There very seldom happens to be a necessity of prohibiting a thing which is not bad under pretence of some imaginary perfection.

There ought to be a certain simplicity and candor in the laws; made to punish the iniquity of men, they themselves should be clad with the robes of innocence. We find in the law of the Visigoths [1691] that ridiculous request, by which the Jews were obliged to eat everything dressed with pork, provided they did not eat the pork itself. This was a very great cruelty: they were obliged to submit to a law contrary to their own; and they were obliged to retain nothing more of their own than what might serve as a mark to distinguish them.

[1691] Book XII, tit. 2, § 16.

17. *A bad Method of giving Laws.*

The Roman Emperors manifested their will, like our princes, by decrees and edicts; but they permitted, which our princes do not, both the judges and private people to interrogate them by letters in their several differences; and their answers were called rescripts. The decretals of the popes are rescripts, strictly speaking. It is plain that this is a bad method of legislation. Those who thus apply for laws are improper guides to the legislator; the facts are always wrongly stated. Julius Capitolinus says [1692] that Trajan often refused to give this kind of rescripts, lest a single decision, and frequently a particular favor, should be extended to all cases. Macrinus had resolved to abolish all those rescripts; [1693] he could not bear that the answers of Commodus, Caracalla, and all those other ignorant princes, should be considered as laws. Justinian thought otherwise, and he filled his compilation with them.

[1692] See Julius Capitolinus *in Macrino.*
[1693] Ibid.

I would advise those who read the Roman laws to distinguish carefully between this sort of hypothesis, and the Senatus Consulta, the Plebiscita, the general constitutions of the emperors, and all the laws founded on the nature of things, on the frailty of women, the weakness of minors, and the public utility.

18. *Of the Ideas of Uniformity.*

There are certain ideas of uniformity, which sometimes strike great geniuses (for they even affected Charlemagne), but infallibly make an impression on little souls. They discover therein a kind of perfection, which they recognize because it is impossible for them not to see it; the same authorized weights, the same measures in trade, the same laws in the state, the same religion in all its parts. But is this always right and without exception? Is the evil of changing constantly less than that of suffering? And does not a greatness of genius consist rather in distinguishing between those cases in which uniformity is requisite, and those in which there is a necessity for differences? In China the Chinese are governed by the Chinese ceremonial and the Tartars by theirs; and yet there is no nation in the world that aims so much at tranquility. If the people observe the laws, what signifies it whether these laws are the same.

19. *Of Legislators.*

Aristotle wanted to indulge sometimes his jealousy against Plato, and sometimes his passion for Alexander. Plato was incensed against the tyranny of the people of Athens. Machiavel was full of his idol, the Duke of Valentinois. Sir Thomas More, who spoke rather of what he had read than of what he thought, wanted to govern all states with the simplicity of a Greek city. [1694] Harrington was full of the idea of his favorite republic of England, while a crowd of writers saw nothing but confusion where monarchy is abolished. The laws always conform to the passions and prejudices of the legislator; sometimes the latter pass through, and only tincture them; sometimes they remain, and are incorporated with them.

[1694] In his Utopia.

BOOK XXX.

THEORY OF THE FEUDAL LAWS AMONG THE FRANKS IN THE RELATION THEY BEAR TO THE ESTABLISHMENT OF THE MONARCHY

1. *Of Feudal Laws.*

I should think my work imperfect were I to pass over in silence an event which never again, perhaps, will happen; were I not to speak of those laws which suddenly appeared over all Europe without being connected with any of the former institutions; of those laws which have done infinite good and infinite mischief; which have suffered rights to remain when the demesne has been ceded; which by vesting several with different kinds of seignory over the same things or persons have diminished the weight of the whole seignory; which have established different limits in empires of too great extent; which have been productive of rule with a bias to anarchy, and of anarchy with a tendency to order and harmony.

This would require a particular work to itself; but considering the nature of the present undertaking, the reader will here meet rather with a general survey than with a complete treatise of those laws.

The feudal laws form a very beautiful prospect. A venerable old oak raises its lofty head to the skies, the eye sees from afar its spreading leaves; upon drawing nearer, it perceives the trunk but does not discern the root; the ground must be dug up to discover it. [1695]

[1695]   *Quantum vertice ad oras*
     Æthereas, tantum radice ad Tartara tendit.—Virgil.

2. *Of the Source of Feudal Laws.*

The conquerors of the Roman empire came from Germany. Though few ancient authors have described their manners, yet we have two of very great weight. Cæsar making war against the Germans describes the manners of that nation; [1696] and upon these he regulated some of his enterprises. [1697] A few pages of Cæsar upon this subject are equal to whole volumes. [1698]

[1696] Book VI.
[1697] For instance, his retreat from Germany.—*Ibid.*
[1698] M. Chabrit expresses his astonishment that Montesquieu dwells upon Cæsar's knowledge of the Germans, and quite ignores the Gauls, with their fund of information upon this subject.—Ed.

Tacitus has written an entire work on the manners of the Germans. This work is short, but it comes from the pen of Tacitus, who was always concise, because he saw everything at one glance.

These two authors agree so perfectly with the codes still extant of the laws of the Barbarians, that reading Cæsar and Tacitus we imagine we are perusing these codes, and perusing these codes we fancy we are reading Cæsar and Tacitus.

But if in this research into the feudal laws I should find myself entangled and lost in a dark labyrinth, I fancy I have the clue in my hand, and that I shall be able to find my way through.

3. *The Origin of Vassalage.*

Cæsar says, [1699] that, "The Germans neglected agriculture; that the greatest part of them lived upon milk, cheese and flesh; that no one had lands or boundaries of his own; that the princes and magistrates of each nation allotted what portion of land they pleased to individuals, and obliged them the year following to remove to some other part." Tacitus says [1700] that, "Each prince had a multitude of men, who were attached to his service, and followed him wherever he went." This author gives them a name in his language in accordance with their state, which is that of companions. [1701] They had a strong emulation to obtain the prince's esteem; and the princes had the same emulation to distinguish themselves in the bravery and number of their companions. "Their dignity and power," continues Tacitus, "consist in being constantly surrounded by a multitude of young and chosen people; this they reckon their ornament in peace, this their defense and support in war. Their name becomes famous at home, and among neighboring nations, when they excel all others in the number and courage of their companions: they receive presents and embassies from all parts. Reputation frequently decides the fate of war. In battle it is infamy in the prince to be surpassed in courage; it is infamy in the companions not to follow the brave example of their prince; it is an eternal disgrace to survive him. To defend him is their most sacred engagement. If a city be at peace, the princes go to those who are at war; and it is thus they retain a great number of friends. To these they give the war horse and the terrible javelin. Their pay consists in coarse but plentiful repasts. The prince supports his liberality merely by war and plunder. You might more easily persuade them to attack an enemy and to expose themselves to the dangers of war, than to cultivate the land, or to attend to the cares of husbandry; they refuse to acquire by sweat what they can purchase with blood."

[1699] Book VI. of the Gallic Wars. Tacitus adds, *Nulli domus aut ager, aut aliqua cura; prout ad quem venere aluntur.*—De Moribus Germanorum.
[1700] *De Moribus Germanorum.*
[1701] Comites.

Thus, among the Germans, there were vassals, but no fiefs; they had no fiefs, because the princes had no lands to give; or rather their fiefs consisted in horses trained for war, in arms, and feasting. There were vassals, because there were trusty men who being bound by their word engaged to follow the prince to the field, and did very nearly the same service as was afterwards performed for the fiefs.

4. *The same Subject continued.*

Cæsar says, [1702] that "when any of the princes declared to the assembly that he intended to set out upon an expedition and asked them to follow him, those who approved the leader and the enterprise stood up and offered their assistance. Upon which they were commended by the multitude. But, if they did not fulfill their engagements, they lost the public esteem, and were looked upon as deserters and traitors."

[1702] De Bello Gallico, lib. VI.

What Cæsar says in this place, and what we have extracted in the preceding chapter from Tacitus, are the substance of the history of our princes of the first race.

We must not therefore be surprised that our kings should have new armies to raise upon every expedition, new troops to encourage, new people to engage; that to acquire much they were obliged to incur great expenses; that they should be constant gainers by the division of lands and spoils, and yet give these lands and spoils incessantly away: that their demesne should continually increase and diminish; that a father upon settling a kingdom on one of his children [1703] should always give him a treasure with it: that the king's treasure should be considered as necessary to the monarchy; and that one king could not give part of it to foreigners, even in portion with his daughter, without the consent of the other kings. [1704] The monarchy moved by springs, which they were continually obliged to wind up.

[1703] See the Life of Dagobert.
[1704] See Gregory of Tours, book VI., on the marriage of the daughter of Chilperic. Childebert sends ambassadors to tell him that he should not give the cities of his father's kingdom to his daughter, nor his treasures, nor his bondmen, nor horses, nor horsemen, nor teams of oxen, &c.

5. *Of the Conquests of the Franks.*

It is not true that the Franks upon entering Gaul took possession of the whole country to turn it into fiefs. Some have been of this opinion because they saw the greatest part of the country towards the end of the second race converted into fiefs, rear-fiefs, or other dependencies; but such a disposition was owing to particular causes which we shall explain hereafter.

The consequence which sundry writers would infer thence, that the barbarians made a general regulation for establishing in all parts the state of villainage is as false as the principle from which it is derived. If at a time when the fiefs were precarious, all the lands of the kingdom had been fiefs, or dependencies of fiefs; and all the men in the kingdom vassals or bondmen subordinate to vassals; as the person that has property is ever possessed of power, the king, who would have continually disposed of the fiefs, that is, of the only property then existing; would have had a power as arbitrary as that of the Sultan is in Turkey; which is contradictory to all history.

6. *Of the Goths, Burgundians, and Franks.*

Gaul was invaded by German nations. The Visigoths took possession of the province of Narbonne, and of almost all the south; the Burgundians settled in the east; and the Franks subdued very nearly all the rest.

No doubt but these Barbarians retained in their respective conquests the manners, inclinations, and usages of their own country; for no nation can change in an instant their manner of thinking and acting. These people in Germany neglected agriculture. It seems by Cæsar and Tacitus that they applied themselves greatly to a pastoral life; hence the regulations of the codes of Barbarian laws almost all relate to their flocks. Roricon, who wrote a history among the Franks, was a shepherd. [1705]

[1706] Nothing definite is known concerning this Roricon; and his works are rather reveries and fables than anything else. See the article in *Mercure* for October, 1741.—Ed.

7. *Different Ways of dividing the Land.*

After the Goths and Burgundians had, under various pretences, penetrated into the heart of the empire, the Romans, in order to put a stop to their devastations, were obliged to provide for their subsistence. At first they allowed them corn, [1707] but afterwards chose to give them lands. The emperors, or the Roman magistrates, in their name, made particular conventions with them concerning the division of lands, [1708] as we find in the chronicles and in the codes of the Visigoths [1709] and Burgundians. [1710]

[1707] The Romans obliged themselves to this by treaties. See Zozimus V. upon the distribution of corn demanded by Alaric.—Ed.
[1708] *Burgundiones partem Galliæ occuparunt, terrasque cum Gallicis senatoribus diviserunt.*—Marius' Chronicle in the year 456.
[1709] Book X, tit. 1, §§ 8, 9, & 16.
[1710] Chapter 54, §§ 1, 2. This division was still subsisting in the time of Lewis the Debonnaire, as appears by his Capitulary of the year 829, which has been inserted in the law of the Burgundians, tit. 79, § 1.

The Franks did not follow the same plan. In the Salic and Ripuarian laws, we find not the least vestige of any such division of lands; they had conquered the country, and so took what they pleased, making no regulations but among themselves.

Let us, therefore, distinguish between the conduct of the Burgundians and Visigoths in Gaul, of those same Visigoths in Spain, of the auxiliary troops under Augustulus and Odoacer in Italy, [1711] and that of the Franks in Gaul, as also of the Vandals in Africa. [1712] The former entered into conventions with the ancient inhabitants, and in consequence thereof made a division of lands between them; the latter did no such thing.

[1711] See Procopius, War of the Goths.
[1712] See Procopius, War of the Vandals.

8. *The same Subject continued.*

What has induced some to think that the Roman lands were entirely usurped by the Barbarians is their finding in the laws of the Visigoths and the Burgundians that these two nations had two-thirds of the lands; but this they took only in certain quarters or districts assigned them.

Gundebald says, in the law of the Burgundians, that his people at their establishment had two-thirds of the lands allowed them; [1713] and the second supplement to this law notices that only a moiety would be allowed to those who should hereafter come to live in that country. [1714] Therefore, all the lands had not been divided in the beginning between the Romans and the Burgundians.

[1713] Licet eo tempore quo populus noster mancipiorum tertiam & duas terrarium partes accepit, &c.—Law of the Burgundians, tit. 54, § 1.

[1714] Ut non amplius a Burgundionibus qui infra venerunt requiratur quam ad praesens necessitas fuerit, medietas terræ.—Art. 11.

In those two regulations we meet with the same expressions in the text, consequently they explain one another; and as the latter cannot mean a universal division of lands, neither can this signification be given to the former.

The Franks acted with the same moderation as the Burgundians; they did not strip the Romans wherever they extended their conquests. What would they have done with so much land? They took what suited them, and left the remainder.

9. *A just Application of the Law of the Burgundians, and of that of the Visigoths, in relation to the Division of Lands.*

It is to be considered that those divisions of land were not made with a tyrannical spirit; but with a view of relieving the reciprocal wants of two nations that were to inhabit the same country.

The law of the Burgundians ordains that a Burgundian shall be received in an hospitable manner by a Roman. This is agreeable to the manners of the Germans, who, according to Tacitus, [1715] were the most hospitable people in the world.

[1715] *De Moribus Germanorum.*

By the law of the Burgundians, it is ordained that the Burgundians shall have two-thirds of the lands, and one-third of the bondmen. In this it considered the genius of two nations, and conformed to the manner in which they procured their subsistence. As the Burgundians kept herds and flocks, they wanted a great deal of land and few bondmen, and the Romans, from their application to agriculture, had need of less land, and of a greater number of bondmen. The woods were equally divided, because their wants in this respect were the same.

We find in the code of the Burgundians [1716] that each Barbarian was placed near a Roman. The division therefore was not general; but the Romans who gave the division were equal in number to the Burgundians who received it. The Roman was injured least. The Burgundians as a martial people, fond of hunting and of a pastoral life, did not refuse to accept of the fallow grounds; while the Romans kept such lands as were properest for culture: the Burgundian's flock fattened the Roman's field.

[1716] And in that of the Visigoths.

10. *Of Servitudes.*

The law of the Burgundians notices [1717] that when those people settled in Gaul, they were allowed two-thirds of the land, and one-third of the bondmen. The state of villainage was therefore established in that part of Gaul before it was invaded by the Burgundians. [1718]

[1717] Tit. 54.
[1718] This is confirmed by the whole title of the code de *Agricolis et Censitis, et Colonis.*

The law of the Burgundians, in points relating to the two nations, makes a formal distinction in both, between the nobles, the freeborn and the bondmen. [1719] Servitude was not therefore a thing peculiar to the Romans; nor liberty and nobility to the Barbarians.

[1719] *Si dentem optimati Burgundioni vel Romano nobili excusserit.* Tit. 26, §§ 1, & *si mediocribus personis ingenuis tam Burgundionibus quam Romanis.—Ibid.* sec. 2.

This very same law says, [1720] that if a Burgundian freedman had not given a certain sum to his master, nor received a third share of a Roman, he was always supposed to belong to his master's family. The Roman proprietor was therefore free, since he did not belong to another person's family; he was free, because his third portion was a mark of liberty.

[1720] Tit. 57.

We need only open the Salic and Ripuarian laws to be satisfied that the Romans were no more in a state of servitude among the Franks than among the other conquerors of Gaul.

The Count de Boulainvilliers [1721] is mistaken in the capital point of his system: he has not proved that the Franks made a general regulation which reduced the Romans into a kind of servitude.

[1721] See *Mercure*, March 1784.—Ed.

As this author's work is penned without art, and as he speaks with the simplicity, frankness, and candor of that ancient nobility whence he descends, everyone is capable of judging of the good things he says, and of the errors into which he has fallen. I shall not, therefore, undertake to criticize him; I shall only observe that he had more wit than enlightenment, more enlightenment than learning; though his learning was not contemptible, for he was well acquainted with the most valuable part of our history and laws.

The Count de Boulainvilliers and the Abbé du Bos [1722] have formed two different systems, one of which seems to be a conspiracy against the commons, and the other against the nobility. When the sun gave leave to Phaëton to drive his chariot, he said to him, "If you ascend too high, you will burn the heavenly mansions; if you descend too low, you will reduce the earth to ashes; do not drive to the right, you will meet there with the constellation of the Serpent; avoid going too much to the left, you will there fall in with that of the Altar: keep in the middle." [1723]

[1722] See M. Thierry in the Introduction to the *Récits Mérovingiens.*—Ed.

[1723]   *Nec preme, nec summum molire per æthera currum;*
     Altius egresses, cœlestia tecta cremabis;
     Inferius terras: medio tutissimus ibis.
     Neu te dexterior tortum declinet ad Anguem;
     Neve sinisterior pressam rota ducat ad Aram;
     Inter utrumque tene.—Ovid, *Metam.* lib. II.

11. *The same Subject continued.*

What first gave rise to the notion of a general regulation made at the time of the conquest was our meeting with an immense number of forms of servitude in France, towards the beginning of the third race; and as the continual progression of these forms of servitude was not perceived, people imagined in an age of obscurity a general law which was never framed.

Towards the commencement of the first race we meet with an infinite number of freemen, both among the Franks and the Romans; but the number of bondmen increased to that degree, that at the beginning of the third race all the husbandmen and almost all the inhabitants of towns had become bondmen: [1724] and whereas, at the first period, there was very nearly the same administration in the cities as among the Romans, namely, a corporation, a senate, and courts of judicature; at the other we hardly meet with anything but a lord and his bondmen.

[1724] While Gaul was under the dominion of the Romans they formed particular bodies; these were generally freedmen, or the descendants of freedmen.

When the Franks, Burgundians, and Goths made their several invasions, they seized upon gold, silver, movables, clothes, men, women, boys, and whatever the army could carry; the whole was brought to one place, and divided among the army. [1725] History shows that after the first settlement, that is, after the first devastation, they entered into an agreement with the inhabitants, and left them all their political and civil rights. This was the law of nations in those days; they plundered everything in time of war, and granted everything in time of peace. Were it not so, how should we find both in the Salic and Burgundian laws such a number of regulations absolutely contrary to a general servitude of the people?

[1725] See Gregory of Tours, book II, chap. 27. Aimoin, book. I. chap. 12.

But though the conquest was not immediately productive of servitude, it arose nevertheless from the same law of nations which subsisted after the conquest. [1726]

Opposition, revolts and the taking of towns were followed by the slavery of the inhabitants. And, not to mention the wars which the conquering nations made against one another, as there was this peculiarity among the Franks, that the different partitions of the monarchy gave rise continually to civil wars between brothers or nephews, in which this law of nations was constantly practiced, servitudes, of course, became more general in France than in other countries: and this is, I believe, one of the causes of the difference between our French laws and those of Italy and Spain, in respect to the right of seigniories.

[1726] See the Lives of the Saints, footnote 1732 below.

The conquest was soon over, and the law of nations then in force was productive of some servile dependences. The custom of the same law of nations, which obtained for many ages, gave a prodigious extent to those servitudes.

Theodoric [1727] imagining that the people of Auvergne were not faithful to him, thus addressed the Franks of his division: *Follow me, and I will carry you into a country where you shall have gold, silver, captives, clothes, and flocks in abundance; and you shall remove all the people into your own country.*

[1727] See Gregory of Tours, Book III., for Montesquieu's deviation from the actual sense of the writer.—Ed.

After the conclusion of the peace between Gontram and Chilperic, the troops employed in the siege of Bourges, having had orders to return, carried such a considerable booty away with them that they hardly left either men or cattle in the country. [1728]

[1728] Ibid., book VI. chap. 31.

Theodoric, King of Italy, whose spirit and policy it was ever to distinguish himself from the other barbarian kings, upon sending an army into Gaul, wrote thus to the general: [1729] "It is my will that the Roman laws be followed, and that you restore the fugitive slaves to their right owners. The defender of liberty ought not to encourage servants to desert their masters. Let other kings delight in the plunder and devastation of the towns which they have subdued; we are desirous to conquer in such a manner that our subjects shall lament their having fallen too late under our government." It is evident that his intention was to cast odium on the kings of the Franks and the Burgundians, and that he alluded in the above passage to their particular law of nations.

[1729] Letter 43, lib. iii. *in Cassiodorus.*

Yet this law of nations continued in force under the second race. King Pepin's army, having penetrated into Aquitaine, returned to France loaded with an immense booty, and with a number of bondmen, as we are informed by the annals of Metz. [1730]

[1730] In the year 763. *Innumerabilibus spoliis & captivis totus ille exercitus ditatus, in Franciam reverses est.*

Here might I quote numberless authorities; [1731] and as the public compassion was raised at the sight of those miseries, as several holy prelates, beholding the captives in chains, employed the treasure belonging to the church, and sold even the sacred utensils, to ransom as many as they could; and as several holy monks exerted themselves on that occasion, it is in the 'Lives of the Saints' that we meet with the best explanations on the subject. [1732] And, although it may be objected to the authors of those lives that they have been sometimes a little too credulous in respect to things which God has certainly performed, if they were in the order of his providence; yet we draw considerable light thence with regard to the manners and usages of those times.

[1731] See the annals of Fuld, in the year 739, Paulus Diaconus, de Gestis Longobardorum, lib. III. chap. 30, and lib. IV. chap. 1, and the Lives of the Saints in the next footnote.

[1732] See the lives of St. Epiphanius, St. Eptadius, St. Cæsarius, St. Fidolus, St. Porcian, St. Treverius, St. Eusichius, and of St. Leger; the miracles of St. Julian, &c.

When we cast an eye upon the monuments of our history and laws, the whole seems to be an immense expanse, a boundless ocean; [1733] all those frigid, dry, insipid, and hard writings must be read and devoured in the same manner as Saturn is fabled to have devoured the stones.

[1733] *Deerant quoque littoral ponto.*—Ovid, lib. I.

A vast quantity of land which had been in the hands of freemen [1734] was changed into mortmain. When the country was stripped of its free inhabitants, those who had a great multitude of bondmen either took large territories by force, or had them yielded by agreement, and built villages, as may be seen in different charters. On the other hand, the freemen who cultivated the arts found themselves reduced to exercise those arts in a state of servitude; thus the servitudes restored to the arts and to agriculture whatever they had lost.

[1734] Even the husbandmen themselves were not all slaves; see the 18th and 23rd law in the code *de Agricolis, et Censitis, et Colonis,* and the 20th of the same title.

It was a customary thing with the proprietors of lands, to give them to the churches, in order to hold them themselves by a quit-rent, thinking to partake by their servitude of the sanctity of the churches.

12. That the Lands belonging to the Division of the Barbarians paid no Taxes.

A people remarkable for their simplicity and poverty, a free and martial people, who lived without any other industry than that of tending their flocks, and who had nothing but rush cottages to attach them to their lands, [1735] such a people, I say, must have followed their chiefs for the sake of booty, and not to pay or to raise taxes. The art of tax-gathering was invented later, and when men began to enjoy the blessings of other arts.

[1735] See Gregory of Tours, book II.

The temporary tax of a pitcher of wine for every acre, [1736] which was one of the exactions of Chilperic and Fredegonda, related only to the Romans. And indeed it was not the Franks that tore the rolls of those taxes, but the clergy, who in those days were all Romans. [1737] The burden of this tax lay chiefly on the inhabitants of the towns; [1738] now these were almost all inhabited by Romans.

[1736] Ibid. book V.
[1737] Ibid. book VIII.
[1738] *Quæ condition universis per Galliam constitutes summopere est adhibita.*—Life of St. Aridius.

Gregory of Tours relates [1739] that a certain judge was obliged, after the death of Chilperic, to take refuge in a church, for having under the reign of that prince ordered taxes to be levied on several Franks who in the reign of Childebert were *ingenui*, or free-born: *Multos de Francis, qui tempore Childeberti regis ingenui fuerant, publico tributo subegit.* Therefore the Franks who were not bondmen paid no taxes.

[1739] Book VII.

There is not a grammarian but would turn pale to see how the Abbé du Bos has interpreted this passage. [1740] He observes that in those days the freedmen were also called *ingenui.* Upon this supposition he renders the Latin word *ingenui*, by the words *freed from taxes*; a phrase which we indeed may use in French, as we say *freed from cares, freed from punishments*; but in the Latin tongue such expressions as *ingenui a tributis, libertini a tributis, manumissi tributorum*, would be quite monstrous. [1741]

[1740] Establishment of the French Monarchy, tom. iii. chap. 14, p. 515.
[1741] See Baluzius II. p. 187.

Parthenius, says Gregory of Tours, [1742] had like to have been put to death by the Franks for subjecting them to taxes. The Abbé du Bos finding himself hard pressed by this passage [1743] very coolly assumes the thing in question; it was, says he, a surcharge.

[1742] Book III. chap. 136.
[1743] Tom. iii. p. 514.

We find in the law of the Visigoths [1744] that when a Barbarian had seized upon the estate of a Roman, the judge obliged him to sell it, to the end that this estate might continue to be tributary; consequently the Barbarians paid no land taxes. [1745]

[1744] *Judices atque præpositi terras Romanorum, ab illis qui occupatas tenent, auferant, & Romanis suâ exactione sine aliquâ dilation restituant, ut nihil fisco debeat deperire.*—Lib. X, tit. 1, chap. xiv.
[1745] The Vandals paid none in Africa.—Procopius, War of the Vandals, lib. I, II. Historia Miscella, lib. XVI, p. 106. Observe that the conquerors of Africa were a mixture of Vandals, Alans, and Franks. Historia Miscella, lib. XIV, p. 94.

The Abbé du Bos, [1746] who would fain have the Visigoths subjected to taxes, [1747] quits the literal and spiritual sense of the law, and pretends, upon no other indeed than an imaginary foundation, that between the establishment of the Goths and this law, there had been an augmentation of taxes which related only to the Romans. But none but Father Harduin are allowed thus to exercise an arbitrary power over facts.

[1746] Establishment of the Franks in Gaul, tom. iii. chap. 14, p. 510.
[1747] He lays a stress upon another law of the Visigoths, book X, tit. 1, art. 11, which
    proves nothing at all; it says only that he who has received of a lord a piece of land
    on condition of a rent or service ought to pay it.

This learned author [1748] has rummaged Justinian's Code [1749] in search of laws to prove that, among the Romans, the military benefices were subject to taxes. Whence he would infer that the same held good with regard to fiefs or benefices among the Franks. But the opinion that our fiefs derive their origin from that Institution of the Romans is at present exploded; it obtained only at a time when the Roman history, not ours, was well understood, and our ancient records lay buried in obscurity and dust.

[1748] Book III, p. 511.
[1749] Leg. iii. tit. 74, lib. XI.

But the Abbé is in the wrong to quote Cassiodorus, and to make use of what was transacting in Italy, and in the part of Gaul subject to Theodoric, in order to acquaint us with the practice established among the Franks; these are things which must not be confounded. I propose to show, some time or other, in a certain work, that the plan of the monarchy of the Ostrogoths was entirely different from that of any other government founded in those days by the other Barbarian nations; and that so far from our being entitled to affirm that a practice obtained among the Franks because it was established among the Ostrogoths, we have on the contrary just reason to think that a custom of the Ostrogoths was not in force among the Franks.

The hardest task for persons of extensive erudition is to seek their proofs in such passages as bear upon the subject, and to find, if we may be allowed to express ourselves in astronomical terms, the position of the sun.

The same author makes a wrong use of the capitularies, as well as of the historians and laws of the barbarous nations. When he wants the Franks to pay taxes, he applies to freemen what can be understood only of bondmen; [1750] when he speaks of their military service, he applies to bondmen what can never relate but to freemen. [1751]

[1750] Establishment of the French Monarchy, tom. iii. chap. 14, p. 513, where he quotes
    the 28th article of the edict of Pistes. See farther on.
[1751] Ibid. tom. iii. chap. 4, p. 298.

13. *Of Taxes paid by the Romans and Gauls in the Monarchy of the Franks.*

I might here examine whether, after the Gauls and Romans were conquered, they continued to pay the taxes to which they were subject under the emperors. But, for the sake of brevity, I shall be satisfied with observing that, if they paid them in the beginning, they were soon after exempted, and that those taxes were changed into a military service.

For, I confess, I can hardly conceive how the Franks should have been at first such great friends, and afterwards such sudden and violent enemies, to taxes.

A capitulary [1752] of Lewis the Debonnaire explains extremely well the situation of the freemen in the monarchy of the Franks. Some troops of Goths or Iberians, [1753] flying from the oppression of the Moors, were received into Lewis' dominions. The agreement made with them was that, like other freemen, they should follow their count to the army; and that upon a march they should mount guard and patrol under the command also of their count; [1754] and that they should furnish horses and carriages for baggage to the king's commissaries, [1755] and to the ambassadors in their way to or from court; and that they should not be compelled to pay any further impost, but should be treated as the other freemen.

[1752] In the year 815, chap. 1, which is agreeable to the Capitulary of Charles the Bald, in the year 844, arts. 1, 2.

[1753] *Pro Hispanis in partibus Aquitaniæ, Septimaniæ, et Provinciæ consistentibus.—Ibid.*

[1754] *Excubias et explorations quas Wactas dicunt.—Ibid.* art. 5. See Marc. form VI. lib. I.

[1755] They were not obliged to furnish any to the count. —*Ibid.*, art. 5.

It cannot be said that these were new usages introduced at the commencement of the second race. This must be referred at least to the middle or to the end of the first. A capitulary of the year 864 [1756] says in express terms that it was the ancient custom for freemen to perform military service, and to furnish likewise the horses and carriages above-mentioned; duties particular to themselves, and from which those who possessed the fiefs were exempt, as I shall prove hereafter.

[1756] *Ut Pagenses Franci, qui caballos habent, cum suis comitibus in hostem pergant.* The counts are forbidden to deprive them of their horses, *ut hostem facere, et debitos paraveredos secundum antequam consuetudinem exsolvere possint.*—Edict of Pistes, in Baluzius, p. 186.

This is not all; there was a regulation which hardly permitted the imposing of taxes on those freemen. [1757] He who had four manors was obliged to march against the enemy: [1758] he who had but three was joined with a freeman that had only one; the latter bore the fourth part of the other's charges, and stayed at home. In like manner, they joined two freemen who had each two manors; he who went to the army had half his charges borne by him who stayed at home.

[1757] Capitulary of Charlemagne, chap. 1, in the year 812. Edict of Pistes in the year 864, art. 27.

[1758] *Quatuor mansos.* I fancy that what they called Mansus was a particular portion of land belonging to a farm where there were bondmen; witness the capitulary of the year 853, *apud Sylvacum*, tit. 14, against those who drove the bondmen from their *Mansus*.

Again, we have an infinite number of charters, in which the privileges of fiefs are granted to lands or districts possessed by freemen, and of which I shall make further mention hereafter. [1759] These lands are exempted from all the duties or services which were required of them by the counts, and by the rest of the king's officers; and as all these services are particularly enumerated without making any mention of taxes, it is manifest that no taxes were imposed upon them.

[1759] See below, chapter 20 of this book.

It was very natural that the Roman system of taxation should of itself fall out of use in the monarchy of the Franks; it was a most complicated device, far above the conception, and wide from the plan of those simple people. Were the Tartars to overrun Europe, we should find it very difficult to make them comprehend what is meant by our financiers.

The anonymous author of the life of Lewis the Debonnaire, [1760] speaking of the counts and other officers of the nation of the Franks, whom Charlemagne established in Aquitania, says, that he entrusted them with the care of defending the frontiers, as also with the military power and the direction of the demesnes belonging to the crown. This shows the state of the royal revenues under the second race. The prince had kept his demesnes in his own hands, and employed his bondmen in improving them. But the indictions, the capitations and other imposts raised at the time of the emperors on the persons or goods of freemen had been changed into an obligation of defending the frontiers and marching against the enemy.

[1760] In Duchesne, tom. ii, p. 287.

In the same history, [1761] we find that Lewis the Debonnaire, having been to wait upon his father in Germany, this prince asked him, why he, who was a crowned head, came to be so poor: to which Lewis made answer that he was only a nominal king, and that the great lords were possessed of almost all his demesnes; that Charlemagne, being apprehensive lest this young prince should forfeit their affection, if he attempted himself to resume what he had inconsiderately granted, appointed commissaries to restore things to their former situation.

[1761] Ibid., p. 89.

The bishops, writing [1762] to Lewis, brother of Charles the Bald, used these words: *Take care of your lands, that you may not be obliged to travel continually by the houses of the clergy, and to tire their bondmen with carriages. Manage your affairs*, continue they, *in such a manner that you may have enough to live upon, and to receive embassies.* It is evident that the king's revenues in those days consisted of their demesnes. [1763]

[1762] See the Capitulary of the year 858, art. 14.
[1763] They levied also some duties on rivers, where there happened to be a bridge or a passage.

14. *Of what they called Census.*

After the Barbarians had quitted their own country, they were desirous of reducing their usages into writing; but as they found difficulty in writing German words with Roman letters, they published these laws in Latin.

In the confusion and rapidity of the conquest, most things changed their nature; in order, however, to express them, they were obliged to make use of such old Latin words as were most analogous to the new usages. Thus, whatever was likely to revive the idea of the ancient census of the Romans they called by the name of *census tributum*, [1764] and when things had no relation at all to the Roman census, they expressed, as well as they could, the German words by Roman letters; thus they formed the word *fredum*, on which I shall have occasion to descant in the following chapters.

[1764] The *census* was so generical a word, that they made use of it to express the tolls of rivers, when there was a bridge or ferry to pass. See the third Capitulary, in the year 803, edition of Baluzius, p. 395, art. 1; and the 5th in the year 819, p. 616. They gave likewise this name to the carriages furnished by the freemen to the king, or to his commissaries, as appeals by the Capitulary of Charles the Bald in the year 865, art. 8.

The words *census* and *tributum* having been employed in an arbitrary manner, this has thrown some obscurity on the signification in which these words were used under our princes of the first and second race. And modern authors [1765] who have adopted particular systems, having found these words in the writings of those days, imagined that what was then called census was exactly the census of the Romans; and thence they inferred this consequence, that our kings of the first two races had put themselves in the place of the Roman emperors, and made no change in their administration. [1766] Besides, as particular duties raised under the second race were by change and by certain restrictions converted into others, [1767] they inferred thence that these duties were the census of the Romans; and as, since the modern regulations, they found that the crown demesnes were absolutely unalienable, they pretended that those duties which represented the Roman census, and did not form a part of the demesnes, were mere usurpation. I omit the other consequences.

[1765] The Abbé du Bos, and his followers.
[1766] See the weakness of the arguments produced by the Abbé du Bos, in the Establishment of the French Monarchy, tom. iii, book VI. 14; especially in the inference he draws from a passage of Gregory of Tours, concerning a dispute between his church and King Charibert.
[1767] For instance, by Enfranchisements.

To apply the ideas of the present time to distant ages is the most fruitful source of error. To those people who want to modernize all the ancient ages, I shall say what the Egyptian priests said to Solon, *O Athenians, you are mere children!* [1768]

[1768] Apud Platonem, in Timæo, vel de natura.—Ed.

15. *That what they called Census was raised only on the Bondmen and not on the Freemen.*

The king, the clergy, and the lords raised regular taxes, each on the bondmen of their respective demesnes. I prove it with respect to the king, by the capitulary *de Villis*; with regard to the clergy, by the codes of the laws of the Barbarians [1769] and in relation to the lords, by the regulations which Charlemagne made concerning this subject. [1770]

[1769] Law of the Alemans, chap. xxii; and the Law of the Bavarians, tit. 1, chap. iv.,
  where the regulations are to be found which the clergy made concerning their order.
[1770] Capitularies, book V. chap. 303.

These taxes were called census; they were economical and not fiscal claims, entirely private dues and not public taxes.

I affirm that what they called census at that time was a tax raised upon the bondmen. This I prove by a formulary of Marculfus containing a permission from the king to enter into holy orders, provided the persons be freeborn, [1771] and not enrolled in the register of the census. I prove it also by a commission from Charlemagne to a count [1772] whom he had sent into Saxony, which contains the enfranchisement of the Saxons for having embraced Christianity, and is properly a charter of freedom. [1773] This prince restores them to their former civil liberty, [1774] and exempts them from paying the census, It was, therefore, the same thing to be a bondman as to pay the census, to be free as not to pay it.

[1771] *Si ille de capite suo bene ingenuus sit, et in Puletico publico censitus non est.*—
  Lib. I, form. 19.
[1772] In the year 789, edition of the Capitularies by Baluzius, vol. i, p. 250.
[1773] *Et ut ista ingenuitatis pagina firma stabilisque consistat.—Ibid.*
[1774] *Pristinæque libertatis donatos, et omni nobis debito censu solutes.—Ibid.*

By a kind of letters patent of the same prince in favor of the Spaniards, [1775] who had been received into the monarchy, the counts are forbidden to demand any census of them, or to deprive them of their lands. That strangers upon their coming to France were treated as bondmen is a thing well known; and Charlemagne being desirous they should be considered as freemen, since he would have them be proprietors of their lands, forbad the demanding any census of them.

[1775] *Præceptum pro Hispanis*, in the year 812, ed. Baluzius, tom. i, p. 500.

A capitulary of Charles the Bald, [1776] given in favor of those very Spaniards, orders them to be treated like the other Franks, and forbids the requiring any census of them; consequently this census was not paid by freemen.

[1776] In the year 844, ed. Baluzius, tom. ii, arts. 1 and 2, p. 27.

The thirtieth article of the edict of Pistes reforms the abuse by which several of the husbandmen belonging to the king or to the church sold the lands dependent on their manors to ecclesiastics or to people of their condition, reserving only a small cottage to themselves; by which means they avoided paying the census; and it ordains that things should be restored to their primitive situation: the census was, therefore, a tax peculiar to bondmen.

Thence also it follows that there was no general census in the monarchy; and this is clear from a great number of passages. For what could be the meaning of this capitulary? [1777] *We ordain that the royal census should be levied in all places where formerly it was lawfully levied.* [1778] What could be the meaning of that in which Charlemagne [1779] orders his commissaries in the provinces to make an exact inquiry into all the census that belonged in former times to the king's demesne? [1780] And of that [1781] in which he disposes of the census paid by those [1782] of whom they are demanded? What can that other capitulary mean [1783] in which we read, *If any person has acquired a tributary land* [1784] *on which we were accustomed to levy the census?* And that other, in fine, [1785] in which Charles the Bald [1786] makes mention of feudal lands whose census had from time immemorial belonged to the king.

[1777] Third Capitulary of the year 805, arts. 20 and 22, inserted in the Collection of Angezise, book III, art. 15. This is agreeable to that of Charles the Bald, in the year 854, *apud Attiniacum*, art. 6.
[1778] *Unducunque legitime exigebatur.—Ibid.*
[1779] In the year 812, arts. 10 and 11, ed. Baluzius, tom. i, p. 398.
[1780] *Unducunque antiquitus ad partem regis venire solebant.—*Capitulary of the year 812, arts. 10 and 11.
[1781] In the year 813, art. 6, ed. Baluzius, tom. i, p. 508.
[1782] *De illis unde censa exigunt.—*Capitulary of the year 813, art. 6.
[1783] Book IV of the Capitularies, art. 37, and inserted in the law of the Lombards.
[1784] Si quis terram tributariam, unde census ad partem nostrum exire solebat, susceperit.—Book IV of the Capitularies, art. 37.
[1785] In the year 805, art. 8.
[1786] Unde census ad partem regis exivit antiquitus.—Capitulary of the year 805, art. 8.

Observe that there are some passages which seem at first sight to be contrary to what I have said, and yet confirm it. We have already seen that the freemen in the monarchy were obliged only to furnish particular carriages; the capitulary just now cited gives to this the name of census, [1787] and opposes it to the census paid by the bondmen.

[1787] *Censibus vel paraveredos quos Franci hominess ad regiam potestatem exsolvere debent.*

Besides, the edict of Pistes [1788] notices those freemen who are obliged to pay the royal census for their head and for their cottages, [1789] and who had sold themselves during the famine. The king orders them to be ransomed. This is because those who were manumitted by the king's letters [1790] did not, generally speaking, acquire a full and perfect liberty. [1791] but they paid *censum in capite*; and these are the people here meant.

[1788] In the year 864, art. 34, ed. Baluzius, p. 192.

[1789] *De illis francis hominibus qui censum regium de suo capite et de suis recellis debeant.—Ibid.*

[1790] The 28th article of the same edict explains this extremely well; it even makes a distinction between a Roman freedman and a Frank freedman: and we likewise see there that the census was not general; it deserves to be read.

[1791] As appears by the Capitulary of Charlemagne in the year 813, which we have already quoted.

We must, therefore, waive the idea of a general and universal census, derived from that of the Romans, from which the rights of the lords are also supposed to have been derived by usurpation. What was called *census* in the French monarchy, independently of the abuse made of that word, was a particular tax imposed on the bondmen by their masters.

I beg the reader to excuse the trouble I must give him with such a number of citations. I should be more concise did I not meet with the Abbé du Bos' book on the establishment of the French monarchy in Gaul, continually in my way. Nothing is a greater obstacle to our progress in knowledge than a bad performance of a celebrated author; because, before we instruct, we must begin with undeceiving.

16. *Of the feudal Lords or Vassals.*

I have noticed those volunteers among the Germans, who have followed their princes in their several expeditions. The same usage continued after the conquest. Tacitus mentions them by the name of companions; [1792] the Salic law by that of men who have vowed fealty to the king; [1793] the formularies of Marculfus [1794] by that of the king's *Antrustios*; [1795] the earliest French historians by that of *Leudes*, [1796] faithful and loyal; and those of later date by that of vassals and lords. [1797]

[1792] Comites.
[1793] *Qui sunt in truste regis*, tit. 44, art. 4.
[1794] Book I, formulary 18.
[1795] From the word *trew*, which signifies faithful among the Germans.
[1796] *Leudes, fideles.*
[1797] *Vassalli, seniores.*

In the Salic and Ripuarian laws we meet with an infinite number of regulations in regard to the Franks, and only with a few for the Antrustios. The regulations concerning the Antrustios are different from those which were made for the other Franks; they are full of what relates to the settling of the property of the Franks, but mention not a word concerning that of the Antrustios. This is because the property of the latter was regulated rather by the political than by the civil law, and was the share that fell to an army, and not the patrimony of a family.

The goods reserved for the feudal lords were called fiscal goods, benefices, honors, and fiefs, by different authors, and in different times. [1798]

[1798] *Fiscalia.* See Marculfus, book I. form. 14. It is mentioned in the Life of St. Maur, *dedit fiscum unum*: and in the annals of Metz, in the year 747, *dedit illi comitatus et fiscos plurimos.* The goods designed for the support of the royal family were called *regalia.*

There is no doubt but the fiefs at first were at will. [1799] We find in Gregory of Tours [1800] that Sunegisilus and Gallomanus were deprived of all they held of the exchequer, and no more was left them than their real property. When Gontram raised his nephew Childebert to the throne, he had a private conference with him, in which he named the persons who ought to be honored with, and those who ought to be deprived of, the fiefs. [1801] In a formulary of Marculfus, [1802] the king gives in exchange, not only the benefices held by his exchequer, but likewise those which had been held by another. The law of the Lombards opposes the benefices to property. [1803] In this, our historians, the formularies, the codes of the different barbarous nations and all the monuments of those days are unanimous. In fine, the writers of the book of fiefs inform us [1804] that at first the lords could take them back when they pleased, that afterwards they granted them for the space of a year, [1805] and that at length they gave them for life.

[1799] See the 1st book, tit. 1, of the fiefs; and *Cujas* on that book.
[1800] Book IX. chap. 38.
[1801] *Quos honoraret muneribus, quos ab honore depelleret.*—Ibid., VII.
[1802] *Vel reliquis quibuscumque beneficiis, quodcumque ille, vel Fiscus noster, in ipsis locis tenuisse nascitur.*—Lib. I, formul. 30.
[1803] Liv. III, tit. 8, § 3.
[1804] *Antiquissimo enim tempore sic erat in Dominorum potestate connexum, ut quando vellent possent auferre rem in feudum a se datam: postea vero conventum est ut per annum tantum firmitatem haberent, deinde statute est ut usque ad vitam fidelis produceretur.*—Feudorum, lib. I, tit. 1.
[1805] It was a kind of precarious tenure which the lord consented or refused to renew every year; as Cujas has observed.

17. *Of the military Service of Freemen.*

Two sorts of people were bound to military service; the great and lesser vassals, who were obliged in consequence of their fief; and the freemen, whether Franks, Romans, or Gauls, who served under the count and were commanded by him and his officers.

The name of freemen was given to those, who on the one hand had no benefits or fiefs, and on the other were not subject to the base services of villainage; the lands they possessed were what they called allodial estates.

The counts assembled the freemen, [1806] and led them against the enemy; they had officers under them who were called vicars; [1807] and as all the freemen were divided into hundreds, which constituted what they called a borough, the counts had also officers under them, who were denominated *centenarii,* and led the freemen of the borough, or their hundreds, to the field. [1808]

[1806] See the Capitulary of Charlemagne in the year 812, arts. 3 and 4, ed. Baluzius, i, p. 491; and the edict of Pistes in the year 864, art. 26, tom. ii, p. 186.
[1807] *Et habebat unusquisque comes Vicarios et Centenarios secum.*—Book II of the Capitularies, art. 28.
[1808] They were called *Compagenses.*

This division into hundreds is posterior to the establishment of the Franks in Gaul. It was made by Clotharius and Childebert, with a view of obliging each district to answer for the robberies committed in their division; this we find in the decrees of those princes. [1809] A regulation of this kind is to this very day observed in England.

[1809] Published in the year 595, art. 1. See the Capitularies, ed. Baluzius, p. 20. These regulations were undoubtedly made by agreement.

As the counts led the freemen against the enemy, the feudal lords commanded also their vassals or rear-vassals; and the bishops, abbots, or their advocates [1810] likewise commanded theirs. [1811]

[1810] *Advocati.*
[1811] Capitulary of Charlemagne, in the year 812, art. 1 and 5, ed. Baluzius, tom. i, p. 490.

The bishops were greatly embarrassed and inconsistent with themselves; [1812] they requested Charlemagne not to oblige them any longer to military service; and when he granted their request, they complained that he had deprived them of the public esteem; so that this prince was obliged to justify his intentions upon this head. Be that as it may, when they were exempted from marching against the enemy, I do not find that their vassals were led by the counts; on the contrary, we see that the kings or the bishops chose one of their feudatories to conduct them. [1813]

[1812] See the Capitulary of the year 803, published at Worms, ed. Baluzius, pp. 408, 410.
[1813] Capitulary of Worms in the year 803, edition of Baluzius, p. 409; and the council in the year 845, under Charles, the Bald, *in verno palatio*, edition of Baluzius, tom. ii, p. 17, art. 8.

In a Capitulary of Lewis the Debonnaire, [1814] this prince distinguishes three sorts of vassals, those belonging to the king, those to the bishops, and those to the counts. The vassals of a feudal lord were not led against the enemy by the count, except some employment in the king's household hindered the lord himself from commanding them. [1815]

[1814] The fifth Capitulary of the year 819, art. 27, edition of Baluzius, p. 618.
[1815] De Vassis Dominicis qui adhuc intra casam serviunt et tamen beneficia habere noscuntur, statutum est ut quicumque ex eis cum Domino Imperatore domi remanserint, vassallos suos casatos secum non retineant; sed cum comite, cujus pagenses sunt, ire permittant.—2nd Capitulary in the year 812, art. 7, edition of Baluzius, tom. i, p. 494.

But who is it that led the feudal lords into the field? No doubt the king himself, who was always at the head of his faithful vassals. Hence we constantly find in the capitularies a distinction made between the king's vassals and those of the bishops, [1816] Such brave and magnanimous princes as our kings did not take the field to put themselves at the head of an ecclesiastic militia; these were not the men they chose to conquer or to die with.

[1816] Capitulary 1 of the year 812, art. 5, de hominibus nostris, et episcoporum et abbatum qui vel beneficia vel talia propria habent, etc., edition of Baluzius, tom. i, p. 490.

But these lords likewise carried their vassals and rear-vassals with them, as we can prove by the capitulary in which Charlemagne ordains that every freeman who has four manors, either in his own property or as a benefice from somebody else, should march against the enemy or follow his lord. [1817] It is evident that Charlemagne means that the person who had a manor of his own should march under the count and he who held a benefice of a lord should set out along with him.

[1817] In the year 812, chap. 1, edition of Baluzius, p. 490, *ut omnis homo liber quatuor mansos vestitos de propria suo, sive de alicujus beneficia habet, ipse se praeparet, et ipse in hostem pergat, sive cum senior suo.*

And yet the Abbé du Bos pretends [1818] that, when mention is made in the capitularies of tenants who depended on a particular lord, no others are meant than bondmen; and he grounds his opinion on the law of the Visigoths and the practice of that nation. It is much better to rely on the capitularies themselves; that which I have just quoted says expressly the contrary. The treaty between Charles the Bald and his brothers notices also those freemen who might choose to follow either a lord or the king; and this regulation is conformable to a great many others.

[1818] Establishment of the French Monarchy, tom. iii, book VI, chap. iv. p. 299.

We may, therefore, conclude that there were three sorts of military services; that of the king's vassals, who had other vassals under them; that of the bishops or of the other clergy and their vassals, and, in fine, that of the count, who commanded the freemen.

Not but the vassals might be also subject to the count; as those who have a particular command are subordinate to him who is invested with a more general authority.

We even find that the count and the king's commissaries might oblige them to pay the fine when they had not fulfilled the engagements of their fief. In like manner, if the king's vassals committed any outrage [1819] they were subject to the correction of the count, unless they choose to submit rather to that of the king.

[1819] Capitulary of the year 882, art. 11, *apud vernis palatium*, edition of Baluzius, tom. ii, p. 289.

18. Of the double Service.

It was a fundamental principle of the monarchy that whosoever was subject to the military power of another person was subject also to his civil jurisdiction. Thus the Capitulary of Lewis the Debonnaire, [1820] in the year 815, makes the military power of the count and his civil jurisdiction over the freemen keep always an equal pace. Thus the *placita* [1821] of the count who carried the freemen against the enemy were called the placita of the freemen; [1822] whence undoubtedly came this maxim, that the questions relating to liberty could be decided only in the count's placita, and not in those of his officers. Thus the count never led the vassals [1823] belonging to the bishops, or to the abbots, against the enemy, because they were not subject to his civil jurisdiction. Thus he never commanded the rear-vassals belonging to the king's vassals. Thus the glossary of the English laws informs us [1824] that those to whom the Saxons gave the name of *Coples* [1825] were by the Normans called *counts*, or *companions*, because they shared the justiciary fines with the king. Thus we see that at all times the duty of a vassal towards his lord [1826] was to bear arms [1827] and to try his peers in his court.

[1820] Art. 1, 2, and the council *in verno palatio* of the year 845, art. 8, edition of Baluzius, tom. ii, p. 17.

[1821] Or assizes.

[1822] Capitularies, book 4th of the Collection of Angezise, art. 57; and the fifth capitulary of Lewis the Debonnaire, in the year 819, art. 14, edition of Baluzius, tom. i, p. 615.

[1823] See the 8th note of the preceding chapter.

[1824] It is to be found in the Collection of William Lambard, de *priscis Anglorum legibus*.

[1825] In the word *Satrapia*.

[1826] This is well explained by the assizes of Jerusalem, chap. 221, 222.

[1827] The advowees of the church (*advocati*) were equally at the head of their placita and of their militia.

One of the reasons which produced this connection between the judiciary right and that of leading the forces against the enemy was because the person who led them exacted at the same time the payment of the fiscal duties, which consisted in some carriage services due by the freemen, and in general, in certain judiciary profits, of which we shall treat hereafter.

The lords had the right of administering justice in their fief, by the same principle as the counts had it in their counties. And, indeed, the counties in the several variations that happened at different times always followed the variations of the fiefs; both were governed by the same plan, and by the same principles. In a word, the counts in their counties were lords, and the lords in their seigniories were counts.

It has been a mistake to consider the counts as civil officers, and the dukes as military commanders. Both were equally civil and military officers: [1828] the whole difference consisted in the duke's having several counts under him, though there were counts who had no duke over them, as we learn from Fredegarius. [1829]

[1828] See the 8th formulary of Marculfus, book I, which contains the letters given to a duke, patrician, or count; and invests them with the civil jurisdiction, and the fiscal administration.

[1829] Chronicle, chap. 78, in the year 636.

It will be imagined, perhaps, that the government of the Franks must have been very severe at that time, since the same officers were invested with a military and civil power, nay, even with a fiscal authority, over the subjects; which in the preceding books I have observed to be distinguishing marks of despotism.

But we must not believe that the counts pronounced judgment by themselves, and administered justice in the same manner as the bashaws in Turkey; in order to judge affairs, they assembled a kind of assizes, where the principal men appeared.

To the end we may thoroughly understand what relates to the judicial proceedings in the formulas, in the laws of the Barbarians and in the capitularies, it is proper to observe that the functions of the count, of the *Grafio* or fiscal judge and the Centenarius were the same; that the judges, the *Rathimburghers*, and the aldermen were the same persons under different names. These were the count's assistants, and were generally seven in number; and as he was obliged to have twelve persons to judge, [1830] he filled up the number with the principal men. [1831]

[1830] See concerning this subject the capitularies of Lewis the Debonnaire added to the Salic law, art. 2, and the formula of judgments given by Ducange in the word *boni homines*.

[1831] *Per bonos homines*, sometimes there were none but principal men. See the appendix to the formularies of Marculfus, chap. 51.

But whoever had the jurisdiction, the king, the count, the *Grafio*, the *Centenarius*, the lords, or the clergy, they never tried causes alone; and this usage, which derived its origin from the forests of Germany, was still continued even after the fiefs had assumed a new form.

With regard to the fiscal power, its nature was such that the count could hardly abuse it. The rights of the prince in respect to the freemen were so simple that they consisted only, as we have already observed, in certain carriages which were demanded of them on some public occasions. [1832] And as for the judiciary rights, there were laws which prevented misdemeanors. [1833]

[1832] And some tolls on rivers, of which I have spoken already.

[1833] See the law of the Ripuarians, tit. 89; and the law of the Lombards, book II, tit. 52, § 9.

19. Of Compositions among the barbarous Nations.

Since it is impossible to gain any insight into our political law unless we are thoroughly acquainted with the laws and manners of the German nations, I shall, therefore, pause here awhile, in order to inquire into those manners and laws.

It appears by Tacitus that the Germans knew only two capital crimes; they hanged traitors, and drowned cowards; these were the only public crimes among that people. When a man had injured another, the relatives of the person injured took share in the quarrel, and the offence was cancelled by a satisfaction. [1834] This satisfaction was made to the person offended, when capable of receiving it; or to the relatives if they had been injured in common, or if by the decease of the party aggrieved or injured the satisfaction had devolved to them.

[1834] *Suscipere tam inimicitias, seu patris, seu propinqui, quam amicitias, necesse est: nec implacabiles Durant; luitur enim etiam homicidium certo armentorum ac pecorum numero, recipitque satisfactionem universa domus.*—Tacitus, *De Moribus Germanorum*, 21.

In the manner mentioned by Tacitus, these satisfactions were made by the mutual agreement of the parties; hence in the codes of the barbarous nations these satisfactions are called compositions.

The law of the Frisians [1835] is the only one I find that has left the people in that situation in which every family at variance was in some measure in the state of nature, and in which, being unrestrained either by a political or civil law, they might give freedom to their revenge till they had obtained satisfaction. Even this law was moderated; a regulation was made [1836] that the person whose life was sought after should be unmolested in his own house, as also in going and coming from church and the court where causes were tried.

[1835] See this law in the 2nd title on murders; and Vulemar's addition on robberies.
[1836] *Additio sapientium*, tit. i, § 1.

The compilers of the Salic law [1837] cite an ancient usage of the Franks, by which a person who had dug a corpse out of the ground, in order to strip it, should be banished from society till the relatives had consented to his being re-admitted. And as before that time strict orders were issued to everyone, even to the offender's own wife, not to give him a morsel of bread, or to receive him under their roofs, such a person was in respect to others, and others in respect to him, in a state of savagery till an end was put to this state by a composition.

[1837] Salic Law, tit. 57, § 5; tit. 17, § 2.

This excepted, we find that the sages of the different barbarous nations thought of determining by themselves what would have been too long and too dangerous to expect from the mutual agreement of the parties. They took care to fix the value of the composition which the party wronged or injured was to receive. All those barbarian laws are in this respect most admirably exact; the several cases are minutely distinguished, [1838] the circumstances are weighed, the law substitutes itself in the place of the person injured and insists upon the same satisfaction as he himself would have demanded in cold blood.

[1838] The Salic laws are admirable in this respect, see especially the titles 3, 4, 5, 6, and 7, which related to the stealing of cattle.

By the establishing of those laws, the German nations quitted that state of nature in which they seemed to have lived in Tacitus' time.

Rotharis declares, in the law of the Lombards, [1839] that he had increased the compositions allowed by ancient custom for wounds, to the end that, the wounded person being fully satisfied, all enmities should cease. And indeed as the Lombards, from a very poor people had grown rich by the conquest of Italy, the ancient compositions had become frivolous, and reconcilements prevented. I do not question but this was the motive which obliged the other chiefs of the conquering nations to make the different codes of laws now extant.

[1839] Book I, tit. 7, § 15.

The principal composition was that which the murderer paid to the relatives of the deceased. The difference of conditions produced a difference in the compositions. [1840] Thus in the law of the Angli, there was a composition of six hundred sous for the murder of an adeling, two hundred for that of a freeman, and thirty for killing a bondman. The largeness therefore of the composition for the life of a man was one of his chief privileges; for besides the distinction it made of his person, it likewise established a greater security in his favor among rude and boisterous nations.

[1840] See the law of the Angli, tit. 1, §§ 1,2, and 4; *ibid.* tit. 5, § 6; the law of the Bavarians, tit. 1, chap. 8, 9, and the law of the Frisians, tit. 15.

This we are made sensible of by the law of the Bavarians: [1841] it gives the names of the Bavarian families who received a double composition, because they were the first after the Agilolfings. [1842] The Agilolfings were of the ducal race, and it was customary with this nation to choose a duke out of that family; these had a quadruple composition. The composition for a duke exceeded by a third that which had been established for the Agilolfings. *Because he is a duke*, says the law, *a greater honor is paid to him than to his relatives.*

[1841] Tit. 2, chap. xx.
[1842] Hozidra, Ozza, Sagana, Habalingua, Anniena.—*Ibid.*

All these compositions were valued in money. But as those people, especially when they lived in Germany, had very little specie, they might pay it in cattle, corn, movables, arms, dogs, hawks, lands, &c. [1843] The law itself frequently determined the value of those things; which explains how it was possible for them to have such a number of pecuniary punishments with so very little money. [1844]

[1843] Thus the law of Ina valued life by a certain sum of money, or by a certain portion of land. *Leges Inæ regis, titulo de villico regio de priscis Anglorum legibus.*— Cambridge, 1644.
[1844] See the law of the Saxons, which makes this same regulation for several people, chap. xviii. See also the law of the Ripuarians, tit. 36, § 11; the law of the Bavarians, tit. 1, §§ 10 and 11. *Si aurum non habet, donet aliam pecunian, mancipia, terram, &c.*

These laws were therefore employed in exactly determining the difference of wrongs, injuries and crimes; to the end that every one might know how far he had been injured or offended, the reparation he was to receive, and especially that he was to receive no more.

In this light it is easy to conceive that a person who had taken revenge after having received satisfaction was guilty of a heinous crime. This contained a public as well as a private offence; it was a contempt of the law of itself; a crime which the legislators never failed to punish. [1845]

[1845] See the law of the Lombards, book I, tit. 25 § 21; *ibid.*, book I, tit. 9, §§ 8, 34; *ibid.*, § 38, and the Capitulary of Charlemagne in the year 802, chap. xxxii, containing an instruction given to those whom he sent into the provinces.

There was another crime which above all others was considered as dangerous, when those people lost something of their spirit of independence, and when the kings endeavored to establish a better civil administration; this was the refusing to give or to receive satisfaction. [1846] We find in the different codes of the laws of the Barbarians that the legislators were peremptory on this article. [1847] In effect, a person who refused to receive satisfaction wanted to preserve his right of prosecution; he who refused to give it left the right of prosecution to the person injured; and this is what the sages had reformed in the institutions of the Germans, whereby people were incited but not compelled to compositions.

[1846] See in Gregory of Tours, book VII. chap. 47, the detail of a process, wherein a party loses half the composition that had been adjudged to him, for having done justice to himself, instead of receiving satisfaction, whatever injury he might have afterwards received.
[1847] See the law of the Saxons, chap. iii, § 4; the law of the Lombards, book I, tit. 37, §§ 1 and 2; and the law of the Alemans, tit. 45, §§ 1 and 2. This last law gave leave to the party injured to right himself upon the spot, and in the first transport of passion. See also the Capitularies of Charlemagne in the year 779, chap. xxii, in the year 802, chap. xxxii, and also that of the year 805, chap. v.

I have just now made mention of a text of the Salic law, in which the legislator left the party offended at liberty to receive or to refuse satisfaction; it is the law by which a person who had stripped a dead body was expelled from society till the relatives upon receiving satisfaction petitioned for his being re-admitted. [1848] It was owing to the respect they had for sacred things that the compilers of the Salic laws did not meddle with the ancient usage.

[1848] The compilers of the law of the Ripuarians seem to have softened this. See the 85th title of those laws.

It would have been absolutely unjust to grant a composition to the relatives of a robber killed in the act, or to the relatives of a woman who had been repudiated for the crime of adultery. The law of the Bavarians allowed no compositions in the like cases, but punished the relatives who sought revenge. [1849]

[1849] See the decree of Tassillon, *de popularibus legibus*, art. 3, 4, 10, 16, 19; the law of the Angli, tit. vii. § 4.

It is no rare thing to meet with compositions for involuntary actions in the codes of the laws of the Barbarians. The law of the Lombards is generally very prudent; it ordained [1850] that in those cases the compositions should be according to the person's generosity; and that the relatives should no longer be permitted to pursue their revenge.

[1850] Book I, tit. ix, § 4.

484

Clotharius II made a very wise decree; he forbad the person robbed to receive any clandestine composition, and without an order from the judge. [1851] We shall presently see the motive of this law.

[1851] *Pactus pro tenore pacis inter Childebertum et Clotarium, anno 593, et decretio Clotarii 2 regis, circa annum 595*, chap. xi.

20. Of what was afterwards called the Jurisdiction of the Lords.

Besides the composition which they were obliged to pay to the relatives for murders or injuries, they were also under a necessity of paying a certain duty which the codes of the barbarian laws called *fredum*. [1852] I intend to treat of it at large; and in order to give an idea of it, I begin with defining it as a recompense for the protection granted against the right of vengeance. Even to this day, *fred* in the Swedish language signifies peace.

[1852] When it was not determined by the law, it was generally the third of what was given for the composition, as appears in the law of the Ripuarians, chap. lxxxix, which is explained by the third Capitulary of the year 813.—Edition of Baluzius, tom. i, p. 512.

The administration of justice among those rude and unpolished nations was nothing more than granting to the person who had committed an offence a protection against the vengeance of the party offended, and obliging the latter to accept of the satisfaction due to him: insomuch that among the Germans, contrary to the practice of all other nations, justice was administered in order to protect the criminal against the party injured.

The codes of the Barbarian laws have given us the cases in which the *freda* might be demanded. When the relatives could not prosecute, they allowed of no *fredum*; and indeed, when there was no prosecution there could be no composition for a protection against it. Thus, in the law of the Lombards, [1853] if a person happened to kill a freeman by accident, he paid the value of the man killed, without the *fredum*; because, as he had killed him involuntarily, it was not the case in which the relatives were allowed the right of prosecution. Thus in the law of the Ripuarians, [1854] when a person was killed with a piece of wood, or with any instrument made by man, the instrument or the wood were deemed culpable, and the relatives seized upon them for their own use, but were not allowed to demand the *fredum*.

[1853] Book I, tit. 9, § 17, ed. Lindembrock.
[1854] Tit. 70.

In like manner, when a beast happened to kill a man, the same law established a composition without the *fredum*, because the relatives of the deceased were not offended. [1855]

[1855] Tit. 46. See also the law of the Lombards, i. chap. xxi, § 3, Lindembrock's edition, *si caballus cum pede*, &c.

In fine, it was ordained by the Salic law, [1856] that a child who had committed a fault before the age of twelve should pay the composition without the *fredum*: as he was not yet able to bear arms, he could not be in the case in which the party injured, or his relatives, had a right to demand satisfaction.

[1856] Tit. 28, § 6.

It was the criminal that paid the *fredum* for the peace and security of which he had been deprived by his crime, and which he might recover by protection. But a child did not lose this security; he was not a man, and consequently could not be expelled from human society.

This *fredum* was a local right in favor of the person who was judge of the district. [1857] Yet the law of the Ripuarians [1858] forbade him to demand it himself: it ordained that the party who had gained the cause should receive it and carry it to the exchequer, to the end that there might be a lasting peace, says the law among the Ripuarians.

[1857] As appears by the decree of Clotharius II in the year 595, *fredus tamen judici in cujus pago est reservetur*.
[1858] Tit. 85.

The greatness of the *fredum* was proportioned to the degree of protection: thus the *fredum* for the king's protection was greater than what was granted for the protection of the count, or of the other judges. [1859]

[1859] *Capitulare incerti anni*, chap. 57, in Baluzius, tom. i p. 515, and it is to be observed, that what was called *fredum* or *faida*, in the monuments of the first race, is known by the name of *bannum* in those of the second race, as appears from the Capitulary *de partibus Saxoniæ*, in the year 789.

Here I see the origin of the jurisdiction of the lords. The fiefs comprised very large territories, as appears from a vast number of records. I have already proved that the kings raised no taxes on the lands belonging to the division of the Franks; much less could they reserve to themselves any duties on the fiefs. Those who obtained them had in this respect a full and perfect enjoyment, reaping every possible emolument from them. And as one of the most considerable emoluments was the justiciary profits (*freda*), [1860] which were received according to the usage of the Franks, it followed thence that the person seized of the fief was also seized of the jurisdiction, the exercise of which consisted of the compositions made to the relatives, and of the profits accruing to the lord; it was nothing more than ordering the payment of the compositions of the law, and demanding the legal fines. We find by the formularies containing confirmation of the perpetuity of a fief in favor of a feudal lord, [1861] or of the privileges of fiefs in favor of churches, [1862] that the fiefs were possessed of this right. This appears also from an infinite number of charters [1863] mentioning a prohibition to the king's judges or officers of entering upon the territory in order to exercise any act of judicature whatsoever, or to demand any judiciary emolument. When the king's judges could no longer make any demand in a district, they never entered it; and those to whom this district was left performed the same functions as had been exercised before by the judges.

[1860] See the Capitulary of Charlemagne, *de villis*, where he ranks these *freda* among the great revenues of what was called *villæ*, or the king's demesnes.

[1861] See Marculfus, book I, form. 3, 8, 17.

[1862] See Marculfus, book I, form. 2, 3, 4.

[1863] See the Collections of those charters, especially that at the end of the 5th volume of the historians of France, published by the Benedictine monks.

The king's judges are forbidden also to oblige the parties to give security for their appearing before them; it belonged therefore to the person who had received the territory in fief to demand this security. They mention also that the king's commissaries shall not insist upon being accommodated with a lodging; in effect, they no longer exercised any function in those districts.

The administration therefore of justice, both in the old and new fiefs, was a right inherent in the very fief itself, a lucrative right which constituted a part of it. For this reason it had been considered at all times in this light; whence this maxim arose, that jurisdictions are patrimonial in France.

Some have thought that the jurisdictions derived their origin from the manumissions made by the kings and lords in favor of their bondmen. But the German nations, and those descended from them, are not the only people who manumitted their bondmen, and yet they are the only people that established patrimonial jurisdictions. Besides, we find by the formularies of Marculfus [1864] that there were freemen dependent on these jurisdictions in the earliest times: the bondmen were therefore subject to the jurisdiction, because they were upon the territory; and they did not give rise to the fiefs for having been annexed to the fief.

[1864] See the 3rd, 4th, and 14th of the first book, and the charter of Charlemagne, in the year 771, in Martene, tom. i. Anecdot. collect. 11, *præcipientes jubemus ut ullus judex publicus . . . . hominess ipsius ecclesiæ et monasterii ipsius Morbacensis tam ingenuos quam et servos, et qui super eorum terras manere, &c.*

Others have taken a shorter cut; the lords, say they (and this is all they say), usurped the jurisdictions. But are the nations descended from Germany the only people in the world that usurped the rights of princes? We are sufficiently informed by history that several other nations have encroached upon their sovereigns, and yet we find no other instance of what we call the jurisdiction of the lords. The origin of it is therefore to be traced in the usages and customs of the Germans.

Whoever has the curiosity to look into Loyseau [1865] will be surprised at the manner in which this author supposes the lords to have proceeded in order to form and usurp their different jurisdictions. They must have been the most artful people in the world; they must have robbed and plundered, not after the manner of a military nation, but as the country justices and the attorneys rob one another. Those brave warriors must be said to have formed a general system of politics throughout all the provinces of the kingdom, and in so many other countries in Europe; Loyseau makes them reason as he himself reasoned in his closet.

[1865] Treatise of village jurisdictions, Loyseau.

Once more; if the jurisdiction was not a dependence of the fief, how come we everywhere to find that the service of the fief was to attend the king or the lord, both in their courts and in the army? [1866]

[1866] See Ducange on the word *hominium*.

21. *Of the Territorial Jurisdiction of the Churches.*

The churches acquired very considerable property. We find that our kings gave them great seigniories, that is, great fiefs; and we find jurisdictions established at the same time in the demesnes of those churches. Whence could so extraordinary a privilege derive its origin? it must certainly have been in the nature of the grant. The church land had this privilege because it had not been taken from it. A seignory was given to the church; and it was allowed to enjoy the same privileges as if it had been granted to a vassal, it was also subjected to the same service as it would have paid to the state if it had been given to a layman, according to what we have already observed.

The churches had therefore the right of demanding the payment of compositions in their territory, and of insisting upon the *fredum*; and as those rights necessarily implied that of hindering the king's officers from entering upon the territory to demand these *freda* and to exercise acts of judicature, the right which ecclesiastics had of administering justice in their own territory was called immunity, in the style of the formularies, of the charters, and of the capitularies. [1867]

[1867] See Marculfus, book I, form. 3, 4.

The law of the Ripuarians [1868] forbids the freedom of the churches [1869] to hold the assembly for administering justice in any other place than in the church where they were manumitted. [1870] The churches had therefore jurisdictions even over freemen, and held their *placita* in the earliest times of the monarchy.

[1868] *Ne aliubi nisi ad ecclesiam, ubi relaxati sunt, mallum teneant*, tit. 58, § i. See also
    § 19. Lindembrock's edition.
[1869] *Tabulariis.*
[1870] *Mallum.*

I find in the Lives of the Saints [1871] that Clovis gave to a certain holy person power over a district of six leagues, and exempted it from all manner of jurisdiction. This, I believe, is a falsity, but it is a falsity of a very ancient date; both the truth and the fiction contained in that life are in relation to the customs and laws of those times, and it is these customs and laws we are investigating. [1872]

[1871] *Vita S. Germeri, Episcopi Tolosani apud Bollandianos* 16 *Maii.*
[1872] See also the life of St. Melanius, and that of St. Deicola.

Clotharius II orders the bishops or the nobility who are possessed of estates in distant parts, to choose upon the very spot those who are to administer justice, or to receive the judiciary emoluments. [1873]

[1873] In the council of Paris, in the year 615. Episcopi vel potentes, qui in aliis possident regionibus, judices vel missos discussores de aliis provinciis non instituant, nisi de loco qui justitiam percipiant et aliis reddant, art. 19. See also art. 12.

The same prince regulates the judiciary power between the ecclesiastic courts and his officers. [1874] The Capitulary of Charlemagne in the year 802 prescribes to the bishops and abbots the qualifications necessary for their officers of justice. Another capitulary of the same prince inhibits the royal officers [1875] to exercise any jurisdiction over those who are employed in cultivating church lands, except they entered into that state by fraud, and to exempt themselves from contributing to the public charges. [1876] The bishops assembled at Rheims made a declaration that the vassals belonging to the respective churches are within their immunity. [1877] The Capitulary of Charlemagne in the year 806 ordains that the churches should have both criminal and civil jurisdiction over those who live upon their lands. [1878] In fine, as the capitulary of Charles the Bald [1879] distinguishes between the king's jurisdiction, that of the lords, and that of the church, I shall say nothing further upon this subject. [1880]

[1874] Ibid., art. 5.
[1875] In the law of the Lombards, book II, tit. 44, cap ii. Lindembrock's edition.
[1876] *Servi Aldiones, libellarii antique, cel alii noviter facti.—Ibid.*
[1877] Letter in the year 858, art. 7 in the Capitularies, p. 108. *Sicut illæ res et facultates, in quibus vivunt clerici, ita et illæ sub consecration immunitatis, sunt de quibus debent militare vassalli.*
[1878] It is added to the law of the Bavarians, art. 7. See also art. 3. Lindembrock's edition, p. 444. *Imprimis omnium jubendum est ut habeant ecclesiae earum justitias, et in vita illorum qui habitant in ipsis ecclesiis et post, tam in pecuniis quam et in substantiis eorum.*
[1879] In the year 857, *in synodo apud Carisiacum*, art. 4, edition of Baluzius, p. 96.
[1880] See the letter written by the bishops assembled at Rheims, in the year 858. art. 7, in the capitularies, Baluzius's edition, p. 108. *Sicut illæ res et facultates, in quibus vivunt clerici, ita et illæ sub consecration immunitatis sunt de quibus debent militare vassalli, &c.*

22. *That the Jurisdictions were established before the End of the Second Race.*

It has been pretended that the vassals usurped the jurisdiction in their seigniories, during the confusion of the second race. Those who choose rather to form a general proposition than to examine it found it easier to say that the vassals did not possess than to discover how they came to possess. But the jurisdictions do not owe their origin to usurpations; they are derived from the primitive establishment, and not from its corruption.

"He who kills a freeman," says the law of the Bavarians, "shall pay a composition to his relatives if he has any; if not, he shall pay it to the duke, or to the person under whose protection he had put himself in his lifetime." [1881] it is well known what it was to put oneself under the protection of another for a benefice.

[1881] Tit. 3, chap. xiii. Lindembrock's edition.

"He who had been robbed of his bondman," says the law of the Alemans, "shall have recourse to the prince to whom the robber is subject; to the end that he may obtain a composition." [1882]

[1882] Tit. 85.

"If a *centenarius*," says the decree of Childebert, "finds a robber in another hundred than his own, or in the limits of our faithful vassals, and does not drive him out, he shall be answerable for the robber, or purge himself by oath." [1883] There was therefore a difference between the district of the centenarii and that of the vassals.

[1883] In the year 595, arts. 11 and 12, edition of the Capitularies by Baluzius, p. 19. *Pari conditione convenit ut si una centena in alia centena vestigium secuta fuerit et invenerit, vel in quibuscumque fidelium nostrorum terminis vestigium miserit, et ipsum in aliam centenam minime expellere potuerit, aut convictus reddat latronem,* &c.

This decree of Childebert [1884] explains the constitution of Clotharius of the same year, which being given for the same occasion and on the same matter differs only in the terms; the constitution calling *in truste* what by the decree is styled *in terminis fidelium* nostrorum. Messieurs Bignon and Ducange, who pretend that *in truste* signified another king's demesne, are mistaken in their conjecture. [1885]

[1884] *Si vestigius comprobatur latronis tamen praesentia nihil longe mulctando; aut si persequens latronem suum comprehenderit, integram sibi compositionem accipiat. Quod si in truste inavenitur, medietatem compositionis trustis adquirat, et capital exigat a latrone*, Arts. 2 and 3.
[1885] See the Glossary on the word *trustis*.

Pepin, King of Italy, in a constitution that had been made as well for the Franks as for the Lombards, [1886] after imposing penalties on the counts and other royal officers for prevarications or delays in the administration of justice, ordains that if it happens that a Frank or a Lombard, possessed of a fief, is unwilling to administer justice, the judge to whose district he belongs shall suspend the exercise of his fief, and in the meantime, either the judge or his commissary shall administer justice. [1887]

[1886] Inserted in the Law of the Lombards, book II. tit. 52, §14. It is the Capitulary of the year 793, in Baluzius, p. 544, art. 10.
[1887] *Et si forsitan Francus aut Longobardus habens beneficium justitiam facere noluerit, ille judex in cujus ministerio fuerit, contradicat illi beneficium suum, interim dum ipse aut missus ejus justitiam faciat*. See also the same law of the Lombards, ii, tit. 52, § 2, which relates to the Capitulary of Charlemagne of the year 779, art. 21.

It appears by a Capitulary of Charlemagne, [1888] that the kings did not levy the *freda* in all places. Another capitulary of the same prince shows the feudal laws [1889] and feudal court to have been already established. Another of Lewis the Debonnaire ordains that when a person possessed of a fief does not administer justice, [1890] or binders it from being administered, the king's commissaries shall live in his house at discretion, till justice be administered. I shall likewise quote two capitularies of Charles the Bald; one of the year 861, [1891] where we find the particular jurisdictions established, with judges and subordinate officers; and the other of the year 864, [1892] where he makes a distinction between his own seigniories and those of private persons.

[1888] The third of the year 812, art. 10.

[1889] The second of the year 813, arts. 14, 20, Baluzius' edition, p. 509.

[1890] *Capitulare quintum anni* 819 art. 23, Baluzius' edition, p. 617. *Ut ubicumque missi, aut episcopum, aut abbatem, aut alium quemlibet honore praeditum invenerint, qui justitiam facere noluit vel prohibuit, de ipsius rebus vivant quamdiu in eo loco justitias facere debent.*

[1891] *Edictum in Carisiaco* in Baluzius, tom. ii, p. 152, *unusquisque advocates pro omnibus de suâ advocatione quos invenerit contra hunc bannum nostrum fecisse . . . . castiget.*

[1892] *Edictum Pistense*, art. 18, Baluzius' edition, tom. ii, p. 181. *Si in fiscum nostrum vel in quamcunque immunitatem aut alicujus potentis potestatem vel proprietatem confugerit,* &c.

We have not the original grants of the fiefs, because they were established by the partition which is known to have been made among the conquerors. It cannot, therefore, be proved by original contracts that the jurisdictions were at first annexed to the fiefs: but if in the formularies of the confirmations, or of the translations of those fiefs in perpetuity, we find, as already has been observed, that the jurisdiction was there established, this judiciary right must certainly have been inherent in the fief and one of its chief privileges.

We have a far greater number of records that establish the patrimonial jurisdiction of the clergy in their districts than there are to prove that of the benefices or fiefs of the feudal lords; for which two reasons may be assigned. The first, that most of the records now extant were preserved or collected by the monks, for the use of their monasteries. The second, that the patrimony of the several churches having been formed by particular grants, and by a kind of derogation from the order established, they were obliged to have charters granted to them; whereas the concessions made to the feudal lords being consequences of the political order, they had no occasion to demand, and much less to preserve, a particular charter. Nay the kings were oftentimes satisfied with making a simple delivery with the scepter, as appears from the Life of St. Maur.

But the third formulary of Marculfus sufficiently proves that the privileges of immunity, and consequently that of jurisdiction, were common to the clergy and the laity, since it is made for both. [1893] The same may be said of the constitution of Clotharius II. [1894]

[1893] Lib. 1. *Maximum regni nostri augere credimus monimentum, si beneficia opportune locis ecclesiarum aut cui volueris dicere, benevola deliberation concedimus.*

[1894] I have already quoted it in the preceding chapter, *Episcopi vel patentes.*

23. General Idea of the Abbé du Bos' Book on the Establishment of the French Monarchy in Gaul.

Before I finish this book, it will not be improper to write a few strictures on the Abbé du Bos' performance, because my notions are perpetually contrary to his; and if he has hit on the truth, I must have missed it.

This performance has imposed upon a great many because it is penned with art; because the point in question is constantly supposed; because the more it is deficient in proofs the more it abounds in probabilities; and, in fine, because an infinite number of conjectures are laid down as principles, and thence other conjectures are inferred as consequences. The reader forgets he has been doubting in order to begin to believe. And as a prodigious fund of erudition is interspersed, not in the system but around it, the mind is taken up with the appendages, and neglects the principal. Besides, such a vast multitude of researches hardly permits one to imagine that nothing has been found; the length of the way makes us think that we have arrived at our journey's end.

But when we examine the matter thoroughly, we find an immense colossus with earthen feet; and it is the earthen feet that render the colossus immense. If the Abbé du Bos' system had been well grounded, he would not have been obliged to write three tedious volumes to prove it; he would have found everything within his subject, and without wandering on every side in quest of what was extremely foreign to it; even reason itself would have undertaken to range this in the same chain with the other truths. Our history and laws would have told him, *Do not take so much trouble, we shall be your vouchers.*

24. The same Subject continued. Reflection on the main Part of the System.

The Abbé du Bos endeavors by all means to explode the opinion that the Franks made the conquest of Gaul. According to his system our kings were invited by the people, and only substituted themselves in the place and succeeded to the rights of the Roman Emperors.

This pretension cannot be applied to the time when Clovis, upon his entering Gaul, took and plundered the towns; neither is it applicable to the period when he defeated Syagrius, the Roman commander, and conquered the country which he held; it can, therefore, be referred only to the period when Clovis, already master of a great part of Gaul by open force, was called by the choice and affection of the people to the sovereignty over the rest. And it is not enough that Clovis was received, he must have been called; the Abbé du Bos must prove that the people chose rather to live under Clovis than under the domination of the Romans or under their own laws. Now the Romans belonging to that part of Gaul not yet invaded by the Barbarians were, according to this author, of two sorts: the first were of the Armorican confederacy, who had driven away the emperor's officers in order to defend themselves against the Barbarians, and to be governed by their own laws; the second were subject to the Roman officers. Now, does the Abbé produce any convincing proofs that the Romans, who were still subject to the empire, called in Clovis? Not one. Does he prove that the republic of the Armoricans invited Clovis; or even concluded any treaty with him? Not at all. So far from being able to tell us the fate of this republic, he cannot even so much as prove its existence; and notwithstanding he pretends to trace it from the time of Honorius to the conquest of

Clovis, notwithstanding he relates with most admirable exactness all the events of those times; still this republic remains invisible in ancient authors. For there is a wide difference between proving by a passage of Zozimus [1895] that under the Emperor Honorius, the country of Armorica [1896] and the other provinces of Gaul revolted and formed a kind of republic, and showing us that notwithstanding the different pacifications of Gaul, the Armoricans formed always a particular republic, which continued till the conquest of Clovis; and yet this is what he should have demonstrated by strong and substantial proofs, in order to establish his system. For when we behold a conqueror entering a country, and subduing a great part of it by force and open violence, and soon after find the whole country subdued, without any mention in history of the manner of its being effected, we have sufficient reason to believe that the affair ended as it began.

[1895] History, lib. vi.
[1896] *Totusque tractus Armoricus aliæque Galliarum provinciæ.—Ibid.*

When we find he has mistaken this point, it is easy to perceive that his whole system falls to the ground; and as often as he infers a consequence from these principles that Gaul was not conquered by the Franks, but that the Franks were invited by the Romans, we may safely deny it.

This author proves his principle by the Roman dignities with which Clovis was invested: he insists that Clovis succeeded to Childeric his father in the office of *magister militiæ*. But these two offices are merely of his own creation. St. Remigius' letter to Clovis, on which he grounds his opinion, is only a congratulation upon his accession to the crown. [1897] When the intent of a writing is so well known, why should we give it another turn?

[1897] Tom. ii, book III, chap. 18, p. 270.

Clovis, towards the end of the reign, was made consul by the Emperor Anastasius: but what right could he receive from an authority that lasted only one year? it is very probable, says our author, that in the same diploma the Emperor Anastasius made Clovis proconsul. And, I say, it is very probable he did not. With regard to a fact for which there is no foundation, the authority of him who denies is equal to that of him who affirms. But I have also a reason for denying it. Gregory of Tours, who mentions the consulate, says never a word concerning the proconsulate. And even this proconsulate could have lasted only about six months. Clovis died a year and a half after he was created consul; and we cannot pretend to make the pro-consulate an hereditary office. In fine, when the consulate, and, if you will, the proconsulate, were conferred upon him, he was already master of the monarchy, and all his rights were established.

The second proof alleged by the Abbé du Bos is the renunciation made by the Emperor Justinian, in favor of the children and grandchildren of Clovis, of all the rights of the empire over Gaul. I could say a great deal concerning this renunciation. We may judge of the regard shown to it by the kings of the Franks, from the manner in which they performed the conditions of it. Besides, the kings of the Franks were masters and peaceable sovereigns of Gaul; Justinian had not one foot of ground in that country; the western empire had been destroyed a long time before, and the eastern empire had no right to Gaul, but as representing the emperor of the west. These were rights upon rights; the monarchy of the Franks was already founded; the regulation of their establishment was made; the reciprocal rights of the persons and of the different nations who lived in the monarchy were admitted, the laws of each nation were given and even reduced to writing. What, therefore, could that foreign renunciation avail to a government already established?

What can the Abbé mean by making such a parade of the declamations of all those bishops, who, amidst the confusion and total subversion of the state, endeavor to flatter the conqueror? What else is implied by flattering but the weakness of him who is obliged to flatter? What do rhetoric and poetry prove but the use of those very arts? Is it possible to help being surprised at Gregory of Tours, who, after mentioning the assassinations committed by Clovis, says that God laid his enemies every day at his feet, because he walked in his ways? Who doubts but the clergy were glad of Clovis's conversion, and that they even reaped great advantages from it? But who doubts at the same time that the people experienced all the miseries of conquest and that the Roman government submitted to that of the Franks? The Franks were neither willing nor able to make a total change; and few conquerors were ever seized with so great a degree of madness. But to render all the Abbé du Bos' consequences true, they must not only have made no change among the Romans, but they must even have changed themselves.

I could undertake to prove, by following this author's method, that the Greeks never conquered Persia. I should set out with mentioning the treaties which some of their cities concluded with the Persians; I should mention the Greeks who were in Persian pay, as the Franks were in the pay of the Romans. And if Alexander entered the Persian territories, besieged, took, and destroyed the city of Tyre, it was only a particular affair like that of Syagrius. But, behold the Jewish pontiff goes forth to meet him. Listen to the oracle of Jupiter Ammon. Recollect how he had been predicted at Gordium. See what a number of towns crowd, as it were, to submit to him; and how all the satraps and grandees come to pay him obeisance. He put on the Persian dress; this is Clovis' consular robe. Does not Darius offer him one half of his kingdom? Is not Darius assassinated like a tyrant? Do not the mother and wife of Darius weep at the death of Alexander? Were Quintius Curtius, Arrian, or Plutarch, Alexander's contemporaries? Has not the invention of printing afforded us great light which those authors wanted? [1898] Such is the history of the 'Establishment of the French Monarchy in Gaul.'

[1898] See the preliminary discourse of the Abbé du Bos.

25. Of the French Nobility.

The Abbé du Bos maintains that at the commencement of our monarchy there was only one order of citizens among the Franks. This assertion, so injurious to the noble blood of our principal families, is equally affronting to the three great houses which successively governed this realm. The origin of their grandeur would not, therefore, have been lost in the obscurity of time. History might point out the ages when they were plebeian families; and to make Childeric, Pepin, and Hugh Capet gentlemen, we should be obliged to trace their pedigree among the Romans or Saxons, that is, among the conquered nations.

This author grounds his opinion on the Salic law. [1899] By that law, he says, it plainly appears that there were not two different orders of citizens among the Franks: it allowed a composition of two hundred sous for the murder of any Frank whatsoever; [1900] but among the Romans it distinguished the king's guest, for whose death it gave a composition of three hundred sous, from the Roman proprietor to whom it granted a hundred, and from the Roman tributary to whom it gave only a composition of forty-five. And as the difference of the compositions formed the principal distinction, he concludes that there was but one order of citizens among the Franks, and three among the Romans.

[1899] See the Establishment of the French Monarchy, vol. iii, book VI, chap. 4, p. 304.
[1900] He cites the 44th title of this law, and the law of the Ripuarians, tit. 7 and 36.

It is astonishing that his very mistake did not set him right. And, indeed, it would have been very extraordinary that the Roman nobility who lived under the domination of the Franks should have had a larger composition, and been persons of much greater importance than the most illustrious among the Franks, and their greatest generals. What probability is there that the conquering nation should have so little respect for themselves, and so great a regard for the conquered people? Besides, our author quotes the laws of other barbarous nations which prove that they had different orders of citizens. Now it would be a matter of astonishment that this general rule should have failed only among the Franks. Hence he ought to have concluded either that he did not rightly understand or that he misapplied the passages of the Salic law, which is actually the case.

Upon opening this law, we find that the composition for the death of an Antrustio, [1901] that is, of the king's vassal, was six hundred sous; and that for the death of a Roman, who was the king's guest, was only three hundred. [1902] We find there likewise that the composition [1903] for the death of an ordinary Frank was two hundred sous; [1904] and for the death of an ordinary Roman, was only one hundred. [1905] For the death of a Roman tributary, [1906] who was a kind of bondman or freedman, they paid a composition of forty-five sous: but I shall take no notice of this, any more than of the composition for the murder of a Frank bondman or of a Frank freedman, because this third order of persons is out of the question.

[1901] *Qui in truste dominicâ est*, tit. 44, § 4, and this relates to the 13th formulary of Marculfus, *de regis Antrustione*. See also tit. 66, of the Salic law, §§ 3 and 4, and tit. 74; and the law of the Ripuarians, tit. 11, and the Capitulary of Charles the Bald, *apud Carisiacum*, in the year 877, chap. xx.
[1902] Salic law, tit. 44, § 6.
[1903] Tit. 44, § 4.
[1904] Tit. 44, § 1-7.
[1905] Tit. 44, § 15.
[1906] Tit. 44, § 7.

What does our author do? He is quite silent with respect to the first order of persons among the Franks, that is the article relating to the Antrustios; and afterwards upon comparing the ordinary Frank, for whose death they paid a composition of two hundred sous, with those whom he distinguishes under three orders among the Romans, and for whose death they paid different compositions, he finds that there was only one order of citizens among the Franks, and that there were three among the Romans.

As the Abbé is of opinion that there was only one order of citizens among the Franks, it would have been lucky for him that there had been only one order also among the Burgundians, because their kingdom constituted one of the principal branches of our monarchy. But in their codes we find three sorts of compositions, one for the

Burgundians or Roman nobility, the other for the Burgundians or Romans of a middling condition, and the third for those of a lower rank in both nations. [1907] He has not quoted this law.

[1907] *Si quis qualibet casu dentem optimati Burgundioni vel Romano nobili excusserit, solidos viginti quinque cogatur exsolvere; de mediocribus personis ingenuis tam Burgundionibus quam Romanis si dens excusses fuerit, decem solidis componatur; de inferioribus personis, quinque solidos,* arts. 1, 2, and 3, of tit. 26, of the law of the Burgundians.

It is very extraordinary to see in what manner he evades those passages which press him hard on all sides. [1908] If you speak to him of the grandees, lords, and the nobility, these, he says, are mere distinctions of respect, and not of order; they are things of courtesy, and not legal privileges; or else, he says, those people belonged to the king's council; nay, they possibly might be Romans: but still there was only one order of citizens among the Franks. On the other hand, if you speak to him of some Franks of an inferior rank, [1909] he says they are bondmen; and thus he interprets the decree of Childebert. But I must stop here a little, to inquire farther into this decree. Our author has rendered it famous by availing himself of it in order to prove two things: the one that all the compositions we meet with in the laws of the Barbarians were only civil fines added to corporal punishments, which entirely subverts all the ancient records; [1910] the other, that all freemen were judged directly and immediately by the king. [1911] which is contradicted by an infinite number of passages and authorities informing us of the judiciary order of those times. [1912]

[1908] Establishment of the French Monarchy, vol. iii, book VI. chap. 4, 5
[1909] Ibid.; vol. iii. chap. 5, pp. 319, 320.
[1910] Ibid., vol. iii, book VI, chap. 4, pp. 307, 308.
[1911] Ibid., p. 309, and in the following chapter, pp. 310, 320.
[1912] See the 28th book of this work, chap. 28; and the 31st book, chap. 8.

This decree, which was made in an assembly of the nation, [1913] says that, if the judge finds a notorious robber, he must command him to be tied, in order to be carried before the king, *si Francus fuerit*; but if he is a weaker person (*debilior persona*), he shall be hanged on the spot. According to the Abbé du Bos, *Francus* is a freeman, *debilior persona* is a bondman. I shall defer entering for a moment into the signification of the word *Francus*, and begin with examining what can be understood by these words, *a weaker person,* In all languages whatsoever, every comparison necessarily supposes three terms, the greatest, the less degree, and the least. If none were here meant but freemen and bondmen, they would have said *a bondman,* and not *a man of less power.* Therefore *debilior persona* does not signify a bondman, but a person of a superior condition to a bondman. Upon this supposition, *Francus* cannot mean a freeman, but a powerful man; and this word is taken here in that acceptation, because among the Franks there were always men who had greater power than others in the state, and it was more difficult for the judge or count to chastise them. This construction agrees very well with many capitularies [1914] where we find the cases in which the criminals were to be carried before the king, and those in which it was otherwise.

[1913] *Itaque colonia convenit et ita bannivimus, ut unusquisque judex, criminosum latronem ut audierit, ad casam suam ambulet et ipsum ligare faciat; ita ut si Francus fuerit, ad nostram præsentiam dirigatur; et si debilior persona fuerit, in loco pendatur.*—Capitulary, Baluzius's edition, tom. i, p. 19.

[1914] See the 28th book of this work, chap. 28; and the 31st book, chap. 8.

It is mentioned in the Life of Lewis the Debonnaire, [1915] written by Tegan, that the bishops were the principal cause of the humiliation of that emperor, especially those who had been bondmen and such as were born among the Barbarians. Tegan thus addresses Hebo, whom this prince had drawn from the state of servitude, and made Archbishop of Rheims: *What recompense did the Emperor receive from you for so many benefits? He made you a freeman, but did not ennoble you, because he could not give you nobility after having given you your liberty.* [1916]

[1915] Chapters 43, 44.

[1916] *O qualem remunerationem reddidisti ei! fecit te liberum, non nobilem, quod impossibile est post libertatem.—Ibid.*

This passage, which proves so strongly the two orders of citizens, does not at all confound the Abbé du Bos. He answers thus: [1917] *The meaning of this passage is not that Lewis the Debonnaire was incapable of introducing Hebo into the order of the nobility. Hebo, as Archbishop of Rheims, must have been of the first order, superior to that of the nobility.* I leave the reader to judge whether this be not the meaning of that passage; I leave him to judge whether there be any question here concerning a precedence of the clergy over the nobility. *This passage proves only*, continues the same writer, [1918] *that the free-born subjects were qualified as noblemen; in the common acceptation, noblemen and men who are free-born have for this long time signified the same thing.* What! because some of our burghers have lately assumed the quality of noblemen, shall a passage of the Life of Lewis the Debonnaire be applied to this sort of people? "And perhaps," continues he still, [1919] *Hebo had not been a bondman among the Franks, but among the Saxons, or some other German nation, where the people were divided into several orders.* Then, because of the Abbé du Bos' *perhaps*, there must have been no nobility among the nation of the Franks. But he never applied a *perhaps* so badly. We have seen that Tegan distinguishes the bishops, [1920] who had opposed Lewis the Debonnaire, some of whom had been bondmen, and others of a barbarous nation. Hebo belonged to the former and not to the latter. Besides, I do not see how a bondman, such as Hebo, can be said to have been a Saxon or a German; a bondman has no family, and consequently no nation. Lewis the Debonnaire manumitted Hebo; and as bondmen after their manumission embraced the law of their master, Hebo had become a Frank, and not a Saxon or German.

[1917] Establishment of the French Monarchy, vol. iii, book VI, chap. 4, p. 316.

[1918] Ibid., p. 316.

[1919] Ibid.

[1920] *Omnes episcopi molesti fuerant Ludovico, et maxime ii quos e servile conditione honoratos habebat, cum his qui ex barbaris nationibus ad hob fastigium perducti sunt.—De Gestis Ludovici Pii, chap. 43, 44.*

I have been hitherto acting offensively; it is now time to defend myself. It will be objected to me that indeed the body of the Antrustios formed a distinct order in the state from that of the freemen; but as the fiefs were at first precarious, and afterwards for life, this could not form a nobleness of descent, since the privileges were not annexed to an hereditary fief. This is the objection which induced M. de Valois to think that there was only one order of citizens among the Franks; an opinion which the Abbé du Bos has borrowed of him, and which he has absolutely spoiled with so many bad arguments. Be that as it may, it is not the Abbé du Bos that could make this objection. For after having given three orders of Roman nobility, and the quality of the king's guest for the first, he could not pretend to say that this title was a greater mark of a noble descent than that of Antrustio. But I must give a direct answer. The Antrustios or trusty men were not such because they were possessed of a fief, but that they had a fief given them because they were Antrustios or trusty men. The reader may please to recollect what has been said in the beginning of this book. They had not at that time, as they had afterwards, the same fief: but if they had not that, they had another, because the fiefs were given at their birth, and because they were often granted in the assemblies of the nation, and, in fine, because as it was the interest of the nobility to receive them it was likewise the king's interest to grant them. These families were distinguished by their dignity of trusty men, and by the privilege of being qualified to swear allegiance for a fief. In the following book [1921] I shall demonstrate how, from the circumstances of the time, there were freemen who were permitted to enjoy this great privilege, and consequently to enter into the order of nobility. This was not the case at the time of Gontram, and his nephew Childebert; but so it was at the time of Charlemagne. But though in that prince's reign the freemen were not incapable of possessing fiefs, yet it appears, by the above-cited passage of Tegan, that the emancipated serfs were absolutely excluded. Will the Abbé du Bos, who carries us to Turkey to give us an idea of the ancient French nobility; [1922] will he, I say, pretend that they ever complained among the Turks of the elevation of people of low birth to the honors and dignities of the state, as they complained under Lewis the Debonnaire and Charles the Bald? There was no complaint of that kind under Charlemagne, because this prince always distinguished the ancient from the new families; which Lewis the Debonnaire, and Charles the Bald did not.

[1921] Chapter 23.
[1922] Establishment of the French Monarchy, vol. iii, book VI. chap. 4, p. 302.

The public should not forget the obligation it owes to the Abbé du Bos for several excellent performances. It is by these works, and not by his history of the Establishment of the French Monarchy, we ought to judge of his merit. He committed very great mistakes, because he had more in view the Count of Boulainvilliers' work than his own subject.

From all these strictures I shall draw only one reflection: if so great a man was mistaken, how cautiously ought I to tread?

BOOK XXXI.

THEORY OF THE FEUDAL LAWS AMONG THE FRANKS, IN THE RELATION THEY BEAR TO THE REVOLUTIONS OF THEIR MONARCHY

1. *Changes in the Offices and in the Fiefs.*

The counts at first were sent into their districts only for a year; but they soon purchased the continuation of their offices. Of this we have an example in the reign of Clovis' grandchildren. A person named Peonius was count in the city of Auxerre; [1923] he sent his son Mummolus with money to Gontram, to prevail upon him to continue him in his employment; the son gave the money for himself, and obtained the father's place. The kings had already begun to spoil their own favors.

[1923] Gregory of Tours, book IV. chap. 42.

Though by the laws of the kingdom the fiefs were precarious, yet they were neither given nor taken away in a capricious and arbitrary manner: nay, they were generally one of the principal subjects debated in the national assemblies. It is natural, however, to imagine that corruption crept into this as well as the other case; and that the possession of the fiefs, like that of the counties, was continued for money.

I shall show in the course of this book, [1924] that, independently of the grants which the princes made for a certain time, there were others in perpetuity. The court wanted to revoke the former grants; this occasioned a general discontent in the nation, and was soon followed by that famous revolution in French history, whose first epoch was the amazing spectacle of the execution of Brunehault.

[1924] Chapter 7.

That this queen, who was daughter, sister and mother of so many kings, a queen to this very day celebrated for public monuments worthy of a Roman ædile or proconsul, born with an admirable genius for affairs, and endowed with qualities so long respected, should see herself of a sudden exposed to so slow, so ignominious and cruel a torture, [1925] by a king whose authority was but indifferently established in the nation, [1926] would appear very extraordinary, had she not incurred that nation's displeasure for some particular cause. Clotharius reproached her with the murder of ten kings; but two of them he had put to death himself; the death of some of the others was owing to chance, or to the villainy of another queen; [1927] and a nation that had permitted Fredegunda to die in her bed, [1928] that had even opposed the punishment of her flagitious crimes, ought to have been very different with respect to those of Brunehault.

[1925] Fredegarius, Chronicle, chap. 42.
[1926] Clotharius II, son of Chilperic, and the father of Dagobert.
[1927] Fredegarius, Chronicle, chap. 42.
[1928] See Gregory of Tours, book VIII. chap. 31.

She was put upon a camel, and led ignominiously through the army; a certain sign that she had given great offence to those troops. Fredegarius relates that Protarius, [1929] Brunehault's favorite, stripped the lords of their property, and filled the exchequer with the plunder; that he humbled the nobility, and that no person could be sure of continuing in any office or employment. The army conspired against him, and he was stabbed in his tent; but Brunehault, either by revenging his death, or by pursuing the same plan, [1930] became every day more odious to the nation. [1931]

[1929] *Sæva illi fuit contra personas iniquitas, fisco nimium tribunes, de rebus personarum ingeniose fiscum vellens implore . . . . . ut nullus reperiretur qui gradum quem arripuerat potuisset adsumere.*—Fredegarius, Chronicle, chap. 27, in the year 605.
[1930] Ibid., chap. 28, in the year 607.
[1931] Ibid., chap. 41, in the year 613. *Bergundiæ Farones, tam episcopi quam cæteri Leudes, timentes Brunechildem et odium in aem habentes, consilium inientes*, &c.

Clotharius, ambitious of reigning alone, inflamed moreover with the most furious revenge, and sure of perishing if Brunehault's children got the upper hand, entered into a conspiracy against himself; and whether it was owing to ignorance, or to the necessity of his circumstances, he became Brunehault's accuser, and made a terrible example of that princess.

Warnacharius had been the very soul of the conspiracy formed against Brunehault. Being at that time mayor of Burgundy, he made Clotharius consent that he should not be displaced while he lived. [1932] By this step the mayor could no longer be in the same case as the French lords before that period; and this authority began to render itself independent of the regal dignity.

[1932] Ibid., chap. 42, in the year 613. Sacramento a Clothario accepto ne unquam vitæ suæ temporibus degraderetur.

It was Brunehault's unhappy regency which had exasperated the nation. So long as the laws subsisted in their full force, no one could grumble at having been deprived of a fief, since the law did not bestow it upon him in perpetuity. But when fiefs came to be acquired by avarice, by bad practices and corruption, they complained of being divested, by irregular means, of things that had been irregularly acquired. Perhaps if the public good had been the motive of the revocation of those grants, nothing would have been said; but they pretended a regard for order while they were openly abetting the principles of corruption; the fiscal rights were claimed in order to lavish the public treasure; and grants were no longer the reward or the encouragement of services. Brunehault, from a corrupt spirit, wanted to reform the abuses of the ancient corruption. Her caprices were not owing to weakness; the vassals and the great officers, thinking themselves in danger, prevented their own by her ruin.

We are far from having all the records of the transactions of those days; and the writers of chronicles, who understood very nearly as much of the history of their time as our peasants know of ours, are extremely barren. Yet we have a constitution of Clotharius, given in the council of Paris, [1933] for the reformation of abuses, [1934] which shows that this prince put a stop to the complaints that had occasioned the revolution. On the one hand, he confirms all the grants that had been made or confirmed by the kings his predecessors; [1935] and on the other, he ordains that whatever had been taken from his vassals should be restored to them. [1936]

[1933] Some time after Brunehault's execution, in the year 615. See Baluzius's edition of the Capitularies, p. 21.
[1934] *Quæ contra rationis ordinem acta vel ordinate sunt ne in antea, quod avertat divinitas, contingent, disposuerimus, Christo præsule, per hujus edicti nostri tenorem generaliter emendare.—Ibid.*, art. 16.
[1935] Ibid., art. 16.
[1936] Ibid., art. 17.

This was not the only concession the king made in that council; he enjoined that whatever had been innovated, in opposition to the privileges of the clergy, should be redressed; [1937] and he moderated the influence of the court in the election of bishops. [1938] He even reformed the fiscal affairs, ordaining that all the new censuses should be abolished, [1939] and that they should not levy any toll established since the deaths of Gontram, Sigebert, and Chilperic; [1940] that is, he abolished whatever had been done during the regencies of Fredegunda and Brunehault. He forbad the driving of his cattle to graze in private people's grounds; [1941] and we shall presently see that the reformation was still more general, so as to extend even to civil affairs.

[1937] *Et quod per tempora ex hoc prætermissum est vel dehinc perpetualiter observetur.*
[1938] *Ita ut episcopo decedent, in loco ipsius qui a Metropolitano ordinary debet cum provincialibus, a clero et populo eligatur; et si persona condign fuerit, per ordinationem principis ordinetur; vel certe si de palatio eligitur, per meritum personæ et doctrinæ ordinetur.—Ibid.*, art. 1.
[1939] Et ubicumque census novus impie additus est, emendetur.—Art. 8.
[1940] Ibid., art. 9.
[1941] Ibid., art. 21.

2. How the Civil Government was reformed.

Hitherto the nation had given marks of impatience and levity with regard to the choice or conduct of her masters; she had regulated their differences and obliged them to come to an agreement among themselves. But now she did what before was quite unexampled; she cast her eyes on her actual situation, examined the laws coolly, provided against their insufficiency, repressed violence, and moderated the regal power.

The bold and insolent regencies of Fredegunda and Brunehault had less surprised than roused the nation. Fredegunda had defended her horrid cruelties, her poisonings and assassinations, by a repetition of the same crimes; and had behaved in such a manner that her outrages were rather of a private than public nature. Fredegunda did more mischief: Brunehault threatened more. In this crisis the nation was not satisfied with rectifying the feudal system; she was also determined to secure her civil government. For the latter was rather more corrupt than the former; a corruption the more dangerous as it was more inveterate, and connected rather with the abuse of manners than with that of laws.

The history of Gregory of Tours exhibits, on the one hand, a fierce and barbarous nation; and on the other, kings remarkable for the same ferocity of temper. Those princes were bloody, iniquitous and cruel, because such was the character of the whole nation. If

Christianity appeared sometimes to soften their manners, it was only by the circumstances of terror with which this religion alarms the sinner; the church supported herself against them by the miraculous operations of her saints. The kings would not commit sacrilege, because they dreaded the punishments inflicted on that species of guilt: but this excepted, either in the riot of passion or in the coolness of deliberation, they perpetrated the most horrid crimes and barbarities where divine vengeance did not appear so immediately to overtake the criminal. The Franks, as I have already observed, bore with cruel kings, because they were of the same disposition themselves; they were not shocked at the iniquity and extortions of their princes, because this was the national characteristic. There had been many laws established, but it was usual for the king to defeat them all, by a kind of letter called *precepts*, [1942] which rendered them of no effect; they were somewhat similar to the rescripts of the Roman Emperors; whether it be that our kings borrowed this usage from those princes, or whether it was owing to their own natural temper. We see in Gregory of Tours, that they perpetrated murder in cool blood, and put the accused to death unheard; how they gave precepts for illicit marriages; [1943] for transferring successions; for depriving relatives of their right; and, in fine, marrying consecrated virgins. They did not, indeed, assume the whole legislative power, but they dispensed with the execution of the laws.

[1942] They were orders which the king sent to the judges to do or to tolerate things contrary to law.
[1943] See Gregory of Tours, book IV, p. 227. Both our history and the charters are full of this; and the extent of these abuses appears especially in Clotharius' constitution, inserted in the edition of the Capitularies made to reform them. Baluzius's edition, p. 7.

Clotharius' constitution redressed all these grievances: no one could any longer be condemned without being heard: [1944] relatives were made to succeed, according to the order established by law; [1945] all precepts for marrying religious women were declared null; [1946] and those who had obtained and made use of them were severely punished. We might know perhaps more exactly his determinations with regard to these precepts, if the thirteenth and the next two articles of this decree had not been lost through the injury of time. We have only the first words of this thirteenth article, ordaining that the precepts shall be observed, which cannot be understood of those he had just abolished by the same law. We have another constitution by the same prince, [1947] which is in relation to his decree, and corrects in the same manner every article of the abuses of the *precepts*.

[1944] Ibid., art. 22.
[1945] Ibid., art 6.
[1946] Ibid.
[1947] In Baluzius's edition of the Capitularies, tom. i. p. 7.

True it is that Baluzius, finding this constitution without date and without the name of the place where it was given, attributes it to Clotharius I. But I say it belongs to Clotharius II, for three reasons: 1. It says that the king will preserve the immunities granted to the churches by his father and grandfather. [1948] What immunities could the churches receive from Childeric, grandfather of Clotharius I, who was not a Christian, and who lived even before the foundation of the monarchy? But if we attribute this decree to Clotharius II, we shall find his grandfather to have been this very Clotharius I, who made immense donations to the church with a view of expiating the murder of his son Cramne, whom he had ordered to be burned, together with his wife and children.

[1948] In the preceding book I have made mention of these immunities, which were grants of judicial rights, and contained prohibitions to the regal judges to perform any function in the territory, and were equivalent to the erection or grant of a fief.

2. The abuses redressed by this constitution were still subsisting after the death of Clotharius I and were even carried to their highest extravagance during the weak reign of Gontram, the cruel administration of Chilperic, and the execrable regencies of Fredegunda and Brunehault. Now, can we imagine that the nation would have borne with grievances so solemnly proscribed, without complaining of their continual repetition? Can we imagine she would not have taken the same step as she did afterwards under Childeric II, [1949] when, upon a repetition of the old grievances, she pressed him to ordain that law and customs in regard to judicial proceedings should be complied with as formerly. [1950]

[1949] He began to reign towards the year 670.
[1950] See the Life of St. Leger.

In fine, as this constitution was made to redress grievances, it cannot relate to Clotharius I, since there were no complaints of that kind in his reign, and his authority was perfectly established throughout the kingdom, especially at the time in which they place this constitution; whereas it agrees extremely well with the events that happened during the reign of Clotharius II, which produced a revolution in the political state of the kingdom. History must be illustrated by the laws, and the laws by history.

3. *Authority of the Mayors of the Palace.*

I noticed that Clotharius II had promised not to deprive Warnacharius of his mayor's place during life; a revolution productive of another effect. Before that time the mayor was the king's officer, but now he became the officer of the people; he was chosen before by the king, and now by the nation. Before the revolution Protarius had been made mayor by Theodoric, and Landeric by Fredegunda; [1951] but after that the mayors [1952] were chosen by the nation. [1953]

[1951] *Instigante Brunihault, Theodorico jubente, &c.*—Fredegarius, 27, in the year 605.
[1952] *Gesta regum Francorum*, chap. 36.
[1953] See Fredegarius, Chronicle, chap. 54, in the year 626, and his anonymous continuator, chap. 101, in the year 695, and 105, in the year 715. Aimoin, book IV. chap. 15, Eginhard. Life of Charlemagne, chap. 48. *Gesta regum Francorum*, chap. 45.

We must not therefore confound, as some authors have done, these mayors of the palace with such as were possessed of this dignity before the death of Brunehault; the king's mayors with those of the kingdom. We see by the law of the Burgundians that among them the office of mayor was not one of the most respectable in the state; [1954] nor was it one of the most eminent under the first Kings of the Franks. [1955]

[1954] See the Law of the Burgundians, *præfat.* and the second supplement to this law, tit. 13.
[1955] See Gregory of Tours, book. IX. chap. 36.

Clotharius removed the apprehensions of those who were possessed of employments and fiefs; and when, after the death of Warnacharius, [1956] he asked the lords assembled at Troyes, who is it they would put in his place, they cried out they would choose no one, but suing for his favor committed themselves entirely into his hands.

[1956] *Eo anno Clotarius cum proceribus et leudibus Burgundiæ Trecassinis conjungitur, cum eorum esset sollicitus si vellent jam Warnachario discesso alium in ejus honoris gradum sublimare: sed omnes unanimiter denegantes se nequaquam velle majorem domûs eligere, regis gratiam obnixe petentes, cum rege transgere.*— Fredegarius, Chronicle, chap. 44, in the year 626.

Dagobert reunited the whole monarchy in the same manner as his father; the nation had a thorough confidence in him, and appointed no mayor. This prince, finding himself at liberty and elated by his victories, resumed Brunehault's plan. But he succeeded so ill that the vassals of Austrasia let themselves be beaten by the Sclavonians, and returned home; so that the marches of Austrasia were left to prey to the barbarians. [1957]

[1957] *Istam victoriam quam Vinidi contra Francos meruerunt, non tantum Sclavinorum fortitude obtinuit, quantum dementatio Austrasiorum, dum se cernebant cum Dagoberto odium incurrisse, et assidue expoliarentur.*—Fredegarius, Chronicle, chap. 68, in the year 630.

He determined then to make an offer to the Austrasians of resigning that country, together with a provincial treasure, to his son Sigebert, and to put the government of the kingdom and of the palace into the hands of Cunibert, Bishop of Cologne, and of the Duke Adalgisus. Fredegarius does not enter into the particulars of the conventions then made; but the king confirmed them all by charters, and Austrasia was immediately secured from danger. [1958]

[1958] *Deinceps Austrasii eorum studio limitem et regnum Francorum contra Vinidos utiliter defensasse noscuntur.*—Fredegarius, Chronicle, chap. 75, in the year 632.

Dagobert, finding himself near his end, recommended his wife Nentechildis and his son Clovis to the care of Æga. The vassals of Neustria and Burgundy chose this young prince for their king. [1959] Æga and Nentechildis had the government of the palace; [1960] they restored whatever Dagobert had taken; [1961] and complaints ceased in Neustria and Burgundy, as they had ceased in Austrasia.

[1959] Fredegarius, Chronicle, chap. 79, in the year 638.
[1960] Ibid.
[1961] Ibid., chap. 80, in the year 639.

After the death of Æga, Queen Nentechildis engaged the lords of Burgundy to choose Floachatus for their mayor. [1962] The latter dispatched letters to the bishops and chief lords of the kingdom of Burgundy, by which he promised to preserve their honors and dignities forever, that is, during life. [1963] He confirmed his word by oath. This is the period at which the author of the Treatise on the Mayors of the Palace fixes the administration of the kingdom by those officers. [1964]

[1962] Fredegarius, Chronicle, chap. 89, in the year 641.
[1963] Ibid. chap. 89. *Floachatus cunctis ducibus a regno Burgundiæ seu et pontificibus, per epistolam etam et sacramentis firmavit unicuique gradum honoris et dignitatem, seu et amicitiam, perpetuo conservare.*
[1964] *Deinceps a temporibus Clodovei qui fuit filius Dagoberto inclyti regis, pater vera Theodorici, regnum Francorum decidens per majorem domûs, cœpit ordinary.—De Majoribus Domûs Regiæ.*

Fredegarius, being a Burgundian, has entered into a more minute detail as to what concerns the Mayors of Burgundy at the time of the revolution of which we are speaking, than with regard to the mayors of Austrasia and Neustria. But the conventions made in Burgundy were, for the very same reasons, agreed to in Neustria and Austrasia.

The nation thought it safer to lodge the power in the hands of a mayor whom she chose herself, and to whom she might prescribe conditions, than in those of a king whose power was hereditary.

4. Of the Genius of the Nation in regard to the Mayors.

A government in which a nation that had an hereditary king chose a person to exercise the regal authority seems very extraordinary; but, independently of the circumstances of the times, I apprehend that the notions of the Franks in this respect were derived from a remote source.

The Franks were descended from the Germans, of whom Tacitus says [1965] that in the choice of their king they were determined by his noble extraction, and in that of their leader, by his valor. This gives us an idea of the kings of the first race, and of the mayors of the palace; the former were hereditary, the latter elective.

[1965] *Reges ex nobilitatem, duces ex virtute sumunt—De Moribus Germanorum.*

No doubt but those princes who stood up in the national assembly and offered themselves as the conductors of a public enterprise to such as were willing to follow them, united generally in their own person both the power of the mayor and the king's authority. By the splendor of their descent they had attained the regal dignity; and their military abilities having recommended them to the command of armies, they rose to the power of mayor. By the regal dignity, our first kings presided in the courts and assemblies, and enacted laws with the national consent; by the dignity of duke or leader, they undertook expeditions and commanded the armies.

In order to be acquainted with the genius of the primitive Franks in this respect, we have only to cast an eye on the conduct of Argobastes, [1966] a Frank by nation, on whom Valentinian had conferred the command of the army. He confined the emperor to his own palace, where he would suffer nobody to speak to him, concerning either civil or military affairs. Argobastes did at that time what was afterwards practiced by the Pepins.

[1966] See Sulpicius Alexander, in Gregory of Tours, book. II.

5. *In what Manner the Mayors obtained the Command of the Armies.*

So long as the kings commanded their armies in person, the nation never thought of choosing a leader. Clovis and his four sons were at the head of the Franks, and led them on through a series of victories. Theobald, son of Theodobert, a young, weak, and sickly prince, was the first of our kings who confined himself to his palace. [1967] He refused to undertake an expedition into Italy against Narses, and had the mortification of seeing the Franks choose for themselves two chiefs, who led them against the enemy. [1968] Of the four sons of Clotharius I, Gontram was the least fond of commanding his armies; [1969] the other kings followed this example; and, in order to entrust the command without danger into other hands, they conferred it upon several chiefs or dukes. [1970]

[1967] In the year 552.
[1968] Leutheres vero et Butilinus, tametsi id regi ipsorum minime placebat belli cum eis societatem inierunt.—Agathias, book I. Gregory of Tours, book IV. chap. 9.
[1969] Gontram did not even march against Gondovald, who styled himself son of Clotharius, and claimed his share of the kingdom.
[1970] Sometimes to the number of twenty. See Gregory of Tours, book V. chap. 27, book VIII chap. 28 and 30, book X. chap. 3. Dagobert, who had no mayor in Burgundy, observed the same policy, and sent against the Gascons ten dukes and several counts who Lad no dukes over them.—Fredegarius, Chronicle, chap. 78, in the year 636.

Innumerable were the inconveniences which thence arose; all discipline was lost, no one would any longer obey. The armies were dreadful only to their own country; they were laden with spoils before they had reached the enemy. Of these miseries we have a very lively picture in Gregory of Tours. [1971] "*How shall we be able to obtain a victory,*" said Gontram, [1972] "*we who do not so much as keep what our ancestors acquired? Our nation is no longer the same.*" . . . Strange that it should be on the decline so early as the reign of Clovis' grandchildren!

[1971] Gregory of Tours, book VIII. chap. 30, and book X. chap. 3. Ibid. book VIII. chap. 30
[1972] Ibid.

It was therefore natural they should determine at last upon an only duke, a duke invested with an authority over this prodigious multitude of feudal lords and vassals who had now become strangers to their own engagements; a duke who was to establish the military discipline, and to put himself at the head of a nation unhappily practiced in making war against itself. This power was conferred on the mayors of the palace.

The original function of the mayors of the palace was the management of the king's household. They had afterwards, in conjunction with other officers, the political government of fiefs; and at length they obtained the sole disposal of them. [1973] They had also the administration of military affairs, and the command of the armies; employments necessarily connected with the other two. In those days it was much more difficult to raise than to command the armies; and who but the dispenser of favors could have this authority? In this martial and independent nation, it was prudent to invite rather than to compel; prudent to give away or to promise the fiefs that should happen to be vacant by the death of the possessor; prudent, in fine, to reward continually, and to raise a jealousy with regard to preferences. It was therefore right that the person who had the superintendence of the palace should also be general of the army.

[1973] See the second supplement to the law of the Burgundians, tit. 13, and Gregory of Tours, book IX. chap. 36.

6. Second Epoch of the Humiliation of our Kings of the first Race.

After the execution of Brunehault, the mayors were administrators of the kingdom under the sovereigns; and though they had the conduct of the war, the kings were always at the head of the armies, while the mayor and the nation fought under their command. But the victory of Duke Pepin over Theodoric and his mayor [1974] completed the degradation of our princes; [1975] and that which Charles Martel obtained over Chilperic and his mayor Rainfroy confirmed it. [1976] Austrasia triumphed twice over Neustria and Burgundy; and the mayoralty of Austrasia being annexed as it were to the family of the Pepins, this mayoralty and family became greatly superior to all the rest. The conquerors were then afraid lest some person of credit should seize the king's person, in order to excite disturbances. For this reason they kept them in the royal palace as in a kind of prison, and once a year showed them to the people. [1977] There they made ordinances, but these were such as were dictated by the mayor; [1978] they answered ambassadors, but the mayor made the answers. This is the time mentioned by historians of the government of the mayors over the kings whom they held in subjection. [1979]

[1974] See the Annals of Metz, years 687 and 688.
[1975] *Illis quidem nomina regum imponens, ipse totius regni habens privilegium, &c.*—Ibid., year 695.
[1976] Ibid., year 719.
[1977] *Sedemque illi regale sub sua ditione concessit.*—Ibid. *anno* 719.
[1978] *Ex chronico Centulensi*, lib. 2, *ut response quæ erat edoctus vel potius jussus, ex sua velut potestate redderet.*
[1979] Annals of Metz, year 691. *Anno principatus Pippini super Theodoricum . . .* Annals of Fulda, or of Laurishan, *Pippinus dux Francorum obtinuit regnum Francorum per annos* 27, *cum regibus sibi subjectis.*

The extravagant passion of the nation for Pepin's family went so far that they chose one of his grandsons, who was yet an infant, for mayor; [1980] and put him over one Dagobert, that is, one phantom over another.

[1980] *Posthæc Theudoaldus filius ejus (Grimoaldi) parvulus, in loco ipsius, cum prædicto rege Dagoberto, major-domus palatii effectus est.* The anonymous continuator of Fredegarius, chap. 104, in the year 714.

7. Of the great Offices and Fiefs under the Mayors of the Palace.

The mayors of the palace were little disposed to establish the uncertain tenure of places and offices; for, indeed, they ruled only by the protection which in this respect they granted to the nobility. Hence the great offices continued to be given for life, and this usage was every day more firmly established.

But I have some particular reflections to make here in respect of fiefs: I do not question but most of them became hereditary from this time.

In the treaty of Andeli, [1981] Gontram and his nephew Childebert engage to maintain the donations made to the vassals and churches by the kings their predecessors; and leave is given to the wives, daughters, and widows of kings to dispose by will, and in perpetuity, of whatever they hold of the exchequer. [1982]

[1981] Cited by Gregory of Tours, book IX. See also the edict of Clotharius II, in the year 615, art. 16.
[1982] *Ut si quid de agris fiscalibus vel speciebus atque præsidio pro aritrii sui voluntate facere aut cuiquam conferre voluerint, fixa stabilitate perpetuo conservatur.*

Marculfus wrote his formularies at the time of the mayors. [1983] We find several in which the kings make donations both to the person and to his heirs: [1984] and as the formularies represent the common actions of life, they prove that part of the fiefs had become hereditary towards the end of the first race. They were far from having in those days the idea of an unalienable demesne; this is a modern thing, which they knew neither in theory nor practice.

[1983] See the 24th and the 34th of the first book.
[1984] See the 14th formula of the first book, which is equally applicable to the fiscal estates given direct in perpetuity, or given at first as a benefice, and afterwards in perpetuity: *Sicut ab illo aut a fisco nostro fuit possessa.* See also the 17th formula, ibid.

In proof hereof we shall presently produce positive fact; and if we can point out a time in which there were no longer any benefices for the army, nor any funds for its support, we must certainly conclude that the ancient benefices had been alienated. The time I mean is that of Charles Martel, who founded some new fiefs, which we should carefully distinguish from those of the earliest date.

When the kings began to make grants in perpetuity, either through the corruption which crept into the government or by reason of the constitution itself, which continually obliged those princes to confer rewards, it was natural they should begin with giving the perpetuity of the fiefs, rather than of the counties. For to deprive themselves of some acres of land was no great matter; but to renounce the right of disposing of the great offices was divesting themselves of their very power.

8. *In what Manner the Allodial Estates were changed into Fiefs.*

The manner of changing an allodial estate into a fief may be seen in a formulary of Marculfus. [1985] The owner of the land gave it to the king, who restored it to the donor by way of usufruct, or benefice, and then the donor nominated his heirs to the king.

[1985] Book I, formulary 13.

In order to find out the reasons which induced them thus to change the nature of the allodia, I must trace the source of the ancient privileges of our nobility, a nobility which for these eleven centuries has been enveloped with dust, with blood, and with the marks of toil.

They who were seized of fiefs enjoyed very great advantages. The composition for the injuries done them was greater than that of freemen. It appears by the formularies of Marculfus that it was a privilege belonging to a king's vassal, that whoever killed him should pay a composition of six hundred sous. This privilege was established by the Salic law, [1986] and by that of the Ripuarians; [1987] and while these two laws ordained a composition of six hundred sous for the murder of a king's vassal, they gave but two hundred sous for the murder of a person freeborn, if he was a Frank or Barbarian, or a man living under, the Salic law; [1988] and only a hundred for a Roman.

[1986] Tit. 44. See also tit. 66, §§ 3, 4; and tit. 74.
[1987] Tit. 11.
[1988] See also the law of the Ripuarians, tit. 7; and the Salic law, tit. 44, art. 1 and 4.

This was not the only privilege belonging to the king's vassals. We ought to know that when a man was summoned in court, and did not make his appearance nor obey the judge's orders, he was called before the king; [1989] and if he persisted in his contumacy, he was excluded from the royal protection, [1990] and no one was allowed to entertain him, nor even to give him a morsel of bread. Now, if he was a person of an ordinary condition, his goods were confiscated; [1991] but if he was the king's vassal, they were not. [1992] The first by his contumacy was deemed sufficiently convicted of the crime, the second was not; the former for the smallest crimes was obliged to undergo the trial by boiling water, [1993] the latter was condemned to this trial only in the case of murder. [1994] In fine, the king's vassal could not be compelled to swear in court against another vassal. [1995] These privileges were continually increasing, and the Capitulary of Carloman does this honor to the king's vassals, that they should not be obliged to swear in person, but only by the mouth of their own vassals. [1996] Moreover, when a person, having these honors, did not repair to the army, his punishment was to abstain from flesh-meat and wine as long as he had been absent from the service; but a freeman [1997] who neglected to follow his count was fined sixty sous, [1998] and was reduced to a state of servitude till he had paid it.

[1989] Salic law, tit. 59 and 76.
[1990] *Extra sermonem regis.*—Ibid.
[1991] Ibid., tit. 59, § 1.
[1992] Ibid., tit. 76, § 1.

[1993] Ibid., tit. 56 and 59.
[1994] Ibid., tit. 76, § 1.
[1995] Ibid., tit. 76 § 2.
[1996] *Apud vernis palatium*, in the year 883, art. 4 and 11.
[1997] Capitulary of Charlemagne, second of the year 812, art. 1 and 3.
[1998] *Heribannum*.

It is very natural, therefore, to believe that those Franks who were not the king's vassals, and much more the Romans, became fond of entering into the state of vassalage: and that they might not be deprived of their demesnes, they devised the usage of giving their *allodium* to the king, of receiving it from him afterwards as a fief, and of nominating their heirs. This usage was continued, and took place especially during the times of confusion under the second race, when every man being in want of a protector was desirous of incorporating himself with the other lords, and of entering, as it were, into the feudal monarchy, because the political no longer existed. [1999]

[1999] *Non infirmis reliquit hæredibus*, says Lambert d'Ardres in Ducange, on the word *alodis*.

This continued under the third race, as we find by several charters; [2000] whether they gave their allodium, and resumed it by the same act; or whether it was declared an allodium, and afterwards acknowledged as a fief. These were called *fiefs of resumption*.

[2000] See those quoted by Ducange, in the word *alodis*, and those produced by Galland, in his Treatise on Allodial Lands, p. 14, ff.

This does not imply that those who were seized of fiefs administered them as a prudent father of a family would; for though the freemen grew desirous of being possessed of fiefs, yet they managed this sort of estates as usufructs are managed in our days. This is what induced Charlemagne, the most vigilant and considerate prince we ever had, to make a great many regulations in order to hinder the fiefs from being demeaned in favor of allodial estates. [2001] It proves only that in his time most benefices were but for life, and consequently that they took more care of the freeholds than of the benefices; and yet for all that, they did not choose rather to be the king's vassals than freemen. They might have reasons for disposing of some particular part of a fief, but they were not willing to be stripped of their dignity likewise.

[2001] Second Capitulary of the year 802, art. 10; and the seventh Capitulary of the year 803, art. 3; the first Capitulary, *incerti anni*, art. 49; the fifth Capitulary of the year 806, art. 7; the Capitulary of the year 779, art. 29; the Capitulary of Lewis the Pious, in the year 829, art. 1.

I know, likewise, that Charlemagne laments in a certain capitulary, that in some places there were people who gave away their fiefs in property, and redeemed them afterwards in the same manner. [2002] But I do not say that they were not fonder of the property than of the usufruct; I mean only, that when they could convert an allodium into a fief, which was to descend to their heirs, as is the case of the formulary above-mentioned, they had very great advantages in doing it.

[2002] The fifth of the year 806, art. 8.

9. *How the Church Lands were converted into Fiefs.*

The use of the fiscal lands should have been only to serve as a donation by which the kings were to encourage the Franks to undertake new expeditions, and by which, on the other hand, these fiscal lands were increased. This, as I have already observed, was the spirit of the nation; but these donations took another turn. There is still extant a speech of Chilperic, [2003] grandson of Clovis, in which he complains that almost all these lands had been already given away to the church. *Our exchequer,* says he, *is impoverished, and our riches are transferred to the clergy;* [2004] *none reign now but the bishops, who live in grandeur while we are quite eclipsed.*

[2003] In Gregory of Tours, book VI. chap. 46.
[2004] This is what induced him to annul the testaments made in favor of the clergy, and
    even the donations of his father; Gontram re-established them, and even made new
    donations.—Gregory of Tours, book VII. chap. 7.

This was the reason that the mayors, who durst not attack the lords, stripped the churches; and one of the motives alleged by Pepin for entering Neustria [2005] was his having been invited thither by the clergy to put a stop to the encroachments of the kings, that is, of the mayors, who deprived the church of all her possessions.

[2005] See the Annals of Metz, year 689. *Excitor imprimis querelis sacerdotum Dei, qui*
    me sæpius adierunt ut pro sublatis injuste patrimoniis, &c.

The Mayors of Austrasia, that is the family of the Pepins, had behaved towards the clergy with more moderation than those of Neustria and Burgundy. This is evident from our chronicles, [2006] in which we see the monks perpetually extolling the devotion and liberality of the Pepins. They themselves had been possessed of the first places in the church. *One crow does not pull out the eyes of another;* as Chilperic said to the bishops. [2007]

[2006] See the Annals of Metz.
[2007] In Gregory of Tours.

Pepin subdued Neustria and Burgundy; but as his pretence for destroying the mayors and kings was the grievances of the clergy, he could not strip the latter without acting inconsistently with his cause, and showing that he made a jest of the nation. However, the conquest of two great kingdoms and the destruction of the opposite party afforded him sufficient means of satisfying his generals.

Pepin made himself master of the monarchy by protecting the clergy; his son, Charles Martel, could not maintain his power but by oppressing them. This prince, finding that part of the regal and fiscal lands had been given either for life, or in perpetuity, to the nobility, and that the church by receiving both from rich and poor had acquired a great part even of the allodial estates, he resolved to strip the clergy; and as the fiefs of the first division were no longer in being, he formed a second. [2008] He took for himself and for his officers the church-lands and the churches themselves; thus he remedied an evil which differed from ordinary diseases, as its extremity rendered it the more easy to cure.

[2008] *Karolus plurima juri ecclesiastico detrahens prædia fisco sociavit, ac deinde militibus dispertivit.*—From *Chronica Centulensi*, lib. II.

10. *Riches of the Clergy.*

So great were the donations made to the clergy that under the three races of our princes they must have several times received the full property of all the lands of the kingdom. But if our kings, the nobility, and the people found the way of giving them all their estates, they found also the method of getting them back again. The spirit of devotion established a great number of churches under the first race; but the military spirit was the cause of their being given away afterwards to the soldiery, who divided them among their children. What a number of lands must have then been taken from the clergy's *mensalia!* The kings of the second race opened their hands, and made new donations to them; but the Normans, who came afterwards, plundered and ravaged all before them, wreaking their vengeance chiefly on the priests and monks, and devoting every religious house to destruction. For they charged those ecclesiastics with the destruction of their idols, and with all the oppressive measures of Charlemagne by which they had been successively obliged to take shelter in the north. These were animosities which the space of forty or fifty years had not been able to obliterate. In this situation, what losses must the clergy have sustained! There were hardly ecclesiastics left to demand the estates of which they had been deprived. There remained, therefore, for the religious piety of the third race, foundations enough to make, and lands to bestow. The opinions which were spread abroad and believed in those days would have deprived the laity of all their estates, if they had been but virtuous enough. But if the clergy were actuated by ambition, the laity were not without theirs; if dying persons gave their estates to the church, their heirs would fain resume them. We meet with continual quarrels between the lords and the bishops, the gentlemen and the abbots; and the clergy must have been very hard pressed, since they were obliged to put themselves under the protection of certain lords, who granted them a momentary defense, and afterwards joined their oppressors.

But a better administration having been established under the third race gave the clergy leave to augment their possessions; when the Calvinists started up, and having plundered the churches, they turned all the sacred plate into specie. How could the clergy be sure of their estates, when they were not even safe in their persons? They were debating on controversial subjects while their archives were in flames. What did it avail them to demand back of an impoverished nobility those estates which were no longer in possession of the latter, but had been conveyed into other hands by different mortgages? The clergy have been long acquiring, and have often refunded, and still there is no end of their acquisitions.

11. *State of Europe at the Time of Charles Martel.*

Charles Martel, who undertook to strip the clergy, found himself in a most happy situation. He was both feared and beloved by the soldiery; he worked for them, having the pretext of his wars against the Saracens. He was hated, indeed, by the clergy, but he had no need of their assistance. [2009] The Pope, to whom he was necessary, stretched out his arms to him. Everyone knows the famous embassy he received from Gregory III. [2010] These two powers were strictly united, because they could not do without each other: the Pope stood in need of the Franks to assist him against the Lombards and the Greeks; Charles Martel had occasion for the Pope, to humble the Greeks, to embarrass the Lombards, to make himself more respectable at home, and to guarantee the titles which he had, and those which he or his children might take. It was impossible, therefore, for his enterprise to miscarry.

[2009] See the Annals of Metz.
[2010] *Epistolam quoque, decretio Romanorum principum, sibi prædictus præsul Gregorius miserat. Quod sese populus Romanus, relicta imperatoris domination, ad suam defensionem et invictam clementiam convertere voluisset.*—Ibid., year 741. *Eo pacto patrato, ut a partibus imperatoris recederet.*—Fredegarius.

St. Eucherius, Bishop of Orleans, had a vision which frightened all the princes of that time. I shall produce on this occasion the letter written by the bishops assembled at Rheims to Lewis, King of Germany, who had invaded the territories of Charles the Bald; [2011] because it will give us an insight into the situation of things in those times, and the temper of the people. They say [2012] that "St. Eucherius, having been snatched up into heaven, saw Charles Martel tormented in the bottom of hell by order of the saints, who are to sit with Christ at the last judgment; that he had been condemned to this punishment before his time, for having stripped the church of her possessions and thereby charged himself with the sins of all those who founded these livings; that King Pepin held a council upon this occasion, and had ordered all the church-lands he could recover to be restored; that as he could get back only a part of them, because of his disputes with Vaifre, Duke of *Acquitaine*, he issued letters called *precaria* [2013] for the remainder, and made a law that the laity should pay a tenth part of the church-lands they possessed, and twelve deniers for each house; that Charlemagne did not give the church-lands away; on the contrary, that he published a capitulary, by which he engaged both for himself and for his successors never to make any such grant; that all they say is committed to writing, and that a great many of them heard the whole related by Lewis the Debonnaire, the father of those two kings."

[2011] Year 858, in Carisiacus; Baluzius's edition, ii, p. 101.
[2012] Ibid., ii, art. 7, p. 109.
[2013] *Precaria, quod precibus utendum conceditur*, says Cujas, in his notes upon the first Book of Fiefs. I find in a diploma of King Pepin, dated the third year of his reign, that this prince was not the first who established these *precaria*; he cites one made by the Mayor *Ebroin*, and continued after his time. See the diploma of the king, in the Historians of France by the Benedictines, tome v, art. 6.

King Pepin's regulation, mentioned by the bishops, was made in the council held at Leptines. [2014] The church found this advantage in it, that such as had received those lands held them no longer but in a precarious manner; and moreover that she received the tithe or tenth part, and twelve deniers for every house that had belonged to her. But this was only a palliative, and did not remove the disorder.

[2014] In the year 743, see the 5th book of the Capitularies, art. 3, Baluzius's edition, p. 825.

Nay, it met with opposition, and Pepin was obliged to make another capitulary, [2015] in which he enjoins those who held any of those benefices to pay this tithe and duty, and even to keep up the houses belonging to the bishopric or monastery, under the penalty of forfeiting those possessions. Charlemagne renewed the regulations of Pepin. [2016]

[2015] That of Metz, in the year 736, art. 4.
[2016] See his Capitulary, in the year 803, given at Worms; Baluzius's edition, p. 411, where he regulates the *precarious* contract, and that of Frankfort, in the year 794, p. 267, art. 24, in relation to the repairing of the houses; and that of the year 800, p. 330.

That part of the same letter which says that Charlemagne promised both for himself and for his successors never to divide again the church-lands among the soldiery is agreeable to the capitulary of this prince, given at Aix-la-Chapelle in the year 803, with a view of removing the apprehensions of the clergy upon this subject. But the donations already made were still in force. [2017] The bishops very justly add that Lewis the Debonnaire followed the example of Charlemagne, and did not give away the church-lands to the soldiery.

[2017] As appears by the preceding note, and by the Capitulary of Pepin, King of Italy, where it says, that the king would give the monasteries in fief to those who would swear allegiance for fiefs: it is added to the law of the Lombards, book III, tit. 1, § 30; and to the Salic Law, Collection of Pepin's Laws in Echard, p. 195, tit. 26, art. 4.

And yet the old abuses were carried to such a pitch, that the laity under the children of Lewis the Debonnaire preferred ecclesiastics to benefices, or turned them out of their livings [2018] without the consent of the bishops. The benefices were divided among the next heirs, [2019] and when they were held in an indecent manner the bishops had no other remedy left than to remove the relics. [2020]

[2018] See the constitution of Lotharius I, in the law of the Lombards, book III. law. 1, § 43.
[2019] Ibid., § 44.
[2020] Ibid.

By the Capitulary of Compiègne [2021] it is enacted that the king's commissary shall have a right to visit every monastery, together with the bishop, by the consent and in presence of the person who holds it; [2022] and this shows that the abuse was general.

[2021] Given the 28th year of the reign of Charles the Bald, in the year 868. Baluzius's edition, p. 203.

[2022] *Cum consilio et consensus ipsius qui locum retinet.*

Not that there were laws wanting for the restitution of the church-lands. The Pope having reprimanded the bishops for their neglect in regard to the re-establishment of the monasteries, they wrote to Charles the Bald that they were not affected by this reproach, because they were not culpable; [2023] and they reminded him of what had been promised, resolved and decreed in so many national assemblies. In point of fact, they quoted nine.

[2023] *Concilium apud Bonoilum*, the 16th year of Charles the Bald, in the year 856, Baluzius's edition, p. 78.

Still they went on disputing; till the Normans came and made them all agree.

12. *Establishment of the Tithes.*

The regulations made under King Pepin had given the church rather hopes of relief than effectually relieved her; and as Charles Martel found all the landed estates of the kingdom in the hands of the clergy, Charlemagne found all the church-lands in the hands of the soldiery. The latter could not be compelled to restore a voluntary donation, and the circumstances of that time rendered the thing still more impracticable than it seemed to be of its own nature. On the other hand, Christianity ought not to have been lost for want of ministers, churches, and instruction. [2024]

[2024] In the civil wars which broke out at the time of Charles Martel, the lands belonging to the church of Rheims were given away to laymen; *the clergy were left to shift as well as they could,* says the life of Remigius, Surius, tom. i, p. 279.

This was the reason of Charlemagne's establishing the tithes, [2025] a new kind of property which had this advantage in favor of the clergy, that as they were given particularly to the church, it was easier in process of time to know when they were usurped.

[2025] Law of the Lombards, book III, tit. 3, §§ 1 and 2.

Some have attempted to make this institution of a still remoter date, but the authorities they produce seem rather, I think, to prove the contrary. The constitution of Clotharius says [2026] only that they shall not raise certain tithes on church-lands; [2027] so far then was the church from exacting tithes at that time, that its whole pretension was to be exempted from paying them. The second council of Mâcon, [2028] which was held in 585, and ordains the payment of tithes, says, indeed, that they were paid in ancient times, but it says also that the custom of paying them was then abolished.

[2026] It is that on which I have descanted in the 4th chapter of this book, and which is to be found in Baluzius's edition of the Capitularies, tom. i, art. 11, p. 9.

[2027] *Agraria et pascuaria vel decimas porcorum ecclesiæ concedimus, ita ut actor aut decomator in rebus ecclesiæ nullus accedat.* The Capitulary of Charlemagne in the year 800, Baluzius's edition, p. 336, explains extremely well what is meant by that sort of tithe from which the church is exempted by Clotharius; it was the tithe of the swine which were put into the king's forests to fatten; and Charlemagne enjoins his judges to pay it, as well as other people, in order to set an example: it is plain that this was a right of seigniory or economy.

[2028] *Canone 5, ex tomo 1, conciliorum antiquorum Galliæ opera Jacobi Sirmundi.*

No one questions but that the clergy opened the Bible before Charlemagne's time, and preached the gifts and offerings in Leviticus. But I say that before that prince's reign, though the tithes might have been preached, they were never established.

I noticed that the regulations made under King Pepin had subjected those who were seized of church lands in fief to the payment of tithes, and to the repairing of the churches. It was a great deal to induce by a law, whose equity could not be disputed, the principal men of the nation to set the example.

Charlemagne did more; and we find by the capitulary *de Villis* [2029] that he obliged his own demesnes to the payment of the tithes; this was a still more striking example.

[2029] Art. 6, Baluzius's edition, p. 332. It was given in the year 800.

But the commonalty are rarely influenced by example to sacrifice their interests. The synod of Frankfort furnished them with a more cogent motive to pay the tithes. [2030] A capitulary was made in that synod, wherein it is said that in the last famine the spikes of corn were found to contain no seed, [2031] the infernal spirits having devoured it all, and that those spirits had been heard to reproach them with not having paid the tithes; in consequence of which it was ordained that all those who were seized of church lands should pay the tithes; and the next consequence was that the obligation extended to all.

[2030] Held under Charlemagne, in the year 794.

[2031] *Experimento enim didicimus in anno quo illa valida fames irrepsit, ebullire vacuas annonas a dæmonibus devoratas, et voces exprobrationis auditas,* &c. Baluzius's edition, p. 267, art. 23.

Charlemagne's project did not succeed at first, for it seemed too heavy a burden. [2032] The payment of the tithes among the Jews was connected with the plan of the foundation of their republic; but here it was a burden quite independent of the other charges of the establishment of the monarchy. We find by the regulations added to the law of the Lombards [2033] the difficulty there was in causing the tithes to be accepted by the civil laws; and as for the opposition they met with before they were admitted by the ecclesiastic laws, we may easily judge of it from the different canons of the councils.

[2032] See among the rest the capitulary of Lewis the Debonnaire in the year 829, Baluzius's edition, p. 663; against those who, to avoid paying tithes neglected to cultivate the lands, &c., art. 5. *Nonis quidem et decimis, unde et genitor noster et nos frequenter in diversis placitis admonitionem fecimus.*

[2033] Among others, that of Lotharius, book III, tit. 3, chap. 6.

The people consented at length to pay the tithes, upon condition that they might have the power of redeeming them. This the constitution of Lewis the Debonnaire [2034] and that of the Emperor Lotharius, his son, would not allow. [2035]

[2034] In the year 829, art. 7, in Baluzius, tom. i, p. 663.
[2035] In the law of the Lombards, book III, tit. 3, § 8.

The laws of Charlemagne, in regard to the establishment of tithes, were a work of necessity, not of superstition—a work, in short, in which religion only was concerned. His famous division of the tithes into four parts, for the repairing of the churches, for the poor, for the bishop, and for the clergy, manifestly proves that he wished to give the church that fixed and permanent status which she had lost.

His will shows that he was desirous of repairing the mischief done by his grandfather, Charles Martel. [2036] He made three equal shares of his movable goods; two of these he would have divided each into one-and-twenty parts, for the one-and-twenty metropolitan sees of his empire; each part was to be sub-divided between the metropolitan and the dependent bishoprics. The remaining third he distributed into four parts; one he gave to his children and grandchildren, another was added to the two-thirds already bequeathed, and the other two were assigned to charitable uses. It seems as if he looked upon the immense donation he was making to the church less as a religious act than as a political distribution.

[2036] It is a kind of codicil produced by Eginhard, and different from the will itself, which we find in Goldastus and Baluzius.

13. *Of the Election of Bishops and Abbots.*

As the church had grown poor, the kings resigned the right of nominating to bishoprics and other ecclesiastic benefices. [2037] The princes gave themselves less trouble about the ecclesiastic ministers; and the candidates were less solicitous in applying to their authorities. Thus the church received a kind of compensation for the possessions she had lost.

[2037] See the Capitulary of Charlemagne in the year 803, art. 2, Baluzius's edition, p. 379; and the edict of Lewis the Debonnaire in the year 834, in Goldast, Constit. Impérial., tom. i.

Hence, if Lewis the Debonnaire left the people of Rome in possession of the right of choosing their popes, it was owing to the general spirit that prevailed in his time; [2038] he behaved in the same manner to the see of Rome as to other bishoprics.

[2038] This is mentioned in the famous canon, *ego Ludovicus*, which is a palpable forgery; it is Baluzius's edition, p. 591, in the year 817.

14. *Of the Fiefs of Charles Martel.*

I shall not pretend to determine whether Charles Martel, in giving the church-lands in fief, made a grant of them for life or in perpetuity. All I know is that under Charlemagne [2039] and Lotharius I [2040] there were possessions of that kind which descended to the next heirs, and were divided among them.

[2039] As appears by his Capitulary, in the year 801, art. 17, in Baluzius, tom. i, p. 360.
[2040] See his constitution, inserted in the code of the Lombards, book III, tit. 1, § 44.

I find, moreover, that one part of them was given as allodia, and the other as fiefs. [2041]

[2041] See the above constitution, and the Capitulary of Charles the Bald, in the year 846, chap. xx. *in Villa Sparnaco*, Baluzius's edition, tom. ii. p. 31, and that of the year 853, chap. iii and v, in the Synod of Soissons, Baluzius's edition, tom. ii, p. 54; and that of the year 854, *apud Attiniacum*, chap. x. Baluzius's edition, tom. ii, p. 70. See also the first Capitulary of Charlemagne, *incerti anni*, art. 49 and 56. Baluzius's edition, tom. i, p. 519.

I noticed that the proprietors of the allodia were subject to service all the same as the possessors of the fiefs. This, without doubt, was partly the reason that Charles Martel made grants of allodial lands as well as of fiefs.

15. *The same Subject continued.*

We must observe that the fiefs having been changed into church-lands, and these again into fiefs, they borrowed something of each other. Thus the church-lands had the privileges of fiefs, and these had the privileges of church-lands. Such were the honorary rights of churches, which began at that time. [2042] And as those rights have ever been annexed to the judiciary power, in preference to what is still called the fief, it follows that the patrimonial jurisdictions were established at the same time as those very rights.

[2042] See the Capitularies, book V. art. 44, and the edict of Pistes in the year 869, art. 8 and 9, where we find the honorary rights of the lords established, in the same manner as they are at this very day.

16. *Confusion of the Royalty and Mayoralty. The Second Race.*

The connection of my subject has made me invert the order of time, so as to speak of Charlemagne before I had mentioned the famous epoch of the translation of the crown to the Carlovingians under King Pepin; a revolution, which, contrary to the nature of ordinary events, is more remarked perhaps in our days than when it happened.

The kings had no authority; they had only an empty name. The regal title was hereditary, and that of mayor elective. Though it was latterly in the power of the mayors to place any of the Merovingians on the throne, they had not yet taken a king of another family; and the ancient law which fixed the crown in a particular family was not yet erased from the hearts of the Franks. The king's person was almost unknown in the monarchy; but royalty was not. Pepin, son of Charles Martel, thought it would be proper to confound those two titles, a confusion which would leave it a moot point whether the new royalty was hereditary or not; and this was sufficient for him who to the regal dignity had joined a great power. The mayor's authority was then blended with that of the king. In the mixture of these two authorities a kind of reconciliation was made; the mayor had been elective, and the king hereditary; the crown at the beginning of the second race was elective, because the people chose; it was hereditary, because they always chose in the same family. [2043]

[2043] See the will of Charlemagne, and the division which Lewis, the Debonnaire, made to his children in the assembly of the states held at Quierzy, related by Goldast, *quem populus eligere velit, ut patri suo succedat in regni hæreditate.*

Father le Cointe, in spite of the authority of all ancient records [2044] denies that the Pope authorized this great change; and one of his reasons is that he would have committed an injustice. [2045] A fine thing to see a historian judge of that which men have done by that which they ought to have done; by this mode of reasoning we should have no more history.

[2044] The anonymous Chronicle in the year 752; and Chronic. Centul. in the year 754.
[2045] *Fabella quæ post Pippini mortem excogitata est, æquitati ac sanctitati Zachariæ papæ plurimum adversatur.*—Ecclesiastic Annals of the French, tom. ii. p. 319.

Be that as it may, it is very certain that immediately after Duke Pepin's victory, the Merovingians ceased to be the reigning family. When his grandson, Pepin, was crowned king, it was only one ceremony more, and one phantom less; he acquired nothing thereby but the royal ornaments; there was no change made in the nation.

This I have said in order to fix the moment of the revolution, that we may not be mistaken in looking upon that as a revolution which was only a consequence of it.

When Hugh Capet was crowned king at the beginning of the third race, there was a much greater change, because the kingdom passed from a state of anarchy to some kind of government; but when Pepin took the crown, there was only a transition from one government to another, which was identical.

When Pepin was crowned king there was only a change of name; but when Hugh Capet was crowned there was a change in the nature of the thing, because by uniting a great fief to the crown the anarchy ceased.

When Pepin was crowned the title of king was united to the highest office; when Hugh Capet was crowned it was annexed to the greatest fief.

17. *A particular Circumstance in the Election of the Kings of the Second Race.*

We find by the formulary of Pepin's coronation that Charles and Carloman were also anointed, [2046] and blessed, and that the French nobility bound themselves, on pain of interdiction and excommunication, never to choose a prince of another family. [2047]

[2046] Vol. 5th of the historians of France by the Benedictins, p. 9.

[2047] *Ut unquam de alterius lumbis regem in aevo præsumant eligere sed ex ipsorum.* Vol. 5th of the historians of France, p. 10.

It appears by the wills of Charlemagne and Lewis the Debonnaire, that the Franks made a choice among the king's children, which agrees with the above-mentioned clause. And when the empire was transferred from Charlemagne's family, the election, which before had been restricted and conditional, became pure and simple, so that the ancient constitution was departed from.

Pepin, perceiving himself near his end, assembled the lords, both temporal and spiritual, at St. Denis, and divided his kingdom between his two sons, Charles and Carloman. [2048] We have not the acts of this assembly, but we find what was there transacted in the author of the ancient historical collection, published by Canisius, and in the writer of the annals of Metz, [2049] according to the observation of Baluzius. [2050] Here I meet with two things in some measure contradictory; that he made this division with the consent of the nobility, and afterwards that he made it by his paternal authority. This proves what I said, that the people's right in the second race was to choose in the same family; it was, properly speaking, rather a right of exclusion than that of election.

[2048] In the year 768.
[2049] Tom. ii, *lectionis antiquæ.*
[2050] Edition of the Capitularies, tom. i, p. 188.

This kind of elective right is confirmed by the records of the second race. Such is this capitulary of the division of the empire made by Charlemagne among his three children, in which, after settling their shares, he says, [2051] *That if one of the three brothers happens to have a son, such as the people shall be willing to choose as a fit person to succeed to his father's kingdom, his uncles shall consent to it.*

[2051] In the 1st Capitulary of the year 806. Baluzius's edition, p. 439, art. 5.

This same regulation is to be met with in the partition which Lewis the Debonnaire made among his three children, Pepin, Lewis, and Charles, in the year 837, at the assembly of Aix-la-Chapelle; [2052] and likewise in another partition, made twenty years before, by the same emperor, in favor of Lotharius, Pepin, and Lewis. [2053] We may likewise see the oath which Lewis the Stammerer took at Compiègne at his coronation. *I, Lewis, by the divine mercy, and the people's election, appointed king, do promise* [2054] . . . What I say is confirmed by the acts of the Council of Valence, held in the year 890, for the election of Lewis, son of Boson, to the kingdom of Arles. [2055] Lewis was there elected, and the principal reason they gave for choosing him is that he was of the imperial family, [2056] that Charles the Fat had conferred upon him the dignity of king, and that the Emperor Arnold had invested him by the scepter, and by the ministry of his ambassadors. The kingdom of Arles, like the other dismembered or dependent kingdoms of Charlemagne, was elective and hereditary.

[2052] In Goldast, Constit. Impérial., tom. ii, p. 19.
[2053] Baluzius's edition, p. 574, art. 14. *Si vero aliquis illorum decedens legitimis filios reliquerit, non inter eos potestas ipsa dividatur, sed potius populus partier*

520

conveniens, unum ex iis quem dominus voluerit eligat, et hunc senior frater in loco fratris et filii suscipiat.

[2054] Capitulary of the year 877. Baluzius's edition, p. 272.

[2055] In Father Labbe's Councils, tom. ix, col. 424; and in Dumont's Corp. Diplomat., tom. ii, art. 36.

[2056] By the mother's side.

18. *Charlemagne.*

Charlemagne's intention was to restrain the power of the nobility within proper bounds, and to hinder them from oppressing the freemen and the clergy. He balanced the several orders of the state, and remained perfect master of them all. The whole was united by the strength of his genius. He led the nobility continually from one expedition to another, giving them no time to form conspiracies, but employing them entirely in the execution of his designs. The empire was supported by the greatness of its chief; the prince was great, but the man was greater. The kings, his children, were his first subjects, the instruments of his power and patterns of obedience. He made admirable laws; and, what is more, he took care to see them executed. His genius diffused itself through every part of the empire. We find in this prince's laws a comprehensive spirit of foresight, and a certain force which carries all before it. All pretexts for evading the duties are removed, neglects are corrected, abuses reformed or prevented. [2057] He knew how to punish, but he understood much better how to pardon. He was great in his designs, and simple in the execution of them. No prince ever possessed in a higher degree the art of performing the greatest things with ease, and the most difficult with expedition. He was continually visiting the several parts of his vast empire, and made them feel the weight of his hand wherever it fell. New difficulties sprang up on every side, and on every side he removed them. Never prince had more resolution in facing dangers; never prince knew better how to avoid them. He mocked all manner of perils, and particularly those to which great conquerors are generally subject, namely, conspiracies. This wonderful prince was extremely moderate, of a very mild character, plain and simple in his behavior. He loved to converse freely with the lords of his court. He indulged, perhaps, too much his passion for the fair sex; a failing, however, which in a prince who always governed by himself; and who spent his life in a continual series of toils; may merit some allowance. He was wonderfully exact in his expenses, administering his demesnes with prudence, attention, and economy. A father might learn from his laws how to govern his family; and we find in his capitularies the pure and sacred source whence he derived his riches. [2058] I shall add only one word more: he gave orders that the eggs in the bartons on his demesnes, and the superfluous garden-stuff, should be sold; [2059] he distributed among his people all the riches of the Lombards, and the immense treasures of those Huns that had plundered the whole world.

[2057] See his third Capitulary of the year 811, p. 486, art. 1, 2, 3, 4, 5, 6, 7, and 8; and the first Capitulary of the year 812, p. 490, art. 1; and the Capitulary of the year 812, p. 494, art. 9 and 11, etc.

[2058] See the Capitulary *de Villis* in the year 800; his second Capitulary of the year 813, art. 6 and 19; and the fifth book of the Capitularies, art. 303.

[2059] Capitulary *de Villis*, art. 39. See this whole Capitulary, which is a masterpiece of prudence, good administration, and economy.

19. *The same Subject continued.*

Charlemagne and his immediate successors were afraid lest those whom they placed in distant parts should be inclined to revolt, and thought they should find more docility among the clergy. For this reason they erected a great number of bishoprics in Germany and endowed them with very large fiefs. [2060] It appears by some charters that the clauses containing the prerogatives of those fiefs were not different from such as were commonly inserted in those grants, [2061] though at present we find the principal ecclesiastics of Germany invested with a sovereign power. Be that as it may, these were some of the contrivances they used against the Saxons. That which they could not expect from the indolence or supineness of vassals they thought they ought to expect from the sedulous attention of a bishop. Besides, a vassal of that kind, far from making use of the conquered people against them, would rather stand in need of their assistance to support themselves against their own people.

[2060] See among others the foundation of the Archbishopric of Bremen, in the Capitulary of the year 789. Baluzius's edition, p. 245.
[2061] For instance, the prohibition of the king's judges against entering upon the territory to demand the *freda*, and other duties. I have said a good deal concerning this in the preceding book, 20, 21, 22.

20. *Lewis the Debonnaire.*

When Augustus Cæsar was in Egypt he ordered Alexander's tomb to be opened; and upon their asking him whether he was willing they should open the tombs of the Ptolemies, he made answer that he wanted to see the king, and not the dead. Thus, in the history of the second race, we are continually looking for Pepin and Charlemagne; we want to see the kings, and not the dead.

A prince who was the sport of his passions, and a dupe even to his virtues; a prince who never understood rightly either his own strength or weakness; a prince who was incapable of making himself either feared or beloved; a prince, in fine, who with few vices in his heart had all manner of defects in his understanding, took into his hands the reins of the empire which had been held by Charlemagne.

At a time when the whole world is in tears for the death of his father, at a time of surprise and alarm, when the subjects of that extensive empire all call upon Charles and find him no more; at a time when he is advancing with all expedition to take possession of his father's throne, he sends some trusty officers before him in order to seize the persons of those who had contributed to the irregular conduct of his sisters. This step was productive of the most terrible catastrophes. [2062] It was imprudent and precipitate. He began with punishing domestic crimes before he reached the palace; and with alienating the minds of his subjects before he ascended the throne.

[2062] The anonymous author of the Life of Lewis the Debonnaire in Duchesne's Collection, tom. ii, p. 295.

His nephew, Bernard, King of Italy, having come to implore his clemency, he ordered his eyes to be put out, which proved the cause of that prince's death a few days after, and created Lewis a great many enemies. His apprehension of the consequence induced him to shut his brothers up in a monastery; by which means the number of his enemies increased. These two last transactions were afterwards laid to his charge in a judicial manner, [2063] and his accusers did not fail to tell him that he had violated his oath and the solemn promises which he had made to his father on the day of his coronation. [2064]

[2063] See his trial and the circumstances of his deposition, in Duchesne's Collection, tom. ii, p. 133.

[2064] He directed him to show unlimited clemency (*indeficientem misericordiam*) to his sisters, his brothers, and his nephews. Tegan in the collection of Duchesne, tom. ii, p. 276.

After the death of the Empress Hermengarde, by whom he had three children, he married Judith, and had a son by that princess; but soon mixing all the indulgence of an old husband, with all the weakness of an old king, he flung his family into a disorder which was followed by the downfall of the monarchy.

He was continually altering the partitions he had made among his children. And yet these partitions had been confirmed each in their turn by his own oath, and by those of his children and the nobility. This was as if he wanted to try the fidelity of his subjects; it was endeavoring by confusion, scruples, and equivocation, to puzzle their obedience; it was confounding the different rights of those princes, and rendering their titles dubious, especially at a time when there were but few fortresses, and when the principal bulwark of authority was the fealty sworn and accepted.

The Emperor's children, in order to preserve their shares, courted the clergy, and granted them privileges till then unheard. These privileges were specious; and the clergy in return were made to warrant the revolution in favor of those princes. Agobard [2065] represents to Lewis the Debonnaire his having sent Lotharius to Rome, in order to have him declared emperor; and that he had made a division of his dominions among his children, after having consulted heaven by three days fasting and praying. What defense could such a weak prince make against the attack of superstition? It is easy to perceive the shock which the supreme authority must have twice received from his imprisonment, and from his public penance; they would fain degrade the king, and they degraded the regal dignity.

[2065] See his letters.

We find difficulty at first in conceiving how a prince who was possessed of several good qualities, who had some knowledge, who had a natural disposition to virtue, and who in short was the son of Charlemagne, could have such a number of enemies. [2066] so impetuous and implacable as even to insult him in his humiliation and to be determined upon his ruin: and, indeed they would have utterly completed it, if his children, who in the main were more honest than they, had been steady in their design, and could have agreed among themselves.

[2066] See his trial and the circumstances of his deposition, in Duchesne's Collection, tom. ii, p. 331. See also his life written by Tegan: *Tanto enim odio laborabat, ut tæderet eos vita ipsius,* says this anonymous author in Duchesne, tom. ii, p. 307.

21. *The same Subject continued.*

The strength and solidity for which the kingdom was indebted to Charlemagne still subsisted under Lewis the Debonnaire in such a degree as enabled the state to support its grandeur, and to command respect from foreign nations. The prince's understanding was weak, but the nation was warlike. His authority declined at home, though there seemed to be no diminution of power abroad.

Charles Martel, Pepin, and Charlemagne were in succession rulers of the monarchy. The first flattered the avarice of the soldiers: the other two that of the clergy. Lewis the Debonnaire displeased both.

In the French constitution, the whole power of the state was lodged in the hands of the king, the nobility, and clergy. Charles Martel, Pepin, and Charlemagne joined sometimes their interest with one of those parties to check the other and generally with both; but Lewis the Debonnaire could gain the affection of neither. He disobliged the bishops by publishing regulations which had the air of severity, because he carried things to a greater length than was agreeable to their inclination. Very good laws may be ill-timed. The bishops in those days, being accustomed to take the field against the Saracens and the Saxons, had very little of the spirit of religion. [2067] On the other hand, as he had no longer any confidence in the nobility, he promoted mean people, [2068] turning the nobles out of their employments at court to make room for strangers and upstarts. [2069] By this means the affections of the two great bodies of the nobility and clergy were alienated from their prince, the consequence of which was a total desertion.

[2067] The anonymous author of the Life of Lewis the Debonnaire in Duchesne's Collection, tom. ii, p. 298.
[2068] Tegan says that what seldom happened under Charlemagne was a common practice under Lewis.
[2069] Being desirous to check the nobility, he promoted one Bernard to the place of chamberlain, by which the great lords were exasperated to the highest pitch.

22. *The same Subject continued.*

But what chiefly contributed to weaken the monarchy was the extravagance of this prince in alienating the crown demesnes. [2070] And here it is that we ought to listen to the account of Nitard, one of our most judicious historians, a grandson of Charlemagne, strongly attached to Lewis the Debonnaire and who wrote his history by order of Charles the Bald.

[2070] *Villas regias quæ erant sui et avi et tritavi, Fidelibus suis tradidit eas in possessions sempiternas; fecit enim hoc diu tempore.*—Tegan, de *Gestis Ludovici pii.*

He says, "that one Adelhard for some time gained such an ascendant over the Emperor, that this prince conformed to his will in everything; that at the instigation of this favorite, he had granted the crown lands to everybody that asked them, [2071] by which means the state was ruined." [2072] Thus he did the same mischief throughout the empire as I observed he had done in Aquitaine; [2073] the former Charlemagne redressed, but the latter was past all remedy.

[2071] *Hinc libertates, hing publica in propriis usibus distribuere suasit.*—Nitard, lib. iv, *prope finem.*
[2072] *Rempublicam penitus annullavit.*—Ibid.
[2073] See book XXX. chap. 13.

The state was reduced to the same debility in which Charles Martel found it upon his accession to the mayoralty; and so desperate were its circumstances that no exertion of authority was any longer capable of saving it.

The treasury was so exhausted that in the reign of Charles the Bald, no one could continue in his employments, nor be safe in his person without paying for it. [2074] When they had it in their power to destroy the Normans, they took money to let them escape: [2075] and the first advice which Hincmar gives to Lewis the Stammerer is to ask of the assembly of the nation a sufficient allowance to defray the expenses of his household.

[2074] Hincmar, let. 1, to Lewis, the Stammerer.
[2075] See the fragment of the Chronicle of the Monastery of St. Sergius of Angers, in Duchesne, tom. ii, p. 401.

23. *The same Subject continued.*

The clergy had reason to repent the protection they had granted to the children of Lewis the Debonnaire. This prince, as I have already observed, had never given any of the church-lands by precepts to the laity; [2076] but it was not long before Lotharius in Italy, and Pepin in Aquitaine, quitted Charlemagne's plan, and resumed that of Charles Martel. The clergy had recourse to the Emperor against his children, but they themselves had weakened the authority to which they appealed. In Aquitaine some condescension was shown, but none in Italy.

[2076] See what the bishops say in the synod of the year 845, *apud Teudonis villam*, art. 4.

The civil wars with which the life of Lewis the Debonnaire had been embroiled were the seed of those which followed his death. The three brothers, Lotharius, Lewis, and Charles, endeavored each to bring over the nobility to their party and to make them their tools. To such as were willing therefore to follow them they granted church-lands by precepts; so that to gain the nobility, they sacrificed the clergy.

We find in the Capitularies [2077] that those princes were obliged to yield to the importunity of demands, and that what they would not often have freely granted was extorted from them: we find that the clergy thought themselves more oppressed by the nobility than by the kings, It appears that Charles the Bald [2078] became the greatest enemy of the patrimony of the clergy, whether he was most incensed against them for having degraded his father on their account, or whether he was the most timorous. Be that as it may, we meet with continual quarrels in the Capitularies, [2079] between the clergy who demanded their estates, and the nobility who refused or deferred to restore them; and the kings acting as mediators.

[2077] See the synod in the year 845, *apud Teudonis villam*, art. 3 and 4, which gives a very exact description of things; as also, that of the same year, held at the palaces of Vernes, art. 12, and the synod of Beauvais, also in the same year, art. 3, 4, and 6, in the Capitulary in *Villa Sparnaco*, in the year 846, art. 20, and the letter which the bishops assembled at Rheims wrote in 858, to Lewis, King of Germany, art. 8.

[2078] See the Capitulary in *Villa Sparnaco*, in the year 846. The nobility had set the King against the bishops, insomuch that he expelled them from the assembly; a few of the canons enacted in council were picked out, and the prelates were told that these were the only ones which should be observed; nothing was granted them that could be refused. See art. 20, 21 and 22. See also the letter which the bishops assembled at Rheims wrote in the year 858 to Lewis, King of Germany, art. 8, and the edict of Pistes, in the year 864, art. 5.

[2079] See this very Capitulary in the year 846, *in Villa Sparnaco*. See also the Capitulary of the assembly held *apud Marsnam* in the year 847, art. 4, wherein the clergy reduced themselves to demand only the restitution of what they had been possessed of under Lewis the Debonnaire. See also the Capitulary of the year 851, *apud Marsnam*, art. 6, and 7, which confirms the nobility and clergy in their several possessions, and that *apud Bonoilum*, in the year 856, which is a remonstrance of the bishops to the king, because the evils, after so many laws, had not been redressed; and, in fine, the letter which the bishops assembled at Rheims wrote in the year 858, to Lewis, King of Germany, art. 8.

The situation of affairs at that time is a spectacle really deserving of pity. While Lewis the Debonnaire made immense donations out of his demesnes to the clergy, his children distributed the church-lands among the laity. The same prince with one hand founded new abbeys and despoiled old ones. The clergy had no fixed state; one moment they were plundered, another they received satisfaction; but the crown was continually losing.

Toward the close of the reign of Charles the Bald, and from that time forward, there was an end of the disputes of the clergy and laity concerning the restitution of church-lands. The bishops indeed breathed out still a few sighs in their remonstrances to Charles the Bald, which we find in the Capitulary of the year 856, and in the letter they wrote to Lewis, King of Germany, in the year 858, [2080] but they proposed things, and challenged promises, so often eluded, that we plainly see they had no longer any hopes of obtaining their desire.

[2080] Art. 8.

All that could be expected then was to repair in general the injuries done both to church and state. [2081] The kings engaged not to deprive the nobility of their freemen, and not to give away any more church-lands by *precepts*, [2082] so that the interests of the clergy and nobility seemed then to be united.

[2081] See the Capitulary of the year 851, art. 6 and 7.

[2082] Charles the Bald, in the Synod of Soissons, says, *that he had promised the bishops not to issue any more precepts relating to church-lands.* Capitulary of the year 853, art. 11, Baluzius's edition. tom. ii, p. 56.

The dreadful depredations of the Normans, as I have already observed, contributed greatly to put an end to those quarrels.

The authority of our kings diminishing every day, both for the reasons already given and those which I shall mention hereafter, they imagined they had no better resource left, than to resign themselves into the hands of the clergy. But the ecclesiastics had weakened the power of the kings, and these had diminished the influence of the ecclesiastics. In vain did Charles the Bald and his successors call in the church to support the state, and to prevent its ruin; in vain did they make use of the. respect which the commonalty had for that body, [2083] to maintain that which they should also have for their prince; [2084] in vain did they endeavor to give an authority to their laws by that of the canons; in vain did they join the ecclesiastic with the civil punishments; [2085] in vain to counterbalance the authority of the count did they give to each bishop the title of their commissary in the several provinces; [2086] it was impossible to repair the mischief they had done; and a terrible misfortune, which I shall presently mention, proved the ruin of the monarchy.

[2083] See the Capitulary of Charles the Bald, *apud Saponarias*, in the year 859, art. 3. "Venilon, whom I made Archbishop of Sens, has consecrated me; and I ought not to be expelled the kingdom by anybody," *saltem sine audientia et judicio episcoporum, quorum ministerio in regen sum consecrates, et qui throni Dei sunt dicti, in quibus Deus sedet, et per quos sua decernit judicia, quorum paternis correctionibus et castigatoriis judiciis me subdere fui paratus et in præsenti sum subditus.*

[2084] See the Capitulary of Charles the Bald, de *Carisiaco*, in the year 857, Baluzius's edition, tom. ii, p. 88, §§ 1, 2, 3, 4, and 7.

[2085] See the synod of Pistes in the year 862, art. 4, and the Capitulary of Lewis II, *apud Vernis palatium*, in the year 883, art. 4 and 5.

[2086] Capitulary of the year 876, under Charles, the Bald, *in synodo Pontigonensi*, Baluzius's edition, art. 12.

24. *That the Freemen were rendered capable of holding Fiefs.*

I said that the freemen were led against the enemy by their count, and the vassals by their lord. This was the reason that the several orders of the state balanced each other, and though the king's vassals had other vassals under them, yet they might be overawed by the count, who was at the head of all the freemen of the monarchy.

The freemen were not allowed at first to do homage for a fief; but in process of time this was permitted: [2087] and I find that this change was made during the period that elapsed from the reign of Gontram to that of Charlemagne. This I prove by the comparison which may be made between the treaty of Andely, [2088] by Gontram, Childebert, and Queen Brunehault, and the partition made by Charlemagne among his children, as well as a like partition by Lewis the Debonnaire. [2089] These three acts contain nearly the same regulations with regard to the vassals; and as they determine the very same points, under almost the same circumstances, the spirit as well as the letter of those three treaties in this respect are very much alike.

[2087] See what has been said already, book XXX, last chapter, towards the end.

[2088] In the year 587, in Gregory of Tours, book IX.

[2089] See the following chapter, where I shall speak more diffusely of those partitions; and the notes in which they are quoted.

But as to what concerns the freemen, there is a vital difference. The treaty of Andely does not say that they might do homage for a fief; whereas we find in the divisions of Charlemagne and Lewis the Debonnaire express clauses to empower them to do homage. This shows that a new usage had been introduced after the treaty of Andely, whereby the freemen had become capable of this great privilege.

This must have happened when Charles Martel, after distributing the church-lands to his soldiers, partly in fief, and partly as allodia, made a kind of revolution in the feudal laws. It is very probable that the nobility who were seized already of fiefs found a greater advantage in receiving the new grants as allodia; and that the freemen thought themselves happy in accepting them as fiefs.

THE PRINCIPAL CAUSE OF THE HUMILIATION OF THE SECOND RACE

25. *Changes in the Allodia.*

Charlemagne in the partition [2090] mentioned in the preceding chapter ordained that after his death the vassals belonging to each king should be permitted to receive benefices in their own sovereign's dominion, and not in those of another; [2091] whereas they may keep their allodial estates in any of their dominions. [2092] But he adds [2093] that every freeman might, after the death of his lord, do homage in any of three kingdoms he pleased, as well as he that never had been subject to a lord. We find the same regulations in the partition which Lewis the Debonnaire made among his children in the year 817.

[2090] In the year 806, between Charles, Pepin, and Lewis, it is quoted by Goldast, and by Baluzius, tom. ii, p. 439.

[2091] Art. 9, p. 443, which is agreeable to the treaty of Andely, in Gregory of Tours, book IX.

[2092] Art. 10, and there is no mention made of this in the treaty of Andely.

[2093] In Baluzius, tom. i, p. 174. *Licentiam habeat unusquisque liber homo qui seniorum non habuerit, cuicunque ex his tribus fratribus voluerit, se commendandi,* art. 9. See also the division made by the same emperor in the year 837, art. 6, Baluzius's edition, p. 686.

But though the freeman had done homage for a fief, yet the count's militia was not thereby weakened: the freeman was still obliged to contribute for his allodium, and to get people ready for the service belonging to it, at the proportion of one man to four manors; or else to procure a man that should do the duty of the fief in his stead. And when some abuses had been introduced upon this head, they were redressed, as appears by the constitutions of Charlemagne, [2094] and by that of Pepin, King of Italy, which explain each other. [2095]

[2094] In the year 811, Baluzius's edition, tom. i, p. 486, art. 7 and 8, and that of the year 812, *ibid.* p. 490, art. 1. *Ut omnis liber homo qui quatuor mansos vestitos de propria suo, sive de alicujus beneficia habet, ipse se praeparet, et ipse in hostem pergat sive cum senior suo, &c.* See also the Capitulary of the year 807, Baluzius's edition, tom. i, p. 458.

[2095] In the year 793, inserted in the law of the Lombards, book III, tit. 9, chap. ix.

The remark made by historians that the battle of Fontenay was the ruin of the monarchy, is very true; but I beg leave to cast an eye on the unhappy consequences of that day.

Sometime after the battle, the three brothers, Lotharius, Lewis, and Charles, made a treaty, [2096] wherein I find some clauses which must have altered the whole political system of the French government.

[2096] In the year 847, quoted by *Aubert le Mire*, and Baluzius, tom. ii, page 42. *Conventus apud Marsnam.*

1. In the declaration [2097] which Charles made to the people of the part of the treaty relating to them, he says that every freeman might choose whom he pleased for his lord, [2098] whether the king or any of the nobility. Before this treaty the freeman might do homage for a fief; but his allodium still continued under the immediate power of the king, that is, under the count's jurisdiction; and he depended on the lord to whom he vowed fealty, only on account of the fief which he had obtained. After that treaty every freeman had a right to subject his allodium to the king, or to any other lord, as he thought proper. The question is riot in regard to those who put themselves under the protection of another for a fief, but to such as changed their allodial into a feudal land, and withdrew themselves, as it were, from the civil jurisdiction to enter under the power of the king, or of the lord whom they thought proper to choose.

[2097] *Adnunciatio.*

[2098] *Ut unusquisque liber homo in nostro regno seniorem quem voluerit in nobis et in nostris Fidelibus accipiat,* art. 2, of the Declaration of Charles.

Thus it was that those who formerly were only under the king's power, as freemen under 'the count, became insensibly vassals one of another, since every freeman might choose whom he pleased for his lord, the king or any of the nobility.

2. If a man changed an estate which he possessed in perpetuity into a fief, this new fief could no longer be only for life. Hence we see, a short time after, a general law for giving the fiefs to the children of the present possessor: [2099] it was made by Charles the Bald, one of the three contracting princes.

[2099] Capitulary of the year 877, tit. 53, art. 9 and 10, *apud Carisiacum, similiter et de nostris vassallis faciendum est,* &c. This Capitulary relates to another of the same year, and of the same place, art. 3.

What has been said concerning the liberty every freeman had in the monarchy, after the treaty of the three brothers, of choosing whom he pleased for his lord, the king or any of the nobility, is confirmed by the acts subsequent to that time.

In the reign of Charlemagne, [2100] when the vassal had received a present of a lord, were it worth only a sou, he could not afterwards quit him. But under Charles the Bald, the vassals might follow what was agreeable to their interests or their inclination with entire safety; [2101] and so strongly does this prince explain himself on the subject that he seems rather to encourage them in the enjoyment of this liberty than to restrain it. In Charlemagne's time, benefices were rather personal than real; afterwards they became rather real than personal.

[2100] Capitulary of Aix la Chapelle, in the year 813, art. 16, *quod nullus seniorem suum dimittat post quam ab eo acceperit valente solidum unum*; and the Capitulary of Pepin, in the year 783, art. 5.

[2101] See the capitulary *de Carisiaco*, in the year 856, art. 10 and 13. Baluzius's edition, tom. ii, p. 83, in which the king, together with the lords spiritual and temporal, agreed to this: *Et si aliquis de vobis talis est cui suus senioratus non placet, et illi simulate ut ad alium seniorem melius quam ad illum acaptare possit, veniat ad illum et ipse tranquillo et pacific animo donet illi commeatum . . . et quod Deus illi cupierit et ad alium seniorem acaptare potuerit, pacifice habeat.*

26. *Changes in the Fiefs.*

The same changes happened in the fiefs as in the *allodia*. We find by the Capitulary of Compiègne, [2102] under King Pepin, that those who had received a benefice from the king gave a part of this benefice to different bondmen; but these parts were not distinct from the whole. The king revoked them when he revoked the whole; and at the death of the king's vassal, the rear-vassal lost also his rear-fief: and a new beneficiary succeeded, who likewise established new rear-vassals. Thus it was the person and not the rear-fief that depended on the fief; on the one hand, the rear-vassal returned to the king because he was not tied for ever to the vassal; and the rear-fief returned also to the king because it was the fief itself and not a dependence of it.

[2102] In the year 757, art. 6, Baluzius's edition, p. 181.

Such was the rear-vassalage, while the fiefs were during pleasure; and such was it also while they were for life. This was altered when the fiefs descended to the next heirs, and the rear-fiefs the same. That which was held before immediately of the king was held now mediately; and the regal power was thrown back, as it were, one degree, sometimes two; and oftentimes more.

We find in the books of fiefs, [2103] that, though the king's vassals might give away in fief, that is, in rear-fief, to the king, yet these rear-vassals, or petty vavasors, could not give also in fief; so that whatever they had given, they might always resume. Besides, a grant of that kind did not descend to the children like the fiefs, because it was not supposed to have been made according to the feudal laws.

[2103] Book I, chap. 1.

If we compare the situation in which the rear-vassalage was at the time when the two Milanese senators wrote those books, with what it was under King Pepin, we shall find that the rear-fiefs preserved their primitive nature longer than the fiefs. [2104]

[2104] At least in Italy and Germany.

But when those senators wrote, such general exceptions had been made to this rule as had almost abolished it. For if a person who had received a fief of a rear-vassal happened to follow him upon an expedition to Rome, he was entitled to all the privileges of a vassal. [2105] In like manner, if he had given money to the rear-vassal to obtain the fief, the latter could not take it from him, nor hinder him from transmitting it to his son, till he returned him his money: in fine, this rule was no longer observed by the senate of Milan. [2106]

[2105] Book I, of fiefs, chap. 1.
[2106] Ibid.

27. *Another change which happened in the Fiefs.*

In Charlemagne's time they were obliged, [2107] under great penalties, to repair to the general meeting in case of any war whatsoever; they admitted of no excuses, and if the count exempted any one, he was liable himself to be punished. But the treaty of the three brothers [2108] made a restriction upon this head which rescued the nobility, as it were, out of the king's hands; they were no longer obliged to serve him in time of war, except when the war was defensive. [2109] In others, they were at liberty to follow their lord, or to mind their own business. This treaty relates to another, [2110] concluded, five years before, between the two brothers, Charles the Bald and Lewis, King of Germany, by which these princes release their vassals from serving them in war, in case they should attempt hostilities against each other; an agreement which the two princes confirmed by oath, and at the same time made their armies swear to it.

[2107] Capitulary of the year 802, art. 7, Baluzius's edition, p. 365.
[2108] *Apud Marsnam*, in the year 847, Baluzius's edition, p. 42.
[2109] *Volumus ut cujuscumque nostrûm homo in cujuscumque regno sit, cum senior suo in hostem, vel aliis suis utilitatibus, pergat, nisi talis regni invasion quam* LAMTUVERI *dicunt, quod absit, acciderit, ut omnis populus illius regni ad eam repellendam communiter pergat*, art. 5, ibid., p. 44.
[2110] *Apud Argentoratum*, in Baluzius, Capitularies, tom. ii, p. 39.

The death of a hundred thousand French, at the battle of Fontenay, made the remains of the nobility imagine that by the private quarrels of their kings about their respective shares, their whole body would be exterminated, and that the ambition and jealousy of those princes would end in the destruction of all the best families of the kingdom. A law was therefore passed that the nobility should not be obliged to serve their princes in war unless it was to defend the state against a foreign invasion. This law obtained for several ages. [2111]

[2111] See the law of Guy, King of the Romans, among those which were added to the Salic law, and to that of the Lombards, tit. 6, § 2 in *Echard*.

28. *Changes which happened in the great Offices, and in the Fiefs.*

The many changes introduced into the fiefs in particular cases seemed to spread so widely as to be productive of general corruption. I noticed that in the beginning several fiefs had been alienated in perpetuity; but those were particular cases, and the fiefs in general preserved their nature; so that if the crown lost some fiefs it substituted others in their stead. I observed, likewise, that the crown had never alienated the great offices in perpetuity. [2112]

[2112] Some authors pretend that the County of Toulouse had been given away by Charles Martel, and passed by inheritance down to Raymond, the last count; but, if this be true, it was owing to some circumstances which might have been an inducement to choose the Counts of Toulouse from among the children of the last possessor.

But Charles the Bald made a general regulation, which equally affected the great offices and the fiefs. He ordained, in his capitularies, that the counties should be given to the children of the count, and that this regulation should also take place in respect to the fiefs. [2113]

[2113] See his Capitulary of the year 877, tit. 53, art. 9 and 10, *apud Carisiacum.* This Capitulary bears relation to another of the same year and place, art. 3.

We shall see presently that this regulation received a wider extension, insomuch that the great offices and fiefs went even to distant relatives. Thence it followed that most of the lords who before this time had held immediately of the crown, held now mediately. Those counts who formerly administered justice in the king's *placita,* and who led the freemen against the enemy, found themselves situated between the king and his freemen; and the king's power was removed farther off another degree.

Again, it appears from the capitularies, [2114] that the counts had benefices annexed to their counties, and vassals under them. When the counties became hereditary, the count's vassals were no longer the immediate vassals of the king; and the benefices annexed to the counties were no longer the king's benefices; the counts grew powerful because the vassals whom they had already under them enabled them to procure others.

[2114] The third Capitulary of the year 812, art. 7, and that of the year 815, art. 6, on the Spaniards. The collection of the Capitularies, book 5, art. 288, and the Capitulary of the year 869, art. 2, and that of the year 877, art. 13, Baluzius's edition.

In order to be convinced how much the monarchy was thereby weakened towards the end of the second race we have only to cast an eye on what happened at the beginning of the third, when the multiplicity of rear-fiefs flung the great vassals into despair.

It was a custom of the kingdom [2115] that when the elder brothers had given shares to their younger brothers, the latter paid homage to the elder; so that those shares were held of the lord paramount only as a rear-fief. Philip Augustus, the Duke of Burgundy, the Counts of Nevers, Boulogne, St. Paul, Dampierre, and other lords declared [2116] that henceforward, whether the fiefs were divided by succession or otherwise, the whole should be always of the same lord, without any intermediation. This ordinance was not generally followed; for, as I have elsewhere observed, it was impossible to make general ordinances at that time; but many of our customs were regulated by them.

[2115] As appears from Otho of Frissingue, Of the Actions of Frederic, book II. chap. 29.
[2116] See the ordinance of Philip Augustus in the year 1209, in the new collection.

29. *Of the Nature of the Fiefs after the Reign of Charles the Bald.*

We have observed that Charles the Bald ordained that when the possessor of a great office or of a fief left a son at his death, the office or fief should devolve to him. It would be a difficult matter to trace the progress of the abuses which thence resulted, and of the extension given to that law in each country. I find in the books of fiefs, [2117] that towards the beginning of the reign of the Emperor Conrad II, the fiefs situated in his dominions did not descend to the grandchildren: they descended only to one of the last possessor's children, who had been chosen by the lord: [2118] thus the fiefs were given by a kind of election, which the lord made among the children.

[2117] Book I, tit. 1.
[2118] *Sic progressum est, ut ad filios deveniret in quem Dominus hoc vellet beneficium confirmare.—Ibid.*

In the seventeenth chapter of this book we have explained in what manner the crown was in some respects elective, and in others hereditary under the second race. It was hereditary, because the kings were always taken from that family, and because the children succeeded; it was elective, by reason that the people chose from among the children. As things proceed step by step, and one political law has constantly some relation to another political law, the same spirit was followed in the succession of fiefs, as had been observed in the succession to the crown. [2119] Thus the fiefs were transmitted to the children by the right of succession, as well as of election; and each fief became both elective and hereditary, like the crown.

[2119] At least in Italy and Germany.

This right of election [2120] in the person of the lord was not subsisting at the time of the authors [2121] of the book of fiefs, that is, in the reign of the Emperor Frederick I.

[2120] *Quod hodie ita stabilitum est, ut ad omnes æqualiter veniat.*—Book I, of fiefs, tit. 1.
[2121] Gerardus Niger and Aubertus de Orto.

30. *The same Subject continued.*

It is mentioned in the books of fiefs, that when the Emperor Conrad set out for Rome, the vassals in his service presented a petition to him that he would please to make a law that the fiefs which descended to the children should descend also to the grandchildren; and that he whose brother died without legitimate heirs might succeed to the fief which had belonged to their common father. [2122] This was granted.

[2122] *Cum vero Conradus Romam proficisceretur, petitum est a Fidelibus qui in ejus erant servitio, ut, lege ab eo promulgatâ, hoc etiam ad nepotes ex filio producer dignaretur, et ut frater fratri sine legitime hærede defuncto in beneficia quod eorum patris fuit, succedat.*—Book I, of fiefs, tit. 1.

In the same place it is said (and we are to remember that those writers lived at the time of the Emperor Frederick I) [2123] "that the ancient jurists had always been of opinion [2124] that the succession of fiefs in a collateral line did not extend farther than to brothers-german, though of late it was carried as far as the seventh degree, and by the new code they had extended it in a direct line *in infinitum*." It is thus that Conrad's law was insensibly extended.

[2123] Cujas has proved it extremely well.

[2124] *Sciendum est quod beneficium advenientes ex latere, ultra fraters patrueles non progreditur succession ab antiquis sapientibus constitutum, licet moderno tempore usque ad septimum genuculum sit usurpatum, quod in masulis descendentibus novo jure in infinitum extenditur.*—*Ibid.*

All these things being supposed, the bare perusal of the history of France is sufficient to demonstrate that the perpetuity of fiefs was established earlier in this kingdom than in Germany. Towards the commencement of the reign of the Emperor Conrad II in 1024, things were upon the same footing still in Germany, as they had been in France during the reign of Charles the Bald, who died in 877. But such were the changes made in this kingdom after the reign of Charles the Bald, that Charles the Simple found himself unable to dispute with a foreign house his incontestable rights to the empire; and, in fine, that in Hugh Capet's time the reigning family, stripped of all its demesnes, was no longer in a condition to maintain the crown.

The weak understanding of Charles the Bald produced an equal weakness in the French monarchy. But as his brother, Lewis, King of Germany, and some of that prince's successors were men of better parts, their government preserved its vigor much longer.

But what do I say? Perhaps the phlegmatic constitution, and, if I dare use the expression, the immutability of spirit peculiar to the German nation made a longer stand than the volatile temper of the French against that disposition of things, which perpetuated the fiefs by a natural tendency, in families.

Besides, the kingdom of Germany was not laid waste and annihilated, as it were, like that of France, by that particular kind of war with which it had been harassed by the Normans and Saracens. There were less riches in Germany, fewer cities to plunder, less extent of coast to scour, more marshes to get over, more forests to penetrate. As the dominions of those princes were less in danger of being ravaged and torn to pieces, they had less need of their vassals and consequently less dependence on them. And in all probability, if the Emperors of Germany had not been obliged to be crowned at Rome, and to make continual expeditions into Italy, the fiefs would have preserved their primitive nature much longer in that country.

31. *In what Manner the Empire was transferred from the Family of Charlemagne.*

The empire, which, in prejudice to the branch of Charles the Bald had been already given to the bastard line of Lewis, King of Germany, [2125] was transferred to a foreign house by the election of Conrad, Duke of Franconia, in 912. The reigning branch in France, being hardly able to contest a few villages, was much less in a situation to contest the empire. We have an agreement entered into between Charles the Simple and the Emperor Henry I, who had succeeded to Conrad, It is called the Compact of Bonn. [2126] These two princes met in a vessel which had been placed in the middle of the Rhine, and swore eternal friendship. They used on this occasion an excellent *middle term.* Charles took the title of King of West France, and Henry that of King of East France. Charles contracted with the King of Germany, and not with the Emperor.

[2125] Arnold and his son Lewis IV.
[2126] In the year 926, quoted by Aubert le Mire, *Cod. donationum piarum,* chap. 27.

32. *In what Manner the Crown of France was transferred to the House of Hugh Capet.*

The inheritance of the fiefs, and the general establishment of rear-fiefs, extinguished the political and formed a feudal government. Instead of that prodigious multitude of vassals who were formerly under the king, there were now a few only, on whom the others depended. The kings had scarcely any longer a direct authority; a power which was to pass through so many other and through such great powers either stopped or was lost before it reached its term. Those great vassals would no longer obey; and they even made use of their rear-vassals to withdraw their obedience. The kings, deprived of their demesnes and reduced to the cities of Rheims and Laon, were left exposed to their mercy; the tree stretched out its branches too far, and the head was withered. The kingdom found itself without a demesne, as the empire is at present. The crown was, therefore, given to one of the most potent vassals.

The Normans ravaged the kingdom; they sailed in open boats or small vessels, entered the mouths of rivers, and laid the country waste on both sides. The cities of Orleans and Paris put a stop to those plunderers, so that they could not advance farther, either on the Seine, or on the Loire. [2127] Hugh Capet, who was master of those cities, held in his hands the two keys of the unhappy remains of the kingdom; the crown was conferred upon him as the only person able to defend it. It is thus the empire was afterwards given to a family whose dominions form so strong a barrier against the Turks.

[2127] See the Capitulary of Charles the Bald, in the year 877, *apud Carisiacum,* on the importance of Paris, St. Denis, and the castles on the Loire, in those days.

The empire went from Charlemagne's family at a time when the inheritance of fiefs was established only as a mere condescendence. It even appears that this inheritance obtained much later among the Germans than among the French; [2128] which was the reason that the empire, considered as a fief, was elective. On the contrary, when the crown of France went from the family of Charlemagne, the fiefs were really hereditary in this kingdom; and the crown, as a great fief, was also hereditary.

[2128] See above, chapter 30.

But it is very wrong to refer to the very moment of this revolution all the changes which happened, either before or afterwards. The whole was reduced to two events; the reigning family changed, and the crown was united to a great fief.

33. *Some Consequences of the Perpetuity of Fiefs.*

From the perpetuity of fiefs it followed that the right of seniority or primogeniture was established among the French. This right was quite unknown under the first race; [2129] the crown was divided among the brothers, the allodia were shared in the same manner; and as the fiefs, whether precarious or for life, were not an object of succession, there could be no partition in regard to those tenures.

[2129] See the Salic law, and the law of the Ripuarians, in the title of *allodia*.

Under the second race, the title of emperor, which Lewis the Debonnaire enjoyed, and with which he honored his eldest son, Lotharius, made him think of giving this prince a kind of superiority over his younger brothers. The two kings were obliged to wait upon the emperor every year, to carry him presents, and to receive much greater from him; they were also to consult with him upon common affairs. [2130] This is what inspired Lotharius with those pretences which met with such bad success. When Agobard wrote in favor of this prince, [2131] he alleged the emperor's own intention, who had associated Lotharius with the empire after he had consulted the Almighty by a three days' fast, by the celebration of the holy mysteries, and by prayers and almsgiving; after the nation had sworn allegiance to him, which they could not refuse without perjuring themselves; and after he had sent Lotharius to Rome to be confirmed by the Pope. Upon all this he lays a stress, and not upon his right of primogeniture. He says, indeed, that the emperor had designed a partition among the younger brothers, and that he had given the preference to the elder; but saying he had preferred the elder was saying at the same time that he might have given the preference to his younger brothers.

[2130] See the Capitulary of the year 817, which contains the first partition made by Lewis the Debonnaire among his children.
[2131] See his two letters upon this subject, the title of one of which is *de divisione imperii*.

But as soon as the fiefs became hereditary, the right of seniority was established in the feudal succession; and for the same reason in that of the crown, which was the great fief. The ancient law of partitions was no longer subsisting; the fiefs being charged with a service, the possessor must have been enabled to discharge it. The law of primogeniture was established, and the right of the feudal law was superior to that of the political or civil institution.

As the fiefs descended to the children of the possessor, the lords lost the liberty of disposing of them; and, in order to indemnify themselves, they established what they called the right of redemption, whereof mention is made in our customs, which at first was paid in a direct line, and by usage came afterwards to be paid only in a collateral line.

The fiefs were soon rendered transferable to strangers as a patrimonial estate. This gave rise to the right of lord's dues, which were established almost throughout the kingdom. These rights were arbitrary in the beginning; but when the practice of granting such permissions became general, they were fixed in every district.

The right of redemption was to be paid at every change of heir, and at first was paid even in a direct line. [2132] The most general custom had fixed it to one year's income. This was burdensome and inconvenient to the vassal, and affected in some measure the fief itself, It was often agreed in the act of homage that the lord should no longer demand more than a certain sum of money for the redemption, which, by the changes incident to money, became afterwards of no manner of importance. [2133] Thus the right of redemption is in our days reduced almost to nothing, while that of the lord's dues is continued in its full extent. As this right concerned neither the vassal nor his heirs, but was a fortuitous case which no one was obliged to foresee or expect, these stipulations were not made, and they continued to pay a certain part of the price.

[2132] See the ordinance of Philip Augustus, in the year 1209, on the fiefs.
[2133] We find several of these conventions in the charters, as in the register book of Vendôme, and that of the abbey, in St. Cyprian in Poitou, of which Mr. Galland has given some extracts, p. 55.

When the fiefs were for life, they could not give a part of a fief to hold in perpetuity as a rear-fief; for it would have been absurd that a person who had only the usufruct of a thing should dispose of the property of it. But when they became perpetual, this was permitted. [2134] with some restrictions made by the customs, which was what they call dismembering their fief. [2135]

[2134] But they could not abridge the fiefs, that is, abolish a portion of it.
[2135] They fixed the portion which they could dismember.

The perpetuity of feudal tenures having established the right of redemption, the daughters were rendered capable of succeeding to a fief, in default of male issue. For when the lord gave the fief to his daughter, he multiplied the cases of his right of redemption, because the husband was obliged to pay it as well as the wife. [2136] This regulation could not take place in regard to the crown, for as it was not held of any one, there could be no right of redemption over it.

[2136] This was the reason that the lords obliged the widow to marry again.

The daughter of William V, Count of Toulouse, did not succeed to the county. But Eleanor succeeded to Aquitaine, and Matilda to Normandy; and the right of the succession of females seemed so well established in those days, that Lewis the Young, after his divorce from Eleanor, made no difficulty in restoring Guienne to her. But as these two last instances followed close on the first, the general law by which the women were called to the succession of fiefs must have been introduced much later into the county of Toulouse than into the other provinces of France. [2137]

[2137] Most of the great families had their particular laws of succession. See what M. de la Thaumassière says concerning the families of Berri.

The constitution of several kingdoms of Europe has been directed by the state of feudal tenures at the time when those kingdoms were founded. The women succeeded neither to the crown of France nor to the empire, because at the foundation of those two monarchies they were incapable of succeeding to fiefs. But they succeeded in kingdoms whose foundation was posterior to that of the perpetuity of the fiefs, such as those founded by the Normans, those by the conquests made on the Moors, and others, in fine, which were beyond the limits of Germany, and in later times received in some measure a second birth by the establishment of Christianity.

When these fiefs were at will, they were given to such as were capable of doing service for them, and, therefore, were never bestowed on minors; but when they became perpetual, the lords took the fief into their own hands, till the pupil came of age, either to increase their own emoluments, or to train the ward to the use of arms. [2138] This is what our customs call *the guardianship of a nobleman's children*, which is founded on principles different from those of tutelage, and is entirely a distinct thing from it.

[2138] We see in the Capitulary of the year 817, *apud Carisiacum*, art. 3, Baluzius's edition, tom. ii, p. 269, the moment in which the kings caused the fiefs to be administered in order to preserve them for the minors; an example followed by the lords, and which gave rise to what we have mentioned by the name of *the guardianship of a nobleman's children*.

When the fiefs were for life, it was customary to vow fealty for a fief; and the real delivery, which was made by a scepter, confirmed the fief, as it is now confirmed by homage. We do not find that the counts, or even the king's commissaries, received the homage in the provinces; nor is this ceremony to be met with in the commissions of those officers which have been handed down to us in the Capitularies. They sometimes, indeed, made all the king's subjects take an oath of allegiance; [2139] but so far was this oath from being of the same nature as the service afterwards established by the name of homage, that it was only a ceremony of less solemnity, occasionally used, either before or after that act of obeisance; in short, it was quite a distinct thing from homage. [2140]

[2139] We find the formula thereof in the second Capitulary of the year 802. See also that of the year 854, art. 13, and others.
[2140] M. Ducange in the word *hominium*, p. 1163, and in the word *fidelitas*, p. 474, cites the charters of the ancient homages where these differences are found, and a great number of authorities which may be seen. In paying homage, the vassal put his hand on that of his lord, and took his oath; the oath of fealty was made by swearing on the gospels. The homage was performed kneeling, the oath of fealty standing. None but the lord could receive homage, but his officers might take the oath of fealty.—See Littleton, §§ 91, 92, faith and homage, that is, fidelity and homage.

The counts and the king's commissaries further made those vassals whose fidelity was suspected give occasionally a security, which was called *firmitas*, [2141] but this security could not be an homage, since kings gave it to each other. [2142]

[2141] Capitularies of Charles the Bald, in the year 860, *post reditum a Confluentibus*, art. 3, Baluzius's edition, p. 145.

[2142] Ibid., art. 1.

And though the Abbot *Suger* [2143] makes mention of a chair of Dagobert, in which according to the testimony of antiquity, the kings of France were accustomed to receive the homage of the nobility, it is plain that he expresses himself agreeably to the ideas and language of his own time.

[2143] *Lib. de administratione sua.*

When the fiefs descended to the heirs, the acknowledgment of the vassal, which at first was only an occasional service, became a regular duty. It was performed in a more splendid manner, and attended with more formalities, because it was to be a perpetual memorial of the reciprocal duties of the lord and vassal.

I should be apt to think that homages began to be established under King Pepin, which is the time I mentioned that several benefices were given in perpetuity, but I should not think thus without caution, and only upon a supposition that the authors of the ancient annals of the Franks were not ignorant pretenders, [2144] who in describing the fealty professed by Tassillon, Duke of Bavaria, to King Pepin, spoke according to the usages of their own time. [2145]

[2144] Year 757, chap. xvii.
[2145] *Tassilo venit in vassatico se commendans, per manus sacramenta juravit multa et innumerabilia, reliquis sanctorum manus imponens et fidelitatem promisit regi Pippino.* One would think that here was an homage and an oath of fealty. See note 2139.

34. *The same Subject continued.*

When the fiefs were either precarious or for life, they seldom bore a relation to any other than the political laws; for which reason in the civil institutions of those times there is very little mention made of the laws of fiefs. But when they became hereditary, when there was a power of giving, selling, and bequeathing them, they bore a relation both to the political and the civil laws. The fief, considered as an obligation of performing military service, depended on the political law; considered as a kind of commercial property, it depended on the civil law. This gave rise to the civil regulations concerning feudal tenures.

When the fiefs became hereditary, the law relating to the order of succession must have been in relation to the perpetuity of fiefs. Hence this rule of the French law, *estates of inheritance do not ascend,* [2146] was established in spite of the Roman and Salic laws. [2147] It was necessary that service should be paid for the fief; but a grandfather or a great-uncle would have been too old to perform any service; this rule thus held good at first only in regard to the feudal tenures, as we learn from Boutillier. [2148]

[2146] Book IV, *de feudis*, tit. 59.
[2147] In the title of *allodia.*
[2148] *Somme Rurale*, book I, tit. 76, p. 447.

When the fiefs became hereditary, the lords who were to see that service was paid for the fief, insisted that the females who were to succeed to the feudal estate, and I fancy sometimes the males, should not marry without their consent; insomuch that the marriage contracts became in respect to the nobility both of a feudal and a civil regulation. [2149] In an act of this kind under the lord's inspection, regulations were made for the succession, with the view that the heirs might pay service for the fief: hence none but the nobility at first had the liberty of disposing of successions by marriage contract, as Boyer [2150] and Aufrerius [2151] have observed.

[2149] According to an ordinance of St. Lewis, in the year 1246 to settle the customs of Anjou and Maine; those who shall have the care of the heiress of a fief shall give security to the lord, that she shall not be married without his consent.
[2150] Decision 155, No. 8; and 204, No. 38.
[2151] In Capell. Thol., decision 453.

It is needless to mention that the power of redemption, founded on the old right of the relatives, a mystery of our ancient French jurisprudence I have not time to unravel, could not take place with regard to the fiefs till they became perpetual.

Italiam, Italiam . . . [2152]

[2152] Æneid, lib. III, 523.

I finish my treatise of fiefs at a period where most authors commence theirs.

THE END

CPSIA information can be obtained
at www.ICGtesting.com
Printed in the USA
LVOW03s1421191117
556905LV00002B/387/P